21X 5/19

PUTTIN' ON THE RITZ

ALSO BY PETER J. LEVINSON

Trumpet Blues: The Life of Harry James

September in the Rain: The Life of Nelson Riddle

Tommy Dorsey: Livin' in a Great Big Way, a Biography

PUTTIN'
ON THE RITZ

FRED ASTAIRE
and the Fine Art of Panache

A BIOGRAPHY

PETER J. LEVINSON

ST. MARTIN'S PRESS ❦ NEW YORK

www.stmartins.com

Design by Susan Yang

Library of Congress Cataloging-in-Publication Data

Levinson, Peter J.
  Puttin' on the Ritz : Fred Astaire and the fine art of panache / Peter Levinson.—1st ed.
     p. cm.
   ISBN-13: 978-0-312-35366-7
   ISBN-10: 0-312-35366-9
  1. Astaire, Fred.   2. Dancers—United States—Biography.   3. Motion picture actors and actresses—United States—Biography.   I. Title.
   GV1785.A83L48 2009
   792.802'8092—dc22
   [B]

                                                         2008035765

First Edition: March 2009

10   9   8   7   6   5   4   3   2   1

FOR GRACE—

THE LIGHT OF MY LIFE
FOR THE PAST 25 YEARS

CONTENTS

ACKNOWLEDGMENTS

F RED ASTAIRE AND I share two important passions. We both like well-made, stylish clothes, and we share an appreciation for jazz. The producer C. B. Dillingham first made a sartorial impression on Fred during his early years of dancing with his sister, Adele, in Broadway musicals. But the Astaires' subsequent excursions to London's West End, where Fred propitiously encountered the debonair and trendsetting Edward, the Prince of Wales, had the most far-reaching influence on Fred's fashion sense. After that, he was well on his way to becoming established as one of the best-turned-out men in public life, exhibiting a decidedly English bent.

Astaire first took to jazz through his excursions to Harlem to check out its unique tap dancers during the late 1920s. However, in the 1930s the swing bands of Benny Goodman, Artie Shaw, Jimmie Lunceford, and Count Basie—especially Basie, whose music Fred became enamored with—influenced his work. Such important jazz musicians as the late Oscar Peterson, Fred's collaborator on the essential *Fred Astaire Story* album; John Pizzarelli; and Louis Bellson; as well as the record producers and arrangers Neal Hefti, Buddy Bregman, and Jackie Mills, expressed their keen observations on how jazz was an integral part of Astaire's musical outlook. Fred's stunning dancing partner on his well-remembered NBC-TV specials Barrie Chase astutely observed, "Jazz was in his bones."

Johnny Mathis called Astaire "the perfect singer." Andy Williams; Michael Feinstein; the late Ahmet Ertegun; the late Fayard Nicholas; Joel Grey; Leslie Bricusse; John Williams; Art Garfunkel; the critics Stephen Holden, Nat Hentoff, Don Heckman, Stanley Crouch, and Richard Schickel; the songwriter Alan Bergman; and the late Bobby Short—all applauded his understated but somehow *perfect* way of interpreting a popular song. This stemmed from his first learning to sing tunes that were integrated into the book of Broadway musicals he starred in, which led to his ability to convey their intrinsic meaning. For many years Astaire has been considered one of the essential pop singers in the history of American music.

All of that, however, pales in comparison with his vast contributions to the dance. If ever a performer deserved his stupendous success, it was Fred Astaire. His supreme dedication to his art seemingly never existed in any other dancer. Perfection is what he constantly strived for, and it became his norm. The results were staggering and enabled him to become America's most popular and stylish dancer and a major film star.

I was fortunate to be guided through the dance world by a number of dancers and choreographers. I must, however, salute especially the untiring efforts of Larri Thomas, whom I justifiably nicknamed the Great One; Jerry Jackson; and the late Becky Vorno. No question of mine ever lacked an answer from them, and they were always available and eager to be of help.

Barrie Chase explained how she first met Fred while dancing in film musicals and described his rigorous rehearsals with her, before by necessity he transferred his dancing and singing from films to television and chose her to star with him on his four specials. Chase was grateful for the opportunity he provided her, though sometimes critical of his work, particularly in the fourth special. Highly opinionated, Chase is never far from the mark.

With respect to Astaire's constantly evolving fashion sense, I interviewed such men's fashion experts as Alan Flusser; Joe Barrato; G. Bruce Boyer; Richard Merkin; and George Christy; the writer Budd Schulberg; along with the bespoke tailor John Hitchcock, the managing director of Anderson & Sheppard, and Norman Halsey, who looked after Astaire at that Savile Row firm for many years. Also, San Francisco's Wilkes Bashford; Cliff Grodd, the longtime president of Paul Stuart; Claudio Del Vecchio, the CEO of Brooks Brothers; John Carroll, who owns Carroll's in Beverly Hills; along with the well-dressed actors Dick Van Dyke and Robert Wagner, who were influenced by Astaire.

So much more was involved in attempting to tell the *compleat* Fred Astaire story. Fred had several incarnations: vaudeville and Broadway performer with his sister; his establishing the movie musical as an art form while dancing with Ginger Rogers; maintaining his superstardom in many other movie musicals; character actor; recording artist; and later distinguished Hollywood senior citizen.

On-screen he presented a likable and shy, very American persona. His grandparents were originally Austrian Jews, who converted to Catholicism; he wound up an Episcopalian. He learned exactly how the wicked world of show business worked and always kept ahead of the curve.

So many people were of great assistance in suggesting interview subjects, making introductory phone calls, offering advice, and in countless other ways. These benefactors include Peggy Alexander, Ray Arnett, Paul Block, G. Bruce Boyer, Jon Burlingame, Vince Calandera, "the other" Ray Charles, Iris Chester, the late Warren Cowan, Fred Curt, Jim Curtis, Dr. Ronald L. Davis (of SMU), Paul de Barros, Jessica Diamond, Margie Duncan, the late Mort Fega, Bert Fink, Ross Firestone, Dan Fortune, Eddie Foy III, Jim Gavin, the late Hal Gefsky, Julie Graham and Lauren Buisson of the Performing Arts Special Collections at the UCLA Library, Lee Hale, Barbara Hall of the Margaret Herrick Library, Marian Hall, Jay Harris, Jimmy Haskell, Tad Hershorn, Katherine Hopkins, Kevin Kennedy, Ann King, Kim Kopf, Jack Lawrence, Randy Malone, Leonard Maltin, Connie Martinson, Ginger Mason, Dottie McCarthy, Joe McFate, Lee Miller, Marianne Moloney, Dan Morgenstern, Audrey Morris, Joseph Morrison, Budd Moss, Ed O'Brien, Roberta Olden, Bob Palmer, Jim Pierson, Bob Podesta, Jess Rand, Peter Rausch, Betty Rose, Jeff Rose, Gene Schwam, Reinhold Schwarzwald, Robert Scott, Paul Shefrin, Marti Spaninger, Roger Vorce, Betty Walsh, Jim Watters, and Rob Wolders.

Further, I want to single out a group of individuals who from the beginning of my work on this project were unceasing in their attempts to be of assistance: Ned Comstock, librarian at the Cinema-Television Archive at USC, Michael Russell, Roger Mayer, Joe Barrato, Al Schwartz, Bill Self, Stacey of the Margaret Herrick Library, and film historian Rudy Behlmer, Dale Olson, and the late Dick Martin.

I can't forget the professionalism exhibited by my literary agent, Al Zuckerman of Writers House, and Diane Reverend, who signed me to St. Martin's Press. I would also like to thank Vicki Lame and Regina Scarpa at St. Martin's Press. John Morrone proved to be a thorough production editor with a keen knowledge of the musical film. Most of all, however, the care and inspiration of Michael Flamini, my editor, made writing the life of Fred Astaire such a pleasurable experience. And far from least, I must thank the supreme efforts and dedication of Petra Schwarzwald, the best assistant one could ever find. In researching my book, I screened all of Astaire's movies with the exception of *Midas Run,* which seemingly is not available. This is in addition to viewing the bulk of his vast array of television appearances.

I interviewed the following people in researching my book: Berle Adams, Ray Aghayan, Corey Allen, Sheila Allen, Donna Anderson, Ray Anthony, Ava Astaire, Jean Bach, Bob Bain, Ken Barnes, Joe Barrato, Mary Ellin Barrett, Mikhail Baryshnikov, Wilkes Bashford, Louis Bellson, Alan Bergman, Harry Betts, Michael Black, Betsy Blair, Ed Blau, Peter Bogdanovich, Bonnie Borne, Elyse Borne, Rose Borne, G. Bruce Boyer, Buddy Bregman, Leslie Bricusse, Carol Bryan, Gary Burghoff, Bea Busch, John Byner, Vince Calandra, Joe Campo, Hoagy Bix Carmichael, John Carroll, Jack Carter, Mike Casey, Dick Cavett, Marge Champion,

Charles Champlin, Martin Charnin, Barrie Chase, George Christy, Dick Clark, Petula Clark, Sterling Clark, Charlie Cochran, Fred Cohn, Buddy Collette, the late Betty Comden, the late Pete Condoli, the late Alexander "Sandy" Courage, Bob Cranshaw, Arlene Croce, Stanley Crouch, Fred Curt, Arlene Dahl, Michael Dante, Hal David, Buddy DeFranco, Claudio Del Vecchio, Pat Denise, Dante DiPaolo, Gerald Di Pego, Peter Duchin, Dominick Dunne, Jane Earl, Ruth Earl, Barbara Eden, Linda Emmet, Ahmet Ertegun, Harvey Evans, Michael Feinstein, George Feltenstein, the late Mel Ferrer, Sean Ferrer, the late Freddie Fields, Allen Flusser, Hugh Fordin, Eddie Foy III, Al Freeman Jr., Terri Fricon, Art Garfunkel, Betty Garrett, Greg Garrison, Larry Gelbart, Art Gilmore, Sam Goldwyn Jr., Ellen Graham, Joel Grey, Cliff Grodd, Earle Hagen, Jack Haley Jr., Brett Halsey, Norman Halsey, Chico Hamilton, Bill Harbach, Don Heckman, Neal Hefti, Nat Hentoff, Maurice Hines, John Hitchcock, Stephen Holden, Red Holt, Tab Hunter, John Irwin, Jerry Jackson, Anne Jeffreys, Alan Johnson, Hal Kanter, Mickey Kapp, Al Kasha, Stanley Kay, the late Michael Kidd, Shelah Hackett Kidd, Robert Kimball, Anna Kisselgoff, Miles Kreuger, Howard Krieger, Alice Krige, Michelle Lee, Ruta Lee, Dr. Jeni Le Gon, Micheline Lerner, Joan Leslie, Monica Lewis, Art Linkletter, A. C. Lyles, Carol Lynley, Dr. Lonnie MacDonald, Bob Mackie, Randal Malone, Andrea Marcovicci, Rose Marie, the late Dick Martin, Leslie Martinson, Johnny Mathis, Roger Mayer, Dan Melnick, Sergio Mendes, Richard Merkin, Eddie Merrins, Alison Miller, Lee Miller, Walter C. Miller, Jackie Mills, Marianne Moloney, Pete Moore, Terry Moore, the late Spud Murphy, Patricia Neal, Miriam Nelson, Phyllis Newman, the late Fayard Nicholas, David Niven Jr., Jamie Niven, Harry Northrup, the late Louis Nye, Margaret O'Brien, Robert Osborne, Janis Paige, the late Oscar Peterson, John Pizzarelli, Bob Podesta, Noah Racey, Uan Rasey, Rex Reed, Charlie Reinhart, Debbie Reynolds, Christopher Riordan, John Rockwell, Alex Romero, Betty Rose, Michael Russell, Donald Saddler, Jay Sandrich, Robert Scheerer, Richard Schickel, Budd Schulberg, Al Schwartz, Bernie Schwartz, Pippa Scott, Bill Self, Dan Selznick, the late Artie Shaw, the late Sidney Sheldon, Karen Sherry, the late Bobby Short, Kirk Silsbee, Maureen Solomon, Allen Sviridoff, Russ Tamblyn, Ned Tanen, Dow Thamon, Larri Thomas, Dick Van Dyke, Becky Vorno, Robert Wagner, Robert Walker Jr., Barbara Walters, Craig Wasson, Burt Weissbourd, Betty White, the late Onna White, Margaret Whiting, Andy Williams, John Williams, Jane Withers, Rob Wolders, Lana Wood, Bud Yorkin, Peg Yorkin, the late Eldee Young, and Efrem Zimbalist Jr.

PREFACE

E ARLY ONE WEEKDAY EVENING in March 1962, I was broiling a hamburger in my studio apartment on Hacienda Place, below Fountain Avenue, in what is now called West Hollywood. For me, at the time, cooking a hamburger required the highest concentration. I was interrupted by the sudden ringing of the telephone and picked up on the third ring.

On the other end, an older-sounding voice said, "Hello, is this Mr. Levinson? This is Fred Astaire." The shock of getting this unexpected phone call from one of the iconic figures in American entertainment should have sent me sailing downward through several floors of a normal apartment building. That was impossible, however, since my apartment was only one floor above the carport of the small building I lived in.

Mr. Astaire got right to the point. "I understand you are scheduled to come over to my house tomorrow afternoon to see my daughter, Ava. Would you please tell me, Mr. Levinson, what is this about?"

I tried to allay Mr. Astaire's fears by explaining I had an assignment from *Cosmopolitan* magazine's editor, Lyn Tornabene, to deliver an article entitled "Daughters of Famous Fathers." Ava was one of the young women who had been chosen to be included. Mr. Astaire was not at all pleased upon hearing this.

"Mr. Levinson, I don't want my daughter to take part in this magazine article. You don't seem to understand. I've just finished a picture called *The Notorious Landlady,* and I'm planning to retire. Anything my daughter says or does reflects on me. I don't like publicity."

I made a further fruitless attempt to get Mr. Astaire on my side: "But, Mr. Astaire, your daughter is a young woman. This story will discuss her hopes and dreams and elaborate on what she hopes to accomplish in her life in the years ahead."

"Mr. Levinson," said the even more determined-sounding Fred Astaire, "I don't want you to bother coming over to my house tomorrow afternoon. Is that clear?"

I finally realized I was getting nowhere and concluded, "I guess I shouldn't plan to do that."

He interjected, "I think that's a good idea."

I said thank you and hung up.

The next morning, just after 9:00 A.M., Ava Astaire called and in a laughing voice exclaimed, "I understand you had a little problem with Daddy last night. Don't worry; I talked him out of it. It's all right. I'll see you this afternoon as planned."

"Daughters of Famous Fathers" did indeed appear in the July 1962 issue of *Cosmo*. Ava Astaire was part of it, along with the daughters of Dean Martin, Harry James and Betty Grable, Dick Haymes, Ann Sothern, and others.

The next time I saw Ava was in May 2004 at the pied-à-terre she and her long-time husband, Richard McKenzie, share in the Knightsbridge section of London, when not living in county Cork, Ireland. Despite having seen Fred Astaire, identified by his famous walk, on the streets of Beverly Hills, and while shooting a song-and-dance number on the set of *Finian's Rainbow,* I never did meet him.

Even if I had, would I ever have discovered that behind the image of the top-hat-and-white-tie, Anglo-Saxon bon vivant stood another man, a shy and retiring person who was the result of many influences both cultural and artistic?

I saw Fred Astaire dance with his sister, Adele, in *Funny Face* at the Apollo Theatre in Atlantic City in 1927—and I've never been the same since!

—GLADYS LEVINSON (MY MOTHER), 1948

PUTTIN' ON THE RITZ

CHAPTER ONE

PAYING DUES

I IS PERHAPS no surprise that Friedrich Emanuel Austerlitz, the father of Fred and Adele Astaire, was a musician—a piano player and singer in his native Austria. As a young man he had grown up attending operettas and concerts in Vienna. As he once related to his two children, "There are two kinds of Austrians . . . rascals and musicians. I belong to the second group."[1] Friedrich had been born in Linz and baptized on September 8, 1868, as part of a Roman Catholic family of beer brewers in Vienna.

What is astonishing is that Friedrich's father, Stephan Austerlitz, a self-employed trading agent living in Prague, Czechoslovakia, who had been born Salomon Austerlitz, and his wife, Lucia Marianna Heller (Friedrich's mother), were Jewish. Despite their Czech background, the Austrian/Bohemian family spoke German.

Salomon Austerlitz and his wife, Lucia, their oldest child, Adele (baptized as Josepha); and Otto, Friedrich's older brother, converted to Catholicism on September 20, 1867, at St. Michael's Church in Leonding, Austria. (This was while the family was living in nearby Linz). Friedrich and his younger brother, Maximilian Ernest (later changed to Ernst), were baptized at birth. (Ironically the parents of Adolf Hitler, the Austrian-born dictator who raised the centuries-old Austrian hatred of the Jews to a demonic level, are buried in the church's cemetery.) Salomon became Stephan Johann Nep, taking the name of his godfather, but retaining his surname of Austerlitz.

At that time, a blatant anti-Semitic atmosphere pervaded Austria. Ingo Preminger, the late literary agent and brother of Otto Preminger, who grew up in Austria, observed, "There had always been anti-Semitism in Austria, but it is not the same brand as in this country, which is *social* anti-Semitism. In Vienna, there was a very different contempt for Jews for which the Church was responsible. It was the Church that taught over and over that the Jews killed Jesus Christ. Hatred for

Jews was always present, in the capital as well as in the provincial towns and cities."[2] This helps to explain the religious conversion from Judaism to Catholicism
of Salomon Austerlitz and his family.

Joseph II, Holy Roman Emperor, authored the Edict of Tolerance in 1781. Its
terms demanded that all Jews residing within the borders of the Empire were to
henceforth assume a new surname, which would become the family's official
name. The amount of the required fee to register that name was determined by
how much each family could afford to pay, that is, the Jewish families of means
could afford to pay a considerable fee. Their newly adopted names (for example,
Goldstein) had a connotation of wealth or something equally becoming (such as
Rosenthal, with its reference to a rose).

Families of lesser wealth were given names like Eisen, meaning iron. The poor
were strapped with names that often reflected "nonsense syllables." The most
frequent Jewish names were those like Richardson (son of Richard), and some
were based on a local city or a place, such as Austerlitz.[3]

The village of Austerlitz had been renamed because the prominent Austerlitz
family had lived there for generations. On December 2, 1805, it was the site of one
of Napoléon's major victories when his army won a valiant battle against the Russian and Austrian armies.

The many restrictions placed on Jews by the Edict of Tolerance in 1781 and
'82 fundamentally allowed them no religious freedom and included forbidding
the use of Hebrew except for ritualistic purposes. Secular transactions were required to be in the languages of the regime. To learn these languages, Jews were
encouraged to attend Christian schools and universities and encouraged to learn
new trades and occupations. The Hofkanzlei (Court Chancellery) went even further by suppressing Jewish admission to Catholic schools and their learning new
trades.

As pointed out by the historian Bruce F. Pauley in his book *From Prejudice to
Persecution: A History of Austrian Anti-Semitism,* "Jewish survival depended on
the protection of the Austrian rulers—whenever it was removed, expulsion or at
least harsh social and legal discrimination was the likely result." Nor did the devastating effects of war help. Again to quote Pauley, "Jewish-gentile relations were
tolerable during periods of prosperity but rapidly deteriorated during social and
economic crises brought on by bad harvests, plagues, wars or revolutions."[4]

The strictly enforced anti-Jewish feeling was slightly altered by the second
Edict of Tolerance, passed in 1782, which affected the Jews living in Vienna and
Lower Austria. It brought few substantial improvements but did attempt to improve the prevailing public feeling toward them. The stated goal of the edict was
to "make the Jewish nation useful and serviceable to the state."

Researchers are unable to probe further back in time, but acknowledge that Stephan's father (Fred Astaire's great-grandfather), Simon Juda Austerlitz, was born in Prague in 1790. Their inability stems from a 1784 patent of Joseph II's that replaced the rabbinate circumcision book (birth book) by standard record books similar to Catholic parish books. The once precisely chronicled dates of births and deaths in Jewish families were thus lost to posterity. Apparently, however, earlier generations of the Austerlitz family (or of its former surname) that came from Alsace, the province located between France and Germany, were Jewish as well.

MICHELINE LERNER, a former lawyer, who grew up in Paris and was married to Alan Jay Lerner, the celebrated lyricist and playwright, longer than any of his eight wives, has devoted herself to a lifelong study of Napoléon Bonaparte. Lerner pointed out that when Napoléon had reached the pinnacle of his success as a conqueror and had created a French empire, he enacted the Civil Code of 1804, which granted liberty, equality, and fraternity to Jews, Protestants, and Freemasons. Following that, on January 31, 1807, he called the Grand Sanhedrin, a meeting in Paris of prominent Jewish leaders. During this conference, which lasted two months, he expressed his admiration for the intelligence and determination of the Jewish people and decried their being forced to live in ghettos. The law that gave them equality was fine-tuned at this conference.

In late 1949 and early '50, Lerner became acquainted with Fred Astaire at the time her husband was writing the screenplay of *Royal Wedding* at MGM, in which Astaire costarred with Jane Powell. After discussing the significance of the Grand Sanhedrin with Lerner, he openly admitted his Jewish heritage to her. Yet nine years later, in his autobiography, *Steps in Time,* the only reference, and it is erroneous, that Astaire made to his family's ancestry was that his father was born in Vienna, where he had indeed lived in the early 1890s before emigrating to America.

Not long after having taped two ninety-minute ABC-TV talk shows with Astaire, comedian and television personality Dick Cavett began hearing various accounts of Astaire's Jewish roots. Cavett asked his friend George Bailey, author of *Germans,* if this could be true. Bailey's study of the Germanic people included extensive historical research on the history of the entire region. Bailey firmly believed the reports of Astaire's Jewish ancestry, exclaiming, "Undoubtedly. There were villages which were renamed using the names of prominent Jewish families. Austerlitz was likely one of them."

Cavett was asked by George Stevens Jr., then coproducer of *The Kennedy*

Center Honors, and son of the director of arguably the most outstanding of the ten Astaire/Ginger Rogers film musicals, *Top Hat,* to conduct an in-depth interview with Astaire for the Kennedy Center Archives. (Astaire had in 1978 been among the first group of artists awarded the prestigious Kennedy Center Honors.)

En route to the interview in a limousine, from the Beverly Hills Hotel with Astaire, Cavett briefly discussed various talking points that might be covered during their interview. Cavett queried Astaire about his Jewish background. Astaire demurred, remarking, "Dick, I'd rather we not get into that." Cavett was stunned and silenced.

FRIEDRICH AUSTERLITZ, like his brothers, Otto and Ernst, became an officer in the Austro-Hungarian army. According to an often-repeated family story, one day, upon failing to salute Ernst, who was his superior officer and very much a martinet, Friedrich was jailed for misconduct. Upon his release, he became disillusioned with life in the military and decided to leave for America, never to return to his homeland.[5]

He arrived at Ellis Island on the SS *Westernland* from Antwerp, Belgium, on October 26, 1892, when he was twenty-four. (This conflicts, however, with Astaire's account, which gave the year as 1895.) He listed his given name as "Fritz" (a nickname), and the ship's manifest recorded his occupation as "clerk."

After a short time in New York, Fritz headed west to Omaha, Nebraska, to start a business with two Austrian friends, Morris Karpeles and Huber Freund, who had emigrated earlier from Austria. Their company was called the International Publishing and Portrait Company. Its aim was to become established as a portrait-photography firm and also as an alternative to the *Omaha Street Directory.* Fritz would be the salesman for the company.

Omaha then had a population of about one hundred thousand, yet still had a small-town flavor. Its being the home of many German-speaking immigrants gave a decided impetus for the company to succeed. Unfortunately, the economic downturn known as the Panic of '93 caused the company to fold, leaving Fritz in desperate straits. He was compelled to take a job as a cook in a saloon run by another immigrant, Fred Mittnacht, a Lutheran.

Fritz became a popular figure at parties among the younger set. Many were intrigued by his mustache, his jovial personality, and his German accent. At a Lutheran social event, he met Johanna Geilus, a shy, dark-haired, bright-eyed schoolteacher at the Lutheran church school.

Her parents were David Geilus and Wilhelmina Klaatke, German-speaking

Lutherans, who hailed from East Prussia and Alsace, respectively. Johanna, who had never ventured outside her Omaha environs, found Fritz worldly with his often embroidered tales of Vienna and military life. He further regaled her by playing piano and singing ballads and drinking songs. Almost immediately, the young couple fell in love.

The Geiluses were troubled by the almost ten-year age difference between Fritz and Johanna, but their daughter's subsequent pregnancy forced them to accept Fritz. A marriage was quickly arranged, for November 17, 1894, at the Erste Lutheran Kirche, officiated by the Reverend Julius Freese. Fritz was twenty-six and Johanna only sixteen. The marriage license revealed "consent given by the father."

Johanna's first child was stillborn, a not uncommon occurrence at the time. But on September 10, 1896 (incorrectly stated as September 10, 1897, on her tombstone), the Austerlitzes announced the birth of a daughter, Adele Marie, who was called Dellie.[6] She was named after Johanna's two sisters and Fritz's sister. Exactly thirty-two months later, on May 10, 1899, a son, Frederick, whose name was Americanized from his father's name by adding a "k," was born at the family's small, nondescript home located at 2326 South Tenth Street in Omaha.

At the age of one, Freddie, as he was called, tottered around, and at two he began to walk and to participate in his sister's impromptu dances around the house. On May 16, 1903, just a few days after his fourth birthday, he joined his vivacious sister in attending the Kellom School. Freddie, small and elfin, looked up to Adele and followed her around as she ran her errands. At this young age, a closeness between the brother and his older sister had already been established.

Given her obvious aptitude for dance, Adele was enrolled by her parents at the Chambers Dancing Academy when she was four. A few years later, Johanna decided that Freddie should tag along with her. According to her, at the academy, he enjoyed trying on his sister's dancing pumps and imitated her beginning ballet steps on her pointed toes, though he didn't remember having done so.[7] This exercise was also beneficial in helping to build up Freddie's slight physique. Looking back on those formative years, Adele recalled, "He tried his best. He was a little thing, a cute little boy."[8]

Almost immediately, Willard E. Chambers was taken by Adele's natural ability. She already exhibited a decided grace and spontaneity and gaiety in her dancing. He made it clear to Fritz that his daughter, who was fast approaching age seven, had the potential to become a star. Fritz recognized her talent as well and noted, "Maybe Freddie will come around to it someday, too."[9] Displaying the precociousness that remained with her for the rest of her life, stagestruck Adele exclaimed to her father that she was going to be a famous dancer when she grew up. "And so am I," her already determined brother chimed in.

Freddie recalled that their mother was always ready to play with them, but she was also strict. "I don't remember any spankings, but I think we got a slap or two occasionally just to level things off a bit. And why not?"[10] Without consciously trying to indoctrinate his children into pursuing a life in show business, but rather to satisfy his own deep interest, Fritz would have them accompany him and Johanna on visits to the local vaudeville theater. Fritz delighted in watching the happiness on his children's faces as they watched the singers, dancers, and acrobats perform. The Austerlitz children were both bright, open to new experiences, with Freddie the more serious child.

But a harbinger of what loomed ahead in the lives of the two dancing school pupils was the sudden interest in trains that Freddie developed. This stemmed from the move the family made to 1421 North Nineteenth Street, close to the railroad. He and Adele became intrigued by the beat and syncopation of the mighty locomotives as they chugged through the neighborhood several times a day. They adapted that to their daily routine by playing at actually being trains and tapping their feet to accompany their own hissing and clattering sounds.

When he was only five, Freddie broke his arm while turning a cartwheel, and it was firmly strapped to a wooden splint. His injury kept him out of dancing school and prevented him from playing in the streets for two months. This incident left a lasting impression on his later professional career, as he developed an intense dislike for including acrobatics in his dance routines.[11]

MORE THAN TWO DECADES LATER, when they costarred in *The Band Wagon* on Broadway, Fred and Adele were interviewed about their early childhood. Fred candidly admitted, "There was a time, I was six . . . when I used to think of her with contempt. She couldn't play ball, or chin herself, or whistle through her teeth. She couldn't even spit! I used to pray at night for God to turn her into a brother. . . . Then when we had the first contest at dancing school, Adele, I remember, put in some crazy little jiggers that we hadn't prepared at all. I was primed for murder until the judges gave us the first prize, with special mention for Adele. It began to dawn on me that she had her way of getting results, and I had mine. Gradually that idea sank in, until I understood that we got along together best if we admitted that we were two separate people."

Adele summed up their early-childhood behavior by explaining, "From that first sock in the eye, I realized you could never be a sister for me. I decided to first accept you as a brother and let it go at that."[12]

*   *   *

FRITZ HAD MOST RECENTLY worked as a salesman for the Omaha Brewers Association. In 1902, the Storz Brewery absorbed the company. This upset Fritz, and he began drinking heavily and turned to other women. Johanna looked the other way as she was innately gentle and soft-spoken, but she was becoming increasingly unhappy. At twenty-five, she was looking for an escape from her hollow and confining domestic existence.[13]

The Austerlitz children were establishing a formidable local reputation as an inspired brother and sister act after appearing at church socials and other events. Adele was seven and a half and Freddie five when they rehearsed and rehearsed, as became their wont, for the Knights of Ak-Sar-Ben ("Nebraska" spelled backward) competition to be crowned in the organization's Coronation of the King and Queen. Formidable as they were as dancers, they lacked the stylish clothes of the wealthier children whose parents helped fund the Ak-Sar-Ben operation. Johanna tried to shield them from disappointment, but their failure to win made her decide that this must not happen again to her children.[14]

Fritz and Johanna become increasingly convinced that Willard Chambers was correct when he said that Adele required more advanced dance training, which she couldn't get in Omaha. Over several months, Johanna and Fritz made an important decision: The children must go to New York, and Johanna would go with them. They firmly believed that there was always a place for gifted youngsters in vaudeville; they had seen that firsthand. Talent was the true barometer in achieving success for young people. New York was not only the hub of the vaudeville business but also the home of many established dance schools.

Fritz was enthusiastic about Adele's chances to succeed. Going to New York with her two children provided Johanna with a way out of her unhappy provincial life. In New York, if they could work in vaudeville, she would be their chaperone, seamstress, and tutor.

When the idea of going to New York was first broached to Adele, she audaciously remarked, "Can we go now?" Fritz would at first have to finance this bold venture by sending money from his earnings as a salesman. In time, he would be able to join them in New York.

In truth, Adele had little chance of making it as a dancer in New York. The competition was simply too strong, and besides, they had absolutely no connections in New York. This reality didn't seem to fit into their plans. Freddie couldn't be left behind, but ostensibly he went along for the train ride; Adele's quest to achieve stardom was the focal point of their parents' dream.

Chambers, in his continuing interest in helping to design a career path for Freddie and Adele, suggested a professional dance teacher named Claude Alvienne. Fritz had also seen Alvienne's card in the *New York Clipper,* a theatrical trade journal. Fritz arranged to send a check to cover the tuition for the first several months of his children's dance study at the Alvienne School.

Their adventure began with Fritz driving Johanna and their two children to the train depot in the family horse and buggy. The parents lugged their baggage onto the train and deposited it on the seats. Freddie, dressed in a winter coat, hat, and scarf, yelled out, "I don't care if anybody gets to New York as long as I do." Adele, in a similar outfit, couldn't hide her pigtails. She addressed her momentarily boisterous little brother with a "Oh, shut up!" retort. As their train pulled away, Freddie looked back at his father waving.

Their two-day, two-night journey, which included changing trains in Chicago, ended at New York's Pennsylvania Station on a cold, windy, gray day in January 1905. So many people dashed by, all in a terrible hurry.[15] Johanna then led her charges to a hansom cab that took them to the inexpensive Herald Square Hotel, only a few blocks away, which had been suggested by Claude Alvienne as a suitable place for them to live. Their hotel room was spartanly equipped with three cots and a small kitchen.

Their first few days were spent sightseeing—the elevated trains, the Flatiron Building, and the subway. The following Monday morning, as planned, Freddie and Adele, clinging to their mother's outstretched hands, arrived at the Grand Opera House Building, located at Eighth Avenue and Twenty-third Street. Climbing up the narrow staircase, Johanna opened the door to Claude Alvienne's Dance School. Its unimposing layout consisted of one large room styled like a small ballroom, complete with three mirrored walls with cane chairs and a small stage at one end of the room. The cream-colored walls were peeling, and the mirrors were equally seedy. This was the dance school they had traveled almost fifteen hundred miles to attend.

The fatherly, white-haired Alvienne directed his pupils by beating the time with a stick, hitting the back of one of the dusty cane chairs. The two neophytes from Omaha happily joined in with the other pupils, young, more experienced New Yorkers, as they practiced theory, drama, music, and dance. When Johanna returned at the end of the day to pick them up, her children rejoiced in relating all they had learned that day.

They would then return to the hotel, where, following up on her background as a schoolteacher, Johanna would assume her other role as tutor, leading them through their paces in the three R's. In his spare time, Freddie would work at his newly discovered hobby by practicing the piano, perhaps a residual from his father, at the Alvienne School by running down scales.

*   *   *

AN ENTIRELY NEW ENVIRONMENT faced them at the Herald Square Hotel, which was essentially a boardinghouse. There they encountered many diverse people—all kinds of transients and senior citizens—and overcoming their initial shyness, they befriended them. Their newly adopted cosmopolitan city intrigued them. As an integral part of their overall education, Johanna, who had shortened her first name to Anna, took them to Broadway to see plays starring John Drew Jr., Lillie Langtry, Laurette Taylor, Maud Adams, and Ethel Barrymore. In their first exposure to a major professional dancer, they made repeat visits, encouraged by their mother, to witness the greatness of the Danish ballerina Adeline Genée, in *The Soul Kiss.* (Freddie claimed to have seen it twenty-eight times.)

In material cut from his autobiography, *Steps in Time*, which Fred Astaire personally handwrote in a perfectly legible script, he admitted he didn't get to play much with kids his own age in the Eighth Avenue and Twenty-third Street area near the opera house. "Mother wouldn't let us leave the stoop. If we did play outside the front door, we were not allowed out in the street." Despite waxing enthusiastic about the various friends he made, Anna evidently recognized the lurking evils of the big city and maintained a tight rein over her children.

Anna and her children had every intention of eventually returning to Omaha. Years later, when they played there, she described their New York venture in a local Omaha newspaper article. "There was no idea of a career. We were just trying to give the children the best possible start. It was plain that Adele had real ability. We just made sure she used it."[16]

Alvienne and his wife, a former dancer, known professionally as La Neva, made Freddie and Adele feel comfortable in their school, never scolding but patiently correcting them when they made mistakes.[17] That they showed a keen aptitude for learning was of equal importance. As they began to progress in their training, it was suddenly Freddie who took their work much more seriously. Rhythm and movement especially interested him. Every new step and dance routine he and Adele learned caused him to want to repeat it over and over until it was perfect.[18] "Mr. Alvienne is going to make a big star out of me," he exclaimed. Adele countered with "Don't be silly. That's me."[19]

A PROMINENT NEW YORK psychiatrist, Dr. Lonnie MacDonald, who has treated countless artists as part of an over forty-year practice, made a study of Fred Astaire's career and noted his seemingly limitless need to excel. "Fred obviously had a powerful drive for self-expression. His drive for affection and self-expression manifested itself in the dance, and it was his outlet to discover the unique individual truth within himself. It would suggest that his relationship with Adele was a fascinatingly cooperative one for the most part. He was able to subjugate himself not just in the work, but he also saw to it that he didn't get involved in any kind of egoism.

"The mother must have been the key. More than a pushy stage mother, she was nice to her children and made them work hard. The father was at home earning the bread, constantly in touch with his wife and the kids on the road, encouraging them.

"Fred was learning, and he was learning because of his genius. I am using the term now, where an individual can really penetrate and know how something works. This entailed his being able to have a relationship with his sister where they were able to cooperate. It's not that usual for siblings to have the kind of relationship they had. He had a lot of self-doubt in him, but his capacity to learn and overcome and a want to practice and express to himself, 'Yes sir, that's beautiful to me.' To him, the work was what was important. Nothing else was."

TO SHOW WHAT they had learned thus far, Adele and Freddie appeared in a showcase at the Alvienne ballroom. Adding a bulbous putty nose, Adele assumed the title role in a scene from *Cyrano de Bergerac*, with Freddie, adorable in a blond wig and a satin gown, playing Cyrano's dream girl, Roxane. Switching genders in the casting wasn't the least bit bizarre as Adele was then three inches taller than Fred. She claimed, "Freddie was quite the most adorable thing."[20]

The karma of New York elegance manifested itself in a bride-and-groom sketch a few months later, in which, for the first time, Fred was dressed in a top hat, white tie, and black satin knickerbockers for a twelve-minute sketch designed by Alvienne. (Tails were too difficult for Anna to make; an oversized black overcoat took their place.) Two large wedding cakes were fitted with bells that could be played with their hands and feet plus electric lightbulbs that flashed on and off. Fred and Adele played "Dreamland Waltz" on the bells as they danced on and around the cakes in a zany routine. On its conclusion, the duo returned for solo spots, Fred tap dancing and playing the piano briefly, followed by Adele performing a short ballet routine. The finale found Fred in a bright red costume playing a lobster, and Adele in a billowing skirt as a glass of champagne. The lobster and the glass of champagne danced another eccentric duet, then played more tunes on the musical cakes. They bowed off to generous applause.

The name "Austerlitz," as a stage name, bothered both Anna and Alvienne. With Fritz being consulted on this matter, a protracted search for a new surname was begun. "Auster" was the first name given a brief consideration before being rejected. "Astier" then seemed right. Adele and Freddie used it in their next few appearances at Alvienne's ballroom. "Astier," however, was thought to sound too French, and any semblance of a foreign name seemed inappropriate. As a compromise, they tried the name "Astaire." (According to Fred, the name probably derived from the family's uncle from Alsace-Lorraine, named L'Astaire.) The name "Astaire" was remindful of the wealthy Astors, an important family in New York society, dating back to the post-industrial-revolution period. It had the aura of success. To Alvienne, "Astaire" brought to mind Astarte, the goddess of productive energy.[21] By now the informality of Adele and Freddie had also been transformed into the more urbane billing of "Fred and Adele," and in turn, Anna had become Ann.

Dick Cavett noted, "Marlon Brando, who hailed from Nebraska, told me that Jews had been treated with distain for many years in Omaha. Marlon also said that he always understood that Fred had come from a Jewish heritage." Perhaps this influenced Fritz Austerlitz's decision to agree to change the family name. One can never know for sure, but the zeitgeist in Omaha at the time seemed to favor the change.

Looking back on that time, Fred claimed he was so young that he never even remembered having any last name but Astaire. He did, however, acknowledge hearing his mother discussing a name change. He recalled believing that "Austerlitz" sounded too much like a battle. Looking back on the name change, Adele concurred that Austerlitz "was a clumsy name. We needed something simpler and shorter that would fit on theater marques."[22]

Although they were now six and a half and nine, the dance act of Fred and Adele Astaire was too good not to go on the road. In addition, money was getting tight. Retired CIA agent Michael Russell, perhaps as a result of his investigative training, discovered that Fred and Adele actually made their vaudeville debut in Newport, Rhode Island, rather than Keyport, New Jersey, as has been credited. On a postcard, contained in Russell's vast trove of Astaire memorabilia, Ann reported on a successful engagement in Newport that predated the North Jersey booking.

Regardless of which engagement marked Fred and Adele's first professional engagement, it seems apparent that Claude Alvienne made the Keyport booking at the Pier Theatre in November 1905 possible. They were merely the opening act, as "Juvenile Artists Presenting an Electric Musical Toe-Dancing Novelty."[23] They repeated their successful routine with the two wedding cakes. The notoriously exacting Keyport audience, who had seen a plethora of young vaudevillians breaking in their acts, applauded them wildly. The local newspaper reviewer went so far as to label Fred and Adele as "the greatest child act in vaudeville."[24] Looking back on this gig, Fred said, "I think if two words had been added, 'in Keyport,' this might have been more accurate."

For their split-week engagement they were paid $30. Fritz, reading the favorable notice, was duly impressed and began coming to New York more often for consultation with his troupers. He enjoyed the wide spectrum of entertainment that New York offered, but, in addition, his outgoing personality brought him into contact with agents and producers.[25]

Soon, the Astaires played theaters in Atlantic City, Perth Amboy, Passaic, Paterson, Newark, and Union Hill in New Jersey, and Philadelphia, Shamokin, Pottstown, and Lancaster in neighboring Pennsylvania, and they ventured out to St. Paul, Minnesota, as well. Following this extensive tour, they opened their first professional New York engagement at the Broadway Theatre on New Year's Eve 1907. That booking, however, was cut short by the Gerry Society, the watchdog agency that closely enforced child labor laws. Child performers were supposed to be at least fourteen (in some states sixteen) to appear onstage—a law that was frequently winked at throughout vaudeville.

This setback led to almost six months of unemployment before a nine-city tour during the summer and fall of 1908. Fred and Adele kept up with their dancing lessons and Ann's tutoring. Fred was still the more serious student. Adele was quicker in learning but didn't enjoy studying. She paid more attention to her paper dolls.

Fred fondly remembered their mother as "one of the most lovely persons you could ever imagine. She was very gentle and very amusing. Her sense of humor was always there."[26] (Ava Astaire McKenzie, Fred's daughter, remarked that even when Ann was in her eighties, "She would suggest things to Daddy and Aunt Dellie, and they would listen intently to what she said.")

Ann quickly learned how things worked in vaudeville. A resourceful woman, she picked up extra money sewing costumes for other performers and working as a cue-card reader in theaters. Unlike the stereotypical stage mother Mama Rose, the mother of Gypsy Rose Lee and June Havoc, as depicted in *Gypsy,* the Broadway musical, Ann developed a reputation as "a terribly nice mother," which helped the young Astaires gain a favorable reputation with fellow performers and aided her in dealing with agents and theater managers.

It was Fritz, however, who scored a major coup by getting his children a spot on the prestigious Orpheum Circuit. This happened by his inducing Frank Vincent, the booker for the Orpheum Circuit, to see them perform in Paterson, New Jersey. The Orpheum contract guaranteed them an astounding $150 a week for a twenty-week tour with rail transportation for Fred and Adele and Ann included.

(The average skilled worker in the United States was then making less than $2 a week.)[27]

Their cross-country journey—Pennsylvania, Iowa, Colorado, Washington, California, Utah, Nebraska, Minnesota, Wisconsin, with a stop in Omaha, was of primary importance in learning what life on the road was all about. They appeared as the opening act on bills comprising everything from musicians to dog acts in a series of two- or three-a-day performances over grueling one-week, split-week, and one-night bookings, often under the worst conditions—"the headaches, the heartaches, the backaches, the flops, the audience that lifts you when you're down" (lyrics from Irving Berlin's "There's No Business Like Show Business," copyright April 24, 1946, Irving Berlin Music Company). Yet Fred enjoyed the entire experience (including, of course, traveling by train), and in recalling this tour he was hopelessly upbeat. While not onstage, he began to pursue his lifelong study of other performers, concentrating in particular on acrobats, jugglers, and tap dancers, watching their work from the wings or the back of the theater, while Adele remained in the dressing room.[28]

Another team they appeared with on the Orpheum Circuit was George Burns and Gracie Allen, who would costar with Fred decades later in the RKO film musical *A Damsel in Distress*. This tour gave Fred and Adele the foundation for everything that lay ahead in their careers. By the time the Orpheum tour was completed, they were suddenly qualified vaudevillians whose song-and-dance act showed an understanding and appreciation of their craft.[29]

"I was more of a singer than a dancer at that time," Fred recalled. ". . . I had developed from nowhere a big voice. Pray don't ask me how or where it went. . . . I had sung 'My Big Brother Sylvester,' in an Italian dialect, and there had been comment by theatre managers that, 'They'd better not tinker with his pipes or they'll ruin his voice.' "[30]

At this juncture, the obvious differences in their respective personalities began to assert themselves. Adele was an ingenious practical joker, who relished improvising outrageously onstage while exhibiting her often outlandish behavior. This was in stark contrast to Fred, who grew more and more immersed in his stage work. Adele reflected, "When he was off dancing by himself, he sort of invented things. I was the clown . . . I liked to be funny. I couldn't be bothered learning all those steps."[31]

In their December 1908 engagement at the Orpheum Omaha Theatre, where they had once been part of the audience, they were a triumph. As Fred glowingly stated, "One huge basket of flowers for Adele contained a lime white poodle," a gift from the Geilus family. Despite the enthusiastic reaction of those who come to see them perform, their newspaper reviews were brief and the *World-Herald* referred to Fred as Harry! The National Corn Show at the City Auditorium got more attention.

THE MIDWEST WAS THEN RAMPANT with dry laws and blue laws, which predated Prohibition. As a result of this antialcohol stance, the Storz Brewery in Omaha had to diversify by making ice, near beer, and other nonalcoholic drinks. This downswing in the beer business forced Fritz to take a cut in salary, but that wasn't all that was going wrong. A Geilus cousin, Helene Geilus, and a local historian, Herold Becker, reported that Fritz was living with another woman in the family household. He continued to make trips to New York once or twice a year, but the marriage to Ann was in disrepair. Somehow, she managed to shield the truth from Fred and Adele.

After the completion of the Orpheum tour, Fritz joined the family for a vacation in Asbury Park, New Jersey. They made plans for the act, taking stock of Fred's having grown a few inches, as had Adele, who was still taller than her brother. In addition, she had developed a sophisticated air. Ann feared that theater managers would soon notice the serious differences between her offspring.

The Gerry Society came back into the picture. To get around it, but still having to deal with their being underage performers, Fred wore long pants offstage and had his hair slicked down, while Adele began wearing lipstick and rouge. A representative from the local branch had come to investigate the act during their appearance at the Orpheum in Los Angeles. Ann did some fast talking by explaining that her son was a late bloomer and expressed complete surprise when questioned why his high-pitched voice hadn't changed.

To compound this problem, Adele adopted the mannerism of dancers several years her senior and inevitably began looking completely ludicrous working with her kid brother. One day a theater manager delivered the ultimate insult to Ann: "The girl seems to have talent, but the boy can do nothing!" She reluctantly informed Adele but pledged her to secrecy. Unfortunately, due to their closeness, Adele then told Fred, which both shocked and angered him. Ann attempted to placate him, but it was to no avail. In a few days he recovered, but Ann foresaw the problems ahead.

This was the watershed moment in the early years of Fred Astaire's career. Dr. MacDonald observed, "Like most great artists he was racked with insecurities. Over the next several years, he had to constantly deal with an often indifferent reaction to his work. His sensitivity was nurtured in ways from his early childhood that enabled him to avoid being wounded by various life experiences. This spurred him into concentrating even more in developing his talent—the long hours working on new steps, turns, the proper arm movements—just some of the many facets that eventually contributed to his becoming the compleat dancer.

"It seems apparent that Fred also took stock of his shy and retiring nature and saw this as an asset, not a liability. He believed, 'Everyone relates to Adele—she is much more outgoing—but if I can continue working hard on my dancing and eventually make my own valuable contribution, people will start paying attention to me. We'll be equals in the act. Mother will like that, too.' This is where his never-ending need and drive to seek perfection found its roots. Though he was the male lead in the act, he was still walking in Adele's footsteps."

Ann decided to retire the act temporarily—or until Fred could catch up to his faster-maturing sister so that the Gerry Society would no longer pose a threat to their future. The wedding-cake act, which had served them well, was permanently retired. Money from the Orpheum Circuit tour enabled them to settle in an inexpensive house in Highland Park, the residential section of Weehawken, New Jersey, for two years.

For the first time, Fred and Adele began formal schooling. As Fred entered the fifth grade at the Highland Park School, he began learning French and started to play baseball, which was to become one of his favorite pastimes. Adele at first found life a bit dull after life on the road, but soon settled into the usual life of an adolescent schoolgirl. Their musical endeavors were restricted to playing triangles in the school orchestra.

In Highland Park, Ann drew several admirers, including a wealthy widower who wanted to marry her and adopt her children, but she declined, explaining that her husband would soon be coming for a visit. She saw no future without her children and her independence.

But once again, money eventually became an important issue. Ann wanted Fred and Adele to attend a vaudeville school that would put them back in the business. With the estrangement from Fritz, she had now assumed the role of personal manager of her children as well. As often happened with the Astaires, it took time for a serious decision to be made, but as usual, it turned out to be the right one. In 1911 the young dance team enrolled at Ned Wayburn's school on New York's West Forty-fourth Street, a ferry ride across the Hudson River.

Wayburn had a thorough knowledge of dance as shown by his frequent assignments as a choreographer for the eminent Broadway impresario Florenz Ziegfeld. Fred and Adele learned musical-comedy dancing, "tap and step dancing" (a phrase Fred coined),[32] acrobatic dancing, exhibition, and modern American ballet.[33] They claimed years later that in the six months they spent at Wayburn's school they learned more than at any other stage of their early career. Wayburn, too, saw a future for Adele, but wasn't at all sure if Fred really had one.

For a short time, Ann seriously considered bringing in an already written act so that Adele could work as a solo dancer, and perhaps Fred could have his own act as well. Wayburn instead saw them as a double act based on his own concept. The cost would be $1,000, a substantial fee, but in addition Wayburn would rehearse the act and secure work so that he could be paid for his services.

Fred and Adele referred to their new act as either "A Rainy Saturday" or "The Baseball Act." Wayburn's idea was for Fred to appear in a gray pin-striped New York Giants baseball uniform with a logo identifying THE LITTLE GIANTS while Adele wore a summer dress. A rainstorm compels them to stay indoors. They while away the time discussing how Adele's first beau will propose to her. Ann supplied an offstage voice. This is followed by Fred in a top hat (which never quite fit him), playing "Father," stumbling home dead drunk. (This segment was supposedly based on Fritz and Ann.)[34] He is immediately harangued by his "wife," played by Adele. The twelve-minute act included two song-and-dance numbers, one being "When Uncle Joe Plays a Rag on His Old Banjo," which Fred played on the piano. The finale featured Adele playing piano.[35] The act jelled and finally they had a fully professional routine with a future.

Wayburn suggested that Fred discontinue his study of ballet to develop his tap-dancing skills. This decision had important implications in the future direction of Fred's dancing. Wayburn later commented that Fred was the first American tap dancer to consciously employ the full resources of his arms, hands, and torso for visual ornamentation. "He dances to American rhythms and with an air of gay spontaneity that consummation reflects the folk origins of his art. Debonair, exultant, amused, he has imported to the tap dance an elegance and mobility of which the cloggers and minstrels of the last century never dreamed."

This sudden flurry of activity necessitated the family's moving to Manhattan. They found a boardinghouse close to Wayburn's school. Weeks of rehearsal preceded Wayburn's plan to debut the act in a Sunday-night benefit program he was producing at the Broadway Theatre. The *Morning Telegraph* observed, "Fred and Adele Astaire are a clever singing and dancing team." Their grown-up presentation was so well received that they were booked for a week, opening on February 19, 1912, at Proctor's Fifth Avenue Vaudeville Theatre at Broadway and Twenty-sixth Street, their first important New York engagement.

At Proctor's, the Astaires encountered the debonair stage star and soon-to-be Hollywood leading man Douglas Fairbanks, who was the headliner, appearing in a sketch called "A Regular Business Man." (In those days legit stars often made brief vaudeville tours between plays.) Fred had previously seen Fairbanks appear on Broadway and regarded him as a model for someone to emulate with his dashing and elegant manner that complemented his stylish clothes. This chance meeting inspired Fred to seek a new direction in his personal style, one that would soon have a far-reaching effect on his entire career.

Unfortunately, for their first performance at Proctor's, the Astaires were the opening act. "How can they do this to us?" Fred complained to Adele. "People will be walking in and they'll miss all our dialogue." Adele tried to buoy her brother's emotions by saying, "Oh, come on, Freddie, we'll just have to be so terrific that the manager will just have to give us a better spot for the evening show." They received an indifferent response to their jokes, songs, and dances, however, from a spare audience during the afternoon performance and were summarily fired. Adele later recalled the desperate feeling that followed: "We had been a couple of cutesy kids, and we were fine, but then we'd got bigger and we weren't so cute anymore."[36]

News of their failure in New York spread throughout the vaudeville business. On a date at a New Jersey theater, they were barraged with coins from the balcony.[37] This downturn resulted in a paucity of bookings during the late winter, spring, and summer of 1912. They were forced to work for lower-echelon vaudeville circuits such as the United Booking Office and the Gus Sun circuit beginning that fall. Fred reminisced, "We opened more shows for Keith [the Keith Circuit] than any other act." Working frequently, however, allowed them to hone aspects of their act.

In all of 1913, they worked only five five-day engagements. But by the beginning of 1914, their bookings improved. Adele then began calling her brother Moaning Minnie, reflecting his constant anxiety. This became the moniker she constantly used in describing him for the rest of his life.

Their years in vaudeville had instilled in Fred an appreciation for ragtime, one of the precursors to jazz. He watched in awe as the black tap dancers danced to ragtime. As part of his study, he became friendly with "Bojangles" Robinson, a star on the Keith Circuit. "Bill Robinson was a buck dancer. He plays turns with his feet as effortlessly and as accurately as a fine drummer plays a snare drum. I admired him, but I didn't do what he did—the wooden shoes up and down stairs. I like to get my feet in the air and move around," Astaire remembered.[38] "John 'Bubbles' Sublett was different. I don't know whether he used tap shoes or not, but he was stylish. I used to meet him occasionally, and we'd try steps together, but at that point in my career I wasn't doing much tap dancing."

Despite the increasingly favorable acceptance from audiences and house managers, the reviews in the press kept emphasizing the same old saw—Fred was the weak link in the act. The *Detroit Free Press* wrote, "For her personality and charm, Adele Astaire outshines anyone who has appeared here in months." The *Philadelphia North American* noted, "The bill began with a pair of excellent dancers, the girl, who was also the possessor of remarkable good looks, being especially graceful of movement." The *Boston Record* said, "Fred and Adele Astaire gave a fine exhibition of whirlwind dancing, although it would be wished that the young man gives up some of the blasé air which he carries constantly with him. He is too young for it and deceives no one."[39]

Fred, now in his teens, was still driven to seek an identity that would bring attention to his own ability, out of the shadow of the consistently glowing notices afforded his sister. For Fred, ballet was not the answer. His aversion to ballet would endure for the duration of his career as a dancer. Though he had greatly admired Adeline Genée on Broadway, he had had only a few weeks of ballet training. He had developed an aversion to the stiff postures that were so much an essential ingredient of ballet. In addition, he felt ballet was effeminate.

Nijinsky brought a strong male presence to ballet, but Fred had never seen him perform. As much as he admired Vernon and Irene Castle, whom he had seen dance together on Broadway, he didn't want to become a ballroom dancer.[40]

ANN SAVED SOME MONEY so that they could enjoy a summer vacation in 1914 at the Delaware Water Gap in Pennsylvania. Fred learned to play golf, which became a passion of his that lasted until his final years. He admitted, "I was so crazy about golf I couldn't sleep nights. It was a sporty little nine-hole course at [the] Water Gap—big rocks in the middle of the fairways. . . . I used to tour it in about forty blows and sometimes under, which the pro told me was pretty good for a kid of fifteen. . . . I had a terrific desire to be a golf pro, and, of course, it all vanished in the wintertime when I went back to my vaudeville hoofing."[41]

Adele spent her time swimming, riding horses, and dancing with socialites. The Delaware Water Gap was then a prominent Eastern society resort. Exposure to the swells led the Astaires to begin to think that the carefree life of the smart set appealed to them—a total departure from living in Omaha or life on the road in vaudeville. During these years, the act worked infrequently in the summer. They often split those months between the Gap and Atlantic City.

Mary Pickford, the foremost female film star of the silent era, arrived to shoot a short subject, *Fanchon, the Cricket,* at the Delaware Water Gap. Tim Satchell's Astaire biography contends that this was the only film Fred and Adele appeared in together, although it was merely a bit part. (Fred had absolutely no recollection of their ever working in the film.) This second exposure to a major star in such a short time fascinated them as they were awestruck by moviemaking.

By now, "The Baseball Act" was passé, as the two participants had simply become too old for it. When Fritz, now living in Detroit, arrived at the Delaware Water Gap for a visit, he also recognized that a new direction was needed. Fred had grown tired of dancing on his toes, calling it "sissy stuff," and made a fateful change in his dancing presentation. He realized that tap dancing had become commercial, and he adopted from Bojangles Robinson and John Bubbles as well as the elegant routines of Vernon and Irene Castle as the basis of his new inspiration.

Once again, Fritz took charge of the situation and contacted Aurelia Coccia, through reading about him in the theatrical press. Coccia and his wife, Minnie Amato, were veteran vaudevillians, well-known for their flash act "The Apple of Paris." Coccia became a mentor who was instrumental in the development of the children's talent. Fred called Coccia "the most influential, as far as dancing goes, of any man in my career." The Coccias also taught the Astaires the tango, but concentrated foremost on developing their showmanship.

One day Fred, who blanched at even the most trifling criticism, overheard Coccia informing Ann that "the kids would have to forget everything they had ever learned and start over," which absolutely horrified him and Adele. Coccia's observation was apparently intended as a "pep talk." Their six months of intensive study with the Coccias was specifically designed to create a much more adult presentation for the youngsters.

The new, more streamlined act trimmed unnecessary dialogue that had slowed down "The Baseball Act." It also incorporated fresh song-and-dance elements, plus some of their old routines, including again a spot for Fred to play piano.[42] It was rightfully dubbed "New Songs and Smart Dances."

Fred brought in his own thoughts about musical selections, trying out various current pop songs on the piano.[43] This followed his making the rounds of various music publishers seeking new material. He acknowledged, "At one point, I really wanted to give up every other side of show business to concentrate on composing."[44]

Being half of an unknown act, however, made it extremely difficult for him to be offered anything of real value. (At that time, songs were usually given out by music publishers on an almost exclusive basis.) Only after several approaches to Irving Berlin's partner Ted Snyder was Fred given use of Berlin's "I Love to Quarrel with You" and "I've Got a Sweet Tooth Bothering Me," as well as Snyder's "Love Made One a Wonderful Detective." The latter was a rather typical vaudeville tune that perfectly fit the act.

"New Songs and Smart Dances" opened in a blackout with Fred offstage yelling, "Stop! Stop! Don't you dare move! You're under arrest!" Adele, also offstage, sang in reply, "What have I done to you?" Fred answered, "Stop, stop! I've got you covered! See that badge on my chest?" Fred pulled Adele onstage as the lights came up and the pair went into "Love Made Me a Wonderful Detective." They continued with tap dances and "I Love to Quarrel with You," sung by Adele, and an adagio number.[45]

In the few recorded examples of their singing together, Adele has the more theatrical voice and a more spirited and zesty approach to a song. Fred was well aware that in his postadolescence he didn't have much of a voice and had only a limited range. His rather tentative delivery concentrated on the lyric content of the songs with an obvious bent toward sincerity. His primary interest was in expressing the truth of a song, but, in addition, the rhythms inherent in dance had contributed to his exacting sense of time.

When they took their more sophisticated song-and-dance act on the road, success on the East Coast followed. In Woonsocket, Rhode Island, however, Adele stuck her tongue out at an audience that wasn't responding to them. This led to a tongue-lashing from the theater owner. She abruptly called him "a stupid fucker."[46] In New Haven and Boston, Yale and Harvard students were quite taken by the sassy Adele, while Fred admired their sport cars, raccoon coats, and blue blazers. This reciprocal admiration led to their developing a college following as well.

After almost a decade of pursuing a vaudeville career, the traveling Astaires underwent some changes within their family relationship. Not surprisingly, Fred took complete charge of the material for the act and rehearsals. His choreography was designed to make Adele the focal point of the act.

In a 1975 interview he said, "Mother always thought she was the better dancer."[47] Ann continued to take care of all the traveling arrangements. Adele was distinctly antirehearsal. She was much more interested in cultivating the attention of her suitors and in generally having a good time. Only reluctantly would she find time to work on new routines with her brother.

The theatrical tradition was not inbred in Adele. As she later described it, "It was an acquired taste—like olives." Adele started referring to Fred as "my big brother," which reflected his now being the taller, but this was in time interpreted as his being the elder. Fred started calling Adele "my young sister" as a protective gesture. Their respective ages became lost in the shuffle. Fred's serious demeanor from being in charge of the act and feeling responsible for his mother and sister was the antithesis of Adele's constant let-the-good-times-roll attitude.

With all of these on- and offstage changes, it was time to seek new representation from an agent who really believed in them. Lew Golden, a small-time agent, and his associate Max Hayes, did the job. They moved quickly and booked the act on the Orpheum Circuit, only this time for $175 a week.[48]

Fred, Adele, and Ann set out on tour across Canada and then down to Detroit, where a vaudeville strike called the White Rats left them stranded. Ann was compelled to pawn a diamond lavaliere and a fur coat to allow them to eat. Fred vividly remembered that one day Ann was compelled to cut up hard-boiled eggs for him and his sister to share.

In Detroit, continuing his constant search for new songs, Fred spent time at the Jerome H. Remick music publishing office. There he became friendly with Richard Whiting, the father of singer Margaret Whiting, and the composer of "Japanese Sandman," "Beyond the Blue Horizon," "Louise," "She's Funny That Way," "Sleepy Time Gal," "Hooray for Hollywood," and other standards. Taking stock of the family's dire financial situation, Fred somehow believed that he could write a hit song on the spur of the moment. At that time, the shy and self-effacing dancer and singer was ill-equipped to write a song of any consequence, and despite Whiting's tutelage, his dream of writing a hit song would have to wait for almost a quarter century.

In desperation, the Astaires worked a nonunion show with many other acts that Margaret Whiting believes his father booked for them. This time they were pelted with flour, eggs, tomatoes, and a barrage of insults. The show closed immediately thereafter. They spent weeks moping around the city, walking everywhere. Finally, the strike ended, and Lew Golden got them work on the Deep South Circuit.[49]

The constant ups and downs caused Fred to become even more determined to present the act in the best possible light. His fast-developing perfectionism came to the forefront. This included his insistence that their music be correctly played by house bands that could range from a pianist and a drummer to a ten-piece band. He saw to it that particular attention was paid to tempos and cues.

Now that they were reestablishing themselves, important headliners looked at them in a new light. In Davenport, Iowa, Bill Robinson watched their act and remarked to Fred, "Boy, you can dance!" Fred had recently begun playing pool and billiards, which led to Robinson's inviting him to spend an evening with him at a pool parlor. Fred marveled at how deftly the famous tap dancer could entice a group of pool hustlers into playing several games with him, then systematically trouncing them with ease.[50]

In New Orleans, at the Orpheum, the Astaires were a last-minute substitute. In the fifth position on the bill, they were a smash. This engagement proved they could handle a key spot in a long-running vaudeville show.

They resumed playing the entire Orpheum Circuit except for Los Angeles and San Francisco, where only the foremost acts worked. By then their weekly salary had been raised to $225 a week. Even after being stuck once again as the opening act, at the Majestic in Chicago, they stopped the show and took six bows before the stage manager insisted on still another one. At last, after years of constant struggle, a future with steady bookings finally seemed probable.

During the Orpheum tour, they appeared on the same bill with two well-established family acts. The first was Eduardo and Elisa Cansino. Fred called Eduardo, "a beautiful dancer who was really an ideal of mine." Adele was equally taken with the sleek Spaniard, but much to Ann's relief nothing came of her infatuation. (A quarter of a century later, Fred would costar in two films opposite Cansino's daughter, Rita Hayworth.) Fred also praised "The Seven Little Foys" as wonderful kids. "We made a very big hit, and they were very nice to us about the success we made."[51]

In Chicago, during a week at the Palace Theatre, they were switched from opening act to third on the bill. The renowned comedian Eddie Cantor was the headliner. One day the nervous Cantor watched them performing and paced up and down, waiting to go on, and shouted out, "What is this—the Gans-Nelson fight?"[52] (The celebrated 1908 battle between two lightweight boxers, one white and one black.) This appearance was a major breakthrough and was part of a fourteen-city tour. They were routed back to New York for two back-to-back weekly engagements to end the year 1915.

Fred continued to pursue finding new songs for the act. Again visiting the Jerome H. Remick office, he met a young piano player named George Gershwin, who was demonstrating the firm's new songs. Fred was dazzled by Gershwin's upbeat personality and the fast runs of the pianist. They struck up on immediate friendship. Fred exclaimed how much he and his sister yearned to appear in musical comedies. Gershwin then offered a prophetic suggestion to his newfound friend: "Wouldn't it be great if someday I would write a musical and you'd be in it?"[53]

Fred selected songs by Jerome Kern ("They Wouldn't Believe Me") and Cole Porter ("I've a Shooting Box in Scotland"), which were perfectly suited to the growing sophistication and lively spirit of the "New Songs" act. In the spring of 1916 the Astaires reached their peak in vaudeville, according to Fred.[54] They played the choice metropolitan circuit in New York—the Colonial, the Alhambra, the Royal in the Bronx, the Orpheum in Brooklyn, and Keith's Washington for the second time.

Continuing their momentum, their 1916–17 tour encompassed some twenty-five cities. They were now commanding $350 a week wherever they performed and were a hit almost everywhere. Their ability and versatility as dancers, plus their style and gaiety, coupled with their closeness as siblings who perfectly complemented each other, were the ingredients that made them such a perfect combination.

A booking at the Palace in New York at Forty-seventh and Broadway was the dream of every vaudeville act. An offer to play the vaunted theater, however, never materialized for the Astaires. As a calculated career move, in June 1917, Fred reserved the back cover of *Variety,* at a cost of $150, to display for the eyes of the industry their most recent glowing notices. The title of the advertisement was DOING BIG IN THE WEST, WHAT WILL THE EAST SAY?

Though today such trade-paper advertisements are for the most part a relic of the past, certain important theatrical figures read the Astaires' notice with keen interest. One of them was Lee Shubert, who, with his brother Jake, had launched Al Jolson on Broadway and, as a result, had become important impresarios. The Shuberts showed an interest in having the brother and sister act appear in their forthcoming musical *The Nine O'Clock Revue.*

A week after the *Variety* advertisement appeared, the agent Rufus Le Maire notified Fred with a short but pithy statement, "Lee Shubert wants to see you." On hearing the news, Adele shrieked in ecstasy, while her more reserved brother broke into a wide grin. "We're going to have to polish up the act," he said cautiously. Adele was suddenly not so reluctant to rehearse.[55]

Ann picked out the proper wardrobe for the meeting with Lee Shubert. They signed a contract to appear in their first Broadway show. Vaudeville was now behind them. A dozen years of paying dues was at last over for Fred and Adele Astaire.

CHAPTER TWO

"THE RUNAROUND"

O N NOVEMBER 28, 1917, the Astaires opened on Broadway as featured players in a Shubert revue. This is just one indication of how far they had come and how much they offered as performers. Fred was eighteen and Adele was twenty-one. Vaudeville had been the training ground. Broadway was indeed "the Main Stem." It was where all young performers who played vaudeville yearned to be accepted, and the Astaires were the latest in a tradition of Broadway greats.

Former vaudevillian Will Rogers, then thirty-eight, was already an established Broadway headliner starring in *The Ziegfeld Follies of 1917.* Also starring in that same production were other former vaudevillians such as twenty-six-year-old comedienne Fanny Brice, as well as fellow comedians Bert Williams, forty, Eddie Cantor, twenty-five, and thirty-eight-year-old W. C. Fields.

Broadway headliners weren't at that time considered celebrities the way they are today. What was important for young performers was to make a good impression on fellow performers and producers. For the Astaires, having the good fortune to be able to establish a permanent home, which they did at the Hotel Woodward at Fifty-first and Broadway, and having the opportunity to perform on Broadway were satisfying in themselves.

The score for the Shubert revue was written by the celebrated composer Sigmund Romberg. The former Ziegfeld beauty Justine Johnston and Mary Eaton were the leads.[1] Starting out in New Haven, after six weeks of rehearsal in New York, the Astaires reveled in having a sizable claque of Yale students wildly applauding their nightly performance. After the opening-night performance, the Yalies stormed onstage and took the pair to supper at the Taft Hotel next to the Shubert. They were soon invited to attend various fraternity parties on the campus. The Shuberts took notice of the Astaires' collegiate following by placing this amazing phrase in the show's program to introduce them: "To make the lucidity of the libretto conspicuous, the following musical interpretations take place . . ." Fred and Adele did three numbers together in the show and also participated in comic sketches.

As often happens with out-of-town tryouts (especially with musicals), the New Haven engagement had its problems. Replacing T. Roy Barnes in New Haven was the veteran vaudeville comedian Ed Wynn, whose friendship with Fred was cemented by their common passion for golf and Wynn's penchant for telling an array of jokes. The title of the show, *The Nine O'Clock Revue,* was changed as its starting time became 8:30 instead of 9:00 P.M., and it was now called *Over the Top.*

The Forty-fourth Street Roof Theater audience for the patriotic-themed extravaganza was looking for an escape from the news of the stalemate of trench warfare in France during World War I. Despite its name change and its theme, the show was not destined to endure as a Broadway hit, lasting only seventy-eight performances.

But as Louis Sherwin of the *New York Globe* saw it, "One of the prettiest features of the show is the dancing of the two Astaires. The girl, a light, spirit-like little creature, has really an exquisite flooding style in her capering, while the young man combines agility with humor."[2] Richard Henry Little of the *Journal of Commerce* observed, "Fred Astaire materially assists in passing the time in *Over the Top.* He is a nimble, graceful dancer of the whirlwind variety, with a few new kinks and gyrations that he is pioneering." The hard work of the male half of the partnership was causing the critics to take notice.

Over the Top went out on tour. Sometimes, being a part of a mediocre production can yield an unexpected dividend. One night in Washington, at the Garrick Theatre, the producer Charles Dillingham caught the show, and the Astaires caught his eye. Dillingham wanted them for his next show, but they were committed to the Shuberts for their next production, *The Passing Show of 1918.*[3]

The Astaires would have much preferred to have been given an offer from Ziegfeld to appear in the *Follies,* but no offer was forthcoming, "although, we had heard rumors that he was interested in our work," Fred commented. Before rehearsals began for *The Passing Show,* at eighteen, Fred became eligible for military service. He got his draft card, but the war ended before he was called.

Adele was constantly besieged by would-be suitors. Fred's innate shyness, however, had long since made it difficult for him to develop serious female relationships. He was surrounded by good looks and glamour in the theatrical world, but his long chin, prominent ears, swiftly receding hairline, and overly thin frame made him shy.[4]

He developed a crush on Jessie Reed, one of the chorus dancers in *The Passing*

Show. Fred had a difficult time getting past merely gaping at her because she, too, had many admirers. Unhappily for Fred, the next year she went to work for Ziegfeld, where she became one of his famous featured beauties.

After a week in Atlantic City, at the Globe Theatre, the production headed to Broadway for a July 25 opening at the vaunted Winter Garden, where Al Jolson's triumphs had helped put it on the theatrical map. *The Passing Show of 1918* ran for 125 performances, but the featured Astaires performed only two song-and-dance numbers, one a tango and the other a comedy routine, which unfortunately called for them to appear in bird costumes singing, "Twit, twit, twit, you'd better do your little bit, bit, bit."

Their having to perform this kind of mundane material didn't, however, dull the critics' enthusiasm. Alan Dale of the *New York Journal* said, "Fred Astaire, with Adele of the same name, danced all evening in knots, and it made one swelter to look at them. Fred is an agile youth, and apparently boneless, like that nice brand of sardines." Heywood Broun of the *New York Tribune* noted, "Fred Astaire stood out. He and his partner, Adele Astaire, made the show pause early in the evening with beautiful ease-limbed dance . . . it almost seemed as if the two young people had been poured into the dance."[5]

As part of their contract with the Shuberts, Fred and Adele participated as the opening act, without being paid, in Sunday-night concerts at the Winter Garden where Jolson, Fanny Brice, and Willie and Eugene Howard from *The Passing Show* were the headliners.[6] Jolson wanted the Broadway community to see how good he was on their night off. The youngsters marveled at Jolson's dynamism. His schmaltzy, over-the-top presentation played to an audience like few others. "Jolie" was, however, completely devoid of any semblance of subtlety, which perhaps served as an example to the Astaires of what *not* to do to appeal to an audience.

In advertising *The Passing Show,* flagrant showmanship, not subtlety, was on the mind of the Shuberts. An ad read, "It's a Whale—Without Jonah, a Huge, Whipping Entertainment, a Brilliant Array of Talent with the Winter Garden's Famous Wiggling Wand of Winsome Witches—150 People, 2 Acts, and 25 Scenes."

Despite their usual billing of "Fred and Adele Astaire's New Songs and Smart Dances," the constantly dissatisfied Fred often felt that Adele's performances in *The Passing Show* were not up to par. He would immediately sense when she wasn't giving her all or when she missed a step or two. He would insist on their rehearsing immediately after the show was over. More than once, he stayed up all night working on perfecting new steps for them to rehearse.[7]

It wasn't all work and no play, however, during the run of *The Passing Show.* In dressing room eighteen, on the ground floor of the Winter Garden, Fred shot craps and learned how to play poker. He also began to explore the excitement of Thoroughbred racing with excursions to Belmont Park with Gordon Dooley (of the famous Dooley family from vaudeville), Charley Foy (of "The Seven Little Foys"), or Lou Clayton (soon to become the partner of comedian Jimmy Durante), who were fellow performers in the show. The first horse Fred bet on, Tiger Rose, won and paid four to one. A devotee of the "sport of kings" was born; two decades later he would become the proud and successful owner of several racehorses.

The Passing Show enjoyed a five-month run, but more important, it did wonders for the Astaires' reputation as Broadway performers. The friendships they developed with fellow performers and new acquaintances also helped them to become attuned to the fast-paced life in New York.[8]

Frank Fay left the show when it went on the road, and Fred replaced him. This significant development meant that Fred had to learn how to handle long passages of dialogue, an important element in his learning to excel while appearing in sketches.[9]

In Detroit, where the Astaires had encountered hard times only a few years before, Fred overslept in his hotel room between the matinee and evening performances. Awakening at 8:15 P.M., he was compelled to run down four flights of stairs when he realized that the elevator was nowhere near the eighteenth floor, where his room was. He finally caught up to the elevator, flashed a $5 bill, and told the elevator operator not to stop for anybody. He then ran the six blocks to the theater and went right onstage in his street clothes, entering the opening scene, already in progress. An hour later, he was able to change into his bird costume and put on makeup.

Returning to Chicago, the site of their earlier triumph at the Palace Theatre, Fred began to indulge himself in the trappings of the "smart set" and form an image of himself as the dapper bon vivant. He bought a spiffy used Mercer sports car (which lasted until the end of the tour in 1918) and bought suits from Brooks Brothers, the celebrated haberdashers who had set the style adapted by Ivy League students. As a sign of his increasing interest in developing a personal style, he began wearing Brooks Brothers' familiar 346 model button-down shirts, which would endure as an essential staple of his wardrobe that somehow on him worked in combination with his later choice of sedate, custom-tailored English suits.[10]

Douglas Fairbanks had triggered Fred's initial interest in clothes. For a time George M. Cohan, the highly successful Broadway song-and-dance man, became his sartorial model. He copied Cohan's walk, his clothes, and his sassy, wisecracking manner. Excelling as a pool player, another talent that he had seriously worked at since witnessing Bojangles Robinson's prowess at the game, was an added ingredient.[11]

Doing publicity was one of the basic requirements of a Broadway performer. Fred, however, found himself uncomfortable doing interviews, which stayed with him for the remainder of his career. He felt his job was to perform at a high standard; relating to a newspaperman caused him to stammer and become withdrawn, self-conscious at his lack of education. Adele, however, dealt with the press with joy. Her vivacious personality and willingness to speak candidly and often outrageously came to the fore with the press.[12]

IN THE FALL OF 1919, Charles Dillingham made use of the Astaires' talents. He had waited almost two years for the opportunity. Dillingham now rivaled Flo Ziegfeld and the Shuberts as a major producer of musicals. However, the Astaires were now no longer "little Freddie and Dellie," as he had called them, but rather a polished dance act that was on the brink of achieving Broadway stardom.

Adele recalled their first meeting with Dillingham to discuss their appearance in his forthcoming production: "It was a hot day, and I remember him mopping his head with a piece of blotting paper. And he said, 'Now, you kids, what do you expect to get a week for being in *Apple Blossoms*?' And my brother said very bravely, 'five hundred dollars a week—excuse me, five hundred fifty.' So Dillingham said, 'I can understand the five hundred. What's the fifty for?' 'The fifty is for our agent.' "[13]

Before starting rehearsals for *Apple Blossoms,* Fred and Adele vacationed at Galen Hall, a resort in Wernersville, Pennsylvania. They found themselves increasingly at ease in socializing with the upper classes. Among them was the Altemus family, who were members of Philadelphia society. A lifelong friendship began with Jimmy Altemus, who was attracted to Adele, and his sister Liz, who became Fred's first serious romantic infatuation.[14] Being fascinated by the rich, Fred was amused by Jimmy's referring to the Altemus mansion, which Fred visited several times, located on the outskirts of Philadelphia at the Falls of Schuylkill, as "the dump." He was also quite taken by Jimmy's Super Six Hudson, a four-passenger, open car with wire wheels, and his stylish wardrobe. That Liz was an accomplished horsewoman (she later ran the very successful Llangollen Farm racing stable) was also a catalyst in bringing them together.[15]

THE JOVIAL DILLINGHAM was an urbane and sophisticated showman. He enjoyed having the Astaires ride around New York in his chauffeur-driven Rolls-Royce.

Adele told her brother, "We ought to get one." Dillingham looked upon them as not just a promising show-business investment but almost as his stepchildren. His elegant clothes, jaunty air, and amusing personality appealed to them equally. In *Apple Blossoms'* first pre-Broadway engagement in Atlantic City, C. B. (as Fred and Adele called him) took them to dinner at the best hotel, the Ritz Carlton. Going a step further, Eileen Dillingham, C. B.'s wife, designed the dress Adele wore in one of the dance numbers in the show.

The eminent classical violinist Fritz Kreisler cowrote the score for the operetta *Apple Blossoms* with Victor Jacobi. John Charles Thomas, the opera singer, was the male lead. It was a chance undertaking for Dillingham to produce an operetta with the Austro/German animosity lingering from the recently concluded World War. The Astaires had no part in the book of the show but offered two outstanding dance numbers, one of which was a tango Kreisler and the English choreographer Edward Royce tailored to Kreisler's popular composition "Tambourin Chinois."

George Gershwin, a friend of Kreisler's, replaced him as rehearsal pianist for the show. George renewed his friendship with Fred and repeated his desire to write a musical for him and his sister.[16] (The budding composer's first Broadway endeavor, *La, La Lucille,* had been a failure that summer.) George and Fred enjoyed playing dual pianos after the show's rehearsals. Challenging each other, they came up with new chords; in turn, Fred showed George new dance steps. Their camaraderie extended to attending nightclubs together looking for talented people they figured would one day make good.

The November 17, 1919, opening-night notice for Dillingham's revue from the renowned *New York Times* critic Alexander Woollcott read, "Fred and Adele Astaire, who romp off with a very considerable portion of the honors in 'Apple Blossoms,' are actually brother and sister. When a pair of dancers calling themselves 'The Astaires' came out of vaudeville, it is customary to discover that one of them is named McGuan and the other Lieblich." Speaking further about Fred, Woollcott said, "He is one of those extraordinary persons whose senses of rhythm and humor have been all mixed up—whose very muscles of which he seems to have an extra supply—are downright facetious." For a change, Adele was short-changed by a review when Woollcott noted, "In addition to her skill as a dancer, the girl of the team possessed vocal ambitions, which she is unable to further in 'Apple Blossoms.'" Charles Darnton of the *Evening World* contended, "Fred Astaire and his pretty sister danced as though they were twins and scored the biggest hit they've ever made."[17]

After the New York opening-night notices had brought them to the attention of serious theatergoers, the next step was for the young dance team to promote themselves and the show by making appearances at parties given by members of New York society. This was an easy task for Dillingham since his family was among the city's elite. Being invited to so many nightclubs eventually led to Fred's hatred of frequenting them. He disliked socializing with people he didn't particularly care for.

With their newfound success, Adele attracted even more fervent male admirers. Fred, however, insisted on serving as the go-between. Adele admitted in a 1975 interview that until she was twenty-three she had never been out with a young man without her brother being along on a date![18]

AS USUAL, Fred was restless and seemingly unable to enjoy the security of being in a hit show. "You started thinking, 'What're we gonna do next? What's it gonna be?' " was the way he expressed his dilemma. "There were always things happening in live shows. In a musical, you didn't have time to get down about it. I just worried about the work. I'd say, 'I didn't do this or that so well tonight; I'd better come in tomorrow and rehearse it.' "[19]

Ann was still close to her children. With their new Broadway salary, they were able to move into a suite at the Hotel Majestic at Seventy-second Street and Central Park West. Fritz remained in Omaha, refusing to accept any money from his children. He finally came to New York in 1919 while *Apple Blossoms* was playing on Broadway and was pleased that the show's composers were both Austrian. He attempted unsuccessfully to make a go of several business ventures.[20] A series of setbacks had had an adverse effect on his normally exuberant outlook, and he often found himself depressed.

Apple Blossoms had a run of 256 performances and lasted until the early summer of 1920. Business had fallen off as the inevitable heat and humidity of June in New York took hold; in those years there weren't even any "air-cooled" theaters. Fred and Adele went on a vacation split between Atlantic City with the Dillinghams and a return to Galen Hall. The *Apple Blossoms* tour started in September and extended until April 1921. Fred and Adele were now making $750 a week.

IN SPITE OF BASKING in two successive personal triumphs on Broadway, the Astaires had also long since been inured to failure, especially after their difficult apprenticeship in vaudeville. Dillingham followed one operetta starring John Charles Thomas with another operetta starring Thomas, with Victor Jacobi as the composer along with William Le Baron, and featuring the Astaires. This time, it simply didn't work; *The Love Letter* lasted a paltry thirty-one performances. Fred described the show as "one of those cumbersome vehicles, very well meant and planned, but it had a concept that couldn't be conquered for musical purposes." Still, *The Love Letter* was of significant importance in the Astaires' overall development. They were the hit of the show. Fritz remarked, "You surprised me. I didn't know you two could do all those things."[21]

Once again "Teddy" Royce was the choreographer. He came up with "The Runaround," which was to become one of the Astaires' most important dance routines. It was incorporated into a "nut" dance called "Upside Down," which Jacobi and Le Baron wrote overnight, which opened the show. In "The Runaround," Royce instructed Adele to put her arms in front of her as if she were on a bicycle holding the handlebars. She then ran around in a large circle looking as if she were grimly intent on getting somewhere. Fred was then instructed to join her, shoulder to shoulder, then they simply trotted around four or five times, their faces expressionless, to the accompaniment of a series of oompahs from the orchestra pit.[22] Then they'd run off, and the audience would want an encore. They would return and find a way of getting into "The Runaround" again.[23]

Fred referred to "The Runaround" as "a dumb number. It was as simple as hell. My sister is the one who was really the reason it became so good. . . . She was a good comedienne."[24] "The Runaround," however, was successfully featured in every one of their subsequent shows except for *The Band Wagon,* and Fred had Gracie Allen revive it in the film musical they starred in together, *A Damsel in Distress.*[25]

A *New York Herald* critic said, "Next to the star (John Charles Thomas), the Astaires, once more dancing around him like fireflies, make the high score of the evening, getting encores from their entertaining singing and 'nutty' dancing to "Upside Down" and revealing in this and other whirlwind numbers that they have developed a penetrating comedy touch with their lips as well as their always ambitious feet."[26]

ONE OF THE MOST PROMINENT theatrical figures of the 1920s was surely Noël Coward—the actor, playwright, composer, and lyricist. In spite of his coming from a middle-class background in the village of Teddington in Middlesex, after his early successes in London's West End, starring in several of his droll drawing-room comedies, he quickly assumed the sophistication of those to the manor born. Coward came backstage with some friends after seeing *The Love Letter* and told the Astaires that they should come to London to perform, predicting enormous success for them with British audiences.[27] When Fred explained the show was closing soon, Coward remarked, "Good, then you can come to London at once."[28] An enduring and meaningful relationship between "the Master" and the Astaires began with that initial meeting. They respected his taste and his never-ending theatrical know-how.

During the final days of *The Love Letter,* Fred, trying to boost his spirits, purchased a necktie at Finchley's, a popular men's store on Fifth Avenue. A salesman began giving Fred career advice: "I think you ought to get out of these revues and operettas and do a real musical comedy like *Oh, Boy,*" referring to composer Jerome Kern's current hit. The salesman explained that he was part owner of Finchley's and had been the producer of George Gershwin's musical, *La, La Lucille.*

Fred thought little about this brief meeting until the salesman/producer, named Alex A. Aarons, sent him a telegram after the tour of *The Love Letter* ended. Aarons wanted him and his sister to appear in his forthcoming show, *For Goodness Sake.* Since Dillingham had nothing to offer the Astaires at the time, he agreed to release them to Aarons until 1922. (Such noblesse oblige would be unexpected in today's Broadway, much less during the decades starting in the 1950s, when David Merrick became the dominant producer of Broadway musicals.)

Although Aarons told Fred to free himself from appearing with Adele in revues, *For Goodness Sake* was just that, a revue. George Gershwin with his lyricist brother, Ira, contributed only three songs to the show as they were committed to George White's *Scandals.* The Astaires received sixth billing while playing the best friends of the leads, a married couple. It also marked the first time that they had speaking roles on Broadway.[29] Once again they stole the show.

On its February 20, 1922, opening at the Lyric Theatre, the critics, who had highly praised their work in their three previous Broadway outings, continued to do so. Alan Dale of the *American* said, "The two Astaires are the principal assets of 'For Goodness Sake.' They can speak a little, act a little, and dance quarts. . . . Miss Astaire is a pleasant little body, with a sense of humor, and Mr. Astaire has the lank lissomeness necessary for his 'line of work.' " Charles Darnton of the *Evening World* wrote, "Here are those young favorites, the gangling Fred and the pert Adele . . . they don't look like as though they were anything more than somebody's children. But when they dance—oh, boy and likewise girl! With ease, grace, rhythm, charm, and humor, youth becomes a wonderful thing, and you realize all this in watching the Astaires. They happen to be the best of their kind."

Robert Benchley, then the critic of the leading picture weekly, *Life,* said, "When they dance, everything seems brighter and their comedy alone would be good enough to carry them through even if they were to stop dancing (which God forbid!)."

As though it had happened overnight, suddenly the effervescence they brought to their freewheeling dance routines thrilled audiences as never before. Working closely with dance director Allan Foster, Fred began creating and choreographing their own dances. Their featured number, facetiously titled "The Whichness of the Whatness and the Whereness of the Who," was derived from "The Runaround" and got a similar response. *For Goodness Sake* had a moderate run of 103 performances.[30] This show was also forced to close because of a summer heat wave, which kept audiences away from sweltering theaters.

One night in Bridgeport, Connecticut, during the tour that followed the Broadway closing, Fred and Adele reached an unexpected high point in their performance. That afternoon Fred had indulged in some shopping, by now well established as one of his favorite pastimes. Among his purchases was a snappy red-and-green-plaid bathrobe. Proudly putting it on after the performance, he got the distinct yet completely irrational feeling that his new bathrobe had something to do with their astounding performance that evening. It suddenly acquired epic importance. Never allowing himself to believe that perhaps talent was responsible for the newfound success, Fred preserved the "lucky" bathrobe and wore it for years afterward on the day of every theatrical opening and on the day of the first screening of his film musicals.[31]

Fred and Adele's growth as performers at last earned them star billing above the title in C. B. Dillingham's *The Bunch and Judy* with a musical score by Jerome Kern. Dillingham raised his prodigies' salary to $1,000 a week now that his new show had been built around them. "Moanin' Minnie," however, was unhappy with several aspects of the show. For one thing Kern's songs were mediocre; one of the songs that Fred was given to sing, "Pale Venetian Moon," was arranged in a key too high for his voice. For another, he was required to wear a white wig with a knot hanging down his back. Strangely enough, the plot of the show proved prophetic as it centered on an American dancing star who gives up her career to marry an English aristocrat.

Problems arose when the show tried out in Philadelphia. The show's book needed fixing. The Astaires' costar, Joseph Cawthorn, fell down a flight of stairs en route to the stage and broke his kneecap. The brother and sister team of Johnny and Ray Dooley (part of the vaudevillian Dooley family) were brought in to replace Cawthorn with the requisite script changes. Another mishap occurred during a dress rehearsal when Fred and Adele were being carried on a table by six youngsters. The "Six Brown Brothers," as they were called, tripped and they crashed to the stage floor. Fortunately, they weren't seriously injured.[32]

On opening night, one of their most consistent admirers from the critics circle, Heywood Broun, wrote, "Fred and Adele Astaire are the most graceful and charming young dancers in the world of musical comedy. . . . Once they begin to dance, they are among the immortals." Nevertheless, *The Bunch and Judy* lasted seven weeks on Broadway following a brief tour.

Dillingham had gradually lost his infatuation with the young song-and-dance team and decided not to renew their contract for future productions.[33] This devastating turn of events caused Fred and Adele to seriously question their future as Broadway headliners. "This was a major flop," Fred recalled in *Steps in Time.* "Our first attempt at stardom turned out to be a conspicuous failure." It took a good bit of time, but they would eventually laughingly refer to the show as *The Bust and Judy.*

Various job offers came their way. They turned down a booking to dance at the Knickerbocker Grill in New York. An offer from the Palace came through, but that meant going backward into vaudeville. Fortunately, they had saved enough money so that they didn't have to rush into anything right away.

They were compelled to take a serious look at exactly where they were in their career. They were justifiably disillusioned about what the future might hold for them. In five years they had been featured players in four Broadway revues and had been given star billing in the fifth production, but it had failed miserably. Among critics, producers, and fellow performers, they had developed a formidable reputation. Commercially, however, the question remained, "Can the Astaires carry a Broadway production?"

At their lowest ebb since the fiasco at Proctor's eleven years before, out of nowhere Alex Aarons approached Fred with an offer he and Adele couldn't possibly refuse, the opportunity to go to London to inaugurate the West End production of *For Goodness Sake,* presented by Sir Alfred Brett, an important English producer. As part of the deal, Ann joined her two offspring, along with Aarons and his wife, as they sailed for Southampton aboard the Cunard ocean liner the *Aquitania,* in March 1923. Fritz had taken ill and insisted on remaining in New York, promising to come to London when his health improved.[34]

During the voyage, Fred and Adele were asked to perform a benefit for the Seaman's Fund amidst difficult conditions. The rough seas, synonymous with winter in the North Atlantic, caused the ship to roll unmercifully as they danced. Having to deal with the elements only added to the hilarity of their performance. Never able to discard a salable idea, Fred made use of this experience by adapting it for a memorable scene in MGM's *Royal Wedding,* in which he danced with Jane Powell.[35]

On their arrival in London, the Astaires met with Sir Alfred, and he took them to see Jack Buchanan, the leading West End musical comedy star, in *Battling Butler.* The Americans were amazed to see how boisterous British audiences were. It couldn't help but remind them of a few vaudeville audiences they had encountered and caused them to wonder what would happen once *they* opened in London.[36]

The script of *For Goodness Sake* required various bits of dialogue as well as jokes to be anglicized, which Fred Thompson was assigned to do. The title of the show also changed, to *Stop Flirting.* A Gershwin song, "I'll Build a Stairway to Paradise" (later revived successfully by Georges Guétary in MGM's *An American in Paris*) was added. Five weeks of rehearsal and back-to-back engagements in Liverpool, Glasgow, and Edinburgh preceded the May 30, 1923, opening at the Shaftesbury Theatre.

On opening night, in the middle of the second act, the Astaires grabbed the audience's attention with their song-and-dance number "Oh Gee, Oh Gosh, Oh Golly, I Love You." "Encore, encore" was shouted out throughout the theater, but it was "The Runaround," derived "The Witchness of the Whatness and the Whereness of the Who," that made them instant stars in Great Britain.

The stupendous reception Fred and Adele enjoyed on Broadway in essentially the same show, slightly over a year earlier, paled in comparison to the way the London audience accepted them. They got a cheering standing ovation, and the crowd demanded that they give curtain speeches. Adele ad-libbed, "My brother and I thank you from the bottom of our hearts—and we want you all to come and have tea with us tomorrow."[37] They were the most popular American attraction to play a London theater since Edna May appeared in *The Belle of New York,* twenty-five years earlier.

Their triumph was reflected by the magnificent critical acclaim they received in the *Nation* and *Athenaeum.* Francis Birrell observed, "In their tireless high spirits, their unfailing delight in their own concerns, their litheness and unceasing activities, Fred and Adele Astaire ceased to be human beings to become, as it were, translated into denizens of the Elizabethan forest." Sydney Carroll of the mighty *London Times* said, "Columbus may have danced with joy at discovering America, but how he would have cavorted had he also discovered Fred and Adele Astaire. They typify the primal spirit of animal delight that could not restrain itself—the vitality that burst its bonds in the Garden of Eden. . . . They are as light as blades of grass, or light as gossamer, and as odd as golliwogs."[38]

Their newfound friend Noël Coward ran backstage, his face beaming. He proudly reminded them how he had predicted exactly how warmly British audiences would receive them. He remarked, "Freddie, when I see you dance, it makes me cry."[39]

Coward and producer André Charlot asked Fred to choreograph two dances that weren't coming together during rehearsals in their forthcoming musical, *London Calling,* in which Coward danced with his close friend and costar, Gertrude

Lawrence. Fred also wound up staging Noël's solo number, "Sentiment." Coward suggested to Fred that he join him in enrolling at the Guildhall School of Music for formal musical education. Coward took the full course while Astaire only studied sight reading, which would be of considerable importance in the years ahead as he further developed his piano playing, singing, and songwriting.

The show moved to the Queen's Theatre, shut down for a short time during Christmas, then returned for an engagement at the Strand Theatre. During the run, audiences would yell out, " ''Core," meaning "encore," and "Oompah," "Oompah," "Oompah," during "The Runaround."[40] However, equally as important, among the tricks of performing that Fred had learned in vaudeville was "Always think of the exit. The exit's the thing that kills 'em. You can make your whole show by your exit." [41]

Never in their wildest dreams could Fred and Adele have imagined that this incredible success would take place not in America, but in the West End of London. This was everything they had worked for in their sixteen years as professionals. Fans and critics were intrigued by the "American drawl" of the young stars. Stars of the London theater toasted them. They were weekend houseguests of titled English families in their stately, historic mansions. Sir Alfred took Fred along to experience the English horse-racing scene, where Fred felt quickly at home with jockeys, trainers, and bookies. The Astaires found themselves so well established so quickly that they became the focal point of major print-advertising campaigns for such items as toothbrushes and pick-me-up remedies.[42] Everything was geared to making them a favorite of the English from the royals to those who frequented racetracks.

After his second visit to the Queen's Theatre to see the show, Edward, Prince of Wales, invited Fred and Adele to supper after their performance. Fred couldn't help but be completely taken by the way the dapper prince dressed. Edward's brother, Prince George, the Duke of York (later to become George VI, king of England), also became a close friend of the Astaires' and another sartorial role model for Fred. As Fred expressed it succinctly, "They were just 'it.' " Edward took Fred to his Savile Row tailor and other specialty clothing stores such as Kilgour, French & Stanbury, and Turnbull & Asser.

Adele indulged the prince's interest in tap dancing by teaching him some complicated steps and danced with him at the Riviera club one night.[43] A fine exchange took place: Fred learned the importance of dressing well, which would have far-reaching effects on his developing an elegant sense of style. In return, in becoming close friends of the two amazing performers, the prince indulged his passion for show business.

Adele adored life in London. Now, she had more admirers than ever before. She indulged her love of clothes by buying new dresses for the frequent tea dances at the Savoy, where they were staying.[44]

Edward wound up attending *Stop Flirting* ten times. This led to Edward's introducing Fred and Adele to other members of the royal family, such as the Duchess of York and Lord and Lady Mountbatten, who also came to see the show. One night, the Mountbattens brought Douglas Fairbanks and Mary Pickford, then married, two major stars whom Fred and Adele had known separately in less prosperous times, to see them perform. Between acts, Fred and Adele visited with Doug and Mary in their private box.[45]

Fred was delighted by the elegance in the dress code of the London theatergoers. He observed, "I was amazed to see an audience where all the men wear white ties. This would not only be on opening night. . . . Not a dinner jacket, but white tie, full dress. Ladies in their jewelries and gowns. It was quite exciting." He also noted that when a show was declining in attendance, black tie replaced white tie on the men.[46] The way of life in London really got to Fred and Adele—the innate kindness of the people and especially the good manners, the reserved comportment, and the overall respect given them by the wealthy, with whom they spent so much time.

They found themselves immersed in a social sphere they enjoyed tremendously but had never imagined could be theirs. Their previous introduction to Philadelphia and New York society by Jimmy and Liz Altemus and C. B. and Eileen Dillingham had led to this moment. This sudden involvement with royalty, however, was something entirely different and completely overwhelming. Not only Fred, but Adele as well, realized they had found the missing element. Henceforth, elegance and sophistication became the byword of their lives and their existence.

They moved to the fashionable Carlton Hotel to settle in for the remainder of the show's run. Along with his Savile Row wardrobe, Fred had also acquired an English accent.[47] As the late bandleader Artie Shaw, who years later costarred with Fred in the film *Second Chorus,* viewed it, "Fred was a rather accomplished American song-and-dance man when he went to London to work with his sister. He came back an English gentleman."

Shortly before Christmas of 1923, Ann left for America as Fritz was now seriously ill in New York. She saw how happy Fred and Adele were in their new milieu and felt they were being looked after properly. During the three-week break before the show reopened at the Strand, they went to Paris for the first time and caught performances by Maurice Chevalier and Mistinguett, the foremost French music-hall performers, along with the American act the Dolly Sisters.

One night soon after, Sir Alfred came backstage between acts to inform them that their father had passed away from cancer. They struggled to complete their performance. The months of frivolity ended with this tragic news. In her letters, Ann hadn't wanted to trouble them with the seriousness of Fritz's illness. She had taken him to Wernersville, where she helped him to try to recuperate, but he passed away there.[48] Sir Alfred offered to close the show for several weeks but suggested to them that the best way to overcome their loss was to keep performing. They agreed that the show must go on.

Fritz had set the direction for his children's entry into show business and backed his plan financially. In his children's early years as performers, he had cultivated friendships with influential agents, and while the children were struggling, he had consistently provided important career advice and support. He had lived long enough to hear from Ann in her letters about their success in London, but sadly his illness prevented his witnessing their triumph in person. He had prepared them well for the show business career that he had always wanted for himself.

Fred had few recollections of his early years in Omaha. His father had been only an occasional presence in his life. He never got to really know him as a father. During the brief times Fritz lived with his family, he was often going through difficult times. Now, Fred and Adele were grown up, and Fritz was gone.

On her return, after burying Fritz in the Bronx, Ann herself became ill and was compelled to spend time at Sir Douglas Shields's nursing home. While there, she met fellow patient James Barrie, who requested to meet Fred and Adele. When they met, Barrie told Adele that he wished she would one day play in his theatrical creation *Peter Pan*.[49] It never happened, but Dellie's gamine charm would have been perfect for the title role.

Stop Flirting, though still selling out after 418 performances, closed by mutual agreement of Sir Alfred and the Astaires. Had it not closed, it might have shattered the London record for the longest-running musical, held by *Chu Chin Chow*. On closing night, the audience sang the songs along with Fred and Adele, then broke into "Auld Lang Syne" and shouts of "Hurry back!" as the final curtain came down.[50]

A YEAR AND A HALF was a long time to stay away from Broadway, and since the media didn't deliver news nearly as rapidly as it does today, many New Yorkers weren't even aware of their great success in London. Fred, therefore, contacted

Alex Aarons to line up a new show. Aarons was by now partnered with Vinton Freedley, who had been the male romantic lead in *For Goodness Sake* and who had also helped finance the show. Aarons wired back that George and Ira Gershwin wanted the Astaires to star in their new show, then called *Black Eyed Susan.*

Without wasting any time, upon the Astaires' arrival in New York on the SS *Homeric,* Aarons got them to sign their contracts on top of one of their trunks just after docking and while they were still in customs. The press badgered them with questions about Adele's dancing with the Prince of Wales, which Fred modestly deflected. They were immediately rushed to George Gershwin's apartment to hear the music, marking the first time George and Ira had written the entire score for a Broadway musical.

Due to Fred's versatility, which now included not only performing and choreographing and playing piano, but also writing songs and playing drums, he was asked to get involved in the show's creation. At that time, performers rarely worked with the composer, lyricist, and bookwriter as part of the writing team. Four weeks of rehearsals started a few days later, then the company was off to Philadelphia to open at the Forrest Theatre.[51]

Three songs that would become synonymous with the Gershwins were in the show: "Fascinating Rhythm," "'The Half of It, Dearie' Blues," and "Lady Be Good." When the latter song was introduced by comedian Walter Catlett, it became instantly popular and caused the show to be renamed in its honor. (Another song, a melodic offshoot of Gershwin's "Rhapsody in Blue" theme, assigned to Adele during the Forrest Theatre engagement, was tossed out, only to surface eventually as "The Man I Love.")[52]

The December 1, 1924, opening night of *Lady Be Good* introduced the second consecutive Fred and Adele Astaire smash hit and the beginning of a highly successful association with the Gershwins. After numerous curtain calls, Adele gave another impromptu speech. Arthur Hornblow of *Theatre* magazine raved, "Adele is, if anything more piquant and impish and her brother Fred, more blushed and joyous. Their nimble feet twinkle faster than ever, and they came near carrying off all the honors of the sprightly new show." The *Times* critic offered, "Miss Astaire in the new piece is as charming and entertaining a musical comedy actress as the town has seen on display in many a moon. Fred Astaire, too, gave a good account of himself."

Adele's zany sense of humor and high spirits on- and offstage made her the epitome of a flapper, a prototype of "the Roaring '20s." Authors Marshall and Jean Stearns, in their book, *Jazz Dance,* wrote that her effervescence led Fred to develop an "outward appearance of amused superiority, a pretence of nonchalance and insouciance. . . . [He] gave the impression of thinking, 'Okay, Adele's the star, so I'll help her out, but I'm bored to death.' And, of course, it influenced the development of his style of dancing, the fine art of understatement."[53]

Fred and Adele found themselves full-fledged Broadway stars playing brother and sister. Their previous roles of playing young sweethearts in a comic vein were now history. Guy Bolton and Fred Thompson's book, as inane as that of most musicals of the time, nevertheless offered Adele the chance to once again showcase her natural talent as a comedienne and also provided Fred with the number "'The Half of It, Dearie' Blues."

Interestingly enough, the characters Fred played throughout the 1920s shied away from saying, singing, or dancing any out-and-out declaration of love. The Gershwins recognized this and purposely provided him with a sufficiently oblique singing and dancing vehicle in "'Dearie' Blues," which was written in a slangy lingo.[54] Originally designed as a song for Fred to sing, Fred devised a tap-dance routine, the first solo dance in his career. It evolved further through Fred's working closely with George Gershwin; they extended this tap routine to include former vaudeville star Cliff Edwards, and it turned out to be a showstopper.

"Fascinating Rhythm," sung and danced by Fred and Adele, was singled out by the *Herald Tribune* in an unusual manner: "The callous Broadwayites cheered them as if their favorite halfback had planted the ball between the goalposts after an 80-yard run. Seldom has it been our pleasure to witness so heartfelt, spontaneous, and so deserved a tribute."[55] The song was introduced early in the second act by Cliff Edwards, who entered as Fred's and Adele's characters were arguing. Accompanied by his famed ukulele, Edwards's singing caused them to stop quarreling. They broke into a dance, the culmination of a perfect amalgam of words, music, and movements.[56] Gershwin often spoke of wanting to express the feverishness of New York in his music, to which people could hardly sit still.[57] "Fascinating Rhythm" was just that.

More important, "Fascinating Rhythm" was one of the earliest examples of a jazz song on Broadway.[58] New York was Gershwin's canvas. Jazz was his muse.

Lady Be Good's Broadway run of 330 performances and its subsequent tour introduced a new kind of American song and dance to musical comedy as well as a higher level of musical-dramatic integration. More fluent and sophisticated than what had come before, it set the standard for what was to follow.[59] Given all that, *Lady Be Good* hasn't endured as a significant musical.

But the show did wonders for the team. The Astaires were now solidly ensconced at the top of the heap, getting a hefty salary of $1,750 a week.[60] *Lady Be Good* was a huge success in an absolutely incredible season that included such hit musicals as George White's *Scandals; Rose Marie; The Student Prince;* Richard Rogers and Larry Hart's first Broadway musical, *Garrick Gaieties;* Eddie Cantor in *Kid Boots;* and Al Jolson in *Big Boy.* This was in addition to such undeniably brilliant dramas as Sidney Howard's *They Knew What They Wanted;* Eugene O'Neill's *Desire Under the Elms;* George S. Kaufman and Edna Ferber's *Minick;* and Maxwell Anderson and Laurence Stallings's seemingly out-of-place antiwar play, *What Price Glory?*[61] Without question, this was the golden age of Broadway.

The musical shows of the 1920s were indeed a patchwork of the older, pre–World War I stars such as Al Jolson, and the emerging younger element made up of the Astaires and English imports such as Gertrude Lawrence and Beatrice Lillie.[62] And what songwriters—Cole Porter, Rodgers and Hart, Jerome Kern, Irving Berlin, and now the Gershwins—to supply them with sparkling melodies!

All of this notoriety and success had no effect on Fred's never-ending pursuit of excellence. The late *Hollywood Reporter* gossip columnist Radie Harris said, "Fred first came into my life when he and Adele were doing *Lady Be Good.* I remember Fred telling me he was always the first one in the theater, and Dellie was the last one out. He always came in and practiced before the show, and Dellie would arrive at just about curtain rise. They couldn't have been more opposite, but he adored her, and she adored him."[63]

On occasion, Adele would rebel against Fred's frequent yen to rehearse after the show. This was when she had a heavy date, usually with a young man from the Social Register. Fred was constantly concerned with her welfare. As he described it, "Adele was being pursued by several young men whom I didn't care for and suddenly loomed as a menace. . . . She laughed, 'Don't be silly—I'm not serious about anybody.' Well, that wasn't quite true, but nothing really developed."[64]

Fred continued dating actresses and showgirls but had few serious relationships. Performing and rehearsing were most important to him. He enjoyed hanging out with old friends such as Jimmy Altemus and John Hay "Jock" Whitney, a friend of Jimmy's from Yale. These friendships would reap unexpected rewards for Fred. He and Jimmy would collaborate on writing one of Fred's songs, "Shake Your Feet"; Jock became an investor in several of the Astaires' subsequent Broadway shows. Fred's interest in horse racing was further nourished by his meeting Mrs. Payne Whitney, Jock's mother, who owned the prestigious Greentree Stable. Fred had become so immersed in the sport of kings that when he wasn't at the track, he placed bets with bookies. He even went so far as to cable London to bet on races there.[65]

In telling the Fred Astaire story, it is necessary to clarify an important point. Hugh Fordin, author of the highly informative study *MGM's Greatest Musicals; The Arthur Freed Unit* and president of DRG Records, contends that Astaire was a homophobe. I never heard this from any of the gay men I interviewed for this book. Though many disagree with this theory, growing up surrounded by two women, a strong father figure, and having spent much of his young manhood in a dancer's environment, there would, perhaps, be reason for him to have been homosexual, but the truth is otherwise. He did, however, have trouble expressing affection. Throughout his life, his mother and his sister were the only ones with whom he could easily express deep emotion.

THE IMPORTANCE OF A CLEVER and resourceful talent agent to finally establish the Astaires' career in vaudeville was exemplified by the work of Lew Golden and Max Hayes in reestablishing them on the Orpheum Circuit in 1915 and '16. Now that New York was at their feet, they once again needed the guidance of a capable agent. They received countless offers for personal appearances away from *Lady Be Good.* One such offer was brought to them by a fellow Nebraskan, a failed publicist and screenwriter turned agent named Leland Hayward.

While making the rounds of New York nighteries when unemployed, Hayward met with a friend of his, Mal Hayward (no relation), who complained about the lack of business at the Trocadero nightclub he ran with Frank Garlasco. The ballroom dance team of Moss and Fontana were a big hit at the rival Mirador club.[66] Leland suggested hiring Broadway's hottest act, Fred and Adele Astaire. He brought the Astaires an offer of $5,000 a week to headline at the Trocadero. Despite Fred's aversion to nightclubs, this was too good to pass up.

The engagement, which took place nightly after the *Lady Be Good* curtain came down, was another smashing success for the Astaires and put the Mirador out of business. Fred remembered that on opening night, "All the swells were there. A nightclub was an atmosphere we had never worked on before, and we didn't like it. . . . Our dances went fine that night—it was okay, but we were really out of our element and the general feeling was that we were doing it for a lark and that, it wouldn't last."[67]

Leland Hayward found himself representing a pair of highly satisfied clients, and as a result he started his own talent agency. In a few years, he built a highly respected agency that represented such major film stars as Greta Garbo, Henry Fonda, Marlene Dietrich, and significant others. The intelligence and resourcefulness he displayed in furthering the stage career of the Astaires and in ultimately plotting the movie career of Fred Astaire would be of considerable importance in Fred's achieving major stardom.

Although the nightclub business was new to Fred, he was smart enough to see that after two sell-out weeks business had cooled. Rather than having to face being asked to take a *cut,* he suggested reducing their salary to $3,000 a week for the last two weeks of the engagement. He bought a cigarette can for Mal and a flask for Frank. His kind gestures were appreciated by the owners, but the experience caused Fred and Adele to never work a nightclub again.[68]

Fred was already looking toward Hollywood. He gave actor-turned-agent Ben Lyon photographs of himself to take with him to Hollywood to see if the film industry had any interest in him. (Films were then still silent.) Lyon gave the photos to John McCormack, a studio general manager, then married to the actress Colleen Moore. McCormack and a fellow executive laughed at the very thought of Astaire's appearance in films.

AN "OUT OF TOWN" engagement in Liverpool, and *Lady Be Good* was off to London. At the dress rehearsal prior to opening night, Ann showed that she was still in the picture when she voiced her unhappiness at the way Fred was performing, pointing out, "Sonny [her occasional nickname for her son], how cross you looked and your forehead was wrinkled." Encouraging words from Vinton Freedley counteracted Ann's remarks, and an unexpected congratulatory cable from C. B. Dillingham further raised Fred's spirits.[69]

The second time around for the Astaires in London on April 14, 1926, this time at the Empire Theatre, was even more triumphant than the first time. On the opening night, as soon as they made their entrance onstage, they were wildly cheered. The audience then squealed as they danced a newly installed Gershwin song-and-dance number, "I'd Rather Charleston."

Among the spate of excellence notices the *Evening Standard* declared, "Miss Adele Astaire is the most attractive thing on any stage." The *Daily Sketch* critic acknowledged the show's pedestrian look but predicted a year's run. The review included such praise as "the Astaires' dancing was uproarious. Fred's solo dance was one of the biggest things of the night."

As with *Flirting, Lady Be Good* had been revised to sound more British. Fred and Adele's initial entrance onstage was purposely delayed so that the notoriously late royals and society people would be in their seats.[70] The Prince of Wales again came to see the show several times and was a frequent visitor backstage, as was Prince George ("P.G." as Fred called him), and his wife, Elizabeth, the Duchess of York, who would later become queen and finally the queen mother.[71]

A personal note sent to Adele at the theater from the duchess asked if she and her brother would like to pay a visit to meet "the baby" at their home in Mayfair. The Astaires did so and made a suitable fuss over the four-month-old girl, who would decades later become Queen Elizabeth II.

The Astaires' every move, such as Fred's purchase of a half interest in the racehorses Dolomite and Social Evening, generated immediate and prominent press attention. Their purchase of a black "baby" Rolls-Royce, complete with a chauffeur, with the money they had made at the Trocadero engagement in New York made even more news. The combination of their youth, performing magic, and personal style garnered them equal coverage in the entertainment as well as the society pages.

The equally erudite and daft playwright George Bernard Shaw even paid a social call on Adele. Shaw referred to her as "one of the most beautiful women I have ever met." She asked him, "What do you think of actors, Mr. Shaw?" "Nothing," replied the garrulous Shaw. "If it weren't for authors, there wouldn't be any." "I should have said dancers," Adele demurred. Her overall reaction to Shaw was "I feel my stay in England is complete. If it didn't make any difference to Mr. Shaw, I'd like to follow him around all day."[72]

The Astaires' success in *Lady Be Good* became so ingrained that the English people thought of them as their own.[73] The spirited boys from Oxford and Cambridge became regulars at the Empire Theatre and sang along with their songs. George Gershwin came over to record several songs from the show that featured Fred and Adele for Columbia Records. The biggest tribute to the "American darlings" took place on August 9, 1926, however, when King George V and Queen Mary, then the reigning monarchs, made an extremely rare visit to the theater specifically to see them perform.

The show could have gone on indefinitely, but the Empire Theatre was about to be torn down to make way for a new cinema. As it was, *Lady Be Good* played for over nine months, which encompassed 326 performances. The Prince of Wales and a capacity crowd of other celebrated figures, which included Adeline Genée, the Danish ballerina who had been the Astaires' first inspiration, attended the closing-night performance.[74] A joyous party at St. James Palace followed the final curtain, to which Edward invited the Astaires and their friends. At the late-night party, Fred's close friend Jock Whitney, then an Oxford graduate student, demonstrated the "Black Bottom" dance.[75]

Adele waxed nostalgically about their nonstop glorious reception in London when she said, "We were one of the first Americans to invade England, and I think that as entertainers we were a little different from what they had seen. I know that a few years later everyone started copying the things we did."[76] (Unfortunately, no film footage is currently available of the Astaires onstage to remind us of just how much they contributed in those years.)[77]

After touring England, Scotland, and Wales, the Astaires returned to New York, bringing their Rolls-Royce with them. Another Aarons/Freedley production with the Gershwins, tentatively titled *Smarty,* was set to go. The producers had done so well with two Gershwin shows that they combined their first names to name the Alvin Theatre on Fifty-second Street west of Broadway to debut their new production. Robert Benchley and Fred Thompson were signed to cowrite the book.[78]

Problems beset *Smarty* when it opened its tryout booking in Philadelphia. The inevitable difficulties with the book were joined by problems with scenery, cues, musical tempos, and costumes. The public wanted no part of the troubled production and business was light.[79]

In Washington, the reception was worse. Benchley was replaced by Paul Gerard Smith. As Fred explained it in a *Collier's* article, "We were playing one version and rehearsing another. Every performance was different from the one before it. There were times when I used to carry my lines typed on cards. I'd have to look down into my hand before I dared open my mouth. . . . Honest, I never thought we'd make it to New York. . . . But that's where Alex Aarons and Vinton Freedley were keen managers. They knew, even when we didn't, that we had something, and instead of junking it, they kept working over it and working it."

A week in Atlantic City at Nixon's Apollo Theatre, commencing on November 7, 1927, revealed lingering script problems, but the musical numbers were beginning to take shape. During a three-day booking in Wilmington, Delaware, that followed, the show got a new title, *Funny Face.* (This became Fred's nickname for Adele.) The addition to the cast of the scratchy-voiced comedian Victor Moore; and new songs that included the comedy number "The Babbitt and the Bromide," choreographed in the vein of "The Runaround," turned things around.

With all of these significant changes, Fred, however, was characteristically dubious about the ultimate fate of the show and sounded off to Adele and their dressers. "I hate flops, and this is one," he said. "We might as well face it. This damn turkey hasn't got a prayer." Adele chimed in, "Oh, let him moan. He loves it. This is the first chance he's had in years. Go ahead, Minnie! You remind me of William Jennings Bryan."[80]

Despite Fred's grave misgiving, on its November 22, 1927, Broadway opening, *Funny Face* got the same rousing reception that *Lady Be Good* had received three years earlier. Alexander Woollcott, now the critic of the *New York World,* wrote, "I do not know whether George Gershwin was born into this world to write rhythms for Fred Astaire's feet or whether Fred Astaire was born into this world to show how the Gershwin music should be danced. But surely they were written in the same key." The *Judge*'s judge, the critic and George Jean Nathan, handed down the verdict: "The Astaire team lifts the evening as they had lifted equally dubious vehicles in the past and sends the show gaily over."[81] Not to be outdone, Gilbert Gabriel of the *New York Sun* said, "They are a sort of Champagne cup of motion those Astaires. They live, laugh, and leap in a world that is all bubbles."[82]

The Gershwins gave the show's title song to Fred and Adele to sing; " 'S Wonderful" for Adele (only to have the song later associated with Fred); "He Loves and She Loves" for Adele and her romantic interest in the show, Allen Kearns, to duet on; and "My One and Only" for Fred to sing with Gertrude McDonald and Betty Compton. In 1929, "My One and Only" as a solo vehicle for Fred was his first hit recording for Columbia Records, reaching #18 on the *Billboard* Pop Chart.[83] "High Hat" was an important vehicle for Fred, dressed in black tie, a custom-tailored double-breasted tuxedo and top hat, to create an even more elegant image onstage. Fred's astounding tap number was backed by a black-tie chorus of two dozen male dancers repeating his steps.[84] "The Babbitt and the Bromide," seemingly tailor-made for Fred and Adele with its sophisticated Ira Gershwin lyrics, described the meeting of two friends who exchange a bevy of clichés, only to meet a decade later, then two decades after that in heaven, where they continue to spout the same tired phrases.[85]

Funny Face established Fred Astaire at last as a truly formidable solo performer as both a singer and a dancer. According to Fred, his development had begun with *Lady Be Good,* when, "in the last week, I had a solo number with the ingénue, not Dellie. Suddenly, after fiddling around with tap, I made up my own way of doing it. I remember the first night I tried it out—it stopped the show. . . .

"We went to London . . . and I did it over there. Then I did more and more of it. I didn't do so much with my sister because she wasn't a tap dancer. I did solos. It was kind of my own way of handling that form. It came in handy in all of the shows I did after that.

"It was strictly a sideline. I did so many other kinds of dance. When I'm called a tap dancer, it makes me laugh. I happened to have some outstanding successful numbers in the tap so people remember. . . . I had a little different treatment of how to apply it. I didn't just set out and hop into 'the buck,' I'd move around and do things."[86]

But a new world had opened up for musical performers with the early-November premiere of Al Jolson in *The Jazz Singer.* Suddenly movies "talked," sang, and the sound of dancing feet could be heard. As we have been unable to miss, Fred Astaire was not a bastion of optimism; he felt that this important innovation would quickly pass into obscurity.

Walter Wanger, then head of the New York office of Paramount Pictures and later producer of such memorable and diverse films as *Stagecoach, Foreign Correspondent, Invasion of the Body Snatchers, I Want to Live!,* and *Cleopatra,* convinced the studio that he should set up a screen test for the Astaires, as they might star in the film version of *Funny Face,* which the studio had purchased. Fred and Adele weren't happy with the results. "We looked awful on-screen," Fred recalled.[87] Despite Wanger's enthusiasm over their test, this was not destined to be Paramount's first excursion into a talking musical. The Paramount film of *Funny Face,* which starred Fred and Audrey Hepburn, wasn't made until almost thirty years later. Many of the songs remained from the original stage musical, but the plot was completely different.

The Astaires' stardom made them more sought after than ever before. After their first waiting for an offer from Flo Ziegfeld back in 1917, the master showman finally approached Fred and Adele ten years later about starring in his next production, set for the 1928–29 season. But Fred knew that *Funny Face* would last at least through the season, followed by the inevitable London engagement that Alex Aarons had already booked. Fred told Ziegfeld, "Adele and I would love to do a Ziegfeld show. Maybe after we get back from London."[88]

Funny Face lasted close to a year and chalked up 250 performances. It shuttered again due to another summer heat wave. Taking refuge from the weather, Fred and Dellie spent a Long Island weekend with Dellie's serious admirer William B. Leeds. Dellie suffered a serious accident when the motor in Leed's $75,000 motorboat, *Fan Tail,* exploded as burning oil and smoke shot into the boat. Adele suffered burns to her face, neck, and shoulders. The London opening was canceled, and an immediate rumor surfaced that Adele would never perform again. Fortunately, she made a complete recovery without any lasting physical damage.

The London run, which finally began on November 8, 1928, was their third hit in a row there. *The Sketch* intoned, "There is no mistaking the fact that London is about to enjoy another outbreak of 'Astairia' this winter. Adele's personality has still the same naïve and easy-going grace, humor, and simplicity. Fred Astaire—that mild and intellectual looking young man—is still the mind of the dance." The West End run exceeded the Broadway run by thirteen performances.[89]

Sir John Gielgud, one of the most distinguished of all English actors, saw one of the Astaires' performances in *Funny Face.* He astutely observed, "I think he [Fred] was obviously the leading spirit. As in as many partnerships, like for instance the Lunts, there was a curious feeling that the man had given the woman the feminine side of his talent, and developed it for her, and then became a wonderful partner. I always think the best dancers are the best showers-off of a woman. Obviously, everyone has a kind of mixture of the two temperaments and when it comes to the dancer, it's a wonderful thing."[90]

Gielgud's perceptive comments seriously delved into the intricate nature of the Astaires' performing relationship with emphasis on their interdependence.

When one of the partners pulls away, the partnership is in danger. On the last night of *Funny Face* in London, Adele was introduced to Lord Charles Cavendish, who had come to the theater that night with the infamous Muslim playboy Prince Aly Khan. Adele's meeting with Lord Cavendish would have a serious effect on the future of the brother-and-sister team.[91]

FUNNY FACE was one of the last of its kind to play the West End. The format for musicals was about to change, although subtly. The climate in America in the 1920s, when excess and frivolity ruled the nation, was coming to a close. No longer was a hopelessly contrived plot, a lively and shapely chorus line, a generous helping of tap dancing and singing, and plenty of comedy the recipe for a surefire Broadway musical hit.[92]

The Astaire/Gershwin show was the final London production in which Fred and Adele would appear as a team, and it also marked Adele's final London appearance.[93] Their several-years-long yo-yo-like existence—the delicious feeling they enjoyed in creating a hit on Broadway, taking it to London for a similar reception, then back to New York to open still another new musical—was about to end. They returned to New York, but this time their new show was a flop.

This show was originally called *Tom, Dick and Harry,* in which Ziegfeld wanted them to star, but despite his purchasing an idea from Noël Coward, which was then given to Louis Bromfield to write the book, then rewritten by William Anthony McQuire, "nothing seemed right from the start," as Fred described it.[94] Vincent Youmans's "Time on My Hands" was a standout song, but that wasn't nearly enough. The real problem was the plot, which concerned a playboy in love with a female Salvation Army worker, who was played by the celebrated Broadway torch singer Marilyn Miller. (Its plot resembled that of *The Belle of New York,* a Broadway musical from 1900, which, ironically, became an Astaire film musical in the early 1950s.)

The Boston tryout at the Colonial Theatre was a disaster. Ring Lardner was hired to rewrite some of the lyrics. Vincent Youmans had a drinking problem and was unreliable, therefore Walter Donaldson was hired and brought in a new song, "You're Driving Me Crazy," for Adele and Eddie Foy Jr. to sing. Fred did a number with Marilyn Miller and four with Adele. Strangely enough, Ziegfeld hired Ned Wayburn, creator of "The Baseball Act" for Fred and Adele in vaudeville, as the show's choreographer. Due to the success Miller had had in previous musicals using her character's name as the title (*Sally, Sunny,* and *Rosalie*), the title of the show was changed to *Smiles.*[95]

Given the glowing reception that the "High Hat" number had received in

Funny Face, Fred searched for a sequel. Soon, the germ of an idea came to him. Waking up at 4:00 A.M. one night in his and Adele's apartment at 875 Park Avenue, he fantasized about a number having a large male chorus of dancers with himself in front using his cane like a gun. He substituted an umbrella for the cane. The commotion of his tapping awakened Adele, who asked, "Minnie, what in hell are you doing?" When he explained he had an idea for a Manhattan number, Adele characteristically replied, "Well, hang on to it, baby—you're going to need it in this turkey!"[96]

Again, doing it *his* way—the only way Fred knew how to make dance numbers come alive—he put it in through constant rehearsals. The final outcome, "Say, Young Man of Manhattan," was a marvel. Resplendent in white tie, top hat, and carrying a cane, he performed a fast tap-dance routine. Using this cane as a weapon, he aimed it at the accompanying chorus of twenty-four male dancers similarly attired. With a series of sharp taps, he "gunned down" one member of the chorus, then another, then another. Finally, with his feet rat-a-tat-tating, he machine-gunned each of the "surviving" members of the chorus. This number was later duplicated in arguably Astaire's most significant film musical, *Top Hat,* directed by George Stevens. Irving Berlin wrote a title song specifically to accommodate the dance routine.[97]

Over the years, Fred has widely been quoted about how much he disliked wearing tails, much as he was born to wear them. As he explained it, "I worked in them a lot, and they were difficult to wear. You see, when you're in tails, the collar melts. If you're working in a picture under all those hot lights, you simply wilt in a heavy, stiff shirt. It shows up badly, and you have to stop, dry off, change, come back, and get all sweated again." Noting that tails were no longer in vogue, Fred added, "For two ballroom dancers to come out and do a waltz in tails and all that—time goes on, and they just don't do that anymore."[98]

The November 18, 1930, opening was equally as exciting as those of previous shows. Photographers were everywhere shooting celebrities as they arrived at the Ziegfeld Theatre, located at Sixth Avenue and Fifty-fourth Street. Returning to his original alter ego as a drama critic, Robert Benchley, in his *New Yorker* piece, damned the show with faint praise: "No show with Fred and Adele Astaire in it could be really considered a *complete* bust. . . . Adele is a fine little comedian, and I don't think it will plunge the nation into war by stating that Fred [Astaire] is the greatest dancer in the world."[99] Brooks Atkinson, the longtime *New York Times* drama critic, didn't care much for the show, but observed, "Slender, agile and quick-witted, the Astaires are ideal for the American song-and-dance stage."

The strong notices for the Astaires couldn't overcome the obvious deficiencies in the book. *Smiles* lasted for only a trifling sixty-three performances. Ziegfeld reportedly lost more than $500,000, a huge sum for a Broadway investment at that time. Fred was owed $10,000 when the show closed; through an arbitration hearing, he collected half the amount.[100]

TWO REPORTED INCIDENTS that took place during the *Smiles* run illustrate exactly how fiercely devoted and sensitive Fred was toward Adele. In the first incident, the accomplished harmonica player Larry Adler, who was featured in the show, was Adele's accompanist on Alexander Woollcott's radio show, *The Town Crier.* The self-taught musician could, however, only play in two keys, which seriously affected Adele's singing. Fred was furious that she was made to sound bad. When Adler returned to the theater afterward, Fred's faithful valet, Walter, warned Adler, "Don't mess around with Mr. Fred today, he'll kill you." The next day an envelope was slipped under the door of Adler's dressing room. In letters cut out from the *New York Herald Tribune* headlines was the message "Larry Adler is a cunt."[101]

In a related incident, Adele again was a guest on another popular radio show, the *Rudy Vallee Show.* Fred reached a critic shortly after the show and said to him, "If you ever take a rap at us, direct it at me, not at Adele, will you?"[102]

As a respite from the on- and offstage turmoil that surrounded *Smiles,* Fred was approached by Alex Aarons, who was then producing still another Gershwin show, *Girl Crazy,* a musical set on a dude ranch in the West. Fred was asked to choreograph the "Embraceable You" number in the show, danced by the lead, Allen Kearns, who Fred knew from their having worked together in *Funny Face,* and Ginger Rogers. Fred went over to the Alvin Theatre to meet Kearns and the young actress to work on the number, but instead of trying it out onstage, where another rehearsal was taking place, they used the foyer of the theater.[103] This was the first time Fred Astaire danced with Ginger Rogers.

As Rogers recalled in her refreshingly candid 1991 autobiography, "Our choreographer wasn't very good, and Fred was able to change and tighten some valuable moves. He was easy to follow, and I fell right in step with him. But to me he was just a man summoned to polish a few rough spots. This was no reason to be particularly impressed."

Ginger Rogers was the stage name for the Independence, Missouri, native-born Virginia Katherine McMath. As a teenager, she had adopted her stepfather's surname and won a Charleston contest. The name Ginger referred to her red hair as well as being a nickname for Virginia. She formed an act called Ginger Rogers and the Red Heads, which toured in vaudeville on the Interstate Circuit in Texas, just as Fred and Adele had. Like them, she had her mother, Lela, on the road with her. Although Lela had a physical resemblance to Ann Astaire, she was a much more aggressive and assertive stage mother than Ann.[104]

Leaving vaudeville to go to New York, she sang with Paul Ash's orchestra, and at eighteen she was the leading lady in the Broadway musical *Top Speed.* A member of the singing chorus in that show was Hermes Pan, a Tennessee-born dancer, born Hermes Panagiotopoulos, who, three years later, would figure prominently in her performing life three thousand miles from Broadway. Ginger's role in *Top Speed* led to her making her film debut in *Young Man of Manhattan,* filmed in Astoria, Long Island. A memorable line in the movie was "Cigarette me, big boy."[105]

Pan recalled, "She was the John Held Jr. girl. She used to be billed that way in vaudeville, and it was her style at the time. She had those John Held legs and short, dark red, bobbed hair, and she used to sing sort of gaga."[106]

As a supreme example of irony, the popularity of *Young Man of Manhattan* inspired Vincent Youmans to write the song, adding the introductory word "Say," which became the showstopping "Say, Young Man of Manhattan" number for Fred Astaire in *Smiles.* Similarly, Ginger's work in *Top Speed* led to her landing the leading-lady role in *Girl Crazy.*[107]

The romantic Gershwin songs such as "Embraceable You" and "But Not for Me" were perfect for Rogers's voice. The more up-tempo, lively tunes, however, were given to newcomer Ethel Zimmerman, who had shortened her name to Merman. Her songs were "Sam and Delilah," "Boy! What Love Has Done to Me," and "I Got Rhythm," which overnight established her not only as a Broadway star, but also made the show a resounding hit.[108]

Several weeks after completing his work on *Girl Crazy,* Fred asked Ginger for a date. "I was really caught off-balance," she said. "We only had [had] a brief professional encounter during my rehearsals." Ginger added, "I didn't know whether he was a good ballroom dancer. Just because a person dances well on the stage doesn't automatically mean he is delightful on the dance floor. . . . I made the discovery that as wonderful a dancer as Fred was on the stage, he was equally as a partner on the dance floor. He really knew how to lead a girl on the floor and used each rhythm to introduce different footwork."[109]

Fred and Ginger went out together several more times, including nights spent dancing to Eddy Duchin's band at the Casino in Central Park. According to Ginger, one night, as they were dancing, Duchin, with a twinkle in his eye, said, "Fred, you and Ginger really look good together." But no serious romance developed. Yet Ginger remembered that another evening, while en route to her apartment, after dancing at the Casino, "Fred held me in his arms, and the kiss we shared would never have passed the Hays Office code!"[110]

* * *

SEVERAL MONTHS AFTER the *Smiles* debacle, the producer Max Gordon brought the songwriting team of Howard Dietz and Arthur Schwartz to Fred's attention. Songs such as "I Guess I'll Have to Change My Plan" and "Something to Remember You By" had been recent hits of theirs. In addition, they had proven themselves equally adept as creators of smart, sophisticated revues. The show was *The Band Wagon.* The supporting cast was led by three talented and versatile performers in Frank Morgan, Helen Broderick, and Tilly Losch. Tying together the entire package was the brilliant playwright turned director George S. Kaufman, who wrote the sketches with the assistance of Howard Dietz.[111]

Fred and Adele signed up, then headed to Europe with stops in London and Paris, booking passage on the German ship *The Bremen.* Committing themselves to the new show before they went on holiday pleased them and gave them every reason to think that their luck was about to change.

On their return, they plunged into rehearsals, learning the witty lines and first-rate songs such as "New Sun in the Sky," wherein Fred put on his now trademark top hat, white tie, and tails. The starring brother-and-sister combination did "Hoops"; "I Love Louisa," which ended the first act with all the leading players singing in a Viennese accent while swirling around on a carousel; and "White Heat." With the Austrian ballet star Tilly Losch, Fred danced "The Beggar's Waltz," in one of his rare displays of balletic achievement. One ingredient was missing—there was no variation on "The "Runaround," although the oompahs were retained in "I Love Louisa." The affable Howard Dietz convinced Fred to play an accordion (which he admitted he had once played in vaudeville), strapped around his neck as he danced with Adele to "Sweet Music (To Worry the Wolf Away"). "Dancing in the Dark," another song often mistakenly attributed to Fred as having introduced it, was, in fact, sung by John Barker in the show as Tilly Losch danced to the rich melody on a mirrored floor.

Albertina Rasch was listed as the choreographer of *The Band Wagon,* but Fred was the major architect of the Astaires' dance numbers. He explained their creation in some detail: "Sometimes the songwriters give us a number and we work from that. The words may suggest the routine, or the music may give us the inspiration. Incidentally, it has always been impossible for us to work up anything with a poor piano player. . . . We listen to the song as it is played over and over again. Our feet move. We find new steps or combinations. Against the wall must be a big, full-length mirror. We watch our feet do this or that, and we say it's good or bad."[112]

"Gradually we do the same steps as the same bar repeats itself. After hours, we may have half a dance. We can't get the rest. Our brains go rum-tum-tum with the music even when the piano stops. Our feet keep moving, hunting for the right thing, but the mirror tells us we are wrong. It is an impasse.[113]

"A terrible feeling of desperation attacks us. We know there must be steps to fill into the holes, but nothing we do looks right. Our tempers fray. Our dispositions sour. Then it is time to go to bed. The music keeps pounding through our heads and our feet twitch under the sheets. These are the hours when most of the difficult spots are licked, for it is during the night that the inspiration we need comes to us. Early in the morning one of us may jump out of bed and find what has eluded us. The new day begins on a happy note if the mirror shows us we have what we want. But this is not the end. There are other dances, too. Day after day for as long as two months, we hammer our way through the problems. It can never be called fun. It is work of the hardest kind, requiring all day with never a thought of anything else. The grind is awful."[114]

The June 3, 1931, opening of *The Band Wagon* at the New Amsterdam Theatre on Forty-second Street took place with the severity of the Great Depression highly visible in Manhattan with Hoovervilles (shantytowns) plaguing Central Park. Brooks Atkinson took note of all this when he said in his *Times* review, "Mr. Schwartz's lively melodies, the gay dancing of the Astaires, and the colorful merriment of the background and staging begin a new era in the artistry of the American revue. When writers discover light humors of that sort in the phantasmagoria of American life, the stock market will rise spontaneously, the racketeers will all be retired or dead, and the perfect state will be here."[115] Richard Lockridge in the *New York Sun* was equally laudatory: "There is a lightness and that ability and dash in whatever they do . . . they are in any case incomparable."[116]

The Band Wagon is remembered as one of the most original revues in Broadway history for its superb Dietz and Schwartz score. But it is also memorable as the last starring vehicle for the team of Fred and Adele Astaire. Its run of 260 performances qualified it as a solid commercial hit. In addition, Fred, who had switched his recording affiliation to Victor, enjoyed a two-sided hit record of "I Love Louisa" and "New Sun in the Sky," which reached #4 and #10, respectively, on the *Billboard* Pop Chart.[117]

Before the closing, Ginger Rogers and an escort came to see the show, just as Ginger was about to leave for Hollywood to make more movies. She called *The Band Wagon* "a sheer delight. I just sat there enraptured with the joy that his [Fred's] dancing brought to my eyes and heart. Tilly was a graceful partner for Fred, but Adele was the crowd-pleaser." A few nights later, Fred and Ginger met

again at a party where she complimented him on his performance. She speculated, "If I [had] stayed in New York, I think Fred Astaire and I might have
become a . . . serious item. We were different in some ways but alike in others.
Both of us were troupers from an early age, both of us loved a good time, and for
sure, both of us loved to dance."

AS HAD HAPPENED IN LONDON, the impact of Fred and Adele's stardom was illustrated by a full-page advertisement for Chesterfield cigarettes that appeared in
Life magazine during the run of *The Band Wagon*. The main graphic shouted out,
"Good, . . . they've got to be good!" It featured the Astaires in top hats, white
scarves, and tuxedos, with their white-gloved hands extended forward for emphasis. Adele's words were "They're milder, Fred," as Fred pointed out, "Tastes better, too."

They also appeared in a two-reel short subject made in New York for Vita-
phone. It was apparently of minor importance to them since Fred never even
mentioned it in *Steps in Time*.

They were living the good life in New York with Ann in a Park Avenue penthouse, a sure indication of their preference for living among the wealthy.[118] A
baby Rolls-Royce complete with chauffeur was still at their disposal (reportedly
the first one in New York).[119] They were constantly sought after to attend parties
in New York and weekend excursions to estates on the north shore of Long Island
by "The 400," the name then associated with New York's high society.

Fred spent a great deal of his leisure time pursuing his love of horses with his
pals Jimmy Altemus, Jock Whitney, and others at Belmont Park, and playing golf
as a guest at exclusive golf clubs. At the Lambs Club, he enjoyed shooting pool
and playing gin and bridge with veteran performers such as Charles Winninger
and William Claxton.[120] He continued buying custom-tailored Savile Row clothes
long-distance by contacting the London tailor Anderson & Sheppard, which kept
his measurements on file. Adele was busy dating Lord Cavendish, attending parties, romantic dinners, and dancing in nightclubs. The charmed life they were
leading was their version of the lifestyle they admired that the upper class led in
London.

In an unconventional departure from this existence, Jock Whitney gave Fred
a pair of big-wheel roller skates as a present. Fred took to learning to skate immediately, but he was afraid that someone from the press might catch him skating
down Park Avenue by daylight. Instead, he confined his skating to nightly excursions after the theater. Ann was terrified he would break an ankle, but he shrugged

off her worries.[121] A few years later, his prowess on roller skates would serve as the basis of one of his most important dance numbers on film.

ADELE'S ROMANCE WITH THE TALL, stately, and quiet lord, the second son of the ninth Duke of Devonshire, several years her junior, proceeded at a deliberate pace after their initial meeting on the closing night of *Funny Face* in London.[122] They were immediately so taken with one another that they spent several days in Paris together before Adele joined Fred in Cherbourg, France, before they sailed home to America. Shortly after that, Charles came to New York to begin to work in the stock brokerage business with the J. P. Morgan & Company. Fred liked Charles immediately and came to realize that he was someone worthy of his sister.

For centuries, the Cavendish family had maintained a close bloodline with England's royal family. As a little boy, Charles had carried the queen's crown at the coronation of George V in 1910. The family owned a town house in Carlton Gardens and spent their summers in county Waterford, Ireland, at the two-hundred-room Lismore Castle, which dated back to William the Conqueror. Sir Walter Raleigh had lived there at one time.[123] Seventy people took care of its four-hundred-acre spread.

Previously, no Cavendish had married outside the nobility. Charles, however, was absolutely set almost from the beginning on making Adele his bride, but it was Adele who actually proposed. As Adele recalled, "I was at '21,' which in those days was a speakeasy. I'd had one drink because I don't drink very much, and I said, 'Do you know we get along so well, I think we ought to get married.' 'Right-ho,' he says, and I thought no more about it. Next morning, he wakes me up and he says, 'You proposed to me last night, and I accepted. If you don't go through with it, I'll sue you for breach of promise.' I think that was cute."[124]

Anna Kisselgoff, the dance critic of the *New York Times* from 1977 to 2005, said that the London *Daily Telegraph* was an anti-Semitic newspaper of the time. The paper published several attacks on Lord Cavendish's choice of a bride, pointing out the unforgivable: Adele was both American and her grandparents had been born as Jews in Austria. Adele's engagement to Cavendish brought the issue of the Astaires' Jewish heritage to the fore.

This did not alter the young lovers. Adele was mad for Charlie and looked forward to the thought that at the age of thirty-five she would become Lady Cavendish living in an Irish castle. She was tired of the traveling and the constant rehearsals. The theatrical life never fully got to her. It took away from having a good time. It was the right moment to retire the act. She was determined to go out with a hit. As planned, *The Band Wagon* was the perfect way to end it all.[125]

The final performance of Fred and Adele in the show was in Chicago at the Illinois Theatre on March 5, 1932. A group of their friends came out from New York to catch the finale of their act after twenty-seven years of working together. Naturally, it was a bittersweet evening. Ann spent most of the performance in Adele's dressing room brushing back her tears.[126]

Adele was left with some doubts. As she expressed it, "I wasn't sure at the time I was doing the right thing, but it did have to be done. I could see that we would have to go our separate ways even though I would miss his moaning."[127]

The next day Adele and Ann left for New York, then on to England, where Adele married Lord Charles Arthur Cavendish at a lavish ceremony in the private chapel of Chatsworth House in Devonshire on May 5. Adele wore a beautiful plain white gown created by the noted New York fashion designer Mainbocher. In a distinct departure from English tradition, Ann gave her daughter in marriage.[128]

Fred was committed to the show and couldn't attend the wedding. Adele's capable understudy, Vera Marsh, took her place for the remainder of the tour.[129]

Fred once again took a serious look at his life and career. At the outset, and through most of their years in vaudeville, he had been in Adele's shadow, but through complete dedication and extremely hard work, coupled with his own ability and an intense desire to succeed, throughout their work on Broadway and in the West End, he had become her equal. They had been a vital part of Broadway in the 1920s.[130] And though very different people, they both appreciated elegance, style, and sophistication, which, along with their incredible talent, had enabled them to achieve the sterling reputation they had carved out as a team.

Fred said he was never upset by the loss of Adele, although this was pure rationalization. As he expressed it in his autobiography, "I knew I'd have to face it sooner or later." Inwardly, he, too, wasn't so sure. He was losing his longtime partner, but a life partner as well as a new dancing partner were in his immediate future.

CHAPTER THREE

IN SEARCH OF A PARTNER

FRED WAS NOW about to enter an entirely new chapter in his life, one that would in time bring him worldwide fame and great wealth. As Adele was preparing to retire from their act, Fred, after several short-lived infatuations, was suddenly involved in the only serious romantic relationship of his life thus far. The object of his affection was indeed his idea of perfection, an American aristocrat named Phyllis Potter.

Fred met Potter on a Sunday in the summer of 1931 during the run of *The Band Wagon.* He had driven out to Long Island for a golf luncheon hosted by Virginia Graham Fair Vanderbilt. He found himself at a table with several other socialites, including Potter, a twenty-three-year-old, dark-haired, petite, doll-like young woman, five feet three inches tall (the same height as Adele).[1] She had a slight speech impediment that caused her to pronounce the letter "r" like a "w." He had noticed her on another occasion at Belmont Park, sitting in a box with Henry W. Bull, the president of the exclusive Turf and Field Club.[2]

Phyllis was born in Boston, the daughter of Dr. Harold W. Baker, a Boston gynecologist, and founder of the city's Free Hospital for Women. On her mother's side, Robert Livingston, governor of New York, helped draft the Declaration of Independence. After the death of her father and her mother's remarriage, she was brought up by her mother's sister, Maud Livingstone, and Maud's husband, Henry W. Bull. A senior partner in the New York financial firm of Harriman and Company, Bull had homes in Manhattan; Islip, Long Island; and Aiken, South Carolina.

In 1926 Phyllis came out as a debutante, and in December 1927 she married a prominent New York socialite, Eliphalet Nott Potter III. A year later Eliphalet

Nott Potter IV was born; fortunately, for him, he was called Peter. Even though both of his parents realized that the marriage had been a mistake, their separation was not an amicable one as Phyllis was the only one who wanted a divorce, but the marriage was dissolved.[3]

THAT SUMMER AFTERNOON in 1931 on Long Island, as the champagne flowed under a broiling sun, Phyllis revealed that she was separated from her husband and intended to bring their three-year-old son, Peter, up in a quiet country atmosphere. Although she had never heard of him or his sister, Fred was charmed nevertheless. Before he left the luncheon, he asked her if he could call her in New York. She said yes, explaining that she was going away but would be returning in a few days.[4]

They met after the theater one night for a drink with mutual friends. Soon after that, Fred came around for tea and also to meet Peter. Several more dates followed, during which Fred became increasingly attracted to Phyllis.[5] He also discovered that Phyllis had several other admirers. He thought that perhaps the way to her heart was to offer tickets to see him perform in *The Band Wagon*. After the show, he hoped he had impressed her with his performance. She responded, "Oh, Fwed, you were vewy good." "To me that was the most valued praise of all time," he recalled.[6]

Phyllis returned to see the show, this time bringing along a drunken escort. During the performance Fred spotted them in the fourth row. He could see how bothersome he was, which made him even more furious. When they came back after the show, he asked Phyllis, "Where did you dig up this snail?" She explained that she had known him for years and rationalized, "He's just a bit tight." She got him to leave, and she and Fred left the theater together.[7]

Fred pursued Phyllis at this uncertain pace for two years. He was absolutely convinced, however, that Phyllis was absolutely the right girl for him and vowed to do anything to win her. The same determination Fred brought to perfecting a new dance step came to the fore in the way he pursued Phyllis. Looking back on their courtship, he described it, "I had to mow them [her many admirers] down one by one." This was despite her seeming inattention, which was coupled with her reluctance to proceed with a new relationship, an unfortunate but natural residue of her recently concluded unhappy marriage. Besides all of that, her entire background was completely out of sync with a show business life.

As Adele recalled, "At the time of *The Band Wagon,* he was nutty for Phyllis. Moping about and behaving just like he had a flop on his hands when we were out of town. He was very funny about it all. But it was really just a matter of seeing if they could sort out all the dreadful legal complications which were upsetting Phyllis so much."

One would assume that Ann would be thrilled that her thirty-two-year-old son had at last found someone he thought he could have a future with, but instead she stated her opposition clearly. Ann was worried about the complicated involvement with a woman with a young son, going through a difficult divorce. The very mention of the word "divorce" was anathema to her. She figured many other attractive young society girls had lives much less complicated for Fred now that he was completely on his own.[8] However, Fred had fallen in love; he wasn't bothered by his mother's less than subtle adverse comments.

During the summer of 1932, Phyllis decided to get away from it all by accompanying the Bulls to London, where Henry was planning to attend the Derby. Her trip to England "just happened" to coincide with Fred's sailing to England and then to county Waterford, Ireland, to visit with the newlyweds Adele and Charles at Lismore Castle.[9] The two couples seemed to be a perfect fit when they subsequently got together in London. His good friends there found Fred and his new love a most charming couple. Enjoying London as much as he ever did in his glory days with Adele, Fred was in no hurry to return to New York.

With romance very much on his mind, Fred never lost sight, however, that he had to decide on just the right show to establish his solo career. He dare not expose himself to the talk among some on Broadway that he would fade away without Adele. Phyllis impressed upon him, "Fweddie, I think you should go back and investigate your career." Since they had finally begun to discuss the possibility of getting married, she reminded him, "You'll have to work, won't you?"[10]

Before leaving for Europe, Fred had entered into discussions with Cole Porter, another Midwesterner, who hailed from Peru, Indiana, about Porter's next show. Porter and his two producers, Dwight Wiman and Tom Weatherly, wanted Fred to star in *Gay Divorce*. Fred, however, was reluctant to commit himself to the project.

On his return to New York, he was in a more serious frame of mind. Cole had recently returned from Hollywood, where his musical *Fifty Million Frenchmen* had gone into production. *Gay Divorce* was based on an unproduced play by J. Hartley Manners.[11] The show required some rewriting as its premise was rather shallow. Fred was to play a man who pretended to be a gigolo in order to act as a corespondent for an Englishman who was trying to get a divorce. What helped tip the scales for Fred was that he had known Cole for a few years, and Phyllis was a distant cousin of Porter's wife, Linda.

The songwriter played the first song he had written for the show, "After You, Who?" for Fred. That was the clincher; he decided to commit to the show.[12] (Strangely enough, this song never registered as an essential of the Porter canon except for being a favorite of the singer Mabel Mercer. It was revived in the 1980s as a staple of the repertoire of another popular cabaret performer, Bobby Short.)

Fred returned to Europe for a few weeks in Tourquet on the Côte d'Azur, where Phyllis was enjoying a holiday with her family. She allayed his fears about going it alone. She wouldn't, however, set a date for their marriage, pointing out he had to devote himself to his upcoming show.

As he started rehearsals for *Gay Divorce* in September 1932, he still had to overcome a series of inner doubts. Although his brilliance had been singled out by the critics, Adele had been the more adored one by audiences as well as by many critics. Adele had made it clear: "He was always staying in the background. I was the one who was pushed forward by him. If there was a laugh to be had, he'd stand back for it. That is the truth, and [yet] people wondered if he could make it alone. They thought he couldn't do without me, but the minute I left that man, he went ahead." In a moment of self-derision she added, "So I must have been a drawback for years, that's all I can think of."[13]

But with all the uncertainty that went along with making an impression as a solo song-and-dance man, he would also have to contend with working alongside a new leading lady. Whatever she had to offer, she simply wasn't Adele—none of his other dancing partners really ever were—despite their various virtues as performers. He and Adele had shared too many performances together, too much personal history on- and offstage together, on top of their closeness as brother and sister.

In *Gay Divorce,* he was given a lithesome blond actress and dancer who had started out as a cigarette girl in nightclubs, before becoming a Ziegfeld star, named Claire Luce, who was then married to the millionaire playboy Clifford Warren Smith.[14] The role called for a genteel siren-type, and Luce was much more glamorous than Adele, with none of her pixie quality. Luce had been working in Hollywood, most recently in director John Ford's 1930 film *Up the River,* in which she was cast opposite Spencer Tracy.

For Luce to come up to the impossible level as a dancer that Fred required in his costar was a tough challenge. She worked diligently, but as she recalled, "I felt sorry for Fred, despite the tremendous schedule of rehearsals that he kept up. . . . I think he missed Adele. I tried awfully hard to be as bright, as cheerful as I could, so I stuck that smile on and tried as hard as I possibly could."

As usual, problems ensued in the first tryout city, which was Boston, with a booking at the Wilbur Theatre. Phyllis wanted to join Fred, but he sensed the problems facing the show. The music worked but Dwight Taylor's book didn't. Fred commented, "I've always felt that my presence in a story makes it tough on a writer. I tend to ruin a book because everybody expects me to hop into a dance every minute."

The director was Howard Lindsay, later cowriter of *Life with Father,* which held the record for many decades as the longest-running nonmusical play in Broadway history. Two important craftsmen on the show, who would go to countless successes on Broadway in later years, were the scenic designer Jo Mielziner and the arranger and orchestrator Robert Russell Bennett. In addition, two superb comic actors, Eric Blore and Erik Rhodes, made an immediate impression with audiences. The *Boston Transcript* critic, however, took a cheap shot at Fred in his opening-night review: "As Astaire must dance and still does very well—but not for the general good as he is now sisterless."

The only really strong selling point in the show was an intensely romantic ballad Porter had written specifically for Fred called "Night and Day." Contrary to his usual procedure, Porter had written the melody first. Monty Woolley, the veteran character actor (famous for playing the title role in *The Man Who Came to Dinner*) and close pal of Porter's since their days at Yale, on hearing the song played by Cole on the piano, remarked, "I don't know what this is you are trying to do, but whatever it is, throw it away. It's terrible."[15]

Porter had been born into wealth, but it was his smart, sophisticated, and often suggestive lyrics, along with his rich and sometimes exotic melodies, that endeared him to high society. His inspiration came from many different quarters. While Porter was writing the score of *Gay Divorce,* he spent a weekend with Mrs. Vincent Astor at her estate in Newport. The grande dame had insisted that they eat off trays away from the dining room table so that their conversation would not to be interrupted by the servants. They sat on the porch during a steady rain, which caused his hostess to complain, "I must have that eave mended at once. The drip, drip, drip is driving me mad."[16] This displeasure of Astor's became "the drip, drip, drip of the raindrops when the summer shower is through," an important phrase in the verse of Porter's "Night and Day" lyrics.[17]

When the song was initially brought to Fred, he complained to Tom Weatherly that his voice would crack if he was forced to sing it in such a high key. (Porter admitted he had widened the voice range to form notes over an octave.)[18] Weatherly suggested to Porter that the song be cut, but Cole insisted on keeping it in as he had the intuitive feeling it would be important to the show. The number proved to be the highlight of the show and became strongly identified with Astaire, chiefly because it became a smash hit record for him on Victor, enjoying ten weeks as the number one record in the country.[19] The passion and the complete conviction with which he interpreted the song along with a rather patrician delivery gave it a highly romantic aura. Working with a choreographer he admired, Carl Randall, Fred developed a romantic and flowing approach to the song that was the complete antithesis of what he would have done with Adele.

Some old stage habits, however, were hard to break, as when he and Claire in a Fred-and-Adele-type routine performed "I've Got You on My Mind." Fred recorded it alone, and it, too, was another hit record from the show, with Leo Reisman's orchestra supplying the backing as it had for Fred's previous hit records.[20] Fred and Claire waltzed around the stage over tables and chairs in other numbers and occasionally stumbled, which, when repeated, generated additional rounds of applause. Fred missed the opportunity to talk over the dance numbers with Adele. Ann was of some help, and Phyllis was understanding, but he missed the counsel of his former dancing partner.

Adele was not entirely out of the picture. At Lismore Castle, she was made aware of some of the problems that Fred was encountering through letters from Ann. She knew Claire Luce, whom she felt was a good choice to work with Fred, but she also knew how difficult it would be for him to adapt to a new and quite different partner only months after her retirement. She and Charlie sent an apt and amusing cable on opening night: NOW MINNIE, DON'T FORGET TO MOAN.[21]

The late-arriving, boisterous, yet at certain intervals blasé opening audience for *Gay Divorce,* on November 29, 1932, at the Ethel Barrymore Theatre, made it that much more difficult for Fred in working with a new costar. Immediately after the final curtain, Phyllis came backstage to sympathize with him and declared, "What a dweadful audience!" Fred responded, "So is the show." Phyllis added, "I liked some of it."[22] At that moment of grave uncertainty, he was pleased that as a "civilian" she wouldn't be apt to deliver a series of opening-night platitudes.[23]

The Broadway critical establishment used the occasion to further comment on the loss of Adele. One reviewer, no doubt reaching a bit to make his point, said that Fred was staring at the wings "as if his titled sister, Adele, would come out and rescue him." Another commented, "Two Astaires are better than one." Harold Lockridge of the *Sun* made the devastating assertion, "When Fred wasn't dancing, he gave a curious impression of unemployment." Perhaps the most unfortunate critique dismissed his future as a romantic leading man with the words "He hasn't the hair for one thing," alluding to Fred's rapidly receding hair.[24] Even one of his champions, Brooks Atkinson, who praised Claire Luce's dancing, said, "But some of us cannot help feeling the joyousness of the Astaire team is missing now that the team has parted."[25]

Fred was not the least bit surprised that the critics noted Adele's absence. "I'd have been disappointed if they hadn't," he recalled.[26] If that wasn't enough, the ineptness of the plot was singled out. Walter Winchell, the most widely read of the Broadway gossip columnists, wrote, "The personable and talented brother of Lady Cavendish never before seemed so refreshing and entertaining—but 'Gay Divorce' has a tendency to go flat for more than two minutes at a time—too often."[27]

Little mention was given by the critics to "Night and Day," which received only a tepid response from the opening-night audience. The forty-eight-bar arrangement, replacing the usual sixteen-bar version for popular songs of the time, made it seem endless. Yet Irving Berlin, a good judge of what constitutes a great song, wrote Porter, "I'm mad about 'Night and Day,' and I think it is your high spot."

Within three months of the show's opening, song pluggers (now called "radio promotion men") succeeded in getting Astaire to record the song and made it so popular on the by now well-established medium of radio that it became a huge standard. It went on to become Porter's most popular song. The success it enjoyed, plus some rewriting and the restaging of certain scenes in the weeks following opening night, led *Gay Divorce* to limp along and last a full season with a run of 244 performances.[28] (This was only two performances less than that of *Funny Face,* which was a certifiable hit.)

Most important, Fred Astaire had helped transform a weak musical into a reasonable hit. He had carried the show himself. This moment proved that his appeal transcended Broadway, that he was a full-fledged musical star.

Not surprisingly, boredom had settled in. Fred remarked to Lucius Beebe of the *Herald Tribune* that Broadway was losing its luster for him. "The stage is beginning to worry me a bit," he admitted. "Just why, I cannot say, only perhaps it's getting on my nerves. I don't know what I'm going to do about it either. I feel that I ought to dance just as long as I'm able to do it and get away with it. Lots of people seem to like it and would be disappointed if I should turn to anything else."[29]

Gay Divorce was Fred's final appearance on Broadway. The noted chronicler of classic popular music, Robert Kimball, in a 1971 interview, asked Astaire why he never returned to Broadway. His answer: "There was a wonderful feeling in New York at Christmastime—the bright lights and the gaiety—and the car shows, et cetera. I think New York was wonderful in the '20s and early '30s. That's not there anymore."

That meant he had only one place to go to expand his audience, and that was Hollywood. Getting there, however, didn't prove easy. The director Mervyn LeRoy, then signed to Warner Bros., where he had just completed *Little Caesar* with Edward G. Robinson and was about to direct the memorable musical *Gold Diggers of 1933,* stopped Fred on a New York street, weeks after the opening, and mentioned how much he had enjoyed Fred's performance in *Gay Divorce.* LeRoy suggested that the show might well make an ideal film musical.[30]

Soon after that, Leland Hayward approached David O. Selznick, then head of production at RKO Radio Pictures, about a movie deal for Astaire.[31] Selznick believed the dancer and singer definitely had a film career ahead.[32] He called Astaire "one of the greatest artists of the day, a magnificent performer." He also referred to him as "unquestionably the outstanding young leader of American musical comedy," adding, "Next to [the English actor] Leslie Howard, Astaire is the most charming man in the New York theater." In a production meeting, RKO producer Merian C. Cooper mentioned that he had seen *The Band Wagon* and found Astaire "a helluva dancer—there wasn't anybody in his class."[33]

In January 1933, Selznick assigned Kay Brown—then a RKO executive, later one of the first important female talent agents, who, at MCA, represented many important talents, such as Ingrid Bergman, Arthur Miller, Paul Newman, and Joanne Woodward—to arrange a screen test for Astaire in New York. For years, the name of the individual who conducted this screen test was never mentioned. Then Debbie Reynolds, in her autobiography, *Debbie: My Life,* announced that it was Burt Grady. On its completion, Grady sent a wire to Selznick conveying his now infamous appraisal of Fred Astaire: CAN'T ACT, SLIGHTLY BALD, ALSO DANCES.

After this less than superlative report, the mood at RKO was anything but jubilant. Selznick admitted, "I am a little uncertain about the man, but I feel, in spite of his enormous ears and bad chin line, that his charm is so tremendous it comes through even on this wretched test." Despite his uncertainty, Selznick moved quickly to sign Astaire before the other studios knew that he was available.[34]

FOR MANY DECADES, Hollywood has taken immediate notice of a successful picture (whether it is a musical comedy, adventure, romance, whatever), then tries to make an exact duplicate in that genre. The cycle is broken after a succession of box-office failures in trying to duplicate the success of the original film. Then it's on to the next film flavor of the moment.

After *The Jazz Singer* a succession of poorly conceived musicals were box-office failures. But perhaps because in 1933 the United States was smack-dab in the middle of the Great Depression, with 12 million unemployed, audiences had a renewed interest in escapist musicals. Maurice Chevalier and Jeanette MacDonald had scored with *Love Me Tonight* for Paramount, and Eddie Cantor in *The Kid from Spain* had been a hit for Samuel Goldwyn in 1932. Darryl F. Zanuck, at that time a Warners producer, had just completed the musical *42nd Street,* choreographed by Busby Berkeley.[35] Musicals again were in fashion, with a void for a younger musical performer to take the lead.

Selznick signed Astaire to a contract through Leland Hayward calling for Fred to be paid $1,500 a week by RKO for his first film. If his option was picked up by the studio, his next two movies after that would pay him $1,750 a week. If he continued to make films for the studio, his salary would be raised to $3,000 a week by his sixth film. Naturally, the first film assigned to him was a musical, called *Flying Down to Rio.*

Production plans in Hollywood often don't run smoothly. First, the start date on *Flying Down to Rio* was delayed. Then, in February 1933, a mere month after signing Astaire to RKO, David O. Selznick left RKO to work for his father-in-law, Louis B. Mayer, "the Lion of Hollywood,"[36] who ran Metro-Goldwyn-Mayer. Selznick, along with Walter Wanger and several other producers had been sought by Mayer to take up the production slack caused by the severe heart attack suffered by MGM's head of production, Irving Thalberg.

Selznick's first MGM movie was a black-and-white backstage musical called *Dancing Lady*. He found a place for Fred to make his debut in the movie as a guest star (as was another stage performer, singer Nelson Eddy). Yet in a Columbia University oral history interview, Astaire claimed, "Joan Crawford asked if I could go over and do a number with her in *Dancing Lady,* which followed on the heels of the Busby Berkeley film musicals. I thought it would be a good idea to get a little film experience before I did this other picture." By negotiating with RKO, MGM got Astaire on a loan-out for $2,500 a week, with RKO making $1,000 a week on the deal.

What has never publicly been known until now is that Fred tried hard to have a part written for Adele in *Dancing Lady*. The movie producer and journalist Dan Selznick, David and Irene Selznick's son, recalled, "I have the distinct memory that my father scheduled a screen test for Adele before she swore off a career. You can see it in Marshall Flaum's wonderful documentary, *Hollywood: The Selznick Years.* Adele was absolutely delightful. To me, she was reminiscent of Imogene Coca. She was so friendly and cute—a little gentile version of Fanny Brice.

"As far as I know, there was no role that was already written that went to another actress. I suspect DOS would have had to perhaps create a role for her, perhaps a sister to the character Fred played. It was too small a part. I doubt Adele would have taken it, but rather waited for her own better opportunity. It's easy to imagine that Fred would have felt more secure if his sister could have joined him in the film."

Before Fred ventured westward for the shooting of *Dancing Lady,* it was time for pleasure. At long last, Phyllis agreed to marry Fred. As he explained it, "Phyllis figured, 'If you go away to Hollywood, you'll start running around with some of those girls out there, and whether you do or not, I'd always think you did, so we'd better get married right now as soon as possible.'"

On July 12, 1933, at 6:00 P.M., Justice Selah B. Strong performed the marriage in his chambers in Brooklyn at the county courthouse. Earlier, Justice Strong had been the presiding judge when Phyllis petitioned and won custody of her son, Peter, for eleven months of the year. According to available reports, Ann Astaire was not present at her son's wedding. She had temporarily returned to Omaha to see her family and to register Fred's birth, since he had no birth certificate and needed it to get a marriage license. Henry W. Bull gave the bride away.

The twenty-five-year-old bride and the thirty-four-year-old groom spent a one-day honeymoon aboard the yacht the *Captiva,* owned by their good friend Jock Whitney's mother, Mrs. Payne Whitney, cruising the Hudson River.[37] Leaving Peter with his nurse in Manhattan, Fred and Phyllis boarded a TWA (Transcontinental Western Airways) Ford trimotor plane in New York that took twenty-six hours, which included several stopovers, to reach Burbank, California. They were goin' Hollywood!

The Astaires were met at the airport by Andy Hervey, a MGM publicist. Hervey arranged for a pair of freelance photographers to shoot them as they disembarked from the airplane. Fred was resplendent in a white straw hat with a striped band, a glen-plaid suit, with a button-down Brooks Brothers shirt complete with a checked necktie and a collar pin, while Phyllis wore a chic blue dotted-print dress with a matching scarf and a small hat. The caption on the picture read ASTAIRE AND BRIDE HERE FROM EAST. The newlyweds were whisked off to a suite in the Beverly Wilshire Hotel, where Wilshire Boulevard and Rodeo Drive intersect in Beverly Hills.[38]

Within a few days, Fred reported to MGM. The plot of the film was a rather typical Depression-era tale (heavily influenced by *42nd Street*)[39] of a hard-bitten "dancing lady," which was supposedly based on Claire Luce's early days in the theater.[40] Joan Crawford, in the title role, was coming off two failures. A great deal of her real-life persona was in her portrayal of the tough, young showgirl/dancer. The elegant Franchot Tone played her wealthy lover. The male lead was Clark Gable, whose ill-defined role was as the determined, irascible director of a musical-within-the-musical who crosses swords with Crawford. When she replaces the original female lead in the show, under Gable's tutelage she becomes a Broadway star and falls in love with him. (This also happened in real life.)

As soon as they arrived in Beverly Hills, the Astaires discovered that Crawford had blanketed the sitting room of their hotel suite with all kinds of white flowers. Playing the role of the hospitable star, she entertained them several times at her home for dinner. But obviously Fred's utmost attention was devoted to the few weeks of rehearsals (never enough for him!) that preceded his three weeks of filming.[41]

The stock market crash in the fall of 1929 had taken away a great deal of Fred's and Adele's savings. He had, however, starred in three Broadway musicals since then, two of which were hits, plus the successful London engagement of *Funny Face.* He was also signed to reprise his role in *Gay Divorce* in London that

November. Now, however, he was intent on registering in movies. His faithful valet, Walter, came out from New York to assist him.

Dressed in a turtleneck, blazer, slacks, and stadium shoes, the nervousness that Fred was experiencing in his first scene in *Dancing Lady* was absolutely palpable. His debut took place in the last half hour of the movie. He was introduced by Patch Gallagher (Clark Gable) as a candidate to play the leading man in the musical in rehearsal. Patch announces to Janie Barlow (Joan Crawford), "Here is Freddie Astaire," then instructs Astaire, "Show Miss Barlow the routine for the opening number, will you?" Fred replies, "I'd love to." After further pleasantries, Fred instructs the orchestra leader in the pit, "Oh, Harry, give us the pickup on the 'Gang' number, will you please? Thanks."[42]

Despite his visible lack of confidence, Fred quickly transformed himself into the assured tap dancer he was. (When he finally saw the movie in London, while starring in *Gay Divorce,* Fred contended he looked "knifelike" in his debut scene.) The "High-Ho the Gang's All Here" number is terminated in the middle when Janie collapses with a sprained ankle.

There was more Astaire to be seen. The climax of the film takes place on the Broadway musical's opening night, in which he dances two completely disparate numbers.[43] Picking up the "High-Ho the Gang's All Here" number, the formally dressed male and female chorus sing the lyrics as they dance around a circular bar. Astaire, in tails, and Crawford, in a white dress, enter arm in arm to perform a strutting routine. All at once, the two stars are amazingly elevated onto a platform and zoom across the sky. The dance mood is abruptly changed as they suddenly land in Bavaria dressed in native costumes, Fred looking rather gauche in a hat, pencil mustache, and wearing lederhosen, as is Crawford in a flaring skirt, peasant blouse, and blond pigtails! They perform "Let's Go Bavarian," a number obviously based on the "I Love Louisa" number from *The Band Wagon.* They leave the stage with a rousing "oompah" ending.[44]

The small role in *Dancing Lady* (a box-office hit) enabled Fred to gain an understanding of the slow and intricate shooting of a Hollywood musical. He had less than fifteen minutes on camera, but his appearance made a definite impression. His superlative dancing ability and shy but natural charm were captured by the camera.

Dancing Lady was just the beginning. *Flying Down to Rio* was finally about to commence production. With all of his considerable moaning, the best was yet to come.

CHAPTER FOUR

FRED AND GINGER

LMOST A MONTH BEFORE Fred and Phyllis were married, RKO announced it was sending a camera crew to Brazil to film background and aerial scenes for its forthcoming musical production *Flying Down to Rio*. A succession of casting notices followed in the film press. The volume of publicity was designed to alert the movie audience that *Rio* was going to be a major film musical.[1]

RKO was an acronym for the combination of the Radio Corporation of America and the theater chains of Keith and Orpheum. The film company was established in 1928 when Joseph P. Kennedy (yes, that Kennedy) persuaded David Sarnoff, the chairman of RCA, to venture into the movie business. The company, at first, showcased RCA's sound on film. However, by 1933 its yearly film slates were extremely unpopular, and RKO was teetering on the brink of bankruptcy.

Merian C. Cooper had replaced David O. Selznick as production chief at RKO. While trying to move *Flying Down to Rio* and other films into production, Cooper was heavily involved in putting together an adventure film about a giant ape captured on a small South Pacific island who wreaks havoc while being held captive in New York. It was to be called *Kong*.

Earlier in 1933, Cooper had signed Ginger Rogers to the studio. By then, Rogers was a film actress, having appeared in twenty-five films. She had recently made a significant impression in *Gold Diggers of 1933,* still considered rather a milestone musical of the Depression period.[2] Her rendition of "We're in the Money" was one of the highlights of the movie.

When Fred reported for work, he had no idea who had been assigned to work with him since the final casting for the picture was still incomplete. For a time Dorothy Jordan was seriously considered by Cooper as Astaire's dancing partner. She had been Adele's understudy in *Funny Face*. Jordan, however, ultimately married Cooper and left with him for Europe on their honeymoon as the picture moved into production.[3]

On the third day of filming, Astaire was informed that Ginger Rogers might be appearing in the film, but he still wasn't at all sure if she was going to be dancing with him since of late Ginger had concentrated on playing several dramatic parts.[4] He questioned whether she was that interested in a dancing role. When it was ultimately decided that she would be cast opposite Fred, they had a joyful reunion and looked forward to working together, this time as dance partners. Ginger helped him to become more comfortable working with the camera.[5] Already a seasoned actress, she possessed tricks of the trade that Astaire was not yet familiar with.

Dave Gould was assigned as dance director for the movie, but Fred found himself drawn to the keen, forward-looking ideas of Hermes Pan, Gould's assistant, who had a great physical resemblance to Fred, although Pan was slightly taller. Pan had, of course, worked with Ginger in *Top Speed* on Broadway. He had never seen Fred perform but remembered, "He was already famous for doing broken-rhythm dancing . . . on the beat, off the beat, back and forth."[6]

On the first day of shooting, their rapport was immediate when Pan showed Fred the way out of a troubling bit of choreography by suggesting he execute a tap "break." At that moment, whether he realized it or not, Fred Astaire had found his muse. Basically, they thought exactly alike about film dancing. A lifetime association was born. Fred once referred to Pan as "the rock. . . . He doesn't make any fuss about anything."[7]

Pan reflected on their association by saying, "I didn't influence his style because he was already a star when I was starting out. People naturally influence each other whether it's unconscious or not. Later on, I could see certain moves or attitudes he would never have done before."[8]

Fred was called Fred Ayres in the *Flying Down to Rio* screenplay. It was a halfhearted attempt to establish his name with moviegoers. He was signed for $1,500 a week and due to overtime wound up making $10,000 on the film.

The movie opens in a Miami hotel where Fred appears as the best friend of Gene Raymond, the bandleader/songwriter/aviator. (Vincent Youmans wrote the film's score.) Raymond has on-camera romance with the Mexican beauty Dolores del Rio, who entices him to fly her to Rio de Janeiro for the grand opening of the Hotel Atlantico.[9] In Miami, in a scene that was originally tinted in a rose color, but never released in that form, Fred and del Rio dance a tango together. Unfortunately, no sparks flew in their number.

Ginger was billed fourth and Fred fifth in the film. Their roles were incidental to the plot and their characters have no interrelationship. While Ginger sang "Music Makes Me" as the vocalist in Raymond's band, Fred is seen playing the accordion in the band. Fred's version of "Music Makes Me," along with the title song, supplied Fred with another two-sided hit record. He also led the band in the spectacular, well-remembered title number in which a bevy of leggy chorus girls pose seductively and then dance while strapped atop the wings of the biplanes flying in formation above the Atlantico Hotel.[10] Though this sequence was the essence of camp, made possible by rear projection and process shots, film audiences marveled at how vivid and absolutely incredible it was.

What excited movie audiences even more, however, was Fred and Ginger dancing together to "The Carioca," shot at a cost of $600 as a major production number in a mere three days on a set representing the Carioca Casino in Rio.[11] Buoyed by Ginger's suggesting, "Let's show them a thing or three," Fred grabs Ginger's hand and they sprint determinedly onto the dance floor. The impact of their dance causes the other dancers to back away to give them more room. This is followed by twenty-five couples in Brazilian costumes, then a group of black northern Brazilians, who add even more variations to the Latin dance number. Fred and Ginger return for a spectacular finale, dancing atop seven pianos, arranged to form a circular dance floor.[12]

"The Carioca," absolutely defined chemistry in dancing between two partners. Here were two well-trained dancers thrown together for the first time on film, who shared a real passion for the dance. Vitality underlined their every movement on the dance floor. They danced with a precision that made it appear as though they had been working together for years. The screen had never witnessed a dance team that combined so many performing virtues.

Fred explained that although he was far from having artistic control of his dance numbers in *Rio,* "the dances were written . . . into the places for the musical numbers, and then it was up to us to decide what kind of a dance we wanted to do in those spots." Hermes Pan's thoughts jibed perfectly with Fred's ideas, along with Ginger's suggestions, in helping make "The Carioca" such a standout.[13]

Fred's work was singled out by the film critic of the *Los Angeles Times,* Philip K. Scheuer, who wrote, "Astaire, being hailed as a 'find,' electrifies in a top specialty and in the rumba-like 'Carioca' (with Miss Rogers)." Thornton Delahanty in the *New York Post* declared, "The chief point of interest is that [the movie] has Fred Astaire in the cast. Then to that, and to that alone, the picture is worth seeing." Syd Silverman of *Variety* similarly stated, "The main point of *Flying Down to Rio* is the screen promise of Fred Astaire. . . . Not that Astaire threatened to become the ocean to ocean rage, but here he shows enough to indicate what he could do with good material. He's already a bet after this film for he's distinctly likable on the screen, the mike kind to his voice, and as a dancer he remains in a class by himself."[14]

For a picture conceived by its producer and screenwriter, Louis Brock, as a romantic vehicle for Dolores del Rio set in an exotic locale, with one dance number Fred Astaire and Ginger Rogers had stolen the picture. It didn't quite figure—how could a shy, lanky dancer with a prominent forehead, a pointed chin, and large hands have any appeal on the screen? But there it was. His incredible ability as a dancer and easygoing charm were captured by the camera much more vividly than they appeared in a Broadway theater.[15] Indeed, 1933 had been an extremely eventful and satisfying year for Fred; he had acquired two new partners—the perfect wife and the perfect dance partner.

Arlene Croce, the foremost observer of the Fred and Ginger phenomenon, put *Flying Down to Rio* into real perspective, however. Referring to *Rio,* Croce, a longtime dance critic of the *New Yorker,* wrote, "It's an Astaire-Rogers movie only in the sense that the two of them are in it. It really belongs to prehistory along with *Dancing Lady,* and the twenty-odd films that Rogers made before it."[16]

BY A PREARRANGED CONTRACT, Fred was now to return to the scene of his earlier triumphs by reuniting with Claire Luce in *Gay Divorce.* The show opened at the Palace Theatre in London on November 2, 1933, after a break-in engagement in Birmingham, England. On his arrival in Southampton with Phyllis and Peter, Fred sadly learned that Adele had suffered a miscarriage.

The West End first-nighters, however, lifted his spirits with the overflowing warmth with which they greeted both him and Luce. The Duke of York, Prince George, was there, applauding his old friend. *Punch,* the English humor magazine, enthusiastically observed, "He [Fred] is at the top of his form. There is an inspired puckishness about his dancing which pleases one very much, and behind it his technique of almost mechanical perfection."

During one of their dance flights, Luce fell and severely injured her hip. She recovered sufficiently to finish the 180-performance run, but it ultimately led to the end of her acting career. She and Fred gave a royal-command performance of "Night and Day" at the Drury Lane Theatre before the show ended its run.[17]

Dellie recovered sufficiently from her miscarriage within a few weeks and came to the theater with Charlie (or Chas, as she called him) for the first time as a member of the audience to see her brother perform. Ann came over as well from New York.[18] Fred proudly showed them some new steps to indicate he hadn't stood still. The enthusiastic audience applauded Adele at intermission. She stood up and bowed to acknowledge their kind gesture.

A few years later, she reminisced about the experience. "It was the first time I realized that Fred had sex appeal. Wherever did he get it? He's so unconceited-looking. He's always had what he's got now, but he never got the chance to show till I left. So when I finished, things came out he didn't know he could do himself."

Since neither *Dancing Lady* nor *Flying Down to Rio* had as yet opened when Fred opened in *Gay Divorce* in London, he was extremely leery of what lay ahead for him in Hollywood. He figured his option wouldn't be picked up, and he would probably be compelled to return to the theater. A cable arrived early in December, however, alerting him of the impact he had made in *Rio*. It came from a young RKO producer, Pandro S. Berman, who expressed with perfect 1930s enthusiasm, "You were a swell success in premiering *Flying Down to Rio* last night." A flow of subsequent cables revealed that the picture had opened at the perfect showcase for film musicals, New York's Radio City Music Hall, and was emerging as one of the top box-office films of the year.

Perhaps the most surprising compliment that Fred received was from Douglas Fairbanks. One night at the Savoy Grill, Fairbanks greeted him with "What do you mean by revolutionizing the movie industry? I've just seen *Flying Down to Rio,* and you've got something absolutely new. It's terrific!"

Berman flew to London specifically to see *Gay Divorce.* He had purchased the film rights for $20,000.[19] He informed Fred that his option had been picked up by the studio and that *Gay Divorce* was going to be made into a RKO movie starring him and Ginger Rogers. Berman also proudly announced that he would be the film's producer.

It was fitting that Astaire's stage career would officially end in London.[20] With and without Adele, the English adored his talent and charm. His appeal bridged the differences between the fish'n'chips common folks and the champagne-preferring royals. His daughter, Ava, observed, "I think he *loved* those years in London. He said that the English were mad, all mad."[21] Although he didn't yet realize it, he had, however, now found a new and permanent home in Hollywood.

Remembering how disappointed he was in seeing himself on the screen in *Dancing Lady,* he turned down the opportunity to attend a private screening of *Flying Down to Rio* before he, Phyllis, and Peter sailed for New York. They stopped off in Aiken, South Carolina, to spend time with Phyllis's family. There, he and Phyllis saw the movie in a local theater. A young man recognized Fred as they were leaving, and a crowd surrounded him. He was at last convinced that perhaps he had made a decided impression in the film.

A young man named Stanley Donen, then attending high school in Columbia, South Carolina, before heading to Broadway to work as a dancer, witnessed this scene. He remembered that Fred was so taken by the crowd's response to him that he broke into an impromptu tap dance. Donen in the 1950s would direct him in two of his foremost film musicals, *Royal Wedding* and *Funny Face.*

* * *

WHILE GINGER ROGERS had certainly meshed perfectly with Astaire in "The Carioca," Fred retained a vision of her as being fundamentally a Charleston dancer, a feeling that stayed with him for decades. He wasn't sure she possessed the right kind of sophistication required for the female lead in the film version of *Gay Divorce* and felt her very American sensibilities ruled against her playing a spirited Englishwoman. Perhaps that was a pretext, however, for he was still fighting being forced to work with a new dance partner.

A letter to Leland Hayward revealed a tormented, demanding star. Astaire wrote, "What's all this talk about me being teamed with Ginger Rogers. I will not have it, Leland. I did not go into pictures to be *teamed* with her or anyone else, not if that is the program in mind for me. I will not stand for it. I don't mind making another picture with her but so far as for this *team* idea it's out! I've just managed to live down one partnership, and I don't want to be bothered with it any more. I'd rather not make any more pictures for Radio if I have to be teamed up with one of those movie 'queens.' "[22]

Pandro S. Berman overruled Fred's deep-set convictions, pointing out that this was Hollywood and box-office appeal was paramount. Given the financial success of *Rio* and the highly flattering press notices Fred and Ginger's work as a team had garnered, the public apparently wanted to see more of them. The matter was settled.

As a contract player, Rogers had been paid $11,476.66 for her role in *Flying Down to Rio*.[23] Leland Hayward took a calculating look at the *Rio* box-office figures and asked for a significant raise for Astaire. Berman instead offered a percentage of the film's profits, something extremely rare in the 1930s movie business. ("Creative accounting" had not yet become a byword of the studio system, which for years has cheated stars out of considerable money.) Hayward's astute agenting would by the midthirties begin to make Astaire wealthy, as his films with Rogers were worldwide hits despite that in those years speaking English was far from universal in the rest of the world.

What was perhaps equally important to Fred, however, was that Hayward had also negotiated to gain him complete approval of the staging of all his dance numbers—quite a feat after three pictures with only the current film providing him with star billing above the title! Through Fred's suggestions, he and Ginger were henceforth photographed in extended dance sequences in full figure with few camera tricks. He was a terror in the cutting room, insisting on the exact synchronization of picture and sound. He insisted that no longer were dance numbers on film to be cut short.[24] Fred and Ginger's routines would move the plot along with romance as the key element. As part of his new deal, he got an unprecedented six weeks of rehearsal for himself and Ginger before *The Gay Divorce* started production.

Sexual mores being what they were, *Gay Divorce* would never work as a film title, according to the edict of the Hays Office, which governed censorship in the movie business. In 1934 terms, a divorce could never be considered gay. A "gay divorcée," however—that was perfectly acceptable.[25] (A modern source, however, contends that the new title was instigated by the studio itself.)[26] Although the plot was somewhat risqué, the innocence and lack of reality in the acting made the picture acceptably tasteful.[27]

In adapting the property from the stage, the profession of the character played by Fred in the play was changed from a novelist to a dancer. He managed to combine high style with a certain street authenticity.[28] The studio also decided to throw out Cole Porter's entire Broadway score except for "Night and Day." Herb Magidson and Conrad Gordon were hired as lyricists and Con Conrad and Harry Revel as songwriters.

From that association came "The Continental," which Magidson and Revel wrote to fulfill the need for an additional dance number. This truly spectacular effort was a bit long (over seventeen minutes), with various participants, including a chorus of thirty-two men and thirty-two women. It culminated with Fred and Ginger in another romping number, combining a tango and a Russian dance routine.[29] "The Continental" also won the first Oscar awarded in the category of Best Original Song from a Motion Picture. ("The Carioca" was runner-up). *The Gay Divorcée* also got a Best Picture nomination, one of its five Oscar nominations.[30]

An important ingredient in the film's mix was its director, Mark Sandrich, who had directed some second-unit work in *Flying Down to Rio*. With this background, his work was methodical. He always came to the set fully prepared. A refugee from directing short films, Sandrich had been rescued from obscurity by winning the Oscar in 1933 for the short musical comedy *So This Is Harris!*

Almost from the beginning, he and Astaire developed a mutual respect that was to extend over eight years and encompass the direction of six of Fred's film musicals. Fred readily acknowledged the importance of Berman and Sandrich in his success with Ginger. Sandrich had a talent for cleverly intertwining the plot and the dance numbers, such as in "A Needle in a Haystack" and in "The Continental." Another of his key innovations was to film the dance numbers to a prerecorded sound track.[31]

Erik Rhodes and Eric Blore re-created their comedic Broadway roles and were aided by the remarkable Edward Everett Horton as the buffoon lawyer. (Rhodes and Blore were about to become stock company players in the Astaire/Rogers movies.) Another noteworthy performance in the film was that of a seventeen-year-old blond dancer named Betty Grable, who was later to become a major star in film musicals. Grable's truly legendary legs were hidden by her white satin culottes when she danced a comedy duet with Horton in "Let's K-nock K-nees."

Though once again Dave Gould was in charge of staging the dance numbers with an eye on their cinematic aspects, Sandrich allowed Pan and Astaire to work out the intricacies of the dance routines in complete seclusion. Pan became the liaison between Astaire and Gould. He would inform Berman and Sandrich of the length of each number and what other ingredients (musicians, ensemble dancers) were needed. Before getting into the planning of the numbers, Fred was aware of how much time he would have on the set and how much time in the script.[32] Before Rogers reported for work, Pan took her place, dancing with Fred as the choreography was being worked out. He would then prerecord all of Ginger's taps. Fred insisted that Pan view the daily rushes as Fred was unsure of how the dance routines photographed. He still wasn't completely satisfied even when Pan (dubbed the Little Bear by Liz Whitney) would assure him of how much he approved of what he had just seen.[33]

This elaborate preparation and perfectionism translated into both enthusiastic critical acclaim and box-office success for the film. The studio's marketing campaign, which labeled Astaire and Rogers "The King and Queen of Carioca," was extraneous; *The Gay Divorcée* easily outgrossed *Flying Down to Rio*. Suddenly, style was "in" as Fred and Ginger brought a new elegance and sophistication to the Hollywood musical.

These were the elements that caused Katharine Hepburn to describe their on-screen magic as "He gives her class, she gives him sex." (When Dick Cavett quoted Hepburn's famous remark to Astaire many years later, Astaire, off camera, remarked in a stinging manner, "Katharine Hepburn is full of shit.")

Andre Sennwald of the *New York Times* summed up Fred and Ginger's appeal in *The Gay Divorcée* by saying, "Both as a romantic comedian and as a lyric dancer, Mr. Astaire is an urban delight, and Miss Rogers keeps pace with him even in his rhythmic flights over the furniture." In fact, the solo Astaire/Rogers dance numbers took only ten minutes of screen time.

"This incomparable dance of seduction is a movie in itself," Arlene Croce said of the "Night and Day" number, romantically set in an outdoor ballroom on the ocean. Croce continued, "Astaire adopted his stage choreography and no more thrilling or more musical dance had ever been presented on the screen. . . . Like all great choreographers, Astaire frequently works against the music. The steps are in perfect counterpoint, and the tension builds like a dramatic undertow. . . . They don't act when they should be dancing."[34]

With all of that, Rogers, rather obviously, was still not up to Astaire's caliber as a dancer. Dressed beautifully, accomplished as an actress, and an adequate singer, she exudes style, but her dancing is at times stiff and mechanical. At one salient moment in "Night and Day," when Fred is doing a dip with her, she looks up at him and all but blurts out, "What do I do next, Fred?"

Looking back on this period of their dancing association, Astaire damned her with faint praise: "She hadn't done the type of thing that I'd do. And we [he and Hermes Pan] had to work on her, and she was such a clever performer that she could fake a lot of things and make it look great. And as she did it, she didn't have to fake so much. . . . I mean, she was just terrific as a personality and as a performer, and she made her dancing look the best."[35]

It didn't much matter. Fred Astaire and Ginger Rogers, two dissimilar people, had combined to create a screen magnetism that saved RKO from financial ruin. Their work presaged a new type of intimate musical comedy that was another RKO contribution. Warner Bros. specialized in displaying large dancing choruses of shapely showgirls who were squeezed into Busby Berkeley's universal geometric shapes. Paramount and MGM stressed singing stars such as Maurice Chevalier and Jeanette MacDonald and later Nelson Eddy and MacDonald, respectively.[36] Fred and Ginger overshadowed them all. They were simply unique and charismatic as well.

BEFORE STARTING WORK on the Jerome Kern musical *Roberta,* which Pandro S. Berman had bought for $65,000, Fred enjoyed some time off to play golf with Phyllis. They had settled into a leased Italian Riviera–type house on North Alpine Drive in Beverly Hills.[37] With Berman once again as producer, Fred confessed that he was at last convinced that he actually rather liked the movie business.[38]

In *Roberta,* due to the studio's inability to yet consider him as the sole male lead,[39] Fred combined the parts played by Bob Hope and George Murphy in the original Broadway production. The lantern-jawed, stalwart-looking Randolph Scott and the exquisite Irene Dunne were the leads in *Roberta.* And as in *Flying Down to Rio,* Fred and Ginger's roles in the movie were secondary, but the two leads unfortunately failed to display any chemistry between them. Fred revealed a newly honed deftness as a rapid-fire comedian in several of his scenes with Scott, in addition to showing how easily his recently acquired English brand of drawing-room sophistication fit into the plot of the film.

This film solidly established Fred and Ginger as a successful team, providing them an ebullient air in contrast to the more sedate nature of their previous film. That *The Gay Divorcée* had opened to such acclaim that some audiences were even applauding at the conclusion of some of their dance numbers no doubt supplied a decided impetus as they filmed their *Roberta* dance numbers.[40]

The plot, set in the Parisian fashion world, concluded with a former football player (Scott) fighting with a Russian princess (Dunne, an American in disguise) over the look of an evening gown! Dunne hauntingly sang three of Jerome Kern's most memorable ballads—"Yesterdays," "Smoke Gets in Your Eyes," and "Lovely to Look At." But the lively dance team easily ran away with the picture.

Rogers displayed her inimitable sex appeal in "I'll Be Hard to Handle," before Astaire joins her as they romp across the screen in a whirlwind routine complete with constant breaks and turns. More than any other previous dance number, this scene turned them into superstars. One can actually *feel* how much sheer fun they are having dancing with one another.

Arlene Croce described Fred's "ratcheting tap clusters that fall like loose change from his pockets infuriating Ginger into an all out effort to dance as hard as she could."[41] It seems readily apparent that Rogers was now on par with Astaire as a dancing partner.

Their "Lovely to Look At" number spelled perfection in ballroom dancing. John Mueller contended, "Rogers, more than any of Astaire's partners, conveyed the impression that dancing with him is the most thrilling experience imaginable."

Then there was "I Won't Dance," which the author Wilfried Sheed contends was adopted from a previous Kern show in London that never made it to Broad-way.[42] It gave Fred a rare opportunity to display his chops as piano player before Ginger shimmies into the scene in a formfitting gold-lamé gown. She sings to him, "When you dance you're charming and you're gentle, 'specially when you do 'The Continental.'" Two Cossacks then carry Fred, intent on not dancing, to the dance floor. He suddenly changes his mind and embarks upon his longest solo dance spot on film thus far with a series of astonishing tap steps interspersed with flashing pirouettes. He and Ginger also reprise "Smoke Gets in Your Eyes" in an elegant ballroom dance.[43]

Deservedly, Hermes Pan was credited as the dance director of a film for the first time. He and Hal Borne, Astaire's rehearsal pianist for all of the RKO films, worked closely together in creating the magnificent dance arrangements that added so much to the success of the various dance numbers.[44]

Another rarely discussed aspect was the dance floor. Astaire recalled, "I always would have to discuss the floor and see that it wasn't too sticky or too slippery or too light or too dark or something that scuffing would show up too much. . . . I found out a light floor showed up less than a dark floor. . . . Then we used to put paint designs on the floor. Finally ended up by getting something—nothing showed like that, but these are little things you have to go through."[45]

Roberta also demonstrated Astaire's further insistence on the use of several cameras to shoot a dance number from various angles. He rightfully contended that with a dance sequence shot in one take, editing the scene would result in a continuity of movement on film. Heretofore, most musical-film directors cut quickly to facial close-ups, dancing feet, and audience-reaction shots to manufacture the feeling of action. Astaire correctly believed that the dancers should supply the excitement.[46]

Charles L. Reinhart has been a central figure in the dance movement for over five decades and is the president of the American Dance Festival. He strongly believes, "Astaire did a hell of a lot for the dance because he refused to allow himself to be cut up in the movies. That had a lasting effect on all film and television dance. You show the body; that's what it's all about. We all owe that to Fred Astaire."

At the beginning of shooting, Astaire would prepare and shoot four or five of the most difficult dance numbers. If they didn't satisfy him, they would be reshot at the end of production. His own solos would be done last.

ALL THROUGH THE FILMING OF *ROBERTA*, Mark Sandrich kept Fred informed of the plans that loomed for *Top Hat,* their next movie, which would include an entire score written by Irving Berlin. This was a treat that Fred could hardly wait to see move into production.

After completing *Roberta,* shortly before Christmas of 1934, he, Phyllis, and Peter went East to enjoy a richly deserved holiday. Like Fred's preceding two pictures, *Roberta* opened at Radio City Music Hall and enjoyed another successful run. Over the years, almost every Astaire film musical would have its world premiere there.

To most keen Astaire observers *Top Hat* is the apex of the Astaire/Rogers musicals. Mel Brooks, the comedian, film director, screenwriter, and playwright, was asked offhandedly by Dick Cavett, on a TCM (Turner Classic Movie) interview special to name his favorite all-time movie. Brooks turned serious for a moment and said, "A lot of people would think I would answer *Grand Illusion* by Renoir or *Citizen Kane,* but I would say my favorite was *Top Hat*—or maybe *Swing Time.*"

The high esteem this film has maintained over more than seventy years attests to its having transcended the category of film musical to the status of high art. Astaire and *Top Hat* serve as perfect examples of the eminent actress and drama coach Stella Adler's statement, "The art, architecture, and clothes of an era were crucial to shaping a role."[47]

One of the unsung factors in the success of *Top Hat* was Dwight (*Gay Divorce*) Taylor and Allan Scott's breezy screenplay. This was the first of six scripts for Fred and Ginger films that Scott wrote or cowrote. His zany dialogue, complete with double entendres, in the Lido sequence was an unexpected highlight of the movie.

Scott, however, had his problems with Astaire. "In the beginning, he worried a little bit about the way I wrote. I was ironic, but without making jokes. You know, I never gave him a joke. I'd been used to stage dialogue. But also, let's face it, he's a helluva snob. He could be perturbed very easily by the wrong reference. His sister, Adele, had married a British peer, and that was one reason he didn't take my cracks about nobility. . . . Freddie as a man was not romantic. His love scenes were all dances."

Irving Berlin's brilliant score of five songs introduced such enduring standards as "Cheek to Cheek," "Isn't This a Lovely Day," and the title song, "Top Hat, White Tie, and Tails." The latter song defined Astaire's image on film forever more. More than any of his four previous musical films, *Top Hat* established him as a *song* as well as dance man. His plainspoken singing style with its concentration on the lyric content added considerably to the popularity of these songs. One reason for the spectacular success of Berlin's songs in the movie was that they were specifically written for Astaire and/or Rogers. Perhaps just as important, they were specifically conceived to fit within the plot. Mark Sandrich explained, "Irving Berlin sat in on all the conferences with the result that all the songs grew out of the scene structure itself."[48]

It was a far cry from Astaire's having had to beg for permission from Berlin's partner, Ted Snyder, back in 1915 to sing "I Love to Quarrel with You" in the act with Adele, during their struggling years in vaudeville, to this moment two decades later. With Astaire's first exposure to Berlin's syncopated jazz songs, another association was established that transcended business and became a long-standing warm personal friendship. Berlin's respect for Astaire was conveyed in his statement "He knew the value of a song before his feet took over." A year after the release of *Top Hat* Berlin told George Gershwin, "There is no setup in Hollywood that can compare with doing an Astaire picture."[49]

Mary Ellin Barrett, author of *Irving Berlin: A Daughter's Memoir,* said, "Truly, the core of the friendship between my father and Fred Astaire was professional, but there was also an affinity of the kind of men they were. They were both not only perfectionists, which is part of professional, extraordinary hard workers, but they were both very fastidious men. They shared a self-mocking state of humor. In their clothes and personally, they were totally luxurious. They were happily married and devoted to their wives. One of the bonds of their friendship beyond professional, beyond simply liking each other, was that their wives, Ellin Berlin, and Phyllis Astaire, and Frances Goldwyn, became friends. It became a family friendship. There would be family occasions with the two wives and their children."

Barrett illustrated her point by telling of a reluctant visit made by her father and Astaire with their wives and children to an amusement park in Ocean Park, then a suburb of Los Angeles, in 1937. "Once they got there, they had an absolutely great time. What everybody remembered was the picture of Fred Astaire in the fun house. . . . I am not saying that it was before or after *Damsel in Distress.*" (Astaire's next movie, which featured a hilarious scene set in a fun house at an amusement park.) Barrett assured me, "Irving Berlin had no part in *Damsel in Distress.*"

When "Cheek to Cheek," the longest hit song Berlin ever wrote,[50] was played and sung initially for Astaire by Berlin in his reedy voice, Fred didn't particularly like it.[51] Just as with "Night and Day," he had problems with the song as it taxed his limited range. Yet this song formed the basis of one of the most scintillating dance numbers of the Astaire/Rogers partnership. Fred, with Pan's help, devised a romantic, flowing dance that was the epitome of what a smooth, romantic dance number should be and even included some tap steps as well.[52] The pink, ostrich-feathered dress Rogers wore, however, was a serious problem. As shooting began, the feathers kept flying off the dress into Fred's mouth, ears, and nose and all over his tails. This happened in take after take.

When Astaire was not getting exactly what he wanted on the set, his quick temper often came to the fore. He lashed out at Ginger. Her protective mother and manager, Lela, charged after Fred. After a while order was restored. The dress designer Bernard Newman stayed up all night to sew the feathers individually to the dress.[53] On the third day of shooting, the scene was at last captured on film.

For years afterward, Astaire frequently affectionately referred to Rogers as Feathers. He and Pan coauthored a parody on "Cheek to Cheek" that began, "Feathers—I hate feathers / And I hate them so [that] I can hardly speak / And I never find the happiness I seek / With these chicken feathers dancing / Cheek to cheek."[54] Henceforth, he insisted on inspecting his dancing partners' costumes before their dance numbers commenced shooting.

Not to be overlooked was the "Isn't This a Lovely Day" number, an additional Astaire/Pan creation, set in a park.[55] It immediately follows Astaire's zealous and amusing pursuit of Rogers, disguised as a hansom-cab driver, complete with a cockney accent, galloping through London. Their nonstop singing and dancing, while dressed in matching sports jackets and Ginger in jodhpurs and a cap, is never interrupted despite a passing shower as Berlin's lyrics underline that "The weather is frightening / The thunder and lightning / Seem to be having their way / But as far as I'm concerned, it's a lovely day." The two performers, obviously delighted in what they're doing, light up the screen as they challenge each other. Ginger is now the compleat dancer. This brilliantly conceived number closes with a spirited tap dance by the dynamic duo, inspired even further by the sound of constant thunderclaps.

The pure elegance of the "Top Hat" number is still the pièce de résistance in the picture and one of the trademark scenes of Astaire's career. Berlin, in a 1976 interview, called it "the best of the songs I wrote for the Astaire films."[56] Indeed, it reeked with class! In the film, it is the hit production number in the London stage musical in which Astaire's character is starring. Sandrich makes vital use of the plot to set up a vocal or dance number. In this case, Fred's character is traumatized by reading a telegram just before going onstage that informs him that the Rogers character has gone off to Venice, where she is being courted by the buffoonish continental Erik Rhodes. This device highly effectively leads Astaire into singing the verse of "Top Hat," "I just got an invitation through the mails," as he saunters onstage.

In another of Hermes Pan's inventive strokes, Astaire holds the telegram in one hand while hitting it with the head of his cane in his other hand. He starts off with a rhythm step (right heel in place with toes tapping right and left). The top-hatted male chorus struts behind him. Subsequently, they leave the stage, but as they reemerge, he "shoots them down" with his cane exactly as he had previously done in *Smiles* and similarly in his number with a top-hatted chorus in *Funny Face* on Broadway.[57] The blistering pace set by Astaire and his backup chorus's tap-dance routine is truly a marvel to behold.

Maurice Hines, the highly talented dancer and choreographer, while fully realizing Astaire's genius, insisted that Hermes Pan never really got his just due. "Pan came up with the concept so Fred could do it and add to it. But what is he adding to the concept? The concept man is the man. But to me, Fred was effortless; that was his greatness. I loved the end of his numbers. When he would end them, he would not end them so big. Fred could end a number by slowly sitting down or slowly leaning on a thing."

When the "Top Hat" number was being filmed, Jimmy Cagney watched off camera. Cagney, a hoofer himself, admired Astaire's work and had sent him a series of telegrams praising it. His arrival on the set, however, made Fred nervous. After the third take, Cagney whispered to Fred, "Don't shoot it again, kid—you got it on the second take. You'll never top that one." But Fred, always the perfectionist, asked Mark Sandrich for one more take. The next morning, when Fred saw the rushes, he discovered that Cagney was right—the second take was ideal.[58]

The extraordinary dancer the late Fayard Nicholas, half of the renowned dance team the Nicholas Brothers, remembered, "Just before my brother and I left for Los Angeles to make our first movie, *The Big Broadcast of 1936,* we were headlining at the Cotton Club with Cab Calloway's band in Harlem. Ed Sullivan [then a Broadway columnist] gave us a note to take to Fred. When we got there, we called the studio and told Fred's secretary we had a little note from Ed Sullivan. We had our chauffeur drive us over in our limousine. My brother, my mother, and I went to the recording room where Fred was synchronizing his tap piece for the movie *Top Hat* as he watched it on the screen. It was wonderful.

"After he finished, I gave him the note. When he read it, he said, 'Oh, yeah, my friend Ed Sullivan.' I said, 'Why don't we go outside. I have a movie camera that takes home movies. My mother will take us as we're doing the time step.' As we went outside, and we started doing the time step, Fred was in the middle, my brother on one side, and I'm on the other side. 'Yeah, oh, yeah.' We did about eight bars. When we finished we shook hands and we were friends ever since."

Fayard added, "Fred tapped, and he did a lot of things like that, but he was at his best dancing with a lady. With Ginger he felt better. He looked better. There was romance, and he could glide forth. He had so much class. He was the greatest dancer America ever had."

THE FINAL PORTION of *Top Hat,* set in Venice, shows the denouement of the love triangle. Astaire and Rogers reunite for a foolish but somehow fitting ending. The art deco setting predominates and perfectly conveys the inspired look and feel of opulence that this spectacle demanded.

Pandro Berman, referring to the art deco look that had been created by the art directors, Van Nest Polglase and Carroll Clark, said, "They established that look in *Flying Down to Rio.* It proved so effective and different from other musicals that we kept it. I don't think the pictures would have been any better if we'd had more money to spend, except for one thing: color. But then color films were still in their infancy."[59]

The magnificent "Piccolino" number, a further study in art deco, is one of the most incredible production numbers in the history of Hollywood musicals. Ginger sings the song while the camera captures the dancers as they indulge in several pseudo–Busby Berkeley formations. Fred and Ginger's dance interlude is exuberant, carefree, and yet courtly. It's the perfect device to set up the movie's romantic conclusion.

The retired Jay Sandrich, son of Mark Sandrich, himself a successful director, primarily in television, related an unusual incident that took place after *Top Hat*'s first preview, in July 1935 in Santa Barbara. In a perfect example of screenwriter William Goldman's often quoted remark about the motion picture business, "Nobody knows anything!," Sandrich recalled, "My mother told me how everyone met in the projection room afterward. Pandro Berman came in and said, 'I have to pay all that money for this lousy score.' Of course, this was Irving Berlin's first movie score. Berman continued, 'How dare he write this terrible score!' My father said, 'You can say everything you want about the direction, but don't you dare say anything about the music because it's a great score!' "

TOP HAT DEBUTED on August 19, 1935, at Radio City Music Hall and set a new record for the theater, grossing $3,160,000 in its run.[60] Its production budget for the six-week shooting schedule was slightly over $620,000. Astaire, Berlin, and Berman each got 10 percent of the substantial profit. Berlin made $300,000 for his share, which was three times his original asking price.[61] The New York *Daily News,* in an editorial, added the film to the list of the all-time best American movies, saying, "*Top Hat* is the best thing yet done in a movie musical comedy."[62]

It's really no surprise that *Top Hat* captured the hearts and minds of American filmgoers and critics, desperate for escape from the reality of a country still enduring almost 25 percent unemployment. The glorious music, extravagant settings, and overall feeling of romance with two tremendously talented singing and dancing leads was the perfect tonic for people's misery.

Michael Wood in his *America in the Movies* wrote, "The movies did not describe or explain America. They invented it, dreamed up an America all their own and persuaded us to share the dream. We shared it happily, because the dream was true in its fashion—true to a variety of American desires—and because there weren't all that many other dreams around."

Gene Kelly, Astaire's only serious competitor as the screen's foremost male dancer, well defined the appeal of the Fred and Ginger movies: "Fred had an elegance that aligned itself with what I guess you'd call high society. In the 1930s, in the poor years in America, it was very much needed. People said, 'Oh, look at those people dancing!' Visiting Venice or some place, in rooms that were all a-glitter with chrome and silver and white. The girls were all beautiful. No sweatshirts or jeans. It was a great escape for people. I do think the psychological portion is underrated here. People wanted to see this sort of thing very much."

But what was perhaps most significant was that Astaire and Rogers had brought pure art to popular movie entertainment. The mating of two kindred souls was expressed by the dance as never before on-screen. They embodied the belief in the transfiguring power of love. Romance combined with style, which they projected like no other dancing couple ever had before on film, was an irresistible combination.

A. T. Baker in *Time*, in a 1973 review of Arlene Croce's book on Astaire and Rogers, described them by writing, "He had an undernourished clown's face, an indeterminately skinny body, and a sophistication that he wore with uncertainty—even in white tie, top hat and tails. She was soft and sunny looking, not beautiful or exotic, but pretty in a way that suggested both sexual challenge and the sisterly virtue of the girl next door.

"But somehow, somewhere, he always got them to dance. Suddenly, this long, nervous little man became masterful. Invariably the scornful, the superior, the prickly Ginger Rogers responded. Their dances, begun as wary fencing, ended on mesmerized fascination."

THAT ASTAIRE AND ROGERS'S on-screen characters lived an entirely frivolous existence never bothered the film audience a whit. They had truly become America's sweethearts. The Hollywood trade magazine *Motion Picture Herald* designated them the fourth most popular movie stars in the country behind Shirley Temple, Will Rogers, and Clark Gable.[63]

The box-office gross of the four Astaire/Rogers movies released thus far for each of them was between $9 million and $10 million, an extraordinary figure when one considers that the price of movie tickets was then in the neighborhood of fifty cents. Women made up a substantial part of that audience. Though Clark Gable was already a full-fledged star who exhibited his macho sex appeal in such films as *It Happened One Night*, America had discovered a very different kind of leading man in Fred Astaire. He brought a gentility that had never been a part of pop culture before him.

Essentially, his screen image combined the sophistication of the British upper class, America's wealthy, a small helping of Omaha, and the training of vaudeville.[64] No trace of his Eastern European Jewish heritage was to be found. The dignity and natural charm of a masculine song-and-dance man provided a much different kind of romantic appeal to women.[65] Their fantasies were perhaps best described generations later by Beatle George Harrison, when he expressed it so beautifully: "Something in the way she moves / Attracts me like no other lover."

Autobiographer, retired dancer, and actress Betsy Blair, formerly married to Gene Kelly, remembered, "As a young dancer growing up in north Jersey, I saw all of Fred's movies believing he was English." A few others, though, guessed differently. The mother of Anna Kisselgoff, the *New York Times*'s dance critic from 1977 to 2005, saw these movies in France and recognized Astaire's Eastern European Jewish ancestry from his facial features.

IN THE OSCAR COMPETITION, *Top Hat* lost to *Mutiny on the Bounty* in the Best Picture category. Among its three other nominations, Hermes Pan was nominated for Best Dance Direction for "The Piccolino" and the title song "Top Hat." He lost to his former boss on the previous Astaire/Rogers musicals, Dave Gould, who won for his staging work in both *Broadway Melody of 1936* for "I've Got a Feelin' You're Foolin'" and *Folies Bergère de Paris* for "Straw Hat." "Cheek to Cheek" lost in the Best Song category to "Lullaby of Broadway" from *Gold Diggers of 1935*.

With the incredible critical acclaim and the spectacular box-office figures of his last three movies with Ginger, Fred was at last secure that he was now a real movie star. He began spending considerable free time, at Santa Anita, playing the horses, just as he had while working on Broadway and in the West End. He devised various "surefire" betting schemes based on careful study of the history of the horses, placing bets with bookies weeks before if the odds were good. He brought his London theater dresser George Griffin to Los Angeles. One of Griffin's betting systems centered on counting the number of letters in the name of the last horse in a racing form, then counting up the number of horses, and choosing that particular horse.[66]

The inevitable next step was for Fred to join such Hollywood film personalities as Bing Crosby in becoming an investor in the Del Mar Racetrack, just above San Diego. Several of his East Coast friends such as Jock Whitney and Alfred Gwynne Vanderbilt brought their horses West to race there. That led to Astaire's buying a ranch in the area.

Though his fellow Broadway performers first got him interested in the sport of kings, and his passion was rekindled by the royals in England, one has to wonder if in addition to the love of the track and the thrill of gambling, the intrinsic beauty of racehorses roaring down the stretch didn't somehow cause him to compare that to the intricate movement of dancers.

Phyllis was interested in real estate, but with her finely honed Eastern upper-class background, she was taken aback by the sprawling suburban look of homes in the Hollywood/Beverly Hills area. She convinced Fred they should build their own home, which they did in the spring of 1936 on four acres they purchased just off Benedict Canyon in Beverly Hills. Located between Pickfair, the historic Mary

Pickford mansion, and the home of Charlie Chaplin, it was on the same street as that of David O. Selznick.[67]

Dan Selznick described the Astaires' home as "the sort of house that you see in a magazine showing neocolonial houses. There was kind of an oval driveway where you could come in one side and go out the other. It was a real country house."

Selznick said of Phyllis, "I found Mrs. Astaire a sweet and gracious English lady. I caught her mid-Atlantic accent. She was someone very poised and well mannered and very clean, very well scrubbed with a terribly sweet smile. She projected an upper-class quality and had a classic voice that one sees with many actresses of the 1930s. They wore very little makeup and were beautifully spoken. You found yourself drawn to them."

As youngsters, Dan and Freddie (Fred Astaire Jr.) were close friends. Freddie would come down to play in the Selznick front yard and swim in the Selznick's swimming pool. Dan Selznick recalled, "Either Mrs. Astaire or Freddie's governess brought him over. Our home was bigger than their house. Then, once in a while, I'd be invited up there. I think the reason we did not see more of Mr. and Mrs. Astaire socially among my parents' friends was that Fred was so shy. He didn't really want to come to large parties or medium-sized parties. When I saw the Astaires, over a four- or five-year period, it was usually at their house. I would generally see Mrs. Astaire because Mr. Astaire I guess was out working."

Early on, while living in their new home, the Astaires became acquainted with the film industry pioneer Sam Goldwyn and his wife, former Broadway actress Frances Howard. The Astaires and the Goldwyns soon became close friends. According to Fred and Phyllis's daughter, Ava, her mother enjoyed showing off her devastating imitation of Goldwyn's unique way of speaking.[68]

After *Flying Down to Rio,* Goldwyn, the master of outrageous statements on a myriad of subjects (in reality his press agent's brilliant creation), had loaned out David Niven, whom he had under contract, to Pandro Berman for a movie for $5,000. In return, Goldwyn offered "to take the dancer Astaire" off his hands for a film on the same loanout terms. At the time Fred was grateful someone wanted him for a movie. Berman, however, knew what a potentially valuable property Astaire was and turned Goldwyn down.[69]

Niven, the London-born actor, biographer, wit, and all-around charmer, a little more than ten years younger than Astaire, became a close friend. He discovered that the Astaires had moved in next door to him in their newly built home at 1211 Summit Drive. One day, returning from playing tennis at the Hollywood Cricket Club, Niven came over to meet Fred, informing Phyllis that he had known

Adele in London. Terrified, Phyllis told Fred, "There's a half-naked man at the door!"

David Niven Jr., a former William Morris agent and movie producer, said, "As far as Daddy was concerned, Fred was like his older brother."[70] He believes their friendship was primarily based on that they both had extraordinary style and were voracious readers. This may have had a delayed effect since both stars wrote their own autobiographies without the aid of a ghostwriter. David wrote three successful books, starting with *The Moon's a Balloon*.

Niven junior remembered one of the first times Astaire came to the Niven home to pick his father up before the two stars headed out to Malibu for a fishing expedition. "Between the two of them, they didn't own a pair of blue jeans," Niven said, laughing. "They wore gray flannel trousers and white [shoes]. Let's not even call them sneakers because they wouldn't have worn sneakers! And long-sleeve shirts, rolled up, little ascots, and hats, and their fishing rods. And off they go with maybe fifty total strangers out there on the Malibu pier on a hot day."

Through Niven, Fred and Phyllis met Irving Thalberg, the esteemed production head of MGM and his wife, actress Norma Shearer. (It was Thalberg who said, "In Los Angeles everyone has two businesses, their job and the movie business.") At the Thalberg home, the Astaires viewed upcoming films in the screening room with Gary Cooper; Claudette Colbert; Fred's old friend Douglas Fairbanks and his new wife, Sylvia; and Charlie Chaplin and his then companion, Paulette Goddard.

Phyllis's guardians, Henry and Maud Bull, enjoyed visiting with her and Fred and enjoyed their common interest in playing golf and horse racing. In time, they decided to disengage themselves from their Eastern roots and became Southern Californians as well. This led to an even closer foursome.

Phyllis's presence formed a cocoon around the Astaires' home life. She was completely devoted to Fred and became a vigilant doorkeeper such that they saw only select friends so that he could fully concentrate on his work. Fred enjoyed a structured life.[71] Phyllis took over the family finances and invested his already considerable earnings wisely. Fred trusted her judgment implicitly.

Years later, he told writer Howard Thompson, "My wife was a wise, remarkable woman. Never around the studio, always there at home when I needed her. . . . I always needed her judgment."[72]

Joan Crawford noted, "They reinforced each other. Fred was a shy man. Phyllis has always been shy. . . . He treated her like the lady she always was. . . . He's kept himself intact and could because he's been so fulfilled in his personal life. I've never seen two people work with such minimum effort at happiness."[73]

Before Fred started his next picture, he and Phyllis visited Adele and Charlie in Ireland before moving on to London. There, Phyllis discovered that she was pregnant. They immediately headed back to America. Months later, when Fred and Phyllis reciprocated and had Adele and Charlie stay with them in Beverly Hills, Adele saw firsthand how completely Fred had adapted to marriage and having a stepson.

Adele discovered she was pregnant with twins during her California visit. Fred was overjoyed at the thought of being a father and an uncle almost simultaneously. On her return to Ireland, on October 27, 1935, however, Adele gave birth prematurely to stillborn twin boys. Writing to Fred, she reasoned she was unfortunately now too old to have a baby.[74]

Now that he had become an important screen personality, Fred branched out into radio, doing six fifteen-minute radio shows, *Your Hit Parade,* sponsored by Lucky Strike cigarettes, for $4,000 a show. The first two shows originated from New York before a move back to California.[75] Backed by Lennie Hayton's orchestra, Fred sang and tap-danced. *Variety* raved, "It was to be expected that he would be a smash hit with his tapping, and he was. But it was Astaire's singing that really connected and surprised."[76]

Radio and records provided the perfect showcase for his singing that heretofore the screen really never had. From August '35 to September '38, Fred amassed an astounding total of twenty-four hits on Brunswick Records, all of them songs from his movies, five of them from the *Top Hat* score. These included four #1 records: "I'm Putting All My Eggs in One Basket," "The Way You Look Tonight," "A Fine Romance," and "They Can't Take That Away from Me." Performing in these two mediums, his adroit approach to interpreting lyrics was more fully appreciated. In movies, his singing was usually a device to set up the dances.

RKO, however, claimed his radio appearances were in breach of this contract with the studio. This, of course, angered Fred. Leland Hayward argued that his client wanted the freedom to do more radio shows. He pointed out that Fred and Ginger's movies had saved the studio and maintained that RKO was ungrateful. He seized the moment to demand a new contract for Astaire that called for a raise to $4,000 a week, payable fifty-two weeks a year, plus a percentage of the gross. Still trying to extricate himself from his association with Ginger, Astaire demanded that she not appear in more than three of his next five pictures—unless he consented in writing. RKO quickly capitulated and insured him for $1 million with Lloyd's of London.

With all of this good news, there was even more—Phyllis gave birth to Fred junior on January 21, 1936, at Good Samaritan Hospital in Los Angeles. She had a quick recovery, but in the meantime she dispatched Fred to Santa Anita during the day. Irving Berlin came by in the evenings for gin rummy, which often lasted late into the night.

DESPITE HIS PREVIOUS TREPIDATIONS after the first preview of *Top Hat,* Pandro Berman realized the public was primed for more of the music of Irving Berlin, along with the combination of Fred Astaire and Ginger Rogers, as well as the rapid-fire dialogue of Dwight Taylor and Allan Scott. Besides that, the studio wanted to put its second Fred and Ginger picture into release in a year's time as had become the practice.

The repercussions of Adolf Hitler's armed buildup in Europe had caused a renewed interest in the American military. Putting Fred Astaire in a sailor's suit in *Follow the Fleet* seemed like a good idea at the time, a respite from his more spiffy formal attire. Astaire concurred. The plots of two previous movies, *Shore Leave* and *Hit the Deck,* were reworked for Astaire and Rogers.[77]

Follow the Fleet was the most self-conscious of any of their films to date. Part of the problem was the awareness that their lengthening history together made it easy to acknowledge Astaire and Rogers as a dance team and to draw on their familiarity with each other.[78] The results, however, were merely so-so, with a few terrific dance numbers barely able to circumvent a skimpy, unserviceable plot. In retrospect, Astaire agreed the movie was not theatrical, yet it grossed a hefty $2,685,000.

Fred's friend, golf partner, fellow poker player, and marlin fisherman Randolph Scott, who had costarred with him and Ginger in *Roberta,* was pressed into service to play Fred's navy buddy. The romantic plot of *Follow the Fleet* essentially copied *Roberta.* In a departure from their previous films, Fred's character is rather callous and a gum chewer, while Ginger's is sentimental, a former vaudeville partner with Fred, now a sailor.[79]

Berman, asked how he kept the Fred and Ginger films fresh, answered, "That was why we did the two formulas that we did. We didn't want to do them all alike. I first made *Gay Divorcée* with Fred and Ginger alone. Then I did *Roberta,* and I decided on having Irene Dunne and Randy Scott in with them, and we broke it up so that it was a four-person picture. . . . Then we decided we'd do *Top Hat* with Fred and Ginger alone. Then we went back to the other formula in *Follow the Fleet,* where we used Harriet Hilliard who later became Harriet Nelson of *Ozzie and Harriet* fame. And Randy Scott again to break up the thing, so that there weren't only the same two people carrying the story."[80]

In the one significant song-and-dance number in *Follow the Fleet* (and one of Fred and Ginger's all-time best), "Let's Face the Music and Dance,"[81] Fred and

Ginger perform on an art nouveau terrace in elegant finery during a show staged on the deck of the ship. And despite Fred's wariness concerning Ginger's dresses, her sleeve in this number "slapped me right in the face. . . . And we kept going and got off and finished, and I was sort of half-groggy, because I was, you know, out of breath. We took about eighteen takes of that thing and finally quit at eight o'clock in the evening.

"We looked at the rushes in the morning. So we got it in the very first take, the one that slapped me in the face. . . . And we never saw it on the screen. It happened when I guess I was in back of her, maybe—as we were turning around. . . . So we wasted that whole day knocking ourselves out."[82]

As the scene unfolds, Fred is about to commit suicide after a bad night at the gambling casino in Monte Carlo. Similarly, Ginger is about to throw herself off a ledge. Here is a perfect illustration of an Astaire/Rogers routine in which Fred's interpretation of Berlin's remarkable "There may be trouble ahead / But while there's moonlight and music and love and romance / Let's face the music and dance" leads directly into the resolution of their individual troubles. This sinuous, passionate dance number is extremely theatrical but with a plot.[83]

Earlier in the movie, Fred in his bell-bottom sailor outfit and Ginger in a satin pants suit, perfectly in sync, dive into another freewheeling tap war in "Let Yourself Go." Ginger displays her solo tap-dancing technique with a tad of a Spanish traveling step.[84] In the reprise, she and Fred compete with several dance-contest winners that Pan had discovered at the Palomar Ballroom, where two months before Benny Goodman had first become the toast of the swing dancers.

Fred exhibited his rollicking piano-playing with a cigarette stuck firmly in the side of his mouth while singing "I'm Putting All My Eggs in One Basket," as Ginger joins in, leading to another tap-dancing exhibition, often comical, requiring a series of complicated steps. This amusing routine appears spontaneous; in reality, in true Fred Astaire/Hermes Pan fashion, it required two weeks of rehearsal.[85] Eager to get things right, Astaire began dance rehearsals in early September, almost two months before production began on the film.

IT WAS TIME for them to get back into a more natural groove, which *Swing Time* provided. Arlene Croce said, "If you put *Swing Time* in a glass ball like a paperweight and turned it upside down, it would be *Swing Time*." It was said to be Ginger Rogers's absolute favorite of the ten films in which she costarred with Astaire. The respected filmmaker and film historian Peter Bogdanovich agreed, "It was the best musical Fred ever made." Allan Scott and Howard Lindsay, under George Stevens's firm direction, made a lively script come alive.

Swing Time was chock-full of moments designed to spoof the by-now-well-established screen legend of Fred and Ginger, although it removed them from their chichi world and transplanted them into a middle-class life. While Jerome Kern turned out another superb group of romantic ballads, he also explored jazz idioms in his songwriting.

The movie opened with Fred, playing the part of John "Lucky" Garnett, a gambler, missing his wedding because his tailor had failed to cuff his trousers on time! Astaire, in top hat and morning suit, soon leaves comedian Victor Moore and jumps onto a freight car heading for New York, a strange comical allusion to those who rode the rails during the Great Depression. Another memorable and hilarious scene finds Fred singing one of Jerome Kern and Dorothy Fields's four songs, "The Way You Look Tonight," to Ginger in a deliberately antiromantic setting complete with soap suds in her hair![86] (The soap suds consisted of soap, egg whites, and whipped cream.)[87]

Perhaps the most amusing moment takes place early in the movie when Fred arrives in New York and takes a dance lesson from Ginger. He poses as a complete klutz, and after several of his falls, Ginger sings "Pick Yourself Up" to him. She then proclaims, "Listen, no one could teach you to dance in a million years. Take my advice and save your money." *Naturally,* he segues into an energized series of dazzling tap steps and ends with a fast-paced ballroom-dance sequence with Ginger that includes their twice hopping over a low fence on either side of the room. This device launches the plot of the picture.

The "Waltz in Swing Time" number is divided into three sections but is incorporated into one shot. It ranks among the most astounding dance numbers ever put on film. Fred's cross-rhythms with constant intricate surprise moves were arranged, at his insistence, at a continuous fast tempo by the arranger, Robert Russell Bennett. The number culminated with a tap dance. Ginger is a vision of femininity dressed all in white.

An additional, offbeat, and humorous approach is brought to the treatment of "A Fine Romance." Fred sings Dorothy Fields's downbeat approach to romance with Ginger in the midst of a snowstorm with a pipe clamped firmly between his teeth. The song is divided into two parts with Ginger then accusing him of being "cold as yesterday's mashed potatoes." As they are about to come to an understanding, and Fred is about to kiss her, their fine romance is interrupted by a well-thrown snowball by Victor Moore.

Al Jolson was one of many important male film stars who appeared in blackface in musicals. The one time Astaire ever appeared in blackface on film is his tribute to his onetime mentor Bill "Bojangles" Robinson in the well-remembered jazz waltz "Bojangles of Harlem," contributed by the combination of Robert Russell

Bennett and Hal Borne. Writer Stanley Crouch stressed, "Fred's tribute was real and showed a definite respect for Bill Robinson—none of that minstrel-type thing Bing Crosby did when he put on blackface. The dignity in the number was extended to the way the chorus dancers performed."

Astaire's homage to Robinson is actually more influenced by his even greater regard for John Bubbles. Fred's costume, derby, and white gloves are close to what Bubbles wore playing Sportin' Life in *Porgy and Bess,* which debuted the year before. Astaire considered Bubbles more inventive than Robinson.

In an interview in the 1960s, Bubbles revealed that he once gave Astaire a tap-dance lesson. "It was on the stage at the Ziegfeld Theatre. He paid me four hundred dollars. He couldn't catch the dancing as quick as Ann Miller, though, so I taught her so she could teach him to save time for them [presumably before shooting commenced on *Easter Parade*]. He was such a nice guy, and I didn't want to teach him for an hour without him getting anything. . . . I gave them heely-toes, cramps, stomps, heely-toe turns, and cramp rolls."[88]

Diana Vreeland, the flamboyant onetime fashion editor of *Harper's Bazaar* and later *Vogue,* whom Kay Thompson essentially portrayed in *Funny Face,* remembered going to Harlem one evening in the 1920s with Fred and Adele. "Fred was going to have a lesson from Bojangles, whom he admired tremendously. Bojangles taught Fred a shuffle: six steps up and six steps down."[89]

Astaire felt Bojangles was a one-trick artist who was mainly adept in this ability to tap up and down flights of stairs. John Mueller stressed that Robinson's dances were foot-oriented with a basically immobile carriage of the upper body, whereas Astaire was intent on expressing his entire body.[90]

Fayard Nicholas told me, "Robinson boasted, 'Fred can't pick up his feet fast enough to ever work with me.'" Such an integrated duel between the two tap masters would never have taken place in a 1930s musical anyway.

Writer Kirk Silsbee maintained, however, "Robinson was the first great tap dancer that we know of, but Robinson was a simple tap dancer; Fred's tapping was anything but simple. Fred's was more dimensional—through speed, rhythmic subdivision, accents—he was far more elaborate. Comparatively, John Bubbles was Einstein compared to Robinson's Isaac Newton."

Robinson and the Nicholas Brothers displayed their truly astounding dancing in several Twentieth Century–Fox musicals, but they were never given romantic parts. Fayard said, "It didn't bother me because what we did in movies made us famous all over the world."

Fred's tap-dance solo had a cocky, jaunty, rhythmically complex feel to it. And instead of the blackface makeup adopted by most white performers, Fred only had his lips highlighted in white. Pan's absolutely brilliant staging of the number incorporated an intriguing use of silhouettes as Astaire danced in and out of shadows.[91]

Astaire remembered, "It was difficult to achieve. It was another one of those tough-trick things. Once again, it was using different screens . . . there were three fellows in back of me. You remember the three shadows? Well, they were all separate shots processed into one. I remember one thing—one of them walked off while the others kept on dancing."[92] Toward the end of the number, the sudden addition of a female dance chorus in sepia makeup so inspires Astaire that his dancing becomes as inventive as something George Balanchine might have created.[93] Peter Bogdanovich remembered the one meeting he had with Astaire: "I came up to his home in Beverly Hills. I found him very reserved and dour. That was, until he began discussing the 'Bojangles' number. Then he became very animated. It seemed like he flew across the room as he described his dancing in that scene."

"Never Gonna Dance," originally one of two titles seriously considered for the movie, until it was thought to be a box-office risk, is a dance of desperation. Fred's and Ginger's characters realize their love affair is over. Resigned to his fate, Fred sings "Never Gonna Dance, Never Gonna Love." The mood is downbeat until their genuine love for each other surfaces, only to end in an inevitable parting. This was one of the most intimate and romantic numbers of their career together.

Richard Corliss, the veteran *Time* art critic, called it "an eight-minute ballet of seduction and parting. The quarreling lovers won't dance; they must dance. Their bodies sway helplessly to the music and then surrender to embrace. Retreating, touching, whirling across the ballroom floor, they try to fight the magnetism of their love, their shared art. The only way to escape its pull is to play the game to its climax. And so they glide up a winding staircase and into the spiraling ecstasy of a dozen dizzying pirouettes. Suddenly she is gone. He is alone. The dance is over."[94]

It has long been reported that Rogers's feet bled after undergoing long and arduous rehearsals for her dance numbers with Astaire. The "Never Gonna Dance" number required forty-seven takes.[95] In the middle of shooting, Ginger's feet did indeed begin to blister and then bleed. Allan Scott's daughter, Pippa, the veteran TV actress turned documentary filmmaker, actually saw it take place.

Scott recalled, "I would sit in the corner of the rehearsal hall and watch Astaire and Pan dance. The person I remember the most is Pan because he was supposed to be Ginger. And then they would bring in Ginger. Hermes would teach her the number first. Then Fred and Ginger got together and danced. I remember watching with horror. She would take her shoes off, and her feet were covered with blood. I not only saw that, but I also saw the doctor come in and inject her feet. For a four-year-old, it was terrifying."

Rose Borne, Hal Borne's widow, recalled Hal's telling her, "Ginger's shoe was cut open at the sole and they used makeup to cover the blood on the satin part of the shoe. George Stevens said, 'Let's cut and come back tomorrow,' but Ginger said, 'Absolutely not! We should just keep going tonight until it's over, and we get it!' And they did."

Reflecting on Fred and Ginger's on-screen chemistry, Scott noted, "Watch her listening to him during a song. That turned the focus on him. Ginger was totally glued to him, and it turned the audience's attention to him and what he sang. We are as mesmerized as she is, and I think that was very powerful. It was very supportive of her, and it made him look all the better.

"She was smaller than he was. That was far more important than you realize. It made him sexy, and he was not very [sexy]. She had this joyous ability to listen carefully and be beautiful, but be small."

John Rockwell, the former dance critic of the *New York Times,* summed up the Astaire/Rogers approach when he said, "They made a new kind of dancing that was acting all by itself. Their dancing was formal and reserved, like Fred. It was ballroom dancing mixed with swing and jazz and tap. But though some of the virtuosity remains remarkable, it was never vulgar and flashy like ballroom today, at least as epitomized by reality TV shows like *Dancing with the Stars.*"

SWING TIME IS ALSO NOTEWORTHY for being the first time Fred and Ginger kissed on film. It happened twice. The first was behind a door conveniently opened to block the camera angle. The second was at the end of the picture when Fred had his back to the camera. Fred firmly believed that the romance was evident in the dance sequences, implying that, as stated in the lyrics of "The Continental," "you tell of your love while you dance." Phyllis concurred with Fred that intimate love scenes with Ginger were unnecessary. He called them "mushy." This was contrary to what Ginger felt, however.

In her autobiography *Ginger,* she candidly revealed, "I still believe Phyllis Astaire was a powerful force. You would never suspect it to see her. . . . I really felt, however, that Mrs. Astaire exerted pressure on her husband, subtly or unconsciously. She would come on the set and sit on the sideline with her knitting, clicking her needles. I found her presence disconcerting, especially during dialogue takes. Fred was uneasy at these times, too. One thing's for sure, she never warmed up to me . . . and she didn't want her husband to either."

After the completion of the movie, Fred and Phyllis headed to Ireland to see Adele and Charlie, then on to London and Paris. Before embarking for Europe, Fred wrote to Berman expressing how much he hoped the "Bojangles" number would register with the movie audience, noting, "I think my taps were okay for sync."[96]

On his return, Fred began work on an hour radio show that was aired for thirty-nine weeks on Tuesday nights for Packard. The car company desperately wanted him, believing he supplied the perfect image to sell its product to its wealthy clientele. Listening to a tape of the November 3, 1936, broadcast of *The Packard Hour,* with its constant interruptions for updates on the national election—"Roosevelt is ahead with twenty percent of the votes tabulated!"—one is struck with the immediacy and power that radio possessed at the time.

The bandleader on *The Packard Hour* was an old friend, the pianist and composer Johnny Green, who arranged and conducted the extraordinary recordings for Fred of "Top Hat, White Tie, and Tails," "Isn't This a Lovely Day," and three other hits that were released on Brunswick Records. On the show, Fred tap-danced on the wooden studio floor; exchanged patter with the comic actor Charles Butterworth, who was later to appear with him in the movie *Second Chorus;* sang songs from his Broadway shows and movies; introduced new tunes, such as Bert Kalmar and Harry Ruby's "Getting Away with Murder"; and sometimes sang a few of his own songs. Eventually, a conflict arose between Astaire's having to rehearse for the show and making movies. The situation became impossible, and the show ended.

President Franklin D. Roosevelt's New Deal boasted a strong following among Hollywood stars. Astaire was not one of them. With the strong conservative influence the English royals had made on his life, and with Phyllis's wealthy upbringing, he rebelled at the thought of paying the higher income taxes that Roosevelt authorized to underwrite his various alphabet social programs. A lifelong Republican was born.

Fred's politics notwithstanding, a few years later he joined an elite group of Hollywood actors who met at the home of Edward G. Robinson, a fervent Democrat, to discuss the grave situation in Europe. The purpose of the meeting was to put together a "declaration of independence," which called on President Roosevelt and Congress to sever all diplomatic relations with Germany—"a boycott that should last until such time as Germany is willing to re-enter the family of nations in accordance with the principle of international law and universal freedom." Such an internationalist stance was at odds with that of the Republican Party at the time, but Fred had long since formed a strong allegiance to this country and its immediate future.[97]

THE SATIRICAL EDGE of *Swing Time* wasn't completely accepted by two of the leading film critics. Frank S. Nugent of the *New York Times* noted, "The picture is good, of course, but after *Top Hat, Follow the Fleet* and the rest, it is a disappointment. Blame it primarily on the music . . . we could not even whistle a bar of 'A Fine Romance,' and that's about the catchiest and brightest melody in the show." Howard Barnes of the *New York Herald Tribune* was equally critical, but of the plot. He wrote, "It is high time that Fred Astaire and Ginger Rogers were relieved of the necessity of going through a lot of romantic nonsense. The vast success of *Swing Time* is more of a tribute to them than to the material of their latest song and dance carnival."

Still, most of the press reaction was favorable. Shortly after another smash opening at the Radio City Music Hall, the *Hollywood Reporter* named Fred and Ginger the country's number one box-office attraction. However, the picture's ultimate gross was slightly less than that of its predecessors. Their wall of success suddenly had a visible crack. The studio thought that following their next picture, *Shall We Dance,* they should perhaps undergo a temporary parting.[98]

Shall We Dance brought into the picture a dear friend of Fred's and Ginger's from Broadway, George Gershwin, who was also a sometimes beau of Ginger's. Doubtlessly, Fred was consulted about working with the Gershwins. He knew how much George and Ira's music had contributed to the success that he and Dellie had enjoyed on Broadway. This film marked Gershwin's second movie score; previously, he and Ira had written songs for the 1931 musical *Delicious,* starring Janet Gaynor.

Pandro Berman observed, "In the case of Gershwin and Porter, I didn't have their properties. I created properties for them, and they created music for the properties. I hired them because of my experience with Kern and Porter being so good; I thought, 'What the hell, I'll give ten percent of the profits to Irving Berlin and Gershwin and get the best rather than the second-raters.' And it worked."[99] Having the opportunity to introduce the melodies of these pop music deities doubtlessly was a valuable contribution to Astaire's escalating stardom.

Strangely enough, Gershwin's various excursions into writing more serious music such as his "Rhapsody in Blue," *Concerto in F, An American in Paris,* and *Porgy and Bess* had left the impression, at least in Hollywood, that his work was too highbrow. He was also thought to be incapable of writing hit songs that would launch movie musicals.[100] In reaction to such misguided judgments, George wired his agent, Arthur Lyons, RUMORS ABOUT HIGHBROW MUSIC RIDICULOUS STOP AM OUT TO WRITE HITS.[101]

The Gershwins were paid $55,000 for *Shall We Dance* (originally called *Watch Your Step*), although George and Ira had sought $100,000. A consolation was an option at $70,000 for their next film. Berlin, however, had received $100,000 for *Top Hat* plus a percentage of the gross.

The *Shall We Dance* screenplay was cowritten by Allan Scott and Ernest Pagano, directed by Mark Sandrich, and once again featured the comic regulars

Edward Everett Horton and Eric Blore, plus the valuable contribution of Jerome Cowan. It brought Astaire and Rogers "back home" to their native element among the affluent. This time, however, Fred was cast as a ballet star using the Russian name of Petrov and affecting a bad Russian accent. His character's real name was Peter P. Peters, of Philadelphia, who falls in love with a Ginger Rogers–style dancer.[102]

This was not the first time the role of a ballet dancer had been offered Fred. A few years earlier, Richard Rodgers and Lorenz Hart had sent him the outline of a story about a music teacher who composes and performs a work that is produced by a classical ballet company. Fred turned it down because it prevented him from wearing his now patented top hat, white tie, and tails. The property was rewritten for Broadway to star Ray Bolger and opened a successful run as *On Your Toes,* a year before *Shall We Dance* was released.[103]

Unfortunately, Fred was never again offered the opportunity to work with Rodgers and Hart. Hart did include his name, however, in the lyrics to "Do It the Hard Way" in the 1940s Broadway musical *Pal Joey,* which launched Gene Kelly to stardom: "Fred Astaire once worked so hard / He often lost his breath / And now he taps all others to death."[104]

Several of the many dancers I interviewed pointed out how inadequate Astaire was in *Shall We Dance* in attempting to authentically perform ballet routines. He had a long-held aversion to ballet, which, given his insistence on maintaining firm control of his image, makes it surprising that he would even consider accepting a role for which he was basically ill-equipped.

The Gershwins' score was chock-full of gems, but for some unforeseen reason several of them didn't resonate strongly with filmgoers on the movie's release. "Beginner's Luck" and "Slap That Bass" both employed mechanical objects (a phonograph and an ocean liner's engines). Astaire briefly taps to the former tune as the phonograph record sticks; he starts at a fast tempo, then dances in slow motion before stopping.

Set in the chromium-plated engine room (which provided almost an art deco look), "Slap That Bass" finds a number of black engineers at work on the chugging machines singing the song's verse, "Zoom, zoom." In stark contrast to some of the engineers, sporting their prominent pectorals, Fred is dressed in a white shirt, tie, trousers, and white bucks. This leads directly into the melody, sung by Mantan Moreland, Astaire, and a chorus, backed by a bassist and a drummer, and concludes with Fred's breaking into a rocketing tap routine along the catwalk of the engine room.

John Rockwell contends, "When you look at those Astaire/Rogers movies, they are so white. One is from Nebraska, one of them is from Missouri. We got

Middle American white people. Looking at 'Slap that Bass,' you have all those blacks on the plantation banging out the rhythm on the pipes. 'Bojangles of Harlem' looked like a minstrel show. Even though it was kind of racist looking, in a way, by doing these numbers you could argue it was part of the process of opening up black culture to mainstream America. The point is that by having scenes like these maybe it's exactly the opposite of what he wanted, but it was part of a process of destroying the very world he was epitomizing or at least of transforming it." Pan believed that Astaire possibly got the idea for the "Slap That Bass" number from watching a cement mixer on the lot. The idea might also have been influenced by the machine-shop scene in Charlie Chaplin's famous film *Modern Times*. (Chaplin roller-skated in *Modern Times,* and some of *his* moves were lifted from Fred's dance steps in *Top Hat.*)[105]

Ira Gershwin initially got the idea for the song "They All Laughed" from an advertisement that contained the tagline "They all laughed when I sat down at the piano." Ira was known as the Jeweler for the precision with which he set words to music. The prolific lyricist (seven hundred songs), who studied classical literature, idolized Gilbert and Sullivan and dreaded writing love songs. "He eschewed using [the word] 'love' whenever possible. . . . Ira loved puns and word games but disparaged the notion of himself as a poet."[106]

"They All Laughed" is set in a New York nightclub where Fred brings Ginger out of the audience while he's performing. She sings the melody, which causes Fred to try some exaggerated ballet leaps around her. These moves completely dazzle Ginger and lead her to break into a fierce tap step, which ultimately results in Fred's becoming competitive as they swirl around the room. The song ends with a leap onto two white pianos, reminiscent of "The Carioca" number from *Flying Down to Rio.*[107]

"Let's Call the Whole Thing Off" finds Fred and Ginger dancing on roller skates in a Central Park rotunda. This is without a doubt one of their most imaginatively conceived novelty dance numbers and contains only one cut in the entire scene. Pan came up with this most original idea, although one might conclude that it was a follow-up to Fred's nightly posttheater roller-skating flights on Park Avenue.[108] At first, however, Fred was very much against the concept. Eventually, he agreed to do it, but it reportedly took thirty-four hours of rehearsal, four days of shooting, and over 150 takes to get it perfect.

This number is also reminiscent of "Isn't This a Lovely Day" from *Top Hat,* complete with Fred and Ginger dressed in matching tweeds. Their tap dialogue on wheels follows the "I'll Be Hard to Handle" routine from *Roberta.* It begins with an argument centered on the classic Ira Gershwin lyric "You say eether, while I say either."[109] As the number progresses, a sudden apprehension comes over the viewer: "When are they going to fall down?" Of course, they didn't until they conclude by crashing onto a lawn.[110]

With each succeeding picture, the pressure mounted to come up with more brilliant and unusual ideas. Fred was adamant about never repeating himself in a dance routine. He and Ginger knew the public would be comparing what they did now with what they had done before.[111]

Ginger was so exhilarated by "Let's Call the Whole Thing Off" number that she scheduled her own roller-skating party, cohosted by her then serious admirer, Alfred Vanderbilt, at the Rollerdome in Culver City on March 6, 1937. The guests included the crème de la crème of Hollywood society—Cary Grant, Joan Crawford, Franchot Tone, George Gershwin, Harold Lloyd, George Murphy, Humphrey Bogart, as well as Lela Rogers and Hermes Pan. The menu consisted of spaghetti, chili, tamales, Boston baked beans, sliced ham, and hot dogs and hamburgers cooked to order. Casual dress was required. *Life* magazine covered it in its *"Life* Goes to a Party" section. The magazine reported that it was unique among Hollywood parties: "This one was so much fun, nobody got drunk."

Conspicuous by their absence were Fred and Phyllis Astaire. This was a perfect example of how Fred and Ginger kept their business and social lives completely separate. They preferred it that way.

"They Can't Take That Away from Me" was surprisingly the Gershwins' only song nominated for an Academy Award. The song is one of their masterpieces, and Astaire delivers one of his most meaningful vocal renditions. It has been synonymous with him over the years, so much so that in the 1990s Robyn Smith, Astaire's widow, informed Rosemary Clooney, then planning a Gershwin tribute at the Hollywood Bowl, that Fred considered it his favorite song.

In the movie, the song is sung by Fred to Ginger on the deck of a ferryboat going from New Jersey to New York during a fog. The song is a device for Astaire to reminisce about his bachelorhood at a time when Fred's and Ginger's characters were to be married. The song is reprised, but instead of having Ginger dance the ballet with Astaire, Harriet Hoctor, a ballet dancer and contortionist, takes her place!

The finale, "Shall We Dance," makes use of a circular stage atop a New York hotel showroom that resembles the Waldorf-Astoria roof. Fred is dressed in a premier danseur tunic. He and Hoctor do a graceful pas de deux surrounded by a corps de ballet. They are suddenly replaced by a chorus of fourteen female dancers all wearing masks with Ginger's image. (Astaire's character, Pete, came up with this idea after a spat with Linda, Ginger's character; he had vowed, "If I can't dance with one Linda, I'll dance with dozens!")

Fred returns dressed in white tie and tails. Following a solo turn by Hoctor, he breaks into the compelling invitation "Shall We Dance," as the chorus reappears in their masks plus one addition, the real Linda (Ginger). She at last realizes she loves him. Pete dances up to each girl in turn, but Linda's "Otchi Tchornya" turns him around. They rush into each other's arms, dance joyously, and end the movie on a perfect lyrical phrase: "They all said we'd never get together / They laughed at us and how! / But ho, ho, ho, / Who's got the last laugh now!"[112]

Critic Joseph Arnold Kaye of *Dance* magazine saluted Astaire's attempts to further the art of film dancing in *Shall We Dance*. He wrote, "Astaire and Rogers are the picture. Everything else seems to have been put in to fill the time between swings. Dance routines are fresh and interesting, dancing is superb. When will Hollywood learn to make a dance picture as good as the dancing, we cannot even guess."

Bob Podesta, currently a professor of international law at the China Foreign Affairs University in Beijing, recently obtained DVD copies of *Top Hat* and *Shall We Dance* that he screened for some of his students. Zhong Li, who also goes by the English name of Mariana, remarked, "Before I watched these movies, I was not familiar with tap dancing, and I knew nothing about Fred Astaire, who must be extraordinarily famous in the West, as I found later on the Internet. . . . I noticed that there was virtually no change of scene when he dances, which means that the lens focused on him during all the dancing process without any unnatural techniques added to it. . . . The most proper words that I could find to describe Astaire are resourceful, humorous, elegant, self-confident, optimistic, versatile, and attractive."

It's noteworthy that a young Asian, exposed for the first time to American film musicals and the style of dancing of seventy years ago, can so easily appreciate the talent of Fred Astaire. Apparently brilliant talent translates easily to any culture.

Podesta subsequently reported that Zhong Li and several other of his students, as a result of viewing Fred and Ginger movies, began to attempt some of Astaire's dance routines, just as many Americans had after seeing the films back in the 1930s, and later in the 1940s and 1950s. At that time suddenly, at every socioeconomic level, fees were extracted from ambitious parents speculating on dance careers for their children.[113]

I HAVE PURPOSELY REFRAINED from discussing the plots of the Fred and Ginger movies in much detail. With rare exceptions, they were fundamentally similar and often inane, with Fred finding the girl of his dreams in Ginger, her rejecting his advances, and finally his charming her into falling in love with him. Astaire's presence elevated the most meager scripts. They essentially supplied a romantic setting to frame song-and-dance numbers for the by then famous combination to strut their musical wares in a manner the screen has never witnessed before or since. As Arlene Croce saw it, "In an Astaire-Rogers film the dancing is often the only real, the only serious business."[114]

Fred's leading ladies, starting with Ginger Rogers, often suffered from having to depend on his whims as the leading man, although Rogers's characters were often independent and sometimes headstrong. She seemed to be angry at him at some point in most of their movies. The roles of Astaire's 1930s and 1940s leading ladies were in no way comparable, however, to the strong, more driven female characters played by such formidable actresses as Bette Davis, Joan Crawford, Katharine Hepburn, Barbara Stanwyck, or Rosalind Russell.

Several talented and amusing comic actors helped the Fred and Ginger movie plots move along at a gingerly (no pun intended) pace and in many cases served as aides-de-camp to Fred in his determined attempts to woo la Rogers. That is, with the exception of the dastardly and camp shenanigans of Erik Rhodes, which were specifically designed to turn over the romantic apple cart.

The *Shall We Dance* screenplay had one of the most complex, and, at the same time, silliest plots of all the Fred and Ginger movies. Puritanism pervades the entire script. Romance is never permitted to surface. Marriage is the ultimate goal. Yet, examples of Allan Scott's sterling wit break through the bland maze, such as during Fred and Ginger's hurried wedding in New Jersey. When Fred asks the officiating judge, "What are the grounds for divorce in this state?" the judge peers over his rimless glasses and replies, "Marriage."[115]

Factors took place behind the scenes that the filmgoer had no knowledge of. In the case of *Shall We Dance* Joseph I. Breen, as head of the Production Code Administration, which had replaced the Hays Office as the industry censor, had serious problems with the original script. Breen advised RKO, "The attempt to make comedy out of the suggestion of—even though such a suggestion is quite untrue—of an unmarried woman, who is pregnant, is in our judgment highly offensive. . . . This element will have to be completely and entirely removed before the picture can be approved by this office." Some nineteen deletions were ordered made. This included the line "But Cleopatra had an asp."

"Throughout this production," Breen continued, "greatest possible care will have to be exercised in shooting dance scenes, especially where dancers are shown in costumes. Please keep in mind that the Code ordains that the intimate parts of the body must be fully clothed at all times. This applies in particular to shots of the breasts of woman." As a result of Breen's edict, the Scott-Pagano script went through several additional rewrites. Astaire wound up appearing in a screenplay with a veneer of sophistication that was negated by his having to play a naive, straitlaced performer whose romantic desires were aimed specifically toward getting married. He and Ginger first encounter one another on an ocean liner where the fellow passengers quickly mistake them for husband and wife. The rest of the film is devoted to their attempt to disprove that belief. They finally come to the conclusion that the only way people will believe them is to get married in order to get a divorce![116]

Allan Scott stressed, "There were so many naughty things in those pictures, actually, and never once did the Breen Office catch it or say, 'You can't do that.' It never occurred to them to ask what Ginger was doing with those men on the Riviera, who was paying her way. . . . Some of the reviewers pointed these things out, but as long as you stayed firmly subtle about these things, the office didn't catch it."[117]

Pippa Scott pointed out, "For my dad, dialogue was absolutely his thing. He was always on the set. He not only had to be there, but Mark Sandrich wanted him there because they always improvised lines."

Despite the various script difficulties, George Gershwin was basically satisfied by the movie's final cut. In a letter to Mark Sandrich, he offered several musical suggestions for sound and camera tweaks, as only an accomplished craftsman could provide, e.g., "Ginger seems to sing slightly off key at the beginning of the verse" in "They All Laughed." Referring to "They Can't Take That Away from Me," which he called "You Can't Take That Away from Me," he remained concerned about putting in the foghorn notes at the end of the song. At the end of the picture, he suggested, " 'Who's Got the Last Laugh Now' [sic] should be done with a mixed big chorus as the harmony Fred and Ginger do at the finish seems weak to me."

The renowned writer Budd Schulberg called Astaire "the classless aristocrat. If you look at the people who were foils for him in his movies, they were all these South American wealthy guys or England dupes. My favorite line in *Shall We Dance* is when Ginger Rogers puts the thing into real perspective when she said, 'I hope I shall never see a heal clicker again.' Until then, we had been influenced by Europe, which was a classed society. You had to know your place. Taste and style were in the blood. You would inherit that with Daddy's castle. Here comes Astaire, who in essence says, 'That's not true. Aristocracy, talent, style, it's not in the blood. Everybody can have it.'

"Ellen Moer's wonderful book on the history of the dandy points out that during times of great social upheaval like in the Depression or the English regency, when breeding or bloodlines are called into question, new things have to come along. And it's always people who develop a new style who are able to break through and construct a new society. The dandy was a revolutionary style. Astaire had that ability.

"I think of him as the new man—the new American man, who was from the New World like Fitzgerald and Hemingway as writers and Louis Armstrong and Duke Ellington in jazz. . . . Astaire was breaking away from the old country with its inbreeding—where you could not get anywhere. There was no ladder to go up. Britain was not what it was anymore. . . . We were gonna fill up the power gap.

"If you look at the other people who came around at the same time, or before, or later, all those people were tall, dark, and handsome. He was not any of that. He had a pear-shaped face and those big ears, but he danced so easily."

LIKE *SWING TIME, Shall We Dance* had slipped below the box-office figures for the previous Astaire/Rogers movies. That, of course, worried the studio. By then, 1938, the movie industry ranked fourteenth among all business in gross volume, eleventh in total assets.[118]

Besides that, Ginger and Lela Rogers wanted to step outside the confines of her being typecast as Fred Astaire's talented dancing partner. They desired recognition for her as a serious dramatic actress. *Stage Door* was the answer, costarring with Katharine Hepburn. It proved to be a better vehicle for her than the previous nine dramatic film appearances she had interspersed while appearing opposite Fred seven times thus far.[119]

When the studio announced that Ginger would not be appearing opposite Fred in his next musical film, the press was somewhat placated by Fred's declaring that the next picture after that would have Ginger as his costar. The feeling was that they were feuding, confirmed by the rumors that had been printed by gossip columnists and fan magazines for some time. Fred denied them, saying, "There has never been one single second of dissension between Ginger and me." Ginger also denied the reports.[120]

Berman sought an English actress as Fred's new leading lady in a P. G. Wodehouse story, *Damsel in Distress,* that had been converted into a London play. This was after American actress and dancer Ruby Keeler, and Jessie Matthews, the queen of English film musicals, had been rejected. Fred was again to play the by now familiar role of an American dancer in England as he had in *The Gay Divorcée* and *Top Hat.*[121] Again, alternating with Mark Sandrich, it was George Stevens's turn to direct.

Before starting work, Fred and Phyllis were once again off to London for a holiday. They stopped at Claridge's, where Dellie joined them. Charlie was in the midst of one of his several attempts at alcohol rehab. None of them ever worked.

In an attempt to get *Damsel in Distress* preproduction publicity, Dellie was even floated as a candidate for becoming Fred's costar, but Fred would not have it. A year later, she did accept an offer to appear opposite Jack Buchanan in an English film musical that was never finished. After a week of shooting she decided it had been a big mistake. She never performed again.

The glamorous Carole Lombard appeared set for the leading-lady role and would be paid $200,000, which angered the ever vigilant Lela Rogers. Ginger was still under contract to RKO and had been paid $61,193.28 for *Swing Time,* while Fred was now getting $119,000 per picture plus his usual percentage.[122] Lombard didn't think it made sense to wind up as Ginger's successor. Alice Faye and Ida Lupino were also briefly considered, but Olivia de Havilland's sister, twenty-year-old Joan Fontaine, who was signed to the studio, had an English father. She got the job.

One unfortunate major problem was that Fontaine was not much of a dancer. Once again, this brought out the Moanin' Minnie in Fred. Fontaine had had some ballet training and had taken tap-dancing lessons from Ruby Keeler's brother in preparation for her role, but she did no tap dancing in the movie.

Fred and Pan, whom David Niven Jr. correctly referred to as "socks and shoes," felt they could put together a few duets with her.[123] Ultimately, they settled for only one number together, and it was lackluster. The young actress was definitely out of her depth. She came across as fragile and whimpering. Like so many things in Hollywood, her casting made absolutely no sense. Once filming commenced, she was almost replaced by Ruby Keeler. Fontaine told Fred years later that *Damsel in Distress* set her career back five years.

The good news was that the option for the Gershwins was exercised. George Stevens again directed. The score included two songs that became standards, "A Foggy Day" and "Nice Work If You Can Get It," along with "Stiff Upper Lip," "Things Are Looking Up," and "I Can't Be Bothered Now." The addition of the brilliant comedy team of George Burns and Gracie Allen almost, but not quite, saved the picture.

As George Burns recalled, "The deciding factor was whether we could dance with Fred. Gracie was a good Irish-clog dancer, and I could get by; but I was a right-footed dancer. My left leg is a washout. I was afraid to dance in front of Fred Astaire, but the money was good—sixty thousand dollars—and I decided what the hell."[124]

Several dance numbers by Burns and Allen, however, delivered big-time with Fred, especially in the sensational "Stiff Upper Lip." Gracie sings the tune to Fred and George after sliding down a fun-house chute at an English fair, complete with treadmill, a spinning disk, a revolving staircase that turns into a chute, all of which is captured by several distorted mirrors. Astaire obviously enjoyed their dancing as well as their comic brilliance. Pan deservedly won the Best Dance Direction Oscar for his truly innovative staging of this number, which emanated from an old vaudeville routine that had been suggested by George Burns.

"A Foggy Day in London Town" was not set in the city but rather incongruously on the grounds of a castle. Fred "of course" is dressed in white tie and tails. The scene is at least atmospheric as the incoming fog captured Fred strolling the manor while smoking a cigarette with moonbeams shining through the trees. For some reason, Fontaine was not included. She only appears fleetingly as Fred professes his love to her in "Things Are Looking Up." This, too, takes place in a wooded area and was shot on a hill overlooking Malibu.[125]

"Nice Work If You Can Get It" marked one of several times Fred made vital use of a drum in a dance number on film, presumably due to his longtime passion for playing the instrument. The tune was originally a nine-bar theme George Gershwin had written seven years earlier. The lyrical inspiration was derived by Ira from a *Punch* cartoon. The song was first delivered in the movie by Astaire and three harpies in a humorous scene. The second time, an explosive version with Fred playing and kicking a drum serves as the perfect conclusion of the picture.[126]

In a taped interview that the pianist and singer Michael Feinstein conducted with Jo Stafford, one of the truly outstanding pop singers of all time, I learned that Stafford, while working in films at the age of twenty as part of the Stafford Sisters, talked about how she wrote the arrangement and played piano on Astaire's sound-track performance of "Nice Work If You Can Get It." As Stafford recalled, "I received a colossal jolt when Fred couldn't do the 'bump, bump'—'and you can get it if you try,' when we recorded it. It was very strange. The master of the syncopated shoes couldn't sing the syncopated notes."

THE ONE MAJOR DEFICIENCY was the absence of the spark that was always in evidence in a Fred Astaire movie—the electrifying presence of Ginger Rogers. As Regina Crowe in the *New York Journal-American* stated it succinctly, "The missing link between a smash Astaire hit and a just good film is—Ginger Rogers." Frank Nugent returned to the Astaire fold writing, "On the whole, fresh, glib, and agreeable presented. . . . What more can one ask of in an Astaire show? Miss Rogers? Don't be a pig, Willy."[127]

The film opened poorly, which led Fred to consider retiring. His mother had once told him that since he started working professionally at such a young age, he should retire at thirty-five.[128] He was then thirty-eight. He discussed the matter with Phyllis. She suggested he go out and play golf.

During the filming of *Damsel in Distress,* George Gershwin had not been visiting the set as he had while *Shall We Dance* was in production. When Fred spoke to him on the telephone, Gershwin explained that he was furthering his budding talent as a painter. In reality, he was dying.[129]

Gershwin's close friend the pianist Oscar Levant was upset that George was missing notes at a subsequent Hollywood Bowl performance of the Concerto in F. His piano playing had always been perfect. The next day George complained about a burning smell in his nose. A series of severe headaches followed.

He remained in seclusion in his Beverly Hills home and began writing the score for his next movie, *Goldwyn Follies,* from which posthumously emerged his last important song, "Love Is Here to Stay." He had an operation for a brain tumor and died shortly afterward at the age of thirty-eight. This prompted the well-known novelist John O'Hara to write a magazine article that famously began, "George Gershwin died on July 11, 1937, but I don't believe it if I don't want to." Hollywood legend has it that the last word Gershwin was heard to utter as he was rushed to the hospital had been "Astaire."[130]

On September 8, 1937, at a Hollywood Bowl concert carried on CBS radio, Astaire joined other Gershwin devotees, Levant, Todd Duncan, Lily Pons, Edward G. Robinson, and George Jessel, at a performance scheduled as part of the regular summer season that turned out to be a memorial tribute. Fred had listened to Gershwin preview his songs from the forthcoming musical film *Goldwyn Follies* at the Garden of Allah earlier that summer, which included "Love Walked In" and "Love Is Here to Stay." Now his monumental contributions ceased at the age of thirty-eight.[131]

Fred was one of the first visitors to console Ira and his wife, Lenore, at the Gershwin home on North Roxbury Drive in Beverly Hills. Fred's grief was enormous. The two had shared some important history together. On their first meeting, they had immediately recognized the talent of the other at a time when they were both going through the growing pains of establishing their respective careers. In addition to their bonhomie, musically they had similar career sparks in trying to hone and develop various erratic rhythms.[132] Gershwin was an integral member of the American royalty of songwriters who had contributed immeasurably to Fred's success on Broadway and in films.[133] Fred would remain close to Ira Gershwin for the rest of his life.

* * *

PRIVACY WAS EXTREMELY IMPORTANT to Fred and Phyllis. He once said, "My private life is not under contract."[134] He spent considerable time with his new son. "It's the best thing that ever happened to me in my life," he said to a reporter in a departure from his usual reserved manner. He gave Freddie swimming lessons and took him on fishing trips. On returning from work at the studio, he would devote time to play with him. Fred also took up gardening, which, like everything he worked at, he took seriously. He purchased a ranch in Chatsworth in the San Fernando Valley, to replace the ranch he had above San Diego. He dubbed his new property the Blue Valley Ranch, where the family often spent weekends.

Mary Ellin Barrett's sister, Linda Emmet, who along with Robert Kimball compiled *The Complete Lyrics of Irving Berlin,* while growing up spent a summer in Los Angeles. Emmet observed Fred and Phyllis: "I found them so unpretentious; they were not at all like Hollywood people were thought of as being."

Fred and Phyllis made frequent trips to see Peter in Tucson, where he attended boarding school. Liking everything English, Fred had brought Enid Dickens Hawksley, the granddaughter of Charles Dickens, to work as governess for Fred Jr.[135] "Life Is Beautiful," the title of the most successful song Astaire ever wrote, which contained lyrics by Tommy Wolf, well described Astaire's home life of the late 1930s.

Still, Fred could have his occasional temperamental outbursts. Hermes Pan recalled having dinner with the Astaires at their home, after which Phyllis asked Fred to do the dishes. Fred dutifully headed for the kitchen. "A moment later, we heard a terrible clatter. She rushed into the kitchen and found Fred breaking the dishes, one at a time. He said to Phyllis, 'Never ask me to do dishes again.' A million women would have blown their top over that, but Phyllis just burst out laughing. Then she pitched in and helped break the rest of the dishes."

THE ABSENCE OF GINGER ROGERS would not be repeated in the next two Astaire musicals. Their next film was the rather ludicrous *Carefree,* which was really a vehicle for Ginger—a screwball comedy with music with Fred playing a psychiatrist. Written by Pagano and Scott, it was directed by Mark Sandrich. Thankfully, it came in at a brief eighty-three minutes.

Months before filming began, Fred was upset over an interview Sandrich conducted with the London *Daily Express,* which Adele had sent to Fred. The director had speculated about the future of the Fred and Ginger combination, saying,

"I don't think it will go on very much longer. You see the snag we're up against is that we have to keep to the same story formula. Not because we want to, but because the public squawks at the slightest deviation." He also was quoted as saying that Fred and Ginger "were scared of losing their identities." He added, "Fred is a genius, and an old worryguts. . . . Ginger Rogers is a darling. She is just a hard-working little girl as genuine as they come. Her only fault is an inferiority complex. She doesn't know how good she is."[136]

Fred seemingly got over Sandrich's interview quickly. Shortly after that he wrote a letter to him, while en route East, on the California Limited, before heading to Aiken for Christmas. It explained how diplomatic Fred was in dealing with Irving Berlin, especially when Irving approached him to demonstrate songs for a forthcoming film. In this case, it was the score for *Carefree*.

Fred wrote Sandrich, "Of course, it is impossible to judge songs at such a session and especially after 'our Irv' gets through building them up etc. There's nothing to do but scream—jump—and yell 'Marvelous' anything less than such a reaction from me breaks his heart—as you know. I swear to you—Irving was so nervous and excited playing the songs for me that he fell off *the piano stool* twice, got so out of breath he had to stop in the middle of a couple of songs from choking, and his fingers were bent back double from that pressing down business of his."

Astaire wrote how much he liked Berlin's "I Used to Be Color Blind," "Change Partners," and "A Hell of a Lot." Fred also said, " 'Carefree' I didn't like at all [which never appeared in the film]. I don't think it means a thing and is like many of those easygoing ideas I had so often." He ended by suggesting, "Better not quote me to Irving except when I'm crazy about that stuff—you know what I mean!!!"

The final score consisted of only four song-and-dance numbers. The first, "Since They Turned Loch Lomond into Swing," was, justifiably, a particular favorite of Fred's, perhaps because it gave a completely different look at him, this time as the possessor of an incredible golf swing. As the scene opens, he's ridiculed by the psychologically disturbed Ginger, Fred's patient, as he begins practicing his golf stroke. Suddenly, he breaks into a tap dance while simultaneously playing a harmonica in swing tempo! It took ten days to rehearse this amazing sequence and two days to shoot it.[137]

Ralph Bellamy, who costarred with Fred and Ginger in a humorous role in the picture, said, "I recall there were eighteen to twenty golf balls teed up, maybe three or four feet apart, and he danced all over the balcony, the furniture, one of those fantastic creative dances and ended with a golf club, still dancing. Then to the rhythm of the music, he hit the golf balls, and when they went to fetch them, they were within eight feet of each other, which to me is quite remarkable—absolute control of every muscle of the body, every second. He knew what he was doing, and it seemed so easy. It looks as if you could do it yourself, but it was that kind of perfection that comes from constant practice."[138]

Reportedly, Fred spent two weeks on this perfectly synchronized routine, using up six hundred golf balls.[139] Not to be outdone, Katharine Hepburn, in a "Babe" Didrikson Zaharias–type role, playing a golf pro, copied this number in the 1952 MGM comedy *Pat and Mike,* one of her last costarring films opposite Spencer Tracy. In this instance, Hepburn's imitation fell short of being flattering.

"I Used to Be Color Blind" is actually a dream sequence devised by Astaire and Pan. It was sung by Fred before he and Ginger transformed it into a swing-dance tune performed in slow motion. To convey the impression that Ginger is floating on air, Fred lifts her several times, something entirely new for them. Their duet was first considered to be shot in color, but Pandro Berman vetoed its cost. If it had been shot in Technicolor, it would greatly have enhanced the impact of what was already one of the duo's truly most outstanding dance sequences.

"The Yam," said to be based on Southern blacks selling yams,[140] starts out as an instrumental played at a country club by a jazz band. According to Astaire expert Michael Russell, Fred thought the song was so silly that it was assigned to Ginger to sing. Another freewheeling traveling dance, reminiscent of "The Big Apple" and "The Lambeth Walk," two staples of the swing era, followed from there. The dance starts on the dance floor of a country club, moves outdoors, proceeds through a neighboring lounge, then moves back to the main dance area. Once again, the having-a-wonderful-time feeling of the two principals in executing the dance is very much in evidence.[141]

The "Change Partners" number, also set at the country club, again makes use of lifts and is another Sandrich device toward a final resolution of the plot. It begins with Ginger dancing with her fiancé, Ralph Bellamy. (Surprisingly, Irving Berlin had actually written the song a few years earlier when Astaire was about to change dancing partners.) Astaire arranges to have Bellamy called off the dance floor to take a phone call. This gives Fred the opportunity to woo Ginger anew in another of their patented graceful romps around the dance floor. The song was the highlight of the picture, and it got an Academy Award nomination but lost out to Bob Hope and Shirley Ross's well-remembered duet on "Thanks for the Memory."[142]

Mary Ellin Barrett pointed out, "Certain Berlin songs tell a story. 'Change Partners,' also 'Isn't It a Lovely Day,' 'Let's Face the Music and Dance,' were prophetic. Some of his songs like these are character songs. Fred is affirming he is a bachelor who doesn't want any entanglements. Also, it sets up the dance. But 'Change Partners,' that's a story."

Another unusual feature of *Carefree* was that at long last Astaire consented to do a love scene with Ginger, even if shortened, without resorting to distorted camera angles. It was the tag to the "I Used to Be Color Blind" number. Phyllis came to the studio specifically to see the rushes of the scene. Fred recalled, "We *used* a kiss and then put it in slow motion. . . . I said to Phyllis, 'Well, we finally got that out of the way,' and she said, 'I'll say you did, and you certainly emphasized it enough. My goodness.' I said, 'Well, it only took about four seconds to do. When you slow it down, it just seems that many seconds more.' And Phyllis said, 'I know how long it was, you don't have to tell me.' "[143]

Ginger's wardrobe in *Carefree* reflected the upcoming 1940s—the witch hats, the snoods, the splashy antiques. The lighting, cinematography, and the luxury were all toned down. Instead of concentrating on capturing the captivating art deco interiors—to emphasize one of the key glamorous elements that were such important aspects of the Astaire/Rogers movies—much of *Carefree* took place outdoors.[144]

Many consider *Carefree* marks the twilight of Fred and Ginger's RKO era. Perhaps this was because it actually wound up losing money—$48,000.[145] Henry Brandt, president of the Independent Theatre Owners of America, on the basis of *Damsel in Distress* and *Carefree,* in an advertisement that appeared in the *Hollywood Reporter* and picked up by *Time* in a subsequent story, labeled Astaire "Box Office Poison." Joan Crawford, Marlene Dietrich, Greta Garbo, and Mae West completed the list.[146] Fred and RKO went ballistic and threatened legal action; Phyllis convinced Fred to forget about it.[147]

Looking for a new approach to successfully showcase their moneymaking team, RKO decided on a movie biography based on the famous dancing duo of Vernon and Irene Castle. Fred and Adele had actually staged Irene Castle's act in 1922, after Vernon's death.[148] The Castles had been an inspiration to them in the early days of their career.[149] This movie was following the trend of another studio, in this case Twentieth Century–Fox, which specialized in musical film biographies, such as *Alexander's Ragtime Band,* starring Alice Faye. For the Castle film, Hermes Pan was the choreographer. The director was H. C. Potter. It took three screenwriters, including Oscar Hammerstein II, to bring Irene Castle's stories, *My Husband and My Memories of Vernon Castle,* to the screen under the title *The Story of Vernon and Irene Castle.* Fred wanted the picture to be filmed in Technicolor, but again RKO decided against it.[150]

Irene Castle was hired as "technical adviser" for the movie, a term that studios believed translated into a factual film biography that would resonate with the public. The widow Castle turned into more than a handful, with the studio regretting that she was so closely involved with the production.

Castle was the stepmother of Jean Bach, one of New York's true sophisticates, and a woman of undeniable charm. As Bach explained it, "Irene was my father George Enzinger's last wife, and he was her last husband. He was Irene's fourth husband. Vernon Castle was her first. Daddy had only two wives, my mother and Irene."

Bach continued, "Vernon was an idol of Fred's. The Castles were the first entertainers to be sought after by society people the way Bobby Short was [and Fred was]. You know Bobby was in the Social Register. Irene had all kinds of jewels from the Grand Duke Dimitri of Russia and from various socialites. She and Vernon were really a class couple. That appealed to Fred. I think Vernon gained something from working with the comedy team of Weber and Fields in vaudeville [Lew Fields appeared in the movie], where he learned to shape the little comedy touches that eventually had an effect on Fred's work. Irene said that Fred was crazy about Vernon for a number of reasons, one of which was that they both adored playing the drums, as did the Prince of Wales. When the time came to make the movie, which I think was probably Fred's idea, it seemed worth it, but Irene became a pain in the neck. Pandro Berman wanted her thrown off the set, but he didn't succeed.

"There were so many falsehoods in the movie. When Vernon and Irene became international stars and went to Paris, the place they were supposed to play closed. They were out of funds. They had taken their black valet [Walter Ash] with them. He shot dice with Parisian car drivers and came back with a lot of money. They were able to buy Irene a little Dutch cap that became famous. Walter Brennan got the part of the valet. That was the first glaring error." (Irene later claimed this was done to satisfy movie exhibitors in the South.)

"Ginger Rogers had trouble getting her hair the length it was, which wasn't terribly long. But she had bleached it so much it would never grow. Irene's major claim to fame at this point, since her dancing career was long over by 1939, was that she invented bobbed hair. Ginger refused to cut her hair or wear a wig. She and Irene had a feud over that and her costumes. Irene also didn't think Ginger was right to portray her. Fred implied he was on Ginger's side, but he never stepped in to balance it out because he was a pacifist."

Instead of dancing as lovers, as they had in their previous musicals, this was Fred and Ginger's opportunity to showcase the various dances the Castles had inaugurated, but with their own technique—the soft shoe mixed with clog dancing, slides, and big leg swings; the Texas Tommy, a forerunner of the Lindy Hop; the Castle Walk; the turkey trot; the tango; the polka; and the maxixe. The latter was the highlight of the movie. In a sense, looking back at the history of modern dance provided perhaps the perfect coda for their nine films together during the 1930s.

By the time of *The Story of Vernon and Irene Castle,* according to the studio papers on the production, Fred was being paid $155,000 while Ginger was getting $130,000. Her wardrobe for the picture cost $2,775, a reasonably high sum for the time. (This overshadowed the price of Fred's toupees, which were budgeted at between $150 and $550.)[151]

The story goes that when Fred saw the film during its world-premiere engagement at Radio City Music Hall, he immediately realized that something was wrong. The sound that emanated from the loudspeakers behind the screen reached his ears a second late, which was too late for him. He rushed to make a telephone call to the studio in Hollywood. "Get someone out here right away," he screamed. "The film is five frames out of sync!"[152]

Partly due to the many continued scenes in the plot, plus the film's being such a departure from Fred and Ginger's lighthearted contemporary musical comedies, the New York movie critics were mixed in their reaction. *Time,* however, contended, "To say that Fred Astaire and Ginger Rogers are well fitted to fill the Castles' dancing slippers is an understatement. Astaire and Rogers symbolize their era just as completely as the Castles symbolized theirs." *Newsweek* was equally favorable, saying, "Rogers and Astaire brilliantly re-create the famous couple's inspired contributions to the dance world. The result is not only a refreshing musical but a haunting screen biography."

THE TRUE NATURE of the Astaire/Rogers relationship has been speculated about for many years. In her autobiography, Ginger made it abundantly clear they had practically no relationship away from the studio. She said, "Well, I think when you work with somebody all day long for ten movies, you become good friends, though he was delighted as not to see me at night over dinner as I was."[153]

A well-known Hollywood actor who knew Rogers personally and was aware of her reputation as a very sexual woman, believed that there might at one time or another have been a liaison with Fred. I tend to think not. The actress Sylvia Sidney said, "Astaire would have strayed as far as his toenails."[154] Fred's life was compartmentalized. He was completely happy with Phyllis at home. Ginger Rogers represented a perfect work situation; he fully recognized that their association had helped to establish him as a major film star. He would do nothing to endanger it.

Slim Keith, the former wife of the highly regarded film director Howard Hawks, and of Leland Hayward, and who had an important presence in New York and Hollywood society for many years, said, "Maybe there was a flirt. I don't know. There wouldn't have been any more than that—it would never have been anything consummated."[155]

The well-known writer Dominick Dunne explained, "I got to know Ginger when I was the stage manager on a live TV special in the late fifties. It was *Tonight at 8:30,* the Noël Coward thing. . . . I got to know her very well. She and Fred were never friends. I mean, they weren't pals, they weren't soul mates. I think it was a slightly snob thing. Ginger was never in the same set, shall we say?"[156]

Ava Astaire McKenzie, speaking of Ginger, said, "Daddy never had any feuding thing with her—they were not particularly friends. She was just different from Daddy." The veteran television character actress Betty White, who was a close friend of Fred's in his last years, said, "I remember one night he really started to dish about Ginger."

Pandro Berman, as producer of all the RKO Fred and Ginger films except for *Flying Down to Rio* and *The Story of Vernon and Irene Castle,* had to frequently deal with Fred's seeming reluctance to continue working with Ginger. As Berman recalled, "The stories you may have heard are absolutely true. After not wanting to work with Ginger in *The Gay Divorcée,* the next picture [*Roberta*] I talked him into doing it again because he had Irene Dunne with him, even though she wasn't playing opposite him. Then in the next one, *Top Hat,* I persuaded him that his ten percent of the profits was worth thinking about, and if he didn't have Ginger, he . . . you know, he made a fortune out of those pictures. So he finally acceded to that one. And every picture was a terrible struggle. And finally I had to promise him if he'd use her in a certain picture, I would give him another girl in the next one. And that's how it came about that we had Joan Fontaine . . . and it was our worst picture."[157]

One day Berman ran into Fred on the studio lot. Fred remarked, "I want to thank you." "What for?" the producer asked. Fred replied, "I've been thinking. Sam Goldwyn, Jack Warner, and David Selznick are good friends of mine, but they don't hire me. You've made pictures with me, and they've been good. So I want to thank you!"

As Fred walked away, Berman stared at him in complete astonishment. Their relationship had been strictly professional. This was the first time Fred had ever said anything personal.[158]

ONCE THE FRED and Ginger phenomenon became established, Ginger resented playing the other dancer to Fred. The famous statement attributed to her—whether in fact she actually said it—"I don't know why everyone makes such a fuss about Fred Astaire's dancing. I did all the same steps, only backwards and in high heels," more than subtly expresses her true feelings. In 1987, after decades of being asked about her relationship with Fred, she told a BBC documentary interviewer, "We were a team. He didn't do it by himself, Fred was not my Svengali. A lot of people think he was. I was very much my own woman."[159]

Ginger's crafty and assertive mother, Lela, was even more aware of how much less of the credit for the grand success of Fred and Ginger went her daughter's way. Lela's aggressive manner constantly irritated Fred. She was forever negotiating with Berman attempting to get significant salary raises, the best costumes, the best roles in dramatic pictures away from Fred, and other perks from RKO. In 1940, Ginger won the Best Actress Oscar playing the title role in *Kitty Foyle*.

In addition to having to compete with Fred's emergence as a superstar, Ginger, despite Mark Sandrich's interview in London praising her, was constantly in conflict with Sandrich. Since Mark directed five of the Fred and Ginger movie cycle, their confrontations took place over four years.

In an April 21, 1938, letter to Sandrich, Pandro Berman wrote, "Her [Ginger's] reluctance to report for this picture [*Carefree*] has been her aggravation at the fact that she is being asked to work under your direction." Berman praised Sandrich for his abilities as a director but pointed out, "Ginger Rogers, like every other actress, is a person who will respond most completely to careful attention and generous pampering . . . ," then chastised him for telling Lela, "If Ginger did not learn to improve her singing and dancing she would at some future date find herself in great difficulties in the picture business." Berman concluded, "Don't take this in the nature of a criticism of you, because as I said before you have been entirely unconscious of many of your actions."

As Berman had stated, even after the public embraced Fred's spectacular work with Ginger, Astaire still had a real problem with having a steady female dance partner. For the most part this was a residual of the troublesome aftermath of Adele's decision to end their act by getting married. The movies with Ginger set a romantic image he couldn't escape and forced him to realize that he had to have a dancing costar if he was going to continue making commercial movie musicals.

Astaire often referred to Ginger as the Wasp. His nickname was based less on her being a White Anglo-Saxon Protestant and considerably more on her often feisty persona both on- and offscreen. Ginger had patiently tolerated Fred's tireless penchant for rehearsal and his unceasing demands to achieve perfection. They were equally aware of the idiosyncrasies the other brought to the dance floor, but the magic they generated together on-screen translated into something too important to discard.

The box-office figures for their last few movies had, however, seriously fallen off, but perhaps just as important the budgets of their movies had considerably increased. *Carefree* had cost $1,253,000 and *The Story of Vernon and Irene Castle* cost $1,196,000. They grossed $1,731,000 and $1,200,000, respectively.[160] The lack of a significant profit was the deciding factor.

Obviously, the public's fascination for their dazzling work together had waned. Berman remarked that their nine films together represented six years of mutual aggression.[161] They both had extraordinary career opportunities in front of them. After seven years, it was indeed time for a change. From this moment on, Fred would never commit himself to another series of movies with the same dance partner.

CHAPTER FIVE

CHANGE PARTNERS AND DANCE

NOT LONG AFTER *The Story of Vernon and Irene Castle* wrapped, Leland Hayward began having discussions with Louis B. Mayer about Fred's starring in a film musical at MGM with Eleanor Powell. Powell admitted to author Bob Thomas that one day shortly afterward, on orders from Mayer, she reported to director Mervyn LeRoy's office at the studio. She hid behind a door when Fred and Hayward arrived to meet with Fred's old friend LeRoy. During the meeting, Fred expressed his anxiety that Powell was perhaps too tall for him and also mentioned that he had heard she was as much of a perfectionist as he was. LeRoy then announced, "Ellie, you can come out now."

"I was so embarrassed, my face was beet red," Powell recalled. After some further chitchat, LeRoy suggested that the two stars stand up, back-to-back. Upon doing so, Powell related, "He was taller than I was by about two inches." An agreement was signed soon after that for Astaire and Powell to work together.

MGM, fresh from amassing a considerable profit from *The Wizard of Oz* and its investment in David O. Selznick's independent production of *Gone with the Wind,* had high hopes for the movie. By this time, the fall of 1939, the studio had begun its unsurpassed reign as the dominant force in film musicals.[1] Cole Porter was hired to write the score. George Murphy, the studio's leading male dancer, was cast as Fred's partner in a nightclub act. The picture was going to be marketed with typical studio flamboyance as "The World's Greatest Dancers in the World's Greatest Musical Show."[2] Preliminary plans were to shoot the film in color, but ultimately the idea was abandoned—it was thought color films didn't always assure big profits. The concern over the impending war (which began fifteen days before shooting commenced) and its possible bad economic effect might have been another reason for this decision.[3]

After a brief holiday in Ireland, Fred began work with Powell, probably the most talented and finished dancer he ever worked with. The new film was called *Broadway Melody of 1940*, the last of a series of four *Melody* films at MGM. Fred and Powell shared costar billing. With all the preparation for the dance numbers alone, Fred decided that beginning with *Broadway Melody*, he would henceforth make only one movie a year.[4]

Eleanor was his equal in every area of the dance, and most assuredly as a tap dancer. That didn't necessarily translate into screen chemistry with him, however, despite their three weeks of rehearsal experimenting with various tap steps.[5] Accomplished as she was, and despite her ready smile, Powell lacked a magnetic and feminine screen personality.[6]

At first, they addressed each other as "Mr. Astaire" and "Miss Powell." This formality seems to have unfortunately extended into the finished picture in their dancing and acting.[7] Romance was never a part of the movie's plot, which basically was another trite backstage musical with the requisite mistaken-identity device. Their attraction for one another was merely implied as the film predominantly showcased their spectacular dancing.

This was Porter's first score for an Astaire film. "I've Got My Eyes on You" gave Astaire the chance to express his love for Powell, singing the song while playing rollicking piano, which ended with his dancing with the sheet music. The reprise was a dance number featuring the three principals.[8] "I Concentrate on You" wasn't sung but provided the background for a lavish balletic Harlequin number that found Fred in tights, an ill-fated venture attempting once again to establish his ballet credentials.

The Astaire/Powell duet on Porter's 1935 hit, "Begin the Beguine," was conceived by Bobby Connolly, the dance director for the film (Pan was then signed exclusively to RKO), and endures as one of the most brilliant dance numbers in the Astaire dance lexicon. It was an exhibition of the two best tap dancers dancing in syncopation to an arrangement of the tune based on the familiar Artie Shaw hit record. In introducing this number in *That's Entertainment!*, the first of three potpourris of magical moments from MGM musicals, Frank Sinatra said, "You can wait around and hope, but you'll never see the likes of this again."

The spectacular set for this number cost $120,000 and consisted of mirrored floors surrounded by mirrored stars and palm trees. The two masters displayed the wide range of their dancing technique in three segments (West Indies plus Polynesia, tap and Spanish elements, and finally jazz tap, dipped in swing), interrupted by a lame pseudo–Andrews Sisters group singing the chorus. An Artie Shaw–like clarinet solo introduced Astaire and Powell's joyous tapping conclusion.[9]

The opulent look of the picture could not disguise that it was little more than mediocre.[10] The *New York Times,* however, praised the film more than Fred's last few endeavors with Ginger. The review said in part, "Fred's arabesques seemed even more fascinatingly intricate than ever." The London *Daily Express* notice said of Powell, "She's a nice looking girl from out of town who keeps superb time. But she looks as strong and confident on her own, you just don't care if Fred gets her or not."[11]

Fayard Nicholas, speaking of Powell, exclaimed, "She could stand toe-to-toe with any man. She was that great." During filming, in an interview, Powell explained, "Fred dances on the offbeat and mostly on the ball of the foot, while I am always on-beat and get most of my taps from my heel."[12]

Fayard remembered attending a party at Powell's home. He asked about her working with Fred in *Broadway Melody.* "Oh, we had so much fun," she said. "In between takes we would have a challenge where we'd try and outdo each other. When we finished the picture and had taken off our tap shoes, I looked over and saw Fred sitting in a corner all by himself. He had his arms folded, and he was looking at me. I said to him, 'What are you doing over there? Come over here.' He came over and said, 'Eleanor, I had a great time with you on this movie.' I told him, 'I had a great time, too. It was wonderful.' Then he said, 'But, Eleanor, I don't want to work with you anymore.' I said, 'Why not, Fred? Didn't we have fun?' He said, 'Yes, we had fun, but you worked me too hard.' "

In 1949, he told a *Collier's* interviewer, "I love Eleanor Powell, but she dances like a man. She's a remarkable dancer, but she has a very mannish style and she's a little big for me."[13]

Fayard added, "When Fred Astaire danced with a lady, she would always follow him. But with Eleanor Powell, he was following her. I had never seen him work so hard. They looked so good together. He respected her. They respected each other." Fred echoed Fayard's comments when he said, "She put 'em down like a man, no ricky-ticky sissy stuff with Ellie."[14]

Another important dancer, Maurice Hines, added, "I'm not surprised that Fred never worked with Eleanor again. He saw the limitations that he knew he had. But the Nicholas Brothers would have been great with her because she could do everything that they could do. She did the acrobatics, she did trowels. She did spins like Fayard. Oh, that would have been the greatest number in the world!"

Alan Johnson, two-time Emmy winner and Tony nominee, believes, "A tap dancer is really a percussionist with his feet. They like jazz. They improvise. That was Sammy [Davis Jr.]. That was Gregory [Hines]. That is Savion [Glover]. That was the progression of tap for me. You can just throw them onstage and play something and they go. Astaire was the foundation that everybody built on. Tap has come a long way. The black tappers were the originals. Fred took that and put that in his body, and he became distinctive—the rhythms, the changes. Like all tap dancers, that's their instrument, their feet.

"The Nicholas Brothers didn't have a choreographer. I heard that Eleanor Powell said, 'I never needed a choreographer. I figured out what to do myself!' Fred had Hermes, but that was a collaboration."

ASTAIRE SAW TO IT that the years of being in Dellie's shadow would never be repeated. He was also well aware of the high level of stardom he had established for himself and never ceased making sure that *he* was the main attraction in every one of his following films. Now, more than ever, he was unwilling to share the glory with anyone else, especially with his female dancing partner.

Appreciating the swing bands, whose spirited music had provided a respite from the woes of the Great Depression for the last five years, Fred had become enamored with the jazz artistry of Artie Shaw, then branded the King of the Clarinet. Fred wanted to do a film with Shaw and his band. The result was *Second Chorus,* Fred's ode to swing music, an independent movie released by Paramount. Fred later referred to this film as "the worst picture I ever made." It probably was, at least until *The Amazing Dobermans,* in the twilight of his career.

Second Chorus was completely unlike any of the previous Astaire film musical concoctions. Little dancing and romance was incidental to the plot.[15] The premise was that Fred and his sidekick, Burgess "Buzz" Meredith, were trumpeters in a college band. (At forty, Fred was a bit old to be playing a college student musician!)

The band's manager, Paulette Goddard, is hired away by Shaw to come to New York and become the manger of *his* band. Fred and Meredith try to trump each other to join Shaw's band. Bobby Hackett, who enjoyed commercial success in the 1950s as a soloist on a series of romantic mood albums by Jackie Gleason, dubbed Astaire's trumpet parts, and the equally adept Billy Butterfield, from Shaw's band, played for Meredith.

Goddard was Fred's willing-but-not-in-his-league dance partner (though no Joan Fontaine) in the fast-paced "I Ain't Hep to That Step but I'll Dig It." She hadn't danced professionally since her days as a Ziegfeld girl when she was billed as Peaches.[16] The number was performed as part of a jam session that included the noted jazz cornetist Muggsy Spanier. Hermes Pan, now finished with RKO, choreographed it and was seen on camera as a clarinetist in the college band. Later,

Fred, in tails, at last got his chance to "dance-conduct"[17] the augmented Shaw or-chestra in the spectacular "Poor Mr. Chisholm" ("Hoe Down the Bayou").

The late bandleader well recalled the picture: "I was through with movies af-ter my experience with *Dancing Co-ed*" (during which he married Lana Turner, his third of nine wives). According to Shaw, *Second Chorus* was originally an idea by the renowned director Frank Capra. "We were going to have Julie Garfinkle [John Garfield], who Jack Warner offered to loan us, and the young band singer Doris Day. I read the script, and it wasn't a bad idea. It was about a kid who graduates from Yale and falls in love with the music of [jazz cornetist] Bix Beider-becke. He breaks his dad's heart, who's an old Irishman, by saying he'll work for him for a year but he's determined to return to New York and make it as a musi-cian. He says, 'Look, Dad, if I can't make it, I'll come back.' Boris Morros [later a FBI counterspy in the early years of the Cold War] was going to produce the pic-ture, but he and Jack Warner had a falling out, and we couldn't get Garfield. There goes the movie.

"I saw Morros one day, and he said, 'I've got a star.' I said, 'Who?' He said, 'Fred Astaire.' I said, 'Fred Astaire's a dancer. What's he got to do with this movie? Our guy's not a dancer.' 'Well,' he said, 'it's a good story.'

"Working with Frank Cavett, we began writing a new story. We were writing one day ahead of the shoot, and we barely made it. We wound up making this piece of crap, which became successful. As far as I'm concerned, the movie was a total parody of a movie. [Fred claimed it played better on TV than in theaters.] I had five percent of the net, but I never saw a dime." Shaw proved himself a credible actor playing himself.

Shaw recalled, "He had this carefree, manufactured cloak of debonair casual-ness. He played a musician, but he had this pose of the debonair musician as it were. He played Fred Astaire. I can't give any better description than that. He did that in life. He did it on the screen. Turns out that was to cover up a core of strictly Teutonic practicality and hard work. He did what he did superbly well, but it had nothing to do with what we were doing. So we had to incorporate a dance in which he led my band.

"I had always wanted to take my band, which was then treated as a dance band, to do a real concert. So we had that scene, which I wrote. The music was set in such a way that he could dance to it. And it just got to be a mishmash. I don't know if his dancing was real, or natural, or what. I do know it was very carefully, and with tremendous scrupulousness, worked out. He worked with a fellow named Hermes [Pan]. The fellow wrote some material for him. They worked all day. He'd come back with a dance. Actually, I couldn't believe my eyes.

"I can't say I liked him, but we got along very well. We had a lot of respect for each other. He liked me. And when it was over, we gave each other a parting gift. I know he wanted to have a jeweler make a clarinet tie clasp, I think. I forgot what he gave me. I gave him a clarinet. I never saw him after that. We lived in two different worlds. He was a Hollywood star. I was a musical star. I must say he had no sense of humor, but he was so dapper. He used to wear a necktie as a belt."

"Would You Like to Be the Love of My Life" was a tune cowritten by Shaw and Johnny Mercer, the first of five musicals in which the superb lyricist worked with Astaire. As the loquacious and incisive musician pointed out, "Johnny gave me the title. I went home and wrote the melody to that title. Fred had a nine-note range, from D to G. He sang it to Paulette at the end of the movie. He had a deal with his wife that he wouldn't kiss any woman. He leaned over her, and we shot his head, and that was it.

"You can bet that Fred rehearsed the song at home and probably ran it down about forty times. He played pretty good piano and probably accompanied himself. When he shot the song, he sang it with a knowledge and awareness of the lyrics. He made it his own. He sang the way he knew—very informal, very debonair—like him." (Despite Shaw's reservations, "Love of My Life" wound up receiving an Oscar nomination in 1941 for Best Song.)

When asked if Astaire's talent bordered on genius, Shaw answered, "If genius is the result of total application, yes. And I believe it is. A genius is a person who has the ability to stay with something until all of it is perfect. Or it's as perfect as it can be. . . . He was inimitable. Nobody could do what he did. Fred Astaire was an ingredient. How it came about, do we question how cinnamon came about? We use it.

"He was very studious about the role he played of Fred Astaire. It was a role that was very, very carefully constructed. . . . A lot of people go to England, they come back the same, but not him. He was like a sponge. He absorbed. . . . He was a man who knew what he should do and did it. He was one of a kind, unique in the sense of an antique dealer. You find an object and you sell it for a hell of a price. Why? Because there's not another one in the world like it. That's what unique means. He stood by himself. That thing he did for the director Stanley Donen, dancing on the ceiling [in *Royal Wedding*], you couldn't have done that with anyone else."

BOSLEY CROWTHER IN THE *NEW YORK TIMES* recognized Astaire's brilliance but lamented, "There is no getting around it; Fred Astaire is still badly in need of a new dancing partner. And judging by *Second Chorus,* he is even more in need of a producer, writer, and a director who will again stir up something smart, sleek and joyous for him to do. For seldom has a first class talent been less effectively used." This adverse criticism—the worst film notice Fred had ever received—came out the week after Ginger Rogers triumphed in *Kitty Foyle*.[18]

Although Fred had briefly flirted with retirement after the indifferent critical and commercial response to his last two films with Ginger, after the two post-Rogers movies he now began to give retirement serious thought. As he later looked back on this down period, he wrote, "When I first came to Hollywood and was knocking things over in pretty easy regularity, about eight in a row, I sensed that there would have to be a letdown sometime." He also remembered that his old friend Douglas Fairbanks had told him, "Now you're hitting 'em hard, and it may go on for quite a while yet, but when you run into that slump, just go away, take a breather, get fresh ideas, and you'll get your second wind. Something will inspire you. You'll get new ambitions and find your groove again."[19]

After vacationing in Aiken during the winter of 1940–41, playing many rounds of golf and listening to various offers to return to Broadway, host new radio shows, and make personal appearances, Fred decided that making movies was all he really wanted to do. Producer Gene Markey had been touting a Columbia contract player named Rita Hayworth, who was originally a dancer, and who had already appeared in thirty-three movies. Markey, speaking for the studio, and particularly its notorious vulgarian president, Harry Cohn, who had long suffered an unrequited passion for Rita, firmly believed that Hayworth had true star potential and that appearing opposite Astaire could help make her a major screen personality. Markey soon entered the navy, but the studio offered $100,000 plus his usual percentage for Astaire to costar with Hayworth in two musicals.

Following the long-ingrained Hollywood adage that events come in threes, Paramount wanted him to team with Bing Crosby in *Holiday Inn,* in between the two pictures with Hayworth. That movie would include an Irving Berlin score. Musicals seemed to be thought of as a way to counteract the gloomy atmosphere that pervaded in Hollywood when a world war loomed.

That "something [that] will inspire you" was indeed Rita Hayworth. Her father, Eduardo Cansino, had been one of Fred's main inspirations as a dancer when he worked on the Orpheum Circuit in vaudeville. Rita, born Margarita Carmen Cansino, had been part of the Dancing Cansinos family act and had taken her mother Volga's surname of Hayworth as her professional name. Starting as a thirteen-year-old, she had received a thorough education in the dance, and during those years on tour, according to the well-established biographer Barbara Leaming, was tragically forced into an incestuous relationship with her father. Rita's raw, kinetic energy had been liberated by none other than Hermes Pan, who worked with her in *Blood and Sand,* where she first dazzled screen audiences.[20]

On their first rehearsal for *You'll Never Get Rich* (probably named for a portion of the lyrics contained in the soldier's popular song "You're in the Army Now"), Fred was, as usual, concerned about the height of his dance partner. Rita mentioned that she was five feet six. Fred asked her not to wear high heels while dancing with him. She answered, "I don't have to." To be assured that they looked right together, they danced around the mirrored room in impromptu ballroom fashion.

The dancing combination of Fred Astaire and Rita Hayworth was absolute magnetism on the screen. The erotic quality that Ginger Rogers brought to her association with Fred in their ten films together was surpassed by Rita's innate Latin sensuality. With the nineteen-year difference in their ages, as dancers Rita's youthful exuberance meshed perfectly with Fred's maturity and elegance. It is a travesty that Columbia, whose film product was then mostly B quality, never consented to make the Astaire/Hayworth films *You'll Never Get Rich* and *You Were Never Lovelier* in Technicolor. If so, I believe there would never have been room for rational discussion over who was Astaire's foremost dance partner.

Over the years, Astaire was asked, "Who was your favorite dance partner?" countless times in interviews in the press, on radio, and later on television. He tried not to answer the question, but when he did, his answers varied. However, the characteristically understated manner in which he described the experience of dancing with Hayworth in his autobiography leads me to believe that she may well have been his favorite. He wrote, "Rita danced with trained perfection and individuality." He waxed enthusiastically about her ability to learn new steps quickly and stated what a delight she was to work with, which also obviously endeared her to him. "She was better when she was 'on' than at rehearsal," he noted. Her stupendous beauty and sex appeal were an added bonus, as was her almost equal desire to his for achieving perfection.

Charlie Reinhart contends, "There was a kind of reserve about Fred. It was charming. It carried over to his dancing. With Hayworth there was no reserve. She was very explosive. And that's why I think they really complemented each other."

Years later, while working at MGM, Fred was asked by script supervisor and later director Leslie Martinson, "Who was the most beautiful woman you ever worked with?" Fred quickly answered, "Rita Hayworth. She could be out all night partying and come into the makeup chair next to mine at six A.M., and from the bottom of her instep to the top of her head, there was simply nobody more beautiful."

Alan Johnson was the choreographer of the 1971 NBC special *'S Wonderful, 'S Marvelous, 'S Gershwin,* in which Astaire appeared. According to Johnson, Martin Charnin, the producer, writer, and codirector of the show, while having dinner with Astaire in New York, asked Astaire who was his favorite dance partner.

He answered, "All right, I'll give you a name, but if you ever let it out, I'll swear I lied. It was Rita Hayworth."

Rita was reluctant to show Fred how physically and emotionally draining she found working with him, according to none other than Orson Welles, soon to become her husband. Hayworth would often come home after working with him at the studio and burst into tears.[21]

COLE PORTER WAS BROUGHT BACK to write the songs for his second Astaire musical, *You'll Never Get Rich*. Unfortunately, they were not up to his usual high standard. He nevertheless received a Best Musical Score Oscar nomination, and the pedestrian "I Kissed My Baby Goodbye" was up for Best Song.

The plot of the picture portrayed Fred transforming himself from a Broadway dance director, where he first meets Rita, into an army draftee. (In real life, he was too old and had children, which made him ineligible for the draft). To realistically depict army life, a small facsimile of an actual military base was constructed near Riverside, California. In the film, after dancing with Hayworth again at a rehearsal for an upcoming show at the camp, he suddenly finds himself so enamored with her that he winds up marrying her in front of a tank. This over-the-top production number, "The Wedding Cake Walk," which included a chorus of fifty dancing beauties, was choreographed by Robert Alton.[22]

The noted Broadway choreographer Donald Saddler was part of the male chorus in the opening dance number. In the extravagant finale, Alton showed Astaire the final dance step in the number. Sixty-four years later, Saddler recalled, "We were all standing there at a respectful distance waiting to see Astaire going over and over and over it. Finally, he turned around to all of us and said, 'Ladies and gentlemen, do you mind if we finish on seven instead of eight? I will never get it. I will make a mistake each time. So, could we change it?'

"I learned that everyone has a different drummer. He was so atuned because he was a drummer inside. The basic dance rhythm for us really started with swing. Fred was such a good tapper that even when the music wasn't playing, you could hear the drums through the tap. He and Ginger did that break in *Follow the Fleet*. Of course, in *Broadway Melody* with Eleanor Powell you saw the best white tap dancing ever."

Saddler also stressed, "The port de bras, the movement or carriage of the arms, was something Astaire adapted from ballet. He had studied ballet and had the command of his body that ballet gives you." Saddler's statement jibes with the report that Astaire and Powell supposedly spent considerable rehearsal time on arm movements before filming began.

Saddler made a distinction between Astaire and the Nicholas Brothers and Bill Robinson: "They had a different style, another beat. They were not as sophisticated-looking as he was. They were really hoofers. Astaire's tapping was wider and chicer. If you put up statues, you would put them up equally." Saddler also believed Eleanor Powell was the best female tap dancer ever. "She could do things like back bends and turns even better than Ann Miller." The soft-spoken but authoritative choreographer continued, "The MGM movies of Astaire benefited from all the things from RKO. But the level of performance was not better. It's just that the frame was better, and there were great producers at Metro like Arthur Freed."

ELEGANCE WAS THE PROPER SETTING for Porter's songs; an army base wasn't. The composer was at first amused and then became furious when Harry Cohn insisted on testing his songs on studio workers to gage their appeal to the average listener.[23] Amazingly, Cole Porter never won an Oscar for his songs despite having written the scores for Hollywood musicals for more than two decades.

The popularity of "Dream Dancing" and "So Near and Yet So Far" were hindered by the ASCAP strike, which prevented them from being programmed on radio. This contributed to neither of them becoming trademark songs for Fred.[24] "So Near and Yet So Far," however, was the vehicle for an exhilarating and romantic dance by Fred and Rita, highlighted by Rita's undulating hip swinging during the rumba portion of the number. While dancing, she was full of radiant smiles. Paradoxically, she affected an aloof, often smug quality throughout much of the rest of the film that caused Fred's initial reluctance to becoming attracted to her.[25]

Robert Benchley was hired for the high-level comic relief that he always delivered. Early in the movie, a subplot depicting him as a roving lothario trying to hide his amorous activities from his wife, and later on at the army camp in an elongated bit involving a diamond necklace, are prime examples of his delicious brand of urbane comedy.

In the film, Fred becomes so taken with Rita that he goes AWOL and is thrown into the stockade. In 1941 Hollywood, racism was just as apparent as it was in any other part of the country. Given this, the Hollywood of that era imagined the prison as an abode for blacks, who, of course, all had to be jazz musicians.

Chico Hamilton, former longtime drummer for Lena Horne, and an important figure in the West Coast jazz movement of the early 1950s, played one of the prisoners. Besides Hamilton, the members of the all-black jazz quintet included two other jazz musicians who enjoyed formidable careers, bassist Joe Comfort (who blew into a jug in the movie) and reed player Buddy Collette. The group provided the backing for Astaire to perform "Since I Kissed My Baby" and the "A-Stairable Rag," based on the jazz evergreen "Bugle Call Rag." The latter was an athletic solo performance, an example of jazz dancing that bordered on the acrobatic, which seemed to delight Fred as he was executing it.

Buddy Collette, who played clarinet in the film, remembered that the musicians were paid $100 a day: "We were treated like we were nothing. When we weren't shooting, we ran off and hid under the piano, anywhere, because we were so tired from starting work so early in the morning."

Hamilton, still active as leader of his own jazz group at eighty-six, remembered the scene with decided trepidation: "What bothered me was that those were the days of the plantation. The studios at that time, when they referred to the black thick screen over the camera, the shade that was for lighting purposes, they used the N-word. And I resented that. I remember Rita Hayworth very distinctly clapping because I said something in protest. When I look back on it, it was a black guardhouse—no white people in there, but the guards were white."

Writer Stanley Crouch, who is African-American, commented, "Most people in show business are cowardly. That's not unusual—Fred Astaire not asserting himself, not saying, 'This is wrong.' James Cagney might have, Humphrey Bogart might have, Edward G. Robinson might have, but they were not representative of how most of those people acted. Most of those people were on a high-class plantation. Jack Warner and those people made them understand very clearly that 'I am the plantation, and you are a slave. You have a big car, a big house, and some great clothes. But I don't want to hear your opinions about anything.' "

Hamilton also remembered how much rehearsal Fred wanted before the scene was shot. "Fred Astaire was a screen actor, and he knew where the camera was and what the camera wouldn't pick up. He did all those gestures to keep the camera on him."

The respected drummer also knew something about movies, having started work at the age of seven in several Tarzan films. He later appeared in *The Pirate* with Gene Kelly, and he and his quintet were featured in the memorable *The Sweet Smell of Success,* which stared Burt Lancaster and Tony Curtis.

Hamilton continued, "This guy [Astaire] was talented, but everything he did was [geared to] rehearsal. I would call it practice, not rehearsal. You just go over [it], over and over, you stop and start. He danced. That's all he did. He was a hardworking dude. I had my sticks and played them on a table and on a little Indian drum. I must say, though, he was pleasant to work with."

ONE OF THE PREREQUISITES of becoming a respected Hollywood showman of the time was to be able to establish new stars through publicity. Ballyhoo was essential; it was the name of the game. (In his unforgettable lyrics to "Hooray for Hollywood," Johnny Mercer referred to "that screwy, ballyhoo-y Hollywood.") The launching of Rita Hayworth would today be labeled "a campaign." Whatever it was called, it was primarily through the carefully thought-out plans of Harry Cohn that it all happened. It was Cohn's idea that Hayworth should dye her hair red to enhance her good looks.

During the shooting of *You'll Never Get Rich, Life,* the nation's leading weekly picture magazine, decided that Rita Hayworth's beauty, paired with the song-and-dance master of the movies, made for a provocative story. The result was a cover story, declaring Hayworth the best dancing partner Astaire ever had. He referred to her as a "born dancer." Conveniently, the piece calling Rita "the Love Goddess" broke on August 11, 1941, six weeks before the Radio City Music Hall opening of *You'll Never Get Rich.* With the sensational photo of her kneeling on a bed wearing a black-and-white satin-and-lace negligee, a star was born. The attendant publicity did wonders for the movie, which also helped to reestablish Fred's potency as a box-office star.

The reviews of the film critics recognized Hayworth's newfound stardom and how easily she bonded with Fred. The *Daily Variety* notice read, "Columbia steps into the big time musical with *You'll Never Get Rich,* a happy combination of music, dancing and comedy that spells box office. The teaming of Fred Astaire and Rita Hayworth is also another happy combination. The picture ranks easily with Astaire's best and displays another side of Miss Hayworth's talents, a side that will find much favor. Her work will stand up to any comparison." The *New York Herald Tribune* said, "Filmdom's master of grace and taps, who has been in somewhat of a decline since the cycle of films with Ginger Rogers, finds a glittering partner in Rita Hayworth."

Onna White was a versatile and highly regarded choreographer on Broadway (*The Music Man*) and in Hollywood (*Bye Bye Birdie*). She also won an Oscar for *Oliver!* White was of the opinion "Rita belonged with Fred. With Rita, he used more of his own style, and with Ginger Rogers he resorted more to technique." When asked to name her personal favorite among Rogers, Hayworth, and Astaire's later dance partner, Cyd Charisse, she said, "I would say Rita because it was always a nice surprise in what she did. With the others, you expected it."

The song-and-dance-man combination of Fred Astaire and Bing Crosby as costars in *Holiday Inn* was a natural. The addition of Irving Berlin to compose the songs brought even more to the musical feast. An important third element was the return of Mark Sandrich as director as well as producer of the film.

This film perhaps best embodies a definite American style. The combination of Crosby, Astaire, and Berlin, the critic John Lahr said, "hymned the joys of the modern republic." It also contained elements of patriotism.[26]

But getting the picture made wasn't easy. Berlin and Sandrich wanted Astaire to work with Bing. Sandrich held out against the studio, which insisted signing Fred for the picture would make the budget prohibitive. Sandrich went so far as to say he would abandon the project if he couldn't have Fred, thus putting himself in danger of being put on suspension.[27] He won, and the film went into production.

Bing was the bigger box-office draw, and since he was also signed to Paramount, top billing for him was never an issue. His was the bigger, more sympathetic role. Fred, for the first time, played somewhat of a lout and lost the girl, in this case Marjorie Reynolds, to Bing. Their respective charms—certainly not the script—made them likable characters.[28] Bing, always respectful of Fred, said of him, "As a dancer, Astaire is the greatest that ever lived. I don't see anybody to touch him. He has genius plus hard work. He is indefatigable."

Before production began on *Holiday Inn,* Fred learned of Phyllis's pregnancy. On March 18, 1942, a baby daughter, Phyllis Ava, who was called Ava (pronounced AH-va), named for a close friend of Phyllis's, was born.[29] He was to dote on Ava for the rest of his life, and she returned his love and devotion. As the actor Robert Wagner described it, "Ava was the gem of his life."

The Astaire marriage seemed too good to be true. The privacy that enveloped their union went against the grain of the way stars were supposed to live. For the most part eschewing movie premieres and nightclubs, their socializing continued to be centered on their home or at the homes of a few other stars and various English expatriates.

In his unpublished autobiography, Johnny Mercer well described the good life in Hollywood in those years when he wrote, "Hollywood was funny, really idyllically so, with lots of people in the same business all making big money and living in that gorgeous country with nothing to do between pictures but play tennis and golf and look at the pretty girls passing by."[30]

GETTING TO WORK WITH CROSBY was a distinct pleasure for Fred. They had been friends for several years and shared a passion for golf, which they occasionally played together. Their bond extended to their common desire to live their lives away from the madding Hollywood crowd. Though both were outwardly laidback, retiring sorts, and neither could be described as brilliant conversationalists, in addition to golf they had the love of horse racing in common. Bing had a sizable racing stable while Fred had yet to start his own but was still a serious follower of the sport. Although both were at the top of the heap in their respective fields of music, no semblance of competition appeared between them.[31] Right from the start, Fred was impressed by Bing's habit of showing up early, just as he always did for dance rehearsals before the actual shooting began.[32]

When the film was first released, the unceasingly controlling Berlin demanded that the film's billing appear as "Irving Berlin's *Holiday Inn.*" After all, he reasoned, the original idea for the movie was completely his (it had been planned as a revue), and he had delivered a far-reaching score of thirteen songs. He had brought his story concept to Mark Sandrich, his champion since *Top Hat,* to work on with him, which concerned one-half of a song-and-dance team (played by Bing) who quits the act, intent on working only on holidays.[33] It was perfect typecasting since Bing had long since adopted nonchalance and transformed it into an art form. Irving had enjoyed a substantial hit with his song "Easter Parade," written for the Broadway musical *As Thousands Cheer* in 1933. In turn, *Holiday Inn* offered his classic "White Christmas." Bing Crosby's Decca version of the song became an American recording institution.

TO COMPENSATE FOR CROSBY'S and Astaire's high salaries, Paramount, especially budget-conscious due to the war, settled for Marjorie Reynolds and Virginia Dale to play their love interests. The romantic element, however, was missing; like Fred, Bing didn't much care for love scenes. Bing could be relied on to deliver a basic soft shoe, which he did with Dale in their opening song, "I'll Capture Your Heart Singing." An easy, freewheeling camaraderie is evident between Crosby and Astaire as each of them tries to outdo the other singing and dancing, while competing for the love of Dale.

Fred had his own standout number, "Let's Say It with Firecrackers," in which he punctuated his taps with the blasts of firecrackers and torpedoes. It took three days of rehearsal and thirty-eight takes and two days of shooting. (It was then that Fred met Gene Kelly, who was about to embark on a career in Hollywood.)[34] As Fred exuberantly described the "Firecrackers" experience, "I loved it because there's a certain amount of satisfaction when you wanted to fill in a break. Like da-da-da-da-da pow! pow! Then spin off and do something else and pow! Just like the Fourth of July!"[35]

The songs and the brilliant way Crosby and Astaire interpreted them made *Holiday Inn* a festive and entertaining movie. Nine of the songs made direct reference to various holidays (New Year's Eve was the subject of two of them), with four nonholiday songs. Crosby sang ten of them and Astaire two, with one duet. Fred also had six dance numbers.

The warmth of the interior of the Connecticut inn during a white Christmas is contagious. This feeling begins when Bing sings "White Christmas" to Reynolds while he "plays" the piano, whistles, hums a chorus, then prompts her as she sings the final chorus. Bing and Reynolds sing a duet on the title song, "Happy Holidays," after that. Fred, who has been rejected by Dale, subsequently swings into a round of drunken jitterbugging with Reynolds in a reprise of "You're So Easy to Dance With," which ends with his falling down and passing out.

A studio press release would have us believe that Fred threw down several shots of bourbon before the number was filmed. Given Fred's penchant for multiple takes on dance numbers, always seeking perfection, this pronouncement appears highly unlikely.

If Fred's "Bojangles of Harlem" number in *Swing Time* seems politically incorrect, in accordance with today's standards, Bing's rendition of "Abraham" in commemoration of Lincoln's birthday in blackface and beard, in the guise of an old black preacher, is equally disturbing. His black housekeeper, Louise Beavers, then sings the song to her children. Reynolds is in blackface as well, playing Topsy in *Uncle Tom's Cabin!*[36]

Another unusual but stylish number was Fred and Reynolds, in colonial dress, complete with Astaire in knee britches, dancing a minuet, "I Can't Tell a Lie," in honor of George Washington's birthday. This number finds Bing again on piano as a member of his brother Bob's Bobcats band. He gives Fred a bad time by changing the tempo. Acting out his insecurity with Reynolds, Fred and Reynolds slither as they switch to jazz dancing, complete with several acrobatic turns.[37] The following moment Fred expresses his undying love for her, but she informs him she is going to marry Bing. He immediately conspires to win her for himself.

Strangely enough, "Easter Parade" is sung by Bing to Reynolds during a horse-drawn carriage ride through the snowy countryside. They return to the inn, where they encounter Fred reclining on the porch ready to help out Bing with his upcoming show.

The patriotic fervor so much a part of 1942 America at a time when the country was on the ropes in the early months of World War II is conveyed in "A Song of Freedom," complete with newsreel footage of Franklin D. Roosevelt and General Douglas MacArthur with the Four Freedoms spelled out as a backdrop. "Plenty to Be Thankful For" continued Berlin's proud patriotic bent.[38]

By now, Reynolds is off to seek stardom as an actress in Hollywood and accepts a convenient offer to appear in a movie about the inn, which is arranged by the venerable actor Walter Abel, playing her agent. Reynolds is seen singing "White Christmas." She hears someone whistling the tune in the background of the set and immediately recognizes the familiar sound belongs to Bing. She runs to embrace him. But that's not the ending. The nostalgic feeling of the "white Christmas" she used to know with Fred and Bing causes her to return to Bing and the real Connecticut inn. Fred and Dale reconcile as well. Together, they sing "Let's Start the New Year Right." It couldn't be a happier ending.

The critical reaction also couldn't have been more enthusiastic when the film debuted on June 19, 1942. The *New York Post* called it "the best musical drama [*sic*] of the year." *PM* said, "The film was full of the most tuneful songs any movie score has had in years." The *Times* notice reported, "Both Crosby and Astaire play their respective roles with good-natured humor and honors divided." *Time* wrote, "Crosby's easy banter is just the right foil for Astaire's precision acrobatics, his wry offbeat humor."

Marjorie Reynolds was singled out for praise and naturally had to withstand the inevitable comparison to Ginger Rogers. The *Morning Telegraph* said, "Marjorie Reynolds is as attractive a—leading lady—to come along for Fred Astaire since the departure of Ginger Rogers." "In Marjorie Reynolds, a very fetching blonde lady, Mr. Astaire has a new partner who can hold her own at all speeds," added the *New York Tim*es.

Fred and Reynolds would, however, never again work together in a movie. Perhaps that's because none of their dance numbers were truly romantic, speculated Astaire dance expert John Mueller. Fred always knew precisely what he wanted, and he usually got his way.

AFTER LITTLE TIME OFF, Fred began shooting *You Were Never Lovelier,* set in Argentina, a bow to Franklin D. Roosevelt's "Good Neighbor" policy, which was politically correct at the time. It gave Fred and Rita the opportunity to perform in an exotic setting. The debonair Adolphe Menjou played Rita's father. Jerome Kern delivered an impressive score, and Xavier Cugat and his orchestra were on hand to provide the musical accompaniment for several of the dance numbers. That the convoluted script, concerning a secret admirer of Rita's who sends her anonymous love notes and flowers, didn't make much sense was incidental—the movie was certainly romantic, and America badly needed escapist entertainment at this juncture. "Dearly Beloved," one of Kern's most beautiful love songs, set the mood for the picture, delivered by Fred with a breathless sincerity constrained by the somewhat lethargic tempo of Cugat's orchestra.[39]

One of the major solo dance numbers of the Astaire canon can be found in this film, the absolutely astounding "Audition Dance," which takes place in Menjou's office. When Fred is asked by Menjou's assistant why he wants to see Menjou, he answers almost Harpo Marx–like with a tap step. As Fred waits, he taps while sitting down. When he steps out for a moment to watch Cugat and his band rehearse, he shows his further impatience by drumming his fingers. Upon finally being ushered into Menjou's office, he displays a considerable range of his dancing wares in hopes of getting a job performing at Menjou's hotel. He starts out by explaining, "Now look, this is a matter of pride with me. I don't like to dance, see. As a matter of fact, I came down here to get away from it. Now you're gonna see me dance and like it!"[40]

He cocks his hat over one eye, kicks the rug aside, then breaks into a captivating series of taps before leaping off Menjou's desk onto various chairs and the couch. He grabs a cane to add another aspect of his dancing and taps out a rhythm on Menjou's head. The routine has a perfect ending as he tosses the cane into a barrel. A brief theme from Liszt's Second Hungarian Rhapsody and a medley of Latin American tunes provided the musical background.[41] Precision, precision, talent, talent!

As Fred begins his courtship of Hayworth, he arrives at Menjou's mansion, "naturally" showing up in black tie. He tells Rita, "I can't bat in your league. I'm a plain, ordinary guy from Omaha—just an old-fashioned, everyday Middle Westerner, where my grandfather was a cattle raiser." "So was mine!" Rita briskly replies.[42]

This sprightly exchange leads into Rita's singing (dubbed by Nan Wynn) "I'm Old-Fashioned," a perfect place to introduce a flowing dance routine combining ballroom and rumba steps, which ends with a tap-dance sequence up and down a flight of stairs. Val Raset was the film's choreographer, but Fred in *Steps in Time* claims that he worked out most of the duets with Rita.[43] Since Fred and Rita had shown their agility as swing dancers in "The Boogie Barcarolle" in *You'll Never Get Rich,* why not do it again with variations? The result was "The Shorty George," a sensational number combining limp knees, bent knees, and a shuffle in place, named for George "Shorty" Snowden, a dancing mainstay of the Savoy Ballroom in Harlem, "the Home of Happy Feet."[44]

The charming and talented venerable arranger and composer, the late Lyle "Spud" Murphy, who had written big-band charts for Glen Gray and the Casa Loma Orchestra, Benny Goodman, and Tommy Dorsey, was responsible for "The Shorty George" arrangement as well as several others in the picture. "I was on staff at Columbia Pictures," Murphy recalled. "Morris Stoloff [who ran the music department] needed somebody to write arrangements of whatever they did that was pop music or jazz." He bonded with Astaire in a great big way. "There wasn't anything about him I didn't like. He was an absolute gentleman at all times. If you had something to say, he would politely listen to what you had to say, and he would never interrupt you. I never met anybody who was nicer to people than he was. I never forgot that because in that [movie] business I had a lot of tough back-

and-forth with people I couldn't stand. They were tone-deaf, and I referred to them in that way at all times."

Murphy referred to Astaire as "an honest singer. As far as I'm concerned, honesty will get you everywhere in the arts. He was adored by his contemporaries. His ear was very accustomed to the sounds of the music, and he knew what was good. That's all you have to know, and the rest you can fake if you have to."

IN ONE MEMORABLE SEQUENCE in *You Were Never Lovelier,* Hayworth's beauty causes Fred to remark, "I can't concentrate when you look at me like that," which introduces the strains of the film's title song, which he sings to her. The tune was reminiscent of Kern's "Lovely to Look At" from *Roberta.* This on-screen scene had its antecedent in an incident that took place offscreen during the production of the film.

Helen Hunt, assigned to take care of Astaire's makeup, recalled fitting him with his toupee one day. Astaire suddenly produced a jeweled pin in the shape of a Spanish dancer twirling her skirts, which he wanted to give to Rita as a present. However, he had serious trepidations about doing so. He told Hunt, "I don't want her to feel I'm after her in any way. You know how it is. She's got so many admirers." Hunt assured him his kind gesture wouldn't be misinterpreted. The present was then given and gratefully appreciated by Hayworth.[45]

Deservedly, *You Were Never Lovelier* enjoyed even greater box-office success than *You'll Never Get Rich,* and the notices were generally favorable. The *Newsweek* review asserted, "The film comes closer than any of the latter-day Astaire shows to capturing the casual charm of the Astaire-Rogers musicals. . . . Although the story is hardly original, the dialogue is bright, the scene tuneful and the players expert." *Time,* although not as laudatory, asserted, "Fred Astaire is still a superb dancer and a deft light comedian," and "Rita Hayworth is still the most ambrosial lady he has ever teamed with."

Archer Winsten in the *New York Post* said, "The older Fred gets the lighter he dances. You can't help looking for the invisible wires enabling him to gig with such youthful featheriness." Alton Cook in the *World-Telegram* said, "One thing you can count on with Fred Astaire, you won't catch him in a bad picture."[46]

The Academy of Motion Picture Arts and Sciences again showed its ongoing respect for an Astaire musical. *Lovelier* received nominations for Best Song ("Dearly Beloved"), Best Score, and Best Sound Recording, but the film went home without winning any Oscars.

In a 1970 *New York Times* interview, Hayworth candidly remarked, "I guess the only jewels in my life were the pictures I made with Fred Astaire. They are the only pictures I can watch today, Fred and me dancing, without laughing hysterically." Looking back on Astaire's thirty-five years of starring in film musicals, it is unfortunate that his association with Rita Hayworth didn't continue. Given the excellent musical artisans at their disposal, splendid vehicles were certainly available that would have fit their talents. It was perhaps too much of a good thing. Fred, however, was adamant about never again being linked with a permanent dance partner. Two films with Rita, successful as they were, were enough for him.[47]

Maurice Hines revealed that Fred had told Gene Kelly, who told Maurice's brother, Gregory, that Rita Hayworth was his favorite dance partner. Hines reports Fred said, "Whenever she came to the soundstage, you always knew it. Everybody stopped talking. But she was totally unaware of the effect. He said she was such a natural and so real and so nice. One of the reasons Fred liked Rita was that he loved stop-and-go stuff—dancing full out, fast, and all of a sudden stop. That's very difficult to do."

BY COINCIDENCE, the mother and aunt of Margaret O'Brien, the appealing child star, a big movie-audience favorite during the World War II years, who won an Oscar for her performance in *Meet Me in St. Louis,* had been members of the Cansino flamenco dance troupe when Rita worked with her father. O'Brien, still an active actress, recalled, "When I first started at MGM, Fred would always come over to my mother and say, 'How are the dancing sisters? Are you still keeping it up? Keep it up. It's so good for you.' And when I got the dancing part in *Unfinished Dance,* he was very interested in how I was doing. He called my mother to find out and came over during rehearsals and gave me a few pointers. I certainly thank him for my dancing ability in that movie. He saw to it that I changed from the Russian ballet teacher I was assigned to, to a gentleman from the Ballets Russes, who wanted me to go with the ballet. But my mother knew a dancer's life is short, and what are the alternatives except to be a dance teacher? I was doing so well at MGM. I danced in *Big City* and *Jane Eyre* before that when I was five."

O'Brien and Astaire saw little of each other in succeeding decades. Randall Malone, O'Brien's manager and good friend, was dining with Margaret at Chasen's one night in 1986 when they bumped into Astaire and his second wife, Robyn Smith. Fred insisted they join him and Robyn. Malone remembered, "He was the kind of person who had no time lapse. He asked Margaret, 'Do you still dance? It's so good for you even if you are not dancing onstage professionally.' "

*   *   *

FRED'S HIGH DRAFT NUMBER of 156 provided him with significant national publicity. Although he was not required to go to war, early on he demonstrated a commitment between movies to entertaining at army and navy bases (just as he and Adele had done in World War I) and by appearing at war-bond rallies. Typical of the latter was his twenty to thirty appearances a day on a tour of Ohio over a two-week period with actress Ilona Massey and comedian Hugh Herbert.[48]

In 1943, he took part in the over three-week-long "Hollywood Bond Cavalcade," which brought a trainload of Hollywood celebrities cross-country. Jimmy Cagney, Judy Garland, Kathryn Grayson, Mickey Rooney, Harpo Marx, Greer Garson, Betty Hutton, José Iturbi, Dick Powell, Lucille Ball, Paul Henreid, and Kay Kyser and his band made up the cavalcade. The tour reminded Fred of the years he had spent traveling with Adele and Ann in vaudeville.

The stars were driven through the various cities in jeeps. They made stopovers by day at war plants, civic functions, and theaters. At night, they performed before enthusiastic audiences at football stadiums and arenas. Fred would sing a song, dance a number, then make a sincere pitch for the audience to "dig deep" and purchase war bonds. One night at New York's Madison Square Garden, they raised the staggering sum of $18 million in war bonds.[49]

While traveling to the next city, Fred would watch as Judy Garland sang, José Iturbi played the piano to accompany Kathryn Grayson, Cagney demonstrated his hoofing prowess, and Mickey Rooney played the drums. Mickey's playing particularly grabbed Fred's attention as he was trying to develop his own ability as a drummer.[50]

When Lena Horne, whose talent Fred admired, joined them in Washington, D.C., he was disturbed that as an African-American Lena was forbidden to stay with them at their hotel. The segregation laws were very much upheld, even in the nation's capital. None of the participants in the cavalcade, however, including Lena, made much of an issue out of it. It was the way it was and nobody cared to do anything that distracted from the war effort.

JOAN LESLIE HAS LED a fulfilling life *after* her movie stardom ended. She had a long and successful marriage to the late Dr. Bill Caldwell and gave birth to twin girls. For years she has devoted herself to working with such charities as the St. Anne's Maternity Home, the Our Mother of Good Counsel Church, and the Motion Picture Home. This is in addition to helping establish and maintain a chair in gynecological-cancer medicine at the University of Louisville Medical School in her deceased husband's name.

As a teenager in the early 1940s, while under contract to Warner Bros., she starred in *High Sierra* with Humphrey Bogart, *Sergeant York* with Gary Cooper, followed by three pictures with Eddie Albert, before singing and dancing with Jimmy Cagney in *Yankee Doodle Dandy.* Two years after *The Sky's the Limit,* she would play George Gershwin's long-suffering girlfriend in the Gershwin film biography *Rhapsody in Blue;* Gershwin was played by Robert Alda, Alan Alda's father.

When interviewed by the press, Leslie would often express her ambition to dance with Fred Astaire. "And so I wrote him," Leslie remembered sixty-three years later. "I really think that's how it started. When Fred got the letter, I guess he said, 'Gee, she's up-and-coming and Warner's thinks the world of her. I've got to meet her!' I was told to meet Fred over at Paramount. Of course, here I am at sixteen, everything in Hollywood seemed to fall into place so easily.

"In an enormous, darkened stage there was a pianist and Fred Astaire and Bing Crosby sitting there. After saying, 'How do you do,' Fred said, 'Dance for me. Anything at all,' and I said, 'Wow, what a terrible spot to be in. Dancers dance. We love to dance. I dance in the kitchen right now. There was music, maybe about sixteen bars, then he said, 'Okay, okay, Joan.' He popped up from his chair and came over to me and put his arms around me, and he ballroom-danced with me in the way he used to dance with Ginger Rogers. He was a very strong leader. I put my hand on his back, we turned around so easily. He backed up and looked at me, and he turned to his producer and said, 'Oh, yeah, she can dance.' I certainly took that for a big compliment. And with that, I was whisked away home by my agent, Louis Shurr."

RKO was then undergoing another financial crisis, which eventually caused its sale to Howard Hughes and later to its extinction. The studio's immediate solution was to try to tempt Fred and Ginger back for another smash musical. Fred signed on but Ginger didn't.

Two days after her audition, Leslie got the script for *The Sky's the Limit.* She was to be loaned out to RKO for the movie, but it was close to a year before production began. *Holiday Inn* was filmed in between with Fred with Bing and *This Is the Army* with Ronald Reagan and Irving Berlin for Joan.

Watching *The Sky's the Limit* it's hard to believe Leslie wasn't twenty-seven, rather than seventeen, when the picture commenced shooting. Fred was then forty-three. This caused Fred to remark, "Gosh, the older I get, the younger they get."[51] Leslie observed, "I was not the best dancer he ever had as a partner, but I was the youngest."

Leslie explained, "I can say I was okay in the rhythm dance number, 'A Lot in Common with You.' We did that number in pieces. I learned it rather quickly, and I practiced it at home between rehearsals. The number combined jitterbugging and tap dancing. But there are moves, turns, and stretches, and then Fred jumped over me at one point and then I jumped over him. Routinely, after a take he would go [see the rushes] and he would watch the dance all the way through. And if he wasn't satisfied, we'd do another take."

The score consisted of only three tunes, written by Harold Arlen and Johnny Mercer, which included "My Shining Hour" and the unforgettable "One for My Baby." The latter was memorable because it was the first time Fred's fabled temper was unleashed on film in an unusually dark dance number.

After being jilted by Leslie, and unhappy about having to return to military duty, he saunters into a bar. After taking a swig of a drink, he smashes the glass against the wall. He addresses the bartender by breaking into "Make it one for my baby and one more for the road." He continues singing as he walks into another bar, then returns to the lounge at the banquet hall where he had earlier attended a formal dinner with Leslie. He has more to drink and winds up smashing another glass.

Still feeling completely stymied, he begins tapping, trying to break out of his funk. He jumps atop the bar and unleashes all of his pent-up frustrations as he systematically kicks all the glasses lined up on the mirrored wall behind the bar. He jumps down and as a finale picks up a barstool and heaves it through the mirror.[52]

A much different and certainly violent interpretation of the classic torch song from that of Frank Sinatra's dramatic approach, to be sure. Sinatra's interpretation was "a nugget of personal experience," as Stephen Holden would describe it. Yet Astaire's vision makes its point. The concept was entirely Fred's creation; he was also the film's dance director.

Bernard "Babe" Pearce, who had worked with him on *Holiday Inn,* originally had the job but was fired a few weeks before the movie started production, presumably because of "creative differences" between him and Astaire.

Leslie noted, "Astaire was acting all the time with his body so it was easy for him to swing over and act. I always thought Fred was an extremely good actor because he had all those years acting in his dancing. He was telling a story with the dance. And in order to tell it really well, it had to be perfect, the way he carried his shoulders, his arms, his hands. That's acting. From seeing Sinatra, and noticing the way he sang the song, his interpretation was quite different—he always emoted the song—he told the story."

The completely unaffected Leslie went on to emphasize, "Fred was a natural. He wouldn't do anything phony and was never restricted by the way he looked. You know, there were plenty of good-looking guys who wouldn't wrinkle an eyebrow, much less express emotion, because they wouldn't look good. He didn't care about things like that."

*   *   *

LESLIE CLAIMS that she did her own singing in the movie, which was restricted to "My Shining Hour," backed by Freddie Slack and His Orchestra. The song formed the basis of a solo dance number by Astaire and was given even further exposure as a dancing duet by Astaire and Leslie, as they glide gracefully around the dance floor in a penthouse. Leslie showed herself to be a more than competent dance partner.

Guitarist Bob Bain, then a member of the Slack band and later a much in demand recording-studio musician, contended that the Slack band got the movie gig due to its hit records "Cow Cow Boogie" and "Mister Five by Five" (based on Lil' Jimmy Rushing, Count Basie's wonderful blues singer), but even more so through the intercession of Johnny Mercer, who was then one of the owners of Capitol Records. (The Slack band recorded for Capitol.)

"We wound up playing all of the music contained in the picture, and two songs were cut, one of which was 'Harvey the Victory Garden Man,' sung by Ella Mae Morse. That's a real World War Two song title! Strings were added to 'One for My Baby' to give it a fuller, more dramatic sound," Bain pointed out.

Leslie and Bain shared a January 26 birthday. "I remember shooting stopped, and they wheeled out a birthday cake and champagne," Bain recalled. Leslie added, "That was a very important occasion—my eighteenth birthday. It meant I no longer had to attend school at the studio. Workers at the studio brought the little one-room schoolhouse onto the set on rollers and proceeded to burn it."

Robert Benchley and Eric Blore, two Astaire comedy regulars, were brought back to provide their unique humorous touches in the movie. Blore played Benchley's valet, a part he had often played opposite Fred. Benchley's scene in which he does a brilliant takeoff on a rambling introduction at a testimonial dinner, full of patented clichés and unnecessary facts and figures, is a sterling example of his puckish humor. (Watching this scene it is easy to see where Professor Irwin Corey's comedic approach came from.)

The picture was not a conventional musical but rather a comedy with music with a rather schizophrenic approach. Cast as a Flying Tigers pilot, along with Robert Ryan, then under contract to RKO, Fred displays his ample comedy chops as he skips out on a national tour by heading for New York to have a good time. Along with Astaire and Leslie's song-and-dance numbers, and Benchley's comedy, inside references were made to their previous costars. Fred angers Leslie, playing a nightclub photographer on assignment, when he says to her, "Couldn't I be the fellow who never gets his name mentioned? The one they call 'a friend.' You know, Ginger Rogers and friend." In the conclusion of "A Lot in Common with

You," Leslie asks, "Where's Cagney?" which prompts Fred to inquire, "Where's Hayworth?"[53] Astaire was upset at the way the studio's publicity campaign misrepresented the film, trying to pass it off as a comedy.[54]

Some serious World War II–related moments included a discussion about the importance of freedom, the moving scene of a war widow breaking down, and Fred's attack on the deficiencies in the manufacture of American bombers (an idea that predated the theme of Arthur Miller's *All My Sons* by three years), which further marked the film's inconsistencies.[55]

The astute Leslie recalled about the making of the film, "Fred would be very annoyed with people that preached the idea of propriety. The front office of RKO wanted to come down and watch him rehearse. He said, 'That's out of the question.' When Charlie Koerner, the president of RKO, wanted to come down and see Fred rehearse, finally he said okay, but not to see him rehearse. This was even before the picture started shooting.

"Fred said, 'Joan, when they come in, you can do cartwheels, can't you?' 'Yes,' I said. Then he said, 'I'd like you to do a cartwheel and stand on your head, and I'll hold your feet and I'll stand there when they come in the door. We'll just be standing with you upside down as if it was part of the rehearsal.' I don't know how I got the nerve but I said no. I'm seventeen years old, and I'm telling Fred Astaire I don't want to do this! But that was his idea of a joke."

Leslie stressed that despite her age and lack of experience Astaire was never condescending. "Nor was Jimmy Cagney when I worked with him. Cagney was very direct," she said. "Fred, however, was more gracious, graceful and subtle."

Dance rehearsals for the movie lasted four weeks. That Leslie had already had thirteen years of dance training helped her deal with Astaire's mastery. "We would work all day. The steps were all within my range. I could get up and do them now. Fred was a wizard genius, a creative wizard genius—nothing short of that. You know, unless you're a dancer or an athlete, you just don't know how his body could do what he did.

"I was told he wore a complete set of flannel underwear under his suit. It made his suits look better and it also absorbed perspiration. A layer of fabric underneath a suit makes a difference, and of course, he was so thin—he weighed about one hundred and thirty-four pounds. He didn't eat lunch. I'll bet that he had cottage cheese and a cup of tea so that he could say that he did."

In rehearsing with Fred, Leslie noticed that he had never undergone proper training in ballet. "Feet positions are very special. He told me, 'In order to land and hold your position, if your toe is turned in, don't worry about it. I never worry about turning my toe. Turn your toe in if you feel more secure. When you land with your toe turned out, turn it in.' I thought, 'Oh, my gosh, a dancer who would land with their toe turned in? That doesn't sound like the right thing to do. . . . But, of course, if he told me to do it, I would do it. So what if he didn't have ballet? He's got more in one toe than all the rest of the ballet people in the world. He had style that no one could imitate . . . there'll never be anyone ever to dance like that again. He flew across. He was grace and creativity personified. It's something so unique it cannot be imitated."

THE MOVIE WAS ONLY a moderate success. After the hosannas he had received for the two Rita Hayworth films interspersed with the success of *Holiday Inn, The Sky's the Limit* was a letdown. Bosley Crowther, usually an admirer of Fred's talent, observed, "Mr. Astaire does one solo which is good, but a bit woe-begone and the rest of the time he acts foolish—and rather looks it—in his quick-fitting clothes." This was perhaps the first and only time that the Astaire wardrobe was deprecated in a review, and it rankled Fred. Having received little adverse criticism, he had a problem withstanding it from reviewers.[56]

The respected writer and critic James Agee in the *Nation* focused on the film's deficiencies, yet he was favorable in his review of Fred's work: "Fred Astaire has a lot, besides his Mozartian abilities as a tap-dancer, which is as great in its own way, as the best of Chaplin. It is the walk, the stance, the face, the voice, the cool, bright yet shadowless temper, and it would require the invention of a new character, the crystallization of a new manner, probably the development of a new cinematic form, to be adequately realized."[57]

Suddenly, there seemed to be a shortage of scripts offered Fred that combined a good love story with outstanding music. Now almost forty-five, in the last few years it seemed he was now playing the mentor, not the desirable man-about-town.[58]

And who came to Fred's rescue? None other than Arthur Freed, the producer and songwriter who had also been a friend of Fred's in vaudeville days. Freed had established himself as the doyen of producers of film musicals with his outstanding 1940s MGM productions, such as *Strike Up the Band, Babes on Broadway, Panama Hattie, For Me and My Gal, Cabin in the Sky, Best Foot Forward, Du Barry Was a Lady, Girl Crazy,* and *Meet Me in St. Louis.* He also knew songs from working as a song plugger after leaving vaudeville. As a lyricist, he wrote such outstanding songs, with composers Nacio Herb Brown and Harry Warren, as "All I Do Is Dream of You," "Beautiful Girl," "Pagan Love Song," "Singin' in the Rain," "Temptation," "This Heart of Mine," "You Are My Lucky Star," and "You were Meant for Me." Freed combined taste and perfectionism, two of the major ingredients that had made Astaire a superstar. Their new association at MGM couldn't have happened at a more opportune time.

CHAPTER SIX

THE DREAM FACTORY AND TWO EXCURSIONS TO PARAMOUNT

OUIS B. MAYER ONCE SAID, "The real business of making movies . . . became the business of making idols for the public to have and identify with. Everything else was secondary." The equally tough and sentimental *macher* also commented, "If we had a popular star, we made a little money, and we could build the star up by making more and more pictures."[1]

Fred Astaire, who had begun his film career at MGM, and who had made his first post-Fred-and-Ginger movie at this studio, now returned to the source with a three-year contract. Here was a major movie star set to begin arguably the most important chapter of his thirty-seven-year-long career. He certainly didn't require a studio publicity buildup but instead ready access to first-rate material that could form the basis for artistic and commercial movies. MGM, "the Dream Factory," could certainly provide that. Highly talented specialists in the art of making musicals such as Vincente Minnelli, George Sidney, Roger Edens, Stanley Donen, Conrad Salinger, Johnny Green, and others were under contract to the studio.

What it could also offer Astaire was access to musicals shot in glorious Technicolor. In twelve years of making movies Fred had starred in seventeen musicals but had never enjoyed that luxury and missed it terribly. In a 1976 interview he said, "If we were doing those pictures now, they would be in color like that," snapping his fingers. "I'm glad the black-and-white era passed. The world is made in color, why make it look black-and-white?"[2]

Arthur Freed and his benefactor and father figure, Mayer, knew precisely how to make and market romantic Technicolor film musicals that would make a significant impact with the public. Three production entities were producing musicals at the studio: the Jack Cummings Unit, the Joe Pasternak Unit, and the Arthur Freed Unit. The Freed Unit was the prestigious entity, the one making the best of the genre.

"MGM functioned like General Motors. It was run with such efficiency that it was a marvel," remarked the veteran actor Ricardo Montalban.[3] "The key to the smooth running of this machine was detail. . . . Sophisticates in New York or Los Angeles might scoff at Andy Hardy or the let's-put-on-a-show MGM musicals, but Mayer knew that formula works. Then as now, people—especially Americans— like stars, spectacle, and optimism, if possible, with a little sentiment attached. They do not want to be challenged or instructed but comforted and entertained" was the keen evaluation of the studio's product—and especially its musicals—as described by Scott Eyman in his superb Louis B. Mayer biography. Its musicals were produced in the area referred to as MGM's "musical campus."

As Rex Reed, the enfant terrible of movie journalism of the sixties, who remains an astute observer as the film critic for the influential New York Observer, said, "Fred Astaire was the only great thing in those old [RKO] black-and-white musicals, and that's why people think he is so wonderful. But when he got to MGM, there were more elements involved—glamorous women, beautiful clothes, incredible sets, Technicolor, those wonderful musical arrangements. The whole concept of the narrative of the film had to have a reason."

Betsy Blair recalled with pride, "We all felt consciously superior to Fox or Warner Bros. We were at the best studio for musicals, and we knew it."[4]

Blair's husband, Gene Kelly, had initially been loaned out to Freed by David O. Selznick, who had him under contract but didn't make musicals.[5] Gene first made For Me and My Gal at MGM, in which he appeared opposite Judy Garland, for Freed. He followed that up with starring roles in Du Barry Was a Lady and Thousands Cheer. Then, his appearance at Columbia opposite Rita Hayworth in Cover Girl made a formidable impression with movie critics and audiences alike through his athletic approach to the dance that reflected the sensibilities of the common man. He was soon to become the dancing star of a series of defining MGM musicals. Always respectful of Astaire, he said, "Fred is probably the least aware of the tremendous influence he has exerted upon dancing and motion picture musicals."[6]

At the studio, the thinking was "Why not team the reigning king of the movie musical with the worshipful pretender to the throne?" The movie was the splashy Ziegfeld Follies. It seemed like a good idea at the time. It was, and it wasn't.

The colossal MGM extravaganza Ziegfeld Follies of 1944, its original title, began production in April 1944, but wasn't released until 1946. It was designed to provide Florenz Ziegfeld (William Powell)—looking down from heaven no less—the opportunity to reminisce about his grand career as a Broadway showman making use of MGM's outstanding roster of stars ("More Stars Than There Are in the Heavens") in lavish production numbers and sketches. The picture was billed as the "Greatest Production Since the Birth of Motion Pictures," but it surely wasn't.

Such star-spangled revues were the all the rage during the latter part of World War II. This was the last of them. They, however, were the forerunners of *That's Entertainment!* (1974) and *That's Entertainment, Part II* (1976), the latter in which Astaire and Kelly were essentially the interlocutors of the film and did a short impromptu dance routine together. *That's Entertainment! III* (1994) was the last and least interesting of the three.

The budget for *Ziegfeld Follies* was extraordinary for the time—$3,240,000—and twenty-three individual numbers were shot. Astaire and Kelly collaborated for the first time along with Judy Garland, Kathryn Grayson, Van Johnson, Esther Williams, Lena Horne, Red Skelton, Cyd Charisse, Lucille Ball—well, you get the picture of the picture, and other name stars were featured. The movie made a healthy profit. It opened as a "road show" attraction, playing twice a day at a high ticket price.

Fred brought the picture immediately to life singing Roger Edens/Arthur Freed's "Here's to the Girls," the trademark of all Ziegfeld productions. After a few dance steps, Fred introduces a bevy of showgirls scantily dressed in satin and feathers. Cyd Charisse, in her second film role, her first at MGM, is in a tutu and does a ballet routine before hopping on a carousel of horses and riding away. Lucille Ball arrives on horseback, dismounts, and leads a chorus in a dance pretending to be cats. The delightful deadpan comedienne Virginia O'Brien sang a parody, "Bring on Those Wonderful Men," which was shot weeks later to supply a coda to the scene.[7]

Fred also participated in two dance numbers with the red-haired stunner Lucille Bremer, fresh from making her film debut in *Meet Me in St. Louis*. Bremer had come to Hollywood from New York, where she had been a Copacabana showgirl and a Rockette at Radio City Music Hall. She was discovered at age twenty-seven by Freed while working as a specialty dancer at the Silver Slipper nightclub.

Freed had Astaire and Kelly collaborate by restaging "The Babbitt and the Bromide," written by the Gershwins, which had been a showstopping number for Fred and Adele in *Funny Face* on Broadway in 1927. The new version actually made more sense as a piece for two male dancers who meet one day on the street, encounter each other a decade later, then meet for the third time in heaven.[8] There they are adorned in beards and carry harps. They can only relate to each other by spouting bromides throughout the various routines. They impersonate themselves and indulge in a friendly competition with a slight acidic touch.[9] Their tap dancing together, however, was sublime as they had an obvious chemistry. It's unfortunate that it didn't continue longer.

Only because of Fred's enthusiastic suggestion did this particular number become a part of *Ziegfeld Follies*. Years later, Kelly agreed with the controversial film critic Pauline Kael's observation in the *New Yorker* that it appeared as though he and Astaire were trying too hard to show that they were having a wonderful time together.[10]

Reportedly some behind-the-scenes friction erupted between them since each had devised his own choreography. Neither wanted to foist his particular style on the other, although the finished product was more Astaire-like.[11] Afterward, Kelly thought their bantering approach to the material was too light. Director Vincente Minnelli thought it wound up as it should have. Fred concurred, saying, "Didn't we beat the hell out of the floor together? . . . We weren't trying after all to do *L'Après-midi d'un faune!*"[12]

Newsweek referred to the number as "the dance for the archives." John McCarten in the *New Yorker* exemplified the magazine's subtle sarcasm by stating, "You may be willing to put up with a good deal of spectacular boredom just to watch Astaire and Kelly together." Bosley Crowther, however, dismissed their collaboration, writing, "The number, done by Mr. Astaire with Gene Kelly as his twin, settles one point of contention: Mr. Astaire has the reach."

Kelly, in 1984, looking back on his dancing career, said, "Fred and I both got a bit edgy after our names were mentioned in the same breath. I was the Marlon Brando of dancers and Fred the Cary Grant. . . . My approach was completely different from his, and we wanted the world to realize this and not lump us together like peas in a pod. . . . If there was any resentment on our behalf, it certainly wasn't with each other . . . yet the public insisted on thinking of us as rivals."[13]

Ever since the 1920s, Astaire had yearned to stage a dance number based on "Limehouse Blues." Freed instructed Minnelli and Robert Alton to work on a new production idea for the number.[14] It was choreographed completely in pantomime and required seventeen days of rehearsal. Almost unrecognizable as an inscrutable Chinese coolie, Fred brought a dramatic pathos to several balletic routines that concluded with his death and his unfulfilled love for a Chinese girl sensuously essayed by Bremer.[15] Robert Lewis fulfilled the antagonist role as a mean menace. (The dreamy setting of the number owed considerably to the "Beggar's Waltz" ballet routine Fred had danced in *The Band Wagon*.)[16] Lee Mortimer in the *New York Daily News* declared, " 'Limehouse Blues' is as fine a dance number as anything ever conceived," and *Time* called it "magnificent."

Hugh Fordin, author of *MGM's Greatest Musicals: The Arthur Freed Unit,* is convinced that the "Limehouse Blues" number "is the best thing Fred ever did." It was Fred's favorite, too. At his Lincoln Center Film Society tribute in his acceptance speech, he said it was his favorite dance number.

Bremer's radiant beauty and grace were beautifully showcased in "This Heart of Mine," which takes place at a formal embassy ball. She and Fred glide across the floor to Harry Warren's lush melody, which was skillfully arranged by Conrad Salinger. Unlike almost every other Astaire ballroom dance number, a kiss was an essential element, but in this case it had sinister implications. The kiss revealed Astaire and Bremer as a pair of elegant jewel thieves, yet a necessary element of humor was somehow missing from its conclusion.[17]

Their flawless execution of these two numbers, especially the latter, raised comparisons to Fred's dancing with Rita Hayworth in *You Were Never Lovelier.* The bright color combinations and crane shots, two well-known elements of Minnelli's direction, additionally helped enhance their dance numbers together.[18]

Fred's "If Swing Goes, I Go Too!" was a solo workout in which he played drums and was backed by a twenty-member male chorus. The number was shot by George Sidney at the beginning of production before Vincente Minnelli replaced him as director. The tune has a brisk swing tempo and was certainly lively enough with Fred throwing drumsticks to the chorus, obviously "inspired" by a similar routine Eleanor Powell and the drummer Buddy Rich devised in the 1942 MGM musical *Ship Ahoy.* Written by Fred, the song revealed his shortcomings as a lyricist as words are strained in an attempt to create various rhymes.[19] None of this mattered much; it was one of several numbers excised from the final cut of the movie.

Dante DiPaolo, the widower of Rosemary Clooney, was an accomplished dancer in films, on Broadway, and in television and nightclubs. He is especially proud that Astaire insisted that he show him a particular dance step DiPaolo had come up with one day at an MGM rehearsal. This led to a budding friendship and mutual respect. DiPaolo danced in the "If Swing Goes" number. He recalled, "Fred and I happened to be walking onto the set together when we shot it. He said, 'There must be a mistake. That's not the set. That's all wrong.' He gathered all the brass around him. They had to scrap the entire set and come up with another one. Seventy thousand dollars went down the drain."

DiPaolo never forgot the impact of the number. He kept a letter for almost forty years in which Astaire lamented its being cut from the movie: "I showed Rosemary the letter. She grabbed on to the part where Fred wrote, 'We'll play it in something one of these days!' She put the contents of the letter together with the song and featured it in her concert and nightclub act."

Fred was brought back to dance with Bremer, Charisse, and the ensemble, but this sequence, part of a huge production number, "There's Beauty Everywhere," also was cut from the film. It was just as well.[20] On that day, Fred had taken five shots for his forthcoming USO tour of Europe and was feeling miserable with a temperature of 102.[21]

A bubble machine malfunctioned countless times in the shooting of this scene. Robert Alton had wanted to create a dreamy phantasmagoria, but the machine couldn't be turned off. The foam continued flowing and released a chemical fume that caused several chorus girls to faint and others to flee from the set screaming.[22] Kathryn Grayson sang the song, which ended the movie.

In August 1944, after completing *Ziegfeld Follies,* Fred flew to Europe to entertain the troops. All of his previous U.S. touring, to entertain the troops and sell war bonds, acted as a prelude to *The Big Show* (the English World War II term for the campaign in Europe) in London and on the Continent. As a dedicated Anglophile, Fred had long been dedicated to England's survival.

He was doubly proud of Dellie's serious involvement in the war effort with the Red Cross in London, where she worked seven days a week at the Rainbow Corner canteen. Charlie had encouraged her participation.[23] She danced with GIs, shopped for them, and wrote thousands of letters to their loved ones in America. Her letters were always signed, "Adele Astaire, Fred's sister." Charlie, in ill health with a liver problem, which Dellie had attempted to heal by insisting he ingest a daily dosage of raw cabbage,[24] remained at Lismore Castle, where Ann Astaire looked after him.[25]

Before making the trip Fred was given an army uniform, boots, and an honorary captaincy. Getting there was not half the fun, however, as he and the accordionist Mike Olivieri bounced around in bucket seats abroad a C-54 from New York that stopped in Newfoundland en route to Pickwick, Scotland. Fred also suffered a sprained back from carrying his heavy bags.[26] From there they went on to London, where he had a reunion with Dellie at Rainbow Corner.

Earlier, Ann had cabled Fred that Charlie, whom she was very devoted to, had died in March. Dellie was extremely distraught by her loss. Charlie was only thirty-eight years old.

Dellie continued her work at Rainbow Corner, where she introduced her brother before his appearance at a show there. Fred told his British and American GI audience, "If these old bones can stand the racket, I'm going to do a bit of hoofing for the boys."[27] Members of Glenn Miller's Army Air Force Band backed him; Miller had just left on his ill-fated flight to Paris, from which he never returned.

The West End musical performer Jack Buchanan and Broderick Crawford, the actor, now a sergeant attached to the Glenn Miller band, also performed in the show.[28] Before leaving London, Fred ran into David Niven, who was now a colonel in the British army. David's spontaneous good humor always provided instant pleasure for Fred. He told Fred he had a thrilling experience ahead of him.

Crossing the Channel, Fred worked with the comedian Willie Shore, Olivieri, and four female dancers, performing for troops in various locales near the front lines in France. At the Palace of Versailles, they performed before five thousand soldiers. When Fred's troupe drove through Paris, its streets were littered with burned-out trucks and cars. They continued on to Belgium and Holland with the Third Army.

In Maastricht, Holland, Fred at last played the Palace. The theater was closed, but the manager recognized Fred and agreed to have him and his cohorts perform before an audience of army engineers. The entertainers spent the night on cots on the stage, sleeping through a German air raid.[29] A few days later, they withstood twelve hours of bombing. Fred spent the time writing a song with Shore, appropriately called "Oh, My Aching Back."[30]

In a September 22, 1944, letter to Arthur Freed, Fred wrote, "We are on our way back in a town that is still studded with 'ever-lovin' snipers. We are not allowed to venture out at night. I'm in a room with a bed in a big building and feel pretty secure for a change. It's a relief to get out of that mud. . . . A Jerry plane dropped some bombs around us . . . the other night while we were having dinner in a tent, we heard him coming and brother you never saw twelve people get on their stomachs so fast in your life."[31]

Marian McPartland, the highly respected jazz pianist whose radio program, *Piano Jazz,* has long been a staple of National Public Radio, was touring as a member of a musical group with Astaire at the time. She had a different version of this latter incident: "I remember one afternoon we had to play on a stage made of planks the GIs had put together. Fred did his whole show in combat boots. He tap-danced in combat boots, and he was wonderful. Then we had a dinner one night and there was an air raid, and we heard all this big noise overhead and he was the first guy under the table. I never saw anybody move so fast."[32]

Fred and his performing ensemble were brought back from the combat zone to Paris in a weapons carrier to appear with Free French performers at the vaunted Olympia Theatre. It was the first performance by an American since the liberation.[33] The legendary Gypsy jazz guitarist Django Reinhardt was in the show. Fred greatly appreciated Reinhardt's talent and told him of having seen him perform at the Palladium in London in 1939.[34]

Fred was billeted at the fashionable Ritz, then at a military hotel where he enjoyed the pleasure of his second bath in five weeks; the previous one had been at a Belgian prison.[35] His group then performed shows in hospitals.

A warm and friendly evening was spent with General Dwight D. Eisenhower and his staff at the SHAEF headquarters, twenty-five miles outside Paris.[36] Fred and Olivieri had already given an impromptu performance. While Fred was conversing with General Eisenhower, the general said to General "Tooey" Spaatz, who commanded the Eighth Air Force, "Tooey, go get your guitar." Spaatz played his guitar "expertly," as Astaire recalled, while Eisenhower joined in with the singing.[37]

The USO was also touring Bing Crosby and Dinah Shore in France at the same time. Fred gladly performed alongside them. Earlier, Fred and Bing had reunited in London, and they had appeared together when Fred first arrived on the Continent. Subsequently, they sailed for New York on the *Queen Mary* as it weaved its way across the Atlantic, wary of contact with German submarines. The ship was full of returning GIs and airmen, for whom they gave nightly shows.

Fred gave a press conference at the USO headquarters soon after the ship docked in New York. He talked about the men he had performed before: "The way they go right back in there time and again to hit the Germans is something. It's impossible to forget. They make wonderful audiences, too. After the show, they'd swarm around me and shout, 'Gee whiz! You're the lucky guy who danced with the girls! How does it feel to hold Ginger Rogers and Rita Hayworth in your arms?'" His answer, in typical Astaire fashion, was "Fine, they're beautiful dancers!"[38]

Clearly moved by what he had witnessed in Europe, Fred then described how he had done three or four shows a day in front of audiences ranging from two hundred to twelve thousand GIs, using a six-by-twelve-foot dance mat when possible. On some occasions, he improvised with hastily built platforms on the back of trucks. In hospitals he jumped from the floor to beds to tabletops while performing. Once, during a blackout, he was temporarily blinded when hundreds of soldiers shone their flashlights onto his makeshift stage.

In New York, he stayed overnight at the Ritz Carlton on Park Avenue, where he called Phyllis and the children. He walked a few blocks down Park Avenue to pray at St. Bartholomew's Episcopal Church to give thanks for arriving back safely. He said, "I find great comfort in that magnificent church in the midst of the hurly-burly of city life. I think of everything there—my life, my work, the hidden meaning of the good and the bad things that have happened to me. I come out of these spiritually refreshed."

Phyllis had been visiting friends while awaiting his arrival. She joined him after the *Queen Mary* docked. Before they left for California, he made hundreds of telephone calls to the families of servicemen he had met in Europe.[39]

On his return home, Arthur Freed and Vincente Minnelli were eager to re-team him with Lucille Bremer in the much maligned sophisticated musical fantasy *Yolanda and the Thief.* Though made almost a year after *Ziegfeld Follies,* it was released three months before *Follies.* Conceived as the movie that would launch Bremer to stardom, it failed to do so.

Bremer had startling good looks coupled with first-rate dancing ability. Minnelli called her "one of the finest dancers I ever worked with."[40] A mechanical manner, an occasional look of bewilderment, and a frigidity, however, tended to overwhelm her presence on-screen. In *Yolanda* she was also playing a religiously devout young woman who falls emotionally and erotically in love with a man she believes to be an angel![41]

The plot was an incongruous confection involving two con men (Astaire and Frank Morgan, his compatriot from *The Band Wagon*) who descend upon a mythical South American country. They convinced Yolanda (Bremer) that Fred is her guardian angel, who has come down to earth to help her manage the vast business enterprises she has inherited. A beguiling dream sequence causes a sudden focus upon the unsavory past of Astaire's character. He is forced to deal with it. Ultimately, he reforms himself through his love for Bremer and his newfound respect for her devout religious faith.[42]

A few of the dance numbers staged by Eugene Loring were the movie's saving grace, although dance critics believe that Astaire actually choreographed "Coffee Time," a magical swing-dance number for him and Bremer. The camera perfectly captured the vigor and buoyancy they gave to the number.[43] The rhythmic hand-clapping of a street throng at a carnival drives them to a stomping climax. In a sense, "Coffee Time" was reminiscent of "I'll Be Hard to Handle" from *Roberta* and a sequel to "The Shorty George" from *You Were Never Lovelier.*

The sixteen-minute-long "Dream Ballet" finds Fred in a cream-colored, double-breasted suit walking through the mythical town of Esperado. When a stranger asks him for a cigarette, he lights it for him, only to discover that the man has an unlimited supply of arms and legs, each holding an unlit cigarette. This surrealistic approach shows off Minnelli's unusual sense of fantasy along with his keen appreciation of Salvador Dalí. When Fred comes upon a group of native girls washing clothes and sheets, they break into a brisk Latin American dance and entwine him in their sheets. This leads into Bremer in a billowing dress with coins attached to it. Their growing love is demonstrated by their passionate dance, which leads into Bremer's singing "Will You Marry Me?" to Fred. After trying to flee with Bremer's money, he becomes ensnared in Bremer's veils, only to awaken in his own bed tossing and turning.[44]

The brilliant use of color, the rich yet obtuse scenic touches, and the sense of well-intentioned make-believe, along with the dances, give the picture its limited credibility. In a letter to his cousin, furnished by Michael Russell, Astaire observed, "It's a BEAUTIFUL picture, but such an unwieldy story. It seemed impossible to get it on the screen the way they wanted it. I didn't like MY PART too much. I thought I looked a bit dull—lacking in gaiety. The part was very confining." And in a Southern Methodist University interview, conducted by Ronald L. Davis, decades later, Fred expressed his lack of respect for Loring's choreography.

Yolanda and the Thief was a box-office disaster, losing $1.6 million. The severity of the reviews for the film was typified by the *Hollywood Reporter*'s notice by Jack Grant, which said, "*Yolanda* the picture as entertainment is often downright embarrassing. It is seldom clear what producer Arthur Freed sought to do with this fantasy. . . . Minnelli does not allow the film to come to life."[45]

Vincente Minnelli noted that at that time when "the industry's weekly audience was 80,000,000, no sensibly budgeted film . . . could fail."[46] The war did provoke a windfall for Hollywood. Film production dropped only slightly below the prewar level. Yet, *Yolanda* failed to recoup its production cost when it debuted shortly after the end of World War II.[47]

FRED WAS NOW IN THE PRIME of his life even though his career was certainly in need of a hit musical. He realized how fortunate he was with an adoring wife and growing children. He practiced his Episcopalian faith, making almost weekly visits to All Saints Church in Beverly Hills, and giving thousands of dollars to the church.[48]

Now that he was financially secure, he could indulge his longtime love for horse racing by starting a racing stable of his own. He contacted Clyde Phillips, a prominent New York trainer, about purchasing two horses; this was after fifteen years of discussing such a move with Phyllis. Beginner's luck was with him as the first horse he bought, the three-year-old colt Triplicate, for whom he paid $6,000, won his first outing at Jamaica by five lengths. Phyllis's uncle, Henry W. Bull, gladly provided Fred with the use of his colors—dark blue, yellow sash, and red cap. Fred's second horse, Fag, did well for a while, then was sold for a nominal profit.[49]

Triplicate (or Trip, as Fred called him) would continue his moneymaking ways for several years. Howard Hughes once heard that Fred's favorite jockey, J. D. Jessup, had been suspended, and his alternate, Basil James, was in the East and due to extreme weather was unable to get to California to ride Triplicate at Hollywood Park's $100,000 Hollywood Gold Cup. The eccentric pilot and then new owner of RKO took charge and had James flown in on one of Hughes's private planes.

In spite of not being familiar with Triplicate's ways, James brought the horse out of the pack and came roaring down the stretch to beat Louis B. Mayer's filly Honeymoon by a neck, equaling the track record. Phyllis and Randolph Scott joined Fred in his moment of triumph as the winner's purse was $81,000. In addition Fred made $6,000 on his own wager. He admitted, "That put me about even for life on betting."[50] Triplicate went on to make over $250,000 in prize money, which would be doubled in today's racing stakes.

FREED WANTED ASTAIRE to star in his next musical, *The Belle of New York,* under the terms of the last of his three-picture deal with MGM. He would be cast as a New York playboy who becomes involved with a Salvation Army girl. The script wasn't ready, however, which delayed production. Fred was unwilling to venture into another movie after the adverse reaction at the studio to *Yolanda and the Thief.* Leland Hayward got him out of *The Belle of New York*—at least temporarily.

In his final negotiations on Fred's behalf, under the aegis of the Hayward-Deverich Agency (the company was absorbed by MCA, the foremost talent agency in show business), Leland persuaded MGM to agree to a loan-out to Paramount. Thus he could be included with the already proven winning combination of Bing Crosby, Irving Berlin, and Mark Sandrich, again as producer and director, in the film *Blue Skies.* The movie was planned as a kind of sequel to *Holiday Inn.*

The film had already started production with the erudite classical and modern tap dancer Paul Draper starring opposite Crosby. There were problems on the set, however. Besides suffering from a serious stammer, Draper found his dancing partner, Joan Caulfield, who was romantically involved with Crosby, not up to his high standards as a dancer. Crosby insisted that Draper be removed from the picture.[51]

Following that, after nine days of shooting, Mark Sandrich died suddenly of a heart attack at the age of forty-four. Sandrich's duties were assumed by Sol C. Siegel as producer and Stuart Heisler as director. Their joint decision was to seek Fred Astaire to replace Draper. Fred accepted the role on the condition that Hermes Pan be sprung from his deal at Twentieth Century–Fox, where he was choreographing Betty Grable musicals. As usual, Fred got his way.

Fred was again apprehensive, this time since neither *Ziegfeld Follies* nor *Yolanda and the Thief* had yet been released. He was also very aware that *Yolanda* loomed as a distinct failure.

At forty-six, he suddenly decided that now was the proper time to retire. "There comes a day when people begin to say, 'Why doesn't that old duffer retire?'" he told *Time*. "I want to go out while they're still saying Astaire is a hell of a dancer."

As Dellie had done with *The Band Wagon,* Fred wanted to exit with a winner, however. He announced that *Blue Skies* would be his last movie. Phyllis, never that happy with Hollywood anyway, fully concurred with his thinking.[52] The death of Mark Sandrich at such a young age gave him added justification to leave while the going was good.

Once again, Berlin insisted that his name should be attached to the film's title; on its release it was billed as "Irving Berlin's *Blue Skies.*" The score was a potpourri of his past song successes, with the addition of four new tunes, which included "You Keep Coming Back like a Song," which was nominated for an Oscar in the Best Song category, and "A Couple of Song and Dance Men."

The ridiculous premise of *Blue Skies* was that Bing, playing a veteran hoofer, had a problem settling down. His character had long since developed a penchant for acquiring a nightclub, making a success of it, selling it, then buying another in various locales around the country. The nightclub stages provided the settings for the musical numbers in the movie.

Strange as it may seem, Martin Scorsese has been quoted as saying that *Blue Skies* was the inspiration for his 1977 ode to the big-band era, *New York, New York.* He took note of Bing Crosby's obsessive habit of buying and selling nightclubs and translated it into Robert De Niro's obsession with learning to play the saxophone in the latter film.

In the *Blue Skies* script, Joan Caulfield was Bing's and Fred's common love interest. "A Couple of Song and Dance Men" was Berlin's personal musical valentine to his two favorite male stars. Their routine smacked of vaudeville in its happy-go-lucky approach and was based on Bing's obvious lack of talent as a dancer. In effect it was a continuation of the "I'll Capture Your Heart Singing" number from *Holiday Inn.* While Crosby sings, Fred dances. It seems unnecessary to demonstrate that Fred is much the superior dancer.[53] That leads to their doing a slew of imitations to conclude the number.

For the third time in a film musical, Fred performed a dance number while playing a drunk. This time it was with Olga San Juan performing "Heat Wave," the big production number in this film. Unhappy with Caulfield, Fred, dressed as a sea captain, and San Juan exhibit deep-rooted sexuality, a rarity in an Astaire musical, in their dancing. Usually adamant about never repeating a dance routine from a previous movie, his closing solo, tapping to a boogie-woogie beat, is really a repetition of "The Wedding Cake Walk" from *You'll Never Get Rich*.[54]

But the most memorable number in the movie is the miraculous "Puttin' On The Ritz," a close relative of Fred's famous "Top Hat, White Tie, and Tails." Here was the essence of Fred Astaire on display as the supreme film dancer. Dressed in top hat, ascot, cutaway, striped pants, and spats, he let loose with decided verve while singing the tune. Before completing the final chorus, he pulls out a cane, which becomes his dance partner. Moving to the rear of the stage, he kicks apart two curtains and what appears? None other than eight miniature Fred Astaires tapping in unison behind the original! Using the shadow-and-mirror devices from the "Bojangles" number, plus an early use of a split screen, each of the miniature Astaires launches into his own individual dance steps. Fred insisted upon being photographed eight different times dancing the routine.[55]

Life called this amazing number "the most stupendous tap dance of all time."[56] Bosley Crowther returned to the fold, writing, "Mr. Astaire makes his educated feet talk a persuasive language that is thrilling to conjugate. . . . If this film is Mr. Astaire's swan song, as he has heartlessly announced it will be, then he has climaxed many years of hoofing with a properly superlative must-see."[57]

It took five weeks to create this scene but was certainly worth the effort. When Fred left the soundstage after the final take on the number, he grumbled, "Forty-one years of this! Do you wonder that I'm quitting?" The next day, after completing his last day of dancing, before the entire cast of the film he took off his toupee, threw it on the floor, stamped on it, and declared, "Never, never, never. Never will I have to wear this blasted rug again!"[58] Mel Brooks, an Astaire devotee to be sure, adapted "Puttin' On The Ritz" for a hilarious comedy tap-dance number in his hit film comedy *Young Frankenstein*.

Although Bing had a field day singing the many established Berlin standards in *Blue Skies,* too many of them sounded the same,[59] although perhaps they were arranged too similarly by Joseph J. Lilley. The plot was foolish, acting by everyone was lackluster, and Caulfield was pretty but contributed little. America nonetheless relished seeing Astaire and Crosby together again. The picture did even better at the box office than *Holiday Inn,* becoming the biggest-grossing picture Fred had ever starred in. This picture was, indeed, the right way for him to bow out in style.

FRED FELT GOOD about what lay ahead. Money was not an issue. Triplicate was doing well. He enjoyed playing tennis on his home court, and there was always golf at the Bel Air country club. "The first great shock of retirement," he acknowledged, "was finding there were no days off."[60]

The public certainly hadn't forgotten him. He was still getting close to two thousand fan letters a day. Many of his letter writers wanted to know, "Where could I go to learn how to dance like Fred Astaire?" He answered that they should go to Arthur Murray Dance Studios. Murray had reportedly made $20 million from his dance studio operation.[61] This led Phyllis to suggest that perhaps Fred should open his own dance studio. Her thinking was "Why couldn't you do just as well with your name and reputation?"

In 1947, the first of the Fred Astaire Dance Studios, with the help of RKO publicist Charlie Casanave, was set to open in New York at 487 Park Avenue. Being his usual dutiful self, Fred claimed he personally trained 150 teachers.[62] The construction on the studio's twenty-eight rooms encountered some serious problems, including the ballroom, which was called the Adele Room. January became September before it finally opened.

Life shot a photo spread of the grand opening, which ultimately never ran in the magazine. There was little business. Fred related, "I don't know what happened to all those people who wrote to me, but they certainly weren't at the studio."

Phyllis felt guilty over the debacle, but Fred placated her by saying, "I wanted to go ahead with the project—it was my idea." For the next two years, business continued dismal. He faced closing down the operation or pumping more money into it. He was determined that it succeed and decided to invest more of his savings. This also meant he would have to seriously consider working in movies again.

After a few years, the studios spread to twenty-six cities, and later forty studios were in operation. Fred invented a new dance called the Swing Trot, which was debuted in *The Barkleys of Broadway,* to feature at the studios. By the mid-1950s, however, his financial involvement ended. Eventually the studios failed, mainly due to poor supervision and franchising problems. For years thereafter, lawsuits were filed by people claiming their wish to dance like Fred Astaire had led them to sign up at the studio but that their dreams were never fulfilled by it. The venture wound up costing Fred $120,000, according to an interview he gave to Art Buchwald in 1959.

Adele and Ann returned to America as soon as the war was over after a ten-year absence. Adele announced, "I'm planning to stock up on some essential things. It's wonderful to see all the lovely girdles. You know our posteriors have spread quite a bit over there."[63]

After a joyous visit in New York, Adele and Ann headed for Los Angeles for an emotional reunion with Fred and his family. Adele, too, thought Fred's decision to retire was sensible. She later said, "It was different for me, but show business and dancing and worrying were in my brother's blood—it was not just his work, it was his life."[64]

While in New York, she telephoned Kingman Douglass, a good-looking Army Air Force officer, who had headed intelligence for the Eighth Air Force when they met at Rainbow Corner. Douglass was a widower with three grown sons, who owned an estate in the horse country near Middleburg, Virginia. The boisterous and witty Adele was strangely attracted to the calm and placid investment banker.

On her return to Ireland, she approached Andrew Cavendish, the son of the new duke, with the news that she planned to get married again and to move to America. She was not well-off despite what Charlie had left her. Andrew donated additional money by the new duke and gave her permission to live at Lismore for three months of the year. In exchange, she would pay a reasonable rental fee toward upkeep of the castle.[65]

On April 20, 1947, Dellie, still Lady Charles Cavendish, married fifty-one-year-old Kingman Douglass in Warrenton, Virginia, at the local Presbyterian church. Adele, as usual, shaved two years off her age. In reality, she was now fifty. She said that she had no regrets about leaving the British aristocracy. Some of her friends were amazed at Adele's choice of a man with such a different disposition. They found Douglass's habit of clearing his throat between words disconcerting. "The poor man's got catarrh," exclaimed Dellie.[66]

In 1950, Douglass became assistant director of the CIA. He held the post for two years before resuming his career in finances, becoming a partner in Dillon Read & Company before retiring.

ARTHUR FREED CONTINUED to approach Fred about returning to work. He was thoroughly convinced that if he could team Fred with the right star, such as Crosby, he would have another hit movie. Fred's answer remained the same: "Sorry, Arthur, I'm retired."

Nonetheless, Fred was becoming itchy. One quiet morning in late 1947, he was puttering around his den, practicing some pool shots. He began looking through his record collection. As he recalled, "I began playing a Lionel Hampton record, 'Jack the Bellboy,' and it sent me right through the ceiling. I jumped to my feet and started dancing.[67] I thought to myself, 'I might as well be doing this someplace where it counts.' The urge and inspiration to go back to work had hit me."[68]

To start preparing to dance again in movies at forty-eight would be difficult, but his body was still surprisingly limber. He was not suffering from the usual stiffness and pain from lingering injuries like so many retired dancers. He admitted, "I have a back that through various phases of my career was injured; I don't know any dancer who doesn't. I turned my ankle a couple of times, and I broke my arm when I was a child, doing a cartwheel. Sometimes I fell during a dance, but I could usually get away with making it seem part of the routine."

SUNDAYS WERE ALWAYS A SPECIAL DAY for Gene Kelly and Betsy Blair at their home in Beverly Hills on Rodeo Drive. A group of progressive-thinking film craftsmen were always on hand, which might include Betty Comden and Adolph Green, the lyricists and screenwriters of Broadway and film musicals; André Previn, the brilliant young pianist, composer, and conductor, a refugee from Nazi Germany; the dancer, choreographer, and director Stanley Donen; the comedian Phil Silvers; composers Hugh Martin and Saul Chaplin, along with his wife, Ethel; the actor Richard Conte and his wife, Ruth; the arranger Lennie Hayton and his girlfriend, Lena Horne (later to be married); Kelly's dancing aide and next wife, Jeanne Coyne; and his secretary, Lois McClelland. Blair referred to them as the Bohemians, as opposed to Fred Astaire's group of friends, which she justifiably labeled the Royals.

"The volleyball games were a fixture on Sunday at noon," Blair remembered. "They were serious, as were all the games we played."[69] During one strenuous volleyball game, Gene broke his ankle.

L. K. Sidney, vice president of MGM, called Fred with the news of Gene's injury, which would prevent him from costarring with Judy Garland in *Easter Parade.* This was exactly one day after Astaire had played the Lionel Hampton record that initially gave him pangs of longing to work again in movies. Fred went over to Culver City to discuss the situation further with Sidney. Fred then called Gene, who said he said he wouldn't be ready to dance again for several months. He suggested that Fred take his place.[70]

Gene's injury didn't prevent him and Betsy Blair from joining fellow actors Danny Kaye, Humphrey Bogart, Lauren Bacall, Evelyn Keyes, Marsha Hunt, and Richard Conte in flying to Washington to stand up for "the Hollywood 10" (the screenwriters Dalton Trumbo, John Howard Lawson, Albert Maltz, et al.) when they were brought before the House Un-American Activities Committee for expressing Communist sympathies in their movie scripts.

The timing of Gene's mishap and Fred's restlessness coalesced perfectly. He agreed to go back to work at MGM in *Easter Parade.* Three days after Gene's injury, Fred began rehearsing the dances for the movie with Robert Alton, and five weeks later filming commenced. His two-year retirement was over.

Although it appeared MGM was still prosperous, appearances were deceiving. In 1947–48, sixteen of MGM's twenty-five releases lost money, totaling $6.5 million.[71] This was in spite of Mayer's saying, "There are no bad MGM pictures"![72] Gene Kelly's musical *The Pirate* was one of the losing pictures, but *Easter Parade* wasn't. This bonanza of musical entertainment was rightfully a big success at the box office. It reflected the quintessence of everything that was right about an MGM musical.

Perhaps most important, the movie was an ideal vehicle for Fred. Ava Astaire McKenzie remarked, "So many things in the movie reminded me of Daddy in real life." Judy Garland was at her peak. Besides their musical camaraderie, she and Fred had a natural rapport as actors.[73] In addition, Ann Miller was at her sexy dancing best as the second female lead.

Jules Munshin, who would later star in *On the Town,* Gene Kelly and Stanley Donen's codirected hit musical, had a brief but effective role as a pompous waiter. But the unsurpassed Irving Berlin songs held the picture together. Roger Edens (although unbilled in the film's credits) and Johnny Green won Oscars for their outstanding musical arrangements for the picture.[74]

The original concept was for Kelly and Garland to repeat their triumph in *For Me and My Gal,* with a script not too different from the original. Arthur Freed, however, wanted to build a musical set in 1912 New York with a Berlin score of, in this case, eight old songs and eight new songs, a plan that had certainly worked with both *Holiday Inn* and *Blue Skies.*

Berlin was so anxious to have Garland, the most emotionally gifted female singer who ever lived (of whom Frank Sinatra one said, "Every time she sings, she dies a little"), sing his songs that he turned down an offer from Twentieth Century–Fox for the property. He was paid the staggering fee of $600,000 for the use of his name, the title of the movie, his songs, and as a consultant. (Supposedly Berlin was so concerned about the high taxes he would have to pay from the MGM deal on *Easter Parade* that he discussed his dilemma one day in New York with lyricist Adolph Green, who suggested that maybe he could have the payments spread out. "How about getting a dollar a year, Irving," Green suggested facetiously.) In contrast, Fred got $150,000 and costar billing with Garland, who made $115,000. The film's budget was $2,694,934.[75]

FRED ENJOYED BEING BACK in front of the cameras again. The movie was certainly a dance feast for him. It was his sixth picture with Berlin, and all of the dance numbers were designed with the camera in mind. He had three numbers with Judy and three with Ann Miller, along with two solo spots of his own. He called Miller "a terrific performer."[76] The lithe dancer was forced to wear ballet shoes in their dance numbers so as not to appear taller than Astaire.[77]

The final shooting script owed considerably to George Bernard Shaw's famous play *Pygmalion*. The plot quickly establishes Ann Miller as Astaire's dancing partner who walks out on Fred to work in a Broadway musical. He vows he can train any girl he chooses to replace her. That's when Garland, playing a chorus girl, enters the picture. He plays the Henry Higgins role in molding her into the dancer of his dreams. He and Garland eventually audition for the *Ziegfeld Follies* and get the job. They are the hit of the show and Charles Dillingham's next show as well, which opens just before Easter. Garland, however, feels seriously neglected. She and Fred have a tiff but naturally make up and stroll down Fifth Avenue passing St. Patrick's Cathedral in the annual Easter parade to end the picture. On that shooting day, February 9, 1948, some seven hundred extras and over one hundred period vehicles were used in typical MGM grand style on the spacious facilities of Lot 3.[78]

The recently deceased, affable, and extremely successful novelist Sidney Sheldon, the recipient of a Tony, an Emmy, and an Oscar, was the movie's screenwriter. Sheldon remembered, "I went with my agent to see Arthur Freed in his office. I said, 'I'm here to do *Pride and Prejudice*.' Freed said, 'Not anymore, you were reassigned. We have a script [written by Frances Goodrich and Albert Hackett]. It's dark, and it doesn't work for us. I can't cast it. No one wants to play it. We want a script that's lighter.' So I wrote a script and gave it to Freed over a period of weeks. He told me it was for Judy Garland and Gene Kelly, and that sounded good. The day I handed him the [final] script he said, 'Gene Kelly broke his leg last night.' I thought it was a joke. It only happens in movies that the leading man breaks his leg."

Once Astaire started work on the picture, Sheldon went over to watch him in rehearsal. "No one was there. He was doing turns. It was incredible. I walked over to him very slowly so he didn't know that I was there. I tapped him on the shoulder. He turned around, and I said, 'Fred, [do it] like this.'"

Sheldon found Astaire "very reserved, but very polite. He was also cold and closed in. I never had a problem with him. I had to create and write a new story for him." Sheldon agreed his new script had a strong *Pygmalion* element, which worked well since Astaire was old enough to be Garland's father. This unforeseen element provided instant reassurance to Garland, who was badly in need of it. Musicians Artie Shaw, Oscar Levant, and David Rose, in addition to Minnelli, had previously fulfilled this role in her life.[79]

The sequence in which Astaire teaches Garland, his Eliza Doolittle, various dance steps at Luigi's Bar reveals a rarely seen aspect of his screen personality, while Judy reveals her vulnerability. He suddenly turns domineering, which mirrors the stern demeanor that was his norm during his countless hours of dance rehearsal—according to the observations of many dancers I interviewed. Dancing was his stock-in-trade; he demanded that it be perfect.

Sheldon said, "Freed never commented whether he liked it or not until the cast commented. . . . I remember that I was told, 'Fred wants to see you.' I went down on the set, where Fred took me aside and said, 'This scene—could you change it for me? It's too rough.' It was a scene when he and Ann Miller were a team. I said to him, 'Fred, you don't have to be mean; the character is.' He said, 'You're absolutely right. Now, would you change it.' I reworked it in five minutes. I worked fast."

It's no wonder that Astaire wanted Sheldon to soften the dialogue in this scene. It might have worked for Everyman Kelly, but certainly not for the elegant Astaire. This would have given the movie audience an unfamiliar look at him as ornery and obstreperous. Fred was constantly aware of his screen image and didn't ever want to be seen veering too far afield from it.

GARLAND HAD ALREADY begun her endless trail of troublesome behavior, aided considerably by her addiction to pills and her deep psychological problems. Her psychiatrist, Dr. Herbert Kupper, suggested that it would be beneficial if Vincente Minnelli, then her husband, and with whom she was going through a particularly tense time, did not direct her in *Easter Parade.* Charles "Chuck" Walters, a former choreographer whose directorial debut with *Good News* had been a hit, soon replaced Minnelli.[80]

Throughout the shooting of the picture, Fred maintained a tremendous respect for Judy's extraordinary talent, her showmanship, and her sense of humor. His presence also gave her confidence, which had ramifications in his own outstanding performance.[81] That she occasionally showed up late for work didn't faze him. She absolutely idolized him.[82] There was no problem with her height—a constant source of worry to Fred. Even with her long, shapely legs, Garland stood only four feet ten and a half inches tall.

Fred noticed immediately how quickly she learned new dance steps. When they first started rehearsing together, he wasn't the least intimidated by stories of her telling Chuck Walters and Irving Berlin that she was JUDY GARLAND AND WAS NO ONE TO FUCK WITH! By now, there was little that Fred couldn't handle in dealing with his leading lady, much less a troubled star such as Garland.

Berlin's songs provided the setting for anyone's tastes, from the inventive "Drum Crazy," in which Fred used a cane, drumsticks, plus his hands, feet, and head, while exhibiting his hobby of playing drums; to the exuberant Astaire/Garland dance number "When the Midnight Choo-Choo Leaves for Alabam'"; to Ann Miller's shimmering "Shakin' the Blues Away"; to Astaire's masterful "Steppin' Out with My Baby," with him dressed in a white suit, red socks, and sporting a cane, and dancing with three beautiful girls before switching to a solo tap-dance spot [83]—the perfect confluence of a rich melody, slow-motion photography, and superb dancing, which was in the tradition of "Top Hat, White Tie, and Tails," and "Puttin' On The Ritz." But the major surprise of the picture was the "A Couple of Swells" number, a perfect vaudeville routine in which Astaire and Garland romped around the stage dressed as hoboes in ragged clothes. Despite looking seedy and unkempt, the delightful duo played the scene with élan, spoofing the pretentious behavior of the wealthy, with Astaire kidding his familiar elegance.[84]

"It Only Happens When I Dance with You," which ranks with Berlin's most haunting love songs, was used as the love theme for the underscore of the picture. Astaire and Miller (who replaced Cyd Charisse) blended perfectly in a number that essentially marks the end of their on-screen romantic as well as professional relationship. They get close, then ultimately pull away from each other as they prepare to part. Astaire ends the dance with a kiss, but he fully realizes he has lost Miller forever.

Peter Lawford, then at the height of his days as a handsome young swain, supplied a helpful presence to both stars in the movie. Frank Sinatra was first thought of for the role. It helped that Lawford and Garland were friends. Lawford sings the happy love song "A Fella with an Umbrella" to Judy in a yearning voice, not any better or worse than when he delivered the title song in the musical *Good News*. "A Fella with an Umbrella" exposes his unrequited love for Garland.

Freed insisted that the script be simple and straightforward with no trivial scenes. "Mr. Monotony," with Judy attired in a tuxedo jacket and tights (an outfit she wore three years later in *Summer Stock*), was considered risqué for a film taking place in 1912 and was cut from the picture. That was a mistake as the outstanding number showed the dynamic star at her best. (Berlin installed the number in his next Broadway musical, *Miss Liberty*.)[85] "Mr. Monotony" was made available in edited form in *That's Entertainment! III* and in subsequent DVD releases. It was finally restored in its entirety in the 2005 DVD edition of *Easter Parade*.

Once production was completed, the studio realized it had a big hit. At first, the advertising department wanted to label *Easter Parade* "The *Gone with the*

Wind of Musicals." Berlin suggested, "Let's just call it a very enjoyable picture." A snapshot of the reviews indicates how enthusiastically the New York film critics greeted Astaire's work and the picture on its June 1, 1948, opening. Tom Pryor of the *Times* said, "Fred Astaire, who has no peer dancing, is at the top of his form, and let's hope he will never again talk about retiring." Lee Mortimer in the *Mirror* said, "*Easter Parade* has everything. . . . We are sunk for glossy adjectives to describe the big Metro musical at Loew's State." Rose Pelswick of the *Journal-American*: "Lilting film has everything. . . . Astaire dances with all charm and brilliance." Howard Barnes of the *Tribune*: "Smart and fetching screen carnival . . . Astaire hoofing more superbly than ever." Kate Cameron of the *Daily News*: "Just what moving pictures shoppers on Broadway have been looking for . . . Whole production done with good taste and showmanship." Leo Mishkin of the *Morning Telegraph*: "A major event of summer movie season . . . return of Mr. Astaire is something to be hailed and celebrated." Cecilia Ager of the *Star* wrote, "Solid, bang up show . . . Fred Astaire's dancing is incomparable and inimitable."

After seeing *Easter Parade* Ginger Rogers sent a wire to Arthur Freed in which she called *Easter Parade* "a true American beauty."[86] Bing Crosby wrote Astaire, saying, "For a guy who had retired ostensibly, your comeback represents the greatest event since Satchel Paige."[87] (Paige, a onetime superstar pitcher in the Negro baseball leagues, in his late forties joined the Cleveland Indians that summer and helped them win the American League pennant.) The reception of *Easter Parade* nullified any doubts Fred might have had about his ability to satisfy both the critics and moviegoers. Moanin' Minnie had been silenced—at least for the moment.

A MINOR INCIDENT that took place during the shooting of *Easter Parade* said something about Astaire's racial sensitivities. In vaudeville, his dancing was inspired by black performers such as John Bubbles and Bill "Bojangles" Robinson. Fayard Nicholas testified to Fred's keen appreciation of him and his brother Harold's dancing. But Fred's not objecting to the disrespectful manner in which the jazz group that backed him in the "Astairable Rag" in *You'll Never Get Rich* were treated begins to tell a story of its own.

Dr. Jeni Le Gon had a small featured role in *Easter Parade,* as the maid for Ann Miller, a normal kind of role of the time for an attractive black woman. Le Gon well remembered meeting Astaire at RKO in 1935 when she did her first movie, *Hooray for Love,* which starred Ann Sothern, Gene Raymond, Bill Robinson, and Fats Waller. She appeared with the two other sepia stars (a 1930s and '40s term) in the "I'm Living in a Great Big Way" musical number and built up a reputation for her acrobatic tap dancing. She wound up making twenty-six movies; *Easter Parade* was her ninth film appearance. Her last movie, *Bones,* in which she played herself, was with the notorious hip-hop artist Snoop Dogg, in 2001.

"During the making of *Hooray for Love,* Astaire and Rogers were the stars of the world," Le Gon remembered. "Bill Robinson knew Fred from back East. We would watch them [Astaire and Rogers] rehearse, and then they would come over and watch us rehearse. And sometimes we would all dance together and exchange steps. So I knew Fred and Rogers.

"Now when I did *Easter Parade,* I was on the set with Ann Miller and Fred. It took us maybe a week or two weeks to do the scene. Fred never spoke to me between takes even while doing a short scene with him at the beginning of the picture. He never recognized me as the person who had danced with him in rehearsals years before. At this particular time, I was all over the newspapers. Louella Parsons wrote about me, and the day she wrote the column, she had no space to write *Jennie* so she just wrote *Jeni.* My mother gave me permission to have it legalized."

A young black woman performer in those days would have been considered out of hand or possibly "uppity" to question why she was being shunned by a major star, even someone she had previously known. Asked for a possible reason Astaire wouldn't talk to her, in view of their earlier association, Dr. Le Gon (she was awarded an honorary doctorate, Doctor of Performing Arts in American Dance, by Oklahoma City University), replied, "I have no idea other than there was this black and white thing. That's all I can say about it. I thought I was going to be able to say hello to him and talk to him."

Could one chalk this up as a momentary failure of Astaire's memory, an example of his keen concentration on his work, or perhaps his shyness? Or does this experience of Le Gon's signal that Astaire respected black entertainers exclusively for their talent, but could not relate to them in any other way than as coworkers? The critic Stanley Crouch pointed out, "Fred Astaire . . . became a screen star by often using the Negro pedal percussion of tap dance and performing most of his numbers to Tin Pan Alley songs such as 'Top Hat' that could not have arrived without the inspiration of Negro melody and phrasing."[88]

This incident involving Astaire and Le Gon caused me to recall a *New York Times* interview with Bing Crosby in the early 1970s, shortly after Louis Armstrong's death, when Bing candidly acknowledged his large musical debt to Armstrong. He remarked on how well they related to each other while working together several times in movies, television shows, and on records. When asked if he had ever invited Armstrong to his home over the decades they'd known each other and worked together, Crosby answered, "Why . . . no. Perhaps I should have."

IN THE SUMMER OF 1948, Mayer and his associates in the Thalberg Building looked admiringly at the box-office response to *Easter Parade.* They were again ultrahappy with Garland, who had been one of their own since 1936. The almost $9 million gross of the movie stood out against the many failures that year. They failed to realize, however, that Astaire was also still an important box-office draw.

The losses the studio suffered that fiscal year presaged what lay ahead. The advent of reasonably priced television sets was a serious problem. The nation became addicted to the little box and turned away from its long-established habit of weekly visits to the local movie house. This was despite Mayer's scoffing, "Who in hell is going to look at those pygmy screens?" An added blow to the movie business was the May 3, 1948, Supreme Court decision that for studios to own the theaters in which their films were shown was a violation of antitrust laws.[89] The studios were ordered to sell the theaters.

Meanwhile, the pleasant experience of working with Judy Garland prompted Fred to want to work with her soon again. The studio thought perhaps it had a new winning combination, like Mickey Rooney and Garland—or Astaire and Rogers. Comden and Green were brought out from New York to deliver the screenplay of *The Barkleys of Broadway,* for which they were each paid $24,000.[90] The plot of the movie concerned a constantly bickering veteran dance team. Astaire and Garland were signed almost immediately for the movie.

When Comden and Green, skillful performers in their own right, did a run-through of their script in Freed's office, Judy and Astaire were there eagerly listening. Judy remarked, "If we can only do as well as they did reading those parts, we're okay." Chuck Walters was set to direct and Judy's old friend Oscar Levant and the comedian Billie Burke, Flo Ziegfeld's widow, were added to the cast.

When rehearsals began in June 1948, Judy called in sick. She complained of migraine headaches and insomnia, which led to some calling her "the American Piaf." Mayer and Freed visited her at home and pleaded with her to return to work. After six days, Dr. Kupper advised them that Judy's being required to report to work every day could lead to a serious mental disturbance. Freed wrote an official studio letter telling Garland she would be replaced in *The Barkleys of*

Broadway and that she was suspended. She still was paid $23,000 through the terms of her studio contract. She called Louella Parsons to tearfully admit, "I'm missing the greatest role of my career."[91]

The resourceful Freed moved fast. He had the script of *The Barkleys of Broadway* flown up to Ginger Rogers's four-hundred-acre ranch in Oregon. MGM was willing to more than double the salary Garland had been offered for Rogers to work again with Fred Astaire. A further inducement for Ginger was that for the first time her salary was larger than Fred's—$162,000 as against his $150,000. Ginger was therefore ready if not totally eager to resume their on-screen relationship.[92] Fred, however, was in no hurry to go retro by dancing again with Ginger.[93]

But that was not the last of Garland and *The Barkleys of Broadway*. One day, shortly after Fred and Ginger began shooting, Judy showed up on the set. She posed for photographs with Rogers and Levant and joked with the crew. Her visit unnerved Ginger to the extent that she vowed to stay in her dressing room until Garland left the soundstage. Chuck Walters intervened as Judy hurled insults about Rogers. He took her by the arm, which caused her to shout out, "I've been asked to leave the set. It's because of the great Ginger Rogers. Well, fuck you, Ginger!"[94] Fred missed the entire episode as he walked in as Judy was abruptly departing. He saw how angry Judy was, which caused him to ask, "What are they doing to that *poor kid*?"[95]

The film opened smartly with Fred and Ginger performing "Swing Trot," behind the film credits. One of Ginger's first lines was addressed to Fred as her longtime husband and dance partner, Josh Barkley: "You always did take me for granted." Obviously, Comden and Green were well versed in the sometimes troubled history of the Astaire/Rogers relationship. The crux of the Barkleys' relationship in the Comden and Green screenplay rested on Josh Barkley's firm belief that the success of the team was fundamentally based on *his* dancing ability,[96] and his wife Dinah's wish to become accepted as a dramatic actress. This was an obvious parallel to Rogers's own career trajectory as she attempted to stop being typecast as merely a dancer during the late 1930s.

An author, who requested anonymity, interviewed Astaire years later concerning *Barkleys*. He remembered that Fred had said, "How dare that bitch walk onto the rehearsal set of *The Barkleys of Broadway* in a pair of high heels the first day. I started to show her the first routine for 'Swing Trot,' and she said, 'You haven't done very much in all the years we've been apart.' I just let it bounce right off me. She was pathetic."

According to Chuck Walters, "There was no real rapport offscreen. They met on the set, did their thing, and parted—no animosity, very polite . . . but you'd think they had just met. You know what it boils down to? She's too big. It's that simple. Too tall."[97]

Yet in spite of Fred's age-old problems with Ginger, in their dancing the old magic was still on the screen. They were older and indeed looked it—it had been a full decade since they had danced together, and Ginger was now a full-fledged star. The zest, the bursts of fire, and the ingenuity remained with a perhaps more mature approach—less flash, a bit more substance. Their comedy scenes together were as light and spontaneous as ever, but the picture lacked the light touch and brilliance of the past.

"Bouncin' the Blues," staged as a rehearsal number, backed by a loosely swinging jazz group that included clarinetist Gus Bivona and pianist Mel Powell, for example, showed Fred and Ginger dishing out their tap-dancing chops with the fervor of yesteryear. It was reminiscent of their "That's good, but can you do this?" approach contained in "I'm Putting All My Eggs in One Basket," in *Follow the Fleet*.[98] Now they had Technicolor to highlight their work, something that was unfortunately sorely missing from their earlier work together.

The magnificent gem of the Gershwins' "They Can't Take That Away from Me" was given the correct presentation—as the basis of a smooth and flowing dance number with Fred in white tie and Ginger in a white frothy dress—not as almost a throwaway number as it had been when it was staged on a ferryboat in *Shall We Dance*. (Freed had insisted on using the song, which cost the studio $10,000.) It was a return to their old standard of elegance, although Ginger was noticeably heavier and wasn't given the most flattering hairdo.

The sardonic Oscar Levant introduced their performance at a benefit with the line "They will now brilliantly oppose each other in one of their greatest numbers." His introduction mirrored the Barkleys' competitive relationship. In the script the dance was designed to bring them back together but doesn't succeed.[99]

This time Ira Gershwin was teamed with Harry Warren. In contrast to the moneys Berlin was able to demand from Paramount and MGM, Harry Warren was paid $80,000 for his songs in the picture and Ira Gershwin got $57,000.[100] Nothing of any significance stemmed from their association, however. Among their efforts, "My One and Only Highland Fling"—one of the Barkleys' onstage numbers, a spoof on Fred and Ginger's earlier routines, masked as a Scottish folk song, with Fred and Ginger in matching plaid kilts and dour expressions—was flat. "Weekend in the Country," with Fred, Ginger, and Levant cavorting around a rural setting, failed in its attempt to come off as lively and charming.

Four years earlier, Gene Kelly had delighted movie fans dancing with Jerry the Mouse (from *Tom and Jerry* cartoon fame) in *Anchors Aweigh*. Fred had to come up with something to top that and did with his spectacular "Shoes with Wings On" number that takes place in a shoe-repair store. Hermes Pan collaborated with Fred in designing the many intricacies of this number, which lasted seven minutes and wound up costing $212,000.[101]

After a dancing customer has left a pair of white shoes on the counter, the shoes break into a tap dance of their own. (Fred's disembodied foot did the tapping.) As Fred puts on the shoes and begins to dance, his offscreen voice begins singing, "When I've got shoes with wings on / The winter's gone, the spring's on . . ." Abruptly, two other pairs of shoes start tapping, then a total of five pairs. They circle around Fred and are joined by a pair of ballet slippers. The best way to end the number was for Astaire and Pan to repeat a main ingredient of one of their most famous routines, "Top Hat, White Tie, and Tails." Fred tries to shoot down the unstoppable tapping shoes, this time with a broom instead of a cane. It doesn't work, however. He resorts to drawing a pair of pistols, whereupon all the shoes fall down upon his head.[102]

Speaking of the screenplay, Betty Comden was not loath to acknowledge, "I just didn't think it was distinguished. It was so trite. I don't think it was terrible, but I just didn't think it was a very worthy vehicle for a star because it didn't seem to have the elegance and the kind of atmosphere that belonged with an Astaire film."

Comden added, "We were disappointed because we [she and Adolph Green] never got to work with Judy [Garland]. But we were thrilled working with Astaire. Just to see him walk into a room was a poem. We both really worshipped him because he was the epitome of style, and he was such a unique personality. We went to many of the same occasions, but we were not close personal friends, and I'm sorry about that. Gene [Kelly], of course, we knew before he went to Hollywood. He became a close friend."

Although Rogers had a significant reputation as a dramatic actor, her *acting,* especially in the last half of the film, was a letdown. A scene in which she plays Sarah Bernhardt onstage is truly embarrassing.[103]

The film ended with "Manhattan Downbeat," following the decision of Ginger's character to give up drama for dancing. She and Fred reunite in a brief dance routine with Fred in white tie and tails and Ginger in an unstylish full-skirted dress. It begins in their apartment and ends on the stage of a musical, complete with moving floor panels and a chorus of high-style strutting dancers.[104] As their final number together and the end of their ten pictures as a team, it's regrettable it wasn't more memorable.

The film critics expressed a mixed reaction to *Barkleys.* Otis Guernsey in the *New York Herald Tribune* called the movie "light hearted and fresh as paint." Kate Cameron in the *Daily News* sniffed, "There was nothing original about the story." Bosley Crowther said, "Ginger and Fred are a couple with incorruptible style, they also have that gift of natural timing in absolute union, so that they're always clicking together when dancing or trifling with the plot. . . . Astaire and Rogers have the talent to make us feel young and gay . . . the inroads have done no damage to their cooperative snap and verve."

Archer Winsten in the *New York Post* said of Comden and Green's screenplay, "Actually, they do a bit of carpentering and polishing here and there which lend a gloss of spontaneity to some of the entertainment." *Variety* continued the somewhat less than thrilled consensus by saying, "The songs were ordinary." John McCarten in the *New Yorker,* however, found the movie distinguished chiefly its bringing Astaire and Rogers together once more. Despite *Time*'s earlier pronouncement that Rita Hayworth was Fred's ideal partner, the magazine now declared, "Ginger is still the best movie dancing partner that Astaire ever had."

The Barkleys of Broadway wound up grossing $5,500,000 on a $2,318,000 budget[105]—a goodly profit in the days when marketing costs were almost nil. The sale of television sets by this time numbered over a million. The thinking was that the return of Astaire and Rogers would be a motion picture event that would take people away from watching television and bring them back to the movie theaters in droves. In reality, *Easter Parade* was a much more successful film.

A *Look* magazine article at the time painted a rosy picture of the studio. It reported that Metro-Goldwyn-Mayer had been inaugurated back in 1924. When it appeared, the forty-acre plant, in the Los Angeles–incorporated town of Culver City, had six glassed-in studios, six hundred employees, and six stars under contract. In the next twenty-five years, the studio produced 1,450 feature films that grossed close to $3 billion, making it Hollywood's richest studio. By 1949, it was a self-contained city, covering 174 acres with 135 buildings, 3,500 employees, and 40 major stars signed to the studio.

FRED HAD COMMITTED himself to a picture at Paramount, *Let's Dance* with Betty Hutton. Once again, the script wasn't ready, so he happily took six months off. He returned to work at MGM, however, not Paramount.

Producer Jack Cummings, Mayer's nephew, enticed him with a script that dealt with the lives of the songwriting team of Bert Kalmar and Harry Ruby, both of whom Fred had known in vaudeville. Fred was to play Kalmar and comedian Red Skelton was Ruby in *Three Little Words,* which was more of a singer's movie than a dance musical. Working on the film, however, was one of Fred's favorite experiences.

This was partly because he deeply respected songwriting and had worked hard to excel at it for decades but never quite succeeded. Throughout the 1940s and '50s, the lives of songwriters were favorite subjects of Hollywood as for example the biographical films produced on Jerome Kern, Rodgers and Hart, George Gershwin, Vincent Youmans, Sigmund Romberg, Cole Porter, and Da Silva, Brown, and Henderson.

Red Skelton had to be talked into taking a straight role by Jack Cummings. Skelton could be a handful to work with due to his occasional lack of concentration and discipline, but Fred worked with him easily.

But what really pleased Fred was his new dancing partner, Vera-Ellen Westmeyer Rohe, from Cincinnati, a *Major Bowes* contest winner (the 1930s and '40s version of *American Idol*), which had sent her to New York where she became a Rockette. The dainty and petite young blonde was a born dancer with tremendous versatility, yet had a bland on-screen personality. She could follow Fred quite easily and shared his drive for perfection, but possessed no distinctive dancing style of her own. They collaborated on one humorous number, "Mr. and Mrs. Hoofer at Home."[106] Hermes Pan was the dance director, but the film lacked a really outstanding dance number.

For the most part, the Kalman and Ruby songs never achieved standard status except for "Who's Sorry Now?," sung in the film by Gloria De Haven; "Nevertheless" sung by Astaire and Vera-Ellen (whose singing was ghosted by Anita Ellis); and "Three Little Words" by Astaire. But the zest with which Astaire and Skelton handled such mundane fare as "Where Did You Get That Girl?," "My Sunny Tennessee," "So Long Oo—Long"; along with Debbie Reynolds, then seventeen, singing "I Wanna Be Loved by You" (ghosted by the song's originator Helen Kane); "Thinking of You," danced beautifully by Astaire and Vera-Ellen; and Arlene Dahl, registering with her rendition of "I Love You So Much," were what made the picture so enjoyable.

The irrepressible Debbie Reynolds said she didn't really get to know Astaire on *Three Little Words,* having only two scenes with him. She recalled, however, "I would be walking down the street at MGM, and, as you know, it was like a city within a city. Mr. Astaire would be gliding up toward the commissary. There was a little jaunty lilt in the middle, and he had a towel around his neck. He wore a rope instead of a belt. His pants were a little short because he would show his sock, which showed his feet, that were always in movement. . . . I watched this genius dancer glide by, and he sort of tipped his hand to me, to his forehead, in a little smile. He was just so friendly."

Uan Rasey, one of the most respected trumpet players who ever lived, had a contrary impression of Astaire. Rasey was a featured soloist with the MGM Symphony Orchestra. He recalled that Fred went through five rehearsal pianists in two weeks on *Three Little Words.* "He would rehearse for months on a picture with individual pianists. He was so reserved and icy," said Rasey. "He would come in and work for five, six hours. He would acknowledge the band [when we did prerecording], but that was about it. I worked with him on several movies after that and on his TV specials, too. He was so into his own desire to give a great performance. One time, there was a four-bar break. We came back together, but he wasn't with us. He accused the orchestra of being out of meter! Johnny Green was conducting, but he didn't say anything. Recording with him could take a whole day on a dance number. He would do fewer takes when he was singing. He would find fault with himself more than anybody else."

Rasey was effusive in praising Kelly's outgoing work ethic, however. The well-remembered trumpet solo right after the beginning of the ballet in *An American in Paris,* played by Rasey, caused Kelly to come up and kiss him after the take. "He had all of us come over to the set when he shot that great number," he recalled.

ARLENE DAHL, the eternally beautiful redhead, remembered meeting Astaire when she first came to Hollywood at a cocktail party given by Sir Charles and Elsie Mendl. She next encountered him at a home screening (the forerunner of the so-called Bel Air circuit) of *The Red Shoes* at the Sam Goldwyns. "Fred came alone, and there were about eighteen there for dinner. I discovered that people could be very rude and critical in this very opulent, comfortable place. All the snide comments came from the ladies: 'Oh my God, look at that rear end! Why doesn't she cover it?' Fred turned to me and said, 'This is going to be a classic.' I said, 'Gosh. I'm happy to hear you say that because I think so, too.'" The superstar and the young starlet had tuned in on an artistic level.

Shortly thereafter, Dahl was sent the script for *Three Little Words.* The first day she began work on the "I Love You So Much" number, Fred came up to her and said, "Do you think this [movie] is going to be a hit like *Red Shoes?*"

"I couldn't imagine that a man of his status would say that," Dahl recalled. "Fred was there to wish me good luck. He gave me a big kick and said, *'Merde'* [a show-business equivalent of "good luck"]. He never came on to me, but we were friends. He came to the recording session when the number was prerecorded. He saw me in rehearsal. I made a gesture and he said, 'That's good. Keep that in.' It was something I did naturally. He was very protective of me. I was very grateful to him for that."

Dahl referred to Richard Thorpe, the film's director, as "a very nice man but, as they say in the business, an usher. 'Move this way, that way.' He never gave me any direction at all." She recalled the only time she ever saw Red get upset with Fred was once when he said, 'Oh, for God's sake, let's do it and get it over with.' Fred was a perfectionist. He liked to rehearse, and Red was very spontaneous."

Although *Three Little Words* lacked the obvious production gloss of an Arthur Freed Unit musical, the picture has a warm feeling that comes across even today. The highly romanticized plot didn't dwell too heavily on the struggles of the song-writing team, but it established Kalmar (Fred) as the senior partner. The sincerity and conviction with which Fred and Red sang, backed by only piano or a small group, were among the highlights of the movie.[107] It's no wonder that André Previn received an Oscar nomination for his scoring of the picture.

Fred and Red's effectiveness as partners helped create a favorable critical response to the movie. Otis Guernsey in the *New York Herald Tribune* wrote, "The whole package is made into a cool and breezy diversion." Tom Pryor of the *Times* said, "Mr. Astaire has drawn rich dividends from time and is dancing at peak form." *Variety* contended, *"Three Little Words* was unquestionably Fred Astaire's best picture in years."[108] The London *Evening Standard* went so far as to say, "Vera-Ellen is certainly the best leading lady Astaire has had since Ginger Rogers with the same grace and much the same sense of humor."

In March 23, 1950, less than four months before *Three Little Words* was released, the Academy of Motion Picture Arts and Sciences awarded Fred his first and only Oscar, although an honorary one, "for the artistry that has brought a unique delight to picture audiences and has raised the standard of all musical pictures." The academy had never previously given an Oscar for a singing or dancing performance. Fred chose not to attend the ceremony, most likely because of his fundamental problem with awards and also anything dwelling on his past achievements. He should have received it a decade before, but at age fifty it was certainly still an important honor.[109] Ginger Rogers presented it to Fred's old friend George Murphy, who accepted for him.[110]

DAHL DESCRIBED how she continued to run into Astaire on several occasions: "Fred would sometimes come alone to parties because I guess it was too much bother for Phyllis to get dressed to come. He would come alone if there was a movie he wanted to see. He was very sociable, quietly friendly. He liked the Sam Goldwyns, he liked Jack Warner, he loved the Mendls. Occasionally, I would see him at the farmers' market when Sir Charles would take me to lunch with a few ladies. Fred liked to go there. He was very dapper, and he shopped. I really think he liked to cook because he always had his fresh bread and vegetables."

Speaking of Phyllis Astaire, Dahl commented, "I didn't really feel that warmth and love between them. She was very quiet. I was never invited to their home. I don't think Sir Charles and Elsie were invited there, and they had had Fred to their home numerous times. Phyllis just wanted their married life to be private, and she wanted him all to herself.

"Fred never flirted with beautiful women. He was always a gentleman and beautifully turned out. He always wore the same cologne—I think it was Chanel's Russian Leather. I once asked him, 'What is that beautiful fragrance that you wear?' He said, 'Why, is it too strong?' I said, 'No, it's delightful.' "

Dahl remembered being invited to a dinner party at Jack Warner's home. Warner had discovered her when she was appearing on Broadway in the musical production *Mr. Strauss Goes to Boston,* which brought her to Hollywood. The purpose of the formal dinner party was to convene a small group of prominent male stars who were rabid Republicans, such as Astaire and George Murphy, to discuss backing a certain candidate, the name of whom Dahl couldn't recall, for Congress. Warner was seeking their endorsement and financial support. Over the years, Astaire kept his politics close to his well-tailored waistcoat.

Art Linkletter, the genial veteran TV personality, was there as well. "There were about twelve men around the table. I was the only one who said exactly what I felt, which was 'I'm just meeting this man. I'm not prepared to support anybody yet. I'm going to take all the information we got tonight into consideration.' But when it came to Fred Astaire, he was his usual meek and mild self. He was about as close a person of importance that I've ever come to meet, who was almost a dead duplicate of Mister Rogers. And so when it came to Fred, around the table, he said, 'This is a very worthwhile gentleman, but my [business] manager decides on all the money that I give, and I don't do anything without his doing it.' He just backed off like a grammar-school boy."

Dahl reflected on this fabulous time in Hollywood: "By the end of 1951, I saw the end of the golden age. I had [had] the best of it, but I didn't know that I was a part of it until it came to the end. I saw the end."

Waxing nostalgically, the Minnesota-born actress, of Norwegian descent, said, "I was under contract at MGM from 1948 to 1954. Nothing was as elaborate as Metro. It was like being put on a satin pillow and being manicured and having your hair done, learning the right makeup, the right lessons, and what clothes are best on you. Metro was a finishing school. You learned everything you needed to know about glamour."

LET'S DANCE, the earlier postponed Betty Hutton project, with music by Frank Loesser, beckoned. Hutton, the raucous blonde, was then Paramount's foremost female star. She had recently completed starring in *Annie Get Your Gun,* replacing Judy Garland, at MGM. Combining Hutton with Astaire and Loesser, a song-writer of a goodly batch of popular songs, two of which were Hutton's rambunctious hits "Murder, He Says" and "Poppa Don't Preach to Me," and most recently the composer of the Broadway hit musical *Where's Charley?,* seemed like a natural. But as so often happens, the seemingly star-perfect package did not generate an artistically successful movie with box-office appeal.

Betty Hutton and Fred Astaire were never meant to costar in a musical. This was obvious to the movie audience. Their personal styles of performing were simply incompatible. The master of musical elegance and sophistication was never meant to work opposite the high-volume, frenetic actress, singer, and comedienne. Astaire required his female costar to display some semblance of discretion, which was sorely missing here. Hutton, in addition, revealed no soft side or vulnerability to match Astaire's often understated ways.[111] That made their romantic involvement seem forced. Tom Pryor said it all in his *New York Times* notice: "Of the many partners Mr. Astaire has drawn in the movies, Miss Hutton is the least compatible."[112]

The Hollywood columnist Harrison Carroll, visiting the set one day, was told by Fred that he didn't have to worry nearly as much as he normally did because he knew Betty would worry about everything for him. He spoke to the press glowingly about Betty's energy and talent. Afterward, however, he made it clear to intimate friends how difficult he found working with her.

Fred had certainly worked with nondancers before, but Hutton often wasn't able to deal with his and Hermes Pan's instructions. Having been pampered as the reigning queen of the studio made such a transition an impossibility.[113] More than once she bolted for her dressing room after messing up a dance routine, while Fred was left pacing the set.[114] To add to that, Betty broke the second finger on her left hand during a dance rehearsal when a gun, a prop in the scene, fell out of Fred's hand and hit her hand.[115]

Pan tried hard to duplicate the freewheeling feeling of "A Couple of Swells" in *Easter Parade* in the "Oh Them Dudes" western number. It succeeded in satirizing Easterners who affect Western clothes. The dance, with Astaire and Hutton playing a pair of cowpokes, complete with droopy mustaches, did have its moments as the stars related well to each other in this comical context. But Pan believed, "It was a case of very bad casting. I don't think Fred should have been subjected to a partner who would limit him."[116]

Allan Scott and Dane Lussier adapted a Maurice Zolotow story, "Little Boy Blue," as the basis of *Let's Dance.* The script didn't work and was constantly being worked on, with several rewrites taking place after shooting commenced. The original script, if filmed, would have run 140 minutes; the finished product was 111 minutes. Even at that length, it was full of inconsistencies and incongruous events. The director, Norman McLeod, never did know what to make of it all.

The plot concerned Hutton's unceasing efforts to keep her fatherless child, played by Gregory Moffett, from the clutches of Boston's Back Bay society. This gave Allan Scott the opportunity to take some sarcastic and amusing swipes at high society, with Lucile Watson, amusing as a wealthy dowager, the butt of many of them. Fred played an itinerant hoofer, Hutton's former partner in USO shows during World War II, intent on giving up his dancing career in nightclubs to take up gambling and financial speculating full-time. (The role was reminiscent of Lucky Garnett in *Swing Time*.) In his pursuit of Hutton, he connives to frame her as a gold digger to prevent her from marrying a friend of his, a prominent socialite.

The flawed plot didn't prevent Fred, however, from having two outstanding solo numbers, one of which was the Gene Kelly–like "Piano Dance," conceived by Pan, who convinced Astaire that he could pull off such an acrobatic number. It takes place during a nightclub rehearsal as Fred limbers up while his real-life rehearsal pianist, Tommy Chambers, lays down a bouncy tempo underneath. He starts to tap-dance and leaps atop, inside, and under Chambers's piano. Returning to the piano, he displays his own version of jazz piano. As he begins to wail on the keyboard, the orchestra breaks into "Tiger Rag," which prompts a bevy of cats to jump out from the innards of the piano. Then Fred leaps onto three chairs that topple over gradually.[117] Again, despite his vowing never to repeat himself, this spectacular routine was still somewhat reminiscent of his memorable number in Adolphe Menjou's office in *You Were Never Lovelier*.

In Fred's other solo spot, he sang and danced "Jack and the Beanstalk"—translated into rather clever Wall Street terms while he tells a bedtime story to Hutton's young son. Here's a completely different side of Astaire, relating poignantly to a child. He cleverly made use of a rolled-up newspaper to stand in for the beanstalk. A backward somersault, leading to his falling unconscious onto Gregory Moffett's bed, concludes the number.

Loesser did contribute one winning song, "Why Fight the Feeling." Hutton presented it as a romantic ballad, although her delivery is marred by her overselling the melody. Astaire, then in the throes of his devilish ways, gives her a hot seat by setting her dress on fire! In its reprise, Astaire regrets his history as a ne'er-do-well and realizes at long last he is in love with her. For some reason, their reconciliation dance number lasts less than a minute. Fred demonstrates his suave moves and Hutton appears ready to reciprocate when the scene abruptly ends.

In conclusion, Hutton loses legal custody of her son to Lucile Watson only to have Astaire and Hutton conspire to abduct the boy. They perform in a production number in a tunnel of love aboard a gondola and then on land, dancing jubilantly. Fred pledges his eternal love for her and show business, a strange combination! Watson unexpectedly gives up her claim to Hutton's son. Fred and Betty kiss, and it all ends sort of well.

Astaire kept up his friendship with Bing Crosby by appearing on his radio show. As the uniquely witty veteran comedy writer, and producer, winner of three Emmys, Hal Kanter recalled, "For four years, I was the cowriter of Bing's radio show. When Fred was a guest on the show, I wrote a spot that included one joke. Fred was supposed to say something about their height. Referring to Bing, Astaire said, 'He used to be taller because he used to comb his hair up.' During rehearsals, Bing took me aside and said, 'Let's not make this professionally embarrassing.' It seems that Fred was very annoyed. Bing wouldn't wear his wig around people he knew, but Fred was worried because he thought people believed he really had hair."

AFTER *LET'S DANCE*, Fred needed a first-class movie. He got it in Arthur Freed's production of *Royal Wedding*. The screenplay was written by the extremely talented lyricist of the Broadway smash hit *Brigadoon*, Alan Jay Lerner. Chuck Walters was set to direct the picture. The setting was London just before the royal wedding in 1947 of Queen Elizabeth II and Prince Philip Mountbatten, the Duke of Edinburgh. The film was set for release to coincide with the "Festival of Britain" celebration that began in early 1951. If that weren't enough, the plot concerned a successful brother-and-sister dance team with the light-opera soprano Jane Powell signed to sing and dance opposite Fred.

But before Powell started work on the movie, a series of personal problems beset the picture, centering around June Allyson and again Judy Garland. Allyson, married to actor and singer Dick Powell, was originally signed as Fred's costar and spent ten days rehearsing the dances with him. She soon realized what a taskmaster he could be. She felt weak and nauseous. From her doctor's office, she called Fred to inform him that she was pregnant and couldn't continue. After a brief silence, he asked nervously, "Who is this?"[118]

Freed again moved quickly and replaced her with none other than Judy Garland. Chuck Walters intervened, explaining he couldn't bear to direct Garland again after the difficult experience he recently had with her when she costarred with Gene Kelly in *Summer Stock*. Kelly also explained his unhappiness about having to work with Judy to Dore Schary, then head of production at MGM.[119]

That meant little to the studio, which thought that Garland still had clout at the box office. She was signed for the picture and a new rehearsal schedule was put in place. Garland, however, after working with composer Saul Chaplin on her vocals and enjoying a twenty-eighth birthday party on the set, arranged by Arthur Freed, informed the film's newly installed director, Stanley Donen, the following Monday that she wouldn't be available for rehearsals that week. Freed negotiated with her to rehearse half days, arriving after the lunch break. It didn't matter. Judy didn't show up at all, calling daily with different excuses to explain her absence. She was fired from the picture. The next day she slashed her neck with a broken bottle in a suicide attempt.[120] On June 17, 1950, her career with MGM was officially over.

According to Donen, "It was never Fred's style to complain." One can be sure, however, he was inwardly furious at Garland, especially after having put up with the difficulties she caused during the filming of *Easter Parade*. After eighteen years the shock and hurt of Dellie's leaving the act to marry Lord Charles Cavendish would still not go away.

Actress and singer Kay Thompson, a mentor of Garland's and later of Judy's daughter, Liza Minnelli, contended, "Fred you'll expect is going to be walking in a spring garden, a wonderful man, who's going to be so polite. He was none of that."[121] Thompson's curt observation was perhaps based on Astaire's reported remark to Hermes Pan, regarding Garland, "It's better for that woman to drop out now than when we are actually shooting. I should never have agreed to working with her again."[122]

LERNER CAME UP WITH THE IDEA of having the plot of the film concentrate on Fred and his sister, who was also his dancing partner. This was after Fred reminisced with him at length about the delightful years he had spent with Dellie in vaudeville, on Broadway, and in London. Lerner took this premise one step further and embellished upon it by having art imitate life in arranging for Jane Powell, playing his sister, to fall in love with a dashing English nobleman (Peter Lawford), while Fred simultaneously courts an English redhead, Sarah Churchill, who plays the daughter of a proprietor of a pub, but who in reality was the daughter of Winston Churchill. (The impact of *The Red Shoes* had at first caused Fred to seriously consider the film's lead, Moira Shearer, as his love interest in the movie until he realized the complete disparity in their dancing styles; "I know she's wonderful, but what the hell would I do with her?")[123] The two couples wind up getting married the same day as the nuptials of Elizabeth and Philip. So as not to confuse British audiences into thinking the movie was a documentary, the title of the film was changed in the UK to *Wedding Bells*.

Romance was incidental to the plot. The love affair between Fred and Churchill had none of the traumas in the Ginger Rogers films. *Royal Wedding* didn't even have a song or a song-and-dance number with Fred and Churchill. (Stanley Donen admitted that Sarah "had zero sex appeal. She ended up throwing a wet blanket on the whole movie.") The characters of Tom and Ellen Bowen (Astaire and Powell) succeeded in re-creating the mutual dependency and casual bantering that were key ingredients in the relationship of their real-life counterparts.

Burton Lane, a born melody maker, who had recently triumphed on Broadway in *Finian's Rainbow,* was hired to write the score with Lerner. Shortly before shooting commenced, Fred requested that another vaudeville number be added to the movie, recalling the success of "A Couple of Swells" in *Easter Parade.* Lerner came up with a priceless song title. The result was the highly successful "How Could You Believe Me When I Said I Love You When You Know I've Been a Liar All My Life?" The enjoyment the number brought to Astaire and Powell in performing it is absolutely palpable.

But Lane and Lerner offered much more. Among their other songs were "Too Late Now," a reflective ballad that became a hit record for Jane Powell, and "The Happiest Day of My Life," on which Fred played piano behind Powell. Then there were the other dance numbers: "Every Night at Seven," which opens the movie and establishes Astaire and Powell as a dance team; "Sunday Jumps," a memorable solo piece for Astaire, who romps around a ship's gymnasium exercising and ends by dancing with a hat rack; "I Left My Hat in Haiti," a torrid Latin dance number, which was a prerequisite of practically every 1950s film musical, which spotlighted Astaire backed by a dancing chorus; and "Open Your Eyes," another comical number with Fred and Powell slipping and sliding across the dance floor while performing during a storm aboard a transatlantic liner. This evoked a nostalgic moment for Fred: the same thing had happened to him and Adele while dancing on the *Aquitania* en route to Europe.[124]

Then there was the sophisticated "You're All the World to Me," often not given its due as a formidable song, which could have passed for a Cole Porter composition: "You're like Paris / In April and May / You're New York / On a silvery day." Burton originally debuted the melody in the 1934 Eddie Cantor film, *Kid Millions,* under the title "I Wanna Be a Minstrel Man," which was performed by the Nicholas Brothers. Lerner's lyric was cleverly romantic and sophisticated.

Rightly or wrongly, this number, a great personal favorite of Astaire's, is arguably the most talked about dance number of his entire film career. He literally danced on the ceiling. Though the film's dance director was Nick Castle, it was Stanley Donen who choreographed this epic number. Donen related that the number's inspiration tracked back seventeen years to his first exposure to Astaire in *Flying Down to Rio.* Donen observed, "He performed as though he were without gravity."[125]

Donen contends the idea for the number was Lerner's, but Fred claimed it was his. Lerner, in his autobiography, *The Street Where I Live,* said that it came to him in a dream: "One night I dreamed that Fred was dancing up the wall across the ceiling, and down the other wall. I mentioned it to Arthur [Freed] the next day." Fred wrote in *Steps in Time,* "I found a spot in *Wedding* for my upside-down-on-the-ceiling-and-around-the-walls dance, which I had planned for some time." He also said that the idea had awakened him at 4:00 A.M. (just as the genesis for "Say, Young Man of Manhattan," the antecedent to the "Top Hat" number, had originally come to him in a dream).[126]

The scene was set up by Fred's ripping out Churchill's photograph from the billboard in front of a theater. He returns to his hotel room, removes his jacket, paces the floor, settles into an armchair, snubs out his cigarette, and continues to admire the picture of Churchill. The photograph was magnetized and stuck to a metal floor lamp. In reality, Fred is sitting in a steel-reinforced cylindrical chamber approximately twenty feet in diameter, similar to the spinning barrel at Coney Island. Donen's camera was attached at the base of the revolving cylinder, which the crew referred to as the Squirrel Cage. Fred called it the Iron Lung. Donen said that the camera rotated full circle along the barrel's circumference as Fred performed each step of his 360-degree tap dance.[127] The cameraman, Robert Planck, was strapped to an ironing board, the camera tied to him, and away he went shooting Fred from every angle.[128]

"The room's starting to move now," Donen explained, as he watched Astaire step out of his chair and trot around it. Fred snaps his fingers, slaps the desk, then starts to alight on the sofa across the room before landing on the wall. He switches to the other wall, on the audience's left, bounces back to the right wall, landing higher this time, until he's fully engaged in dancing on the vertical surface. He adds a few bounces on the sofa until he reaches the ceiling, moves around the chandelier, and continues his leaps. He is never acrobatic like his old friend Douglas Fairbanks, but more inventive.[129]

Donen added, "Fred's coat was sewed to the chair, and the chair was screwed to the floor. The draperies were made of wood. There's nothing soft in the shot. There was only one cut during the sequence—while he is at midpoint on the wall necessitated by having to change the roll of film. We rehearsed this [scene] for weeks and filmed it in one morning. . . . We were literally through with the entire sequence by lunch."[130]

* . * *

IN RETROSPECT, Lerner was highly critical of his work in *Royal Wedding,* saying, "My contribution left me in such a state of cringe that I can barely straighten up." Yes, *Royal Wedding* was far from being in the same league as his *My Fair Lady* and *Camelot,* but certainly comparable to *Paint Your Wagon* and *On a Clear Day* and far superior to *Coco.* Donen agreed with Lerner's view of his own work, saying, "The story is not interesting. You look at the movie, and you don't care."

What the movie did offer was well-produced, impressive-looking, escapist entertainment, with good songs and a first-rate performance by Fred Astaire and a very good one by Jane Powell. Keenan Wynn added some needed offbeat humor playing twin brothers, both talent agents on either side of the Atlantic.

During shooting, one afternoon at dusk, Astaire approached Lerner, in an even more serious frame of mind than usual, to say, "Oh, Alan, why doesn't someone tell me I cannot dance."[131] "The tormented illogic of this question made any answer insipid, and all I could do was walk with him in silence" was Lerner's reaction.

Powell, who was paid $15,000 for her role in the movie as against Fred's usual salary of $150,000,[132] became an established leading lady as the result of her performance in *Royal Wedding.* The difference in ages on-screen, however, between Astaire and Powell was undeniable. In a later conversation with Robert Osborne, the host of Turner Classic Movies, Powell said of Astaire, "Yes, he was a perfectionist, but everybody was in those days. They wrote that about Fred because there was nothing else to write about him. He was a rather colorless personality . . . what else can we talk about Fred? Well, he's married, and he doesn't go out, so he's a perfectionist."

Despite Powell's remarking of Astaire, "I hardly knew him. I don't know if anybody really knew him," and her claiming that she had insufficient rehearsal time with him because he was tired of dancing routines he had earlier done with June Allyson, she appeared willing and exuberant in their dance numbers. "When Phyllis was on the set," according to Powell, "she was always Mrs. Astaire. . . . She would sit and watch, but never smile. I think she said hello to me once. Astaire was always very boyish with her, almost nervous, which fascinated me, since he was so authoritative otherwise."[133] Powell also said, "In person he didn't have the vitality that you would expect from him."[134]

That certainly wasn't evident in the "Sunday Jumps" and "You're All the World to Me" numbers. John Mueller, writing of "Sunday Jumps," said, "Many Astaire duets include a beautiful and witty transition step, the Astaire double Helix," referring to Fred's habit of circling his partner as if stalking his prey before they front off and dance. "In this duet, Astaire uses the double Helix to begin the dance as he deftly spins his way around the rotating clothes tree and tenderly takes it in his embrace." Mueller also stated, "Astaire's encounters with the weights [in the ship's gymnasium] . . . has its screwball surprises—as when he belts the punching bag with a high kick."[135]

Stephen M. Silverman, author of *Dancing on the Ceiling: Stanley Donen and His Movies,* in speculating how Judy Garland would have fared in working with Astaire again, wrote, "Garland might only have seemed a fascinating but neurotic intruder, no doubt enhancing the backstage production-number elements of the film which are lacking in the final place, but also furnishing the book portion of *Royal Wedding* with more of the one ingredient it definitely did not require, show business artificiality."

The film grossed a healthy $4 million. The newspaper and magazine film reviewers called it "engaging," "light-hearted," "lightweight," and "pleasant." Bosley Crowther returned to harshly criticizing an Astaire musical by writing, "It has one swell number built on the world's longest-titled song, three or four that are good, a laugh here, a laugh there, colored newsreel of the British royal wedding, and so long pal."

FRED WAS SLOWLY but surely running out of suitable, established dance partners. A further problem was that few young dancers were coming along with real star potential. The difference in ages between him and his dancing costars was becoming serious, something that had become extremely evident on camera. The scripts weren't getting any better, either.

The Belle of New York had been offered to him six years previously (and an earlier version of it had been brought to Van Johnson), but since the script wasn't ready, Fred had done *Blue Skies*. In 1952, *Belle* became his next picture. He had enjoyed working with Vera-Ellen in *Three Little Words* and had admired her dancing ability. Chuck Walters was signed to direct his third movie with Fred.

In addition to his usual fee, Fred was given his choice of costar. However, he showed no more enthusiasm in the project than he had heretofore. Walters shared the same sentiment and said that the real reason the picture didn't work was the lack of chemistry between Fred and Vera-Ellen on-screen.[136]

A turn-of-the-century musical about a young female Salvation Army worker and a Manhattan playboy lacked basic appeal. That problem, multiplied by the absence of any spark between the costars (as in *Let's Dance*), allowed the film little chance to become successful. *Belle of New York,* made at a cost of $2.5 million, grossed under $2 million.[137]

Fred did, however, have some outstanding dance numbers, choreographed by Robert Alton, such as "Seeing's Believing."[138] Dressed in top hat and tails, upon meeting Vera-Ellen, Fred falls hopelessly in love with her at first sight, a vivid example of the fantasy element that was so much a part of the film. Shot against a blue screen background, devised by art director Jack Smith,[139] Fred seemingly flies onto the Washington Square Arch on lower Fifth Avenue, over the rooftops of New York, and then into the clouds with her. (The influence of "You're All the World to Me" was obvious.) "Oops" found him dancing through and on top of a horse-drawn trolley car while unconvincingly playing a conductor in his pursuit of Ellen. "Thank You, Mr. Currier, Thank You, Mr. Ives" was a stylish, picturesque number, shot at a cost of $87,000,[140] with Fred and Vera-Ellen dancing through the four seasons against the backgrounds of the famous paintings, which included an ice-skating sequence in Central Park. "I Wanna Be a Dancin' Man" was staged as a more contemporary solo number in which Fred, in a straw hat, wearing a white suit, and wearing spectator shoes, begins dancing on sand, sprinkled on the floor, and demonstrates the full range of his agility. Conrad Salinger created a swing arrangement of Harry Warren and Johnny Mercer's only noteworthy tune from the score.

I spoke to Alex Romero, then a dancer, and a friend of Astaire's, who watched him rehearse the "Dancin' Man" number. Finding himself stuck, Fred asked Romero, "What am I going to do, Alex?" Romero suggested, " 'Fred, we can do it this way . . . and then that way.' Arthur Freed walked in so Fred asked me to show Arthur what I had come up with. Then he said, 'That's perfect, Alex. Now teach it to me.' He put his arm around me. That made me really feel good. I then became the assistant to Robert Alton on *The Belle of New York.* I worked on 'Oops,' in the part where Fred turns the horse around, and Vera-Ellen begins laughing. Before long I became a choreographer. I went on to *Love Me or Leave Me* with Doris Day and designed the famous 'Jailhouse Rock' number for Elvis Presley. Fred made it all happen for me."

Vera-Ellen, dressed in a sequined gown, stockings, and heels, transforms herself into a coquette while singing (ghosted again by Anita Ellis) "Naughty but Nice." She prances around like the Latin Quarter chorine she once was in this number, which takes place at Weber's Casino, where Fred is now a singing and dancing waiter. (A number like this was often thrown into fifties musicals; rather than sexy, these numbers often turned out to be trashy.) It leads into Fred's "I Wanna Be a Dancin' Man."

In the picture, an argument over her shocking appearance is precipitated by Fred before they finally resolve their problems. Fred, attired in top hat, white tie, tails, and spats, and Ellen, in a wedding dress, suddenly break into a dance and float into the sky to end it all.

All of these various dance numbers, which took up more that half of the film's brief eighty-two minutes, had contributed to its eight months in production. Two pictures with Vera-Ellen as his dance partner was again Fred's limit; they never worked together again.

At the beginning of production, the Joseph I. Breen office, in a letter to L. B. Mayer, had objected to the way the Salvation Army (called the Daughters of Right) was portrayed in the script: "Its activities are travestied almost to the point of burlesque." Breen also wrote, "People are humanized by indulging in drinking, whoring [!], suggestive costumes, dancing and risqué singing which were contrasted with the Salvation Army." By July 10, 1951, however, Breen saw fifty-one pages of the final script and saw that it met the requirements of the Code.[141] His only complaint was that the Currier and Ives number didn't run long enough.

Word of the Breen office's tinkering with the script must have spread to New York. The Broadway musical producers Feuer and Martin wired Arthur Freed objecting to similarities between *The Belle of New York* and their musical production *Guys and Dolls.* Freed assured them the film was quite different. He explained, "Ours is a period picture. The mission girl is the only real similarity."

Astaire's jaunty dance numbers and Vera-Ellen's adaptability disguised the film's various shortcomings. Bosley Crowther found her "as graceful and pleasing a dancer as any that has gone before." *Newsweek* contended, "Possibly none of his opposites has ever matched Astaire's personal style as brilliantly." Hollis Alpert of the *Saturday Review of Literature* had a new slant: "Astaire himself is miraculously good in his dances, adding to one of them the kind of excitement Harold Lloyd used to generate on the side of a skyscraper but always dancing when he was doing stunts." In contrast, the *Hollywood Reporter,* while saying, "Vera-Ellen proves to be the most agile and versatile partner that Astaire has teamed with in many years," also pointed out, "Chuck Walters' direction does little to enhance the weak script." *Variety* called it "a mildly entertaining package of song, dance, and comedy, but the grossing outlook is spotty." Alton Cook of the *New York World-Telegram and Sun* said, "Fred has left so many mellow memories behind him in other pictures. It is painful for an old admirer watching him try to palm off such fare as *The Belle of New York.*" Philip K. Scheuer of the *Los Angeles Times* perhaps summed it up best by saying, "The latest Astaire vehicle from MGM remains horse-drawn rather than walking on air. Like its ageless hero, it is seldom, for all its bright and continuous promise, strong on audience participation."

DEBBIE REYNOLDS WAS MAKING *Singin' in the Rain* when Astaire was working on *Belle of New York*. She was not having a particularly good time working with Gene Kelly, who was intolerant of her lack of experience as a dancer. She remembered, "There was a rehearsal hall between Fred and I. He was with his cane, Hermes Pan, and a drummer busy rehearsing next door. No one was allowed in because there was always a security guard at the door.

"Fred Astaire wasn't a talker, and he wasn't a joke teller. He called himself a businessman, an ordinary man, not a dancer. He felt he was a businessman who danced. He didn't like the word 'star.' He loved his ranch, and he looked after his money well, and he loved his sister, his wife, and his children. He didn't particularly care about the business. This was a business [to him] but not necessarily his favorite business.

"I was very young. I was an athlete, a gymnast, but not a dancer. Mr. Mayer put me in the film, much to Gene's disappointment, because he could have had a young girl from Broadway who was an expert dancer and tapper.

"I was on my lunch break, and I was in tears. I had so much to learn. . . . I was learning Gene's style and Gene's steps. I had to do what he would be using in the dances and to work off those specific steps. I hid in the corner under the concert grand [piano] in the corner of the rehearsal hall sobbing because it just seemed so insurmountable, and I could not get all of this accomplished. I didn't want anyone to see me crying because I was brought up that you never quit, and you had to finish what you started."

At this turning point in her early career, a man walked into the rehearsal hall. "I heard a voice say, 'Who is that? What's going on? Who's crying under there?' I didn't want to answer but I said, 'It's just me, Debbie. I'm just taking a moment for myself. I'm sorry if I upset whoever you are.'

"A hand reached down and a man's voice said, 'Give me your hand. Come out from underneath there.' It was Mr. Astaire," Reynolds recalled. "And so I took his hand and he pulled me up. He stood in front of me and took my chin. He said, 'Now, this is not the way we learn. In order to dance you have to suffer and you must give yourself totally to it. It will finally come. Things that are worthwhile are difficult to accomplish, I tell you. Come with me.'"

Astaire took Reynolds by the hand into the rehearsal hall where he had been working. He said to her, "Now, you sit down there and watch me and see how hard it is for an accomplished dancer, how hard it is to come by really great dancing—finding the steps, the combinations. You'll see how hard it is for even me. You'll see that what you're going through is not anything different. You will always have to work this hard, and you will always have to sweat. If you don't sweat, you're not working very hard."

For the next twenty minutes, Reynolds watched Astaire go through his amazing routine. "And when he threw the cane at the drum in frustration and his face turned beet red, and he had reached a point where he couldn't find the combinations, I felt I should crawl back and leave the room," the veteran actress and performer recalled. "Because he glared over at me, as if I was blocking him, and I might have been. By allowing me to watch, he had taught me a great lesson. And I never did quit. I began work and began practicing, and I cried no more."

THE FINANCIAL LOSS SUFFERED by *The Belle of New York* was an early sign that the MGM musicals, even one produced by the Arthur Freed Unit, were not imperishable and perhaps signaled that the golden years were over.[142] The long reign of the benevolent tyrant Louis B. Mayer was coming to an end. American movie entertainment was moving into a new phase. CinemaScope and 3-D films were sometimes successful at the box office, but not always.

Fred, now a mainstay at MGM, continued living his quiet home life. Although Arlene Dahl recalled having seen him several times at dinner parties, Hermes Pan said, "If you could get Fred to attend a party, it was considered the social event of the year." He preferred staying home in Beverly Hills or on his ranch with Phyllis and the children. There he began growing oranges and grapefruit in addition to housing his racehorses. He had high hopes for Triplicate's younger daughter, Stripteaser. He showed snapshots of his horses to his costars and fellow workers as though they were photographs of his children.[143]

At the Blue Valley Ranch he could relax completely. He played his extensive collection of jazz records and practiced on his set of drums to various big-band and small-group recordings. He was always open to reading new scripts, but he had become leery of working opposite young female stars.

Arthur Freed saw the failure of *Belle of New York* as a good reason to update *The Band Wagon,* a proven success as a revue that Fred and Adele had starred in on Broadway in 1931, in London, and on tour. Freed recruited Comden and Green, and paid them $103,000[144] to alter its original concept to a comedy with Astaire, established at the start as a has-been returning from voluntary retirement (the latter does sound familiar!) who jump-starts his comeback by starring in a Broadway musical. Many script conferences followed, including with Astaire, that led to its final version.[145]

As part of its transformation, Freed wanted to title the film *I Love Louisa,* and in another misguided move, for a moment Johnnie Ray was considered for the part that was eventually played by Jack Buchanan.[146] The backstage problems of a musical breaking in on the road, the premise of the film, were based on Betty and Adolph's own personal observations. It also contained references to Astaire's own career, such as when his character, Tony Hunter, returns to Manhattan for the first time in years and inquires, "Where's the New Amsterdam? I had one of my biggest successes there."[147] (Where he had starred in the original *Band Wagon.*)

Though Astaire found Vincente Minnelli a bit ethereal for his tastes[148] (witness their association on the ill-fated *Yolanda and the Thief*), Minnelli was a hero to the studio, basking in the success of *An American in Paris,* released eighteen months earlier, which had won the Oscar for Best Picture. Dancing had certainly been a keynote of that film. In recent years, Michael Kidd had rightfully emerged as a doyen of modern dance choreographers through his work in *Finian's Rainbow* and *Guys and Dolls* on Broadway. He was sought as choreographer by Minnelli and was paid $22,500.

The box-office successes of "catalog musicals" in the early 1950s, making use of the well-established songs of Jerome Kern, George Gershwin, and Nacio and Freed, continued with *The Band Wagon.*[149] The original Dietz and Schwartz score was retained from the Broadway musical with the exception of four songs, but eight of their other songs were added. "By Myself," an obscure ballad from their 1937 London production of *Between the Devil,* which had starred Jack Buchanan, became a standard when it was reintroduced by Astaire in *The Band Wagon.* "That's Entertainment!," written specifically for the picture, emerged as another important song.

The final cost of the production was $2,169,120. It had an expensive look to it. The scenic designer for the musical numbers, Oliver Smith, put his distinctive touch into developing various bright color combinations that enhanced several of these sequences along with his set ideas. For instance, he built a stark background for "I Guess I'll Have to Change My Plan" so as not to distract from the elegance of the two stars, and the elaborate "Girl Hunt Ballet" set was complete with a strategically designed bar and staircase.[150]

Betty Comden said she and Adolph had to balance the writing so as not to make Astaire overshadow Buchanan, often compared in the West End to Astaire, in this number. "The duet they did [in matching top hats, white tie, and tails] was perfect, just perfect," Comden rightly pointed out. She was also proud of their writing the lead into "Triplets," in which Astaire, Nanette Fabray, and Buchanan, dressed in matching bonnets and baby clothes, performed their priceless and well-remembered comedy dance routine on their knees.

Arranger Alexander "Sandy" Courage was justifiably pleased with his version of "I Guess I'll Have to Change My Plan." He explained, "The whole process started with Fred and the rehearsal pianist in one of the rehearsal rooms that was big enough for a piano and that's all, and enough room for Fred to move around. Fred and Jack sang the chorus, and then they went into this little double dance, very soft shoe. I took down whatever movements they made—where they turn, where they go, stop with the cane, all the patches. I had the sheet music in front of me. The rehearsal pianist made a piano score for me in which all the patches are worked and maybe little things like 'deedle, deedle, deedle' and how long it would last on that bar. I took that home, and I started writing to the rehearsal pianist's sketch, which is what it's always been as far as I know in pictures."

FABRAY AND OSCAR LEVANT'S CHARACTERS were based on the real-life Comden and Green. The scene toward the beginning of the movie in New York's Grand Central Terminal, as Fred comes in off the train and is met by a group of zealous fans carrying signs, was based on Betty's similar welcome of Adolph at Grand Central on his return from California, very discouraged. Comden had greeted him with a placard saying ADOLPH, WE'RE YOUR FAN CLUB.

Comden was a serious admirer of Astaire's singing. "I'd rather listen to him than anybody else," she avowed. "There's a casual beauty to the way he sings. It's very natural and unaffected, and yet it's very theatrical at the same time. You know you're in the presence of a theater personality. He's a great, natural performer, and there's a tremendous amount of artistic skill in back of it." She considered his treatment of "By Myself" a classic. "It was a perfect example of his being able to show his vulnerability. That's what made that song enjoy a new life of its own."

Comden cited some basic differences between Astaire and Kelly, from her experience in working with both of them. "Gene was involved in every department, every detail of the movie, as in *Singin' in the Rain* and *On the Town,* in which he starred and codirected with Stanley Donen. Fred, however, wanted to dance and wanted to know what the songs were about. He wasn't as interested in the script, but in *The Band Wagon* he had a big acting part, so the script certainly concerned him. He was wonderful in the picture. And, of course, Gene was more athletic and more physical. Fred, however, had this unusual quality of grace and lightness." Comden agreed, "I must also say there never was any rivalry between them."

Among the problems on the set of *The Band Wagon,* Oscar Levant was coming off one of his heart attacks, and Jack Buchanan was nervous about working with Astaire. Cyd Charisse, playing a ballet dancer, was her usual shy self. Nanette Fabray thought Fred was equally aloof and remote. She remarked, "He was a dictator who made me work harder and longer than anyone." Fred thought otherwise: "I didn't think she disliked me. I thought we had fun joking around the set with Oscar Levant. I think its kind of funny if someone called me snooty and cool. I don't think I ever had that attitude."[151]

But during the filming of the rousing "I Love Louisa" number, Astaire said to Fabray, in accusing her of scene-stealing, "I've put up with that with Betty Hutton. I'm never going to put up with it again." Fabray, aghast, asked, "With what?" to which Astaire replied angrily, "You know what I'm talking about!" Vincente Minnelli instructed Fabray, "Just play it cold." This was after a month of intense rehearsals.

Jack Buchanan got $20,000 for playing the part[152] of the director of the Broadway musical breaking in on the road after Clifton Webb was sought but turned down the role in order to play John Philip Sousa in *Stars and Stripes Forever* at Twentieth Century–Fox.[153] Buchanan's character was supposedly based on the combination of Orson Welles, the scenic designer Norman Bel Geddes, and actor/director José Ferrer. His clothes and the nervous way he smoked were based on Minnelli.[154] The veteran song-and-dance man was suffering from constant dental problems during filming that made him appear unwell.[155]

For perhaps the first time since the celebrated "feathers" incident on the set of *Top Hat,* during the shooting of "Cheek to Cheek," Fred walked off the set and went to his dressing room. He could not resign himself to Minnelli's constantly changing his mind. When Minnelli was shooting a hotel-room scene with the principal players, Fred became so incensed he said, "That's it, I can't think. I've got to get out of here." The tantrum was brief. Fred approached the director to announce, "All right. I'm ready now." That evening he apologized to him. Minnelli acknowledged that he was complex, saying, "I drove everybody crazy. But frankly I hadn't noticed Fred had stormed off. I was too busy concentrating on the scene."

Minnelli said of Astaire, "He lacks confidence at the most enormous degree of all the people in the world. He will not even go to see his rushes. He'll stay out in the alley and pace up and down and worry and collar you when you come out and say, 'How good was so-and-so?' It would be much simpler if he would go and look at them himself, you know. But he always thinks he is no good."[156]

Fabray was quoted as saying, "It was the coldest, unfriendliest—the most terrible experience as far as being in show business is concerned. Nobody spoke to anybody."[157] Yet out of great turmoil brilliant and enduring art is often created. The unblemished reputation that *The Band Wagon* has earned over more than fifty years is a case in point.

Michael Kidd felt that Fred could and should extend himself beyond all the things he had previously done. As Kidd described it, "He was an interesting guy. He actually had the enthusiasm of a seventeen-year-old, but at the same time a naïveté. He wanted to learn, and he was not critical. He requested they get me for the movie, so Arthur Freed did. That was *his* big talent, accumulating talent. When I met Fred the first time, he said, using very specific, simple language, 'Gee, Mike, I'd like to learn some of these jerky movements.' I said, *'Jerky,* I always thought of them as being syncopated.' Then he said, 'Some of the floor work you do.' Anything that was different from standing up being the elegant, musical tap dancer."

Kidd spoke with decided reverence of the perfectly flowing and poetic duet Fred danced in Central Park with Cyd Charisse: "If you look at it carefully, the entire number has only three shots. Three shots the entire number! And one shot he would have the other dancer, Cyd, in a corner over there, he would pick her up, and we'd call cut from the long shot. The next shot would be a close-up of them doing that same twirl. . . . They're very long sequences."

Kidd added, "On the face of it, they are ill-matched. And each of them had their doubts. They were not sure they could go through with this. I must remind you they were two extraordinary, graceful dancers."

This superlative dance sequence perfectly blended the high art of the ballerina and the hoofer.[158] It also moved the plot along and proved that two dancers from two completely different disciplines and generations could successfully mate styles. The sensuality of the number also reveals they are falling in love. Cyd Charisse said, "I know it was one of Fred's favorites. He loved the *sound* of Connie Salinger's arrangement."

According to Anna Kisselgoff, Kidd had once told her, "Astaire was less interested in the emotional motivation. Technique was [what was] important to him. He would say, 'Let's do the steps, let's add the looks later.'" She also pointed out that Gene Kelly was interested in creating the character onstage through his dancing while Astaire was a character.

"To show what a perfectionist Fred was," Kidd related, "every single move in his mind was important. There was an incident in which I said to him, 'Take her [Charisse] by the hand and move her to the left.' His face fell, and he said, 'I can't do that, Mike.' I said, 'You can't do it. Why not?' Fred replied, 'I did that step with Ginger in *Flying Down to Rio.*'"

Kidd related, "In rehearsal, Astaire wore very casual clothes, loose slacks and a shirt. He would have a bandanna around his waist. He did not wear a wristwatch; he had a kind of ribbon, holding his wristwatch together. To me, the most memorable part was watching him walk down the street, going to lunch. You could not take your eyes off him. He was not putting it on. He had this very easy, jaunting walk; sometimes he would be snapping, sometimes he would be chewing gum. I don't think that walk of his was planned to attract attention in any particular way. I think he walked that way."

Kidd admitted he had little to do with the "Triplets" number, explaining it was all preconceived. "I didn't touch it. It was all Fred." Specially made boots made of saddle leather were molded to fit over the three stars' knees as they "danced" the number. The baby shoes were then added to the bottoms of their boots. Their feet and legs were covered with specially made black velvet stockings.[159]

The shooting of the number was further complicated by Fabray's having torn up her leg the day before while rehearsing the "Louisiana Hayride" number. Her injury required stitches. The "Triplets" number began shooting immediately after she had taken a shot of novocaine.

Kidd's wife, Shelah Hackett, his assistant on *Guys and Dolls* and on several movies including the Julie Andrews movie *Star!*, described her husband as "probably the most energetic, lively dancer of any choreographer I can think of." She observed, "Jerome Robbins had a totally different style; he was much smoother, more balletic. Michael's very sharp and angular with uncontainable energy, quirky and just bursting with edge. It does reflect his personality, and it usually has humor." Hackett added, "There is one movement Fred Astaire did in [the] 'Shine on Your Shoes' [number] that every time I look at it, it looks so much like Michael. Most of what Fred is, is usually Fred Astaire, but [I see] a couple of movements, and then I think that's Michael—the way he kind of leans his head into his arms."

"Shine on Your Shoes" was indeed an inventive number, which takes place in a shoeshine parlor on Forty-second Street. (Fred had suggested to Kidd, "Gee, I would like to do it with a black man.") The bootblack, LeRoy Daniels, was authentic, as his stand was in downtown Los Angeles at Sixth and Main.[160] He was also a good tap dancer. For his one week of work Daniels made $350. His brisk shoe-shining motivates Astaire and lifts up his spirits after he has come into Manhattan and become disillusioned by how much it has changed. His frustration increases as he encounters newfangled machines in an amusement arcade, which Kidd suggested as a set. While singing the song, Fred mounts the shoeshine stand and uses the chair to do a series of short kicks, then inspired by Skip Martin's jazz chart, he tap-dances around the arcade.[161]

Michael Kidd explained, "He loved drums and always had drums at rehearsal. In 'Shine on Your Shoes,' he wanted to do a little break, kick the shoeshine stand, twirl around, and do it. He had the drummer play *ba, bah, bah-bah*. 'Let's try this. Let's try that.' He rehearsed all morning for that."

Watching him shoot this number was none other than the distinguished English actor Sir John Gielgud, then acting in *Julius Caesar,* on a nearby soundstage at MGM. Gielgud remarked, "He had sweated his way through four gray flannel suits that morning doing that number over and over again. . . . The skill was amazing. I was amazed at his painstaking thoroughness and extraordinary accuracy." This was almost thirty years after Gielgud had seen Astaire perform in *Funny Face* in the West End.[162]

CYD CHARISSE'S EARLY YEARS at MGM had been marked by fits and starts. Her career enjoyed a significant boost from dancing with Gene Kelly in *Singin' in the Rain,* playing a sultry vamp. Charisse was working on a number in Rehearsal Hall C for *Sombrero* with Hermes Pan when Fred walked in, wearing a straw hat. He carried on a polite conversation with Charisse but kept looking in the mirror. Twenty minutes after he left, the phone rang in the rehearsal hall. Arthur Freed was calling to inform her he wanted her for *The Band Wagon.* Freed said, "I assured Fred you look taller than you are. He had to see for himself. You passed."[163] Nonetheless, in one scene in the movie Astaire gauges Charisse's height.

After their "Dancing in the Dark" number, there unfortunately was no romantic follow-up between Astaire and Charisse. The element of romance is thrown away. They rejoin by dancing "You and the Night and the Music" in a rehearsal sequence and then onstage as special effects amusingly go awry in the background.

But the delightfully long-limbed dancer Charisse, playing two parts, as a frightened blonde and a slinky dance-hall moll ("more curves than a scenic railway"),[164] was given her screen-defining moment in the famous thirteen-minute-long "Girl Hunt Ballet." Astaire referred to her as "a beautiful mover." In the guise of a hipster—white suit, black shirt, with a white tie, Fred plays Rod Reilly, a take-off on the tough-detective genre patented by novelist Mickey Spillane. It provided Fred with the opportunity to assume a sexy on-screen persona for the first time and was a role he loved.

The concept for the number was devised by Michael Kidd and cost $300,000 to film.[165] Without his taking any writing credit, the amusing tongue-in-cheek dialogue, read as a staccato voice-over by Astaire, was written by Alan Jay Lerner. Michael Kidd described his creation: "I wrote the scenario as a kind of chase in which Fred, following a series of odd clues, would track Cyd in several bizarre locations. The locations were chosen with an eye towards lending themselves to a unique cinematic design. The final scene took place at Dem Bones, a highly frenetic version of a jazz joint. The denizens, all potential killers, moved in their own highly stylized, syncopated manner. Fred, moving to a heavy jazz beat, enters in pursuit of the real killer. I worked out the scene with Fred and Cyd along with Alex Pat Daniel, which ends with a big fight.

"Where we got to the fight, or maybe even before it, I discovered something interesting: Fred wanted me for the picture, but he was uneasy. I wasn't Hermes Pan. He just sat on the bench while I was working out the fight with all the other guys. Everything was happening in rapid succession. Each detail had to be worked out carefully. Fred said to me, 'I don't know if I can do that, Mike.' And then I'd say, 'Suppose you do something like this,' and I would get up and try something on the bar. So finally at five o'clock he would say, 'You gonna do much more, Mike . . . is it okay if I go home now?' I realized I would never get the number done if Fred sat there all the time."

Kidd took matters in hand. He told the other dancers that they had to work on all the movements he desired before Fred came in the next day. When he arrived, Kidd showed him exactly what he wanted him to do. "I showed him by working with the other dancers," the late choreographer recalled. " 'That's a good idea,' he said. 'Okay, now I'm not sure, but maybe something like this.' And [then] I'd do the next part." Kidd instructed the other dancers what to do next. "Fred would say, 'Gee that looks pretty good. I think I'll try it.' So in essence that whole number was set between the hours of five and six [in the late afternoon]. I never worked so fast in my life."

Pat Denise, who was the dance-in for Cyd Charisse on the movie, remarked, "Fred worked from nine to four. Michael made us come to the studio after five. Fred did not like to see something being made or molded. And Michael knew this, so he wanted the stuff to be polished before he showed up the next day."

"With Fred Astaire you could shoot the whole scene intact," Kidd added. "He would learn it so perfectly. There was no improvising. That's the way it was done. By the time we had finished rehearsing, he knew the number so perfectly we could do it over and it would always be exact, and it looked spontaneous." This well-crafted and well-performed number served as the final sequence in the musical within the musical.

Kidd concluded, "Fred was the most natural dancer I've ever seen rather than a studied dancer. Every movement was thought out. It all stemmed from his early training in vaudeville and on Broadway."

"That's Entertainment!" was reprised (in a version written specifically for the movie) by the principal players, moving toward the camera as a curtain call: "A show that is really a show / Sends you out with a kind of a glow / And you say as you go on your way, 'That's Entertainment!' " It certainly was that and provided the perfect ending.

On the film's release, it appeared as though every element—the plot, the witty dialogue, the music, the dancing by Astaire, the launching of Cyd Charisse as a highly sensuous dancing star, and the superlative production values—made *The Band Wagon* the blue-ribbon-prize musical of MGM's golden era of musicals. In the first three weeks of its July 9, 1953, world premiere engagement at Radio City Music Hall, it was the biggest-grossing film ever to play the theater. The picture wound up making a profit of approximately $4 million.[166]

The critical acclaim was in the same vein. *Newsweek* put Fred and Cyd on its cover and called the movie "a gala and witty enterprise with a brisk and funny original script. . . . Astaire is to show-dancing what Léonide Massine was in such elegant ballets as *Blue Danube*—all formal elegance, a steady demonstration of the exquisite restraint which permits the electrifying release." *Collier's* chose the movie as its Picture of the Month. Bosley Crowther's pronouncement said it all: "*The Band Wagon* is a show that respectfully bids for recognition as one of the best musical films ever made." Archer Winsten echoed Crowther's accolade by writing, "No mistake about it, a review of *The Band Wagon* boils down to a collection of superlatives. It is the best musical of the month, the year, the decade, or for all I know, of all time." Otis Guernsey in the *Herald Tribune* called it "a big load of musical comedy pleasure." William Hogan of the *San Francisco Chronicle* wrote, "Comden and Green have come up with the wittiest satire on show business ever to hit the screen."[167]

Some observers felt that Fred's performance was his best since *Top Hat*. It had been a long time since he had performed such a wide range of superb dance numbers as *The Band Wagon* offered. But that was of little importance to the studio. Fred's MGM contract was up, and no new contract was offered him. With the plunge in box-office receipts, Hollywood was panicking. Term contracts were suddenly a thing of the past. Paramount wanted him to again star with Bing Crosby, in *White Christmas,* but Fred was in no hurry to rush into another picture so soon. No other studio came up with individual film ideas for him.

Retirement again became a serious option for Fred. He was quoted as saying, "I would just phase gently out of the action for a while, return minus the old dancing shoes and possibly go into producing when I got the urge."[168]

At that moment, when it appeared he was being forgotten by the movie industry, Harry Friedman at MCA (Leland Hayward had left the agency business for Broadway to produce *Mister Roberts*) called with a firm film offer. Darryl F. Zanuck had seen Fred and Phyllis dining at Romanoff's in Beverly Hills the night before and suddenly had the thought that he should play the lead in Fox's upcoming musical version of *Daddy Long Legs*.[169] There was talk of casting Leslie Caron as Fred's costar, an idea that intrigued Fred even further.

WHILE IN NEW YORK for the opening of *The Band Wagon,* Fred and Phyllis attended the races at Belmont Park. One afternoon, Phyllis complained of a headache. She said she felt dizzy and faint. She requested that they leave early. The next day she was fine and turned down Fred's suggestion of seeing a doctor. In the next months, she suffered similar attacks, one at the Santa Anita racetrack. Soon after that, she failed to attend an event at Ava's school and asked to be excused from a dinner date that she and Fred had made with Cole Porter. She underwent various tests, which indicated that she required major surgery for cancer of the lung.

The first operation lasted five hours and took place at St. John's Hospital in Santa Monica on Good Friday in 1954. Fred's old and dear friends David Niven and Hermes Pan sat with him in the waiting room. Freddie, now in the air force, rushed home on emergency leave from Lackland Air Force Base in San Antonio, Texas. The surgery was deemed successful. An unexpected relapse occurred, however. Phyllis was compelled to undergo five weeks of five-days-a-week radiation treatments in downtown Los Angeles, accompanied by Fred.[170] Feeling a bit better, Phyllis joined Fred in spending weekends at the ranch.

Three months after her first operation, she returned to St. John's for more surgery. Fred visited All Saints Church several times during this challenging time, immersed in prayer. Freddie again flew back to Los Angeles. After her hospital stay, Phyllis returned home. Fred was informed that Phyllis had little chance of living much longer. She died at 10:00 A.M. on September 13, 1954.[171] She was only forty-six years old.

Fred described her passing to David Niven: "She lapsed into a coma for several weeks. I knew she would snap out of it. She didn't. She looked like a beautiful child. She never loses her sweet facial expression. Phyllis . . . slipped away from us."

Dellie arrived from Virginia. Neither she nor Ann, now living in the Summit Drive house after having lived with Dellie in Ireland for almost two decades, could console Fred. Nor could Hermes Pan, Sam Goldwyn, Randolph Scott, David Niven, or Fred's other longtime friends who came to see him at the house. Fred had never before experienced a personal tragedy of this magnitude.[172]

Phyllis had been the perfect life companion for Fred. She had vigorously protected their privacy, raised their three children, and invested his money wisely. Her background, her coming from the Eastern, old-money aristocracy that he cherished, offered him the kind of life he always wanted and thrived on. It was the perfect antidote to the vulgarity of show business, a business he well understood but basically tolerated for what it did for him. Show business had provided him the opportunity to display his superlative talent and had made him wealthy, but most of its members were not the kind with whom he and especially Phyllis enjoyed associating.

He had begun rehearsals for *Daddy Long Legs* in July. He ceased when Phyllis's health worsened. Right after her death, Fred told the producer of the movie, Samuel G. Engel, he couldn't possibly do the movie. He said, "The kids are shattered and I'm shattered. The worst thing is that Phyllis wanted me to do this picture. But I can't."

Engel told him going back to work would be the most therapeutic thing for him to do. William Goetz, a friend of Fred's and a staff producer at Fox, also encouraged him to do the picture. For a moment, Zanuck considered Maurice Chevalier as Fred's replacement. In an unprecedented gesture, Fred offered to reimburse the studio for the costs of the production delay. Engel thanked him for his kindness but refused his offer.[173]

On October 16, Fred tearfully returned to the studio, telling Engel, "I don't know if Old Dad can make it, Sam. But I'll try. I'm reporting for work." Fred realized the show must go on.

CHAPTER SEVEN

THE LAST OF THE GRAND OLD MUSICALS

*D*ADDY *LONG LEGS*, a popular 1912 novel by Jean Webster, and a tearjerker, had been filmed twice earlier with Mary Pickford and Janet Gaynor as the ingenue lead.[1] Twenty-four years later it became the basis of a musical. The plot concerned a young orphan who falls in love with her wealthy anonymous guardian, who sponsors her education at an American university. The title refers to the young girl's physical image of her benefactor. This story made it more acceptable for Fred Astaire to have a much younger costar.

Beginning work on his first picture in almost two years, he admired his twenty-four-year-old costar Leslie Caron's professionalism, her surprising ability as a tap dancer, combined with her constant quest to make their dance numbers perfect. Caron was also in complete awe of his work. Their dancing backgrounds were different, however, as Caron had been steeped in classical ballet, having studied at the Paris Conservatory and at one time been a member of the Ballets de Champs-Élysées.[2] This was certainly in evidence in her dancing with Gene Kelly in her American film debut in *An American in Paris*.

The original story of *Daddy Long Legs* was slightly altered by the husband-and-wife screenwriting team of Henry and Phoebe Ephron, the parents of the writer and director Nora Ephron,[3] to allow for Caron's French nationality, and to have the film take place in Paris, where her benefactor (whose moniker is Jervis Pendleton III) is on a diplomatic mission, and New York, where he resides. Jean Negulesco wasn't a musical director, but a well-established filmmaker. As Henry Ephron pointed out, "Negulesco made beautiful pictures—take a look at *Three Coins in the Fountain*."[4]

Though certainly not a rival of *The Band Wagon* in overall excellence, *Daddy*

Long Legs was, despite efforts to change it, a sentimental musical fairy tale that contained several splendid dance numbers. Sentiment was not a favorite theme of Astaire's, but the essential charm of the script won his approval.

Fred had long admired Johnny Mercer's lyrics. Their association dated back to *Second Chorus* in 1940. *Daddy Long Legs* was the only time Mercer contributed both music and lyrics to a movie, with ten songs, such as the Oscar-nominated "Something's Gotta Give." Fred established the song as one of his many hits through the conviction with which he approached the lyrics and his emphasis on conveying its inherent rhythm. This led to Fred and Caron's dancing romantically to the tune on a hotel balcony. Photographed elegantly by Leon Shamroy, the supreme cinematographer, the scene subtly indicates just how smitten he is with her.[5] They continue dancing against a background of Times Square, El Morocco, the Latin Quarter, and other nightclubs before returning to the balcony.

The "Sluefoot" number was a 1950s dance creation featuring considerable leg jolting, arm jabbing, and shuffling like an old Bert Williams routine. Caron said, "It was my favorite number in the film—so much fun to do. I loved the rhythm and the arrangements." "Sluefoot," was a dance specifically created for the movie, such as "The Carioca," "The Continental," and "The Yam" in previous Astaire musicals. In the various dance numbers in the film, it is again evident how Astaire self-consciously disguises the size of his unusually large hands by curling his fingers.

Former dancer Fred Curt, now the wardrobe supervisor at the Pantages Theater in Hollywood, was a dancer in the film. He remembered having "a couple of weeks" rehearsal with the dancers getting the "Sluefoot" number ready for filming. "There wasn't too much movement involved. Fred and Leslie rehearsed by themselves. We rehearsed with Fred the last week. Shooting took four days." Curt saw that one of Astaire's most important filming techniques from the 1930s was still intact. "I found out that he [still] wanted the whole shot full figure, no cutoff. I must say he worked harder than anybody."

Contrary to what other dancers have said over the years, Curt said, "Fred was never aloof. He would always come over and introduce himself. What other major movie star would come up to you and say, 'Hi, I'm Fred Astaire'? He was so disciplined. And if you were disciplined, he loved you even more. Some people get the word 'perfectionist' mixed up with 'temperamental.' "

RAY ANTHONY AND HIS ORCHESTRA backed up the dance numbers taking place at the college dance. "Sluefoot" was a plot device to establish Astaire's comfort in dancing to the music of Caron's generation. The Fred Astaire Dance Studios naturally latched onto it in hopes of creating a national dance craze, but didn't succeed in doing so as Ray Anthony had done with "The Bunny Hop."

"Dream," a favorite song of Fred's, was a nostalgic dance number at a college prom for the costars. But even further, it was the frequently heard background theme for Caron's fantasies. Fred sings one chorus of it later in the picture as a voice-over, but its most effective use was to conclude the film with Astaire and Caron in a sublime ballroom-dance sequence.

The French choreographer Roland Petit offered two dream ballets, "Daydream Sequence" and "Dancing Through Life." Like Caron he was eager to work with Astaire. Some speculated at the time that Zizi Jeanmaire, who had made an impact starring opposite Danny Kaye in the 1952 Samuel Goldwyn film musical *Hans Christian Andersen,* would get the female lead role. Jeanmaire had starred in several of Petit's ballets and had become his wife in 1954. Previously, Caron had danced to his choreography in the film *The Glass Slipper* and had appeared as a guest star with his Ballet de Paris troupe on Broadway.

During Caron's daydreams as a college student, with background music by the veteran screen composer Alex North, she envisions her sponsor, who is known to her only as John Smith, in many guises. First, he is seen as a Texas oil millionaire, then as a tango-dancing playboy wearing a monocle and a mustache, dancing with her. The former guise allows Fred the rare opportunity to perform a solo comedy dance routine while attired in a cutaway suit, western string tie, ten-gallon hat, cowboy boots, and spurs. He seems to relish dancing bowlegged and on the outside of his feet.[6] (For the first and only time in a musical sequence, his voice was dubbed; the familiar bass voice of Thurl Ravenscroft replaced his.)[7]

Fred's tango display finds him dancing with nine admiring females including a young dancer named Barrie Chase, wearing a blond wig, who was paid $750 a week as a "specialty dancer" on the picture. The number ends with Caron dancing a ballet routine as Fred embellishes several intricate steps and hovers over her as her guardian angel. Although Caron felt this ballet was Petit's best work in the movie, his choreography in the balletic dream sequence was clearly at odds with Astaire's dancing style. With the assistance of David Robel, Astaire designed his own choreographic movements.

Caron's second dream sequence (the so-called "Nightmare Ballet") takes place two years later. It takes on an international aspect as Caron continues to question the true identity of her Daddy Long Legs, though without realizing it she has already met Pendleton and fallen in love with him. Various newspaper stories are shown that chronicle his travels, which causes her to imagine herself as a ballet dancer in the Paris opera, as a slinky siren in a Hong Kong boîte, and lastly as a striking carnival dancer, dressed appealingly in a costume inspired by the pantominist Pierrot, in a Rio de Janeiro street carnival. She is pursued by three exaggerated Daddy Long Legs figures on stilts. No matter where she dances, Astaire's character eludes her.[8] Considering Petit's two extended ballets, one wonders if they were really designed to fit the movie.

Filming began on the second ballet, at a total cost of $120,000, which featured Caron and much less of Astaire, thus allowing him the luxury to slowly grow into his character while grieving. "Fred used to sit down during a rehearsal and put his face in a towel and just cry," Caron said.[9] "He talked about what a sweet person Phyllis was. I think he was grateful to be working. I still remember how he enjoyed talking to the crew about racehorses." He was fully prepared when "Something's Gotta Give" and "Sluefoot" were filmed next, where he was in his element.

Jerry Jackson, for several years one of the leading movie and television chorus dancers and who was Hermes Pan's assistant on several projects, including *Finian's Rainbow,* commented, "For me, Astaire was the gold standard of tap while Caron was an exquisite ballet dancer. Their two styles could not be more diverse. However, as Leslie's guardian angel in the dream sequence, Fred performed Roland Petit's choreography effortlessly. He managed to partner Caron, who was on point, without compromising his signature style. In 'Something's Gotta Give,' the ball was in Fred's court. Although Leslie executed the steps with precision, her movement at times had an influence of the nineteenth century and seemed a bit out of place. I believe she fared better in the delightful 'Sluefoot,' an energetic contemporary number in which she and Fred had a chorus of college students and seem to be on the same page."

The French actress and dancer, however, contended, "Fred was easy to dance with just as it was easy to dance with Gene. It was then a wonderful and inspiring experience working with Fred. Fred danced right on the beat with real élan. I didn't have any trouble working with Fred because I had been trained in modern dance." But she also admitted, "He could be angry and crabby if anything went wrong. For instance, he once stepped on my foot during a number, and he yelled at me. I yelled right back at him."[10]

Caron actually did more dancing than Astaire in the movie, and her work is even more impressive than in *An American in Paris.* In an interview with dance critic Anna Kisselgoff, Caron made an interesting observation concerning Astaire's work: "When you are dancing, you don't have to huff and puff and get out of breath. You have to control your stamina. He [Fred] *phrased* his breath with the dance phrase. That's why he looked so smooth. He was controlling. That's what training gives you. In a sequence, he times his breath to go along with the phrase. He was never out of breath. He had an incredible constitution."

* * *

RAY ANTHONY'S BAND was featured in the movie as a result of its having enjoyed great success with his dance records and having been voted the number one band in the country. He recalled that "Sluefoot" was shot in one day. "We prerecorded our part for Fred, Leslie, and the other dancers. In front of the camera, we had to play exactly what we'd just recorded. No afterthoughts, no improvisations, not a single added hot lick, or you don't synchronize."

Anthony, then referred to as "Cary Grant in B flat" [due to his resemblance to Grant] had worked at Fox in *Sun Valley Serenade* thirteen years earlier as a member of Glenn Miller's trumpet section. Since Astaire had long been especially fond of the swing bands, he enjoyed having Anthony's aggregation play behind him. "He was serious about his love for big bands," Anthony affirmed.

"Working with Fred was easy as pie," Anthony said. "He was an easygoing hard worker, but disciplined for what he had to do. He rehearsed a lot with just a drummer on a lot of things. I believe it was Roy Harte. When I think of Fred Astaire, I think of him dancing and hitting the drums, particularly the bass drum with his feet [*Easter Parade*]. Of course, I get to see quite a few of Fred's old musicals since Hef [Hugh Hefner] sometimes plays them at the Playboy Mansion on Friday and Saturday nights."

Still active at eighty-five, Anthony recalled that the extremely talented arranger Billy May had contributed the sterling arrangement for "Something's Gotta Give" and probably "Sluefoot" as well. May had complained to trumpeter Uan Rasey of the experience, remarking how studious and reserved he found Astaire. Well-known for enjoying himself in the recording studio, May said, "Someday he will become human."

The Emmy-winning and Oscar-nominated composer and arranger the late Earle Hagen, on the other hand, enjoyed dealing with Astaire on the movie. "I first worked with Walter Ruick, Fred's rehearsal pianist. I took down what Walter was doing, and I sketched out what I wanted to do. It was a solo dance number for Fred. I used a big orchestra. I talked it over with Fred. He was knowledgeable and enthusiastic. I basically orchestrated the number exactly the same as I told him I was going to do. He was one of the few dancers I ever worked with who didn't change his mind on the stage."

As we have seen, Astaire had enjoyed showing off his ability as a drummer in previous films. Here he opens the picture singing the verse of "The History of the Beat" before playing the brushes, which establishes his love for jazz and its various progressions, before he breaks into an exuberant but brief tap dance. His drumming is complemented by a pipe clamped tightly in the right of his mouth.

Playing drums somehow establishes him as the wayward son of a snobbish wealthy family. Any relatively experienced observer of jazz can, however, see that his drumming technique is scarcely in line with his other more obvious musical talents.

His drum solo is interrupted by the arrival of his nervous business manager, Fred Clark, a master of double takes in so many comedies of this period, who is constantly attempting to head off Astaire's unconventional ways. The blunt-talking Thelma Ritter, a natural scene-stealer, delivered one of her usual memorable comedic turns, complete with outrageous wisecracks, playing Fred's secretary, who constantly acts as Caron's fervent booster. (Nominated an unprecedented six times for an Oscar, Ritter never took home the prized award.)[11]

One day, while visiting Fred on the set, Noël Coward insisted on meeting Ritter. He said, "That marvelous woman, that superb artist who has never made a wrong gesture in any scene, I'm a devoted fan who wouldn't miss a picture she's in."

Astaire was pleased with the script as well as the entire production. He especially relished the risqué side of his character. He objected, however, to doing a romantic scene Henry Ephron had written for him with Caron to conclude the "Something's Got to Give" number. "That love scene," he said, "I can't play it. Cary Grant can play it. I can't. I don't make love by kissing. I make love by dancing." (Some ingrained habits never cease.) Instead, he ended the scene by some grand improvising. He jumped onto a room-service food cart in the hallway and glided away.

The sophistication of the Ephrons' writing was on display in the scene that follows when Larry Keating, playing the American ambassador in France, disapproves of Pendleton's behavior with his young admirer. This was a cut above the kind of dialogue one usually finds in a musical film of this period. The expertise of the acting by Astaire and Keating also indicates why both succeeded as long-time seasoned actors.

Leslie Caron said of Fred, "He was intelligent, and I think the ones who get carried away with their fame are not the greater thinkers. Fred was of the period when your duty, if you were to be paid, was to entertain. You were not allowed to bore people, to give them something slapdash."[12]

Actress Terry Moore, probably best known as supposedly having once briefly been married to the reclusive billionaire Howard Hughes, was then under contract to Fox. At the time of *Daddy Long Legs,* in which she was the second female lead, Moore was developing a Las Vegas nightclub act with three male dancers. She contends that this training prevented her from being intimidated by a dancing interlude with Astaire in the "Sluefoot" number. Unfortunately, according to Moore, most of this footage was excised from the film's final cut.

She recalled, "Fred was extremely lonely and forlorn during the early part of shooting. He spoke to me at length about how much he missed Phyllis." Moore speculated, "If Fred had approached me at another time in my life, I would have been interested in dating him. Like Howard Hughes, I felt that Fred never totally grew up, but I must say his gentlemanliness and kindness made him one of my all-time favorite people."

When Fred was seventy-two, Caron was in Los Angeles with her then husband, the actor and director Michael Laughlin. She called Fred and asked if she and Michael could come over to meet him. Fred invited them to his home. Fred wanted her to meet Ann. "I couldn't believe his mother was still alive," she remembered. Ann, then ninety-three, was blessed with a healthy complexion that added to her overall beauty. Caron was greeted by Ann's saying, "Oh, you're the little girl that danced with my Fred." The actress recalled, "She talked about him as if he was only a teenager or something like that."[13]

The movie was shot in CinemaScope, a trademark at Fox for its most important film releases, which meant that both sides of the screen had to be filled in, something readily apparent in the dance numbers staged at the college prom. The CinemaScope lens underlined the size of the college gymnasium where the "Sluefoot" number was staged, and the vast expanse of the balcony in "Something's Gotta Give," which allowed Fred and Caron additional space to dance. In one scene in Fred's office, what appears to be a wide-screen TV set is on display. How that got into a 1955 movie is indeed puzzling.

Fox also came up with a new color process called Deluxe, which caused all the colors to appear as pastels, thus preventing the musical numbers from achieving the radiant look that was a highlight of *The Band Wagon*.[14] Jerry Jackson, however, insists, "I remember being so impressed by the remarkable art direction in the dream ballets. The invasion of vivid colors and dynamic shapes was so startling that it influenced several numbers I created for the *Folies-Bergère* in Las Vegas years later."

WHEN THE MOVIE WAS RELEASED, Fred agreed to help sell the picture by doing publicity in New York. This meant television exposure by making nonperforming appearances on the classic panel shows *What's My Line?* (as the mystery guest), and *I've Got a Secret*. His "secret" was that he loved playing drums, which he did with the show's trio. He also took a bow from the audience on the *Ed Sullivan Show* and did a brief tap dance with a golf driver. He was aware that through such exposure 50 million people saw an entirely new side of him along with prominent mentions of the movie.

The usually laudatory New York film critics had slightly disparate views of *Daddy Long Legs.* "At 55, Fred Astaire remains head man among American hoofers. His dancing is as graceful and as effortless as ever" was *Newsweek*'s appraisal. William K. Zinsser in the *Herald Tribune* followed suit by writing, "There's something about Fred Astaire that is always youthful, and he is ideally suited to this bright song and dance version." In contrast to this kind of praise, *Time* said, "Fred and Leslie dance prettily when separated, but when they get together the ballerina looks about as comfortable in a two-step as Fred would in a tutu." John McCarten of the *New Yorker,* who had admired Fred's work previously, contended, "Although a capable enough practitioner of ballet, Leslie Caron is no Ginger Rogers when it comes to picking them up and putting them down in the breezy Astaire style." The respected film critic, however, believed, *Daddy Long Legs* could have given Fred Astaire "one of his best opportunities in ages to display both his *peculiar* charm and his dancing skill," and "with Leslie Caron, Fred Astaire has a dancing partner wholly worthy of his talent."

The picture was profitable domestically, grossing a tidy $7 million on a $2 million investment and did especially well internationally. Fox offered Fred an additional property called *Dry Martini,* but it failed to come together as a movie. He never made another musical at the studio nor another film with Leslie Caron.

Fred took Ava and Ann with him to Ireland, which meant spending considerable time at Lismore Castle resting while Ava went on to Dublin and then London. He had enjoyed wonderful times at Lismore with Phyllis over the years. He was in no hurry to return to California, but he knew he would soon have to go back to making movies to help alleviate the pain of her loss, which was still slow in going away.

Ava perhaps found it easier to get over the loss of her mother. She assumed the role of the lady of the house, looking after her father, while Ann took over running the household. The actor Robert Wagner, Astaire's longtime friend, referred to Ava as "the jewel of his life." Ann, of course, always referred to Fred as Sonny, and she was always Mother to him.[15] Their dueling tempers, however, were sometimes a problem.

After a while, Ann realized the Summit Drive home had too many memories of the past. She convinced her son to put the house up for sale and to purchase a property on San Ysidro Drive, set back from the road, and just around the corner. Dan Selznick said, "I remember learning from my mother that Mr. Astaire was so inconsolable that he couldn't stay in that house any longer because in every room he wept. The house he built in 1959 was a one-story house and had a nice backyard, and Freddie was very sad with all that was going on, but he was also clearly sad to leave the house he grew up in."

The marble house on San Ysidro Drive, off Benedict Canyon, was painted white, was long with two wings, one for Ava and one for him, with Ann's room in the middle, and it included a basement. Three acres surrounded it, and a circular driveway led to the house. Carriage lamps were on either side of the massive door. The library included a backgammon table—a favorite game of the London aristocracy back in the 1920s and '30s—which Fred took pride in playing. The library opened into the billiards room, where he could play pool or billiards. The bookshelves were filled with books on horse racing dating back to 1923, when he had first become addicted to the sport, along with prints and photographs of horses on the walls behind the bar, and bound copies of his movie scripts. His Oscar and Golden Globe, awarded by the Hollywood Foreign Press Association, were interspersed with the Hollywood Park Gold Cup, won by Triplicate. A photograph of his favorite horse hung over the fireplace, along with a small, primitive portrait of a bird wearing a top hat, painted by Irving Berlin.[16]

The dining room chairs were reproduction Sheraton, the silverware was in English Georgian style, and one wall was adorned with Ava's painting of a classically pillared dreamscape. The living room opened onto the swimming pool, which was surrounded by palm trees. A few keepsakes of his past were in the living room—photographs of George and Ira Gershwin and Cole Porter, along with silver-framed portraits of Fred and Phyllis, Fred and Adele, Fred and Ava, Adele and Charles Cavendish. One of the sofas was adorned with a needlepoint cushion, complete with an elegant floral design stitched by Adele. On the reverse side was the delicately stitched inelegant message from its creator: FUCK OFF.[17] Fred's drum set, piano, and record player were installed in the bedroom.[18]

Customarily, Fred awakened at 5:00 A.M. and had one egg for breakfast before working on crossword puzzles. He would then start working on his favorite musical pastime of writing songs at the piano.

He continued his love for golf and was proud of having scored a hole in one with a four iron one afternoon in June 1945 at the Bel-Air Country Club. If he did not have a twosome arranged, he would often play a round by himself. Then there was always the racetrack, Santa Anita or Hollywood Park, where he spent many satisfying afternoons holding court in his box.

He had found a new passion, making nightly radio calls with policemen with whom he had become acquainted through having a shortwave radio license. Ignoring the minor calls, when he heard a call on the emergency frequencies, he would contact the police and join them at the scene of the crime. Hermes Pan said, "He does the damnedest, most unexpected things—and can't explain them. One night, for example, I saw a crowd on a Los Angeles street about four o'clock in the morning. A man had been stabbed and was lying on the sidewalk. A police car drove up, and who should pop out of it but Fred. He had been riding with the cops. When he got lonely or bored at night, he often used to do this—in Los Angeles, New York—in Melbourne, Australia. He really wasn't sure why he did it himself. I asked him once, and he said, 'It's like going on a good hunting trip, and you suddenly run into some excitement.' "[19]

Once, he covered a bank robbery, and the thief was caught hiding in bushes at the back of the building. Astaire was walking back to the police car with the handcuffed thief when the criminal turned to him and said, "Mr. Astaire, can I have your autograph?" So Astaire obligingly scribbled it for him on the same piece of paper he had used to draw the plans for robbing the bank.

Dealing with all kinds of people and situations during his nightly rounds with policemen gave him insights that were later extremely helpful in the latter part of his career as a character actor. It's then perhaps not at all surprising that his step-son, Peter Potter Astaire, later became a policeman in Santa Barbara.[20]

A FIFTY-SEVEN-YEAR-OLD song-and-dance man was becoming an endangered species. Popular music had undergone a radical change beginning in the early 1950s. Teenagers had become enamored with the soulfulness of black music, which was now called rhythm and blues. In January 1956, a former Tupelo, Mississippi, truck driver turned singer, who had carefully and lovingly listened to black music in the Delta, made six guest appearances on CBS-TV's *Stage Show,* hosted by Tommy and Jimmy Dorsey. America suddenly embraced its first and most influential rock 'n' roll (distilled from rhythm and blues) sensation in the person of Elvis Aaron Presley.

Paramount Pictures, however, believed there was still life in musicals using traditional pop-music scores. The studio signed Astaire to a two-picture deal. Another musical starring Fred with Bing Crosby was proposed but never became a reality when Bing departed from the studio.[21] *Papa's Delicate Condition,* a musical based on a story by silent-film star Corinne Griffith about her father,[22] was another film possibility offered Astaire.

Sammy Cahn and Jimmy Van Heusen had become the composer and lyricist of choice during Frank Sinatra's miraculous comeback. They were hired to write the score for *Papa's Delicate Condition.* Cahn, the most frustrated performer of any nonperformer I've ever known, had a lifetime goal to write for Astaire. He came up with a lyric for a tune for which Van Heusen wrote an appealing melody. The song, "Call Me Irresponsible," was geared to the role of the father in the picture, which Astaire would presumably be playing.

"I stood in front of Fred Astaire. It was one of the great moments of my life," said Cahn. "Fred Astaire was one of the single best enunciators. With him the words stand in front of the notes."

As the lyricist was singing the song, Astaire interrupted him. Astaire said, "Stop! This is one of the best songs I've ever heard," according to Cahn. His rejoinder was "Excuse me, Mr. Astaire, this is one of the best half songs you've ever heard. If you'll allow me to finish, please."

When Cahn completed the song, Astaire repeated his enthusiasm. As Cahn got up to leave, Fred said, "Do you know how you [and Jimmy] got this assignment? Because Johnny Mercer wasn't available." Cahn replied, "I consider that a high compliment, Mr. Astaire." "No, I'll give you the compliment. The compliment is that next time Johnny leaves town, I won't be so nervous," said Astaire.

Papa's Delicate Condition wasn't made until 1963, and since the title role called for a drunk, a more natural choice was to cast Jackie Gleason. "Call Me Irresponsible" was awarded the Best Song Oscar the following year. The emerging singer Jack Jones had a big hit with it, outselling Frank Sinatra's version. Fred never recorded the song.[23] In the summer of 2007, Michael Bublé, Canada's pale imitation of Sinatra, revived it.

DURING HIS TWO-YEAR ABSENCE from the screen, one movie script particularly piqued Fred's interest. MGM now owned the rights to *Funny Face,* which he had starred in with Adele on Broadway in 1927, and for which they had originally been screen-tested at Paramount. Arthur Freed and Roger Edens imagined the ideal combination of Astaire and Audrey Hepburn for the movie. *Funny Face,* however, never became a MGM musical. One reason was the recent failure of Gene Kelly's *It's Always Fair Weather,* which caused the studio to pass on another big-budget musical. The consensus at the studio was that the market for musicals was waning fast.

A drawn-out negotiation over *Funny Face* took place. One problem was that Warners owned the rights to the Gershwin songs and had sold them to MGM. The key factor in finally getting the picture made was that Paramount had the unique and refreshing Hepburn under contract. Edens commented, "Coming from *War and Peace* to this, Audrey was all the shrewd businesswoman till the deal was signed . . . but once it was set, she was all for it."

Hepburn was eager to work with Astaire and vice versa. A deal was finally put together at Paramount by her agent, Kurt Frings, to mount the production with Edens and Donen coming over to the Marathon Street studio along with the Gershwin music. MGM was awarded a share of the profits of the film, which turned out to be considerable.

Audrey Hepburn had made her American debut in Philadelphia early in the fall of 1950 in Colette's play, *Gigi,* playing the title role. My mother, Gladys, an astute judge of talent (see her appraisal of Fred Astaire after seeing him in the original *Funny Face* in this book's epigraph), in a telephone conversation said, "Last night, I saw a little girl [she was actually five feet seven inches tall but slender] named Audrey Hepburn, who comes from Belgium. One of the movie studios will certainly sign her up right away. She is going to be a great star." Gladys was right. Paramount signed Hepburn almost immediately, cast her opposite Gregory Peck in *Roman Holiday,* and she won the Oscar in her first starring role. She quickly became a huge box-office star.

What captured America was Hepburn's natural elfin charm, native acting ability, enchanting screen personality, and what is almost nonexistent in a major star—she was genuine. She also had an innate sense of style, something not lost on Fred Astaire. Her initial training was as a ballet dancer. (One of my fondest memories in the theater was watching Hepburn dance over a table when she starred in *Ondine* on Broadway in 1954.)

The script for *Funny Face* was written by Leonard Gershe, a personal friend of Hepburn's, which had been adapted from his unproduced stage musical *Wedding Day,* with a score by Ogden Nash and Vernon Duke, which had originally been sold to MGM.[24] Astaire's role of photographer Dick Avery was based on the majordomo of fashion photography, Richard Avedon, who had been the first important photographer to photograph Hepburn. Gershe and Avedon had been friends in the merchant marine during World War II. *Wedding Day* had been based on Avedon's real-life relationship with a model named Doe he discovered in Greenwich Village, whom he later married. Avedon was retained by Paramount as "visual consultant" on the picture and made Astaire appear convincing as a fashion photographer.

Hepburn played a semibohemian Greenwich Village bookseller who, under Astaire's tutelage, is transformed into a supermodel, decades before the term was conceived. It was basically a Cinderella story with, once again, the *Pygmalion* aspect brought into play to diffuse the issue of the thirty-year age difference between Astaire and Hepburn. (The *Pygmalion* theme was certainly popular that year as the famous Shaw play was transformed into the hit musical *My Fair Lady.*)

Gershe said, "I rewrote *Wedding Day* according to the specifications that

Roger [Edens] felt would be more suitable to the screen. We changed the title to *Funny Face* when Roger Edens came up with the idea of using a Gershwin score. Then Stanley [Donen] came in on it."[25]

A fierce schedule of five weeks of rehearsals and prerecording commenced. An incredible fifty minutes of prerecorded music, composed and conducted by the film's musical director, Adolph Deutsch, was in the final score.[26]

The excesses and superficiality of the fashion world were amusingly satirized by Kay Thompson, in her first costarring role. Thompson's sense of camp was highlighted in one of three Edens and Gershe songs, the zesty "Think Pink," which Donen and Eugene Loring cochoreographed. Jean-Paul Sartre and existentialism, along with "the beat generation," which were threatening the blandness of the 1950s, were also given amusing send-ups as well in Hepburn's "Basal Metabolism" dance number, choreographed by Loring and set naturally in the basement of a smoky Paris bistro.[27]

Funny Face was not the best of the thirty-one film musicals Fred Astaire ever made, but it certainly was the most charming. The reasons for its grand success were many. Its substantial $3,164,000 budget helped pay for the perfect combination of costars; the film featured a stupendous Gershwin score, adapted from the original *Funny Face,* plus "Clap Yo' Hands" from *Oh, Kay!*[28] and "How Long Has This Been Going On" from *Rosalie;* and incredible dance numbers, designed by Loring and Astaire, coupled with superb musical arrangements by Conrad Salinger, Van Cleave, Skip Martin, Adolph Deutsch, and Alexander "Sandy" Courage. That went along with supreme helpings of glamour and sophistication, under Stanley Donen's strong and imaginative direction, collaborating with Roger Edens;[29] and the stylish high-fashion wardrobe worn by Hepburn, designed by Hubert de Givenchy and Edith Head. All of these ingredients gave it the aura of an MGM musical.

Plus we always had Paris, whose milieu was incorporated into the film as a result of three weeks of filming that went overtime due to incessant rain. Donen's quick travelogue of the City of Light, "Bonjour, Paris!," featuring Astaire, Hepburn, and Thompson, duplicated what he had previously achieved in *On the Town.*[30] Footage of the Eiffel Tower, the Champs-Élysées, l'Opéra, the Louvre, Notre Dame, the Seine, Montmartre, and the fountains of Versailles added to the sophisticated look of the film.

IN A UPI INTERVIEW, Edens called Hepburn "a transparency. That's the exact word. I've never been able to find one that suits her. She's the loveliest actress on the screen today."[31]

Fred Astaire and Joan Leslie waltz to Harold Arlen's "My Shining Hour" in RKO's 1943 musical *The Sky's the Limit*. (From the collection of Joan Leslie)

Astaire and his costar Barrie Chase in the foreground during a dance rehearsal with the ensemble during the first NBC special, 1958's *An Evening with Fred Astaire*. (From the collection of Larri Thomas)

Fred dances with Marjorie Reynolds to "Be Careful, It's My Heart" while Bing Crosby accompanies them from the piano in *Holiday Inn* (1942).

Fred wails on the piano while jamming with Freddie Slack's Orchestra on the set of *The Sky's the Limit*. Slack is at right clapping his hands keeping time. The guitarist is Bob Bain. (From the collection of Michael Russell)

The "Sluefoot" number with Leslie Caron, Ray Anthony and His Orchestra in the background, in *Daddy Long Legs* (1955).

Ginger Rogers and Fred Astaire: The "Famous Feathers" scene while dancing to "Cheek to Cheek" in *Top Hat* (1935).

With Helen Hayes in the NBC TV-movie *A Family Upside Down* (1978).

Fred and Barrie Chase rehearse a "dip" number from the fourth
NBC special, *The Fred Astaire Show* (1968). (From the collection of
Sterling Clark)

Left to right: Betty Compton, Adele Astaire,
Gertrude McDonald, and Fred Astaire in *Funny Face*
(1927). (From the collection of Michael Russell)

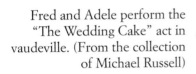

Fred and Adele Astaire in
portraits as young children.
(From the collection of
Michael Russell)

Fred and Adele perform the
"The Wedding Cake" act in
vaudeville. (From the collection
of Michael Russell)

Fred and Adele in *The Band Wagon*
(1931). (From the collection of
Michael Russell)

Fred and Ginger dance to "Pick Yourself Up" from *Swing Time* (1936).

Fred and Ginger recreate one of the dances of Vernon and Irene Castle in the *The Story of Vernon and Irene Castle* (1939), the last of their RKO musicals.

Fred and Ginger in a scene from *Flying Down to Rio* (1933), the first RKO musical to reveal the magic of their dancing.

Fred and choreographer Hermes
Pan (Astaire's longtime collaborator)
confer on the RKO lot over a problem with one of Fred's tap shoes.

Fred Astaire and Gene Kelly, the
masters of film dancing, in *That's
Entertainment, Part II* (1976).

Perhaps the most original number of Fred Astaire's film dancing career: He appears to be dancing on the walls and ceiling in "You're All the World to Me" from *Royal Wedding* (1951).

Astaire dancing with an ensemble that includes Larri Thomas (right rear) in *An Evening with Fred Astaire*. (From the collection of Larri Thomas)

Director Mark Sandrich, a particular favorite of Astaire, kicks up his heels with his star between scenes of one of their films together on the RKO lot. (From the collection of Jay Sandrich)

The dancing chemistry between Fred and Rita Hayworth, especially in *You Were Never Lovelier* (1942), caused Astaire often to label the redheaded star as his favorite dance partner.

Fred and Audrey Hepburn dance the enchanting "He Loves and She Loves" number from *Funny Face* (1957).

Astaire dancing on a stage in Versailles during his 1944 tour to entertain the GIs. Mike Olivieri is the accordionist. (From the collection of Stevie Holland)

Left to right: Hermes Pan, Ginger Rogers, publicist Eddie Rubin, Astaire, and songwriter Hal Borne on the set of *Follow the Fleet* (1936). (From the collection of Rose Borne)

Astaire, Ginger Rogers, and Hal Borne (at the piano) in a scene from *Roberta* (1935). (From the collection of Rose Borne)

Mick Jagger and his then wife, Jerry Hall, and Ahmet Ertegun congratulate Fred after the 1978 Kennedy Center Honors in which Astaire was an honoree. (From the collection of the late Ahmet Ertegun)

Fred and his second wife, Robyn, in their Beverly Hills home, 1980s. (From the collection of Michael Russell)

Fred and his first wife, Phyllis, scan the program at Santa Anita race track, 1948. (From the collection of Michael Russell)

Ava Astaire McKenzie with her father in England, 1976. (From the collection of Richard McKenzie)

The joy that Fred and Ginger communicated while dancing together is depicted in "The Yam" from *Carefree* (1938).

Astaire and Hepburn got along famously, with Hepburn getting first billing. Fred found Audrey "a conscientious, considerate dream angel to work with. . . . No matter what the circumstances, Audrey's always the same kind, vital, but gentle person to everyone. She puts a song over with plus histrionic values and dances up a storm. And as for her acting, well! It's very pleasant to work in something that you really like. I've been fortunate that way in most cases."

He even had four kissing scenes with Hepburn—an all-time record for any of his movies, only to be surpassed in *Silk Stockings.* One wonders, however, if Fred's intense dislike of passionate love scenes ultimately had a longtime negative effect, as he was sometimes criticized for a lack of sex appeal on the screen.

Stanley Donen commented, "What held it [*Funny Face*] together was that both thought the other was near perfection."[32] "Audrey was skillful, and her training helped speed her understanding of what to do."[33] Kay Thompson mentioned, "Stanley had Audrey pretend something from the very start of the picture. He had her do a whole thing of young-girl attitudes towards Fred so she felt, like so many of those actresses, that she was really half in love with him from the beginning."

As part of the 1981 AFI (American Film Institute) tribute to Astaire, Hepburn told of the first day she began rehearsing with Fred at Paramount. "I remember he was wearing a yellow shirt, gray flannels, and a red scarf knotted around his waist, instead of a belt, and the famous feet were clad in soft moccasins and pink socks . . . then suddenly I felt a hand around my waist, and with his inimitable grace and lightness Fred literally swept me off my feet. I experienced the thrill that all women at some point in their lives have dreamed of—to dance just once with Fred Astaire."

Sean Ferrer, Audrey's son, who runs the Audrey Hepburn Children's Fund, told me, "She used to speak a lot about how he was the most elegant guy she'd ever met. She also had this dream of being a dancer that stayed bottled up until she was offered *Funny Face.* She enjoyed making the picture because of her desire to dance, and of course, doing it with Fred made it special. You take that and the love story. I think it was the first time she had to stretch her acting abilities beyond a romantic comedy." Sean also observed, "She was a very insecure person whose shy insecurity made everyone fall in love with her. She was a star who couldn't see her own light."[34]

Rob Wolders, Hepburn's companion for the last thirteen years of her life, said, "I know this from Audrey—that she was more in awe of Astaire than she was of anyone that she ever worked with." Wolders also recalled that she told him as a young woman in Holland she first saw American films shortly after the end of World War II. "Because she was so interested in the dance, everybody was talking to her about this dancer called Freddy 'Ster.' In Dutch, *Ster* means 'star.' She immediately thought Astaire must be Dutch until she saw his films and realized he was an English-speaking performer."

Wolders pointed out, "Astaire was extremely thoughtful of her and aware of her limitations as a dancer. It was strenuous for her, but she wanted that. Astaire allowed her to shine within those limitations. He did not ask her to do anything that they knew she would not be able to do. But I know above all, she didn't want to take the chance of letting down a man like Astaire. So without being prompted, she worked very hard."

Pat Denise, who worked closely with Hepburn on the picture and later as an assistant to the choreographer on the four Astaire television specials, spoke of Hepburn's nervousness. "I taught her Eugene Loring's choreography. She was scared of having to dance with Fred, but she was such an angel you never got the feeling that she was as big as she was. She was a beautiful person. Fred was a gentleman with her."

Eugene Loring, the first dance director of a film to be referred as "choreographer," called working with Audrey "the happiest . . . experience I had . . . with anything. . . . It was just divine working with her."

This mutual respect and admiration Astaire and Hepburn had engendered was evident in their dance numbers together. The rich and sometimes hazy cinematography by Ray June was an example of bold, brilliant, and extensive use of color. A perfect example of Avedon's influence is evident when the title song is sung by Astaire to Hepburn in his darkroom, which leads into an intriguingly staged dance routine. They are bathed entirely in a striking ruby red, except for a white square of glare from an enlarger.[35]

Stanley Donen explained, "Since it was a movie about fashion photography, the use of color became very important, almost of primary importance,"[36] and in a *Los Angeles Times* piece by Philip K. Scheuer Donen said, "There is no real departure in photography, no difference in stock or development, though the Technicolor people gave it special attention."

"Let's Kiss and Make Up" was a tour-de-force solo dance spot for Astaire. It started out as an inspiration of Fred's one stormy morning when he arrived at the studio wearing a raincoat. Looking in the mirror at the rehearsal hall, he began improvising. He quickly saw that his raincoat swayed in an interesting manner as he made a few turns. He began whipping the raincoat around like a matador's cape.[37]

He told a *Newsweek* reporter, "I started with absolutely no ideas until I got to working, or digging, as I call it. . . . I saw how the raincoat looked like a cape! I thought, 'How am I going to get a reason for doing it [making the passes]?' All routines are murder. I'm thinking of the present and the future and not of the past. I don't live in the past. You can't do anything about it anyway. I like to remember it but not feel that I'm still doing it."[38]

In the scene, Astaire attempts to reconcile with Hepburn after he has been turned off by the psychobabble that preceded the "Basal Metabolism" experience. In true Hollywood fashion, he throws a stone against her Left Bank apartment window to gain her attention and climbs up to her second-floor balcony to serenade her. The following dance sequence, a particular favorite of his, reached its climax when he jumped off the balcony onto the courtyard and his umbrella suddenly became both a baseball bat and a golf club.[39] The combination of various elements—a raincoat, an umbrella, and Sandy Courage's dramatic paso doble arrangement—made it all work.

Courage remembered, "We couldn't have the piano play the paso doble because it wasn't going to work. Fred came in when we were recording it. That's when he said that the beginning was too slow, and that was when we fixed it." Asked if he had been complimented by Astaire on the completion of the number, Courage said, "No, no. I don't know if he ever did that with anyone. I can't imagine that.

"Years later, I was watching the Johnny Carson show, and there was Fred as a guest. He was asked what number from his films he would want to do over again, and he said, 'The Spanish number that I did with "Let's Kiss and Make Up."' I was just flabbergasted." Here was a flagrant example of his failure to be satisfied with even something that had been highly praised.

The principal romantic musical moment in the film takes place on the misty grounds of a French chapel. It is preceded by a five-minute sequence of Hepburn being coached and photographed by Astaire as she models several Givenchy gowns against the background of various Parisian locations. At the chapel, Hepburn is radiant in a bridal dress while Conrad Salinger's swooping, romantic string arrangement provides a picturesque backdrop. Fred and Audrey start out strolling as he sings "He Loves and She Loves" to her. They glide onto a raft that floats them downstream. That leads to their dancing, prancing journey through the countryside.

Hepburn had only one dance number of her own, "Basal Metabolism," in which she cavorts with two male patrons of a café and runs the gamut of a lively free spirit. (The silhouette of Hepburn in a Gap TV commercial is lifted from this scene.)

Her singing was an added high point of the picture, as was Astaire's, which helped make a successful sound-track album on Verve Records. Her singing a bit of bebop with Kay Thompson in "On How to Be Lovely" provided a charming moment. Her breathy, English-accented, little-girl voice worked well with the

Gershwin ballads as she sang the lyrics with conviction. (It's unfortunate little of her singing appeared on the sound track of *My Fair Lady,* released seven years later.)

RUTA LEE PLAYED THE ROLE OF LETTIE, Kay Thompson's assistant in the amusing "Think Pink" ("Banish the black, burn the blue, and bury the beige") number. Lee was on the set of *Funny Face* for several weeks and reminisced, "You know, when you're sitting around the set, which is something that does not get done anymore because everything is go, go—you get to see and hear things. I got to know Fred. He was a little remote but very sweet. I had first seen him when he came on the set or into the rehearsal hall of *Seven Brides for Seven Brothers,* my first movie. Usually, he came around with Hermes Pan.

"On *Funny Face,* you had to kind of slide in and just be quiet when Fred and Audrey were rehearsing. Fred didn't want anybody to be there. I sure never thought of him as sexy, except when I saw him move and dance. Then there was something so charming in his sophistication. It was a sophistication that was accessible somehow when you watched him dance. You could feel yourself in his arms. You could place yourself with Fred Astaire, as far as I was concerned. And that part was wonderful. And then to find him more of a sweet and charming man. Perhaps there was an interest in me that I wanted to be recognized. Who knows?

"As a human being, I did find him attractive. As a man I would be interested in romantically—absolutely not. I liked him very much. He patted me on the butt and said, 'That's a nine-bell ass. Ten is for angels.' Now coming from Fred Astaire, that is really something."

THE LINGERING ANIMOSITY KAY THOMPSON had for Fred, based on her belief of his cavalier attitude toward the replacement of Judy Garland in *Royal Wedding,* was reawakened during the shooting of *Funny Face.* Fred had his own problems with Thompson. As Stanley Donen saw it, "Fred never said anything, but it was clear that he hated doing the 'Clap Yo' Hands' number with Kay, and she was uncomfortable. I think the reason is because, [although] he would never express it, he liked women to be extremely feminine like Ginger, girls who were very floaty, and he thought of Kay Thompson as someone he didn't want to be close to. He knew she had an amazing talent; he just didn't want to be near it."[40]

As a postscript to the shooting of the "Clap Yo' Hands" number, Thompson said that Fred objected to Donen, "What is she doing?" while Thompson was "doodling" at the piano as the scene was being set up for shooting. Donen explained that she was doing exactly what he expected her to do. After the scene was completed, Fred grabbed her and said, "Where did you learn balance?" Thompson claimed she made no reply: "It wasn't worth the time. He was just somebody who was frightened. I could have shot Fred but [I] didn't."

According to the film critic Rex Reed, before shooting "Clap Yo' Hands," Thompson told Audrey Hepburn, "I'm going to wipe the floor with that man." And she did. She stole the whole number. Reed also said, "Kay was also a perfectionist who could drive you crazy. She didn't follow orders very well."

Thompson was adamant that Astaire was constantly crotchety during filming in Hollywood, and the situation worsened once the picture moved to Paris for further shooting. Donen maintained that Thompson's contention that Astaire was cranky because "he wanted to be great in front of Audrey" was untrue. His firm belief was that Fred wanted to be great for himself.

Further, Thompson claimed, "After Fred had yelled at Audrey a couple of times, and she was in that white [bridal] dress and her shoes were blackened from the mud, she was smiling, and they were supposed to be in love" (in "He Loves and She Loves"). This caused Hepburn to remark, "I've waited twenty years to dance with Fred Astaire, and what do I get? Mud."

The three of them rode back to Paris in silence. In a subsequent phone call to Hepburn, Thompson admonished her not to listen to whatever Fred said to her while the camera was on her. Hepburn replied, "Yes, well, it is a bit of a strain." "Heaven," said Thompson.[41]

Whether these incidents happened precisely the way Thompson said they did is an open question. The three stars in question are no longer with us. Certainly, Fred did have a reputation on occasion of being "the demanding one," but considering Thompson's predisposition toward him, and his toward her, the true nature of these events is debatable.

Nevertheless, as concerns the soggy grass in this scene, Fred said, "I can't dance in that. Fix it." Stanley Donen answered, "We'll do what we can. But how can we fix it?" Astaire replied, "I don't care! Put down wood and paint it green!"[42]

RICHARD AVEDON HAD ONLY GOOD THINGS to say about Fred: "Every story they tell about Fred is true. The discipline, the graciousness. We were all in awe of him. He was very easy." At the end of filming, Fred gave Avedon a gift, a pair of suede moccasins. He recalled, "I just put them on the mantelpiece for years. They were actually too big."[43] After Avedon and Gershe saw a rough cut of the picture, Avedon turned to his old friend and said, "You know, I've always wanted to be Fred Astaire, and there is Fred Astaire being me." [44]

The late great photographer also mentioned that Astaire showed him a "Fred Astaire–like" step with an umbrella. "It was a complete throwaway . . . almost invisible. It was in the way he walked. As he moved along, he bounced the umbrella on the floor, to the floor, and then he grabbed it. It was effortless. . . . A few years later I was photographing Gene Kelly and told him that Fred Astaire had taught me this trick with an umbrella. And Kelly said, 'Oh, I'll teach you one,' and he did, and the two tricks with an umbrella in some way define the difference between Fred Astaire and Gene Kelly and, in my view, demonstrate who is the greater of the artists. With Gene Kelly, he threw the umbrella way up into the air, then he moved to catch it, very slowly, grabbing it behind his back. It was a big, grandstand play, about nothing." [45]

In the book *Richard Avedon: Made in France,* Judith Thurman writes, "*Funny Face* is an artifact of a remote, lost civilization. Three of its purist pleasures have not dated: Hepburn's face, Givenchy's couture, and Astaire's dancing—all pertinent, the dancing in particular, to Avedon's work. She equates Astaire's buoyancy to Avedon's pictures, the classical discipline with which the dancer, like the photographer, made the artificial and rehearsed seem effervescent and spontaneous." [46]

Donen admitted his most emotional moment as a filmmaker occurred "on the morning we laid out Fred's sequence of the 'Bonjour, Paris!' number. It was a Sunday. We were on the Champs-Élysées. I was directing Fred Astaire, and we had to have extras dressed as policemen to keep away the crowds. . . . We used crumpled-up cigarette packages as Fred's marks, and then I hit the playback and Fred started singing that song. I thought, 'This is it. In my entire life, this is all I ever wanted to do.' " [47]

The instant when Astaire exits from a taxi, catches a glimpse of the Arc de Triomphe over his shoulder, tips his hat, casually slips a hand in the pocket of his trousers, and begins to stroll the boulevard is indeed pure Astaire. Likewise, the entire production of *Funny Face* could be described as summing up Donen's style.[48]

The finale followed another lovers' misunderstanding. It returned Astaire and Hepburn to the romantic setting on the aforementioned raft. No dialogue is necessary to cement their reconciliation. They drifted away to the strains of Fred's singing, "You've made my life so glamorous / you can't blame me for feeling amorous," the chorus from " 'S Wonderful." Writer Joe Goldberg described it well when he said, "Avedon and Donen made this scene into a moving Monet painting." [49]

SOON AFTER RETURNING TO CALIFORNIA, Fred decided to show Paris to Ava, now that her school year at Westlake School for Girls was completed. He proudly showed off his daughter, walking among the summer tourists crowding the streets. They then segued to England, making a stopover to attend the glorious Goodwood races, where Fred's two-year-old filly Rainbow Tie was set to compete.

The queen, who was also attending the event, was informed of Fred's presence. Lord Plunkett, her personal attendant, asked Fred and Ava to come to the royal box between races. It was the first time Fred had seen the queen since attending a luncheon with Elizabeth's parents many years earlier when she was a mere child. He reminisced about once having danced with her mother, the queen mum. The queen corrected him: "You mean she danced with you."

Per her agreement, Adele was back at Lismore, this time with her husband, Kingman Douglass. The whole trip was a dazzling experience for fourteen-year-old Ava. In Ireland she met many old friends of her father's and her aunt's. The beginning of her love affair with Ireland started here. She ventured off to London, while her father remained in Ireland. [50]

THE NOTICES FOR *FUNNY FACE* were as rapturous as any Astaire musical film ever received. Bosley Crowther went so far as to say, "You won't see a prettier musical or one more extraordinarily stylish during the balance of this year—a picture with stars in every department. . . . The eye is intoxicated with sensory thrills . . . acting, singing, and dancing are elegant."

William K. Zinsser in the *Herald Tribune* said, "In the world of movies, there are a few irresistible sights. Their appeal is as certain as the law of gravity, which might be called 'The Astaire-Hepburn Law.' One of the sights is Fred Astaire dancing. Another is Audrey Hepburn doing anything at all."

Kate Cameron in the *Daily News* in her four-star review included such praise as "Fred [Astaire], as a fashion photographer, maintains through the picture the verve, expert dancing technique and flair for comedy that distinguished the musicals which he and Ginger Rogers did so successfully together. . . . Not since *An American in Paris* has color been made an important adjunct of a film."

Archer Winsten's *Post* review included, "Unbelievably as it may sound, Astaire has never danced more gracefully or more originally." He singled out Stanley Donen's essential contribution to the film's success by noting, "Donen has thrown the whole thing together with the dash and slap of a fine, loose-drawing master of draughtsmanship."

Arthur Knight in *Dance* magazine observed, "Astaire reveals the elasticity, the perfection of line, and the sense of pictorial design that have kept him pre-eminent among screen dancers for many years. His fresh *adagio* with Miss Hepburn on points ["He Loves and She Loves"] is easily his most successful creation in this form—tender, wonderfully romantic and wonderfully imaginative."[51]

Once again, an Astaire musical had its world premiere engagement at Radio City Music Hall. A breathless Paramount publicity-department news release heralded its success: "Marking the biggest single week's gross for any theatre anywhere in the world, in the history of the motion picture industry, Paramount's *Funny Face* in its 4th week at Radio City Music Hall took in $214,777 at the box office."

Fred once again made himself available to do publicity in New York in support of the picture. In addition to press interviews, he sang his new Verve recording, "That Face," while appearing on Ed Sullivan's variety show and did an hour-long interview on *Arlene's Home Show,* hosted by Arlene Francis and Hugh Downs.

ROBERT MULLER OF ENGLAND'S *Picture Post* interviewed Astaire during a scene setup in Paris. The encounter provided a brief but revealing character sketch of the shy and lonely dancer as well as a glimpse of his longtime uneasiness at talking about himself.

Muller began his piece by observing, "He sits by himself, away from the glare of the arc lamps, in the grey hall light of the Gare du Nord, looking at nothing in particular with pale eyes, a man much nearer sixty then fifty with a pink shirt and the sad, lined face of a clown in love. When he talks to you, he stares at his shoes, which he taps lightly against a rail. He has not thought of something clever to say. He lacks the assurance of the mediocre. He does not talk in quotes, being questioned by a stranger embarrasses him. Fred Astaire isn't selling Fred Astaire. He speaks haltingly, as if English was a foreign tongue to him. He doesn't volunteer information, but politely answers questions. . . . He displays none of the phony horror of business.

"He said, 'When you work, there's always a terrible fear that you'll dry up; that the new ideas won't come; that you get stale. In 1947, I retired because I thought I had dried up. I enjoyed my private life so much that I thought I could live without dancing. Then I got some new ideas and wanted to start again. And my wife said, 'Sure, go ahead.'"

THE LINGERING PROBLEM of working with leading ladies decades his junior that faced Astaire in the mid-1950s was not his alone. The same fate was shared by other major stars, such as John Wayne, Gary Cooper, Clark Gable, Humphrey Bogart, and Cary Grant. Fred's age had once again been brought to his attention by John Mc-Carten's review in the *New Yorker,* in which the reviewer damned him with faint praise: "Put *Funny Face* down as an amiable bit of seasonal fluff and rejoice that Mr. Astaire's middle-aged bones can still rattle with an infectious beat."

Fred took stock of the age problem that plagued him by paraphrasing General Douglas MacArthur's famous farewell speech to Congress, saying in his 1959 *Steps in Time* autobiography, "Old dancers never die, they just toupée away." He also wrote, "Where are they going to get all the May-December romance stories required for the aging male stars?" In an oblique reference to *Time* (perhaps based on the magazine's unfavorable *Funny Face* notice), he compared the magazine's method of reporting to "a cashmere sledge hammer."

He had the vaudevillian's fear of staying on the stage too long—of failing to move to the wings before the applause died down.[52] Older people were stuck in front of their TV sets. The movie audience was getting younger and wanted new screen heroes and their own music, which was now rock and roll. They saw plenty of music on television variety shows, which kept them away from the movie houses. Always completely aware of the ever-changing trends in show business, Fred once again gave serious thought about the entire situation: Was there really a future now for him in the movie business?

Once again, Arthur Freed came to the rescue. The Arthur Freed Unit was yesterday; Freed was now an independent producer at MGM. Arthur offered Fred the lead in *Silk Stockings,* playing opposite Cyd Charisse. Based on the 1939 Greta Garbo/Melvyn Douglas film, *Ninotchka,* a devastating spoof on communism, which had been a triumph for the renowned director Ernst Lubitsch, it had in 1954 been adapted as a Broadway musical. The show, *Silk Stockings,* contained a Cole Porter score—always a lure to interest Fred. Porter's score, his last one for Broadway, contained such songs as "All of You," "Without Love," "Paris Loves Lovers," and the title song. Such fare was not Porter's best work for films, but the age of the immortal Broadway songwriters turned film-score composers was on its way to extinction.

* * *

ROUBEN MAMOULIAN, himself a Russian émigré, knew what his homeland was all about. He had made *Queen Christina* with Garbo and had an exemplary theatrical background, having directed both the 1927 Broadway play *Porgy* and the Gershwin opera *Porgy and Bess* in 1935, as well as *Oklahoma* in 1943, and *Carousel* in 1945. These credentials, plus Fred's feeling that Mamoulian's directing style resembled that of Lubitsch,[53] led to his being selected to helm *Silk Stockings.* This was despite that Mamoulian's last picture, a musical version of Eugene O'Neill's *Ah, Wilderness!* called *Summer Holiday,* which starred Mickey Rooney, had been a complete failure. Fred had faith in Freed's artistic judgment. He agreed to have lunch with Mamoulian to discuss his approach to the Porter musical.[54]

Mamoulian told Astaire the only reason he had agreed to direct the movie was because of him and Cyd Charisse. The emphasis was to be on the dancing, downplaying the political context,[55] which wasn't fully accomplished. Fred brought up the age difference between him and Cyd, which in this case was "only" twenty-two years. The director was obviously prepared for the star's query. "What kind of nonsense is that?" he said. "I see all the young actors today on the screen and none of them can match you in charm or romantic appeal, so for heaven's sake, get off that peg. You're not too old!"

When he sensed that Fred was still reluctant to commit himself, Mamoulian doubled his efforts by suggesting, "With you, a dancer playing the film producer, and Cyd, a dancer playing the Russian girl, I think we can introduce a new element—pantomime in place of extended dialogue. We'll have high comedy with the three Russian commissars and a love story that is believable and touching."[56] Mamoulian later pointed out in an interview, "The psychological and dramatic development existed only in the dancer."[57]

Leonard Gershe was signed to write the screenplay with Leonard Spigelgass (and Harry Kurnitz, who did some rewriting). Considerable dialogue from *Ninotchka* was retained.[58] As choreographer, Hermes Pan was signed to work with Astaire, and Eugene Loring with Charisse and the other dancers.

Eugene Loring had choreographed the Broadway musical. He was paid $15,000 for his work on *Silk Stockings,* while Pan got $30,000, which was only $4,000 less than Mamoulian's salary. Loring's choreography in *Yolanda and the Thief* had not been to Fred's liking, although they had worked together on other movies, most recently on *Funny Face.* The veteran choreographer was quoted as saying that he preferred not to choreograph for Astaire again: "He's very difficult to work with. By that I mean it's hard to create for him and get something new and fresh that also pleases him. He's very set in his ways."[59] Perhaps the central problem was Loring's penchant for creating dances with an element of ballet, which was diametrically opposed to Fred's wishes. André Previn was the musical director and conductor, working with a staff of arrangers that included other well-established Astaire musical cohorts as Conrad Salinger and Skip Martin.

After these important craftsmen had been added, with Mamoulian's added assurance, and with the changing of his role to that of a glib, suave movie producer, Astaire couldn't say no. Rehearsals began for his thirtieth film appearance in mid-September 1956.[60]

Fred's contract called for him to again get $150,000 over twenty weeks, which included rehearsal time. It also specified, "All wearing apparel necessary under, except 'character' or 'period' wearing apparel, will be furnished by you."[61] As usual, Astaire was natty in 1956 proper Hollywood-producer attire, wearing beautifully cut blue blazers and suits with double vents, years before double vents become fashionable. In a few scenes, his proverbial pink socks were highly visible, for as usual his trousers were purposely cut short enough for them to be seen.

MAMOULIAN STATED IN HIS PREPRODUCTION NOTES, "The love story is the weakest point in the script. If we fail with it, all the shooting is for nothing."[62] "It is abrupt . . . and unbelievable. It also greatly lacks charm."[63] The picture was further hindered by the downbeat manner with which Charisse played Ninotchka. She was not a good enough actress to act the role with any sympathy or much sensitivity. The decision not to deglamorize her in her scenes as a dedicated Communist was another mistake.

Charisse, however, was a perfect fit as Fred's dancing costar. He referred to their compatibility by saying, "That Cyd! When you've danced with her, you stay danced with." Plus, she brought eroticism to her dancing. A key ingredient in her eventual decision to overthrow the bonds of totalitarianism was her discovery of a pair of silk stockings. Her sensuously charged dance to "Silk Stockings" was the cinematic element that resolved the whole story.

As her comical sidekicks, each spying on the other to preserve the venal interests of Marxism, were Peter Lorre, Jules Munshin, and Joseph Buloff. Lorre, playing against type, was a comic revelation and an impish song-and-dance man, particularly in "Too Bad (We Can't Go Back to Moscow)." George Tobias, as the Soviet commissar of the arts, had the distinction of having worked in all three incarnations of the *Ninotchka* story. Another important element was the casting of Janis Paige, who was a standout playing a brassy movie star based on Esther Williams, who had come to Paris to work on a "boiled down" film version of *War and Peace!*[64]

While watching Jack Cole, the flamboyant choreographer, whose modern dance and jazz concepts Astaire greatly admired, rehearse with several dancers on the choreography for Gene Kelly's *Les Girls,* Astaire became reacquainted with Barrie Chase. She was Cole's assistant and Kay Kendall's dance-in. Astaire and Chase had first met at Cole's rehearsal studio, at which time he had recruited her for a dancing spot in *Daddy Long Legs.* They had seen each other around the MGM lot in the interim. This time Astaire asked Cole if he could borrow her to appear in *Silk Stockings* in the "Too Bad" number.

Chase recalled, "When I went over to work with Fred, I said to myself, 'I have to get rid of the pelvic movements. . . . When you dance with Jack that's common . . . that's just part of the style.'" She was paid only $285 a week, but worked several weeks. Besides rediscovering Chase, Fred was intrigued by the way Cole's drummer, Jackie Mills, played the brushes behind Cole's dancers. He, too, would wind up having a future in working with Astaire.

IN A 1965 *LIFE* INTERVIEW with Dave Zeitlin, Astaire discussed his training routine before starting work on a specific project and his approach to the dance. "I harden my legs, get my breathing going, gradually build up my stamina and learn to conserve any energy. I might get winded early in a routine. So I pantomime a little to avoid unnecessary exertion and pace myself to the end. [Barrie Chase said, "He trained like a prizefighter, doing roadwork. I would drop from exhaustion, and he'd keep going for hours."][65]

"I train just like a racehorse. . . . If the [dance] floor is good, I can use ordinary leather shoes. If it is slippery, I wear shoes with rubber on the bottom. Or maybe some resin sprinkled on the floor will do the trick. But whatever I do, I must get a good grip, without slipping or sticking.

"Tougher than a performance itself is working out a number. If I can get started on an idea, I can follow up on it fairly easily, but to get started on a routine, that's the thing. It's hard because you keep feeling that nothing is good enough: I say to myself, 'That's lousy.' It's not always lousy, but that's a good way to think because otherwise you may accept a lot of things you shouldn't.

"I've never yet got anything one hundred percent right. Still, it's never as bad as I think it is. I can remember when I was on the stage and I would say, 'I wish I could throw out tonight's performance and forget it.' People would say afterward that they didn't know the difference. But I did.

"Dancing is a sweat job. You can't just sit down and do it. You have to get up on your feet. When you're experimenting, you have to try so many things before you choose what you want that you may go days getting nothing but exhaustion.

This search for what you want is like tracking something that doesn't want to be tracked.

"I don't know what my dancing style and techniques should be called. I just dance, but with a beat. The beat has always been part of my system. Now the beat has become an indispensable part of modern dances—the jerk and the frug and others I don't even know the words for. I don't think of these dances as vulgar. When two people are on a dance floor and they don't touch each other and are sometimes oblivious of each other, and when they walk around looking in opposite directions and are more concerned about themselves than with whom they are dancing—those dances aren't vulgar. I just think they're nuts."[66]

I asked Don Heckman, who in addition to being a jazz critic is also a practicing psychologist, about his feelings on Astaire's obsessive approach to the dance. He began by saying, "One of the things you find with anyone who has compulsive behavior of that sort is that there are a couple of reasons for it. One might be that they are so obsessed with it that they have to do it. Like people who have to count the steps all the time when they are walking, which doesn't have any productive aspect to it. But with that kind of behavior, when you look at it, it's what is the result that's beneficial in some way or other. . . . You would imagine that someone who is that specific and is a performer, you have to wonder whether or not that was not the trigger that releases him into their creativity. This obsessive thing gave him a freedom."

When I discussed Fred's repetition of his gestures by rehearsing them in front of a mirror during his third NBC special, something that carried over to his dance numbers, Heckman said, "You can make a case that he would not feel comfortable about them freeing himself unless all of the structure was first in place, and that was the liberating force that set him free.

"Did he do them that precisely, was there some aspect to it that was different, or was it simply a matter of energy and enthusiasm? Sometimes, the difference between a good performance and a better performance isn't that any of the pieces are any different—it's the spirit in which they are released. Maybe he did all the gestures in exactly the same places, but there was an energy and a spirit by his doing them only in that safety.

"Cyd Charisse, as a ballet dancer, seems to have come from that same structured background. I am sure in her case choreography was very specific, and you did it the same way every time."

IN THE MID-1950S, MGM was starting to rid itself of leftover contracts, and that meant many of those affiliated with musicals. One of them was the composer Arthur Schwartz, who threw a going-away party for himself. That was where a young actor named Michael Dante, a former Washington Senators shortstop, met Fred Astaire.

"It was a beautiful summer evening in 1955, with the champagne flowing," recalled Dante, now retired but host of a popular radio talk show on KGAM in Palm Springs. "I went alone. I was seated at a table for four with Fred Astaire, Johnny Mercer, and Josephine Baker [the American-born entertainer turned French superstar]. I was the rookie under contract to MGM. They made me feel at home. All of them were fascinated that I had been a big league baseball player."

Astaire had played baseball as a boy and kept up with the game and its principal players over the years. He continued his interest in the following decades when it was fashionable for Hollywood stars to become avid fans of the Los Angeles Dodgers.

"I explained to them about how a shoulder injury ended my baseball career, and how Tommy Dorsey got me signed to MGM. They all expressed their great respect for Tommy. I mentioned how much discipline entered into playing baseball well and said that was part of what made Tommy Dorsey successful. That seemed to really interest Fred, because, of course, he was so disciplined. He went on to speak about the movement of athletes, their ability, and their concentration on eye-hand coordination. He found certain parallels to the dance. He said, 'It's fascinating. Playing shortstop involves foot work and flexing the knees like dancing.' We all talked so long that Arthur came over and suggested that we partake of the food. He later told me it was the first time Fred had gone out socially since the death of his wife."

GIVEN PORTER'S PENCHANT for installing double entendres and racy lyrics into his songs, *Silk Stockings* ran into trouble with the Hollywood Production Code, now presided over by Geoffrey Shurlock. Not for the first time, objections were made over Porter's lyrics. Among them, in his song "Stereophonic Sound" (sung by Janis Paige), the end of the line "If Zanuck's latest pictures were the good old fashioned kind / Look at Monroe's behind" had to be removed, and "Unless her lips are scarlet and her bosoms five foot wide" was deemed highly objectionable. (The latter was changed to a five-foot-wide mouth.) A remark about Ava Gardner playing Lady Godiva was kept, but a line about seeing her in the bare was changed to "they wouldn't even care." "All of You" ("I'd like to make a tour of you") had to be delivered in a "nonsuggestive manner." In the "Satin and Silk" number, caution was addressed to the portion of the lyric that said, "And she's all prepared to make a friend." The phrase in the song "shake like hell" was termed unacceptable. In the "Silk Stockings" number, Charisse was not allowed to appear full figure in the bodysuit she was wearing.[67] The love scenes could not contain open-mouth kissing. Final judgment was reserved until delivery of the final print of the film on February 12, 1957, when the movie passed without any changes.

SILK STOCKINGS NEVER GOT CLOSE to reaching the heights of *Funny Face.* Though both movies were set in Paris, the former was filmed entirely in Culver City, thus eliminating what could have been an important romantic element. The dance numbers in the movie, however, belong in the realm of Astaire's most romantic film dancing, particularly the spectacular Astaire/Charisse versions of "All of You" and "Fated to Be Mated," wherein Fred makes full use of his vast arsenal of dancing technique to woo Cyd. Simultaneously, she shows how easily she is completely tuned in to him. Reportedly "All of You" was her favorite dance number, which was doubtlessly because Ninotchka was her favorite role.

Astaire recalled, "I had a couple of things where I had to lift her and catch her [Charisse] and do things, and it worked out. . . . I'm not that good a lifter of women. You know, dancing—what do you call [it]—ballet type of lifts and things. . . . But I had one thing where she was up on a platform, and she had to leap down into my arms. Pan was the choreographer on that, and if it hadn't been for Pan, I don't think I ever would have done it. . . . He showed me a kind of a way to do it. And I did it. I got her and was so pleased. He always used to beat me down and get me to do something that I thought I couldn't do, which I was grateful for."[68]

In stark contrast to the lack of cutting that was so essential to the success of Fred's dance numbers with Ginger Rogers, considerable cutting took place in *Silk Stockings.* The bulk of it involved going from a full-figure shot to a medium shot of the upper body, rather than the more typical cuts between different full-figure shots. Astaire had used this device before on occasion in having the camera shoot close-ups of the dancers. In *Silk Stockings,* the full-to-medium cut is the standard, not the exception, but that did not lessen the impact of the dance numbers.[69]

The big surprise of the film was the exuberant and refreshing work of Janis Paige. Coming off the Broadway hit *The Pajama Game* as the female lead, Babe, costarring with John Raitt, her scene-stealing in *Silk Stockings* should have led to an important movie career for Paige but didn't. Not that she wasn't able to make an impression in subsequent comedic and dramatic parts for several years, but her talent deserved more than she got. As one example, she lost the *The Pajama Game* movie role to Doris Day, but then Day was a major star at the time.

Paige was informed that she had the role in *Silk Stockings* immediately after her opening-night performance at the Coconut Grove, where the maître d' informed her that Arthur Freed was in the house and wished to speak with her.

Paige recalled, "Arthur said, 'No testing. You're going to have a dance number with Fred Astaire.' " Breathlessly she protested, " 'I'm not a trained dancer,' " to which Freed countered, " 'Don't worry, it's going to be okay. We'll work with you.' " Paige was paid $39,990 plus overtime for her performance in the movie.

Her first day of rehearsal was a nightmare. "I had a shocking-pink Ford," Paige said. "I was stopped by the gate guard for not having a pass to drive into the studio lot. I drove around and around and finally parked by the train station. I ran into the rehearsal studio. Fred looked up and said, 'You're late.' I started to cry because I couldn't catch my breath, and I was so scared. He ran over and said, 'What's the matter?' I said, 'I was forty-five minutes early.' He got me some water and asked me what had happened. 'Where are your car keys?' I gave them to him. He walked over to a fellow, threw him the keys, and said, 'Go get her car and drive it back on the lot.'

"I can still remember what he was wearing—he had on medium gray flannel pants, with the cuffs rolled up. He wore those great black-and-white shoes with the taps. He had on a really white shirt, a soft-blue-and-white ascot, and he had a stripped red tie around his waist, and pink socks. He also wore a gold watch.

"He took my hand and said, 'I'm sorry this happened to you.' 'Oh, Mr. Astaire,' I cried. 'Please call me Fred,' he said. The next day I drove on the lot and was able to park right next to his car.

"Once we started rehearsing, I did everything he told me. Hermes Pan watched me to see my limitations. Fred was always helpful. I never heard a harsh word. I never saw anybody work harder. He never made me feel that I wasn't this great dancer.

"There was an aura about someone like Fred. There really is an energy about those people that transmits to you, and you are different. I noticed that with the great ones that I worked with that you say you don't know them. There is a reason why. There was a kind of imaginary boundary that was there that you didn't cross. . . . I don't know if they are ever aware of it. Maybe it comes from their up-bringing, their discipline, but you just didn't go there."

According to Paige, considerable cuts were made in the final version of the "Josephine" number, which along with "Satin and Silk," in which she exhibited a decided flair, was one of her two featured solo numbers. Paige recalled that Fred had trouble with a particular routine in "Stereophonic Sound," which they performed together. "It was a close-up. He couldn't get it. . . . The more he tried, the more he went blank. He got so frustrated he walked off the set. 'I'll be back in a few minutes. I've just got to get myself together.' He came back and got it down. He turned to me and said to me, 'I got it, kid,' and I said, 'God, yes, it was wonderful.'

"At the end of 'Stereophonic Sound' there was something very cute. We were dancing on this conference table. We had to grab on to this chandelier, swing out, and let go. The morning that we rehearsed it, he said, 'I've got to grab you. I've got a great ending. . . . You know where we swing up to the side of that table and do the side circle, and we turn around, I'm going to have that big chandelier come in on a music cue, and we're going to swing out over the heads of those reporters. We're going to let go and land à la [Al] Jolson.' Then he said, 'Do you think you can do it?' And I said, 'Sure, absolutely. I can do that.' We couldn't rehearse it in the rehearsal hall because there was no way to hook anything up. So we did it."

Paige described Mamoulian as "a very elegant, lovely man" and said, "The age of the gentlemen, it's gone. I don't think we'll ever have it again. They came from a time where we were taught manners first of all. We were taught deportment. We were taught responsibility and discipline. . . . I think that there are probably gentlemen out there in the business today, but I don't find many. I think they're almost forced not to be gentlemen."

The gentlemanly Cole Porter wrote two new songs for the picture, "Fated to Be Mated" and "The Ritz Roll and Rock." The latter was his rather clumsy attempt to combine his elegant world and the music of the young. Despite remarking about "the sameness of rock 'n' roll," Astaire specifically requested his old friend write "a twist on the rock 'n' roll craze"[70] for the picture. Although to have Fred sing a rock 'n' roll song was amusing, to dress him in top hat, white tie, tails, and a red sash, with a cane, was ludicrous. Then, to have him tap-dance to remind the film audience of his past was completely unnecessary. A satirical edge was attempted in this number, but it didn't succeed.

The music changed from mock Tchaikovsky to rock 'n' roll. Fred admitted, "I thought the dance was good, but I didn't like the way I sang it. It just makes you shudder when you see something like that."[71] Fred ended the scene—which was shot in January 1957 and was his last musical number in his last major musical— by fittingly smashing his top hat flat.[72]

A dancer who worked on "The Ritz Roll and Rock," the extremely personable Harvey Evans, has been working steadily in films and on Broadway for an incredible five decades. One of his specialties is acrobatic dance. Harvey recalled, "I picked up the mood of the other dancers. It seemed like Hermes worked very slowly. He was sort of vague about what he wanted. Astaire did not come in much. He would come in a few hours each day. He looked older than I thought he would be. As the number progressed, it was not going to be any kind of great dance number. It was just going to be more Fred Astaire. Fred kept saying, 'Can't the boys be lower?' so a lot of the time we were on the floor. He was impatient but not to the point of annoyance."

Evans noticed a sudden change when the actual shooting of "The Ritz Roll and Rock" took place. "Fred suddenly became younger, more boy than the old Astaire. Pan would design something, but it came alive when Fred stepped in. It was a work process that was so brilliant I could not believe it. Hermes Pan was the nicest guy in the world, and I did appreciate the job. I don't want to cast a shadow about how much I was proud to be in that number, but I remember on breaks we used to go and watch Jack Cole rehearse the girls in *Les Girls*. It was exciting and new. I would say Bob Fosse was more like Cole because Cole was first and Cole and Gwen Verdon were tight, and Carol Haney and Cole were tight. They all became [important] Fosse people."

Harvey went on to say, "I have a friend, Tony Stevens, who is a director/choreographer here in New York. He has a theory that people who are unique and become stars have limitations. They know how to use their limitations to the best advantage so they become so unique that no one else can do what they do. . . . In dance class you learn to point your toe all the time, to keep your leg straight, to make a nice line, not a sharp line. Astaire did not have that ability. He made his own style, whereas Kelly was the best of that kind of dancer. . . . He would do barrel rolls, he would do triple pirouettes, he would do double tours, he would do things you learn in class. Astaire could not do any of that. He didn't [even] try. He was the most flowing, graceful dancer in the entire world, and that's why nobody could duplicate him. . . . That's why he was the greatest dancer of them all. Baryshnikov freaked out when he saw him because he broke his rules and other rules, and he made it work to his advantage. To me, Kelly was the best of the formula, just wonderful, very athletic, but that you could copy. Astaire you couldn't copy."

In 1973, Harvey worked with Ginger Rogers in *No, No, Nanette* in Dallas. He said, "I danced with her in the 'You Can Dance with Any Girl at All,' number, which was based on the Castle walk. She was slow to pick it up and very slow in learning her dialogue. One of the cast brought the Fred and Ginger book for her to sign. She refused to sign it. She said, 'I won't sign anything with me and Mr. Astaire connected.' However, she signed something for me and wrote, 'Young Astaire.' Maybe that's not a compliment, but I took it as a compliment."

RELEASED JUST FOUR MONTHS after *Funny Face, Silk Stockings* also played for six weeks at Radio City Music Hall. Its world premiere engagement commenced there on May 20, 1957, and it was the biggest-grossing musical ever to play the theater.

Its success was in great measure due to the extravagant praise of some of the principal Manhattan movie reviewers. Bosley Crowther selected the movie as one of the best films of 1957. He wrote, "There should be legislation requiring Fred Astaire and Cyd Charisse to appear together in musical pictures every two years."

Wanda Hale in the *Daily News* said *Silk Stockings* was "infinitely better than the Broadway show for the single reason that it has far greater talent participating with acting, singing and dancing. . . . And there is the benefit of the camera, CinemaScope and Metrocolor." Alton Cook in the *World Telegram and Sun* declared, "Janis Paige is one of our best dancers."

Time described the movie as "a lithe version of a fairly spirited musical comedy in turn woven over an old velveteen original." Arthur Knight in the *Saturday Review* commented, "The plot, although simplified to the point of imbecility, still remains too ponderous for a good musical." William K. Zinsser, however, went even further against the grain of some of the press reviews by writing, "When these two amiable people, Fred Astaire and Cyd Charisse, dance across a shiny floor, or sing one of Cole Porter's facile songs, all's well on the screen. It's when they stop to talk that the movie comes to a halt, and they stop to talk very often."

John McCarten, never a certified Astairophile, however, countered Zinsser's review when he concluded his review: "To wrap up the enterprise, Mr. Astaire in the full panoply of top hat and tails does a number called 'The Ritz Roll and Rock.' It has a lot of dash."

The advertising campaign naturally emphasized Cyd Charisse's magnificent legs. In those years, entertainment editors gladly lapped up flowery press handouts from the movie studios. Great Britain's MGM company took a page from Howard Strickling's studio-based flackery department by sending out a news release stating, "Cyd Charisse in *Silk Stockings* wears the world's most expensive stockings. They were laced with diamonds and other jewelry worth £300,000."[73]

Fred was pleased to do his part for MGM by going to New York to do publicity. He took a bow on what was Ed Sullivan's tenth-anniversary show. But his most important appearance was on Edward R. Murrow's highly popular *Person to Person* show, which televised Fred at home.

This was not the kind of probing interview that Murrow had done with Nehru and Robert Oppenheimer.[74] Rather, this interview show was a forerunner to the current *Tonight* show and other talk shows in which a star plugs his or her current project with predetermined talk "areas."

The truly legendary journalist introduced Fred as "the highest-paid dancer in conjunction with *Silk Stockings*." Astaire began by revealing that Fred Jr. was still in the air force and Peter was "in business and lives downtown." Astaire rationalized his 1946 retirement by saying, "I wanted to retire to my dance studios and racehorses." After two years, he glibly remarked, "I came back to movies for a rest." He readily admitted that at long last he was getting used to seeing himself on-screen!

Walking around his San Ysidro property, he stopped off in the garden, which led to the backyard and the swimming pool. Returning to the house, he showed off the photos of his horses and their trophies. He mentioned how being exposed to horse racing in England initially piqued his interest in the sport and led to his wanting to purchase horses of his own.

When Murrow brought up Fred's having been awarded an Oscar for bringing distinction to screen musicals, he suddenly became embarrassed. He acknowledged that he had 120 of his dance studios currently in operation, with openings set in Houston and New Orleans. "They're doing well, everything's fine," he said.

Admiring Cyd Charisse's dancing, he said, "We knocked the floor a great deal." Turning to his hobbies, he mentioned his love for golf and making records "for the great Norman Granz." He told how much playing his jazz records meant to him and admitted he liked "some rock 'n' roll."

He sauntered into his bedroom, where his set of drums was on display. (They were later housed in his bathtub!) He asked Murrow, "Do you want me to play?" "Of course," Murrow replied. Fred showed off his average technique with the brushes as a Benny Goodman Quartet record played in the background. Concluding the number, he blurted out a self-satisfied "Yeah!"

As he got out from behind his drums, he smoothed back the rugs that he had inadvertently kicked over. (Always the perfectionist!) He exclaimed that he was "too busy in pictures to appear on television." With that evasive observation, the curtain came down on Fred's exposing his home to American households.

SILK STOCKINGS CAME IN under budget and made a healthy profit. Still, it was the final dance musical Arthur Freed ever produced. It was the final movie Rouben Mamoulian ever directed. Cyd Charisse never made another musical in Hollywood.[75] Fred would star in one more musical, eleven years later, but it was inferior to the enduring musicals of the Arthur Freed Unit. The golden age of the Hollywood musical had come to an end.

Roger Mayer, the recipient of the coveted Jean Hersholt Humanitarian Oscar in 2005, knows much about both musicals and MGM. The erudite, retired executive (no relation to Louis B. Mayer) spent twenty-five years at Metro-Goldwyn-Mayer, ending up as vice president of administration at the studio. He left MGM for the Turner Entertainment Company to manage the library of films he had been working on at MGM. Eventually, he became the CEO of Turner Entertainment.

Mayer also had the distinction of having had Fred Astaire vote in the garage of his Beverly Hills home, which was used as a polling place, for twenty-five years. Mayer said, "I remember that sort of a sad aspect was that every year I would ask my wife, 'Well, did Fred show up?' And she'd say, 'Yeah, and he's walking more slowly.' And so we watched him age in that regard."

Knowing the studio as well as he did, Mayer noted, "I think that MGM for many years had executives who had the ability to pick both literary material and talent that when put together made first-rate motion pictures and commercial motion pictures. The management kept falling behind the times and was unable to see changes. For example, it was the last studio to get into television and the last to market its features to television. They thought if they could ignore television, it would go away.

"But I think the major problem was that later managements after Mayer and Thalberg—and really starting in the midsixties and after that—didn't have the ability to pick material, and they didn't have the respect for talent that the previous managers had. . . . They were unwilling to make the sort of deals that everyone else was making, such as granting percentage compensations. Therefore, they lost talent and material. The studio system worked beautifully. . . . MGM allowed it to fall apart. I arrived the day Marlon Brando's *Mutiny on the Bounty* went over budget, and it has been downhill ever since."

Mayer delved into the validity of the decision made at MGM, which the entire industry embraced, to cease producing musicals. "It became more and more expensive to produce them, and the market didn't grow. A musical that ten years earlier would have made money now lost money. And whereas the market for other kinds of pictures outside the United States continued to grow, the American musical did not."

I quoted Betty Comden, who had said that there weren't any replacements for Fred Astaire and Gene Kelly. Mayer said, "There might have been. They weren't developed. There were still big musical stars on Broadway. They could have been signed and put into musicals. It just didn't work that way anymore. I still believe if you produce a first-class musical, even though it's much more expensive now, there is a market for it, and *Chicago* was a perfect example of that. . . . Some of the most successful animation films today are musicals like *Little Mermaid, Beauty and the Beast,* and *The Lion King.* The fact that Hollywood has abandoned the musical pretty much I think is an overreaction."

After *Chicago* did extremely well, *Phantom of the Opera* and *Rent* failed to register at the box office. In 2006, *Dreamgirls* was a hit domestically but made no fiscal impression in foreign markets. At Christmas 2007, the Stephen Sondheim musical *Sweeney Todd,* starring Johnny Depp, was a critical success but not a hit at the box office. *Mamma Mia!,* adapted from the popular Broadway musical, containing the songs of ABBA, the popular Swedish rock group, with Meryl Streep attached, came out in the summer of 2008. *Nine,* another Broadway musical, based on the Fellini film *8½,* and starring Daniel Day-Lewis, is scheduled for release in 2009. Though there seems to be a rush to make musicals again with several projects in discussion, the commercial failure of *Sweeney Todd* leaves the future of movie musicals in doubt.

Mayer's comments on what happened to MGM and to musicals has definite credence. In later years at the Turner Entertainment Company he dealt with Robyn Astaire, Fred's widow, acting as a liaison between Turner Entertainment and Warner Video, which distributes the prize RKO and MGM musicals that Astaire helped become national treasures. Mayer believes that the vast trove of Astaire musicals has registered with a new generation because of "the quality of entertainment and the artistry. The commercialization of these pictures hasn't faded. In addition to that, we have not allowed the negatives to fade as the technology for restoration got better. . . . We can [now] make these pictures look better and sound better than they did originally."

We have seen what happened to the stupendous film musicals of yesteryear, but Fred Astaire would not think of quitting. He had another idea about how he could present himself to the American public. The answer he believed, and rightly so, was to present himself on television.

CHAPTER EIGHT

THE CLOTHES THAT MADE THE MAN

AS WE HAVE SEEN, Fred and Adele Astaire became full-fledged stars through their first exposure to British theater audiences in 1923, while making their debut in *Stop Flirting.* This engagement lasted a year and a half. They returned to the West End in 1926 in *Lady Be Good* and triumphed anew. Their third London turn, in 1928, took place with *Funny Face,* which enjoyed a longer run there than it did on Broadway.

Their inescapable appeal was referred to in the English press as "Astairia." The *London Times* gushed, "Columbus may have danced with joy at discovering America, but how he would have cavorted had he also discovered Fred and Adele Astaire."[1] Fred's longtime appeal in Great Britain was commemorated forevermore in the lyrics to the poignant ballad "A Nightingale Sang in Berkeley Square": "Our homeward step was just as light as the tap-dancing feet of Astaire . . ."

In addition to providing an impetus to return to Broadway, each time as more important stars, their triumphant London engagements and related stopovers in various cities in the north of England and Scotland gave the Astaires a genuine appreciation for everything British. They became dedicated Anglophiles. Among other things, the grand acceptance they received from the aristocracy, from Edward, the Prince of Wales; the Duke of York (later King George VI); and others had a profound effect on the political thinking of the young Americans, and as a result they became quite conservative. But an additional and far more lasting effect on them was the attraction they developed for stylish clothes.

Earlier, Fred had been fascinated by the chic manner with which Douglas Fairbanks and C. B. Dillingham dressed. Fred and Dellie had certainly been a part of the social set in New York. Spending time with the Duke of Windsor and his coterie of friends was, however, something completely different and more en-grossing.

Dellie retired from the stage to marry Lord Charles Cavendish in 1932 and lived in Ireland as well as London. Fred made his last London stage appearance three years later starring in *The Gay Divorce.* London was Fred's finishing school. Vaudeville and Broadway had been his grammar school and prep school, respectively.

Fred's primary model in becoming a fashion icon was the Duke of Windsor, himself an ardent admirer of Fred's song-and-dance numbers. Alan Flusser, the well-known men's fashion designer and author of three noteworthy books on men's fashion, most recently *Dressing the Man,* is an expert on the importance of the duke's influence on Astaire. "I think that the Duke of Windsor is the single most important influence in the history of men's clothes," said Flusser with con-viction. His admiration for the duke has extended to his adopting the duke's drape style of tailoring in his own line of men's clothing.

Flusser explained, "The Duke of Windsor broke most of the rules of civilized dress in those days. You have to understand that the duke—by virtue of his obligations—had an enormous variety of styles of dress that he had to wear. He was used to wearing costumes most of his life, starting at a very young age. His grandfather Edward VII was very strict and dressed in the kind of garb expected of a king—very stiff, very formal. But Edward really changed men's clothes. He detested stiff clothes. He introduced soft clothes and helped popularize the din-ner jacket and a pleated-front [formal] shirt with a turndown collar, which was more comfortable. This was seventy years before Armani basically broke down the conventions of the rigidity of male dress from the Victorian age.

"In those days, you had this mixture of high and low society. The Duke of Windsor was one of those people who went out and caroused with people that were not of his class—other theatrical people like Noël Coward and Gertrude Lawrence who were also pretty well turned out. Dressing fashionably then meant that you dressed like him. Fashion was set by the well-to-do or by the people of the upper class.

"I would say that the Duke of Windsor governed over the sartorial world from the early twenties to certainly pre–World War II. It happened that the single most photographed male in the world happened to be a fashion person. There were no designers then. What you wore and how you looked had an enormous impact, especially then."

Liza Minnelli made an extremely valid point when she said, "There were a lot of people in New York who were really under the influence of the Duke of Windsor . . . and I think they brought that style to Hollywood. Hollywood didn't really have that kind of elegance until this whole group of people moved out there—the Gershwins, my dad, Fred Astaire, Vernon Duke, Cole Porter . . ."[2]

Flusser said, "I don't know if everybody would consider Fred Astaire in terms of his being one of the three best-dressed men in the world, but in terms of his influence I think he was. I think if you solicited the opinions of designers like Bill Blass, Giorgio Armani, Ralph Lauren, Oscar de la Renta, and you asked them who would you name as one of the ten best-dressed men in history, Astaire would be one of them. Being on the stage and in front of a camera his clothes were part of Astaire's arsenal of communication. I don't think in the history of mankind there is anybody who looked more effortless on camera."

In *Steps in Time* Astaire wrote that he saw and admired the white piqué, rounded waistcoat that Edward Windsor designed and wore. That caused him to approach Hawes & Curtis in London, but he was informed, "We can't give you something that was made for the Duke of Windsor." He went out and had somebody else make it up for him.

Is it any wonder that the young former vaudevillian from Omaha would be terribly impressed by the look of the clothes worn by the male English aristocrats who came often to see him and his sister perform and praised them to the heavens? In America, he had heretofore been accustomed to associating with fellow performers, whose taste in clothes was often gauche. In addition, what was taking place in London with male fashion had not as yet been imported to New York on a grand scale.

As he grew increasingly enamored with the look of the duke's clothes, he couldn't help but notice how his friend and fashion inspiration introduced new and heretofore unacceptable combinations, as for instance his wearing a pair of suede shoes with a suit. The duke's style was called chic dégagé (free or at ease). Flusser pointed out, "Everything goes through experimentation with clothes if you are interested in clothes. Astaire was no different. In films, this caused Fred to begin tinkering with his own new look after adapting the look of the male English aristocracy. He wore short side vents in his jackets that were cut with a fuller chest and sometimes a button-down shirt with a double-breasted suit. His style changed slightly to become more American. I say American because other than tails it was softer for the most part. Fred Astaire wore soft, casual clothes, cut in a comfortable, unpretentious manner that were not very formfitting."

Flusser added, "Fred didn't like precious stuff like that worn by Anthony Joseph Drexel Biddle [the American diplomat]. In a million years, he wouldn't wear clothes like that. Fred was anything but self-conscious. He is one of those people who had his own feel for clothes and got it. Style is something that you develop from within. When you looked at the way he dressed, the best thing about him was that he tried to make it look not at all self-conscious. You have to practice to make it look unpracticed, so to speak. He once compared dressing well to putting on a show."

One would assume that the Great Depression would have had an adverse effect on men's fashion. Flusser, however, believes, "It eliminated those people who could not afford to dress well from the people who had money. . . . It separated the cream from the cheese. The cream came to the top because they could afford it, so they had a bigger impact on the dressing consciousness at that time when people began to have money. The rich guys were the only people who had the money to continue what the Duke of Windsor kind of started, which was to use tailors and how to dress. In the 1930s, American men were considered to be among the best-dressed men in the world."

This feeling continued and endured for many years. As my Austrian-born assistant, Petra Schwarzwald, pointed out, "In Europe, people dress better than in America when they leave their house. Since living in America, I realize that it might have been as a result of seeing American films because they showed all these well-dressed and well-mannered actors. They were our models. We thought that in America people dressed well, and we looked up to the American culture."

Of course, what Astaire was displaying on-screen, beginning with *The Gay Divorcée,* in the early 1930s, provided men with someone of distinction to emulate. Astaire's clothes sense went hand in glove with his dancing. That he wore custom-made clothes enhanced his development of an elegant image. He was said to have killed dozens of publicity stills because of some near-invisible wrinkle in his coat or trousers.[3]

Early on, while performing in London, he went to Anderson & Sheppard Ltd. to have his clothes made. The firm, established in 1906, already had as its customers celebrated American men of style such as Rudolph Valentino, Douglas Fairbanks, and Gary Cooper, as well as Marlene Dietrich, and Katharine Hepburn, who favored wearing men's suits and tuxedos. (Adam Gimbel, founder of the department store, once said, "No one, except Fred Astaire, can wear white tie and tails as well as Marlene Dietrich does.") Douglas Fairbanks Jr. came soon after, as did Sam Goldwyn. Years later, Astaire brought Norman Granz, the jazz promoter, who in turn brought Duke Ellington to the Savile Row company.

Today, George Hamilton is about the only recognizable Hollywood star who still buys custom-made clothes there; the level of taste among male stars in the film capital has disintegrated considerably over the last several decades. Prince Charles married Camilla Parker Bowles in an Anderson & Sheppard morning suit. Its tailors also made Astaire's suits, tuxedos, tails, and casual clothes. Turnbull & Asser made his shirts, and he bought his ties there.

The more than subtle changes Astaire made in his look over the years included not only wearing button-down Brooks Brothers shirts along with double-breasted suits but also with blue blazers. He supposedly owned over 150 neckties and was said to try on a dozen or so before settling on the perfect one to wear with that day's outfit.[4]

According to Flusser, button-down shirts were introduced in the United States by the Englishman John Brooks, one of the Brooks Brothers, in 1896. Brooks saw English polo players wearing a button-down-collar shirt while playing the game; the buttons helped keep the collar points from flying in the face while moving quickly on a horse. Brooks brought a few shirts back to New York and had them copied for the store.

Sometimes, Astaire topped off his look with a boutonniere in his lapel or a silk pocket square with a pair of suede shoes. This went along with his peculiar habit of wearing neckties as belts tied on the side. (Later he wore scarves as belts.) He also had an odd habit of wearing a collar pin across the wings of a button-down shirt, which Flusser referred to as "one of his eccentricities." Astaire extended his love of jazz to becoming a master of fashion improvisation.

Flusser cited how effectively Astaire could mix patterns, which was ahead of its time. "An example would be donning four patterns, perhaps five where his socks were visible. That's where he got into the habit of wearing a kind of a kerchief over a paisley shirt and a blue blazer and a pattern belt."

NORMAN HALSEY LOOKED after Astaire at Anderson & Sheppard for many years. Halsey observed, "He always seemed very happy, even with the constant pain that he endured from a lifetime of hoofing. He would sometimes get twinges, which he couldn't hide. When he was with you, you got his undivided attention, no sideways glances one notices with some show-business people looking for recognition and admiration. In conversation, he could be very serious and was quite au fait with the UK and the world political scene and informed generally more I suspect than the majority of people in his profession. He was a most easy customer. He knew exactly what he wanted, and that was that. One experienced a feeling of euphoria just being in his presence, and when he left, you were on a high.

"To my mind, the trousers always seemed slightly short; however, that was his choice, and although it is quite common in the police force in Manhattan, he definitely did not look like a New York policeman. He always favored soft materials, flannels, saxonies, and vicuña [whose prohibitive price is now £1,500 per meter]. If in a film, say *Easter Parade,* he wore a clean-cut, hard-finished worsted suit that was not of his choice, but that of the studio's. He was never difficult in the fitting room. The one thing he gave particular attention to was his dress coats, and the way they reacted when he moved.

"The last suit he had from Anderson and Sheppard was a double-breasted two-piece in dark blue flannel. It was a gift from John R. Fell, a senior partner in a Wall Street securities firm. . . . Put Fred in a two-hundred-dollar suit and he would make it sparkle. He could look like a million dollars in an old sack."

When I arrived at Anderson & Sheppard to interview John Hitchcock, the managing director and senior coat cutter, he showed me the Prince of Wales sports jacket (which we would call glen plaid), once a mainstay of Fred Astaire's wardrobe during the 1940s. It was about to be shown in a Savile Row museum exhibit in Milan. The price for this exquisite creation with black, light blue, and white highlights within the plaid was $3,000.

FRED ASTAIRE'S MEASUREMENTS: (IN INCHES)			
∽ Coat ∾		∽ Trousers ∾	
4	slope of shoulder	42½	outside leg
17¼	neck point to waist	32½	inside leg
18½	neck point to waist for dresswear (morning suit or white tie)	9¼	rise—distance from inside leg to the top of the waistband
		29	waist
29½	length of jacket	39	seat
60	neck point to floor	20	circumference of trouser at knee
7¾	half back measurement taken between shoulder blades	16½	circumference of trouser at bottom
21	shoulder to elbow		
31¾	sleeve length		
35	chest		
30	waist		
12¼	across front chest		
25¾	sleeve measurement		
19¾	half waist		

Hitchcock stressed that the Anderson & Sheppard cut was "slightly different from anybody else," referring to the soft natural shoulder cut the firm favored. "It would have been no problem for one of our tailors to make a jacket for Astaire. He was quite slight but in perfect proportion. We could make him look really good," Hitchcock said proudly. The paper patterns of the firm's longtime customers, containing their measurements, are left hanging in the store. Astaire's specifications are still on display.

Hitchcock showed me his long-ago-developed prowess as a cutter by creating a pair of trousers in a mere twelve minutes. He said to fully learn the craft of tailor took ten years.

Budd Schulberg used the Italian phrase *sprezzatura*—the casual, the studied nonchalance—to describe Astaire's success in establishing casual clothing in America. "The Europeans did not have sports clothing. They had suits. Way after World War Two, if an Englishman went to a soccer game, he wore a suit; we would wear a polo shirt.

"The casual jackets and slacks that Astaire wore made a guy think, 'I wish I could be like that.' The other part is that Fred made us feel maybe we could. If we could wear clothes like he does, maybe we might meet a girl like Ginger Rogers."

Schulberg continued, "I used to be an Anderson and Sheppard guy, and for a while I had Astaire's cutter [Charles Bryant, who was the chairman of the company]. He used to tell me that when Astaire came in for a fitting, he would try on the suit, and he would dance up and down the hallway. That was to make sure the suit moved with him.

"Some people would say, 'Well, he had a body for clothes.' No, no, he knew exactly what he was doing, straight down to the last button. My feeling is that a guy who has style wears clothes well no matter what his body looks like. I met Aristotle Onassis because we shared the same shirtmaker at one time. He had a weird build, but he looked fabulous. He knew what looked good on him."

Douglas Fairbanks claimed, "My father used to wear a tie around his waist instead of a belt, too. Fred just made it famous."[5] "The turned-up trousers were more particular to Fred. His style was a studied carelessness."[6]

Slim Keith, a society and sartorial notable on her own, observed, "I don't think Fred ever had any idea he was setting a style; it was just how he liked to look. He used that look in films a lot; in any casual sort of scene, he was always the best casually dressed man."

Audrey Hepburn, herself a paragon of style, offered, "His clothes were always very casual, and terribly, extremely elegant, because he had such taste. Was he good-looking? I think so, because charm is the best-looking thing in the world, isn't it?"[7]

ALAN FLUSSER, in his East Forty-eighth Street showroom, features a large flat television set with video clips of carefully selected scenes from various Fred Astaire movies. I conducted an interview with him as we watched Astaire perform various musical numbers.

Before watching the first clip, the fashion authority said, "I remember one of his practice outfits. He wore baggy, gray flannel pants and a pink Brooks Brothers shirt. The trousers were a little on the short side; he wanted to be able to see his feet because he was always shot full length in a scene with rarely a cut in it. He had a tie around his waist. This was all carefully calculated. The belt replaced suspenders, which he used to wear. The cuffs on his sleeves were rolled back. He wore long underwear so he wouldn't perspire. He wore his pants, like other well-dressed people, on his waist as opposed to his hips. Of course, they were custom-tailored and very full, which enabled him to dance more freely. This also gave him a longer leg line." In later years, a knotted handkerchief adorned his throat in rehearsals, presumably to absorb sweat.

A scene from *Top Hat* finds Astaire in a short cotton jacket. Flusser said, "It was a good length for him. His suit jackets were cut away pretty much in the front. They were like a conductor's coat with high armholes that provided him with more freedom to raise his arms. See how the jacket buttons from the left to the right. He is wearing a Brooks Brothers button-down shirt and a Brooks Brothers striped tie number one. The stripes are going in the opposite direction. And he's wearing suede dancing shoes with some kind of bright color socks."

I was able to trace the origin of Astaire's unique suede dancing shoes, size nine, through the help of Joe Barrato, the well-known fashion consultant.

These shoes are for sale at Battaglia, the men's store on Rodeo Drive in Beverly Hills. They are cross-laced but are actually a slip-on shoe with a higher heel than similar shoes. The instep contains elastic under the tongue that causes the shoe to fit tightly. The shoes had standard tap equipment attached, which consisted of metal plates on the toe and heel, and a loosely embedded steel washer that clinked lightly when the heel hit the ground, which reportedly Astaire hammered in himself. He wore them throughout his dancing career in films and television, keeping seventy to a hundred pairs on hand as each pair usually lasted for only six shooting sessions.[8]

Dow Thamon, the manager at Battaglia, said, "We don't call it the Fred Astaire. We should, but we don't. I wonder if anybody knows they were his shoes. I also wonder if we called it that would it mean anything to young people. We still sell them in the hundreds every year." This is especially interesting because the shoe is priced at $1,100 a pair. (In 1941, they cost $20 a pair.)

The shoes were custom-made in northern Italy and designed by Artioli, who was a close friend of Giuseppe Battaglia's. Battaglia referred Astaire to Artioli, who suggested to him, "I have a shoemaker in Italy, in Tradate, who is very good. He could make up some wonderful dancing shoes for you." Once they were made, Astaire admired them immediately. Battaglia began selling the model shortly thereafter. Today they can be custom-made in any kind of leather a customer might want.

FLUSSER NOTICED THAT IN *ROBERTA,* in which Astaire played dual roles, principally that of the society bandleader "Huck" Haines, he wore the rounded waistcoat, which he had had copied from the Duke of Windsor, along with high-waisted trousers. "The vest is long enough to cover the waistband of the trousers, and he wears one stud button instead of three. You never see that today."

But for Flusser, the apex of Astaire's combining fashion with the dance is the "Dancing in the Dark" number with Cyd Charisse that takes place in Central Park in *The Band Wagon.* "As far as I'm concerned, I don't think any man looked more elegant. He is wearing off-white trousers and some sort of tweed jacket with a red foulard pocket square, a yellow Brooks Brothers button-down shirt, and a yellow silk tie along with his favorite brown-and-white correspondent shoes with yellow socks. The coat is a little longer. [This was two decades after *Top Hat.*] He always wore flat pockets and a ticket pocket. You can see the width in his shoulders."

Continuing his survey of Astaire's clothes in the "Dancing in the Dark" number, Flusser observed, "There is a line from his shoulder to his waist, and then from his waist, an unbroken line right to the bottom of his shoe. That gave him an elongated line and made him look taller. Also, the line is accentuated because the eye goes from the floor up the full pleated trousers, which gives you another illusion of height. It's another reason why short people wear side vents. This is almost the same camera angle as you saw in *Top Hat,* slightly lower, slightly looking up. If you are a student of his clothes, and you watch all the stuff going on, see how his coat sits on his armpits up to his neck. It doesn't move. In ready-made clothes you couldn't do that because the way this coat is cut. And it's without a doubt, in my opinion anyway, the most extraordinary outfit that's ever been put on film."

G. BRUCE BOYER, the former longtime fashion editor of *Town & Country* and a highly respected men's couture writer, as well as the author of *Fred Astaire Style* and other books, said, "When I look at Fred's early movies, starting with *Flying Down to Rio,* what I see in his style is a mid-Atlantic man. He put it all together. It's part Oxford, part London West End, and part Princeton, USA. . . . He picked and chose. If it weren't for Astaire, Cary Grant, and Gary Cooper, half the men in America would have never known what kind of clothes they should wear."

Boyer noted, "American 'cool' started with Astaire's fine art of understatement; he became a hero whose weapon was style. Astaire was the democratic ideal: a classic aristocrat," and "Astaire mixed his dance styles the way he mixed his dress styles: with a spontaneous exuberance in which the hard work was well hidden within the detail and subtlety."

As part of his concentrated study of Astaire's clothes, Boyer discovered that Astaire was a size 36. "To my mind, the entire film of *Swing Time* actually revolves around his clothing. The narrative structure is based on Astaire's necessity to wear proper clothes, as much as by him trying to get the girl. Even during the 'Fine Romance' courtship number, there were lyric references, like Rogers's never having a chance to crease his blue serge pants."

Boyer clarified that King Edward VII, when he was the Prince of Wales, actually invented the glen plaid, but his grandson the Duke of Windsor popularized it. "It went on to become a staple of men's suits and sport jackets. On his wedding day, Fred was photographed in a glen plaid suit with a button-down shirt.

"When he was young, he did all kinds of crazy things like that," Boyer continued. "He would wear long point collars with a pin through it. When he wore a button-down shirt with a pin through it, now that was really fooling around. When he wore an ascot with a big knot, he used a tie bar to hold it in place. Nobody was doing that kind of stuff. In England, they would only wear white bucks for sport, on the tennis court, et cetera. Well, Astaire started to wear them in the thirties with a suit jacket, with suits, and with sports jackets, which is kind of why they started wearing them at Princeton, Yale, and Harvard. He would wear them with a Savile Row suit. Then again, that's another example of his blending things.

"After the First World War, the Duke of Windsor became kind of the 'salesman of the empire' and traveled the world promoting Great Britain. He made half a dozen trips to America with the Oxford polo team. He picked up the habit of wearing suede shoes from soldiers in his regiments, who had been in India. Suedes were really the wrong side of the leather. It was considered flamboyant, but Astaire picked up on it."

Boyer mentioned other innovations of the Duke of Windsor's that became popular, such as Fair Isle sweaters; large knot ties (the Windsor knot, as worn occasionally by Astaire and always by Ronald Reagan); the boater straw hat (seen in several Astaire movies); boldly checked tweed suits (another favorite of Astaire's);

the Brigade of Guards tie (the eternally popular red-and-blue, broad stripes); and spread-collar shirts.⁹ In addition, the popularization of the zipper fly is attributed to the duke. Reportedly, he had his tailor take off the zipper from his luggage and make it into a fly for his trousers.

Speaking of the casual approach Astaire brought to wearing clothes, Boyer said, "I always think of him—even in his most formal outfits, tailcoats—he wears them like you and I would wear pajamas. Everybody else puts on tails and they tend to look like a Prussian general. I must say, too, that he was one of the very few stars who kept the same measurements all his life."

Boyer also observed, "Fred believed that the clothing had to follow you when you dance. At Anderson and Sheppard, they made a lightweight soft coat because there is so little padding in it. That's a good thing for a dancer. The coat molds itself to a person's body. It didn't have a shape of its own."

Boyer also picked up on the difference in Astaire's toupees—another important ingredient in his overall look. From about 1960 on they suddenly had the appearance of an obvious hairpiece, whereas from the thirties through the fifties his hairpiece was slicked back and looked completely authentic. "They suddenly began to look like they were made of thatch and very obvious. I think he was trying to copy young men who were combing their hair to the side, like a Caesar cut. He was trying to be young," Boyer noted. Alan Flusser added, "He wore toupees of different colors. He changed his choice of color to fit his complexion as he got older."

Richard Merkin, another well-regarded fashion writer and jazz observer, admired Astaire's mode of dress but not nearly as much as his colleague Flusser. Merkin thinks that Astaire's basic theatricality had a considerable influence on his style of dressing. "His use of a necktie worn as a belt is a perfect example," Merkin contends.

He also emphasized that like Edward Windsor, Astaire was rich and that enabled him to look elegant by simply buying the best clothes. He concluded that Astaire, like the Duke of Windsor, was a true dandy. He felt this was the principal element in creating his particular fashion style.

In 1959, the English men's fashion magazine *Tailor & Cutter* proclaimed Astaire one of the World's Best Dressed Men. The citation read, "He is one of the few Americans who can wear a suit of tails without looking like they had to throw it on his back to get it on him. . . . He chooses his clothes with an eye to his lack of inches."¹⁰

ASTAIRE KEPT UP a front of total disinterest that on occasion even bordered on disdain when asked by the American press how he felt at being constantly referred to as a fashion icon. A good example of that took place in the fall of 1968 when the veteran journalist George Christy, while on assignment for *Town & Country* magazine, interviewed Astaire in his suite at the St. Regis. He found him anything but happy to address his reputation as a well-turned-out gentleman.

Christy recalled, "I don't know what happened previous to my meeting with him. He cleared his throat disdainfully when I arrived. I asked if he preferred that I come back another day. 'No, no, no,' he said, but he was visibly disturbed. I had to calm him down, so I said, 'You know, I've always admired you. You have such a royal splendor!' 'What are you talking about?' he snapped. I continued by saying, 'You have a certain style. Your clothes are impeccably tailored.' He said, 'That's not true. That's bullshit!' When I said that nobody could wear a top hat and tails like him, he said, 'Oh, well, anybody can do that. I'm an actor.' "

After this rude beginning, Astaire admitted, "I like to make sure that the shoulders are fitted," when asked what he looked for first in a suit. "You have to look at yourself in a three-way mirror to see that everything is right three ways. You have to make sure that the tailoring is neat."

He turned petulant again when Christy brought up his habit of wearing a striped tie as a belt and averred that no one else could carry that off. "That's nonsense," Astaire said. When Christy asked if he recycled his older ties to become belts, he said, "No, whatever tie I like, I just put it on."

The mention of shoes brought the interview back to greater civility. Astaire said, "I think it's worth it to spend extra money on shoes." He told Christy that he bought his shoes at Fenn-Feinstein, then on Fifth Avenue. He admired their brown, wingtip suede models. "They say you shouldn't wear brown shoes with a blue suit. That's nonsense. Brown shoes are perfectly wonderful. I also wear them with a gray flannel suit," he declared.

He discussed his love for straw hats: "I don't think you should ever buy a cheap hat because they don't hold up well. You have to have a good panama hat. It will hold its shape."

The same reaction to his being praised for his fashion prominence occurred eleven years later. "It's all very nice, but I can't say I understand it," muttered Astaire about his election by the International Best Dressed Committee as "the all-time best dresser who's had the strongest influence on masculine elegance in the twentieth century." Did he think of himself as elegant? a reporter from *Listen,* a supplement of the *Los Angeles Times,* asked. "Of course not. I don't think of that sort of thing at all," the song-and-dance man retorted. "Well, we always sort of picture you in white tie and tails," *Listen* persisted. "That's your problem," said Astaire. "I don't like dress suits at all. Especially not white tie and tails. I just grab something out of the closet and wear it."[11]

As ever, Astaire protesteth too much. He was never at all unaware of his importance in men's fashion.

In 2007, Ralph Lauren celebrated his fortieth year in business for himself. The basis of his appeal as a men's clothing designer owes considerably to perpetuating the fashion image created by Astaire. Not long after becoming established, Lauren wanted to honor the importance of Astaire to his own success by designing a Polo jacket appropriately called the Astaire. Not surprisingly it represented Astaire's elegance and became popular. It was available in cotton, wool, and cashmere for prices ranging from $200 to $600 (not to be confused with today's prices of Lauren's best jackets).

In October 1978, the *New York Post,* always eager to elevate a minor dispute into something bordering on a juicy scandal, chronicled the contretemps between Fred's attorney and Lauren in its Page Six section, with the titled FRED ASTAIRE FOILS RALPH LAUREN. It was the lead story that day in the newspaper's lively, much read section.

The *Post*'s anonymous reporter quoted James Taylor (Astaire's attorney) as saying, "Mr. Astaire realized that the label was probably intended as a compliment, but he would prefer not to have his name attached to a clothing line. It looked as though he approved of the label and was perhaps receiving some form of compensation, which is not the case." Taylor wrote a letter to Lauren stating this was a flagrant case of infringement and ordered him to discontinue selling the Astaire. Soon afterward, the Astaire disappeared from Lauren's boutiques.

CLIFF GRODD HAS BEEN the respected president and CEO of Paul Stuart in New York since 1951. Back then, many top male stars such as Cary Grant, Frank Sinatra, and Jack Lemmon were customers. Grodd said, "We became a place where they felt comfortable, and we did not take advantage of who they were." At that time, Paul Stuart was located on a side street in a much smaller shop than its current location at the corner of Forty-fifth Street and Madison Avenue. Business hours then commenced at 8:00 A.M.

Grodd remembered one early morning when Astaire knocked on the door. "I let him in. He was much slighter than I had imagined. He came in about a jacket that had to be snagged. He was very astute, somewhat shy. There was something appealing about him. He had everything and had a certain ease to it. I also remember that he looked at me when I wrote down his name and his address. I asked him if there was an 'e' at the end of his name. I felt foolish asking him that. He must have thought, 'Who is this smart-ass?'

"I always insisted that if you wear your clothes tight, you look bigger; if you are coming out of them, you have more presence. If you wear a size that's a little too large, you look lost in the clothing. It's my own theory, and he subscribed to it, too. Whenever I sold him something, we close-fit it or altered it. He was way ahead of his time in clothing and slimming you down and making it look more sophisticated and elegant."

Grodd was pleased to report that Astaire's belts also consisted of Paul Stuart ties. "In those days, our neckwear—stripes and foulards—was narrow. But I remember how attractive I found it. Now that sort of belt has come back with a vengeance."

Astaire bought only ready-made wear such as jackets, ties, and accessories from the store. These purchases included pink and other-colored socks. "They were loud, a little more sublime. They were eye-catching. He was very definitive," said Grodd, "but he was very mild in his taste. He had panache in whatever he wore. Those fellows develop a personality through their clothing. [The author] Tom Wolfe is another one."

Grodd summed up Astaire's sartorial point of view when he said, "He never wore anything that didn't work with what he was wearing, which I think is the sign of an excellent dresser. He had the ability to dress in a way that when you looked at him, you were struck by the sensitivity of it." He agreed that Astaire's day-to-day look was minutely planned. "It was not as studied as it was in the beginning. It was a comfortable look. He had developed the ability of not being discoordinate."

The genial Wilkes Bashford has run his own well-established men's store in San Francisco for over forty years. Bashford attributed his interest in opening his own establishment to "the sense of style represented by Astaire, Gary Cooper, and other leading male film stars of the thirties and forties that has never been equaled. In addition, when you looked around in that era of the late forties and the early fifties, there were a lot of people well dressed."

Bashford believes Astaire wore his clothes better than any of his Hollywood contemporaries. "His clothes looked totally natural on him, the clothes moved with him, and yet they were fitted. Many people's clothes looked comfortable because they were oversized or they did not recognize the waist in the jackets. Their clothes were big or slouchy, which is the look Armani has done at different times. Fred Astaire's clothes were elegant. Sometimes it is difficult to combine obvious elegance with obvious comfort, but Astaire was so natural, even more than the Duke of Windsor."

Contrary to Flusser's belief, Bashford feels, "The Duke of Windsor's clothes always looked wonderful, but there was a certain stiffness to them. Sometimes, a person as stylish as Astaire was doesn't always get the look that *he* got. The fact that he wore an ascot, which created a very elegant look, was again soft-lined with an open-neck shirt."

One cannot overlook the importance of Brooks Brothers in chronicling Astaire's pursuit of his own inimitable style. The venerable Madison Avenue–based institution, now an international brand, was the source of several of his trademarks, not only for its famous button-down shirts and rep neckties, but also its straw bowlers, felt hats, socks, and other accessories. Astaire was a customer there for over sixty years, starting when he first came to Broadway with Dellie.

Flusser made the interesting point that Brooks Brothers, though different from Anderson & Sheppard, worked for Astaire "because he was much more American and casual and not as formal. It was more genteel and easygoing. Brooks was offering soft, natural-fitting clothes—not clothes that were formal and rigid that pulled a great deal of attention to yourself."

Claudio Del Vecchio, the current CEO of Brooks Brothers, has presided over the company's expansion and the modernization of its stylish clothes without departing from its heritage. Too young to have known Astaire personally, he is highly conversant with his fashion influence and importance to the company's history.

Explaining Astaire's seemingly inappropriate combination of a Brooks Brothers button-down shirt and an English suit, the shy, soft-spoken chief executive contends, "That was that confidence factor again. He was innovative when you think of how he wore his clothes. He was very elegant in *Top Hat,* but he was extremely casual in another film, yet he was elegant in his casual wear. I think it's the little touches, the nuances. They were kind of eclectic, but not contrived. They were natural, free, loose, and easy—like the way he danced.

"I also think the fact that he was in show business gave him the liberty to do the kinds of things that he did. The confidence and the style that he had—that was his statement, his image. He projected that with a lot of authority and panache. And I think the way he walked with his hands in his pockets—he felt clothing. Two men could wear the same jacket. One of them just wears a jacket. When Fred Astaire wore it, it became an extension of himself. It was not just a piece of rag on his back. Everything that he did was a reflection of him, of his style."

Joe Campo, currently a salesman at the highly successful Polo store in Short Hills, New Jersey, waited on Astaire when he worked at Brooks Brothers in 1959, at the age of eighteen. Astaire walked in the store one afternoon, late in the year. "My picture of him now is every picture of Fred Astaire you would ever see. I remember he had a topcoat on. There was only one female salesperson in the store at that time. Her name was Mickey. Fred Astaire was her client. She introduced me to Mr. Astaire and said, "He is going to help you." I remember he wanted five shirts, and they had to be monogrammed. They were all button-down collars, raw Egyptian cotton shirts. The total cost was ninety-four dollars.

"I was making fifty-four dollars a week so to me that was monumental. People who shopped at Brooks Brothers looked like they shopped at Brooks Brothers. Mr. Astaire didn't. He stood out, because he was so elegantly dressed. I remember looking at this guy walking toward me and being mesmerized by him. He could have been an architect. I knew he was a famous personality. And when he was about five feet away he smiled. He was witty."

DURING THE WAR YEARS, of course, Astaire was cut off from his English haberdashers. Beverly Hills tailors took over his custom-tailoring. But the studios were also a source of good clothes then and now for any important star.

Paramount's oldest employee, the eighty-nine-year-old producer A. C. Lyles, remembered meeting Astaire when Lyles was an office boy working for the studio's chairman, Adolph Zukor. RKO was located next to Paramount. "I owned one suit and a coat at that time. I first met Fred when I walked over to RKO. He was such a gentleman. . . . One day I said to him, 'Mr. Astaire, I have to tell you. Someday I hope that I can afford to dress the way you do.' He said, 'I'll tell you something that you should learn. Come in every morning and go to wardrobe and get to know the head of wardrobe.'"

As a result, Lyles said, "So, a lot of the pictures you see of me from when I was ten years old on up, I can look at them and say, 'I borrowed that coat from the wardrobe department.' Astaire would do it. He fascinated me. I admired his having a tie draped as a belt. Now I can afford to have my suits made in England. I couldn't get away with what he did, but I had belts made of the same material as my suit. It's a kickback to Fred."

One of the custom tailors in Beverly Hills that thrived during the 1960s and into the 1970s was Eric Ross, with sixteen tailors in tow. Bernie Schwartz, now also working at the Polo store in Short Hills, ran the establishment. He remembered when Astaire first came into the shop in the early seventies. "It was right in the midst of the long-hair period, which Fred didn't particularly like." Schwartz believed his job was to install a certain confidence in his new customer, showing him politeness and respect but at the same time not trying to oversell him—in fact not selling him at all. As he saw it, he had to make Astaire believe that he knew the clothing business.

"He decided he would let us make a blazer and a pair of gray flannel trousers for him," Schwartz recalled. "What we picked out was beautiful. I think it was a Loro Piana. The other pair was a Carlos Barbera. They are two fine, beautiful mills.

We finally selected a beautiful nice, soft flannel. Fred said, 'I have always been known for being slim. Let's go for the plain front.' At his age, he was showing just a touch of a belly, a tiny, tiny bit. He selected a beautiful blue cashmere for the blazer, one shade lighter than a navy blue. It gave a nice trim look. He was always very body-conscious.

"We made the coat with real buttonholes. He had some gold buttons he gave us with his initials on them, four on each sleeve. After the second fitting, he said, 'This is nice,' which was rare because Cary Grant took eight fittings. All of a sudden, he tore a button off one of the sleeves and we all said, 'What are you doing?' He said, 'Now it looks like it's used a bit. People will get a kick out of saying, 'Mr. Astaire, you are missing a button, and we will have a little conversation.' So, one sleeve had three buttons instead of four. It worked remarkably. If he was gonna look casual, he was gonna look *very* casual. I loved the idea."

CARROLL'S IN BEVERLY HILLS has for many years been a leading men's clothing store and was a frequent haunt of Astaire's. John Carroll took over following the death of his father, Dick Carroll, several years ago. "I came into the business around 1984, although I started first as a stock boy. I saw Fred there a couple of times," Carroll recalled. "It was in the last stages of his life so he wasn't as vibrant, but he was always dashing. He always wore a hat. That's because he wasn't wearing a toupee."

In the September 2000 *GQ,* Dick Carroll reminisced about his longtime customer. "Fred Astaire came to us when Stanley Donen was making *Funny Face.* Stanley came in and bought a white raincoat, and Astaire wore that raincoat in the last scene of the picture. We did a lot of sweaters for Astaire. We made a cashmere sweatshirt that he liked, and he had it in four or five colors. And he used to buy a lot of ties. He used to come in and spend half an hour at the tie bar very quietly; nobody knew who he was or what he was doing.

"But what I remember most about Astaire was that he came in once and bought a beautiful tweed jacket. We had done a lot of work on it, and it was just beautiful. When it was finished and he was in the fitting room in front of me, he put the jacket down on the floor and stamped all over it—the shoulders, the lining, the facing, the vents. And then he picked it up, shook it off, and put in on—and then he felt comfortable. So I guess that tells you something."

John Carroll recalled, "We made some clothes for him for movies in the fifties and sixties. He would mostly buy ties, ascots, and tiepins. I learned that even with small items like that he always requested that he be given a small bag. He didn't want his jacket pockets to show any kind of a bulge. He liked a certain kind of

Caswell-Massey spray cologne. I remember in the eighties, when he wasn't working, he would come in and browse. He was very deliberate. He never returned anything. He probably knew everything that was in his closet, and he knew exactly what would go with what."

His daughter, Ava, said, "He loved to putter around the old Newberry's five-and-ten in Beverly Hills and look for chains that he could sew onto his shoes—just a little glittering something."[12]

BRETT HALSEY, still a handsome man in his seventies, would not be a recognizable name to contemporary moviegoers. Nevertheless, he has carved out a respectable fifty-year acting career in Hollywood and Europe. He had significant roles in such films as *Return to Peyton Place, The Best of Everything,* and more recently *The Godfather Part III,* as well as guest-starring roles in many television series.

Halsey first met Astaire in 1956 while they were getting their Jaguars, his a vintage model, Astaire's a new one, serviced at a Hollywood garage. "Jaguars were terrible in those days," Halsey said. "We talked about cars a lot. It's funny, we never talked about show business.

"The thing that he did that impressed me more than anything was he taught me how to dress. I liked his style, more English than Brooks Brothers. What I learned was that he never changed his style, but he wore beautiful clothes, the best cut. He taught me that I should buy good clothes, and if they fit your body, hang on to them. The way he presented it was 'You don't have to follow the styles; you find out what looks good on you, and if it's well cut, and good stuff, no one will ever accuse you of being out of style.' "

Like Astaire, Halsey was a customer at Carroll's. "They dressed me for roles that were American. When I went to Rome, my clothes were made by Angelo. I went more for British clothes, however. Fred was such an important figure in all our lives. If he handed you something as he did with me about clothes, you had it for a long time. That's how I felt about his advice."

AFTER TALKING WITH a wide assortment of people involved in some manner with men's clothes, I talked with a man with a vast background in men's clothing retailing, Joe Barrato. He was drawn to Astaire as a youngster, at the age of eleven, after seeing *The Band Wagon.*

"I guess it was the combination of music, the style, and this guy Fred Astaire just popping out of that movie which made such an impression," Barrato recalled.

"I like to dance, and I would pretend I was Astaire. I would occasionally wear a tie as a belt. Fred was spontaneous in everything he did. It was the same way with his clothing, understated and unpretentious. It was very simple. He had a very specific point of view, a distinct flair. He had complete confidence. That was his statement. You might call it casual elegance."

While leafing through the pages of *Fred Astaire Style,* showing Astaire in various outfits, Barrato noted that Astaire in his eighties wore garrison belts with big buckles as against wearing belts buckled on the side as he did during the 1930s. "And look at him wearing a scarf with a sport jacket on his way to playing tennis. Those were examples of the Fred Astaire style. You don't duplicate that. You get the influence, but you can't duplicate it.

"I feel Fred Astaire gave me a gift, and I really treasure that. He has given that gift to Ralph [Lauren], Allan Flusser, and Giorgio Armani. Ralph has maintained his point of view like Fred Astaire."

Barrato began taking a serious look at men's fashion when he started out working for Brooks Brothers. It continued while working for Ralph Lauren, in the days when Lauren was starting his own business; when Barrato headed Brioni in North America; and recently when he was in charge of Lauren's two most prestigious lines of men's clothes. *Esquire* once selected Barrato as one of the ten best-dressed men in the industry.

He believes that through the years women had a profound influence on the way important men dressed. He said, "Gary Cooper's style, for instance, was influenced by an Italian *contessa* who turned him into a sophisticate."

I insisted, however, that the English aristocracy served as Astaire's primary fashion inspiration, and that Phyllis Astaire's taste probably had some influence as well. Barrato said, "Fred was very shy. He didn't have that confidence with women," implying that in Astaire's case women had little influence on his quest to develop his personal style.

Barrato still wears Brooks Brothers button-down shirts on occasion. They are always a half size smaller then his other shirts. He believes Astaire did that, too. "It gives you a better roll. The roll on that collar is just amazing."

ROBERT WAGNER REMAINS a long-standing member of Hollywood royalty. He well remembers the era when the important male actors set an example and made a definite statement with their clothes. They were stars and dressed to look like what they were—the standout personalities of their time. Whenever they appeared in public, they dressed with a confidence that exuded the glamour they were selling on-screen.

Wagner emerged as a young leading man after signing on as a Twentieth Century–Fox contract player in the early 1950s. He reflected on that time when he said, "At the time I started out in the business, everybody had an individual style—Cooper, Fred Astaire, Cary Grant—they had their own look. They didn't deal in labels; they created their own style. It was classic—Fred with his knots, Cary with an open shirt or sweater. And women did the same thing. They had their own way of making it happen.

"I don't know how some of these men that are executives and lawyers do it— today it's a tough thing to keep that look up with suits. They're so expensive. But they are going for the trendy. Everything has become trendy . . . I don't think they have any sense of the basics. You have to have a sense of the basics before you can start. When Astaire opened up his jacket and put his hand inside his belt, that was classic. He made it happen. He made the clothes happen for him. You've got to have the man inside the clothes. Clothes don't make the man. The man moves with the clothes."

The look in Hollywood today is quite different. Young actors enjoy being photographed attending fashion shows, but this rarely has any impact on their limited, mostly casual wardrobe. The opposition by male stars to wearing stylish clothes began to be felt after World War II when Marlon Brando burst upon the scene in *A Streetcar Named Desire* wearing a T-shirt and jeans. It became his everyday uniform and also reflected his disdain for the establishment and especially Hollywood. The feeling among young actors was that informal attire gave a sense of freedom, providing a badge of honor for them to be recognized as true artists. The beat movement of the 1950s, Brando's dressing in motorcycle gear in *The Wild One,* and then the punk movement that started in the late 1970s that followed on the heels of the Beatles revolution went even further. The slow death of classic men's clothing started there.

Yet Wagner admires the leather jackets often worn by today's young actors. "They put together a good look. I don't know, however, whether they know how to do the classic stuff. It's a different era, a different time. You and I have seen such changes in everything—in technology, in literature, in computer images. What about *The Bridge on the River Kwai*—when the train comes over that bridge, and they blew up the bridge. That was a real train and a real bridge. That doesn't happen anymore. We who caught that other era were lucky."

Wagner appeared on ABC's *The View* along with the superb character actor Robert Vaughn to promote an episode of the TV series *Hustle,* with a clever script involving two scheming con artists, in which they costarred. Neither actor needed advice on what to wear on *The View.* They were both attired in attractive suits, Wagner's a Ralph Lauren creation suggested by Joe Barrato. The example and the influence of the classic male stars whom they grew up with in the movie business was obvious.

In contemporary Hollywood, male stars are usually dressed in jeans when attending the premieres of their movies. Years ago they would have appeared in black tie or white tie. (Jeans have their place, but in my view they still shouldn't be worn to a film premiere.) If the film deals with a serious subject, they might wear a suit, but rarely a necktie to go with it. That went out a decade ago when the "casual Friday" trend began in New York offices. This once standard element of male attire seems to be rapidly heading for its demise.

This is in stark contrast to how young actors learned about dressing well in the days when the studios ruled the industry, not the stars. As Robert Wagner recalled, "I had a little sense about clothes, but those wardrobe guys at Fox were great. They knew how to make you look good. They knew wardrobe and set you up with some of the greatest tailors."

Dick Van Dyke, long recognized for being a spiffy dresser, said, "I have a picture of Fred and myself together which I have on my wall. It was taken on the set of *Bye Bye Birdie.* I had on one of my very best tailored suits. Standing next to him, I looked like a schmuck."

Van Dyke continued, "You know, most men don't have any idea how they look in clothes. They'll buy something somebody else wears. They'll see something they like, but they have no idea what it looks like on them. Fred's idea of lines, you know, was the same as his dancing. He knew, and he always had a one-button suit with the one button which was at the waistline or perhaps lower that gave him that long 'V.' For a long time, I wore my trousers short, as Fred did, like on the old *Van Dyke Show,* showing a little sock, but people made such fun of me that I had to get my pants lengthened."

Bruce Boyer believes, "Unfortunately, like a blacksmith, a cobbler, or a cooper, in ten years bespoke tailors won't exist." As Flusser intoned, "If there is nobody for men to look at, then where are men going to find out about how to dress well?" Joe Barrato said it all when he remarked, "What has happened to men's clothing? How do you think a woman wants her man to look? Dressed in a T-shirt and a pair of jeans or dressed elegantly? They always say elegantly. I think there has been a total breakdown. We are missing something, and our industry is missing the message here. In the days of Fred Astaire, elegance was a normal thing, except he brought it to another level."

CHAPTER NINE

THE NBC-TV SPECIALS: THREE HITS AND A MISS

IT IS IMPORTANT TO RECOGNIZE that Fred Astaire's career, starting in 1925 with Leland Hayward, was guided by brilliant and carefully executed agency representation. MCA, his agent after the departure of Hayward, was the dominant talent agency in show business for more than two decades. Following its move into representing the leading film stars, Jules Stein, Lew Wasserman, and their minions saw almost immediately the wave of the future, and that was television.

By the mid-1950s, MCA had become an equally powerful force in that lucrative field as well, packaging its own shows for sale to the networks and eventually owning its own production company, Revue Studios, which produced shows with MCA clients. Revue was in turn a branch of Universal Pictures, which MCA had also purchased. MCA's all-encompassing presence led to its appropriately being referred to as the Octopus.

Enter Berle Adams, an MCA vice president and a member of the agency's board of directors, who was a major factor in the company's success in television. Putting musical television shows together was his forte. Harry Friedman, Fred's longtime movie agent, arranged to put Adams and Astaire together for a meeting at MGM. Something of great consequence came from that.

As Adams recalled, "The advertising agencies were always coming to me if they wanted a new idea. Movie stars didn't appear on television. I always felt, however, that Fred Astaire and Gene Kelly would be fresh ideas for television. Fred should be the first."

Adams described Astaire as "a very careful man. He had to know everything that was going on, but he was very relaxed about it. He was not an easy man to convince. I went to see him a couple of times. I had to show him that if he did television, he wouldn't have to make any decisions. I would have to make all the decisions. He decided that he would take that risk, so I sold the show to Chrysler. I said, 'I know who I want for director. I know who I want for the writer of the show, and who I want to decorate the set and all that. It's up to you. You have the approval. It's your show. You own the show.

"The next day he called me up and said, 'Look, I don't know a damn thing about television. I told you I'd do the show for you. You're responsible for all the other elements.' "

Adams told Fred he wanted his old friend from Chicago, David Rose, who had composed and conducted music at MGM for many years, as musical director of the show. Astaire had known him there. Rose was to have a thirty-piece orchestra at his disposal.

Bud Yorkin was set as the producer, director, and writer. Yorkin related that Rose was a close friend of his, whom he wanted to work with him on the show. Yorkin had already established himself in television by directing variety shows starring Dinah Shore, Bud Abbott and Lou Costello, Dean Martin and Jerry Lewis, Tony Martin, George Gobel, and Tennessee Ernie Ford. Herbert Baker wrote special material for the show, Hermes Pan was to be the dance director, and Ed Stephenson was the set director. Adams explained, "The artists owned the packages. We could bring [in] anybody we wanted. We got our commission off the top, below the line and above the line."

WHILE ALL THESE vital backstage business machinations were taking place, Marie Torre, a leading television editor of the time, who wrote for the *New York Herald Tribune,* referred to Astaire's recent promotional appearances on television publicizing *Silk Stockings* as having "sprung hope in the hearts of video pursuers who have been falling over antennae trying to shake loose from the movie lots. Sad to relate, however, any TV man with Astaire in his eyes is merely having a pipe dream."

Torre was wrong. Fred had been offered a few weekly television series but wasn't interested in such a taxing commitment.[1] He carefully "tested the waters" on Sunday, December 1, 1957, by appearing in a humorous part in "Imp on a Cobweb Leash," a CBS half-hour comedy produced by Revue Productions for *General Electric Theater,* hosted by Ronald Reagan. No singing or dancing was involved. Instead, Fred played an executive who showed up at a board meeting in Bermuda shorts and a crew cut![2] The television audience and critics seemed to find his natural charm endearing on the small screen. The show made a sufficient impact to warrant a rerun.

Following that appearance, Astaire began to concentrate on developing his ideas for a possible television special. He knew how important it was to have the right dancing partner. Barrie Chase came back into the focus.

Chase, the bright and highly opinionated retired dancer, recalled, "There was a time lapse of about a year, a year and a half," referring to the interval after she had worked with Astaire in *Silk Stockings*. "There was a bar right next to the studio [MGM] that lots of us, Kay Kendall, and especially jazz dancers, went to after work to get some wine. Gene [Kelly] would sometimes come in. All of a sudden, Fred started coming in. He said to me once, 'Are you really serious about dancing?' I thought that was the dumbest question I had ever heard because with Jack [Cole] you worked very, very hard. I said to Fred, 'There's not a chance in the world that I would be putting myself through this if I were not serious about it.'"

HOAGY BIX CARMICHAEL, son of the famous composer and character actor, who oversees his father's formidable music copyrights, first met Fred as a teenager while playing golf at the Bel-Air Country Club. Soon, a lasting friendship was established. Carmichael remarked, "Fred had a hard chuckle, not as bad as George Bush, when he does that silly head thing. I remember a number of times when he would act out his laughter. He would do a turn, hit a golf club, and smack it down."

Fred felt a closeness with Hoagy. One day, while Hoagy was visiting Fred's home, Fred said to him, "I am working with this young dancer." Carmichael recalled, "Like a fourteen-year-old kid, he looked at me with this sort of 'Gosh, I don't know whether I should be talking about these things,' but, he went on to say, 'Should I date Barrie Chase—take her out? I would really love to. What do you think?' I remember saying, 'Fred, you are sitting at home, for God's sake, why not?' He used to walk around Beverly Hills. Any girl he passed on the street would have been glad to go out with him. He never had a normal childhood. I don't know if he ever matriculated like a lot of us did, chased some girls like teenagers do. He was in vaudeville. Fred grew up very differently."

Astaire did eventually ask Chase to have dinner with him. They spent several evenings "having a great time, a fascinating time," recalled Chase. She acknowledged her chronic lateness. "I said to Fred, 'I can set my watch by you. If we are going to go to dinner at eight o'clock, you are at the door at eight o'clock on the minute. You are so on time all the time.' He said, 'No, you're wrong. I'm early. I sit in the car and wait until eight o'clock.'"

One night, she told him how much she wanted to see the Moiseyev dancers, the Russian folk-dance group, perform at the Shrine Auditorium, but said that she had been unable to get tickets. Fred came through with a pair of tickets, and they attended a performance. "The Moiseyev dancers were sensational," Chase remembered. "It was fabulous. What they did was [perform] one dance number after another. Fred was very influenced by the Moiseyev. That gave him the idea of doing a dance show with one dance number after the other—not like a variety show with a singer, a comic, and acrobats with lots of talk."

One night shortly thereafter Astaire took Chase to dinner at Villa Nova. He said that he was seriously considering an offer to do a television special. He asked if she would be interested in working with him. He said, "We'll work for a while, no chorus, just you and Pan and me."[3]

Chase was signed to Twentieth Century–Fox when Fred asked her to work with him on his television special. On his recommendation, she changed agencies to sign with MCA. Fred helped her obtain a release from her contract with Fox.

Fred conceded, "Barrie was the inspiration for these specials that I did. . . . She had a good sense of humor, very sensitive, and very stylish. She was always putting herself down, but if you ever tried to put her down—look out. She knew what she was doing, but she was just a little shy about learning this and that and the other thing. . . . There was never any question about the difference in our ages because she carried it off so beautifully. I wasn't going to do the specials at all. . . . Then, I found myself a dancer, and I knew I could do it with her. She was new, she was great with me, and we clicked. When the Chrysler Corporation offered me three shows, one a year, I said, 'Yeah, I can do it.' "[4]

Astaire approached the attorney Ed Blau to represent him on his contract with Chrysler for the special. Blau had previously been an MCA lawyer. Blau revealed, "Fred was actually reluctant to do the special; he was reluctant to do all the subsequent ones as well. The contract called for MCA to have exclusive distribution rights for the term of the copyright plus six renewals, which made it fifty-six years. You couldn't change it. It was sacrosanct."

In his dealings with Astaire, which lasted for several years, Blau described Fred as "not very forthcoming. I don't think he laughed a lot. He was a very serious, introverted kind of person. I don't think he was into the money that much. He was more concerned about how hard he would have to work on a project. He was a perfectionist, and that meant that if he did it, and his name's connected with it, if it had to have his stamp of approval, it would have to meet his standards. I formed his corporation, Ava Productions, which produced the specials."

ON MAY 6, 1958, Fred appeared as a guest on a local television show hosted by Oscar Levant with his wife, June. Fred was his usual debonair self, dressed in a double-breasted blue blazer and gray flannel slacks. The hideously neurotic and self-centered pianist introduced Fred to his TV audience by calling him "the greatest song-and-dance man in history" and "an incredibly charming man." Levant's introduction had an immediate effect on Fred's demeanor. He began crossing his arms and holding himself rigidly. The expression on his face read, "What am I doing here? How did I ever allow Oscar to talk me into appearing on this stupid show."

Levant accompanied Fred as he sang a cluster of his old songs, naturally leaning toward several written by Oscar's former sidekick George Gershwin, such as "They Can't Take That Away from Me." Then Oscar began talking endlessly and simultaneously chain-smoking while switching from one unrelated topic to another, causing Fred to scowl even more. After a commercial break, Oscar told his audience that Fred had another engagement that evening and unfortunately had to leave. It was none too soon. This was one television guest spot Fred should never have accepted. Strangely enough, though, in *Steps in Time* he referred to his appearance on Levant's show as "one of my most enjoyable experiences"!

"AN EVENING WITH FRED ASTAIRE" was broadcast "live in living color," with a studio audience, at 9:00 P.M. on NBC-TV on October 17, 1958. The announcer's familiar voice was that of Art Gilmore. The show got a barely acceptable 18.9 share.

I interviewed Bud Yorkin, who had an intimate view of how the show was created. It seemed impossible that Astaire would dare to appear in a live television special at a time when every important film star was terrified of the medium—afraid if he or she appeared on television it would cause irreparable harm to his or her box-office appeal and image. Astaire thought otherwise, in spite of his usual inner doubts. He felt television offered a great opportunity for him.

Yorkin noted, "That was the year Gene Kelly did the first TV show he ever did and Bing Crosby as well. I know because I was offered all three of them. I felt I could do more with Fred. I think Fred was very leery of what might happen on television because he said to me, once we got to know each other really well, that he enjoyed doing some of the movies . . . but he said [speaking of television], 'It's too fast for me in a way.'"

When Astaire and Yorkin first met, at Fred's home, Fred immediately asked Yorkin, "What would you do with me?" The director recalled, "I don't think he was trying to challenge me. I said to him, 'Number one, I would never want to see you open up with a top hat, tails, and a cane.' I thought the opening should be just him with a Count Basie–type vamp in the background to bring him on. He would do his own choreography [with Pan] as the credits went on. For his first dance number with the chorus, I had an idea that everything in the studio should be frozen with him dancing all around the place. I said to him, 'You bring the whole stage to life, to movement.'

"I explained to him, 'The thing to do is we can rehearse this show like a Broadway show.' We had six weeks of rehearsal." (This was at a time when TV specials usually underwent two weeks of rehearsal.) Even though Berle Adams had told Fred that Yorkin should be the director, Yorkin was one of several producer/directors Fred interviewed for the job. Fred intended to make full use of his right of approval. He wanted the show to reflect his personal touch.[5]

Yorkin made it clear to Astaire that everyone thought he should at least dance one number with Ginger Rogers on his special. Peg Yorkin, then Yorkin's wife and now chair of the board of the Feminist Majority Foundation, recalled, "Bud didn't want that. I think that's one of the major reasons Fred chose Bud to do the show. Bud was well-known in the business, but for Fred I think that was a very important issue."

A few days later, Astaire called Yorkin and said, "I hope you'll do it. I really think we're gonna have a great time." Then, as Yorkin recalled, "We took that idea of mine for the opening and finally got him to execute the first number with the idea that all the dancers were like puppets who came to life doing the dancing, all frozen. He and Hermes and I agreed that by having people with that kind of a tempo beat, it would play against them, and he could have more fun. He could do a turn, and then they could do a turn and copy him.

"We spent a lot of time together. I thought to myself, 'How do you make this show different?' I felt that by doing a show that was [really] a one-man show— that was something new at the time. I told him he might have to give in to the sponsor. I explained that Chrysler was putting almost half a million dollars into the show. He said, 'You better get somebody else to do the show.'

"I told Fred to hold tight and went to Detroit and met with Jack Barlow of the advertising agency that represented Chrysler. They wanted Ricky Nelson to be a guest for ratings. I told him we weren't going to have any name guests on the show to get a rating, that if Fred Astaire couldn't hold an audience for fifty minutes, we were all in trouble. I convinced Jack to go along with it."[6]

The two guests were to be Barrie Chase and Jonah Jones, the jazz trumpeter, leading his quartet. Neither was of any name value, but their presence added immeasurably to the artistic, critical, and eventual ratings success the show enjoyed.

As plans moved ahead, Fred learned that Ginger Rogers was scheduled to go on CBS-TV with her own special shortly before his was scheduled to air. He firmly believed Ginger planned it that way. As a result, Chase remembered her fear that everyone would say, "Why doesn't Fred dance with Ginger?" She felt it was the kiss of death. Pat Denise, who was one of Pan's assistants, told her, "Barrie, don't think about it; just go do your job. Put it out of your head."

Strangely enough, Denise, who worked closely with Barrie on the show, informed me, "Hermes did his best to get Fred to use Juliet Prowse on his first special. He had worked with her in Europe. Juliet was more of a jazz dancer than Barrie, who was first a ballet dancer. Hermes had a peculiar attachment to Juliet."

The what-ifs are part of show business legend. It didn't much matter that Pan favored Prowse as Astaire's dance partner for his first TV special. Barrie Chase got the job and did the next three NBC specials as well. Astaire always knew exactly whom and what he wanted before he finally started work on a project. As good a dancer as Prowse was, he must have reasoned, among other things, that she was too tall and rangy for him, and that the television camera would pick up on that.

Knowing that he was dancing with an unknown, who was fundamentally a chorus dancer, meant considerable effort was required to mold her into a compatible dance partner. Fred recognized, "She was difficult, but they were all like that—all the girls when they were learning. They were afraid of me, too."[7]

He wanted Chase to look good. He approved her costumes, makeup, hairstyles, and the camera angles. He recalled past endeavors with other partners; "I always remember their saying, 'You made me cry!' Well, it's true. Everybody cries, including myself, trying to get some jobs done."[8] Jerry Jackson said, "Barrie told me just before they would go on to do a number, Fred would say, 'Sweetie, just go out there and have a good time, and don't make any mistakes.'"

I asked Chase what was the most important thing she learned in her years dancing with Astaire. She quickly replied, "Never to like yourself. Never be satisfied with what you do." (We have seen that this was a fundamental ingredient in Astaire's performing modus operandi.) She also pointed out, "Whenever you watch Fred in anything that he did, you always liked him—acting, dancing, or singing. He had a tremendously likable quality, which is a gift."

Summing up what made Astaire unique, Chase said, "It was his grace, his style, and his moves. . . . He moved like no one else. You could full-frame Fred, and there was never an awkward moment, never. . . . It was incredible. He had his own sense of timing and rhythm. There's no category for the way he danced." She added, "He didn't only influence my work, he made my career."[9]

THE SIXTEEN-MEMBER CHORUS (eight men and eight women) consisted mostly of those who had worked with Fred in movies. Fred was there first at rehearsals, which were held in a loft above a mortuary. He usually began work at 8:30 A.M.; the dancers came in at 10:00 A.M.

Astaire's personal agent at the time, Ned Tanen, recalled, "One day during rehearsals for the show he was kind of giving me a little gas about something. You could tell he was upset. I said to him, 'Fred, why don't you move over a little bit.' He said, 'Why should I move over?' I looked behind him, and there was a stiff lying on the gurney he was leaning against."

One of the members of the chorus was the standout dancer Larri Thomas, who never stopped working in musical films, television variety shows, and specials throughout the 1950s and 1960s. Retired dancer Bea Bush Wilcox, who danced in the chorus of the first three specials, described Thomas as "very stylized and gorgeous, very chic and aristocratic. She had a wonderful air about the way she danced." Thomas is indeed deserving of the moniker the Great One.

Thomas met Astaire for the first time at the rehearsal for the first special. "I did not audition for the job. [Obviously, Hermes Pan knew of her reputation.] I don't think a television show ever had that much rehearsal. It was like six weeks with the dancers, and he must have rehearsed a couple of months with Barrie and Pan before that."

Thomas set out the proper etiquette and a guide for dance rehearsals: "There was to be no talking, chewing gum, or eating. No sitting on the floor. Never any disrespect shown. Music is the most important ingredient in working on the dance. Before you can build a fire, you must have a spark. The edge is where everything happens. There is a particular moment you work for, and when it happens all you can say is 'Aah.' "

In discussing Astaire and Gene Kelly, she said, "I loved Fred as a singer, but he did not knock me out as a dancer, only because I don't like hoofers all that much. Hoofing is laying down iron tap dancing. I loved the Fred-and-Ginger thing. Nobody could do it better. Nobody looked better in a pair of tails. . . . I respected what he did, and how he wanted it to come out on film. I just liked to watch Gene Kelly dance more than anybody else. . . . I can't explain it—charisma, chemistry. Fred was fabulous, but you know I wouldn't wanna jump on his bones."

Thomas recalls being paid somewhere between $130 and $150 a week, plus overtime, for dancing on the special. (According to Wilcox, Astaire paid the dancers above scale.) Rehearsals generally lasted six to seven hours a day, five days a week, which included an hour lunch break. Thomas figures she made all told a little over $2,200 on the show.

She recalled the pressure involved in doing the show live. There were no cue cards, no retakes, yet she never recalled seeing Astaire lose his temper. "You could tell when he was feeling a little bit [annoyed]. He let Pan do the talking. If any yelling had to be done, Hermes's assistant Gino Malerba would do it." Thomas did, however, recall Fred getting furious at Barrie Chase for being constantly late for rehearsal. She also acknowledged that Chase "had beautiful feet" (a comment made by no less than four other dancers), and "she was a good dancer."

BETTY ROSE, the widow of David Rose, who takes care of his extensive music publishing interests, said, "David loved working with Fred because they were both perfectionists. He went over to Astaire's home first to go over tempos before starting on the show. Fred would dance while David would play the piano."

Rose's perfect understanding of tempos was apparent when Astaire opened the show with a perfect Basie-like arrangement, using four drummers, to bring him and the dancers on. Recalling its purpose, Bud Yorkin said, "I just wanted it to be contemporary."

With Rose's arrangement of his tune "Svengali," Yorkin's startling opening, with the dancers in a semicircle, established the format of the show. As the producer/director described it, "It was a dance show, not a comedy show, not a drama—the kind of show that Fred was famous for. It looked like it was black-and-white, which it wasn't. It was done in black and purples. We decided to do the costumes in black and white . . . very sparse—that was the look of the show."

The costume designer for the show was Ray Aghayan, aka the Persian Prince. Part of Aghayan's formidable reputation had been achieved in those years through dressing Dinah Shore during her long-running NBC, Sunday-night TV variety show. He remembered that a certain conviviality pervaded the first Astaire special.

Aghayan designed all of Astaire's clothes except for his tuxedos. "I remember I put him in pants without pleats. In those days, everyone wore pleats, so I had to convince him to go along with it." Contrary to popular opinion, according to Aghayan, Astaire didn't have the jackets he wore in films cut looser when he danced. "You always cut a gusset on a male dancer, an extra fabric so the sleeve is cut with more room. That's so he could raise his arm without pulling the jacket."

To compensate for Barrie Chase's being five feet six inches, he recalled, "We just lowered her heels so as not to appear too tall for Fred. She was exactly the right size for him as a partner. She had a nice dancer's body. Whatever you made looked right because of her proportions. You could do things on her you couldn't do with other girls. When she danced, she was very sexy. But she could be picky with Fred."

YORKIN REPORTED, "Every number was full stage in the sense that we used the whole stage. Three of the four stages in the Burbank studio were utilized for the show, switching from one to the other for each number. There were also a lot of costume changes between the numbers. Seconds before airtime, Fred reached down to straighten the shoelaces of his black-and-white shoes. Most people would be worried about their lines. . . . Fred was worried that his shoelaces wouldn't be right for the close-up on his feet that opened the show."

Astaire's nervousness continued right into his opening talk spot. He was obviously preoccupied by the sheer possibilities of mistakes being made. As usual, he was not at a loss in playing himself. He came across as natural and appealing, which made one feel that everybody watching the show was pulling for him to succeed.

"Change Partners," the Berlin/Astaire chestnut, made an immediate impact as a romantic duet with Fred and Barrie Chase. Chase brought an eroticism to the number that was reminiscent of that sometimes found in Ginger Rogers's dancing partnership with Fred. The studio audience's immediate response seemed to inspire them. In a restaurant, Fred meets Barrie when her escort leaves the table. That leads into her dream-sequence dance. Fred is about to spirit her away when her escort returns, and he is left in the lurch. "We tried to tell a story with every number," said Yorkin.

Fred brought Chase back for a curtain call. He introduced her to the audience, and a short, impromptu conversation ensued between the two. It seemed as though Fred intentionally didn't want her to talk. He wanted a dancing object, an attractive woman who would look good while dancing with him—definitely not someone on a par with him. Perhaps this was the aftereffect of having had to deal with Ginger Rogers years ago.

Jonah Jones, whom Fred personally sought for the show, was given a choice spot playing two tunes, "Baubles, Bangles, and Beads" and "Mack the Knife," back-to-back from his hit Capitol album *Muted Jazz.* Continuing in a jazz realm, David Rose and His Orchestra, featuring Bobby Hammock on piano and Alvin Stoller on drums, contributed "Man with the Blues," a segment that combined Rose's composition "Young Man's Lament" and "Like Young," which he had previously arranged and helped to make into a hit record for André Previn. The interplay between Astaire, portraying a man lost in loneliness, and the dancers was simply stunning. This number was the only one in the entire show in which the music had been prerecorded.

"That number grew right from the music," recalled Yorkin. "I played a recording of what David had done. It motivated Fred. He said, 'Jesus, it's almost like a story. We could do *West Side Story* with it, something like that.' Hermes didn't know what to do with it. I mentioned having seen the Folies Bergère in Paris. There was a scene in it with venetian blinds opening and closing. Every time the blinds opened, there was a nude standing there; we couldn't do that, but we did have Barrie Chase. Each time the blinds opened, there was Barrie, and then she started coming after Fred. That's how we started the number."

"Old McDonald's Trip" delivered a perfect change of pace with Astaire surprisingly at home in a rural setting doing a country hoedown. Aghayan maintained the black-and-white motif of the show with the female dancers wearing black skirts and white tops, along with black-and-yellow headbands. Fred and the dancers then segued from square dancing to Spanish dancing, then to jazz, with complete ease.

Jonah Jones returned with his group to play "St. James Infirmary," a particular favorite of Fred's, which had also been featured on Jones's album. Chase and Fred were sensational as they danced briskly backed by Jones's trumpet solos and vocal rendition. It was arguably the most electrifying number in the entire show and helped establish Chase as one of Astaire's foremost dancing partners. (Yorkin remembered, "We used to laugh and say, 'The mortuary, where we rehearsed, gave us the motivation for 'St. James.'")

As we have seen, Fred never repeated himself in the choreography of his dance numbers and constantly avowed his lack of interest in his past accomplishments. He closed the show with a long medley of songs he had originally introduced or made famous. It would have been a serious mistake if this medley hadn't been a key part of his first special. Perched on a stool, a favorite prop of nightclub singers of the era, he began with "Lady Be Good," which he and Adele had danced to originally on Broadway in December 1924, before moving on through "Cheek to Cheek," "A Fine Romance," "They Can't Take That Away from Me," "Nice Work If You Can Get It," "A Foggy Day," "I Won't Dance," "Something's Gotta Give," "Night and Day," and ending with the inevitable "Top Hat, White Tie, and Tails." (Reportedly, at the completion of "Top Hat," when Fred removed his top hat, he had an especially broad smile on his face, glad that his toupee hadn't come off).

He thanked the Chrysler Corporation for making the hour possible and said good-night. Viewing a tape of the show forty-seven years after it originally aired, Yorkin suddenly blurted out, "Boy, I don't know how he kept it going!" Peg Yorkin recalled Bud's remarking at the time how much weight Fred appeared to have lost in rehearsing for the show.

In a *TV Guide* interview Yorkin called Astaire "the most conscientious man I ever worked with." Still, Yorkin admitted having had some problems with him. Once was when he pointed out that they were doing live television, and a particular dance number could last only seven minutes. "All those years, he was used to looking at a camera . . . now I came in with three crane cameras and a dolly camera.

Fred said, 'What's all this equipment? Why are they there? That camera's centered. That's where I'm dancing.' I told him, 'Fred, I can't shoot it there. . . . You have to take my word on some of this.' So he was a little upset that day. He came into the booth and watched a scene on tape of a dance we had just rehearsed. He was absolutely amazed at what he saw, how we edited as he danced. We became really good friends after that," said Yorkin.

He added, "If you stood back forty or fifty feet, and you watched this man dance, you wouldn't know whether it was Hermes or Fred Astaire. Hermes had every move; he looked like Astaire. He performed like him. Almost every step that Fred made, Hermes would do and turn like Fred would do, and he might embellish it or change it."

CHRYSLER THREW A LAVISH PARTY at the Beverly Hills Hotel right after the show. "Richard Nixon called as Fred walked through the door," Yorkin recalled. "Fred couldn't believe it. He was just blown away. People were waiting in line. Ed Sullivan called from New York." Yorkin described it as "one of those nights that you never have, like the opening night of *My Fair Lady* or something. . . . Fred went away to do *On the Beach* in Australia shortly after that. He wrote me several letters from there. In one of them he said, 'I've never had anything like this in my whole career. I've never had such mail coming in . . . I've never had so many telegrams. Boy, this medium's something. I guess somebody liked *your* show.' "

THE TELEVISION CRITICS, a sour and sometimes severe lot, who don't normally have much to cheer about given the mundane quality of programming, then and now, were anxiously awaiting a show of decided quality. Probably the most influential critical observer of them all, Jack Gould of the *New York Times,* said in the opening lines of his piece, "Television had one of its unforgettable exciting evenings last night—an hour with Fred Astaire. . . . In his first live appearance before the cameras, Mr. Astaire swept all before him in a tour de force of artistry and personality. The home screen was bathed in the glow of true creative theatre as the dancer did one number after another for which any Broadway producer would give his eyeteeth. . . . Mr. Astaire and his colleagues have set a new standard for musical TV."

Gould was so captivated by the show that he wrote a follow-up article, on October 26, which analyzed in some detail the ingredients that made the show such an event. The critic emphasized Astaire's impact and how he treated the medium: "For sixty minutes he also imparted in TV a sense of impeccable taste, a theatrical elegance and dignity that it so seldom captured. Gone were all the tiresome and familiar happenings common to so many specials—the weary procession of guest stars, the interminable introductions, the perfunctory production numbers, the hackneyed camera work.

"Mr. Astaire and his colleagues on the program—Bud Yorkin, the director; Hermes Pan, the choreographer; and David Rose, the conductor—chose to present a small review—a review with point of view, enchanting originality, and beguiling freshness." Further, Gould singled out the "St. James Infirmary" number: "Barrie Chase, dancing the entombed gal who was so cold, frail and fair, made the screen sizzle. It was a camera of mood, to be felt rather than described."

Newsweek heaped additional laurels upon the show: "From the moment the slick-haired old master, 59, showed a chorus of young dancers what it was all about in his opening number till he pulled up a stool and sang a dozen nostalgic tunes in his breathy voice, there wasn't a doubt. This was one of TV's finest hours."

Almost unanimous acclaim for the show spewed forth from the nation's TV critics, as evidenced by the often flinty TV critic of the *Herald Tribune,* John Crosby, who weighed in with "Just about the best television show I ever saw." Six weeks later Crosby wrote, "I don't know why we were so caught by surprise since Astaire on stage and screen has practically never done anything badly."[10] Irving Berlin wired Fred, "You have a whole new career if you want it."[11] Cole Porter, Ira Gershwin, and other old friends called him to praise the brilliance of the show.

To boost the show's rating, and to bring added attention for the Emmy Awards competition, a repeat showing was scheduled for January 26, 1959. The second viewing got a significantly better share of 26.2. The show had been profitable for Chrysler and Ava Productions. NBC had paid Fred $250,000 for the show; it cost $195,000 to produce it. The rerun brought in an additional $150,000.[12] Chrysler gladly picked up the option for a second Astaire special.

A few weeks before the Emmys, Bea Bush Wilcox threw a party at her one-bedroom apartment on Havenhurst Drive in West Hollywood for the cast of the show. "Frank Radcliff was the bartender. Fred Curt was helpful. I didn't expect Fred or Barrie to show up. All of a sudden there was a knock at the door. I opened the door and went blank. It was the day of my divorce. There was Fred and Barrie. Fred said, 'Bea, it's Fred and that's Barrie.'

"They ended up sitting on the kitchen floor drinking beer, playing with my cat, Petrillo, eating chili in a cup, laughing with all the dancers. Fred was totally at home. He was among dancers, among what he loved to do. We had all worked so hard together. We were all so much in love with what we were doing. He knew he was safe. There would be no publicity. He stayed until two A.M. Johnny Mathis was there with Maggie Banks. Johnny sang. Maggie was a dancer, who was like an agent, who had referred me to Hermes Pan."

"AN EVENING WITH FRED ASTAIRE" received an unprecedented nine Emmy Awards at the ceremony, held at the Hollywood Palladium in April 1959. Fred was naturally ecstatic. Never before had he been photographed looking so happy. Not until 1976 when the movie made for television *Eleanor and Franklin,* which concerned Eleanor and Franklin D. Roosevelt, won eleven Emmys was the record established by the Astaire show broken.

"An Evening with Fred Astaire" won Emmys for Most Outstanding Single Program of the Year; Best Special Musical or Variety Program, One Hour or Longer; Best Direction of a Single Musical or Variety Program; Best Writing of a Single Musical or Variety Program; Best Live Camera Work; Best Art Direction in a Live Television Program; Best Musical Contribution to a Television Program; Best Choreography for Television; and Best Single Performance by an Actor.

On winning the Best Actor Emmy, Fred told the television-industry audience, "This is a great night for old dad." Some controversy had been attached to this nomination, however. As part of what has been an interminable dispute between the Los Angeles and New York chapters of the Television Academy, Ed Sullivan, as head of the New York chapter, protested that Astaire was not an actor but a dancer. The Los Angeles chapter supported Astaire's nomination, asserting that Fred had portrayed several different roles in each of the dance numbers he performed. To skirt any semblance of controversy, Fred offered to return the Emmy; his gesture was not accepted by the academy.

After the awards presentation, an orchestra played for dancing. Peg Yorkin had danced with Astaire. As she recalled, "I had also once danced with Jimmy Cagney, so all my dreams were fulfilled. Neither of them were good ballroom dancers." Whether Fred was good or not, the thrill of dancing with Fred Astaire was momentous then and now.

Fred spent the remainder of the evening dancing with others, such as the actress Kim Novak, but principally with Barrie Chase. By then their dancing partnership had developed into a romance. Betty Rose said, "Fred told David that he was crazy about Barrie. He also said that she was the best dancer he had ever worked with since Adele."

Fred admired Barrie's feisty personality. He had long been used to strong women—his mother, Adele, Phyllis, Ginger Rogers, and his daughter, Ava. He consulted with friends, such as Randolph Scott, wondering if they thought Barrie could replace Phyllis in his life. Scott advised, "No one had to replace Phyllis, and no one ever will. But you can find a new dimension with someone else and at least fill part of the gap in your life."[13]

This was Fred's first serious romantic involvement since Phyllis's death four years earlier. (Bud Yorkin said, "Fred talked about Phyllis a great deal.") In time, Fred reportedly asked Barrie to marry him, but those who knew Chase said offstage they lacked chemistry. The thirty-four-year difference in their ages was insurmountable. Chase once told an English writer, "Fred was not a god to me; he was just a guy."

Dellie was quoted on the effect Chase had on her brother: "She vibrated him. As he'd say, she filled him full of vibes—I think that's what happened. She was so inspiring to him and was such a beautiful dancer. And a little temperamental, which he liked. They got on beautifully together."[14]

Bea Bush Wilcox said, "I think Barrie worshipped Fred for giving her the opportunity to work with him. I also think she loved him dearly." When interviewed, Chase didn't care to comment on this aspect of their relationship.

LESS THAN TWO MONTHS after the first special, Fred began filming *On the Beach.* On his return, he began to think about what he wanted to do on his second NBC special. This time the theme was established as "the beat." Barrie Chase and Jonah Jones were signed for repeat performances, along with the addition of the Bill Thompson Singers, who didn't appear on camera.

In the meantime, Fred guest-starred again on *General Electric Theater* on September 3, 1959, in "Man on a Bicycle." Describing his reason for accepting such instantly forgettable fare, he said, "I did it and seemed to get away with it. No one seemed to mind too much, or maybe no one noticed it." The two *General Electric Theater* appearances gave an impetus for him to later accept additional dramatic roles on television.

The quality and the ratings of "An Evening with Fred Astaire," which resulted in the show's being awarded the prestigious George Foster Peabody Award for excellence in broadcasting; his *General Electric Theater* appearances; and the sale of the Fred and Ginger films, as part of a package of RKO films to television, were all a boon to Fred's newfound popularity. He was suddenly being rediscovered on television by a *new* audience. An atmosphere for "Another Evening with Fred Astaire" had been established.

Bud Yorkin returned as producer and director. He remembered, "At first, I didn't want to do it again. It was like being asked to do *Gone With the Wind* a second time. That was an impossible task. I just didn't know where the hell we'd go. We had to do something different."

The second special, which aired on November 4, 1959, opened in much the same way as the first with "The Afterbeat," a rhythmic offering cowritten by Fred and Johnny Mercer establishing "the beat" as the theme of the show. As host, Fred appeared and immediately showed much more assurance than he had in the first special. He was joined by the dancers, who emerged through paneled cubes in the backdrop. They converged for a vigorous dance routine that ultimately ended with all the participants collapsing on the floor.

Fred Curt was part of the chorus of dancers who danced "The Afterbeat." "Any dancer knows that we dance on the beat," said Curt. "Everything is one, two, three, four, and this was afterwards. . . . I missed it [during the first re-hearsal] because if I was not on the afterbeat, I threw all the dancers off. All of a sudden here comes Fred Astaire: 'Okay, I'll show you where it is.' He grabbed me by the waist and goes, 'Bara, bara, ba,' and he pushed me out. And he goes, 'Got it?' I think he did it four times. He said, 'It's hard.' I finally got it. I just thought, 'Here is Fred Astaire helping me out.' Anyone could say, 'If you can't get it—out!' Further down the line other people lost it, and he helped them as well.

"We finished work at six o'clock on the special; Fred would work until seven or eight o'clock on his stuff with Barrie. And even when she would go home, he would work with Pat Denise, her dance-in. A lot of the time he would use Hermes as a partner because Hermes was around watching over Fred's dancing."

Having worked with Astaire and Hermes Pan several times, Curt was in an ideal spot to evaluate the Astaire/Pan connection. He declared succinctly, "Hermes would bake the cake and Fred would come in and put the icing on it."

TO SHOWCASE BARRIE CHASE'S red-haired beauty, the second number in the show, "That Face," began with Fred's discovering her on the cover of a fashion magazine. The fantasy aspect continued as Fred sang and danced to her face, which darted above him before she appeared in the flesh and joined him in the dance. She faded away as the Bill Thompson Singers beautifully re-created the melody.

After charming the audience with his comments about "That Face," Fred felt obliged to once again exhibit his drumming. Years ago, the drum as a rhythm instrument naturally caused Fred to want to learn how to play it. He was paired with a master technician, Alvin Stoller, who had played on *The Fred Astaire Story,* the album that Norman Granz had recorded nine years earlier with Oscar Peter-son. Here Stoller held himself back so as not to completely overshadow the star. Fred executed a dance to Stoller's drumbeat.

Jonah Jones and his quartet played "My Blue Heaven," "A Gal in Calico," and "When the Saints Come Marching In," then Jones bantered lightly with Fred.

Keeping the beat going, with the trumpeter in tow, was a perfect way for Fred to introduce "Night Train," set in a railroad station. Larri Thomas played the part of Fred's old girlfriend, whom he has not seen in years, who is scheduled to arrive on the next train. His spirited dancing reflects his simultaneous happiness and anxiety at meeting her again. On Thomas's arrival, she has her husband and children with her. The amusing finale ends with Fred's suffering a broken heart.

The craze surrounding the beat generation, inspired by Jack Kerouac's bestselling novel, *On the Road,* was the focus of a dance number. Poet Ken Nordine had come up with *Word Jazz,* a short-lived cult-album sensation at the time when poetry combined with jazz was in fashion. Fred and Barrie Chase displayed their enjoyment in spoofing the beats as they danced to Nordine's narration of his "My Baby," the only prerecorded number in the show.

When the opportunity presents itself, cross-promoting a star's current project is an age-old practice. With the release of *On the Beach,* Fred's dramatic-film debut, looming a month later, it was a natural for "Waltzing Matilda," the popular Aussie folk song, to be featured on the special. David Rose supplied another of his patented string arrangements for Fred and his cohorts to dance a swirling routine. Fred's plug for the movie and his appreciation for the Australian people followed.

He proudly told the audience the dancers on the show did things he couldn't possibly do and vowed that perhaps he should take some lessons. The audience loved his humility.

Fred continued his interest in pop culture. Therefore, in maintaining the au courant and topical nature of the special, he appeared in an Alfred E. Neuman (of *Mad* magazine fame) mask throughout the "Sophisticated Lady" number. The mystery of who was behind the mask continued throughout the number. It was one of the most imaginative approaches to a dance routine ever devised, though it somehow bothered Jack Gould, who said it led to a "fatal contradiction in mood." Barrie Chase flirted with several suave gentlemen in black tie in a bar only to settle on Alfred E. Despite the comic intention of the piece, she and Fred performed an amazing dance routine. Fred wryly said, "I always wanted to do a dance where my expression never changes."

To conclude the show, Astaire repeated himself by singing another bevy of standards that he had introduced. The medley consisted of "Fascinating Rhythm," "Dancing in the Dark," "The Way You Look Tonight," "Dearly Beloved," "Steppin' out with My Baby," "Let's Face the Music and Dance." "The Carioca," "The Continental," "One for My Baby," and "By Myself."

"Another Evening with Fred Astaire," though again a favorite of the TV critics, was not the Emmy-winning sensation of its predecessor. It received nominations in the Outstanding Performance in a Variety or Music Program and Outstanding Program Achievement in the Field of Variety Categories, but won no awards. The show had to settle for winning the TV Guide Award.

Larri Thomas, who appeared in three of the specials, and Carole Bryan, another dazzling blonde, who appeared in the second special, discussed a typical rehearsal with Fred and Hermes Pan. Bryan was the only new dancer in this show. She had previously worked with Pan in Italy.

After the dancers arrived carrying their dance bags, then changed from street clothes into leotards for the women and chinos for the men, and before starting to rehearse, the dancers had coffee. The jolt from caffeine unleashed their muscles and limbs.

On the first day of rehearsal, Pan reacquainted Fred with the dancers, and he was briefed on Bryan's dancing background. The dance numbers were usually rehearsed in the same order in which they would be performed on the show. Bryan noted, "By the time we all arrived, Fred and Hermes had been rehearsing various steps for an hour or so." Thomas added, "They had already been working together for weeks, two to four hours a day, before we even started. They concentrated on little segments, not necessarily a whole number."

Bryan added, "They always danced with music—a pianist and a drummer. The routines were not set in stone. Things change when you start to get things going. Fred would learn things fast—they had been working together for hundreds of years. They knew how each other moved, you know.

" 'There is something not quite right over there' was the way Pan would react to an incorrectly executed dance step," according to Bryan. Thomas said, "A lot of times Pan would say, 'Kids, go in the other room while Fred and I work on something.' That's because he didn't like people glaring at him while he was learning new stuff. When he knew what he was doing, he would come out." Thomas referred to Astaire affectionately as "a king."

The first number might take three hours to learn, though the process might sometimes extend over several mornings. Dick Martin, the retired comedian and director, remembered watching Fred work on a dance routine at 9:00 A.M., when Martin arrived early at NBC to rehearse a variety show that he and his partner, Dan Rowan, were doing. "We had a break at four P.M. I peeked in and discovered he was still working on the same number."

On some days, as many as three numbers in sections could be worked on at once. Thomas stressed, "We would do sixteen bars a day." (With all of this preparation, the number might last only a few minutes on the show.) After the number was learned, Pan would call a twenty-minute break. "Maybe just to go out and get a cigarette," Bryan related. Thomas interjected, "Maybe it was because there was something he didn't think was working. Fred kept more or less silent. He was thinking of steps five-six-seven-eight."

"Another Evening with Fred Astaire" was taped in sections. Fred had learned certain things from the first show. Most important, taping the show would allow mistakes to be instantly corrected.

Bryan remembered, "[The dancer] Jerry Stabler was standing behind me. He said, 'Carole, do you think this is gonna be a take?' I said, 'I don't know, how do you feel?' 'Jesus, I don't know,' he said. 'I don't know if I should do it full out or not.' " Conserving one's strength was important to every dancer.

Both women remarked how different Astaire and Pan were as individuals. They loved and admired Pan's warm and outgoing personality. Was the association of Astaire and Pan a case of opposites attract, in view of Astaire's contrasting quiet and shy manner? Bryan remarked, "The thing was, Fred was comfortable with him. I think there was an umbilical cord. They were attached."

Some days the dancers would sit and watch Fred and Barrie work on a particularly intricate routine. Thomas recalled, "Other times, we might be off in the other room playing cards." Bea Bush Wilcox pointed out, "Fred would never rehearse on anything except a hardwood floor. You could kill your legs and your back if you worked on concrete. You need wood."

The choreographer Miriam Nelson, who was working at CBS at that time, confirmed that Fred hated dancing on cement floors. She remembered that she had heard that "Fred wasn't about to dance on concrete, and he made NBC put down a decent floor of wood. Most people probably don't know this—when you put down a wood floor, you don't put it right on the cement, you leave a little space which gives a little cushion for when you dance. You're not hitting so hard. When we heard that they had a new floor at NBC, I called production and had the nerve to say, 'Why can't we have a wood floor . . . we're killing ourselves.' They talked it over, and they said, 'We're going to give you a wood floor.' "

PAN FULLY REALIZED he could get seven numbers done in six weeks with the high caliber of dancers he had hired. After a number was completed, Fred would never approach, for instance, Thomas to say, "Larri, you really did a great job on that number." He was polite and respectful to the dancers, but as she noted, "He was stubborn. If he couldn't get something, he would work until he felt it was absolutely right. He wouldn't give up."

David Rose amusingly related, "I would walk into a rehearsal, and there would be dead silence for five minutes, with Fred and Hermes Pan just staring at each other. Then Hermes would say he had the answer to their problem. He would set off on the left foot instead of the right. They had been debating for fifteen minutes which foot to step out on. Every step he took had to be accounted for."[15]

THE MOST LOQUACIOUS INTERVIEW subject I encountered was the former dancer the late Becky Vorno, who was a longtime associate of Hermes Pan's. Vorno knew considerable about dance. She would often dance with Fred in rehearsal once Fred and Hermes had devised a dance routine. Barrie Chase would on occasion watch them and learn it that way.

As Vorno recalled, "Sometimes she wouldn't even be there, and Fred would tell me, 'I want it done this way, not the other.' I went along with it, and then we did the 'Sophisticated Lady' number, which I thought was very very good. I was the blonde in 'Night Train' sitting on the train bench who sashays over to Fred and then did a kick over his head. I also danced with Fred on 'The After-beat.'"

Vorno observed Astaire and Pan at work up close over several years. "A lot of times, Hermes would make suggestions to Fred, and Fred would say, 'No, I can't do that.' And Hermes would say, 'Yes, you can.' And then Fred would do it and Hermes would say, 'Let me show you how to do it.' This is the way that they worked together.

"Sometimes Fred would watch Hermes and I dancing to see what he had in mind. Fred would never say, "Watch," never offer any real suggestions, never smile, but would just walk over to me and take my hand and say, 'Okay, let's try it.' If it worked for him, he'd use it.

"The biggest thing with Fred that Hermes had to watch out for with his girl partners was the fact that Fred was not a strong man. Gene Kelly could lift anybody. I mean he was a muscle guy, but Fred was [only] strong in the legs. For instance, in 'The Girl Hunt' number in *The Band Wagon* with Cyd Charisse, her back is rigid because she helped take her weight off where he's bent over holding her. Because if she had fallen, let's say, at the waist, he would have dropped her right on her head and on the floor. You had to be the top of the line to dance with him in the first place."

While further focusing on the Astaire/Pan association, Vorno said, "You have to realize that Fred was the star and Hermes the choreographer, but there was never any animosity between them. In the second special, Fred's part in the original concept of the dance numbers would be danced by Frank Radcliff, and I was Barrie. And then Fred and Barrie would take over. As we watched them dance,

I'd say to Frank, 'I didn't see anything wrong.' Sometimes Fred would be tired. They'd take a break. It was just that they had done it so many times that day. We used to say that we could fake it, but Fred would never fake anything. Dancing meant more to him than anything else in the world."

Vorno worked closely for nine months with Pan on the choreography for *My Fair Lady.* "I adored working with Audrey Hepburn on this movie," she said. "Audrey asked about Fred when she first got there from her home in Switzerland." Surprisingly, Astaire, who had relished working with her in *Funny Face,* never came to visit her or Pan on the set. Vorno mentioned, "George Cukor [the director] had been given a ninety-days schedule from Jack Warner to get her work completed." Perhaps given that edict—or because of his own aloofness—Astaire was reluctant to come to the studio. I asked Vorno if she thought Fred saw Hepburn socially during that period. "No, I don't think she did," Vorno said.

HOWARD KRIEGER WAS A MEMBER of the chorus in the third special. Krieger had previously danced alongside the likes of Ginger Rogers, Eleanor Powell, Mitzi Gaynor, and others. He observed, "I worked with all these dancers for so many years. I never saw anybody prepare himself like Fred Astaire. Even when we started, you could see his mind work. And he was almost dead silent while he was thinking of all these things. Before he went onstage, everything went through his mind like a calendar. It was like automation. It was unbelievable. The thing that was probably different with him than with anyone else was that he would laugh. He'd go *ha-ha-ha-ha,* meaning he would psyche himself by laughing. He did it each time—the whole process, the smile. He was like a robot, you know. And, of course, a star doesn't get to be a star without working every second and stay a star."

Krieger further noted, "I don't think anybody has ever passed him by or ever will pass him by. He would see everything that he thought looked good, and he would repeat every gesture. Everything was calculated, studied. There were no mistakes with him."

Speaking of mistakes, Jerry Jackson repeated an incident that was told him by Pan. It took place during a rehearsal with Fred and the dancers for one of the specials, presumably the fourth one when some replacements took place. Fred, ever the perfectionist, kept going over a certain dance to make sure that he not only looked right, but also felt comfortable doing the steps. While trying to concentrate, he was distracted by the mirrored reflection of a chorus member. She was making faces and complaining because it was taking him so long to learn the movement. During the next break Fred pointed the dancer out to Pan and requested that she be replaced by the next day's rehearsal. Fred didn't want to cause a scene, as many stars would have done under the same circumstances. He knew that losing his temper would disrupt the rehearsal. He found it expedient to do it *his way*. He got what he wanted but in a dignified and resourceful manner.

THE THIRD SPECIAL, "Astaire Time," which aired on Sunday, September 25, 1960, at 10:00 P.M., again on NBC, provided Fred with perhaps the moment he had been waiting an entire career for—his guest star was Count Basie and His Orchestra, featuring the magnificent blues singer Joe Williams. The blues-drenched orchestra, with its well-defined four-to-the-bar swing tempo, was ideal for the dance. Basie was in the midst of a second career peak with his New Testament Band.

Fred realized the pitfalls of dancing to the Basie band, where the tempo and horn "licks" could vary with each performance. Therefore, Berle Adams and Fred met to discuss having the music prerecorded on this show. "That's very important," Astaire pointed out. "You may not realize it, but when I dance, I dance not only to the rhythm and beat of the music, but to specific horn riffs and other nuances." Adams, however, insisted, "You won't be able to dance to recorded music. It's television. They won't let you."

Adams had suggested Gil Rodin, the former alto saxophonist, to produce the third special along with Astaire. Rodin's billing, however, was merely "production coordinator."

Rodin and Adams dealt with the musicians' union on Fred's behalf concerning prerecording the music. Adams remembered, "Gil did all the talking. He knew everybody. They finally made a ruling that we could prerecord the music for the show. When the recording of their work was played, and Fred and the other dancers were rehearsing, the musicians had to be in their chairs, and they would be paid on an hourly basis."

Having the recordings for the dance numbers was a significant victory for Astaire. He told Adams, "That's wonderful. Hermes [Pan, who was set as choreographer] and I can work on it." That meant they could plan all the dance routines for the big production numbers at Fred's home before rehearsals began.

Departing from a big-band jazz instrumental as the background for the opening number, this time the show used Tchaikovsky's "Romeo and Juliet Overture," as interpreted by David Rose and His Orchestra. Yet both classical and jazz rhythms were in play.

As Fred Curt, who danced in the show, explained, "Fred always mixed rhythms. He would do a ballroom step to a jazz rhythm while the dancers behind him were doing a ballet or waltz thing—a counterpoint against each other. You have to have the right mentality. You also have to have a lot of musicianship, which Astaire certainly had." This mixing of rhythms in dancing might in some way be connected to Fred's appreciation of Vernon and Irene Castle, who introduced several significant dance rhythms and mixed and matched them in their presentation.

Jerry Jackson, while watching a video copy of the show with Curt and me, commented on the "Romeo and Juliet" opener: "Some of the choreography for Fred and Barrie is very similar to the combinations he performed with Ginger. For instance, there are typical Astaire steps like the body-to-body chaîné turns. Other movements are based on ballet. The freeze element that opened the first special was utilized again here."

"Miss Otis Regrets" was justifiably a favorite number of Fred's. It was full of turns, and once again a combination of ballroom and jazz dancing. He was seen smoking but not inhaling! (According to Curt, Fred had given up smoking during the first special.) Fred played a butler complete with white gloves and a vest. Barrie Chase finally got the chance to really talk. The parody was amusing, with Barrie essaying a stiff Victorian in a purple dressing gown with a sequined top and ballet slippers.

WITHOUT QUESTION, the most fabulous character I encountered in my research was the late Greg Garrison. Garrison knew exactly how to present Dean Martin while producing and directing *The Dean Martin Show* during its nine years on NBC. Martin recognized Garrison's importance and gave him a sizable portion of the show's profits, which made Garrison a rich man.

After being on the television blacklist following a physical confrontation with two network executives in a television control room in New York ("I was a bad boy"), Gil Rodin hired him to direct *The Bob Crosby Show*. Shortly after that, Rodin convinced Fred that Garrison should be the director of his third special. "I owe Gil a lot," Fred acknowledged.

One day, while rehearsing at NBC, the director learned that Ginger Rogers was in the building and wanted to come by and see Fred. "I spoke to Pan about it. He said, 'Barrie's not here. She's not due until two o'clock. Have her come in.' And Ginger arrives. She and Fred did the biggest hello with the hugging. It was one of those hugs you give to your aunt Alice, you know. She's got a big bosom, but you don't get too close. Ginger looked great. When she left, Fred kind of went, 'She's very nice.' But it was pretty obvious that there was nothing there to begin with."

Garrison vividly recalled an incident that took place just before taping the first number with Fred and the Basie band. It was an Astaire moment for the ages and a perfect example of his insistence on planning every gesture: "There was a break, and one of the stage managers came up to me and said, 'Fred wants to see you for a minute.' I went into Fred's dressing room, and he says, 'How many performers would ask the stage manager to have the director come into his dressing room and then say to the director, "Thank you for coming." And I just looked at him and I went, 'Yeah, okay.' He says, 'What do you think of this? "Thank you, Count Basie." He tugs on his nose, pulls his ear, shuffles his foot, and almost crosses his legs and looks down sheepishly. And I go, 'That's Fred Astaire. Sounds pretty good.' He says, 'Wait, wait, how's this?' He drops his head down, looks up to the side, shuffles the foot, crosses the other leg, and goes, ' "Thank you, Count Basie, you were wonderful." What do you think of that?' I said, 'Well, you didn't do "you were wonderful" the first time.' He said, 'You liked the "you were wonderful"? I said, 'Yeah, I like the "you were wonderful." ' He then said, 'What about the pulling the nose and scratching this and turning the head and pulling on the earlobe, 'cause, you know, Perry Como used to do a little pull on the earlobe.' 'Yeah, you're right. Lose the earlobe,' I said, 'but, you know, just push the nose a little bit and do that aw-shucks look, turning your head and looking up into the camera and going, "Thank you, Count, you were . . ." ' He said, 'How about, "Thank you, Count Basie"? They should know . . .' I said, 'Well, we've already introduced him, so you'll be better . . .' 'Well, let's try it again.' So we do it again, and I'm in there for about fifteen minutes listening to a choreographed 'Thank you, Count Basie' and that's *exactly* the way he did it on the air."

It was now time to experience the roar of the Basie band in its instrumental, "Not Now, I'll Tell You When." Fred obviously relished dancing with the mighty jazz machine on "Sweet Georgia Brown." One could feel Basie's music coming right into him. He offered some laid-back hoofing, almost a Bob Fosse–like routine. Their collaboration was a seamless integration of music and dance. First, the famed Basie rhythm section, then the entire band, became Fred's dancing partner.

Jean Sibelius's "Valse Triste" was a beautifully conceived romantic number by Hermes Pan, who was both dance director and associate producer of the show. It was Chase's first solo number in the specials, and something she was justifiably proud of. Supported by the corps de ballet, she demonstrated her superb ballet technique. As the number begins, she is portrayed as an elderly woman. Gazing into her boudoir mirror, she reminisces and is transformed into a youthful, radiant image of herself wearing an Empire chiffon gown. Handsome suitors court her and partner her in an ethereal ballroom. Barrie's point work and filmed lines were flawless.

The forthright Garrison admired her work. He said, "Chase was the difference between a kid coming up from Triple A ball and going against the New York Yankees who doesn't have a ninety-three-mile-an-hour fastball but who knows how to hit the corners. That comes from not being so smart but being totally aware of who she is. She knew what she wanted, and she knew her limitations. The only thing she asked to have done periodically was through quiet moments with Fred when she would make suggestions. She knew what to suggest, it was like a magician doing sleight of hand. 'Am I going to show this leg? How's the turnout?'

"She had the kind of features that you never forget, chiseled features, great legs, and great moves, and that poker face. You never got a smile out of her on camera. It wasn't any of this showbiz stuff. She was one sexy kitten. Fred was hung up on this girl. She helped a lot because he didn't have just me to focus on. He was concerned about her."

Miriam Nelson said, "Barrie danced with me in the chorus in several shows, and one movie in particular. The first time I saw Barrie dance with Fred, I could hardly wait because I knew how well she danced. She had a very sexy body, and she moved in a very sexy way. And that would make Astaire look sexier, too."

"WE HAVE TO DANCE OR ELSE NO PAY," a song-and-dance creation of Pan's, shows the influence of Jerome Robbins and *West Side Story,* as the male dancers, attired in jeans and sneakers, cavort across the screen. This lively number was a perfect example of modern jazz dancing.

The jazz standard "The Sheik of Araby" brought Astaire back to the stage as the dancers faded away. This was essentially a novelty number that showcased the Earl Twins, Ruth and June, which revolved around a full-length mirror.

Jane Earl Barton said, "The dancer John Brascia had told Hermes Pan about us. He had seen us dancing in a little coffeehouse down the street from the American School of Dance on Hollywood Boulevard, where we took jazz dancing from Eugene Loring. We immediately became close friends with Hermes. He loved the way we moved." That led to the Twins working with Pan in the film version of *Can-Can.* Ruth Earl Silva recalled, "We were caught up in the film so we couldn't do Fred's second show. Pan asked us to appear in the third special.

"We worked with Fred and Hermes in choreographing the mirror number. We rehearsed from nine to noon, five days a week, for more or less six weeks, because you try different things. Pan told us about Fred's coming home in his Chrysler and how he would sit in his driveway and fall asleep. The German housekeeper, Zella, would come out and wake him up and get him out of the car. He worked bloody hard.

"In the beginning of our number, we used part of a floor exercise we choreographed in a Judy Garland show we had done at the Flamingo in Vegas. We incorporated some of those moves in front of the mirror, squeezed down. It took a lot of work with us having to do it on the opposite side of the open-framed mirror and within the restrictions of that frame. I guess it was Hermes and Fred's idea to do the mirror thing—what a great idea! After the exercising, we spoke, and then we went to a time step sequence ending up with floor/knee turns. What a fun number it was."

The mirror number was based on pure illusion. Jane Earl was practicing dance combinations, which were reflected in a large rehearsal-hall mirror. Fred is watching with admiration when suddenly the reflection starts to make small moves that the real dancer is not doing. Eventually, Fred and the audience discover that "the reflection" is actually the other twin, Ruth Earl. The number culminates with all three performing some terrific choreography to accomplish this "trompe l'oeil" in dance. The synchronization and precision of the turns had to be perfect, and it was. "Hermes had to kind of keep us in the background as much as possible so the viewing public wouldn't know there were twins in the show," Ruth Earl explained.

Appearing on "Astaire Time" led to the Earl Twins working with Jack Cole in *Let's Make Love,* with Marilyn Monroe, and many other dance gigs such as appearances on *The Bell Telephone Hour,* in the *Irma la Douce* movie, and in a Bob Hope show from the Middle East. This is not to mention Las Vegas nightclub engagements with Frank Sinatra, Dean Martin, Johnny Carson, and Tony Bennett.

THE MOST IMPORTANT part of the show followed with Joe Williams backed by the Basie band singing "Going to Chicago Blues," and their big hit, "Every Day," and "Shake, Rattle and Roll." As Williams sang, Fred entered, wearing a gray hat, a print shirt, and white shoes, with Chase in a slinky, off-the-shoulder dress. They did a magnificent interpretive jazz dance to "Hallelujah, I Love Her So," then broke into a jitterbug to "It's a Lowdown Dirty Shame."

Barrie Chase told of having had difficulties in interpreting her character in the blues medley. "Fred said to me, 'What do you mean you can't get the character? It's you, Barrie. You're just Barrie.' We had been rehearsing to a tape of Basie. Everything was set, but we weren't allowed to use the track on the show. Some kind of union deal.

"And I said, '. . . You've got to give it something to hang on to.' A lot of the stuff was improvised, and they [the Basie band] couldn't repeat it. . . . Well, Fred was going nuts because we had set everything and very specifically. And they could not get it. Fred said, 'Come on, Barrie. Let's show 'em what we've choreographed to this.' In the recording session, Basie said to Fred, as we rehearsed, 'You know, she's hearing stuff I didn't even know was there.' I loved that a lot.

"Late at night, Fred got into the cutting room and took out the questionable sections. He then removed the same sections from the tape we had rehearsed to and spliced them into the newly recorded tape. He came to rehearsal the next day and said, 'Problem solved.' I'm like, 'What the heck?' He started laughing. 'Now you don't tell anybody.' The number had already been choreographed, and with Fred accents were important, not only the beat and the sound. They were written in stone."

A *DIFFERENT* KIND OF A MEDLEY with Fred, once again delivering a potpourri of songs he had introduced in his Broadway and film musicals, came next. It began with the obscure "Thank You So Much, Mrs. Lowsborough—Goodbye." He gave his aw-shucks shrug to the generous round of applause as he moved on through "Funny Face," "I Love Louisa," "Flying Down to Rio," "I'm Putting All My Eggs in One Basket," "They All Laughed," "Lovely to Look At" (while doing one of his familiar gestures of touching his cheek), "Let's Call the Whole Thing Off," then switched from a blue blazer to an Ainsley collar shirt, suede shoes, and a cane to sing and strut "Easter Parade" and "A Shine on Your Shoes." He thanked Chrysler and said good-night.

Greg Garrison referred to Astaire to others as Fearless Fred "because he was just that," he said. He remembered Astaire saying to him, after the first run-through of the show, "You really did a wonderful job. I'm so pleased." He then turned to Pan and said, "There's a sixteenth of a bar that's missing in the cut." Garrison said, "I'd never heard of anything called the sixteenth of a bar in my life, but we found it. It was a frame and a half. He knew."

"Astaire Time" won two Emmys, for Outstanding Performance in Variety or Musical Performance, for Fred, and Outstanding Program Achievement in the Field of Variety. Fred graciously brought Gil Rodin onstage to share in the triumph. But the show did not deliver a good rating. Chrysler had the rights to the sound-track recordings, which were released on long-playing records and made available only to its customers. The company's association with Astaire had come to an end after three shows.

AMERICA UNDERWENT a cataclysmic change between 1960 and 1968, when Fred did his fourth NBC special. An unpopular war that divided the country was taking place in Vietnam. The long-brewing problems of civil rights, women's rights, and the rights of homosexuals, which had been swept beneath the fabric of the bland 1950s, suddenly came into the open. The baby boomer generation that had emerged and wanted its own kind of music, rock 'n' roll, following the arrival of the Beatles in February 1964 to appear on the *Ed Sullivan Show*. They became the muse of a generation. As Wordsworth wrote, "It was good to be alive and to be young was even better."[16] Tin Pan Alley, and the Broadway and Hollywood musicals, had been replaced in importance by London, San Francisco, Nashville, Detroit, and other cities as the principal sources of popular music.

Fred Astaire represented what the baby boomers hated. He was their parents' song-and-dance man. The songs he sang and the elegance he displayed in his dancing bore absolutely no resemblance to rock 'n' roll, the Frug, or the Watusi. That was where it was at.

"The Fred Astaire Show" on NBC, which aired on February 7, 1968, had little resemblance to the three specials that had preceded it. The only way the network and a new sponsor, the Foundation for Commercial Banks, would financially back a Fred Astaire special would be for him to present contemporary recording artists as his guest stars.

As Art Garfunkel well described this period: "The demographics were moving on." Accordingly, the folk rock duo of Simon and Garfunkel, the pop Latin jazz instrumental group Sergio Mendes and Brasil '66, the soul jazz duo Young-Holt Unlimited, and the rock group the Gordian Knott were signed to appeal to the young audience.

Barrie Chase returned as Fred's dancing partner. Fred produced the special with Gil Rodin, and Robert Scheerer was the director. Neal Hefti was the music director. Hermes Pan was absent from his usual post as dance director; Herbert Ross, the Broadway choreographer, took his place.

Chase explained, "Fred didn't want Pan. He came to me and said, 'I don't want Pan on the fourth show.' I don't believe [that] he ever said that to Pan."

I asked Barrie if, perhaps, the network or the advertising agency pressured Fred into having a different kind of dance format and therefore a new choreographer. She said, "Who in the world would ever pressure Fred? Not a chance. He'd have told them to go to hell. Nobody was going to tell Fred."

During the taping of the third special, Pan was also choreographing *Can-Can* at Fox. According to Chase, Fred asked Pan, " 'Can you do the show and the movie at the same time? I don't think you can.' Pan said, 'Yes, I can.' He assured Fred that he could. Well, Pan was out quite a bit when Fred needed him. Pan wasn't asked to do the fourth show. I'm sure Fred would deny that Pan did himself in."

Fred told Chase, "You pick who you want." The advertising agency informed her that Herb Ross was interested in the job. She recalled, "We went for drinks, and we talked. I liked him. I thought he could work with Fred. This was before Herb started doing movies. So, Fred met him, and they got on well."

Ross remarked of Astaire's respect for Chase's talent, "He just worshipped her. He thought she was the best partner he's ever had and one of the best dancers in the world. He never tired of watching her dance, and indeed she was wonderful."[17]

One of the principal reasons "The Fred Astaire Show" didn't succeed the way its predecessors had was that almost all of Astaire's dance numbers were arranged in what was musically au courant in 1968, and that was rock 'n' roll. Not that Fred couldn't execute his numbers in that tempo, but rock 'n' roll was simply not his milieu. Neal Hefti heartily agreed.

Hefti was highly capable of writing adventuresome arrangements. He was the composer of the memorable themes from the TV shows *Batman* and *The Odd Couple,* and the tune "Girl Talk," adopted from his score to *Harlow.* He remembered, "Herb Ross told me, when I came to the first rehearsal, 'If you really want to know what we are trying to do, go down to the Whisky a Go Go and see what's going on down there." Hefti replied, "I go there anyway." Besides being an arranger, he was then in charge of A&R (artists and repertoire) at Frank Sinatra's Reprise Records, which meant an important rock club such as the Whisky was one of his haunts.

Sterling Clark, one of the chorus dancers in the show, who had worked with Fred the previous year in the film musical *Finian's Rainbow,* perhaps supplied the best analysis of what went wrong with the special. Clark remarked, "I hadn't seen the show in thirty-seven years. . . . I wondered why they never show that special. It's obvious Fred was then almost sixty-nine years old. He was at a point where he was not capable of doing what he had done before. And because of this incapability and the difficulty of putting the show together, I am sure it was hard for the director and the choreographer, Herbert Ross, to come up with a concept of how to make him look good. I also realized there was too much improvisation going on." Barrie Chase agreed, "When you're improvising, you actually think you're doing more than the body is doing; I think that happened on that show."

Clark continued, "I don't think by improvising the way Fred did it made him contemporary. . . . In all his movies and almost all of his television shows, he always portrayed a character that had a script to work from. Herbert Ross was very famous for using dancers that would interpret acting without a script and without dialogue. It's obvious that this is what they tried to do, which meant you are a character dancer, and you are acting as you are dancing, and you are acting out a scene or a story or a character, but without a script. . . . If you watch the show, it does not show off Fred at his best for him just to be portraying a character.

"I thought Barrie Chase was fabulous. She looked great. She holds up everything in the show. One of my favorite things is when Fred simply sits on a stool and is himself as he talks to the audience and sings those wonderful songs. He still had tone and pitch. The other thing that I really loved was Simon and Garfunkel because they stood there and sang that wonderful new song, 'Punky's Dilemma.'"

THE KINDLY ROBERT "Bobby" Scheerer at the age of twelve had auditioned for a role as a tap dancer in *Holiday Inn,* which he didn't get. Scheerer had most recently produced and directed Frank Sinatra's 1967 special with guest stars Ella Fitzgerald and Antonio Carlos Jobim. He said, "It was a thrill for me to work with Fred on the special.

"We talked for a long time. Fred explained to me that at RKO, 'We would do everything we could to bury the cuts, bury the edits, never cutting on the beat.' I've since gone back to look at those movies, and it's true. Nothing is cut for effect."[18]

"I still think he was the best tap dancer ever. I'm not putting down the Nicholas Brothers. Astaire had the ability to display humor, style, drama, and class— and to have all the elements come together. With Gene Kelly you could always spot the familiar steps that he would do: the barrel rolls and the hand shaking. I was never aware of that with Astaire. He was original."

Scheerer once asked Fred how many takes it took for him to throw the cane that bounced off the wall and into an umbrella stand in the number in Adolphe Menjou's office in *You Were Never Lovelier.* "He said, 'One. I rehearsed a lot.' That's what Astaire did; he was a worrier. He wanted to get it just so, and he worked and worked and worked. That was exactly Fred Astaire."

Scheerer continued, "Fred was very open to suggestions up to a point. He asked for an advance tape of Simon and Garfunkel's new record of 'Punky's Dilemma' so he and Herb could choreograph the number for the show. When Simon and Garfunkel came into the studio, the first thing Paul Simon did was say, 'There's something in 'Punky's Dilemma' where there is one word that's repeated three times. We remixed it and the version we're putting out only had the one word said once. It doesn't affect the time. . . . It doesn't make any difference.' Fred said, 'No.' Paul Simon, who was a little powerhouse, went to Fred and politely asked him [again] and ended up virtually begging him. Fred said, 'No, it's been choreographed.' That was so unlike the Astaire that I had learned to know. Here's the firmness. Here's the man who knows what he wants and gets it. That was fascinating to me."

Scheerer contended, "Barrie was mean and nasty to Fred, and he took it pretty much. I was very unhappy to see it happen." By this time, the romantic involvement between Astaire and Chase was over.

Chase admitted, "I was unhappy with a lot of stuff, and I made it known. The show didn't go anywhere. I thought Fred with rock 'n' roll was horrific. They should have never allowed him to do it. He was too old. He never did another special."

Scheerer lamented the almost total lack of tap dancing by Astaire in the show. "At his age, he wasn't what he was. I think that's one of the reasons that he wanted the feeling of freedom and improvisation. He didn't want to talk until the final medley. That appalled me. So I demonstrated for him six bars, and then on the seventh bar, *bang!* You'll look into a tight shot and say, 'Good evening.' He said, 'Good,' and we did it. It worked. That pleased me to be able to do that."[19]

As an inspiration, Hefti said that Astaire had brought him a country-and-western record and suggested he "write a tune like this." The entire rehearsal for the musical score was restricted to one day. Again, the music was prerecorded.

According to Scheerer, "Oh, You Beautiful Doll" was Fred's favorite number in the show. It continued right from the theme of "The Fred." Astaire instructed Hefti, "Use your harmony, not mine." Astaire displayed a vigor along with his usual grace and an element of comedy in this lighthearted number. Barrie responded in kind. "You could really see how much Fred enjoyed doing it," Scheerer noted.

ASTAIRE'S DANCING to the jazz of Young-Holt Unlimited was certainly one of the high points of the show. This was the trio co-led by bassist Eldee Young and drummer Redd Holt, two-thirds of the original Ramsey Lewis Trio, which had enjoyed a major pop hit with "The In Crowd." "I did a lot of cutting on the beat in this number because I think it enhanced the music. I did it with the feet. Fred even did a bit of the Swim here," Scheerer commented.

The late Eldee Young remembered, "Bob shot Fred tapping his foot while straddling a chair facing us as we played our hit 'Wack, Wack.' Then we went into 'Mellow Yellow' [the Donovan tune]. He walked over, and I played a little cadenza and then he started dancing his routine. He threw some tap steps in there. He mixed them up with some regular dancing. There were some improvised parts. Don Walker [the group's pianist] reached inside his piano and began strumming the strings. Fred responded to that in his dancing. It was back-and-forth play. For fun, he fell on the floor, then he began swimming away and finally crawled offstage. After doing his show, I thought of him as more of a jazz dancer."

"Fred knew that I came from the era of the show drummer," Redd Holt remarked. "In our one day of rehearsal, he said, 'Catch me, man, catch me.' That meant,

'I'm going to dance around—when I move, you catch me. Dig what I'm doing and then accompany it.' That's when he reached out and touched my snare drum. I went *pow*—'Leave my drums alone.' He snatched his hand back like I was hitting his hand. It was all impromptu—no choreographer was involved. It was all about what he felt."

Lennon and McCartney's "Eleanor Rigby" was Chase's solo number in the show and one of the best examples of her dancing talent and versatility. She had suggested the song to Fred. Herb Ross, and Ross's assistant, his wife, the former ballet star Nora Kaye, conceived the number. Bob Scheerer's soft lighting added to its impact, but he believed, "This was where I thought Herb really connected with Barrie."

Sergio Mendes and Brazil '66 had scored with its rhythmic Latin hit version of Burt Bacharach and Hal David's "The Look of Love." Fred was quite taken by the record and wanted to adapt it as the basis of a dance number. Chase concurred, calling it "romantic music and pretty to dance to," but referred to the resultant version as "a piece of junk."

She said, "I did not like the story of the number at all. Herb put it together." Scheerer said, "We had a lot of girl dancers, and I decided that I wanted to use the girls to keep the music going because it's just a static number. I wanted to make it more visual." On viewing the number on video during rehearsal, Chase wondered, however, "What are we doing? I didn't find it interesting or humorous. I must tell you truthfully there wasn't too much I did love in that show."

In the number, Fred was dressed in a chocolate brown tuxedo with thin trousers, plus a mustache and long sideburns. Chase was in culottes. She took her necklace, wrapped it around his neck, pulled it off, and put it around *her* waist. Then he twirled the necklace and put it around *her* neck. They both fell down as Fred played with his mustache.

This was a rather obtuse attempt at a comedic ballroom number. The several instances of Astaire's falling down and crawling on the floor during the special, which were designed to be humorous, wound up making him look like an old man for the first time in a musical presentation.

Sergio Mendes recalled that the number required two weeks of rehearsals, four or five hours a day. "There was no attempt to change the music. We played it exactly like the record. I was in complete awe in working with Fred because I had seen his films while I was a kid in Brazil."

The perfect sound mix was a highlight of Simon and Garfunkel's rendition of their huge hit "Scarborough Fair," along with "America" and "Punky's Dilemma," a trademark of the folk rock duo's presentation. Fred and Barrie are at first seen sitting on pillows along with a group of young people, who had been brought in to make up the audience for the number (a "hootenanny thing," as Garfunkel described it). Fred and Barrie then began to dance to establish the mood of "Punky's Dilemma." Scheerer described it as "a character number, it's not a dance dance."

Having represented Art Garfunkel at one time, I knew he would have a definite albeit ethereal perspective on working with Astaire. Garfunkel recalled, "I met Fred at a bungalow at the Beverly Hills Hotel. We [he and Paul Simon] had come to Los Angeles to appear on *The Andy Williams Show* at about the same time. He was a total charming pro; he was relaxed, he was California, as opposed to us East Coasters. He had softer shoes; he had a very genteel style. He reminded me of Long Island and sailboats, and blue blazers. I believe he wore an ascot—the Gatsby image. He was wired; his impeccable moves revealed a very fine artist. Like so many professionals in L.A. in the business, he learned to control his act and to enjoy his life in years that were then not his young years."

During rehearsal, Garfunkel remembered, "We didn't schmooze with Mr. Astaire. . . . He was just a gracious gentleman. He came from my father's generation. . . . There was a David Niven thing there. Style does it every time. I find Fred Astaire in my memory as an impeccable gentleman. He dotted every i and crossed every t. He didn't have to fake how hip he was to talk about the Beatles or any of that. It was not part of the gig. He had an honesty [about the fact] that we were meeting across a generational link—'I'm not going to get young for you and make a fool of myself.' He was accommodating the ratings realities. In one sense I'm his guest; in the other sense, I'm my mother's son, watching the great Astaire accommodating the rock 'n' roll era, and yet I'm in the shoes of Mr. Rock 'n' Roll here."

Speaking of himself and Paul Simon, Garfunkel said, "We were rehearsal freaks, some kind of perfectionists. I remember that, so that there was that kind of affinity, and that's why we were so pleased to be on the show. One sensed that Fred Astaire was brilliantly controlled and scripted so that the gestures almost were the brain telling the limbs to do something. This was not going to be TV in its middlebrow sense. This could be really tasty. . . .

"If I could replay any of this, I would say, 'Mr. Astaire, it's such an honor to meet you.' And then I would look for some downtime to see if wit and jokes could lead to a conversation, particularly about old times. My real self is so in awe of Fred Astaire and the era that he represented. To have a window on David Niven or Cary Grant, or any of that, it would be a fabulous thing, but I was too shy in those days to open up to it."

BOB MACKIE HAS EXHIBITED a distinctive glamorous flair in his clothing designs that first became recognized in the 1960s for stars such as Mitzi Gaynor. As a prerequisite for this ability, he long ago developed an acute understanding of pop culture. He was Ray Aghayan's assistant for several years. Now they are partners, who share office space in Studio City. Mackie's reputation for glamour and versatility continues to the present.

He said, "Fred Astaire was never anybody else in any of these movies, except maybe in his later ones. That's a movie-star thing. The movie stars, especially in those days, that really worked were the ones who had a bigger personality. You wanted to see them, and that's what you got. He certainly wasn't movie-star handsome. But he had a great deal of charm. I think the dancing was secondary. He was very creative, and he also had a great deal of style."

Mackie was the costume designer for the fourth special. He remembered, "Fred was always the chicest, the most wonderful person. He would bring stuff from home. He had beautiful clothes, classy. He wore his own clothes on the show and his own pants and blazer. It was a funny time for fashion because fashion had changed, and you either looked young or you looked old. There was no in-between. Fred had to dip into the look of the time.

"I gave him pleats just as Ray had in the first show. He loved it. The girls were very extreme, and he was extreme, like the Russian shirt he wore. As long as you have Fred Astaire as Fred Astaire, and he can have his own moments, that's fun for him."

Mackie had a favorable impression of "The Look of Love" number. He believes, "Fred was playing another character in that number. It looked very good, and the girls [the dancers] were all very extreme high fashion with very high boots, which was late sixties, early seventies. He and Barrie both wore yellow shirts. I don't remember whose concept it was. We had so many meetings. I found Barrie someone who was one to be very modern, cutting-edge, very young in her whole look. She was a wonderful partner for Fred. She didn't take away from him at all."

Mackie had to be extremely conscious of what the show was about—and that was to create a more hip look than in Astaire's three previous specials. In line with that the designer noted, "Each scene was different. I tried to pace the show so we had a look here, and the next look would be different, and this would be very flamboyant, and the next would be very quiet. You always try to make the next thing coming up very interesting or lead into a big contrast. But you still have to maintain the personality for that person."

Mackie readily admitted, "Things that worked in 1968, that were the latest and hottest thing, we have now seen it and heard it a million times. It's not the same when you watch it again. I was very young, and everybody wanted somebody young. It was crazy."

*　*　*

The take of "The Fred Astaire Show" on "Limehouse Blues" by Astaire and Chase differed considerably from what Fred and Lucille Bremer had done in *Ziegfeld Follies* in 1946. Chase thought the movie version was "terrific, but I hated that number in the television show. Fred was not dancing well. He was almost seventy years old, and he was weak. That's why he stopped dancing. There were certain moves in it now, if they were done as caricature, they would be good, but they were done for real. I just said, 'Deliver me from this number. I can't do this.' I've got to tell you something. Fred was charmed because he used to always say, 'But now, don't you like the number better?' And I'd go, 'Who do you think you're talking to?'

"That number was viewed as a satire. They [TV critics] reviewed it as satire. Now this is interesting. It was not created as a satire, but then I thought to myself, 'After this, if you set out to do a satire, the only way you ever do it properly is not to do it as a satire but to do it straight.' You know it's a satire, but you're doing it straight."

Fred was dressed as a gangster in a double-vented suit, black shirt, white tie, and his favorite black-and-white shoes. The dancers enter and perform a jazz dance. Fred and Barrie, in a serious, down mood, take over, then go into a ballroom dance before a semblance of modern ballet took over.

Regardless of one's taste, this is not a number deserving of Astaire's and Chase's talents. Its inadequacies supply an added reason for why there was so much opposition to Herbert Ross's choreography. The absence of Hermes Pan was telling. As Carole Bryan stated, "Herbie was not the sort of choreographer for Fred for this show."

For the finale of the show, which was improvised, Fred delivered still another medley of tunes associated with him: "A Shooting Box in Scotland," "I Love to Quarrel with You," then "Look to the Rainbow," and "When the Idle Poor Become the Idle Rich" (from *Finian's Rainbow*). Fred, in a sport shirt and trousers, with a bandanna tied around his waist, broke into "Top Hat, White Tie, and Tails." All of a sudden, ingeniously, the number dissolved into having Fred appear in his classic white-tie-and-tails song-and-dance man garb as the rock group the Gordian Knot, took over from the forty-piece Hefti orchestra. (Fred had discovered the group one night at the Troubadour, a folk and rock club in West Hollywood.) It continued accompanying him, playing the song in rock 'n' roll tempo, while standing atop a wire tower. This was indeed a novel staging idea, but it underlined that Astaire's television career was unfortunately dependent on rock 'n' roll.

Jack Gould in his review noted, "Except for the last few minutes, Mr. Astaire largely eschewed any singing himself or indulging in the light banter that on his earlier specials engagingly unified the separate parts of his programs. In consequence, the show had a tone of antiseptic detachment that made it considerably less warm and appealing." Nevertheless, Gould concluded, "Mr. Astaire no doubt could dance to the dial tone of a telephone."

IN RETROSPECT, one can state unequivocally that the first three specials were examples of the highest-quality television entertainment. Certainly the variety shows and musical specials of the late 1950s and early 1960s were not of the same stripe. The Astaire shows also deflected Newton Minnow's well-remembered 1961 declaration calling television "a vast wasteland."

Having seen at the Paley Center an evening devoted to clips of Mitzi Gaynor's specials from the 1960s and 1970s, I was immediately taken by the obvious differences between the Gaynor specials and the Astaire specials. Hers supplied a study in highly professional but fundamentally slick entertainment. Astaire's shows were considerably more sophisticated and artistic. His exemplified what could be accomplished by a star of enormous talent whose high standard for performing made an undeniable impression on the quality of the work of all the other participants in his shows.

But by 1968, both America and television had significantly changed. What Fred Astaire had long represented in American entertainment was now suddenly out of fashion. This was not the time for him to make his exit, however. He had considerably more to accomplish. He had already made inroads—this time as a character actor in movies and television. A rewarding second act in this American life lay in the years ahead.

CHAPTER TEN

THE PERFECT SINGER AND THE WOULD-BE JAZZ MUSICIAN

T HAT FRED ASTAIRE was such a nonpareil dancer has long overshadowed that
he was also an outstanding singer. Or is it that a widespread lack of historical
perspective on pop culture has caused us to overlook that fact? Some of the
foremost singers of traditional popular music consider Astaire among the best
there ever was.

"He sang perfectly! That's all there is to it" is how Johnny Mathis described
Astaire's vocal prowess. "And fortunately he had a voice to remember. There are
some of us who are blessed with a sound that God gave us, and the minute we
open our mouths, everybody knows who we are. Fred had a wonderful sound!
That's a very good thing if you're trying to make a profession out of it. Not only do
you remember Fred's voice, but he sang as though he were dancing around and
living the lyrics. His diction and intonation were flawless, and he was bound by
these composers and lyricists. He was also carrying the dialogue of whatever scenario he was doing right into the music. He sang as he spoke, which a lot of people
don't do. He also had a small voice, and that protected him from having a wobble
to it in his later years.

"He had a fair range. In other words, he knew what his range was. He didn't
try and do a falsetto because he couldn't do that. But he really knew what he *could*
do, and he worked at perfecting it."

Michael Feinstein, who lovingly perpetuates the heritage of America's classic
songwriters, referred to Astaire, along with Rosemary Clooney and Bing Crosby,

as "one of my all-time favorite singers." He echoed Mathis when he said, "He had an innate interpretive ability that is remarkable because it sounds conversational, and it is absolutely letter-perfect. He took very few liberties with the songs because he didn't need to. I find the recordings of the standards he introduced from the RKO [Astaire/Rogers] films with [the arranger/conductor] Johnny Green in most instances are the definitive performances of all time of those songs. One of the things I love about those thirties recordings is that his taps are the drums. What I mean is, you don't need drums because you've got Fred's tap dancing. And it's more exciting for me to hear those feet.

"Fred was somebody who trusted these songs. . . . I think he appreciated these songs so much because he himself was a songwriter, even though he always dismissed his own efforts and wished he could have had greater success and, in his estimation, more talent as a songwriter. His appreciation for quality in music and lyrics was supreme. Besides that, his phrasing was sophisticated."

One of the treasured audiotapes in Feinstein's vast collection is that of Astaire making mistakes in his recording of "Shine on Your Shoes" from *The Band Wagon.* The master dancer and singer had encountered pitch problems, necessitating a number of takes, whereupon he began humming the song to himself over and over before he got it right. "It was something like take twelve. It shows how hard he worked on his vocals, and how uncomfortable he was, yet how paradoxically effortless it sounded in the end." Concluding his appraisal of Astaire's prowess as a singer, Feinstein said, "What he worked for in the mediums of dance and film, and the number of songs he inspired—for that alone, every person who ever opened their mouths to sing a note, be it Eminem or the polar opposite—owes a debt to Fred Astaire because he's part of a legacy, a musical legacy for which the world would be much poorer without."

Feinstein related to biographer James Kaplan that at a 1975 salute to Ira Gershwin at the Dorothy Chandler Pavilion in Los Angeles, Frank Sinatra sang "A Foggy Day" and "They Can't Take That Away from Me." After completing "A Foggy Day" he remarked, "Well, it's not as good as Fred Astaire, but it was louder."

Singer Andy Williams brought out an essential ingredient of Astaire's singing style: "He doesn't just sing the notes the way they're written." Williams illustrated his point by singing the opening bars of his own trademark song, "Moon River." "He doesn't sing it that way. He kind of talks like he's dancing, like he moves. . . . I tried to sing like him in some [songs]—in interpreting the words in a different way. I think he sang what the lyrics were rather than singing them the way they're written. He didn't pay any attention to that. He interpreted the words in a different way with a voice that was a little higher than normal."

Williams further demonstrated his view of Astaire's vocal approach by singing the familiar opening lines of Gershwin's "They Can't Take That Away from Me," "The way you wear your hat, the way you sip your tea." Williams made the point that "he brings his rhythm as a dancer into that interpretation. He sings the melody right, but he doesn't sing it with the same rhythmic notation. ["He syncopated the rhythm" is how Michael Feinstein described it.] He sings the lyrics the way he feels them. Songwriters like to hear their songs the way they wrote them. They love Ella Fitzgerald singing the Gershwin songbook because she sang the songs the way they're written. But he wouldn't do that. He sang the way he danced. He wasn't influenced at all by the time as written because he brought his own time to the songs. He's the only one I know who does that. I don't mean that people don't back-phrase and don't do all that, but not in the way he does."

As a postscript to the importance of "They Can't Take That Away from Me," the late Fayard Nicholas, of the revered Nicholas Brothers dance team, after listening to Astaire's 1952 version backed by a sextet led by jazz pianist Oscar Peterson, remarked, "I always liked the way he sang that song more than any other tune. That's because the music flows with him, and he's right there with it. You can tell that he's having a good time, and I'm having a good time, too, in listening to it. But he had fun with every tune he sings."

Another observer who expressed a keen appreciation for Astaire the singer was Ahmet Ertegun, the late record-industry mogul, who years ago started out by producing jazz and rhythm 'n' blues records and established this latter genre by producing important records with Ruth Brown and Ray Charles. In Ertegun's opinion, "Fred's accent was very important. It was an upper-class accent. It's American, but it's American high style, and he has a great understanding and appreciation of the lyric. He delivers them with a great deal of ego so that the meaning is not lost. The lyrics were just like they were with Mabel Mercer. He had his own sense of time, and it's infallible. . . . When he dances, you [can] see that he has great rhythm. The way he sings, he has a different sense of that. He is one of my favorite singers."

Ertegun continued his astute observations about Astaire, which were perhaps influenced by his own privileged upbringing. "Nobody has his great style, nobody who has that command. He has nothing that's street. He's above the street. You see, when you see Sinatra, you know he's still on the street. Astaire is grand and he's aristocratic—an aristocratic showman. Sinatra will take a great lyric and put a little slang in and bring it down to the street. They sang a lot of the same songs. Sinatra did it for the larger crowds—for the masses. Astaire sang it for the upper classes and the songwriters—for the people with taste. Of course, that's because they come from a different time.

"You could make the same comparison between Fred Astaire and Bing Crosby.

Bing Crosby is also more for the masses. In relation to Astaire, he's more of a people's singer, like Frank Sinatra. He comes from the street, also, but a different street."

New York Times movie and music critic Stephen Holden extended the Astaire/Crosby analogy when he said, "Crosby came out of jazz and the crooning tradition that was deliberately intimate and seductive; it came out of the megaphone and the microphone . . . it's seducing with total perfection. Astaire didn't come out of that; he came out of his own persona and out of his dancing. And so when you hear him, hear his recordings, there's dancing on the recordings, many of them. The dancing was either light or fast, and the rhythms are not emphatic at all, they're not hard, they're part of the Astaire personality. He glides and the singing has a kind of easygoing quality that's not about focusing the voice on seduction or on winning points for beauty. It's about a devil-may-care kind of casual, the same devil-may-care casual mastery as his dancing. Astaire's singing had a conversational quality as opposed to a singing quality."

When asked if Astaire could shade his songs in an emotional way like Crosby or Sinatra, Holden said, "His persona didn't have a dark side. If he did, it was a very, very light shade of gray. It was a casual, light downer. He didn't feel suicide was an option. I don't think he was an alcoholic."

Interestingly, Crosby, between 1934 and 1960, introduced more songs that were nominated for Academy Awards (fourteen) than any other singer. Astaire and Sinatra tied for second with eight nominations each.

Holden continued, "Fred Astaire had a lightness or a mystique that projected happiness in songs like 'The Way You Look Tonight' or 'Cheek to Cheek.' He realized their fantasies better than anybody else because of who he was, because of his persona in music. So he created magical, romantic scenarios that nobody else could do."

Holden also brought out a heretofore overlooked point: "Singers were [then] trained with bands or conservatories or vocal coaches until rock came along because they had to have a certain kind of chops. Astaire didn't have obvious chops the way other singers did. In that way he was really ahead of his time."

Holden was referring to Astaire's small, untrained voice. His approach to singing concentrated on the lyrical importance of a song. Although they had much stronger voices, this was something that Crosby and especially Sinatra made a keynote of their singing styles.

FRED ASTAIRE'S SINGING STYLE wasn't built in a year but rather over more than a decade. In duets with his beloved sister, Adele, such as "Oh, Gee! Oh, Gosh!" recorded in 1922, it is obvious how he defers to Dellie, since at the time she was the bigger star. Yet by their 1926 version of "Fascinating Rhythm" with George Gershwin accompanying them at the piano, Astaire elongated the word "be," which becomes "bee." This indicates how he was beginning to explore a fresher, more modern way of phrasing. In the 1931 Broadway cast album of *The Band Wagon,* the way he handled "Dancing in the Dark," later one of his trademark songs, was rather tentative; it was as if he wasn't quite sure of how to handle the Dietz and Schwartz ballad.

As part of this evolution in his singing style, which extended throughout the 1920s, we must keep in mind that his career was then concentrated on the stage, where his voice had to be heard in the uppermost reaches of a theater without a microphone. He had to make his voice resound. In Hollywood, however, when he began prerecording songs for movies, he began exploring a more intimate style of singing. Perfect diction and conveying the intrinsic meaning of the words had gradually become paramount in his musical thinking. Faced with the great differences between stage and screen, he soon adjusted his approach to singing accordingly.

Indeed, the "Fred and Ginger years" (1933–39) were when his unique singing style crystallized. As Will Friedwald wrote in his liner notes to the Rhino boxed set *Fred Astaire & Ginger Rogers at RKO,* "Astaire perfected his [now] familiar staccato style wherein he comes down directly on the beat in a precise, often syncopated fashion." It's also true that his interpretations of the many incredible ballads commissioned for him to sing in these films defined his singing style forevermore.

Such standards as "The Continental," "Top Hat, White Tie, and Tails," "Cheek to Cheek," "Let's Face the Music and Dance," "The Way You Look Tonight," "A Fine Romance," "Fascinating Rhythm," "Nice Work If You Can Get It," "They Can't Take That Away from Me," and "Change Partners" were first introduced by Astaire, usually singing alone, though sometimes in duets with Rogers. The success of their movies and their association with elite composers such as the Gershwins, Kern, also Porter, and one must never overlook Irving Berlin, led to the zenith of the so-called Great American Songbook.

One afternoon during the 1970s, the retired personal manager Jess Rand was having his hair cut at the Beverly Hills Hotel. Astaire was in the next barber chair. Rand reminded Astaire of how they had first met on a few occasions years earlier when Astaire came to visit Irving Berlin at Berlin Music, Irving's music-publishing company. Right away, Astaire extolled the virtues of Berlin's songs, emphasizing what a great talent Irving was.

Rand then asked Astaire if he had a favorite between the Gershwins and Berlin. Astaire answered, "For a rhythm tune, when you're dancing with a lady, there was nobody whose music could compare with Irving's. When Irving knew he was writing for a dance number, every note was a definite tap. When it came to writing a romantic melody and lyrics, though, there was nobody like George and Ira."

A perfect example of what Astaire was citing about Berlin's way with a rhythm tune ("when you're dancing with a lady") is "Cheek to Cheek" from *Top Hat.* The staging of this number also serves as a plot device to get Astaire and Rogers back together after some bumpy moments on their pathway to love. Indeed, tap dancing was a prime ingredient in this scene from a film that many consider the apex of their association.

Berlin never ceased his laudatory feeling about Astaire's importance as a singer. At the age of eighty-eight, he said, "He's as good as any of them—as good as Jolson or Crosby or Sinatra. He's just as good a singer as he is a dancer—not necessarily because of his voice, but by his conception of projecting a song. He sang it the way you wrote it. He didn't change anything. And if he did change anything—he made it better. He might put a different emphasis on the lyric. He'd do things that you hoped other singers wouldn't do."[1]

The critic Richard Schickel emphasized "the casual elegance, the way the thirties songwriters came up with these songs in their heads, and the casual elegance with which Astaire delivered them." Of course, the Gershwins wrote a potpourri of superb ballads that Astaire introduced: "They Can't Take That Away from Me," "Shall We Dance," "How Long Has This Been Going On," " 'S Wonderful," "He Loves and She Loves," "Nice Work If You Can Get It," "A Foggy Day," and others. It's impossible to figure just how many more outstanding songs George Gershwin would have contributed for Astaire had he not passed away in 1937.

ASTAIRE'S FILM APPEARANCES with various leading ladies, following his last 1930s movie with Rogers, *The Story of Vernon and Irene Castle,* led to his introducing the songs of such other first-rate musical craftsmen as Johnny Mercer and Harold Arlen. By the early 1940s he had become recognized as the preeminent song-and-dance man of the time. His decade as an exclusive MGM star, beginning in 1946, solidified his status through his starring roles in several more musicals.

By then, no fundamental changes occurred in Astaire's approach to a popular song. His talk/sing style had been set. However, his MGM years gave him access to various masterful arrangers such as Conrad Salinger, Skip Martin, Alexander Courage, and the young André Previn, all of whose work enhanced his delivery of both ballads and rhythm tunes during this amazing era.

Astaire's bestselling 1930s Brunswick recordings of songs from the Fred and Ginger films (which differed from the movie sound tracks) had previously made him a star on records. His 1935 rendition of "Check to Cheek," backed by the Leo Reisman Orchestra, was one of the biggest hits of the decade, and one of his eight #1 records.

Right from the start, in the recording of "Cheek to Cheek," a strong rhythmic pulse is established that underlines Astaire's rather ethereal first chorus. He sings like a man deeply in love who has at last found "the happiness I seek." The second chorus finds him singing in a much lower register with considerably more verve, almost like a jazz singer. Reisman's swaying strings, muted trumpets, and piano breaks underscore the song's lilting melody line in the ride out. The popularity of this record owes much to Astaire's radiant delivery, which seemingly served as an inspiration to an America going through hard times. While dancing to this record, men felt as if they were Fred Astaire, and women felt as if they were dancing with him.

In 1936, when swing-band records were the rage, two of Astaire's records nonetheless were #1: "A Fine Romance" and "The Way You Look Tonight." The success of "A Fine Romance" is primarily due to the jaunty manner with which Astaire interprets Dorothy Fields's lyric. The combination of a muted trumpet, violin, and piano solos supplies an added romantic aspect to Johnny Green's arrangement. "The Way You Look Tonight" combines another outstanding Kern/Fields tune with one of Astaire's most sublime recorded performances. The delight that he brings to interpreting the rich melody is almost palpable. This became one of his favorite songs, and he recorded it many times throughout the remainder of his career.

Astaire's song "I'm Building Up to an Awful Letdown," which he wrote with Johnny Mercer, perhaps the most compelling song he ever wrote, was another hit record for him in that year. That led to his being given his own thirty-nine-week radio show, *The Packard Hour,* on NBC.

By modern musical standards, it's Astaire's involvement with both the lyrics and the feelings in these songs that has caused them to become enduring pop records, and indeed classics. He overcomes the often intrusive and simplistic arrangements that ruled the day in thirties film musicals and on romantic records as well. Except for "I'm Building Up to an Awful Letdown," all of these songs were prominently featured in the Fred and Ginger musicals and therefore had a ready-made buying audience.

The market for his series of mid- and late-1930s records, backed by various "potted palms" orchestras, inevitably and mercifully ran its course. This led to something more musically challenging. Still, it's rather disconcerting to hear the

1940 Columbia single "Who Cares," in which Astaire was paired with Benny Goodman. Astaire was essentially put into the role of a band singer in what was primarily a dance record. (The Fred Astaire–Johnny Green and Leo Reisman records were essentially three-minute dance records as well.) He sounded extremely uncomfortable singing at a pell-mell tempo despite having the soft cushion of the Goodman reed section underneath him along with the added stimulus of Goodman's twiddling clarinet.

Being offered the chance to dance to Goodman's erstwhile competitor Artie Shaw and His Orchestra was the principal reason Astaire agreed to star in Paramount's *Second Chorus*. Shaw recalled how easily Astaire learned "Love of My Life," a song he had written with Johnny Mercer for the movie. "It wasn't much of a song," said Shaw, "but he knew what he was doing, and he made it work. Everything he did was carefully studied."

Once again, preparation ruled the day. Shaw is correct: "Love of My Life," though an Oscar nominee, wasn't much of a song. But by reason of Fred's constant rehearsing of it at home in one night, Astaire made something of it that worked the next day on film.

The March 18, 1991, PBS special, "The Fred Astaire Songbook," hosted by Audrey Hepburn with understated observations, is the perfect aural and visual document to make the case for Astaire's abilities as a singer. Perceptive comments were contributed on camera by Liza Minnelli, Richard Schickel, Melissa Manchester, Peter Duchin, and Hermes Pan, along with voice-overs by Fred, Dellie, and Will Friedwald.

Hepburn said that working with Astaire in *Funny Face* was a "fantasy come true." She added, "His dancing was out of reach but his singing was somehow within reach."

Minnelli said, "The public never really understood what a marvelous singer he was. He had a pitch and a texture like no other. The best way to hear a song is to have Fred Astaire sing it."

Melissa Manchester marveled at the bravura performance that he gave to "Night and Day." On a voice-over, Astaire, however, again mentioned the trepidation he had in his first attempts at singing it.

Pan brought out the necessary relationship between Fred's singing and dancing. As an example, he mentioned how Fred utilized a dancer's rhythm in singing "Top Hat." Taking that point further, the writer Will Friedwald discussed how Astaire brought the same sense of rhythm to singing "Slap That Bass" in repeating the meter of "zoom, zoom, zoom" in *Shall We Dance*.

Hepburn came up with the interesting tidbit that Ira Gershwin had said to his brother, "I think we could make something out of fog." The result was the beguiling "A Foggy Day" from *A Damsel in Distress*. While speaking of the Gershwins, she told of how delighted she was to sing "He Loves and She Loves" with Fred in *Funny Face*. It showed upon viewing the film clip.

Pan returned to quote Irving Berlin, who once said of Astaire, "His phrasing, time, and diction make him my favorite singer." Fred's version of Berlin's "Cheek to Cheek," in Manchester's opinion, brought the listener into the fantasy element in the song. She also brought out another compelling fact: the minor-key changes in "Let's Face the Music" reflected the pathos of the Great Depression. The red-headed singer compared Fred and Ginger's working ethos to "oil and vinegar," whereas with Judy Garland their hearts go out to each other."

Clips of Porter's "I've Got My Eyes on You" and Berlin's "Drum Crazy" dwelled on Astaire the instrumentalist. On the former tune, his credentials as a jazz pianist were on display as in perhaps no other scene from any of his movies. Hepburn believed, "The variety and depth of his musical talent was endless."

She conveyed another interesting trifle of information, concerning Mercer and Arlen's "One for My Baby." Apparently, various changes in tempo were made before Fred was ready to sing and dance the song in the famous barroom scene in *The Sky's the Limit*. His arm and leg movements had to be synchronized so as to jibe with the tempo of the number.

This led to Minnelli's saying, "Astaire's approach to singing was personal and conversational." In solidifying this statement, she quoted her father, who had told her, "Fred gave so much thought to each song before he attempted to sing it."

Clips of "By Myself," "I Guess I'll Have to Change My Plan" (with Jack Buchanan), and "I Love Louisa" from *The Band Wagon* captured Astaire arguably at his peak as a singer. This was in contrast to having Oscar Levant playing too fast and too loud—two things an accompanist should never do—on "Lady Be Good" during Astaire's ill-fated appearance on Levant's television show.

The composer Burton Lane said, "I never saw anyone like Fred—the way he worked so hard," in describing his association with Astaire in *Royal Wedding*. He also said, "Fred was one of the most astounding [musical] performers ever seen on-screen." Lane mentioned that he originally wrote the melody of "You're All the World to Me" when he was only seventeen years old, though it was first heard in an Eddie Cantor musical. Its later incarnation turned out to be the basis of one of Astaire's signature song-and-dance numbers.

In conclusion, Hepburn said, "Fred could do anything. He was one of the most sophisticated images of all time. He had a genius I was allowed to be part of for one brief moment." The enchanting " 'S Wonderful" with Hepburn and Astaire singing and dancing together ended a worthwhile and highly informative presentation.

I would like to fantasize for a moment and imagine Fred's singing and dancing Billy Joel's famous tune "New York State of Mind." If ever a song seemed tailor-made for him, this is it. I would not, however, advocate his approaching any of Bruce Springsteen's hymns that yearn for a better America. They would have been beyond his scope.

In 1979, Whitney Balliett, then the reigning éminence grise of jazz and mainstream pop music, writing in the *New Yorker,* mentioned a few singers' observations on Astaire's singing: "Anita Ellis, who worked with him on two films, said, 'On the set, every inch of every step was worked out, and when he sang, I always felt that he eased up and became calmer, that his singing was a nice place to be.' Sylvia Sims said, 'He invented lyrical economy. His singing was the shortest distance between two points.' Barbara Lea noted, 'He belonged with the incidental singers like Johnny Mercer. He wasn't trying to sell anything but the song, which he got across with precision, clarity, and humor. There wasn't any ego trip involved. He had no intention of astounding you.' "

Balliett noted, "As Sylvia Sims suggests, the rhythmic intensity and brilliance that governed Astaire's legs and feet certainly controlled his singing. He has a light baritone, and his timbre is smooth. It is an angular, tidy, pure-cotton voice with little vibrato. It arose from necessity, and it is tough and adaptable. . . . His long notes may waver, and he sometimes lands near his notes instead of on them, but he makes every song fresh-faced and as if each were important news. There doesn't seem to be anything between the words and the listener: the lyrics pass directly from the sheet music to the ear."[2]

Barrie Chase observed, "Jazz was in his bones. "Indeed, it was rarely, if ever, out of his musical consciousness. This was part and parcel of his particular rhythmic approach to singing and its effects on his dancing. It is important to note that the standard four/four jazz time signature is also the basic dance tempo." Writer Stanley Crouch said, "Jazz is the most sophisticated musical performing art, it is a music built on adult emotion rather than adolescent passion." Astaire grasped this early on, which helped draw him into it.

In Crouch's 2005 *New Yorker* profile of the jazz tenor saxophonist Sonny Rollins, he alluded to the fact that Rollins and Astaire shared a common musical thread: Neither of these titans ever thought they were good enough. They shared a firm belief that only by devoting countless hours to rehearsing their craft might they ever be *accepted* as true artists. Crouch also quoted Rollins as saying, "I know most of the songs [I play] and most of the lyrics. The story begins with the melody; you keep the story going by using the melody the way you hear it as something to improvise on."

Rollins's approach as an instrumentalist is an apt description of the way Fred Astaire approached the songs he sang. His artistry as a singer at the beginning owed much to his thoroughly learning new songs in the Broadway musicals he starred in by keeping in mind how they fit into the book of the show. His deep concentration on the importance of the lyrics was established here.

LOUIS BELLSON HAS LONG BEEN an important drummer, considered one of the leading jazz practitioners of the art. His sixty-six-year career has included stints in the big bands of Duke Ellington, Count Basie, Benny Goodman, Harry James, and Tommy Dorsey, as well as leading his own big band. He also had an extensive show-business career as the musical director for his wife, Pearl Bailey, until her death in 1990.

Bellson first met Astaire in Los Angeles after Fred performed at a 1955 "Jazz at the Philharmonic" concert, produced by Norman Granz, at the Shrine Auditorium in Los Angeles. (This was during the time when Astaire was recording for Granz.) Bellson said, "I was amazed how much he appreciated the Harlem tap dancers like Baby Laurence, Bunny Briggs, Teddy Hale, the original Bill Bailey, and, of course, John Bubbles. He had gone to see them work when he was in New York during the 1920s and '30s.

"I knew that he was aware that Buddy Rich, Jo Jones, Chick Webb, Gene Krupa, and myself started out as tap dancers. He loved Chick Webb's playing, telling me what great natural ability Chick had."

Although we've noted Astaire's lack of decided prowess as a drummer, Bellson said, "I picked up on what he was doing when he played drums in movies. I noticed there was something in the way he used his feet that influenced me. Buddy and I watched and listened to him when he danced. We picked up on sound and interpretation from him. Those two things were vital for drummers. I think he could have been a great drummer—the way he moved, his hands were right, his knees were right, and he had all of that rhythmical thing."

With his obvious enthusiasm for Astaire's work, it's not surprising that in Bellson's long career as a composer, he would write a piece inspired by Astaire's talent. "I created a piece called 'The Matterhorn' for a big-band album I did on Verve with the drummer Billy Cobham. Billy came up with the title. [Cobham resides in Switzerland; he obviously named it for the Swiss mountain.] Fred was my inspiration in writing it because I thought of him because he danced in different time signatures. Some of the old tap dancers could only dance in the usual four/four rhythm. Fred could go from three/four to six/four, then seven/eight—all over the place. I knew that Billy Cobham was a good sight reader, and he could play all those various time signatures."

Robert Walker Jr., the former actor and Malibu art-gallery owner, is the son of the actor Robert Walker and Jennifer Jones. He met Astaire in 1955 at the home of David O. Selznick when he was married to Jennifer Jones. Once again, the common denominator was drums.

"Fred was strolling around the grounds—maybe they had a croquet tournament going on that day, which they did frequently in those days," Walker recalled. "He must have heard me wailing on my drums in the house. My brother Michael and I lived in our own little boys' house on the property. Fred and I chatted, and then he invited me over to his house by saying, 'I have a couple of sets of drums there, and we can jam together.' We made a date then and there."

The personable entrepreneur felt Astaire was a far better drummer than he was, especially in his ability to listen. "I was only fifteen at the time so I played loud and fast. Fred, being older, was more hip to things. He helped teach me. We began to have a conversation on the drums for a couple of hours rather than my just working out my ego. There was a subtlety in the way he played. And in a sense we danced together. I remember that moment so fondly. I guess when you're young you remember older folks that are kind to you because so many older folks brush off youngsters. But Fred made the time for me. I've had a few people in my life like that who have been mentors in a sense."

Walker later had a solo drum act, and he has kept up his playing over the years. He has ventured away from jazz and now is a devotee of world music. His gallery/gift shop had on display a potpourri of exotic drums from all over the world. Perhaps Astaire's interest had something to do with it all.

As noted with Robert Walker Jr., Astaire's love for jazz extended to his rehearsing at home, which gave him great personal satisfaction. The late actor Mel Ferrer, who recently died, recalled Astaire's asking him if he could show him something one night after he and his then wife, Audrey Hepburn, finished dinner with Fred and his wife, Phyllis, at their Beverly Hills home. "We went up to his attic, whereupon he put on a Woody Herman record—a screamer like 'Apple Honey' or 'Wildroot' or something like that. He got behind his set of drums and began playing. I could see how he got such enjoyment out of doing that."

The choreographer and director Michael Kidd recalled, "I can remember when I worked with him on *The Band Wagon*. He would come in some mornings and tell me how he had played his drums the night before in his house to Count Basie's music. That apparently meant a lot to him."

During Astaire's 1968 NBC special, Irv Cottler was playing drums in Neal Hefti's orchestra. Apparently, Astaire didn't like the way Cottler was playing on his dance numbers. He corrected him several times, even though Cottler was a well-established drummer. He'd started playing drums for Frank Sinatra in 1962 after having worked on many of Sinatra's historic recordings with Nelson Riddle. In retaliation for Astaire's comments, Cottler complained to Neal Hefti, "You think he is a great dancer—he has no time!"

The former jazz drummer Jackie Mills initially met Astaire at MGM when Mills was the drummer alongside pianist Gerald Wiggins (with no bassist) playing for the choreographer Jack Cole's dance rehearsals. One day in the late 1950s, while Astaire was visiting Cole, he shyly asked Mills, "Do you think you could teach me how to really play the drums?" Astaire was obviously not satisfied with his playing and was concerned that the two numbers that had featured him playing drums in the film *Daddy Long Legs* did not appear fully authentic. Ever the worrier, he felt this would leave himself open to criticism from the average movie-goer, not to mention the jazz musicians whom he revered.

As Mills recalled, "He wanted to be able to deal with the high-hat cymbal. He loved Jo Jones's playing so I showed him how Jo used the high hat when Jo played with Count Basie. After that he wanted to know how Sonny Greer was able to get that sound from the big Chinese cymbal that he played with Duke Ellington. Then I showed him how to use the bass drum a little differently, and some little things about tuning up his drums and wetting the bass drum head, something I had learned form the great drummer Dave Tough." Mills continued, "He felt it was easier to master jazz than other kinds of music, which is why he so enjoyed dancing to jazz. He loved all kinds of jazz: Dixieland, bebop, big bands like Benny Goodman, Duke Ellington, Woody Herman, Jimmie Lunceford, and small groups. He was fascinated with the feeling of jazz, where it came from, and how it got to the point where it was at the time. We'd have a cup of tea or go someplace, to a five-and-dime store, and talk about it. He was shocked about the environment for jazz musicians: gangster-owned clubs where they were used to playing. That was a whole new world to him that he loved to hear about it.

"He was a gentleman and treated women with great respect. I learned a lot from him. I learned a lot about focus and how he didn't leave things to chance. If you watched him or heard him talk, after a time you'd understand that focus ruled his life. It was the essence of his attitude towards life."

In his four television specials in 1958, '59, '60, and '68, it was no accident that Astaire insisted on jazz as an important feature. He insisted on booking the Jonah Jones Quartet as a guest on the first two shows and Count Basie and His Orchestra on the third show and Young-Holt Unlimited on the fourth show. The pride with which he introduced Basie showed clearly that Basie was his longtime favorite. He told Jackie Mills he had actually dreamed of that moment.

Astaire's becoming a pupil of Jackie Mills led directly to Mills heading A&R for Choreo Records (later Ava Records), which Astaire financed in 1961 and which lasted four years. The idea for its start-up was simple. "One day," Mills remembered, "Fred asked me, 'How much would it cost to open a record company?' I told him, 'About twenty-five thousand dollars.' He said, 'I can handle that. Let's start a company.' "

According to Mills, Astaire and Hermes Pan were 96 percent owners; Mills and songwriter Tommy Wolf split the remaining 4 percent. The company was most likely conceived as a tax shelter. *Three Evenings with Fred Astaire,* the sound track of his first three TV specials, was the company's first release, along with an album by Carol Lawrence, who had been the female lead in the Broadway version of *West Side Story.*

Milt Bernhart, the jazz trombonist well remembered for his epic trombone solo on the famous Frank Sinatra/Nelson Riddle record of "I've Got You Under My Skin," had been a member of the orchestra that played Elmer Bernstein's music on the sound track of the film *Walk on the Wild Side.* Bernhart told Mills how impressed he was by Bernstein's jazz-influenced theme for the movie. Choreo then bought the rights to the sound-track album. The theme from *Walk on the Wild Side* became the company's first singles release and became a #1 record.

Based on the assumption, long a part of the thinking of the entertainment business, that the sequel to the original will be a hit as well, Choreo released the sound-track album, again of Elmer Bernstein's music, from Astaire's friend Gregory Peck's *To Kill a Mockingbird.* The album was not nearly so successful. Plans for an album of Peck singing folk songs and playing guitar never jelled.

Astaire gave Mills carte blanche to decide the label's recording direction. A crossover album by the classical violinist Eunice Shapiro of Stravinsky's Violin Concerto in D was an ill-fated attempt. Since folk music was then in vogue, presaging the violent change the country was about to undergo, several folk albums were produced. They didn't sell nor did the jazz product, which was then fashionable but soon to lose its importance, with albums by established musicians such as the cornetist Muggsy Spanier. The jazz pianist Pete Jolly had a hit, however, with "Little Bird" during the bossa nova craze.

Ava Records was a victim of the times. Rock 'n' roll was what was hot; what Ava released for the most part wasn't. There were also ongoing problems with MGM Records, its distributor, over the release of jazz records. In 1965, Astaire sold the company. According to Mills, the new owner, Glenn Costen, took possession of all the tapes and the company's catalog of records and never made the final payments to him.

Pianist, composer, and lyricist Tommy Wolf, who with Mills had coproduced the record company's entire recording output, collaborated on writing songs with Fred. Wolf and Mills also served as the accompanists during the dance rehearsals for the third Astaire special. (Fred's songwriting career, which eventually encompassed twenty-seven songs, had begun inauspiciously in 1919 with "She's Got the War Bride Blues.") Over thirteen years Fred and Wolf had two fair-sized hits, "City of the Angels" and "Life Is Beautiful," both of which Fred recorded. The former was often played as the closing instrumental by Doc Severinsen's band on the *Tonight Show* during the Johnny Carson era and was therefore probably Astaire's most successful song. "Life Is Beautiful" also became a popular Tony Bennett record.

Bennett, on the AFI (American Film Institute) CBS special "100 Years . . . 100 Songs," subtitled "America's Greatest Music in the Movies," referred to *The Band Wagon* as his all-time favorite movie and singled out Astaire's contributions to its success. Bennett had devoted an entire 1993 album, *Steppin' Out,* to eighteen songs that Astaire had originally introduced either on Broadway or in films. In the liner notes for this CD, Bennett wrote, "If the composer wrote a gem, Astaire turned it into a diamond."

Perhaps Bennett was indulging in a bit of hyperbole. Obviously, some of the songs Astaire introduced and some that he recorded were better than others. For the most part, however, he personally chose the songs he released, and most of them were derived from his film musicals. He was fortunate to have made his Broadway debut at a time when the best American popular songs were being written. This superior brand of popular music continued into the next decade as he segued into starring in film musicals. In the 1940s and during the war years, this kind of music continued to be popular and furnished him with first-rate material. His last major hit was "Something's Got to Give" in 1955, from *Daddy Long Legs.* The next year, Elvis Presley burst upon the scene and the age of "good music" abruptly ended.

Debbie Reynolds, who also appeared on the AFI special, said, "Fred wasn't noted as a singer, but every song he sang in films remains a standard and all the singers sing it." As an example, one of several important songs missing from the AFI compilation was Dietz and Schwartz's "By Myself" from *The Band Wagon.* Astaire's rendition is screenwriter and lyricist Betty Comden's favorite memory of having worked with him. She declared, "The picture of him walking alongside the train when he comes to New York was just poetic. . . . I loved that part; I love that song." Comden and Green set up a magical moment that revealed Astaire's rarely seen vulnerability. It also reintroduced the song that thereafter became an important standard.

Fred never really managed to wear a ballad like a custom-tailored suit the way Sinatra did. He lacked the intensity, and the sense of intimacy and vulnerability that Sinatra possessed, perhaps because he was not the same tortured soul.

Vulnerability, as exemplified by Sinatra in his classic *In the Wee Small Hours* and *Only the Lonely* albums, was really never part of Astaire's vocal makeup. As an example, Astaire approached Harold Arlen and Johnny Mercer's signature torch song "One for My Baby" in an entirely different way when he introduced it in Paramount's *The Sky's the Limit.* Margaret Whiting, the veteran pop singer, had an interesting take on Astaire's interpretation of the song: "He was carrying the torch when he came into the bar. He said, 'It's quarter to three,' sat down, and talked to Joe, the bartender. Then he got up and kicked the glasses off the bar. He never missed a beat as he sang while he danced and danced as he sang. He didn't do 'It's quarter to three' like Sinatra. The intensity was there in a different way. It came out like an actor. It was a spiritual happening and a masterpiece." Astaire's unusual approach touched on anger rather than vulnerability without sacrificing the song's intrinsic meaning.

Another explanation of Astaire's method of singing mournful ballads was supplied by Mel Tormé in his book *My Singing Teachers.* He called Astaire one of his favorite singers, explaining, "One aspect of Astaire's singing that always impressed me was his handling of torch songs, the ones about loss or unrequited love. Unlike any other singer in memory, Fred approached these tunes with an air of self-ridicule . . . self-sufficient and independent; one got the feeling that he could survive anything and do without anyone."

Bobby Cranshaw has been a well-regarded jazz bassist for over four decades. He has been a member of Sonny Rollins's band for many years. He acknowledged, "My thing is learning tunes. Through [the bassist] Ray Brown and Maurice Hines, and various jazz musicians, I learned that if you want to know the melody to tunes, you listen to Fred Astaire and Ella Fitzgerald. Most kids didn't know the standards. I teach that at the New School here in New York."

Fred Cohn, who wrote the liner notes for the Verve album *Fred Astaire's Finest Hour,* contends that one reason for Astaire's enduring importance as a singer was that his sound was a welcome departure from that of Bing Crosby, Rudy Vallee, Russ Columbo, and the other crooners who had become popular in the early 1930s, "Even by the time of *Ziegfeld Follies* [1946], he sounds much more modern than Tony Martin, and he was a much more adept singer than Tony. His particular sound also does not have the singular flourishes of many of the Broadway singers of this time.

"I would say the long suit of his singing, however, was his absolute rhythmic sense. There was a kind of classiness to it. He was always getting into the deeper meaning of the words. I think he must have spent a long time figuring out his interpretation of 'They Can't Take That Away from Me,' with all that attention to detail. He's giving you the song's emotion rather than his own. There's a wispiness to his voice, a lack of fiber, a lack of affectation, and there's nothing trained about it. Knowing what we know, that very lack of training could have resulted in a lot of preparation."

Speaking of Astaire's version of "Night and Day," Cohn stressed that Porter wrote the familiar line "oh such a hungry yearning" as a kind of springboard for one of Astaire's flights. "You're left with Astaire and his rhythmic genius. It's not about voice, not about expressiveness, it's about the song and the rhythm."

Joel Grey, who made his mark as the emcee in *Cabaret,* went even further: "The influence Astaire had on my work was always his ethic of excellence, a standard. He had this reserve that was very alluring but intimidating. His singing has always been amazing because he didn't have a big voice, but he said so much in his phrasing that was even more pertinent than Frank Sinatra. Astaire for me was always an actor/singer. He told a story that was not motivated by the melody particularly, but the words. So that's an actor's vehicle. I think that in a certain way he was the Duke of Windsor of music—glorious, subtle, aloof, elegant."

"AS A SONGWRITER, I've always felt the literature of popular music would be much poorer without Fred Astaire. He integrated a song and communicated exactly what the writers wanted. That's why the songwriters loved to write for him— rhythmically, romantically, and lyrically, always faithfully," summed up Alan Bergman, who with his colyricist wife, ASCAP president Marilyn Bergman, has won three Academy Awards. "He was a wonderful actor, and he told you the story through his wonderful instrument, although I guess people can criticize that instrument. He had such a persona that when you wrote for him, it was like writing for a character in a play. It fit perfectly."

The tall, lean, and bespectacled Bergman recalled a time in the 1950s: "I was going out with Marilyn, and we had started writing together. I wanted to marry her, but I didn't have a quarter. The composer Lew Spence said, 'I've got an idea for a song called 'That Face,' and I said, 'That's a nice idea. Let's write it up.' Marilyn's favorite singer was Fred Astaire, along with Frank Sinatra, and somehow we got an appointment with Mr. Astaire. We met at his office. He said, 'I don't record anything that's not in my movies, but I'll listen. We sang the song for him, and he said, 'I really like this song. I'm going to record it next week.' We were thrilled."

Listening to Astaire's rendition of "That Face," it seems apparent that the song did have a special meaning for him. Once again, he employs his patented sincere approach in his treatment of this ballad. At the very end of the tune, he delivers a sigh of complete resignation to "That Face," which is completely disarming.

Bergman continued, "He went on *The Ed Sullivan Show* to plug his movie *Funny Face,* but he sang 'That Face.' People thought it was from the movie. He called me from New York to tell me that Dorothy Fields wanted to know who wrote the lyrics."

Two years later, Bergman came home from playing tennis one afternoon and asked Marilyn if anybody had called. "Some guy Fred," she replied facetiously. Bergman said, "I returned the call. Fred said he was going to do the song on his second special. He planned to sing it to Barrie Chase, the dancer he was going with. He asked me to write a couple of more choruses. So, I wrote him a couple more choruses."

"Another Evening with Fred Astaire," in 1959, established "That Face." Barbra Streisand later sang it to Miss Piggy on one of her TV specials. Even Eddie Fisher couldn't destroy the song when he sang it with attendant publicity to his then wife, Elizabeth Taylor, in his Las Vegas nightclub act. Astaire's record was featured in the 1962 William Holden/Audrey Hepburn comedy, *Paris When It Sizzles.* It was the last song Fred introduced that became a standard.

In 1981, shortly after Astaire married Robyn Smith, the former jockey, he was honored by the AFI in a televised tribute. Bergman recalled, "Marilyn and I arrived early. I went over to Fred's table to congratulate him, and he said, 'This is the young man who wrote . . . ,' and he sang 'That Face' to Robyn unaccompanied. When he got through, I said, 'I can go home now. Nothing can top that.' And he laughed."

NEAL HEFTI INTERESTINGLY amplified how Astaire's singing satisfied the wishes of the songwriter. After seeing *De-Lovely,* the Cole Porter film biography, and upon hearing Porter's voice over the film's credits, Hefti compared Porter and Astaire. "The thing that made Fred Astaire a good singer was the same thing that made Cole Porter a good singer. Fred could have been a songwriter rather than a singer. Songwriters sing a certain way, and a lot of people say, 'I would rather hear the songwriter sing than Frank Sinatra because the songwriter, with his limited range, gets every word and every note correct.'"

The respected expert on pop singers Henry Pleasants, in his 1974 survey, *The Great American Popular Singers,* made the rather oblique comment, including Astaire as "another example of an artist [primarily a dancer] who has sung more persuasively than most singers sing. The same may be said of Marlene Dietrich, Walter Huston, and Lee Marvin[!]."

The composer, writer, and Frank Sinatra mentor Alec Wilder considered Astaire one of his musical heroes. In his highly regarded 1972 treatise, *The American Popular Song: The Great Innovators, 1900–1950,"* Wilder said, "I'd like to point out something that has greatly impressed me—every song written for Fred Astaire seems to bear his mark. Every writer, in my opinion, was vitalized by Astaire and wrote in a manner they had never quite written in before: he brought out in them something a little better than their best—a little more subtlety, flair, sophistication, wit and style, qualities he himself possesses in generous measure."

MONICA LEWIS WAS AN ACCOMPLISHED POP SINGER of the 1940s and 1950s who starred on radio and records and appeared frequently on *The Ed Sullivan Show* and in a few MGM musicals. The studio still had Judy Garland under contract at that time. She was their pop singer, and as a result Lewis was never given the right opportunities. Opera was then in at MGM, with Mario Lanza, Kathryn Grayson, and Jane Powell as the centerpieces.

Astaire had his own observations about dancing and singers, which he rarely expressed to other performers. One night at a party at the Waldorf-Astoria, he discussed these subjects with Lewis. She recalled, "He inferred that while dancing involved technique, and there were some marvelous technicians, and also people who had a great look, it was very hard for him to find the balance that suited him. He didn't want to be short on one or the other. With regard to singing, he felt an emotional response was what was really important. And while technique was very important, and the control of what you had was certainly important for singing anything classical or operatic, he felt that if the technique was showing more than the emotion, you had a problem. He said the main thing about singing was connection."

DESPITE HIS TREMENDOUS SUCCESS in film musicals, by 1952 Astaire found himself without a recording contract. That's when Norman Granz, the dynamic jazz-concert promoter and astute self-promoter, who had formed Norgran Records, later changed to Clef and eventually to Verve, decided to act on his admiration for Astaire the singer.

Granz called Astaire one day that fall with an intriguing idea: "Would you be interested in recording all the songs that you've either introduced or made famous, but this time you'd be backed by an all-star jazz sextet led by Oscar Peterson?" "Why not?" Astaire figured. God knows he knew all the songs. Besides that, he had always yearned to sing with a jazz group.

Astaire and Granz came to an almost immediate understanding. The album would be titled *The Astaire Story.* It would, however, have to be done Astaire's way—not in the usual procedure of "Okay, let's try one, 'Cheek to Cheek,' take one." Astaire and Peterson diligently rehearsed all the songs over two days. That way Astaire could listen at home to the tapes to familiarize himself with Peterson's approach. Again, Astaire left nothing to chance.

Granz decided on an ideal combination of stellar musicians to complement pianist Peterson. His cohorts would be Ray Brown on bass, Barney Kessel on guitar, Alvin Stoller on drums, along with two superior horn players, Charlie Shavers on trumpet and Flip Phillips on tenor sax. Knowing that his group was there to accompany Astaire, Peterson recalled, "We didn't want to force him into a corner. We just wanted him to be comfortable. We listened to the way he was interpreting each song and tried to work with that. . . . Norman made it clear to the musicians that it was Mr. Astaire's date, not a jam session." Peterson also acknowledged that he didn't veer too far from the basic 4/4 swing tempo so that Astaire would feel at ease.

Peterson wrote in his autobiography *A Jazz Odyssey: The Life of Oscar Peterson* (Continuum), "The initial rehearsal and talk-through went very well. Although Fred voiced some doubts about his competence as a vocalist, he was very clear on the feel and treatment he wanted on most of the songs; on others he was less sure and would wonder aloud, 'I've never understood why he wrote that kind of lyric for this particular tune' or 'I've never felt comfortable with this passage,' telling you precisely why.

"It would be idle to pretend that the sessions passed without a hitch. For all his rhythmic feel, Fred was not naturally attuned to jazz phrasing, and it was at times perilously easy to throw him via the wrong intro or a misplaced fill. We learned to gauge our ad-lib lines around and behind him very carefully, giving him enough time to hear his place of re-entry coming up; we also stuck firmly to the normal harmonic clusters, as any kind of 'modern' dissonance could phase him or make him worried about his own intonation.

"I found it fascinating to discover how different were Fred's senses of time as vocalist and as dancer. Dancing, his time was so strict that he could make an accompaniment sound early or late; his vocal time, however, was very loose, uninhibited, and unmeasured. I found the best way to accompany him was to give him a long harmonic chord cushion and let him take his natural liberties with metronomic time."

During a rehearsal, Granz and Peterson cajoled Astaire into sitting in with the group by playing drums. As Peterson recalled, "To hear his time in conjunction with Ray [Brown's] vast sound was quite an event, and the look of rapt intent on his face was a joy to behold."

In addition to recording thirty-five songs (two of which Astaire wrote), he tap-danced for two tunes. Peterson and his group improvised two versions of "The Astaire Blues," written especially for the record. Astaire even played a bit of piano for his tune "Not My Girl" before giving way to Peterson while Fred delivered the vocal. At the conclusion of the last session, the dancer now turned jazz singer presented each of the musicians with gold identification bracelets inscribed WITH THANKS; FRED A, and Peterson proudly wears his every day, fifty-five years later.

When I asked Peterson if this album was a milestone in his career, he quickly answered, "By all means! It started out as a challenge and ended up a pleasure. We're very proud of it."

Astaire's long-held affinity for jazz and what it had meant to him as a singer and dancer were incorporated into the feeling of ease that dominates this recording. All of his standard fare is on display here. The tempos were little less stringent than in his earlier big-orchestra recordings of these same songs. The plaintive, yearning quality is evident in Astaire's voice, but with touches of a refinement and a new understanding of such lyrics as those of his song "Not My Girl," which he wrote in 1935 with lyricist Desmond Carter. He is so inspired by the groove established by the ensemble that he delivers a much more exuberant version than his original take on this song. He is not emphasizing the romantic aspect of these songs as he once did. It is rather a straight-ahead-yet-sincere version of these tunes that he is offering.

Alan Bergman believes, "Fred was more relaxed and so easy. It was obvious he was having a very good time. His renditions of the songs were much more intimate. Singing at a slower tempo gave him the chance to articulate and interpret these songs a little deeper. I mean he was one of the great interpreters. It was great to hear 'Cheek to Cheek' played a little slower—much different than the way he had done it many times before."

Ahmet Ertegun held a contrary view. He contended that if he had produced the album, he would have seen to it that Peterson had exhibited less of his jazz chops. I disagree. Peterson's playing was supportive, not obtrusive. To me, *The*

Astaire Story is Astaire's definitive album. He was completely comfortable in a jazz context without trying to phrase like a horn or to exhibit other traits of a jazz singer. He was highly effective using his own dancer's rhythm. It was jazz. And when the musicians joined Astaire in singing "I Love Louisa" with a pronounced Germanic accent, they displayed more natural good humor than that found in the original Broadway cast album of *The Band Wagon,* on which Astaire had been a participant.

Strangely, the critical reaction to *The Astaire Story,* when it was released in 1953, was not favorable. Doug Watt of the New York *Daily News* called the album "mediocre" and was appalled that Astaire thought he could do a jazz record. Peterson believes, "They [the critics] were out of their realm. . . . They were used to criticizing jazz . . . evaluating, supposedly. . . . I don't think the majority of them, to be very frank with you, understood a lot of it either. But when you put the kind of vocalizing Fred was doing with jazz, it really became a befuddling situation for many of them."

On its 1980 rerelease, *New York Post* jazz writer Dick Sudhalter, saw the album in a much different light. "His [Astaire's] feeling for a phrase is faultless, his time impeccable. . . . His voice may not be one of the classic voices—but he is indeed one of the great singers in American music. . . . Astaire and his accompanist seem to have established an easy working rapport right from the start."[3]

In 1989, critic Kevin Whitehead in a review in *DownBeat* wrote, "How did the man with the paper-thin voice do it? By making singing before a mic an act of dancing in the dark; he's so elegant, you can almost see him gliding across the floor. His phrasing was conversational as any jazz musician's—he'd talk his way through a couple of key words, blurring the line between song and natural speech (surely an outgrowth of his theatre years). . . . Even by his own measure, Fred isn't in the greatest voice; his intonation is shaky. . . . The music is highly textured but swings like mad." The review awarded four and a half stars out of five.

Nat Hentoff, always an astute observer, and one who has long maintained an open mind in his jazz criticism, took a new look at the record almost fifty years later in a November 14, 2002, *Wall Street Journal* piece. Among his conclusions were "When I've been asked to define jazz singing, aside from listening to the obvious names, I suggest trying to find *The Astaire Story.* . . . By contrast with carefully constructed, self-conscious attempts at swinging by such current jazz divas as Diana Krall and Jane Monheit, Astaire, without any guideposts but his own instincts and imagination, became one of the swinging improvisers . . . a sort of new addition, as he put it, 'to the Jazz at the Philharmonic group.'"

John Pizzarelli is a well-established jazz-influenced singer and guitarist who has succeeded through the respect and know-how he brings to traditional pop songs. He learned to appreciate them from his father, the jazz guitar master Bucky Pizzarelli. John discovered *The Astaire Story* in 1985 while browsing through a record store in Japan. "My wife [Jessica Molaskey] and I spent a summer listening to it," he recalled. "We were at my friend's house in the Hamptons. We sat and listened to it on the porch. We shook our heads and said, 'How brilliant is his understanding!'" Pizzarelli reminisced about "tagging along with my dad to the Dick Gibson Jazz Party where we were sitting in with Flip Phillips. He had this gorgeous name bracelet on. I think it was twenty-four-karat gold. You see this and we're like whoa. On the back it was inscribed WITH LOVE FROM FRED. And then I saw *The Band Wagon* and Fred had one on."

In discussing *The Astaire Story,* Pizzarelli said, "I noticed that there were a couple of things that Oscar worked out with the guys. . . . On the other songs, they just go. I don't ever feel that Fred is nervous to be singing jazz. He is so inside the songs you never feel this is a Broadway star or a movie star singing with a jazz group. He knows why he is there; he is making this a great record. . . . It would be a master class in how best to communicate those songs. That's why his voice is beautiful to me. He sang with the best musicians in the world going straight ahead. He doesn't have to do any gymnastics, jump over any hoops, or 'scooby dooby doo.'"

As other singers noted, Pizzarelli talked about Astaire's deep understanding of songs, their rhythms and lyrics. "When he sings 'Puttin' On The Ritz,' he does not have to do anything but sing the song because he knows what the song means. His time is ridiculous. He's wiggling in and out of the lyrics, and he's joyful.

"You hear him tap-dance at the end. He's doing with his feet what he could have done with his voice. He can do all that. It's the top. When I hear him sing 'Heaven, I'm in heaven,' he is totally in control of the song, and if you were to hear him sing it, it would make sense to you. 'They Can't Take That Away from Me'— why should he change the melody, why should he do anything but what he does? He already knows George Gershwin wrote it this way. Ira Gershwin wrote this lyric. He knew these guys, and he knew where it came from."

The highly articulate singer and musician's thorough analysis of the album continued with his saying, "He, Fred Astaire's it. He can take it out of the theater and put it in the context of a jazz group, and he understands the difference. It's like Sinatra singing 'In the Wee Small Hours'; the way he understands it emotionally, Sinatra is a different animal—but the way Fred goes in with a small group and delivers the ball. It's like the Count Basie approach to singing, almost. He sang the rhythm tunes and the ballads, and it's wistful that he can laugh in the midst of presenting a song. It's important for any jazz singer to understand how Fred Astaire sings with a group as a starting-off point. I think it's one of the key albums of my development. I have it on my iPod so it's always with me. Every once in a while I put on a track."

Five years after the release of *The Astaire Story,* arranger Buddy Bregman began a musical collaboration with Astaire. Bregman, a formidable raconteur, remembered, "When we first met at the Verve office, Astaire said, 'You write for dancers. I love the way you write those dance beats.' I had done albums with Sammy Davis Jr. and Bob Fosse. I told him, 'I stole that from you, especially from "Silk Stockings." ' " (Bregman explained, "Every album of mine has to have that particular phrase. It's a Fred thing.")

Bregman continued, "Fred had called Norman [Granz] at the office because he had liked some of the albums I had arranged. I was then head of A and R for Verve. Shortly after our first meeting, Fred said, 'You know I'm a songwriter. I'd love to record my songs with you.' I started to listen to them as I played piano for him while he sang. His melodies were kind of mundane."

According to Bregman, when he suggested his interest in arranging an album of Astaire singing his own songs, Granz balked. He told Bregman, "If you record anything with Fred Astaire, you're fired! I paid so much money for that other thing I did with him [*The Astaire Story*]. It didn't sell, God damn it." (The truth is that the cut-down version of this album, entitled *Fred Astaire Sings Irving Berlin,* fifty-five years later remains the second-biggest selling CD in Astaire's vast recording catalog.)

Bregman somehow got Granz to change his mind. Bregman claims that it was he who first had the Bergmans audition "That Face" for him, which led to the meeting with Astaire and the decision to record the song.

As Bregman refers to it, "Thursdays with Fred" began as a weekly retreat at Astaire's home. "We'd talk. Our relationship grew. It had nothing to do with show business. If you don't like or love Fred Astaire, you had to revere him. The musicians revered him. Before we recorded the album, he and I rehearsed for weeks at the Verve office."

Astairable Fred was planned as a showcase for his songs. Five of them were featured in addition to the Bergmans' "That Face," one song by Dietz and Schwartz, two by Berlin, two by Porter, and one by Kern. Porter's "I Concentrate on You" was given a less serious treatment than the song usually receives. Again going against the grain, Astaire brought a different meaning to it—a slower, more concerned approach by concentrating on the subtle nuances in Porter's lyrics. On this and other songs, Bregman's charts were punctuated by a bevy of meaningful solos by such jazz musicians as Ted Nash on tenor saxophone, Harry "Sweets" Edison on trumpet, and Claude Williamson on piano. They significantly influenced Astaire's vocal interpretations.

"The three recording sessions were wonderful," Bregman recalled. "The first take on 'That Face' was just perfect, but we did a second one anyway. Fred's not a singer. We're talking about a visual guy who, when he adds the visual in the voice, it's thrilling; when he just does 'the voice,' there's a kind of a scrim there that you don't always 'see.' But it's Fred Astaire's voice, and it's so distinctive that if he wanted to do one or two or fifteen takes, I couldn't care less. All his singing is heartfelt. You believe everything he says."

Bregman stressed, "He's the meaning of lyrics. With Fred, when he said to a young lady he loved her, you believed it. Bing, with whom I also worked, sang it; Fred meant it. When he sang, and when he talked, he emphasized certain words. He talked the song in a rhythm and a melody that was his own. He did little trill things a couple of times that would give it emphasis, [the kind] that you never heard anybody do before. It was Fred talking with a little music. He swung in a way that obviated what he did with his feet. What he did with his feet was very black. What he did with his voice was very white. From the waist down he was a black man. From the waist up he was a white man.

"Every time I was at the house he was on the drums. He loved Buddy Rich and black artists, but he liked everything white. You could tell he liked me because I was white. Speaking of my arrangements, he said, 'You're the white Basie.' I loved that."

One day, Bregman said to Astaire, "Tell me you're the greatest tap dancer of all time." He said, "I'm definitely not. I've got style. I'm not the best tap dancer of all time." Bregman countered with "Well, who is the best tap dancer?" "Sammy Davis Jr.," said Astaire. "Buddy, for every sixteen steps I do, he can do sixty in the same amount of time. He's the best tap dancer in history."

DURING THE 1960S and 1970s Leslie Bricusse wrote the score for such screen musicals as *Doctor Doolittle, Goodbye, Mr. Chips* (on which he collaborated with John Williams), *Scrooge,* and *Willy Wonka* (which he wrote with Anthony New-ley). In his autobiography, *Music Man,* Bricusse related, "The most treasured fan letter I ever received from anyone in my life—a four-page . . . handwritten, thought-ful and beautifully detailed letter, analyzing and complimenting my songs, one by one, comparing them to Irving Berlin (ye Gods!) and at the foot of page four, the signature of the one human being above all others whom I would have wished to like my songs—Fred Astaire."

Bricusse feels that Gene Kelly's famous rendition of "Singin' in the Rain" was really a Fred Astaire number. He also cited that Astaire and Rex Harrison, who helped Bricusse win the Oscar for Best Music, Original Song ("Talk to the Animals") for *Doctor Dolittle* in 1967, shared a rhythmic feeling that made them both original and convincing musical interpreters.

One evening at Bricusse's home, Astaire was playing pool with Sammy Davis Jr. The flashy entertainer was dressed in an open-neck shirt with a mass of gold trinkets hanging from his neck. This had an immediate effect on Astaire's sartorial sensibility. In the midst of the game, Astaire looked over at a good friend and remarked, "What a vulgar little man!"

IN 1975 came a completely unforeseen offer from a London-based record producer named Ken Barnes, now a successful video producer. Barnes had most recently recorded Johnny Mercer for United Artists Records. Afterward, Mercer requested that Barnes come to Beverly Hills to straighten out some problems Mercer had encountered with his recording studio. While there, Barnes conferred with Marshall Robbins, the professional manager of Mercer's publishing company. Robbins asked Barnes if he would like to meet Astaire.

The affable Barnes picks up the story: "I went up to his house—a sort of circular Greek house all on one floor. I followed him into his bedroom where he played 'Life Is Beautiful' on the electric piano. I said to myself, 'I don't believe this. This is like being in a Fred Astaire musical.'"

Barnes returned to London, where he recorded two albums with Bing Crosby, at a time when no one was much interested in recording older established stars such as Mercer or Crosby. He was asked by Alan Warner of United Artists to inquire if Astaire might be interested in recording for the company. He wrote to Shep Fields, a former bandleader famous for his Rippling Rhythm orchestra, then Astaire's agent at ICM, about his recording plans.

Speaking of Astaire's recording deal, Barnes recounted, "He wasn't expensive, but he wasn't cheap. United Artists went first-cabin with him. They put him up at the Connaught." Crosby's albums had made the pop charts in the UK, one of which became a gold record. The company believed there could be a similar market for Astaire.

Barnes and his associate, arranger Pete Moore, decided to record Astaire (yet again) singing the major songs from his movies in one album, while another would be devoted to contemporary songs along with his own compositions. Crosby had already recorded five albums with Barnes and Moore and had told them, "If you've got any more projects that are interesting, I'm your man." That led them to think, "Let's try and record a third album with Fred—an Astaire/Crosby reunion."

When the two veteran stars agreed to work together again, each wanted to give the other top billing. This lead to Barnes and Moore "naturally" writing a song for them entitled "Top Billing." "I don't think any album was put together quicker than this one," Barnes remembered. Barnes and Moore both felt Crosby's voice was in slightly better shape than Astaire's since he had recently been making a series of personal appearances. A total of three albums encompassing nine recording sessions were scheduled over a three-week period (a modern miracle) in London.

According to Barnes, "Fred treated every vocal like a choreographic routine. He would want to know what happened here, did he hear the brass there—he was really very precise, whereas Bing would just say, 'Well, the tempo's good, the key's fine. I'll leave it to you fellows.' "[4]

Astaire and Crosby, whom Artie Shaw once called "the first hip white man, born in the United States,"[5] had long maintained a genuine admiration for each other's talents. An undeniable, albeit rarely mentioned, nonchalant element in Astaire's singing style, first evident back in the 1930s, was a direct influence from Crosby. The jazz writer Nat Hentoff delivered a succinct summation of Astaire's and Bing Crosby's singing: "Fred had the *feel* of jazz; he and Bing had the pulse of jazz. There's no question that they were jazz singers."

Astaire was concerned, however, about getting Crosby to rehearse with him. Crosby had golf dates in Scotland, a priority for him. However, Fred said that he needed six or seven hours of rehearsal, which Crosby would never agree to—as Crosby saw it, "Fifteen minutes in front of the piano. How sweet it is. No problem." To alleviate the problem Moore suggested to Astaire that he come over to his place where he had the arrangements laid out. Barnes sang Crosby's part with Astaire. An additional problem was that Astaire didn't like the vocal parts and was doubly worried about Crosby's penchant for throwing ad-libs into his songs.

At the prerecording meeting, Crosby arrived armed with his version of the songs, complete with written-out ad-libs on manuscript paper. Astaire found them confusing. As ever, he arrived prepared, armed with colored pencils. He suggested underlining his ad-libs in red and Crosby's in blue. A wavy line in both red and blue would indicate precisely what they were to sing together.

The next morning, as the first recording session was about to get under way, Barnes recalled that Crosby looked over Astaire's shoulder as Moore on piano played the first song before the musicians arrived. "Bing's quite mischievous, you know," Barnes pointed out. "He said, 'You know, Fred, I think it would be better if I sang this line and you sang that line.' Fred panicked. Bing was sending him up a little bit. . . . He added, 'I just think it suits me better.'

"Fred proceeded to take out his blue pencil, scratched out the blue, and replaced it with 'appropriate' red markings. They began singing again, whereupon

Bing uttered, 'Mmmm, no, I think it was better before.' Fred wondered, 'Now, which one is it?' The manuscript was now a mass of blue and red scratchings. 'I can't read anything now,' he [Fred] said. Fred was so scared that Bing would destroy him in the ad-lib department, but, in fact, when you hear Fred's retorts, they were off-the-cuff. He was very funny." Barnes remembered, "That whole thing took about twenty minutes because by then the band and the backup singers had all arrived and were tuning up.

"The entire recording was done live. That's the way Bing liked it. When he came over to London, he said to me, 'I don't want to sing in a cubicle. I didn't come over here to record in a goldfish bowl. Put me with the band.' That's the way Fred liked it, too. They don't dare record like that today."

Barnes, summing up the Astaire/Crosby pairing, said, "The sessions were very freewheeling. Bing had dear Fred figured out because he did make Fred relax. Fred had razor-sharp diction, good intonation, and his own style of phrasing, which seemed to owe nothing to anybody. . . . He had a way of breaking up phrases that only a dancer would do." Moore contended, "Fred had a grudging respect for Crosby, but it was actually a great admiration. He said to me, 'Bing doesn't have to rehearse, after all.' I must say, these sessions were one of the things I came in the business to do. There was never a moment of tension."

One of the central ideas in the approach to the album *A Couple of Song and Dance Men* (the title of an Irving Berlin song they had sung together in the film *Blue Skies* and had recorded for Decca) was that they would sing some of the songs Crosby had originally made famous and some that Astaire was known for, plus seventies songs such as "Roxie" from the Broadway musical *Chicago*. Barnes rewrote the lyric to "Pick Yourself Up" so that Astaire would teach Crosby how to dance in a takeoff of the famous scene in *Swing Time* wherein Ginger Rogers teaches Astaire how to dance. Moore wrote a chart for nine musicians that heightened the interplay between them. Other highlights were their versions of "Change Partners" and "Spring, Spring, Spring," from the MGM musical *Seven Brides for Seven Brothers.*

The sound of tap steps at the end of the title song was initially simulated by the combination of a drum roll on a clog box (a wooden box). This was a substitute for Astaire's refusal to supply his own tap steps. The next day Barnes played Astaire the playback of the tune. He snapped, "That's terrible. That doesn't sound like me at all. Somebody's feet, but not mine, are going in there! Look, I'm seventy-six years old. You're not supposed to dance when you're seventy-six."

Taken aback, Barnes remarked, "You're not supposed to sing love songs either, but you're doing a good job of it." He vowed to get the composer Lionel Blair to fill in the tap steps. "That will give him an after-dinner story for the rest of his life, how he had to do Fred Astaire's dancing for him." The psychology behind Barnes's remark succeeded. Astaire blurted out, "Oh, you son of a gun. All right, roll back the carpet, put the microphone down there, give me some headphones, feed me the track, and I'll do it. But right now—because tomorrow I'll give you an argument!"

"The funniest thing was that the sound engineer had seen Fred do various routines in movies and said to him quite seriously, 'Fred, for Christ sake, when you do the dance, don't dance all across the floor and across the ceiling!' It was wonderful," Barnes remembered with pride. "It was just one bar, but it was the last professional dancing he ever did."

The second Astaire album that Barnes and Moore worked on together, *They Can't Take These Away from Me,* contained Fred's well-remembered movie songs. By 1975, however, while he retained the old moxie in his singing, his vocal quality was fading, and by then he had recorded these songs to death.

The 1970s songs on the album *Attitude Dancing* had charm and sounded as though Astaire felt comfortable singing Pete Moore's contemporary arrangements. His cover of the title song, written by Carly Simon and Jacob Brackman, was a gem. The gentleman songster waxed nostalgic on "Life Is Beautiful," underlining Tommy Wolf's lyric that life had indeed been beautiful for him. He had excelled in vaudeville, on the Broadway and London stages, in movie musicals, on radio, records, and television in a career that had spanned almost seventy years.

Of the three albums, *A Couple of Song and Dance Men* was undoubtedly the pièce de résistance. Unfortunately, they are only available on CD, as a three-disc set, in the UK, but not in America. The merchants of mediocrity felt there was no market for them in the United States in the early 1980s when they could have been transferred to CD, but they never were.

On SoundScan, the official tabulator of sales for record companies, which also serves as the source for the various *Billboard* charts as of May 1, 2007, Astaire has sold a rather astounding total of 209,723 records since 1991. This is particularly interesting in that his 1959 and 1960 albums have never been made available on CD, nor have the last three albums he recorded, as mentioned above.

Upon reviewing Astaire's surprising sales figures, Regina Joskow, vice president of Verve Records, noted, "In a culture largely dominated by here-today, gone-tomorrow teen pop sensations, it is remarkable that Fred Astaire's recording catalog continues to sell as well as it does. His consistent CD sales are a testament to his enduring appeal."

* * *

TODAY, the brand of popular music that Fred Astaire helped establish seventy to eighty years ago is now predominently confined to cabarets that thrive in only a few cities. The late Bobby Short, the most recognized advocate of this music, was a long-established Manhattan musical institution, when he headlined at New York's Café Carlyle, a watering hole for the swells who remembered the heyday of this music.

Short spoke reverently of Astaire, first on his style. "But Fred also had substance to go along with that style. He was a perfect dancer and a marvelous singer. The second thing is arguable because pure singers might object to his being called a singer, but Fred Astaire had an innate sense of rhythm, great tone, great sound, and a wonderful way of using words and making all the words count. He knew just how to punctuate, how to enunciate and make the whole song come to life. A lot of American singers and British singers tried to copy that jaunty, elegant way of his. The voice was very, very daring—daring to reach the notes, daring to make it all come true."

Short brought out the influence that the British musical-comedy star Jack Buchanan had on Astaire. "Jack Buchanan in his top hat, white tie, and tails was really and truly, if ever there was one, a kind of model for Fred Astaire." Short related, "After Fred went to England, it changed his accent. You will hear the long *k*, the long *a*, and other messages of the so-called British pronunciation. Fred was a pretty quick study. I caught myself sounding totally country English after a week in London the first time I went there."

In discussing the songs Astaire wrote, Short contended, "He'd sung the best American popular songs ever composed. And so I would think that a bit of that style and taste would rub off on him. I think it did. I especially liked a song of his called 'You Worry Me.' Unfortunately, we never met, but he and John Bubbles were my two favorite singers."

On Short's passing, on March 21, 2005, Michael Feinstein noted in the *New York Times,* "He single-handedly perpetuated and preserved American popular music in an era when it was quickly fading into oblivion. There could be a similar argument made that Fred Astaire had a great deal to do with keeping this kind of music alive even earlier through his recording and television shows when it first was undergoing its steady but radical change during the mid-'50s to '60s."

ANDREA MARCOVICCI, the classically sculpted chanteuse, has been an annual headliner at the Oak Room of the Hotel Algonquin in New York for more than twenty years. The *International Herald Tribune* has referred to her as "the greatest cabaret star of her generation." One of her recent engagements was entitled "Andrea Sings Astaire."

Marcovicci spoke authoritatively about the virtues of Astaire the singer. "I know why the great songwriters of the first half of the twentieth century wanted him to introduce their songs: It was his ego-less devotion to the song. It's simple. There are no tricks, no frills, there's no extra Bing Crosby 'va-va-va-voo,' there's no 'doobie-doobie-do' or extra syllables à la Mr. Sinatra; and when it comes to the lyrics, they're delivered with heart. There's just that touch. It's light, and it's the same thing about the way he romanced women.

"And he has that round vowel from Omaha, Nebraska, so it gives the round talk quality to the sound. There's no lyricist that wouldn't want to hear that. . . . He also hears things in short phrases because he doesn't like to extend. He didn't sing anything he didn't sing well. Everything was written for him. He didn't attempt to sing something that wasn't a good song for him."

Extending her slightly overheated but nonetheless perceptive prose, Marcovicci said, "To me, Fred Astaire represents everything lost—everything elegant, graceful, and lost in our society. We've lost manners, conversation, letters, beauty, and they're irreplaceable. He makes me ache because they're gone."

I ASKED BOBBY SHORT, who, incidentally, grew up with Dick Van Dyke in Danville, Illinois, if he thought Astaire could emerge as a star today. Realistically he answered, "I don't know. I think that everything's so short today, and the pop culture bag is so overloaded. Ask somebody sixteen years old who Gary Cooper is, they don't know who that is. They wouldn't know who Fred Astaire is. And they're so self-absorbed.

"There's a time for everything. Astaire was so art deco in so many ways—the way he walked, the way he talked, he was debonair—in an old architectural fashion he was debonair. Maybe that just wouldn't be possible to construct in today's society. And let's face it, you go to a dance with people who are [more than] fifty years old, and the band plays 'Cheek to Cheek,' the ladies are all swooning when they hear that song, and the men all want to look like Fred Astaire. But you get those younger than that, and you're in trouble."

Unfortunately, we shall probably never again witness the era of the classic Fred Astaire musicals, just as we shall never again witness the swing era, the age of the great dance bands, when, as writer Gene Lees described it, "a lot of popular music was good, and a lot of good music was popular." The big bands were a kind of musical companion piece to Astaire's film musicals. This period, which Astaire greatly admired, extended from the Ginger Rogers days through the war years. Gone today is an appreciation for extraordinary talent, beautiful music, elegance—and, yes, panache.

Stanley Kay, the personal manager over the years of such talented performers as Buddy Rich, Michele Lee, Gregory and Maurice Hines, who played drums for Josephine Baker, Patti Page, Frankie Laine and The DIVA Jazz Orchestra, remarked, "When people talk about great singers, they talk about stylists like Fred Astaire, Louis Armstrong, Billie Holiday, and Nat Cole. None of them had good chops, but they were all outstanding storytellers. . . . The days of the great musical talents—whether they be musicians, singers, dancers, or choreographers—are gone. Now we have imitators, but no originals."

Shortly after Frank Sinatra's death, Margo Jefferson of the *New York Times* defined stardom of great artists as "the ability to take their gifts, their limitations, and their influences, and mold them into a unified whole called 'My Personality.' "[6] And so it goes. Performers such as Frank Sinatra and Fred Astaire, each of them the ne plus ultra of not only an art but of a historical moment, took worlds with them when they left.[7]

CHAPTER ELEVEN

THE CHARACTER ACTOR EMERGES AS THE SONG-AND-DANCE MAN FADES

NEVIL SHUTE'S 1957 novel depicting the grim aftermath of nuclear war set seven years in the future was a natural subject and a bestselling book during the uncertain years of the cold war. Producer-director Stanley Kramer, in the 1950s, was at the forefront in Hollywood, not fearing to take on controversial subjects in such films as *Inherit the Wind* and *The Defiant Ones*. *On the Beach* followed in the same vein. He referred to it as a "dark symphony."

Kramer observed, "Whether we live or die in the years ahead is the principal hope and fear on the minds of people today. This is the biggest story of our time." Upon buying the film rights to Shute's novel, Kramer went about putting together a dream cast that included Gregory Peck and Ava Gardner as the leads and such supporting actors as Fred Astaire, Tony Perkins, and newcomer Donna Anderson.

Kramer had first sought the distinguished English actors Alec Guinness and Ralph Richardson to play the key part of the scientist. Both were unavailable. Kramer's wife, Anne, saw one of Astaire's old movies on television and said to her husband, "There's your scientist." At first, Kramer demurred, but then realized that in this case casting against type was an absolutely right choice.[1]

Fred Curt remembered that during the rehearsals for "Another Evening with Fred Astaire" Fred had told him, "Stanley Kramer approached me and said, 'Fred, I have this great movie I want you to do. It's called *On the Beach*.' I said to

Stanley, 'I am not doing musicals anymore,' and Stanley said, 'I don't think you would call this a musical.'"

For Astaire, *On the Beach* was a distinct challenge after twenty-seven musicals, nine revues, two inconsequential TV guest-starring acting roles, and a television special. His character, Julian Osborne, an Australian scientist and race-car driver, played a pivotal role in the film, which was shot within the environs of Melbourne, Australia, over three months. Sardonic, philosophical Julian, deeply troubled by the responsibility of science for the annihilation of mankind, finds some measure of relief in drink and in racing his Ferrari—and in railing melodramatically against the stupidity of mankind.[2] The familiar image of Fred Astaire was erased as he completely became the scientist.

After the first run-through with the cast, Kramer remarked, "You'd think Fred had been playing serious drama all his life." As ever, Fred took extreme care in preparing for this very different role by diligently working on the script. He even went so far as to allow his toupee to be mussed up.[3] The triumph of his 1958 special had given him an added confidence.

Gregory Peck remembered just how seriously Fred took his work: "He wanted every move set—the lighting of a cigarette, the body language, every gesture and movement. All good actors do. I like rehearsal myself. Fred and I went over our scenes together in our spare time."[4] Fred called his work in the film "some of the most thrilling moments I've had in my career, because working with Stanley Kramer meant an awful lot to me, and he wanted me so much for that thing, and I think I came off okay in it."[5]

Fred told the Broadway columnist Leonard Lyons on location in Australia, "I'll last a lot longer. I can't become the oldest dancer in the world. Just to be able to dance is not enough. You need something more, around which something of substance can be built. I've seen hundreds of fine dancers disappear."[6]

To begin work, Fred flew to Australia, by way of Tahiti, with the dancer Donna Anderson, making her first important film appearance. "I was not a terribly social person at nineteen," said Anderson. "I don't think we struck up anything that I ever remember, except that he was very considerate of me. . . . He kind of looked after me like an uncle or father would." During a stopover in Honolulu, Fred was surrounded by autograph seekers. He told them, "Better get hers, too."

Anderson well remembered the key scene early in the film as the captain of an American submarine, Peck, and Perkins, playing her husband, an Australian naval officer, and their naval colleagues were extremely anxious about exactly when the atomic fallout coming from the west coast of North America would drift down to Australia. Speculation was rampant that it would take several weeks.

Astaire's character knows otherwise. With one deeply troubled look, he tells the audience that the end is much nearer than they think. His prediction of imminent doom follows, as he explains that he was one of those who had helped develop the bomb and reflects on its destructive capacity. He apologizes for his drinking problem. This scene was surely an example of extraordinary screen acting.

Anderson recalled, "My character, the wife of Tony Perkins, broke in on that speech. [Her lines were "I won't have it, do you hear! There is hope."][7] It caused me to go into the other room. But it was this speech of his that my character played off. I really got something from it." She added, "I don't think he had any trouble doing straight acting. Everyone was very impressed with his work."

Tony Perkins also admired Astaire's acting: "What was he best at as an actor? Standing still. He had a beautiful stillness, an authenticity, a simplicity. Just a little shift of his head in any of his acting scenes would be very eloquent. He was very austere. He wasn't all over the place."

Astaire's role was extensive. He became a sort of scientific cruise director when he joined Peck on board the submarine *Sawfish* on a fact-finding expedition to the California coast to inquire about the degree of atomic radiation in the atmosphere and to search out any remaining signs of life. This made for moody and haunting footage. When it became obvious that the end was near, the vessel returns to Melbourne. Its crew votes to return to America to die.[8]

KRAMER, long astute at creating broad-based publicity for his movies, used *On the Beach* as the focus of a worldwide PR campaign calling for the immediate outlawing of atomic weapons. The movie's premiere was a true event, as the film opened simultaneously in eighteen cities on seven continents. It was said to have been seen by thirty-three thousand movie patrons in one night, a hefty total for that time. Worldwide acclaim followed for the film, but because of its length and harsh sense of reality, it was not a commercial hit.

Gregory Peck flew to Moscow for the opening at the Domkino Theater. It was the first time a modern American picture had opened in the Soviet Union. Peck reported, "They accepted the theme as a dramatic warning and they also agreed that no one is pointing the finger at them . . . that this insanity has to stop."

As a result of working together in *On the Beach,* Peck and Astaire developed a warm bond of friendship. Their close relationship lasted almost thirty years, until the time of Astaire's death. That their political outlooks differed greatly—Peck being an outspoken liberal dating back to his risking exposing anti-Semitism in *Gentleman's Agreement* in 1947 to his backing the Berrigans by producing the film *The Trial of the Catonsville Nine* in 1972, and Astaire having a quiet but nevertheless firm conservative bent—never had any effect on their friendship. The two rare old-time Hollywood gents had formed and maintained a lasting respect for each other.

THE CRITIC ARTHUR KNIGHT, of the *Saturday Review,* saw the movie as "a picture that aims at something big and emerges as something tremendous." John McCarten of the *New Yorker,* however, sniffed, "God forbid we should wind up on the littoral of Australia in the gluey attitudes of the doomed characters."

Bosley Crowther in the *Times* called Astaire's performance "amazing" and also said he "conveyed in his self-effacing manner a piercing sense of the irony of his trade." Arthur Knight went so far as to assert, "Astaire's work is not only reminiscent of but compares favorably to an Alec Guinness performance." *Newsweek* said, "Astaire has never performed better."

This kind of critical reaction to a serious role should have led to a succession of substantial roles in subsequent films. A Best Supporting Actor Oscar nomination was deserved, but it wasn't tendered by the Academy. Fred continued as a character actor for more than two decades, but, unfortunately, he was never given the opportunity to act in a serious vehicle of the importance of *On the Beach* ever again.

DONNA ANDERSON, now assistant to David Pope, the CEO of Danjaq, which produces the James Bond films, supplied a clue to Astaire's casting in *On the Beach.* She explained, "What is interesting is that Stanley Kramer hired many dancers, like Gene Kelly in *Inherit the Wind.* I was put under contract to Stanley because I was a dancer. He had seen me in a demonstration for Eugene Loring, who was choreographing the *Billy the Kid* ballet. Stanley believed that physical ability was transferable to acting. He had a talent for finding actors and surprising people with some other facets of them."

What particularly grabbed Anderson's attention was one day when Fred and she went shopping together in Melbourne. "It was illuminating to me how a man that had so many years of being a celebrity was so unaffected by it, or even the other way, how he was extremely humble. When people came up to him, he was almost embarrassed by it rather than taking it. I have seen performers who expected it. Fred was really shy about it, and that was endearing. But I was also surprised because I thought, 'When is he ever going to get used to it.'

"One time I went to a baseball game with Cary Grant and Dyan Cannon. They walked through Dodger Stadium with people waving at them and yelling at them, and it was like kind of what happens to royalty. It was totally different from people's reaction to Fred Astaire."

RETURNING HOME in the late winter of 1959, besides starting to make plans for his second NBC television special, Fred completed the final draft of his three-years-in-the-works autobiography, *Steps in Time,* for publication by Harper and Brothers. Noël Coward had provided him with the apt title. The book well reflected its author—modest, matter-of-fact, with a noticeable lack of malice toward almost anyone. It was essentially a "and then I sang and danced in . . ." chronicle with little insight into the impact of the grand career he had enjoyed or any semblance of precisely how he had made it all happen. Given the venal nature of show business, his life hadn't been quite as serene as he had painted it.

He wrote the entire book himself in pencil, in longhand, but consulted extensively with the writer Cameron Shipp for literary advice. Ava edited and proofed his work.[9] The *New Yorker* said of it, "His writing was like his dancing, precise and debonair, and his book recalls past gaieties—his own and his audiences—without a trace of wistfulness." It was on the *New York Times* bestseller list for two weeks. With the publication and acceptance of *Steps in Time* and the success of both "An Evening with Fred Astaire" and *On the Beach,* 1959, by any criteria, was a very good year for him.

He was especially proud of himself for the acceptance he received for his first time out in a straight acting part. After finishing the picture, he wrote Kramer, "There wasn't a moment that I wanted to break into a song and dance." All sorts of movie roles were offered him. He considered them all but quickly refused any scripts that would have him playing a retired dancer. He was now finding himself having parallel careers in films and television.[10]

Recording was still important to him. To have an album released simultaneously with his second NBC special, he made a deal with Kapp Records, a small but respected label. Mickey Kapp, who assisted his father, Dave Kapp, in producing the album, recalled, "Fred did a little tap dance on one of the tunes he recorded. We laid out six-by-six pallets on the floor so we'd get a tap sound. The mic was hung down low. He had his tap shoes in one hand, and he was wearing regular shoes. He stood on his left leg, lifted his right leg up, untied the shoe, kicked it and put the tap shoe on, tied the lace, and never wavered. Then he did it with the other foot. You try standing on one foot."

Kapp also learned from Astaire that his toupees were made from nuns' hair woven into Belgian lace. "They were made in a monastery in France," said Kapp. "I don't know if it's true, but I heard they cost thirty-five hundred dollars each."

By the beginning of the 1960s, male superstars such as Fred Astaire, Gary Cooper, Cary Grant, and Jimmy Cagney, who had been important to the movie business of the 1930s and 1940s, were now suddenly "the old men of Hollywood," yet they were still treated with a smattering of respect. Humphrey Bogart had died there years earlier. Cary Grant would act for only five more years. Cooper would die in 1961. Astaire's longtime friend Sam Goldwyn was no longer an important producer.

On his last important film, *Porgy and Bess,* Goldwyn had reportedly first considered the far-fetched casting of Al Jolson, Rita Hayworth, and Astaire, playing Sportin' Life, all in blackface. This was before settling on Sidney Poitier, Dorothy Dandridge, and Sammy Davis Jr. for the principal roles.[11]

Sam Goldwyn Jr. related, "After he retired, my father tried several times at one point to get Fred to produce a movie. He told me, 'I never tried to sell anything so hard.' He felt there was no one who knew more about musicals than Fred because he was so involved in his films. He cared about everything. Dad told Fred that producing would mean a whole new career for him." Goldwyn speculated that Fred turned his father down, thinking, "I'm not sure I could do that." "I do remember that Fred told me he would have loved to do a movie with Bob Fosse. He had tremendous admiration for Fosse."

At this juncture, no star in show business was bigger than Frank Sinatra. According to George Jacobs, then Frank Sinatra's valet, Sinatra "craved class like a junkie" and was simply overawed by Astaire: "Once, when we were on the Warner lot, we saw Fred Astaire walk by. Mr. S was as excited as the schoolgirls used to get excited by him. He insisted we follow Astaire around the lot, hiding in the shadows to make sure he didn't see us. They must have met at the William Goetzes or somewhere. Mr. S didn't think he was worthy to go up to him. 'Look how he moves. Just look at him,' Sinatra whispered to me. 'I feel like a klutz.' He may have had total confidence as a singer, but very little as a hoofer [despite his more than adequate dancing with Gene Kelly in *Anchors Aweigh*]. That's why Astaire was a god to Sinatra, because for him it was natural, just as being cool was natural for Bogart. Astaire never spotted us that day at Warners, but if he had, I'll bet Mr. S would have asked him for an autograph."[12]

IN 1960, Ava came out in the Los Angeles debutante cotillion. Her father, resplendent in white tie, presented her. As Ava recalled, "I did it because I felt my mother would have wanted it." In an area so intertwined with the motion picture industry, as recently as the late fifties film performers and their ilk were frowned upon by old-moneyed Los Angeles.[13]

Fred became a grandfather for the second time in the summer of 1961 when Freddie and Gale had their first of three children, Fred Henry Astaire. Peter and his wife, Janet, had already presented Fred with his first grandchild, Phyllis Maud, the first of their three children. Peter was then a sheriff in the Los Angeles County Sheriff's Department before moving to Santa Barbara in the same position. Later, he became a private detective and is now retired and lives part of the time near Freddie in San Luis Obispo and also on an island off Seattle.[14]

That summer, Broadway producer Ed Padula enjoyed a smash hit with his musical *Bye Bye Birdie,* which starred Dick Van Dyke and Chita Rivera. Gower Champion was the director. Padula's first choice as director, however, was Astaire, who turned it down.[15]

When he later saw the show, Fred sent Champion an enthusiastic letter praising his direction. Maybe it was too late in his life for Fred to consider making his directorial debut by returning to Broadway. From personal experience, he knew how uncertain and frantic life was for a musical breaking in on the road—or as Howard Dietz described it in his lyric to "That's Entertainment," "Everything that happens in life can happen in a show." In addition, the thought of directing a musical comedy concerning a rock 'n' roll star (which satirized Elvis Presley's entry into the army) most likely held no interest for Fred. But perhaps what he told Robert Kimball, when he fondly remembered his years on Broadway, resonated with him and he figured, "Been there, done that."

Dick Van Dyke emerged from *Bye Bye Birdie* as a star. This brought him to Hollywood and his hit comedy show. The first time he ever saw Astaire was when he followed him in line at the $100 window at Santa Anita. He confessed, "I did that, number one, to get the walk down, and, second, to find who he bet on so I could bet my two bucks." As a performer, Van Dyke said, "Comedically, I stole from Stan Laurel; physically, I stole from Fred Astaire. You might as well steal from the best."

Astaire, on the popular Bob Crane radio show, when asked whom he admired among the young dancers, named George Chakiris in *West Side Story* and Dick Van Dyke. "I like the way he moves," he said. This was after the movie version of *Birdie* was released.

"I was in my car when I heard it and almost drove off the freeway," Van Dyke recalled. "I didn't know what to do." He remembered that Astaire had been on the set at Columbia watching him when he was shooting *Birdie* and Fred was working on *The Notorious Landlady.*

Van Dyke brought out something that no one else did: "I think that he made some songs famous that no one else could have done—little songs of Berlin, Cole Porter, and, of course, Gershwin, and Kern." Van Dyke demonstrated what he meant by extemporaneously singing "Isn't it a lovely day." "There was a lightness he had, and he syncopated even when he was singing a ballad. I think some of those songs otherwise would have flopped, like 'Pick Yourself Up,' with Ginger Rogers. I walked out of the theater with that song in my head. Astaire was murder on verses. He made songs out of the verse every time. He'd been on the stage, and he knew how to sell a song."

Van Dyke continued, "One of the reasons he liked Alice Faye, Betty Grable, and Ginger Rogers, he just said they were terrific women, they were hard-core working girls, they showed up, they were on time, they did the job, and they were always prepared. But they had no kind of class. . . . Fred Astaire had acquired this thing, and he wanted to be around it. . . . There wasn't a dancer who had the body grace of Fred. He was a tap dancer, not a hoofer. But the Gregory Hines kind of hoofing has taken over. All the kids want to do that; nobody wants to do Astaire's form. And that grace, that balletic movement, doesn't exist. I was raised on Astaire. My dad did everything he could to emulate him. He tried to dress like him. We went to all the Astaire movies. Fred had panache. He was the living example of that word."

WILLIAM PERLBERG, an established producer at Paramount, offered Astaire the part of the American version of a roué, Biddeford "Pogo" Poole, in the film adaptation of the Broadway playwrights Cornelia Otis Skinner and Samuel Taylor's *The Pleasure of His Company.* Fred told Wanda Hale of the New York *Daily News* that he accepted the part "because I had no romance in it." He played opposite the Austrian actress Lilli Palmer, as his ex-wife, Kate, and Debbie Reynolds was his estranged daughter, Jessica, who was in love with the owner of a horse ranch, Roger, played by Tab Hunter.

The film was a slick version of the original, transformed by Taylor, of what had been a considerably more urbane drawing-room comedy. But after all, this was a Hollywood movie of the early 1960s. The significant breakthroughs in camera technique, characterization, and above all in making cinema more realistic, along with a broadened look at sexuality, were still a few years away from taking hold.

In the original 1958 Broadway production, the English actor Cyril Ritchard was considerably more in character as the droll continental. The part played by Lilli Palmer was played originally by Cornelia Otis Skinner, who over the years wrote several dramatic stage vehicles for herself to star in. The Tab Hunter role onstage had belonged to George Peppard, which resulted in his getting an MGM contract and soon afterward to his starring at Paramount opposite Audrey Hepburn in the magical *Breakfast at Tiffany's.* Charles Ruggles repeated his Broadway performance as the caustic father-in-law.

Astaire was not unaware of the way the movie differed from the Broadway version: "They had a very pretty wife, named Lilli Palmer, for me. She shouldn't have been a pretty wife. She should have been a hawk like she was on the stage. When my character, Pogo, came back, he didn't want anything to do with her. All he wanted was to use her. He moves on . . . and he takes over, and he does all these things, which was funny. But they wanted to warm this picture up. They got a very pretty lady like Lilli for me to come back to and wish that I had never done all those things. And I looked with longing eyes, wishing that my whole family life had been different, which killed the whole piece, it took all the sophistication out of it. Everything . . . It wasn't the picture we started out to do."[16]

Astaire participated in a ballroom-dancing sequence with Lilli Palmer. As a nineteen-year-old refugee in Paris, years earlier, Palmer had auditioned for a job as a chorine at the Moulin Rouge in Paris, during which, while wearing high heels, she had tripped over three dancers. She was afraid to repeat that performance while dancing with Astaire and protested to director George Seaton. Seaton, however, insisted, "We're grateful for every chance to show Fred dancing . . . anybody can dance with Fred Astaire!" In the script, Fred says to her, "I promise not to step on your feet." The actress remembered, "I landed squarely on his, stopping him dead in his tracks." "Good Lord," said the annoyed Astaire, to which Palmer replied, "I warned you." "The second time he swept me off," she said, "he never allowed me to land at all, and I just hung suspended in his arms, trying to remember my lines while bereft of the support of terra firma."[17]

As a postscript to her moment of desperation at an MGM rehearsal studio, when Astaire had cheered her up by explaining the discipline needed to be a dancer, a decade later Debbie Reynolds found herself costarring, and as part of that, dancing with him in a wedding-reception scene, in *The Pleasure of His Company.* "I was so nervous that I couldn't follow him correctly," she remembered. "Fred said to me, 'You don't have to follow me, just dance with me.' That put me at ease. He glided me, and his hand was always on my back and always at my waist and just pushing me, or rather steering me, gliding me around in this little dance that we did together. We didn't even rehearse it. It was quite thrilling, and it was a charming moment. He was the most kind, sweet, and gentle person. That's how I shall always remember him."

During this ballroom scene, Fred sang a bit of Rodgers and Hart's "Lover." This scene was designed to show Pogo as a true sophisticate, but one who had little interest in fatherhood or any semblance of responsibility. He was opposed to Jessica's marrying Roger because that would interfere with his plans to take her back to Europe with him to make up for his years of neglect. But such thoughts wouldn't fly in the movie morality of the time. As a result, Pogo has a change of heart. He tells Jessica to forget their plans, leaving her free to marry Hunter. He departs for Europe by plane with a painting of Jessica as a child and with the family's cook.[18] Problems solved.

While playing it safe in the denouement of the plot, *The Pleasure of His Company* did have its share of risqué, double-entendre dialogue. Reynolds describes her fiancé, Hunter, as having "all sorts of artificial insemination and all that sort of thing," when actually describing Hunter's breeding habits for his horses. When Fred asked Palmer, "What are we going to do tonight while the young are out dancing?" Palmer answered, "We're going to bed." Fred then says, "Is that the best you can offer?" Palmer replies, "It wasn't an offer." Considering the problems faced by MGM regarding the lyrics by Cole Porter in *Silk Stockings* five years earlier, it's surprising that kind of dialogue wasn't censored and the picture wasn't refused a Production Code seal.

Perlberg and Seaton confronted a serious problem when the picture was forced to close down production in March 1960, as a result of the first strike ever called by the Screen Actors Guild, then presided over by Ronald Reagan. Despite having originally helped create the union in the 1930s, Fred commented, "It is violently wrong to interfere with production in the middle." This was following his phone call to Reagan asking if he could intervene and allow *The Pleasure of His Company* to recommence shooting. The future president told him, "There's absolutely nothing I can do."[19]

Perlberg and Seaton's film *The Counterfeit Traitor,* starring Bill Holden and Lilli Palmer, working for them for the third time, was slated for production in Europe. After the strike ended, they began production almost immediately and finished that picture first. Eight months later, returning to California and the San Francisco locations, where the *The Pleasure of His Company* was set, the last two weeks of shooting were finally completed. Fred and Lilli Palmer picked up a kissing scene they'd started months earlier.

THE ALWAYS QUOTABLE REYNOLDS, when asked for her evaluation of Astaire as an actor, answered, "He was a businessman. He said to me, 'I made a buck.' I don't think acting was hard for him. I think he thought of it as a piece of cake. And I think he found it just to be a day's work, and there wasn't any joy in acting. It was in his dancing that there was a happy feeling of accomplishment."

Reynolds continued, "Acting is a part of the dance. It leads to the dance. It leads to the accomplishment. The dance did not lead to the acting accomplishment. He wasn't that interested in it. It was not his forte, and it was not his love.

He was not a gregarious Irishman or had that outgoing personality like Gene [Kelly] had. Gene wanted to be noticed. Fred was a quiet man. He was a man that liked to be left alone."

The veteran actress admitted, "I knew that they were going to give him second billing to me, and I said, 'That is impossible. You put Fred Astaire first.' I wouldn't take top billing. I would have been a conceited fool if I had thought otherwise, because Fred Astaire will go down in history, certainly not Debbie Reynolds. Fred and Gene Kelly were superior talents, and those of us who worked with him were not necessarily by any means equal in talent. We were just fortunate to have worked with them."

Reynolds's keen observations jibed with those of Harvey Evans, the dancer who worked with Astaire in *Silk Stockings*. "As an actor," Evans concluded, "I think Fred used his aloofness as a style of acting. That was him. That was his personality. When he acted with someone, he was always maybe looking down on them instead of having this open face. He always had an air and an attitude that carried on into his acting. In real life he wasn't like, say, Doris Day, who I had just worked with in the movie of *The Pajama Game*. You could go up to Doris and give her a hug. You don't go up to Astaire and hug him because he had that kind of a personality."

TAB HUNTER, a few years ago, published his refreshingly candid autobiography, *Tab Hunter Confidential: The Making of a Movie Star,* in which he admitted his homosexuality, while spending years as a heartthrob for women. His book was a critical and commercial hit. The still blond former actor had never met Astaire, except in passing, before working with him in *The Pleasure of His Company.* "But I got to know Fred's daughter, Ava," he recalled. "I really was terribly impressed with both of them. Fred was such a natural human being. We spent a lot of time talking about horses. I've been involved with horses my whole life."

Turning to Astaire's acting, Hunter said, "I thought he was absolutely wonderfully roguish in the role. Fred was Fred, and that's what you loved about him. That's what he played. I do think that people use themselves. That's a God-given gift to be able to use yourself, and that was the character of Fred. I can still remember that scene where he played the piano, and there was a close-up shot after that. He asked me, 'Was it all right, Tab?' I said, 'You're asking me? I love your work.'"

Hunter summarized his impression of Astaire by saying, "He had such dedication. It was fabulous. *That's why he had such staunch power.*"

Yet with all the movie-star voltage in the film, the film critics were not ecstatic. Rose Pelswick, the film reviewer of the *New York Journal-American,* labeled the movie for what it was, "an amiably featherweight comedy," though surprisingly

Bosley Crowther called it "a lot of fun." He said, "It was hard to imagine anyone else better qualified to play the prodigal parent than Fred Astaire."

The *New Yorker*'s Edith Oliver wrote, "Fred Astaire is as wonderful as ever, which makes it doubly sad that the picture, for all its surface glitter, is a very shoddy piece of work." *Time* attacked the movie for its "undertones of incest and overtones of Andy Hardy" and scathingly attacked Reynolds, saying, "After ten years in pictures and a highly publicized scandal-divorce [from Eddie Fisher], she is still playing the head pom-pom girl at Beverly Hills High."

AS MENTIONED EARLIER, Astaire was in the midst of his ill-fated mission with Ava Records. After eight months, he moved the company's office from what was then the Tin Pan Alley area of Hollywood, on Selma off Vine Street, to the fabled Sunset Strip, the pride of L.A. in the 1960s. The veteran arranger Harry Betts, who began writing for Stan Kenton while playing trombone in his band and has contributed charts for Frank Sinatra, Peggy Lee, the Beach Boys, and Barry Manilow, among others, called his experience of being one of two house arrangers for Ava Records "the most fun I ever had in the music business."

As Betts explained it, "Fred's company would give you the music and say, 'Do it.' What a firm that was! Luckily, I had the same ideas they had." He had heard the sound-track album of the first three NBC specials and told Astaire, "I really like what you did on that album." The president of the company replied, "You know something, I like what you do, too."

They became friends as well as coworkers. "I could call him up anytime and discuss things with him, which was a nice feeling. What he wanted was good music. I did seven or eight albums for the company, including the Carol Lawrence album *The Jazz Soul of Dr. Kildare* and *Bossa Nova at the Movies.* I found Fred very gentle, never pushy. I was really impressed with him. We discussed jazz a lot. He understood how Jimmy Blanton, the bass player, was the key to the wonderful Duke Ellington band of the 1940s. In those years when I worked with him, he went to jazz clubs quite a bit."

Terri Fricon, now an important music publisher in Nashville, began work as the receptionist at Ava Records and eventually worked her way up to office manager and took care of music publishing for the company. Fricon recalled an incident that reflected on Astaire's insistence on a language code in the office. "One day, the program director at KRLA came in the office for a meeting. He was talking rather loud and used a four-letter word. Mr. A just blew his top because I was sitting in on the meeting with two other women, one of which was the bookkeeper. 'You will not talk that way in front of women.' That was very Fred. You didn't see that very often. Most of the time he was in very good humor. He called me 'sweetie.' He had impeccable manners. He was so elegant and yet down-to-earth."

Fricon saw firsthand how he questioned a lot of rock 'n' roll. "He liked lyrics, but it was difficult for him to understand the thoughts of 'Oh baby, oh baby, oh baby.' There was a surf group that he liked, led by Gary Zekley, and Hank [Jones] and Dean [Kay], a folk rock duo. Dean cowrote "That's Life" with Kelly Gordon that was a big hit for Frank Sinatra. Fred also signed a piano player and singer named Charles Cochran. He left a lot of the details in running the operation to Jackie Mills and Tommy Wolf. He wasn't in every day, but he was always aware of everything that was going on.

"He talked about his past and how important his mother was to him. They were very close. I do remember seeing her once. She was a beautiful lady. I don't think he ever talked about his father. I don't ever remember him speaking about vaudeville."

IN RESEARCHING AND WRITING BIOGRAPHIES, I have come to appreciate that invariably the best interview subjects are the least well-known to the public. The pianist and singer Charles Cochran is one of those people. I had enjoyed seeing him perform in the late fifties and early sixties on New York's East Side in such long-gone clubs as the Tender Trap and the Living Room. Cochran met Ava Astaire in Los Angeles after being given her telephone number by Fifi Fell, who had known Fred in New York when he starred on Broadway. "I had recorded an album accompanied by a bassist and guitarist for a small label. Ava liked it a lot and played it constantly at home. One day Fred inevitably entered her room and said, 'Who's that? Oh my God, I would love to put him under contract.' I wound up doing two albums for Ava Records," Cochran recalled.

The first album was entitled *Presenting Charles Cochran.* Fred told Ava, "If it's a hit, Charlie is my discovery, but if it fails, it's yours." "The record company was one of the very few failures in Fred Astaire's professional life," Cochran pointed out.

Fred was in the control room quietly watching when Tommy Wolf produced the album. The album had airplay when it was released, but as Cochran noted, "The company really did not get behind it. I also said a few stupid things in hindsight. I went over to his house one night for dinner and mentioned a couple of songs I did, 'After You' and 'Dream Dancing.' Fred said, 'Oh, listen, you know the songs that I did that were not successful were unsuccessful for a reason,' and then he said of himself, 'I'm not much of a singer.' I think he had a self-image that he thought would be attractive to be that way. He liked quiet and conservative."

Before meeting Astaire, Cochran thought of him as "genial, quite warm, and audacious, but animated. When I met him, there was not anything warm about him at all. Not that there should be. He was friendly, and he was cordial, and he was polite.

"I was invited for dinner at seven fifteen. Ava said, 'Daddy likes to be prompt,' and I was prompt. It was nice, not stilted conversation. There were three or four people there. You were served one drink. And you were at the table at maybe seven twenty. You were served an impeccable little meal. You had consommé, but fancy consommé with julienne vegetables in there, and beautifully cut lamb chops with little veggies, dessert and the café. . . . It was lovely, like being on the East Coast again. It was served by a uniformed maid."

One night Charles Cochran decided to bring Anita O'Day, one of *the* essential jazz singers and one of the most far-out personalities the jazz world has ever known, to the Astaires. Cochran recalled, "I had to go to this big party, which was a dance. And I took her, which was a mistake. She had on a reasonably presentable outfit, and I put on my tuxedo. I thought, 'What a loose canon she is.' She would always do things that were *not* expected of her.

"We walked into the big living room, which was laid out like a ballroom. Immediately, Anita goes up to Fred and says, 'Hey, Fred, you wanna dance?' Which was not his thing, but he knew the job. He did not look particularly startled. He was gracious and danced with her. But I just died one of those deaths. I think at one point, while they were dancing, she said to him, 'Hey, you don't lead, do you?' "

BESIDES HIS INVOLVEMENT with Ava Records, in the next few years Fred devoted himself primarily to dramatic television appearances. These were made during the time he was host-narrator of *Fred Astaire Premiere Theater,* a coproduction of ABC and Revue Productions, sponsored by Alcoa, that began airing on October 10, 1961, with a teleplay he appeared in called "Mr. Crazy." This was one of five shows he acted in until the series ended on September 12, 1963. *Premiere Theater* broadcast a total of fifteen half-hour dramas and fifteen hour shows.

When asked why he could commit himself to a television series at this stage of his career, he answered, "To have nothing to do would drive me crazy. For a film, we do four pages of a script a day. It takes longer to set up the lighting for a movie scene. . . . TV is geared to go faster. We do ten pages of a script a day. Most scenes are shot in one take. For a movie, we always take one more no matter how good the last one was."

Margaret O'Brien reflected, "Fred was a great actor. It was not easy to keep that image going over all those years. He had to create an acting career that went on and on. He could not let down."

In a rare moment of candor, while doing publicity in New York for his upcoming series of dramas, Astaire described himself to Sidney Fields, in his "Only Human" feature column in the *Daily News,* as "impatient, hard to please, and often bad-tempered. . . . I always have to do it the way I want it. And when I see what I do, it gnaws at me how I could have done it better."

Referring to Bing Crosby and Perry Como, Astaire told a *Herald Tribune* reporter, "There's a big difference, you know, between carelessness and casualness, and the showman who is ill-prepared and disrespectful to the audience has no right to be called an entertainer." Astaire defended the state of television, saying, "I can't go along with TV critics. I think they're harsh on TV. I'm impressed that so much of TV is as good as it is. Furthermore, it's something for nothing. Don't think this doesn't make a psychological difference."

Though he long abhorred personal publicity, by this stage of his career he had achieved a mastery of how to sell his current project. That the New York entertainment press had bought the image he had created made his selling job that much easier. He knew that *Premiere Theater* was not going to be anywhere near the high artistic level of his three specials. It was a relatively easy job. Besides the five shows he was obliged to star in over two seasons, all he really had to do were "wraparounds" as host, several of which could be done in one day. This job had little relation to what he had done for most of his career. Still, this anthology series boasted some important guest stars, such as Lee Marvin, Arthur Kennedy, Cliff Robertson, Shelley Winters, Telly Savalas, and even major movie names such as Jimmy Stewart and Charlton Heston.[20]

Typical of what he was up to in acting was a November 7, 1962, show called "Moment of Decision," in which he costarred with Maureen O'Sullivan. He played a Houdini-like escape artist. When he could appear in black tie as he did here, it was always a treat for the audience. (It's hard to say who looked better in a tuxedo, Astaire or Dean Martin.) The plot revolved around Fred's conflict with his greedy landowning neighbor, who wanted to take over his property. A particular favorite of his in the *Premiere Theater* series was "Mr. Lucifer," playing opposite Elizabeth Montgomery, in which he portrayed the devil in six different disguises.[21]

Another show in the series he seemed to enjoy acting in was the drama "Blues for a Hanging." He costarred with Janis Paige, whom he had enjoyed dancing with in *Silk Stockings.* He was cast as a jazz musician, a clarinet player. His fingering on the instrument was professional-looking. His passion for the music showed. The sound of the clarinet seemed to belong to Buddy DeFranco, whose playing along with that of Benny Goodman and Artie Shaw defined the jazz clarinet. I asked DeFranco if he dubbed Astaire's playing. He recalled, "I was so busy in

L.A. in those years. It does stand out in my mind that I once worked with Astaire."
From the sound of the bebop clarinet it had to be DeFranco.

Astaire's character was that of a weak, disillusioned alcoholic, caught up in a
murder in which it appears he was a witness. He quickly establishes the character,
and he and Paige work closely together to untangle him from his dire predica-
ment. Describing Fred's work on the show, Paige said, "It's definitely Astaire—his
walk, the way he wore his clothes, his voice, his mannerisms. . . . He came from
the time when men were gentlemen, and they didn't talk about themselves. They
didn't complain about things, and whatever went on in their lives was checked by
themselves. I don't think he was as complicated as people say he was."

LESS THAN A YEAR after the release of *The Pleasure of His Company,* Fred starred in
the Columbia comedy *The Notorious Landlady,* directed by Richard Quine, and
written by Blake Edwards and Larry Gelbart. The role was somewhat secondary,
yet key, that of an urbane, bon mot–speaking diplomat in the American embassy
in London. The title role belonged to Kim Novak, starring opposite Jack Lemmon. In this film Novak shows herself for once to be a deft comedian.

The story concerns the mysterious death of Novak's husband. Lemmon has
rented a flat in her London home. Astaire, playing Lemmon's boss at the embassy,
orders him to keep a watchful eye on her. Naturally, a romance ensues between
landlady and tenant. Astaire meets her and is equally charmed by her. Lemmon
and Astaire decide they must clear her name from any suspicion over the supposed murder of her husband. A rambling satire that occasionally borders on
farce ends with a Keystone Kops–type chase sequence (a frequent staple of Blake
Edwards's screenplays) accompanied by Gilbert and Sullivan music.[22]

Gelbart authored the bulk of the screenplay, which was a complete overhaul
of the original version by Edwards. It was chock-full of witticisms, with Astaire
rendering his fair share. (Astaire had, of course, long displayed a talent for handling snappy comedy lines dating back to George S. Kaufman's original *The Band
Wagon* on Broadway and the Allan Scott–penned musical comedies with Ginger
Rogers.) When explaining to Lemmon why he must investigate Novak's innocence or lack of, Astaire says, "I said that absolutely heavenly woman killed her
husband—sort of permanent legal separation," or perhaps even better is his subsequent remark: "You will learn, Gridley [Lemmon], that the higher your position,
the more mistakes you are allowed. In fact, if you make enough of them, it's considered your style. Now you happen to be in what I would call a one-mistake position. And you've made it."[23]

To interview Larry Gelbart is to treat oneself to a stream of original and pithy comments. He is never "on" like songwriter Sammy Cahn and most comedians. With him, wit is natural.

Gelbart said admiringly, "I think I'd be safe in taking some credit for suggesting Astaire, though I never did meet him. I thought he had the sophistication to make a credible diplomat. . . . He spoke the way he danced. His timing was impeccable. He was in the pocket—well-tailored pockets, of course. That was his whole life. He couldn't put the accent on the wrong word. He couldn't sound awkward. He knew how to do less, which most people don't know how to do. It was fun to write, knowing he would be delivering the lines that I'd written. He and Jack Lemmon were musicians, Jack a piano player and Fred a drummer. Whether they were dancing, singing, playing piano, acting whatever, I think they fed off each other's rhythm."

The screenwriter added, "The only time I actually ever saw Fred was when he was walking down Vine Street wearing a sports jacket, a bandanna around his neck, and slacks, always a little bit short so you could see the socks. I think the only thing Gene Kelly ever sort of borrowed from Astaire was his wearing athletic socks and always loafers."

Richard Schickel, the noted biographer, film and book critic, as well as film documentarian, witnessed the camaraderie between Astaire and Lemmon one Friday afternoon on a visit to the set of the movie. "I remember Jack saying to Astaire at the end of the day, 'Have a good weekend, Twinkle Toes.' "[24]

The sometimes helter-skelter plot of the film took away from the generally favorable view the film critics held for its comedic impact. *Newsweek* was unduly harsh in contending, "These shenanigans get more involved than Casey Stengel at a press conference, and the mystery's solution is preposterous and underhanded." *Time* saw the movie as a "beguiling if hokey mystery."

And though the film's art director, Cary Odell, supplied the film with a completely authentic English flavor, the picture was shot on the back lot of Columbia with a few scenes filmed at nearby Paramount. As a background theme, "A Foggy Day" was heard, which was reminiscent of Astaire in white tie and tails having sung it to Joan Fontaine in a faux misty-English-estate scene in *Damsel in Distress.*[25]

As noted earlier, after completing the filming of *The Notorious Landlady,* Fred again seriously contemplated retirement. This one, however, was only a momentary whim. Barrie Chase was preparing a Las Vegas nightclub act at the Sands Hotel under Hermes Pan's direction. Naturally, Fred was involved in his continuing mentor role while the romance continued with Chase.

The then twenty-three-year-old dancer and actor Christopher Riordan, known to his friends as Cio Cio San, was a part of Chase's act. He remembered that during rehearsals Pan "was like Fred, working, working, working. Fred was sort of mimicking everything that Hermes did. He came in every day to watch rehearsals. Fred wanted something wonderful to happen for Barrie, even though he was not going to be part of it."

When Chase opened at the Sands, Astaire was there supervising last-minute corrections. "Fred wanted everything to be contemporary," said Riordan. But that wasn't enough. As usual, following Chase's performance, Fred wondered if things couldn't somehow be better.

"After the show," Riordan recalled, "we were walking through the lobby of the hotel. Fred put his arm around me. Everybody knew who Fred Astaire was. They were staring at us thinking, 'Who is this other guy?' He said things to me like 'What do you think about the show? Do you have any suggestions?' I was just blown away. He was interested in my opinion—he was tuned in to the younger age group."

Riordan learned from his association with Pan that Astaire's approach was to take on every new dance partner with the thought that she was the most wonderful dancer in the world. "He tried to do the very best with each one of them," Riordan said. "Fred thought what really mattered was that he had to be the perfect person, and if he was perfect and had it [down] right, then everything else would follow.

"I would not trade having worked with Fred Astaire, Hermes Pan, and Barrie Chase [with whom he is still close] for anything. It was one of the most educational things in my entire life. Fred was the kindest big star I ever worked with." Since then Riordan has worked extensively in movies as an actor, dancer, choreographer, and consultant. He recently said, "When I was choreographing, I was Mr. One More Time. Having worked with Fred Astaire, you knew you were going to do it again and again and again. . . . I am sure I must have picked that up from Fred."

Over the years, Astaire had various offers to headline in Las Vegas. Ned Tanen, then his MCA agent, who later ran Universal and after that was a producer at Paramount, accompanied him to Vegas when one of the hotel talent buyers insisted that money was no object in getting Fred to work at the hotel. As Tanen remembered, "Fred and I were given an elaborate suite, but before the day was through, Fred said to me, 'Let's get out of here. This place is not for me,' so we flew back to L.A." Astaire never worked in Las Vegas.

Ned Tanen said of Astaire, "He had been a hero to me since I was a kid. He became more of a hero to me as I knew him. There was nothing ever over-the-top about him at all. His whole life was under. He was a kind, tough, humorous, and shy individual. Dealing with Fred Astaire was not dealing with a major personality. It was dealing with a really gracious gentleman—something that doesn't exist anymore. He was a gracious good friend to me."

The blunt retired executive described an interesting night at Astaire's home. "I arrived at the house to attend Ava's wedding in the afternoon, in a rented tuxedo. Fred said to me, 'What the hell are you doing here? That was last night! Come on up tonight. I'm shooting pool with Jackie Gleason.' Gleason was a genius, but not the most pleasant human being. He was kicking Fred all over the room and being mean and nasty. Fred gives me a look. He starts running the table on Gleason like seven times in a row. Gleason breaks his cue. He was furious and left. [This must have been a crushing blow to "the Great One" as he had only recently exhibited his finesse as a pool shark, Minnesota Fats, in the hit movie *The Hustler*.] Watching Fred shoot pool was like watching him dance in *Royal Wedding,* but not turning the camera upside down."

Tanen also recalled Fred's asking him one day, " 'What kind of car should we get?' *We.* I said, 'I don't know. I'd get a gull-wing Mercedes.' 'Go get me one,' he said, so I got it for him. I drove it. He didn't want to drive. I was making fifty-five dollars a week. We got a BMW 507 and a Maserati. He'd trade them in. I'd buy the car for him, get rid of it, and buy another one."

ON APRIL 30, 1963, MGM, with great fanfare, announced that *Say It with Music,* a grand musical to be produced by Arthur Freed and based on Irving Berlin's catalog of songs, would, after many delays, soon begin filming. It was planned as a 1964 release with Frank Sinatra and Judy Garland as the leads. Other performers long associated with Berlin such as Astaire, Bing Crosby, and Ethel Merman would join popular singers of the day such as Johnny Mathis, Connie Francis, and Pat Boone in smaller roles. The budget was a healthy $15 million. Berlin wrote ten new songs for the film.

It seems too far-fetched to be true, but the picture was planned to open with the cast of the highly popular TV series *The Beverly Hillbillies* singing one of Berlin's songs. Astaire was to function as some sort of Greek chorus in his role as narrator. His first scene would have him philosophizing, while standing in front of the Plaza Hotel in New York, about how the more things change, the more they stay the same. Freed saw the foolishness of all that and scrapped the two sequences.[26]

The combination of trying to deal with the availability of all these musical stars, the change of screenwriters from Leonard Gershe to Comden and Green and others, plus the spiraling budget, made the picture finally lose its luster. *Say It with Music* was never made.

Doubtless, an equally important reason for its cancellation was the sudden impact of the Beatles' debut in America on *The Ed Sullivan Show* in February 1964. The music had changed. Irving Berlin had abruptly become ancient musical history.

* * *

ASTAIRE'S PROFESSIONAL ASSOCIATION with Barrie Chase continued. The *Fred Astaire Premiere Theater* was off the air by the beginning of the 1963–64 TV season. Chrysler came back into the Astaire TV picture with its sponsorship of an October 2, 1964, episode of *Bob Hope Presents the Chrysler Theatre.* Entitled "Think Pretty," it costarred Astaire and Chase and was written by a phalanx of prominent TV writers, which included the teams of Garry Marshall and Jerry Belson (*The Odd Couple*) and Sam Denoff and Bill Persky (*The Dick Van Dyke Show*). As a pilot for a potential dramatic series, it was an expensive show, with Tommy Wolf writing an original musical score and the now celebrated composer John Williams as arranger. Hermes Pan was the dance director.

With this amalgamation of talent, the show should have been a winner, but it wasn't, although Fred did have some good throwaway lines given him. When Astaire first gave Chase the script, she remarked to him, "It's probably the worst script I've ever read. This is just awful." Fred said, "Well, thanks, because I worked with the writers on it." Chase rightfully said to him, "This show has what I call ingredients . . . it has a dance number at the end of the show, and other ingredients, but that doesn't make a show."

As Chase explained, "My father was a writer [Borden Chase, screenwriter of *Red River,* who worked on Brando's *Mutiny on the Bounty* and also authored a great many television shows and movies], and I lived for six years with Robert Towne before Robert was Robert. I've been around more than a few good writers my whole life."

Fred played the head of a small company, who produced records, in this semi-farcical tale. Chase successfully portrayed the glib and driven personal manager of a comic played by the late Louis Nye, the real-life comedian. Against Chase's wishes, Fred sets up a microphone to record Nye's nightclub act for a future album, but Nye's character is taken ill and winds up in the hospital. Fred plans to record him there! Nye has such ridiculous lines as "I had a TV dinner of leftovers!" To get the hospital's cooperation, Fred offers to donate 10 percent of the record's sales to the hospital.

A few days after Louis Nye arrived for rehearsals at NBC in Burbank, Bob Hope dropped by his mobile dressing room. Nye told Hope whom he was working with, which prompted Hope to ask, "How are you doing with Fred?" "Fine," said Nye. Hope remarked, "It's a nice thing for you to be working with Fred, but you will rehearse till you go insane. This man rehearses, and you can never make up something as you go along. You'll rehearse Monday, Tuesday, Wednesday, Thursday, Friday, and Saturday . . ." Hope was speaking from experience, having worked with Astaire in *Smiles* on Broadway in 1930. In addition, Fred's penchant for rehearsing had long been legendary within the show business community.

Nye noted that after they did a scene together, Fred would ask, "Was it all right?" "God almighty, I felt so terrible because to me this was such a chance to work with this giant," said Nye. "And if I'm supposed to be involved with him in the story, I want to know him. I felt just a bit uncomfortable because I wanted to be more with Fred, but nobody seemed to notice. I didn't have enough guts to say, 'Fred, let's relax and bullshit with this. Let me get angry at you in a scene or something.' In comedy, maybe you shouldn't be a perfectionist. But, Jesus, I was disappointed. I wanted to get something out of it so that it would look like a good show. That was really an unhappy moment in my life."

As for the dancing, Fred and Barrie did a brief frug and later a fox-trot to the Tommy Wolf title song, sung by Astaire in a recording studio, which contained a pseudo–Nelson Riddle arrangement, written by John (then billed as Johnny) Williams. The tune was a device to mellow Chase's character's anger toward Fred Adams, the convenient name of Astaire's character. Later, Chase began a dance number, set in the record-company office, by doing some ballet flourishes, which lead into a lively, romping dance routine with Astaire to conclude the show. It almost, but not quite, made up for the silliness of the plot.

AMERICA WAS IN ANYTHING but a silly mood in the summer of 1965. Black Americans had grown tired of broken promises and being treated as second-class citizens. On August 11, 1965, after a black motorist was pulled over for alleged drunken driving, things quickly spiraled into what became the Watts riot, which led to thirty-four deaths and property damage totaling $35 million.

After the five-day-long civil war ended, writer Budd Schulberg, long dedicated to helping the downtrodden, ventured into the area. He placed a typewritten announcement on a bulletin board at a local clubhouse stating his intention to start a writers' workshop. From this brave endeavor emerged the Watts Writers Workshop, which continues to the present. Such well-known writers as Quincy Troupe and Stanley Crouch have arisen from the workshop.

Schulberg first approached his liberal friends in Hollywood. Gregory Peck and Jack Lemmon each gave him several thousand dollars. Sammy Davis Jr., for years in financial turmoil, pealed off $500 as a donation. In that light, Schulberg decided to telephone Astaire.

"I had met Fred at a gathering one night at Bennett Cerf's town house in the East Sixties years before. I found him extremely standoffish," the author remembered. It is assumed that Cerf, the late book publisher, who had been a panelist when Astaire was the mystery guest on the *What's My Line?* TV show, was probably then courting Astaire, hoping to sign him to Random House for his autobiography. Considering the staunch liberalism of Cerf's friends, it's not surprising that Astaire was uncomfortable in such a setting.

When Schulberg telephoned Fred, he got this reply: "Budd, whatever gave you the impression that I would be interested in giving money to start a workshop to help black kids? You've got the wrong guy."

Astaire's rejection of Schulberg's plea was in stark contrast to the behavior of Jimmy Cagney, who, when asked why in the 1930s he had given money to help defend the Scottsboro Boys, said, "I saw poverty on all sides for a long time. Such a thing leaves its impression. You can't go through life and build a wall around yourself and say, 'Everything is fine for me and to hell with the other fellow.' "[27]

SYDNEY CHAPLIN, Charlie Chaplin's son, was then the male lead in *Funny Girl,* opposite Barbra Streisand on Broadway. Gene Kelly was a close friend of his.

"I remember the night Gene Kelly asked me if I could get a date for Fred Astaire, who was in town. I asked some of the kids in the show. This one cute chorus girl said, 'I can't. My boyfriend wouldn't like it.' I said, 'It's just for one evening. You'd be doing me an enormous favor.' She called her boyfriend, who told her, 'I can't see you tonight,' so I introduced Fred to her. They were like two high school kids. They didn't even look at each other. They were both so shy. I said to Gene, 'What are we going to do?'

"We took them to Trader Vic's and had some of those strong rum drinks. That loosened them up a little. We took them to Goldie's New York [once one of the real treasures of New York]. It used to be my hangout. They had two piano players. [One was Goldie Hawkins, the proprietor; the other was Wayne Saunders.] I sang a few songs, then Gene sang a few of his songs. At three or four in the morning, they closed the place and locked the doors. Fred started up with 'The Way You Wear Your Hat.' "

Phyllis Newman had been Sydney Chaplin's costar a few years earlier in *Subways Are for Sleeping.* She was married to Adolph Green, Fred's old friend and coworker, who had written the book and lyrics with Betty Comden for the show. They were there for the festivities. "That was really a funny night. Fred was drunk and absolutely hilarious. He even danced that night," Newman remembered. Chaplin said, "A lady was sitting in the corner, drunk. She said, 'That guy thinks he's Fred Astaire.' "

Chaplin added, "The next day Fred had to leave for L.A. at seven o'clock in the morning. At eleven o'clock, the doorbell rang. It was a deliveryman. He had a gift of three scarves, shirts, and ties with a note that said, 'Thanks for the lovely evening.' It was signed, 'Fred.' "[28]

SINCE THE FEW GOOD MOVIE roles extended to a character actor now in his mid-sixties seemed to have eluded him, Fred returned to television a year after "Think Pretty" was aired to guest-star in a four-part *Dr. Kildare* during the November sweeps period. To have Astaire as special guest star once again playing a very different character—a negligent father who was a born pool hustler—seemed a good bet. In those days, Richard Chamberlain as Dr. Kildare was, along with Vince Edwards, the reigning prince of television. Astaire's appearance gave the home audience a first-time look at his long-ago-developed skill at the pool table. Again, he successfully portrayed a rather weak character.

He was offered the host plot on the popular ABC variety show *Hollywood Palace*. The lure of being back on home ground was too good to forgo. Having Barrie Chase for two of his four appearances was an added inducement, as was his admiration for the show. Also by 1965, no offers for him to host his own special were forthcoming.

Astaire's first hosting gig on *Hollywood Palace* took place on October 2, 1965. Fred opened the show by providing a brief sampling of contemporary dance steps while vowing modestly that he couldn't do the frug, the twist, or the jerk. This show was a dance fest with the appearance of Rudolf Nureyev and Dame Margot Fonteyn, the stars of the Royal Ballet. Their exhilarating talent as soloists and as a team had given them near rock-star status throughout the world, as was demonstrated that evening. One could readily sense the high regard Fred held for the two titans of ballet, the one field of dance that by choice he had never devoted the proper time or the effort to master.

As host, while ingratiating himself with the audience, he again showed how uncomfortable he was by burying his hand in his dinner jacket as he swayed from one side to the other while delivering his lines and introducing the guests. As the show's coproducer Bill Harbach noted, "He displayed all his gestures and all his nervousness." He was more effusive than usual while introducing the jazz organist Jimmy Smith. He quipped, "You're now going to see a one-hundred-nineteen-year-old man dance" before he sinuously danced to "The Cat," written by Lalo Schifrin, a favorite record of his, which was a jazz-crossover pop hit of the time.

He became so immersed in the two-and-a-half-minute dance that he removed his jacket. At times, it almost appeared as though he didn't quite comprehend what he intended to accomplish in depicting a cat trying to kill a fly, though he admitted it took almost four weeks to prepare the number. He saved face by breaking into a series of glides. Smith said to Astaire on its conclusion, "You killed that fly sixteen bars ago," another good line probably furnished by the show's writers, Jerry Bigelow and Jay Burton.

Fred's second hosting job on *Hollywood Palace* took place on January 22, 1966, with him dressed smartly in a blue blazer and wearing his favorite black-and-white shoes. This was more of an Ed Sullivan kind of a show with a parade of guest stars (Barrie Chase, Mickey Rooney, Petula Clark, etc.), although the *Hollywood Palace* shows were a decided improvement on the often haphazard way Sullivan presented his guests.

Fred opened the show with two Gershwin tunes, "Let's Call the Whole Thing Off" and "They All Laughed," before suddenly turning au courant by reciting a cluster of "in and out" lines: "Pop art is in; Rembrandt is out." "The Mets are in; the Yankees are out." "Bikinis are in; the girls in them are out."

He introduced Chase as "the most artistic young dancer I ever worked with. She had to be a star." The years Chase had spent training as a dancer and the decade of working with Astaire showed in the provocative style and confidence she displayed in her dancing to "The Girl from Ipanema," whose sensuous bossa-nova tempo fit her perfectly.

Fred joined Chase in a number, ingeniously set in a department-store window, that deserved to have been a part of one of the NBC specials. Fred, as a window dresser, works putting a dress on a mannequin. Chase is a mannequin who suddenly comes alive with a jazz movement with her hips. The terrific twosome depart from the confines of the store window and dance a lush routine.

The March 10 show was highlighted by a splendiferous turn by Ethel Merman singing duets with Fred in an extended medley of their Broadway hits. Merman was her usual loud self who overpowered Fred's more subtle singing approach. This served as the basis of a running joke. Toward the end of the songfest, as scripted, Fred actually outshouted Merman, at least for a moment.

On his own, he did a strenuous dance routine to the "Bugle Call Rag." The dance lasted two minutes on camera but took three weeks of preparation. As he told the *Los Angeles Times* entertainment editor, Charles "Chuck" Champlin, "It's more difficult to do than people think. It's like running as fast as you can. You're like a horse going the distance. [This comment perhaps provides the linkage between Astaire's love for horse racing and the dance.] You ask yourself, 'Am I going to last?'"

Champlin described Astaire as "very laid-back and self-effacing. He always seemed vaguely surprised that people thought he could dance as well as he could.

It's hard to believe that he didn't know he was that good. But the world knew, so he kept what he thought to himself." Speaking further of Astaire, the now retired journalist speculated, "It must have disturbing to him in the sense that suddenly you bear almost no relation to what you are and what your origins are. You're lost in space in a way. There are probably a lot of movie people who feel like that. It's sort of like waiting to be found out. But I thought he had a kind of persona that will carry on, whatever. He was one of the great professionals."

On April 30, 1966, the last of the *Hollywood Palace* shows that Astaire hosted was marked by a strutting, sexy dance number Barrie Chase performed with Herb Alpert and the Tijuana Brass to the group's enormous hit, Bacharach and David's "This Guy's in Love with You." It was so spectacular it aided in the show's getting five Emmy nominations that year.

Bill Harbach raved about the modern "Piaget Number," which included an element of an Apache dance, as Chase kicked two guys off the stage. She is intrigued by a man reading a newspaper, sitting on a stool, and breaks into a sexy dance around him. The man, however, won't even look at her. After her series of provocative movements, all in tempo, she becomes immersed in a newspaper article and grabs the newspaper out of his hand and winks at the camera as she strides off.

Bill Harbach is the son of Otto Harbach, the librettist of various Broadway musicals including *Roberta*. Bill Harbach said of working with Astaire, "There was not a hard edge to him at all, but he'd drive you crazy because he was never satisfied with himself. We'd work until sometimes two in the morning on a dance with Barrie Chase or whoever he was working with. Finally, it was perfect, the band's perfect, and it's fine. He'd say, 'Bill, can we do it again?' I'd say, 'Fred, it's perfect. Look.' I'd roll it again on the monitor. He'd see it, and everybody would applaud, and he'd say, 'I think I can do it a little better.' "

All four shows were taped over four weeks. Harbach remembered, "After the solo number Barrie did at the end of the show, she said on camera, 'I'm glad this is over,' because she had spent all week or two weeks working on it. He was in awe of her, and she could really dance."

Having worked with Gene Kelly and Astaire, the erudite retired producer reflected, "Gene was a perfectionist, too, but not as much as Fred. Let's say, Gene would do it seven times; Fred would do it twenty-two times. But Fred was the classiest host we ever had. You don't get any classier than that."

Harbach reflected on the effect the 1960s rock 'n' roll revolution had on musical stars such as Astaire, Kelly, and Crosby, who was the original host of *Hollywood Palace*. "There were no bigger giants than those people, and all of a sudden it was over except for television shows. Boom! You're out of the sketch.

"When we had our first meeting with Fred at his house, which looked like it was in Oyster Bay, Long Island, he agreed with my idea that we should do a spoof on the terrible music of today. . . . That's when we did the thing about the frug, the jerk, et cetera. The whole idea was to make it comfortable for the star.

"He later came over to our house for a dinner party that included my partner, Nick Vanoff, who used to be a dancer. We played some music, and Nick got up and did a dance step. Fred said, 'Where did you get that? Let me see that again.' He and Nick then did some things together."

One night a year or so later, when Hollywood was especially aglitter over an invitation-only gala reception held in honor of Princess Margaret, Fred was apprehensive. He was scheduled to dance with her and was told the princess was quite an adept Watusi dancer. When they took to the dance floor, he mentioned to her what he had heard. The princess, however, said, "I don't know what the Watusi is. You shouldn't believe everything you read in the press." She wanted to do a fox-trot. He admitted that social dancing was actually a bit of a novelty for him. "I don't really care for it that much," he said.[29]

EDDIE MERRINS WAS THE REVERED GOLF PRO at the Bel-Air Country Club for forty years. Now he is the club's pro emeritus. From 1962 to 1974, he gave Fred golf lessons about six times. As Merrins recalled, "I think he valued what he learned in a lesson and pressed it into service." Merrins figured that Astaire's handicap was about fourteen. "At one point, it might have been as low as ten. His score would be in the middle eighties, and in the nineties when it wasn't so good. His was what we term a classic swinger, not a power hitter, but he had a very languid swing. He had beautiful balance, beautiful posture. He had the form to go with it. It looked effortless and it was" (as shown by the famous series of successive teeing-off shots in *Carefree*).

Merrins agreed that Fred's weighing about 135 pounds most of his adult life prevented him from scoring in the upper seventies. "Distance comes from the strength factor," Merrins pointed out. Ben Hogan in the fifties had a similar build, but he had strength." Fred took the game seriously. He could leave his cares and relax. He never talked about show business or about his accomplishments.

The recently deceased comedian and director Dick Martin, who was a long-time member at Bel-Air, knew Astaire for twenty years. "It occurred to me that I don't think Fred Astaire had a friend . . . [yet Fred's friendship with Bill Self started at the club when the producer needed someone with whom he could play a round]. I don't think Fred even played at any of the tournaments. I always wondered about Astaire because you would have thought that he and Bing would have been close enough that he could go up there to the Bing Crosby Tournament held in Pebble Beach. A name like Astaire would have been a magnet for crowds. He reminds me of another member, John Williams, who always plays alone. Fred always played by himself. Now, I don't mean by that that he was not a friendly man or that he was not liked."

AT LAST, a big-budget musical, shot in wide-screen Panavision, *Finian's Rainbow,* was mounted for Fred to star in with Petula Clark at Warner Bros. during the summer of 1967. It was his first movie in six years and the only movie he ever made at Warners. This was a musical with a bite—a satire on Southern racism combined with a generous touch of Irish blarney amid a hunt for gold reserves buried at Fort Knox. Unfortunately, what was thought-provoking for a Broadway musical in 1947 was outdated in the campaign to achieve civil rights twenty years later. As Clark noted, "The mixture of the racial story and the fairy tale was a little bizarre. It's a very difficult cocktail to get right."

Film audiences as well as film historians never did get used to seeing Astaire out of uniform in shabby clothes wearing a modified, battered Rex Harrison–type hat from *My Fair Lady,* along with a permanent stubble while speaking with an Irish brogue in his role of Finian McLonergan, an Irish immigrant. To go one step further, *Finian's Rainbow* was directed by Francis Coppola, in his second film-directing job, with absolutely no credentials as the director of a movie musical.

The Broadway version had played a healthy run of 723 performances and starred David Wayne and Ella Logan. The McCarthyism of the early 1950s prevented Hollywood from tackling such a controversial topic in a film musical, which contained such blatantly political songs such as "When the Idle Poor Become the Idle Rich" and "Necessity."[30] In 1957, an animated version of the property was briefly in production at Warners that was to star Frank Sinatra. The sound track of the score, written by E. Y. "Yip" Harburg and Burton Lane, featuring such standards as "Old Devil Moon," "How Are Things in Glocca Morra?," "Look to the Rainbow," "If This Isn't Love," and "When I'm Not Near the Girl I Love," and sung by Sinatra, Judy Garland, Louis Armstrong, and Ella Fitzgerald, has long been a much-sought-after album by record collectors.

Due to the casting of Petula Clark as Astaire's daughter, the focus in the movie was almost as much on singing as on dancing. Don Francks was the male romantic lead, for which singer Jack Jones had first been considered. Hermes Pan was hired as the dance director, his sixteenth picture working as dance director with Fred, although he contributed unbilled to several others. However, when Pan's contract was not renewed, the choreographer Claude Thompson staged the last two numbers.

After a steady succession of hit records, starting with "Downtown" in 1965, on Warner Bros. Records, Jack Warner naturally wanted to go see Petula Clark perform at the Coconut Grove. He saw her charm and soon signed her as the female lead for *Finian's Rainbow.* Clark was not new to film; she had been under contract to the J. Arthur Rank Organisation when she was eleven years old and had appeared in twenty-two movies previous to *Finian's Rainbow.* Having seen the Fred and Ginger movies as a child made Clark realize, "The idea of working with Fred Astaire was a distant impossibility. When I was told I would be working with Fred, I said, 'Do you really mean *Fred Astaire?*' Perhaps there was another Fred Astaire that I didn't know about."

Clark recalled that Quincy Jones wrote an arrangement of "Old Devil Moon" during the time makeup tests were being conducted for the picture. She was so crazy about the chart that she requested that he be hired for the movie. It's assumed Coppola rejected him because Jones was typecast as a jazz arranger. Ray Heindorf arranged the score for the movie and did a splendid job.

"So here I was in Hollywood," Clark said nostalgically. "It was really quite mind-bending. Fred was so sweet and funny and charming. He seemed to love pop music and knew all my songs. We rehearsed on a stage. I really wish somebody would have taped it."

Clark reminisced about how the summer of 1967 was particularly warm and sticky. "People were passing out while we were dancing under the hot lights. They would disappear and sit around their swimming pools on weekends, but Fred lived in his dressing room so he could rehearse. I think he felt this was the last film he would be dancing on-screen, and he wanted to get it right. Hermes Pan and Fred worked together almost every weekend.

"In the very best way," Clark added, "Fred was a snob. That's to say, he did not like mediocrity, but on the other hand he would never shock anybody. He would never be rude to anybody."

Although opinions vary about Coppola's direction of the film, Clark believed, "He wanted to do a different kind of musical, not a Hollywood musical. He wanted to do something real. . . . There are places where you can feel it, some kind of power and reality, and something a bit tougher than anything we had seen before in musicals. And then you had Tommy Steele playing the leprechaun in this slightly musical kind of fashion."

The sequence where Fred and Petula arrive in America was shot outside San Francisco in Petaluma. Coppola shot "How Are Things in Glocca Morra?" there with a handheld camera à la the contemporary director Steven Soderbergh. All of a sudden Coppola wanted to leave the location and wander off with Astaire and Clark. "We came to a field," Clark recalled. "He said, 'Fred, just dance, dance across the field.' I remember Fred said, 'But that's full of rabbit holes and cow shit. I am not gonna do that.' Francis said, 'That's the real thing,' but Fred said, 'I don't do real things. Build me a field in a studio, and I'll do it.' It was hysterical. We had laughs. We sang all the Beatles songs, hanging out. It was a perfect day not worrying about the people at the studio.

"Little by little, although Fred and Francis were so different, they finished liking each other and respecting each other for their different qualities. It was perhaps a difficult marriage, yes, but I certainly felt, because I was in between them, there was something really good between them."

A particular favorite of Petula Clark's in the picture was Al Freeman Jr., who played the young botanist. His two scenes in which he demonstrated mentholated tobacco along with the proper way to shuffle while carrying a tray to the Southern senator (Keenan Wynn) almost got Freeman a Best Supporting Actor nomination. In the next two years he played key roles in *The Detective* with Frank Sinatra, with Sidney Poitier in *The Lost Man,* and in *Castle Keep* with Burt Lancaster.

Freeman remembered Astaire as being "charming, always smiling, and agreeable." He also noted how astonished he was that Astaire was having trouble getting the tempo right on a dance number set in a barn. "The track had to be sweetened by adding a drum so he could finally dance on the beat."

He said, "Francis's idea of trying to modernize the singing, rather than making it whimsical, was quite something for the 1960s. What he did in the movie was also very unlike the movie of *Brigadoon,* which was shot all misty." Freeman, like Petula Clark, firmly believed the movie could have been infinitely better if it had had three weeks of rehearsal and then performance of the script on a stage before shooting commenced. As he described it, "What took place during rehearsal allowed more of the concept of the personalities and the social comments for the piece to be weaved together. When the film went into production, it became too literal."

As indicated earlier, the majority of the influential film critics had serious problems with the film. *Time* objected to "the simplistic notion of the '40s that Negroes are just like whites beneath the skin is more than an embarrassment now." Joe Morgenstern in *Newsweek* lacerated it by calling it "a shuffling relic that tries hard to be modern." Arthur Knight in the *Saturday Review,* however, offered an enthusiastic minority opinion: "They have not updated it. My, how progressive it all seemed twenty years ago! My, how quaint it all appears today! How well-meaning! How single-minded! . . . This *Finian's Rainbow* transcends time. Like Astaire, it seems ageless."[31]

John Mueller in *Astaire Dancing* offered perhaps the most stinging criticism of the film by observing, "Just about all the film is ill-paced. Virtually all the dialogue scenes (as well as most of the jokes) are belabored. The musical numbers are also tedious." However, he acknowledged, "Astaire gives one of the liveliest and most enduring performances of his career," but went on to say, ". . . All Astaire is given is a brief romp here and a fragmentary jig there. And even this material is dismembered by Coppola's frenetic camera work, which even includes inset shots of Astaire's dancing feet, the first in thirty-five years."

The British press went even further. The *London Evening Standard* film critic wrote, "Now we know. There's schmaltz at the end of the rainbow." The *Daily Telegram* said, "Blarney is to blame."

The dancer and choreographer Jerry Jackson was Pan's assistant on the film. Jackson, looking back on the movie, stated, "Jack Warner said he would do *Finian's Rainbow* if Fred would star in the movie. Coppola did not necessarily want Fred because he thought he was old-fashioned, and Francis was into the new thing and new actors. The studio insisted on Fred, and Fred insisted on Pan. Francis said that I was young, and I knew what was happening. The 'now' kind of thing. As for the dancing, he had some abstract image of what he wanted, but he really didn't know what it was."

Freddie Fields, who then ran ICM, represented both Coppola and Astaire when the company was CMA. He said, "I sold Warners on Coppola based on their getting Fred Astaire, contrary to what Jackson and others contend was the director's reluctance about Astaire's starring in the movie. Coppola would understand right away what Fred Astaire would do with such a movie. Music and some movement, put Fred Astaire in it. Coppola was brilliant, but something did not work in this picture. If he directed it today, it would be a totally different movie."

Coppola in later years called *Finian's Rainbow* "a disaster," but also pointed out that he was brought in to direct a project that had already been cast and structured. "At twenty-nine, I was making an older man's picture."[32] However, he acknowledged, "I had my way, within the limitations of time and money. I was very responsible. I was . . . working in a big studio, in a methodology I didn't understand very well."[33]

The now legendary director referred to the book of the original show as "terrible, sort of ridiculous" yet with "something warm" about it. He explained, "I fought very hard not to change it, which was probably a mistake. I had the idea that if you do *Finian's Rainbow,* you shouldn't rewrite it or update it. I guess I was wrong." Instead, he said, he merely tried to "zip it up."

The film lacked warmth as the audience was never brought into the happenings on-screen. Tommy Steele seemed to be part of a separate movie. The romantic element was almost nonexistent, and once Pan was dismissed, the choreography was improvised.[34] Another huge mistake was that Astaire had few opportunities to dance solo.

Barrie Chase didn't get the role of the mute dancer, Susan, for which she was interviewed. This was probably because Chase was in Coppola's view too connected with Astaire and Pan. Barbara Hancock, who got the job, danced the solo "Rain Dance" number when she discovered the pot of gold and joined Tommy Steele in the over-the-top "When I'm Not Near the Girl I Love."

Jackson believes Pan was paid somewhere around $40,000 for the sixteen weeks he worked on the picture—top money for a dance director on a major film musical. While Astaire was rehearsing the dance number in the barn, Coppola, while sitting on the crane camera, said to Jackson, "I don't like that dance step there. Could you fix it?" Jackson suggested that Coppola talk directly to Pan about it. This exemplified the animosity that prevailed between Coppola and Pan, which led to his contract not being renewed. Jackson left the film when Pan did, although Coppola wanted him to stay on until the end of shooting.

Pan's later comments about Coppola included, "He was a real pain. . . . He would interfere with my work and even with Fred's. Those schoolboys who studied at UCLA [as Coppola did] think they're geniuses, but there is a lot they don't understand."

Coppola's way with actors was evident in the way he translated their personal feelings during the close-ups of musical numbers. As Jackson pointed out, "It was not like we are going into an acting scene and all of a sudden we go into a musical number. He would add to the acting and that would lead right into the musical number. It would work because all the acting was there. I think that's one of the reasons he wanted to do a musical."

Sterling Clark, before dancing with Astaire in the fourth NBC special, danced with him in *Finian's Rainbow*. "Since the movie was a period piece, the choreography and the steps and ideas were more of a period style of dancing. In some of the stuff that Fred does, it's some of this old style and steps, which, of course, Hermes gave to him. If you watch the footwork, there are certain angles, poses, and body languages. What he did in the movie fit the style of an older man. I was proud of what he was doing, even though his energy was not the same."

Visiting the set that August, on the Warners back lot, while representing Al Freeman Jr., I can attest to how frail Astaire appeared. I was amazed that he had to be put in a chair and then hoisted by a boom crane to land on top of a freight car to start shooting the "When the Idle Rich" number. Years earlier, he would nimbly have climbed atop the freight car.

Fred was completely candid in a 1971 interview in his feelings about the movie. His thoughts were indeed well-founded. "I never thought it came off right. Doing it was one of the greatest things to do. I do things because I think I'm going to like them . . . as we did it, we just loved the whole thing. And then the picture came out and got slammed all over the place by various critics, which I'm not saying is wrong. They could easily feel that way about it. . . .

"It was released as a hard-ticket picture [as a road-show attraction]. We finished it in September. . . . Instead of coming out the following Easter or summer, they waited a whole year. . . . I thought it was too long. And the reason it was too long was because they decided to make a hard-ticket picture out of it, and in order to do that they had to have it run two hours and forty minutes or something, with an intermission. You know, this was in the wake of *The Sound of Music.* They thought they had another *Sound of Music.* We just had the worst luck imaginable with that picture. I think if they could have taken twenty minutes out of the picture in the right spots, which easily could have been done, the story would have been different. They would have made money."[35] Later on, the eve of his eightieth birthday, he called *Finian's Rainbow* "my biggest disappointment."[36]

In a further interview concerning the movie that Fred gave to Bob Thomas for *his* Astaire biography, Fred said, "I always thought that the daughter, Petula Clark, and I should have been seen in Ireland. [I was told,] 'We can't afford to spend the money.' I thought, 'Jesus, Warner Bros. can't afford to spend the money. . . . At one point they didn't want Finian to dance because he hadn't danced in the stage version. That's the kind of thinking that was going on. I said, 'Wait a minute, for God's sake, if I don't do a dance, the people will throw rocks at this thing. They'll say, "What's the matter with him—is he sick or what?"'" Fred did dance, in three numbers, "Look to the Rainbow," "If This Isn't Love," and "When the Idle Poor Become the Idle Rich."

FOR AN ACTOR APPROACHING SEVENTY, any role, much less a really good role, is hard to come by. Although this must have bothered Astaire more than he would outwardly admit, he was still working. Freddie Fields noted, "He would like to come over to the office. He would sit outside my office when we had a staff meeting. I would walk in and out of the meeting and talk about different things, and he would listen. Behind his niceness, I sensed a toughness. I never intruded on this toughness or he never exposed me to it. We had a nice relationship, businesslike. We never went to dinner together. We had no social relationship. He was not Judy Garland, he was not Peter Sellers, he was not Steve McQueen, or the other crazy clients. He was Fred Astaire. He had a prominence that was kind of disappearing, and during that time he was kind of becoming more of a legend. It's hard to sell a legend. He had such an image."

Astaire was intrigued enough about going to Europe in 1968 to accept the part of a stylish British Secret Service agent, John Pedley, in *Midas Run.* By sheer coincidence, not too far afield from the premise of *Finian's Rainbow,* he is cast as a cunning mastermind of a scheme to hijack a government shipment of $15 million in gold ingots being transported from Europe to Tanzania via Italy. He was able to show off his Anderson & Sheppard custom-tailored suits in the role.

While in London filming, Fred spent time with his old friend and racehorse consultant, Jack Lewis. They talked of old times, two lonely, aging widowers sharing a long-standing interest in horses. Fred was envious of Jack, who still retained some of his hair. And after completing filming in Italy, Fred headed to Ireland to spend time at Lismore with Dellie, there for her usual summer holiday.

Freddie traveled around the Continent with his father and played a small role as the copilot of the getaway plane in the movie, the only movie role he ever accepted. Ava also arrived for a visit. Location shooting took place in Venice, Terracina, Rome, Milan, Siena, and Florence. For a time, Fred thought he could interest Freddie in getting into film production. Instead, he followed up his air force training and became a helicopter and test pilot before switching to real estate.

Caper films were very much in vogue during the 1960s, perhaps as an offshoot of the James Bond film craze. Fred's cohorts in the picture were the always likable actor Richard Crenna, the attractive English actress Anne Heywood, along with a quartet of fine character actors—Roddy McDowall, Sir Ralph Richardson, Cesar Romero, and Adolfo Celi.

The motivation for John Pedley's scheme was simultaneously to enrich himself and to show the British government how upset he was in being passed over for elevation to knighthood.[37] The plot thickens when his superior (Richardson) orders him to oversee the shipping of the ingots. The hijacking is successful, but Pedley is put in charge of discovering what happened to the ingots. In a save-all climax, he recovers the loot and gets Crenna and Heywood exonerated from any charges by claiming they are in reality government agents. For his good works he is finally given the knighthood he has long coveted.

Selmur Pictures, the film company that produced *Midas Run,* was one of several English-based movie companies that thrived briefly during the 1960s under the Eady Plan, which provided considerable government financing for film production. Raymond Stross, the producer of the film, wanted to showcase his wife Anne Heywood's beauty by featuring her in a few nude scenes that were shot after the film wrapped. Fred remarked, "It was not in the script. I'm not a prude, and I don't mind bad language or anything else, but this gratuitous nudity is stupid."[38] The power of suggestion that was so much a part of his thirties films was now passé; by the late sixties nudity and sex on-screen was in.

On its May 1969 opening, Abe Weiler of the *New York Times* said, "Despite its amiable 14-karat good intentions, *Midas Run* contains more dross than gold." Fred, however, came out relatively unscathed, for as Alan Kriegsman of the *Washington Post* saw it, "What keeps this mishmash from being a total loss is mainly Fred Astaire." *Variety*'s Ronald Gold had a similar view of the picture and Astaire's importance in it by observing, "The film is a spotty effort that is salvaged occasionally by Fred Astaire's ability to overcome a strictly pedestrian script."[39]

Referring to the film, and Astaire's participation in it, the iconoclast George Frazier in *Esquire* wrote, "Style, of course, isn't always forever. Scarcely had my column appeared in print then Fred Astaire proved me correct. One day, we had the remembrance of a very stylish man who endowed our lives with incomparable enchantment, and the next he had opened in a thing called *Midas Run*. There have been pictures more awful than this and nobody was hurt, but it was *Midas Run*'s unique disservice to drag down Astaire."[40]

IN 1968 AVA MARRIED CARL BOSTLEMAN, who owned a Beverly Hills antique shop. The wedding took place on the lawn at the Astaire home with the minister from Fred's church, All Saints Episcopalian in Beverly Hills, officiating. The marriage lasted less than two years and ended in divorce.

On May 17, 1970, Ava married Richard Clayton McKenzie, fourteen years her senior, an artist who owned an art gallery on La Cienega Boulevard in Beverly Hills. McKenzie's wife had died a year earlier, leaving him with two young children. The wedding ceremony was again held at the Astaire home.

Before too long, Ava and Richard moved to London, then to Lumberville in Bucks County, Pennsylvania, and later to County Cork, Ireland, where they reside today. They kept in constant touch with Fred by telephone and visited with him often either in Ireland or in Beverly Hills.[41]

For over forty years, Betty White has enjoyed an enduring career with recurring roles in such shows as *Life with Elizabeth, What's My Line?, Match Game, The Mary Tyler Moore Show, Golden Girls,* and *The Bold and the Beautiful,* plus frequent appearances on talk shows and in commercials. In the late sixties, she and her husband, Allen Ludden, the host of the popular TV game show *Password,* attended a cocktail party where they met Ava and Richard. The two couples clicked and left the party to have dinner together. In their conversation, Richard and Betty discovered they shared a passion for the *Oz* books.

Ava soon arranged for the Luddens to have dinner with her father and Dellie, who was in Beverly Hills for a visit. Fred was a tremendous fan of *Password*. "I had to buy a Fred Astaire dress," White remembered. "Dellie was a dynamite lady with a bawdy sense of humor. We made another dinner date with Ava and Richard along with Fred and Adele.

"Adele invited us to Lismore for a week. One day, when we were there, Fred called to speak to Adele. He also wanted to speak to Allen about a certain clue that had been disallowed in *Password*."

After Betty and Allen returned from Ireland, they had dinner with Fred about every six weeks. The veteran performer Rose Marie told of being a guest for a dinner party at the Luddens'. Fred Astaire, the actor Richard Deacon, and the pianist George Tibbles were also invited. Rose Marie recalled, "Allen asked me to sing. George was at the piano. Fred came over and his foot started going with the tempo.

"I sang several songs. As I started to sing 'The Devil and the Deep Blue Sea,' Fred took my hand, picked me up, and we started to dance. We danced beautifully. I looked at him and said, 'Do you know how to shim sham?—which was a dance that started in Harlem years and years ago.' He said, 'Sure, let's do it.' George started to play, and we did the shim sham. It was one of the biggest thrills in my life.

"Fred's daughter and her husband were in the other room. Betty came out to the kitchen to tell everyone, 'You better come in here and catch this. You'll never see anything like this again.' When Fred and I finished dancing, he said, 'Thank you for the dance.' I said, 'No, thank you.' After that, we all played Dirty Password."

HOLLYWOOD CONTINUED to view Fred as the perfect choice to play a devious, erudite character. With his debonair image, that seemed the perfect role for a sophisticated septuagenarian. So, he was teamed with the handsome leading man Robert Wagner to portray his father, an international superthief, Alistair Mundy, in four episodes of the ABC-TV series *It Takes a Thief* in 1969 and 1970. Having the opportunity to work with Astaire, a close friend, whom he had known since his childhood, was an enriching experience for Wagner.

Wagner recalled, "Fred Astaire was the first movie star I ever met. I was six and a half years old and a boarder at the Hollywood Military Academy. Peter Potter, Fred's stepson, was another one of the students. Fred used to pick up Peter in a cream-colored Packard convertible, on Friday afternoon, and he would put me in his car. I had no idea who he was. He was such a warm, wonderful, caring person.

"My father was a member of the Bel-Air Country Club, and Fred was a member there. My sister and I would be there for dinner, and we would see him there. We lived just off the golf course. In 1936, there was nothing there. I used to see Fred walking around the golf course. I tried to catch up with him. I would say, 'Hi, Mr. Astaire.' As the years went on, I wanted to get into movies. Fred said, 'Gee, this is a great idea.' He was so encouraging. I worked at the club as a caddie. That's how I met Clark Gable, who took me to MGM."

The admiration with which Wagner spoke of the image Astaire projected was enlightening. "Fred was so unique. Fred had this cool kind of style, the manners he had, the way he could be with anybody, talk with anybody, the way people looked at him, the way people cared about him, and the way he cared about people. That was his true success."

I remembered Wagner when he was under contract at Twentieth Century–Fox in the 1950s. I thought of him as "a pretty boy." My opinion of him changed when one of my favorite clients, the late actor and comedian Godfrey Cambridge, raved about what a good friend he had been to him during the sometimes difficult times they shared withstanding the selfish behavior of the emerging star Raquel Welch, on the European location of *The Biggest Bundle of Them All.*

Upon meeting Wagner, I discovered a warm and caring man who just happened to be an actor. By the late sixties, Wagner was in the midst of a comeback in movies when Lew Wasserman, then chairman of Universal (now that MCA had been dissolved by order of Attorney General Robert Kennedy), talked to him about starring in *It Takes a Thief* as a weekly series.

Wagner approached Hughie McFarland, who was also Astaire's valet, who agreed to work with him on the show. At the end of the first season, McFarland suggested to Wagner, "What about getting Fred for the show?" "Oh, Jesus, I don't think he'd do it," replied the actor, afraid that such a request would put Astaire in an embarrassing position because of their longtime friendship.

When Wagner called Astaire, he conveyed the thoughts of the show's producer, Glen Larson: "We're gonna introduce you in Europe as you're 'evacuating' money out of the Lido, the casino in Venice. You would play my father, but you and I have been estranged. I had been caught and sent to prison." Astaire reacted positively: "I like the idea." Wagner noted, "He was the kind of a person who either said yes or no. It wasn't 'Well, let me think about it.'"

MCA executives were at first against the casting of Astaire, afraid of what his financial demands might be as well as of the costs of travel and hotels in sending him to Europe, where shooting was to begin. Wagner stayed at home in Palm Springs on a sit-down strike ("of about five shooting days") until the company capitulated to his wishes and agreed to sign Astaire. Shooting commenced in Venice, then proceeded to Rome.

"Right after Fred arrived, we shot in a villa in Rome. After lunch one day, Fred started dancing around this vast ballroom without music. He kicked the piano a few times, did a couple of things, and the Italian crew, which was watching him, went crazy," recalled Wagner.

"As an actor, he was wonderful. We talked on the phone a great deal at the beginning about the part. We had to improvise, and he was always adjustable to that. We rehearsed a lot. He stepped right into the character and it worked. Fred had courage in everything he did—in his singing, his dancing. He was always trying to do something more. He wanted to be very current. Whatever he took on, he would become very, very interested in it."

David Niven Jr., who produced or coproduced twelve big-screen and TV movies, including the memorable *The Eagle Has Landed,* and received two Emmy nominations for his productions, was not an admirer of Fred's work as a character actor. "I thought it was sad," he said. Regarding Astaire's performance in *On the Beach,* he remarked, "It is almost like in the *Towering Inferno.* You say, 'What is he doing there?'" However, Niven did admire Fred's work in *It Takes a Thief.* "He was wonderful and debonair. He looked like he was more comfortable playing that particular role."

Viewing the four episodes, two shot in Europe and two at Universal Studios, the rapport between Astaire and Wagner was evident. RJ, as he is known, said, "I had such great respect for Fred, and I was so proud to be with him. He really had an affection for me. I think all of that came across. He was proud that I was doing well. We talked about the scenes, what we were going to do, and what we are going for. Then we would throw it all away. It all fell in together."

The easy rapport between the two extended to their playing their roles to a fare-thee-well with tongue planted firmly in cheek. "The Great Casino Caper," their first episode working together, which aired on October 16, 1969, and was re-run the following February, was perhaps the most lively of the shows they appeared in together. Fred, resplendent in a pink neck scarf, blue blazer, and white ducks, is introduced to the series in the perfect setting—at the billiards table—while losing badly to Adolfo Celi, an evil international banker. He cons Celi into a double-or-nothing bet. The fast-moving plot allows father and son to amusingly pull off as intricately staged a robbery as has ever been seen in film or television. Somehow, the two are involved with some sort of secret U.S. government agency. The finale takes place on a yacht, where Edward Binns, their government liaison, is convinced the daring twosome are holding back 90 million lire from their night's work!

Looking back on his friendship with Astaire, Wagner said, "I was so fortunate that I was able to work with him professionally and have my life be part of his and be with him. This was truly a blessing. Fred was very instinctive. He knew what was right for him, and he knew about himself. He was his own man."

As I left Wagner's tastefully appointed former Brentwood estate, he said, "Let me show you something," whereupon he opened the garage door. A smiling photographic cutout of Astaire was standing by the door. "See, F.A. is still with us," Wagner said.

CHAPTER TWELVE

A DECADE OF TRIBUTES

A S THE 1970S CAME ALONG, Fred Astaire assumed an even more elevated station in the Hollywood firmament. He had withstood all of the trends and vagaries of Hollywood over four decades and had established a unique position for himself as the supreme master of style coupled with extraordinary talent. The film industry has always admired class, perhaps because under the vacuous sheen of glamour there was indeed an absence of true elegance. It was now time for the song-and-dance man turned character actor to be honored for his long career and his significant achievements. The respect that came to him in this decade disproved an adage of Artie Shaw's: "Nostalgia ain't what it used to be."

Starting off a decade of tributes was the first of two *Dick Cavett Show*s, on ABC, which aired on November 10, 1970. The thought of being Cavett's only guest over ninety minutes obviously made Fred anxious. The producer on Cavett's staff who had been assigned to deal with him during the pre-interviews found Fred "mean and nasty."

This was Astaire's first in-depth talk show appearance. (The Oscar Levant debacle doesn't really count as a talk show.) Fred had suffered an inner-ear problem earlier that year that greatly affected his balance and caused him to decide sadly that his dancing days were now behind him. Cavett recalled when they taped the show, Fred sat on the very edge of his chair. "I asked him could he sit back. He said he couldn't because he had recently hurt his back and described crawling on the floor in his bedroom when it happened."

After Cavett's introduction, Astaire got a standing ovation when he came on-stage. He began by admitting, "Mr. Cavett, I've never been brainwashed," which was his offhand way of admitting his nervousness about exposing himself on a talk show. The camera revealed his shyness early on when Cavett referred to him as "being known as one of the nicest guys in show business." Cavett had to use all his skills as a talk show host to coax Fred past delivering short answers to questions, so as to make the interview something more than superficial.

When Cavett brought up his prowess as a singer, Astaire declared, "I never thought of myself as a vocalist." From where he was sitting, he sang the first of several Gershwin songs, "They All Laughed," before moving over to a stool and continuing with renditions of "Lady Be Good," " 'S Wonderful," and "A Foggy Day." That was followed by three Berlin standards: "Cheek to Cheek," "Isn't This a Lovely Day" (when he finally began to relax as he got into the music), and "Top Hat." Then the focus shifted to the real reason for Fred's coming on the show, *The Over-the-Hill Gang Rides Again* movie, which was also conveniently on ABC. A film clip was shown, whereupon Fred understatedly but effectively sold the movie. Then he broke into a few dance steps toward the conclusion of the show.

On the second *Cavett Show,* aired on October 13, 1971, Fred seemed far more at ease and even at times spoke with some semblance of authority. Again he sang Gershwin and Berlin medleys to keep the talk spots to a minimum. He vehemently denied that he and Ginger didn't get along, but his argument seemed shallow. He finally referred to her as "an asset to my life." He said, "Let's sing a song for Ginger," which led to "I'm Putting All My Eggs in One Basket," "Easy to Dance With," and "I Used to Be Color Blind."

At Cavett's suggestion, Fred demonstrated a few pointers about dancing the time step. Kneeling down beside Cavett, he amusingly described the host's steps as "a klutz waltz." This final segment seemed to enable him to completely unwind as he again broke into several dance steps of his own as the closing credits rolled.

Looking back on the talk shows he did with Astaire, Cavett remarked, "Why doesn't anybody ever look remotely like him when they're dancing? Nobody can do whatever he did with that body, those features. When he turns, my [late] wife pointed out there is no preparation for the turn. You can't do that from zero, but he did. So maybe he could stand beside this table and in one move jump on it, which he also did."

Cavett speculated whether the friendship that developed between them might have been due to their both being natives of Nebraska. Cavett said, "Marlon Brando [also from Nebraska] called it 'a foolish kinship.' " The talk show host and comedian remembered getting a Christmas card from Astaire. A little snapshot on it showed a deer looking into his living room window. He wrote on the back, "Wild Beverly Hills rose eater."

* * *

THE OVER-THE-HILL Gang Rides Again had a good script by Richard Carr and was a clever spoof on westerns—a most unusual vehicle for Fred Astaire. Fred was suitably groomed in a droopy mustache and beard. It was a movie of the week, a staple of seventies and eighties television, and was produced by Aaron Spelling and Danny Thomas.

The camaraderie Fred exhibited with the rest of the Gang—Walter Brennan, Edgar Buchanan, Andy Devine, and Chill Wills—was both amusing and heart-warming as they rid a small town of a group of desperadoes. Fred was obviously enjoying playing the role of the Baltimore Kid and even had an amusing drunk scene, which he later admitted he prepared for by having a few drinks beforehand. In a way, the "Let's Dance" song and his dancing duet with Betty Hutton in western garb and his solo turn as a Texas oilman in *Daddy Long Legs* had prepared him for this role.

Lana Wood, Natalie Wood's sister, was an actress and was later involved in casting and television production. She played a prostitute in *The Over-the-Hill Gang*. "My first scene in the movie was difficult as I was in jail. Fred arrived on the set. He saw that there was no chair for me and said, 'I'm so sorry.' He dragged a chair for me and one for himself, and we started talking. I mentioned having seen *The Gay Divorcée* recently on television and my favorite song 'A Needle in a Haystack' in *The Gay Divorcée* was cut. We began singing songs together and having a wonderful time. I pride myself on knowing lyrics, but we couldn't come up with the lyrics from 'A Needle in a Haystack.' I really think I got to know this warm, warm man—talking about films, songs, and things. The day before we wrapped, Fred arrived with this big envelope. I opened it up. It was the original sheet music from 'A Needle in a Haystack' with all his little notes on it where he had originally underlined certain words. And then he sent me a lovely handwritten letter about what a thrill it was to work with me."

Wood recalled, "Leslie Bricusse was going to throw a party for me before I went to New York to do a movie. He asked me who I wanted to have invited. I told him, 'Fred Astaire,' but he said, 'He's a neighbor, but I know he won't come.' At eight thirty promptly on the night of the party, he was the first at the door, and he was one of the last two to leave."

Bricusse subsequently bonded with Astaire. One night at dinner at Bricusse's home, as they were playing pool, Astaire suddenly asked the Oscar-winning lyricist and composer, "Leslie, I've been wanting to ask you this for years, but I didn't like to mention it. Why do you suppose it is that they didn't want me to play Willy Wonka?" This film musical, with its score written by Bricusse and Tony Newley, had been a box-office hit, starring Gene Wilder, and received a Best Original Score Oscar nomination. "The Candy Man," contained in the score, was soon recorded by Sammy Davis Jr. and became the biggest record of his career.

Bricusse reflected, "I did not believe what I had just heard. Here was the greatest song-and-dance man in history telling me that he had actually asked to play Willy Wonka and they had turned him down. He was the right age. He looked like he should be Willy Wonka. My heart stopped when I thought of what he would have done with the musical numbers, which for the most part were cumbersomely staged in the film, containing none of the magic that was generated when Astaire was on a set."[1]

Since the age of the great film musicals was long over, Fred was open to another kind of musical—a TV animated musical special, "Santa Claus Is Comin' to Town" featuring puppets and toylike sets. The special aired on ABC on December 14, 1970. Fred was the narrator and played a mailman while starring with Mickey Rooney and Keenan Wynn. The movie was produced and directed by Jules Bass and Arthur Rankin Jr., who were prominent in the animation field. Bass and Maury Laws wrote the musical score.

The plot detailed the early life of Kris Kringle and his journey to becoming the man we know as Santa Claus. Its humor and excellent sense of character registered with the TV audience. Fred closed the hour-long presentation by singing the Christmas classic title song with a decided verve that showed his true feeling for the old standby. Howard Thompson of the *New York Times* referred to the show as "a cute perky bundle for the romper set." It proved so popular that it became a Christmas perennial on the network for the next few years.

The romper set seemed to love Astaire. This led Bass and Rankin to bring Astaire back again in 1977 to play the mailman narrator in "The Easter Bunny Is Comin' to Town." This time the mailman decides to stop a deluge of letters by answering letters to the Easter Bunny.

IN HIS PERSONAL LIFE, Fred was trying to find a new way to live without Phyllis. His brief friendship with Lana Wood (they never saw each other again) was indicative of where his life was in the early 1970s. He had been a bachelor for sixteen years by the time of his shooting *The Over-the-Hill Gang Rides Again.* He wanted to get to know the actress he was working with, but he was also perhaps interested in taking her to dinner. "He was pretty lonely in those years. I think it was fortunate that he had his work. I can tell you that from my own experience," observed Robert Wagner.

ALTHOUGH HIS ROMANCE was long over with Barrie Chase, she and Fred continued to be good friends. At Eastertime in 1977, Barrie married Dr. James Kaufman at the Capitolini in Rome. Chase was then working on an RAI Televisione show. Jerry Jackson, who was choreographer on the show, was the best man at their wedding. Their marriage has continued to the present. They have a son, Jeb, who is a stockbroker. Dr. Kaufman came up with several innovations that were important in modern dentistry and subsequently retired. Chase ceased performing shortly after her marriage.

Clearly, Fred was in search of a new female companion. He had dinner dates with various much younger women, one of whom was Tina Sinatra. Sinatra explained, "I love him [Fred] just like I love my father. People find it difficult to understand this kind of relationship, how two people can be close and yet not be romantically involved and planning marriage."[2]

Jennifer Jones, before her marriage to the financier Norton Simon, pursued Astaire, but Fred had no interest. His good friend Bill Self well described Fred's bachelor status in those years when he said, "I think Fred was in love with Phyllis all his life. I always felt he was dating later for companionship and fun, nothing serious."[3]

The actress whom he was seen with most frequently for more than a decade (although she said their relationship lasted "probably twenty years") was the former successful model, turned actress, Carol Lynley, who referred to Fred as "fragility and steel. By 'steel' I meant discipline. I was late once, and he didn't like it. I was never late again. He had this ability to turn every twenty-four hours into a joyful experience, and that's a genius besides physical genius."[4] Their close relationship endured despite being, according to Lynley, entirely platonic.

"He kind of wanted it to be a romance. He was a father figure to me. I felt it would get in the way of obviously a very long friendship. He used to chase me around the pool table." She laughed as she said, "He loved it when I bent over. . . . His instincts were heterosexual, extremely heterosexual. I probably did make a mistake, but on the other hand I had a very, very long and very meaningful relationship. We never had an argument."

Lynley noted, "Fred would call me up and say, 'Let's go out and get drunk.' And I'd say, 'Oh, all right.' Not that Fred would ever get drunk—he enjoyed cocktails. Then he'd say, 'Let's make it two weeks from Thursday,' and we'd go to the Bistro. I would drink white wine, and he'd have an old-fashioned. He loved those very thirties cocktails . . . and he was not a fancy eater. . . . When we went to Chasen's, he would have chicken potpie; when we went to the Bistro, he also had chicken potpie. He liked apple sauce."

They had initially met in Los Angeles through Allen Delyn, a business associate of the notorious Broadway producer David Merrick, who wanted to bring "an old friend of mine" to dinner with the two of them. "I couldn't believe how lucky

I was. We just hit it off. He had a great sense of humor," Lynley recalled. "Ava has the same thing. It's an Irish point of view. I am half-Irish. We saw the funny side of things. We made each other laugh. That was the key to our relationship.

"He liked everything that was new. He sent me a photograph of himself going down his driveway on a skateboard. Two months later, he sent me a photo with his arm in a sling, holding a martini. He was pissed when his doctor made him stop doing it when he was eighty."

Spending as much time with Fred as she did, Lynley got to know Dellie. Lynley recalled. "I used to have dinner with the two of them. She would say something, and Fred would blush and would roll his eyes—'Oh, God, there she goes again.' But she was funny. She would break out into songs they had done in vaudeville and on Broadway."

Lynley described Dellie's elegance, which extended to "changing her jewelry five times a day. It was all spectacular jewelry. She was very tiny. She had custom-made shoes and custom-made clothes, more so than Fred. He was more casual then Dellie and also more polite."

BY THE EARLY 1970S, rock 'n' roll had long since dominated pop music. A few TV specials, however, still featured classic popular music. Two such shows that Astaire starred in, which were aired in January and September 1972, were " 'S Wonderful, 'S Marvelous, 'S Gershwin" and "Make Mine Red, White, and Blue," both of which were on NBC.

The former show was part of the *Bell System Family Theater* and also featured as host Jack Lemmon, along with guests Ethel Merman, Leslie Uggams, Peter Nero, and others. Getting Astaire to appear on the show took an unusual effort. The producer and writer of the two-hour-long special was Martin Charnin, later the lyricist and director of the Broadway smash *Annie*.

Charnin recalled, "I had just done the Anne Bancroft special, and basically I was sort of the new flavor of the month. Lemmon played all the characters in the show—George Gershwin's father, George's publisher, et cetera. Jack was the only person who spoke in the show. Everybody else sang or played music.

"Elliot Lawrence [the conductor] and I had laid out the songs we thought were identifiably Astaire songs. I spoke to Astaire on the phone. He asked me, 'When are you coming out?' Fred picked me up at the airport in a white Silver Cloud Rolls-Royce that he drove himself [which according to Hoagy Bix Carmichael was left to Fred by Gary Cooper]. His home was close to a Gatsby-like estate. I remember that every floor in the downstairs could have been tapped on; there was no carpeting, or marble, or Formica. There were no scuff marks on the floor. Maybe in Gene Kelly's house, but not in Fred Astaire's house! He had a cabinet in the room where his piano was. The Emmys were displayed in the cabinet. He asked, 'Your [Emmy] is just like that, right?' He asked me if I would like some iced tea. He had a manservant and a piano player. I brought out the medley and explained to him how we wanted this medley to go, and how I was going to use him in the show. He wanted to know if I wanted to shoot pool first.

"He wore a plain yellow tie as a belt, thin pants, and his cuffs didn't meet the tops of his shoes so you could see his socks. Therefore, you could see both the color and the grace of the curve of the arch. But the thing that was most extraordinary was the lack of pretension. He was the most unpretentious human being I ever met in my life, and also the most confident person I have ever met in my entire life. We worked for a good three hours. It was very easy and collaborative. I taped the segues between songs. That's the only day I worked with him.

"He drove me to the airport. I had to take the red-eye back. I was able to call Lemmon from the airport and tell him, 'Jack, I want to tell you that Fred is going to do it.' Jack said, 'Okay, I'll do it.' "

Charnin kept in touch with Astaire by telephone. He asked for his measurements to have a tuxedo made for him. Fred thanked him but said that he would bring his own tuxedo. His sequence was set to be taped on a Friday, but because he wanted to rehearse, the taping date was changed to a Thursday. Charnin picked him up on his 6:00 A.M. arrival at Kennedy Airport, carrying his own garment bag containing his tuxedo. They headed immediately to the Brooklyn studio used by the Bell Telephone Company to tape Astaire's singing to prerecorded orchestra tracks, arranged by Al Cohn.

Charnin described Astaire's work as "absolutely letter-perfect, indefatigable." Fred was concerned, however, about the look of a shot of him rising off a stool in the midst of the twelve-song medley, which lasted twenty minutes. Afterward, Charnin drove with him to the Sherry-Netherland Hotel, where he was staying. That night they went to Sardi's, where Fred requested they have dinner.

"When we walked in, there was silence. Vincent Sardi said, 'Mr. Charnin,' and gave me a gigantic handshake. He seated us in the middle of the room at a table meant for six people. A different set of waiters served us each course." Over dinner, as usual, Fred was again concerned about how he came off in the show. He said to Charnin, "If it's not perfect, I'll come back." He agreed to stay another day so he could do a number with Jack Lemmon.

"I'll never forget it," Charnin added. "When we were driving back in the limousine, we passed a couple of hookers standing on Eighth Avenue. He nudged me and said, 'The way she wears her hat . . .' "

The next day Astaire and Lemmon, playing piano, spent two hours rehearsing and shooting "The Babbitt and the Bromide," which Astaire and Gene Kelly had performed together in *Ziegfeld Follies*. When the show finally aired, Fred sent Charnin a congratulatory wire. The show was awarded sixteen Emmy nominations, ultimately winning an Outstanding Achievement in Music Direction of a Variety, Musical or Dramatic Program Emmy for Elliot Lawrence.

"MAKE MINE RED, WHITE, AND BLUE" was NBC's lame attempt to circumvent the turmoil in the country caused by the Vietnam debacle by illustrating in a musical variety show what was right about America by focusing on its rich history and its people. The program was designed to appeal to what Richard Nixon referred to at the time as the Silent Majority, the predecessor of the Religious Right. But scheduled against *The New Dick Van Dyke Show* on CBS and the Summer Olympics on ABC, which got a huge forty-two share, it got only a sixteen share and was a distant third in the ratings.

The cast of performers was diverse. Besides Fred, as host, it included the 5th Dimension, Michele Lee, Bob Crane, and even the Native American actor of choice in Hollywood during those years, Iron Eyes Cody, who was the subject of a patronizing tribute to the Indians. Fred sang "Fascinating Rhythm" but was also given Earl Robinson's "Ballad for Americans" and Irving Berlin's "Give Me Your Tired, Your Poor" from his 1949 Broadway musical, *Miss Liberty,* which proved to be ill-advised material for him to sing.

Astaire and Lee rehearsed the David Rose–arranged "all-American" song medley given them by carrying around a tape recorder. Lee remembered, when they were finished, "He asked me if I thought his singing was okay. 'Should I do it again?' he said. My God, Fred Astaire, this icon, was asking me if his singing was all right! He meant it. He was so unassuming. He never played star."

The downbeat reviews said it all. *Variety* observed, "Astaire underplayed his host role in his typical low key ingratiating manner to set the tone for the hour. . . . Astaire got a splendid assist from Michele Lee in duets with the Jimmy Joyce singers." *Daily Variety* said, "It was not the music but rather the unimaginative staging of the show which made it a rather pedestrian one." Glenn Lowell of the *Hollywood Reporter* said, "This time around, however, the patriotic reaffirmation is not only sanctimonious and self-satisfied, but also disappointingly slipshod. . . . Astaire tells us Americans learn from their mistakes. Let's hope NBC learns from this one."

To end the year, Fred and Dellie attended the late-November opening of the Uris Theatre in New York. Broadway's Hall of Fame was unveiled on the wall of the theater's huge lobby. Their names were rightfully included among the 123 names on the gold-lettered list.

ON NEW YEAR'S DAY 1973, at Santa Anita, in the fifth race, Exciting Divorce was slowly emerging out of the pack, in eighth position out of twelve horses at the quarter mark. But on the turn, the horse, ridden by jockey Robyn Smith, took charge and was running behind only two horses, Lost Moment and Lady Broadcast, the latter whose rider was the famous jockey Willie Shoemaker, using his whip. With a roaring crowd cheering her on, in the final stretch the determined Smith passed Shoemaker, who had been in the lead by half a length, and won the race by a neck. Smith's grim look melted into a half smile at her significant achievement as she entered the winner's circle.[5]

Watching Smith's extraordinary exhibition was Exciting Divorce's owner, fifty-eight-year-old Alfred Gwynne Vanderbilt II, then the president of the New York Racing Association; the horse's trainer, Bobby Lake; and Vanderbilt's old friend of almost forty years, Fred Astaire. Many years earlier, the Bromo-Seltzer heiress, Margaret McKim, had taken Vanderbilt, then a teenager, to see the hit Broadway musical *Funny Face,* and afterward they'd met Fred and Adele Astaire backstage.

On this occasion, despite learning in the racing form that Exciting Divorce had in December been seventh out of eight horses and lost in its last two outings at Aqueduct, Astaire placed $200 on his old friend's filly based on their longtime friendship. He wound up winning $1,600 on the race!

That night Vanderbilt asked Smith if she would come to join him and Astaire for dinner at Chasen's in Beverly Hills. She conversed with Fred over dinner. Fred was amazed that such an attractive young woman could deport herself so well as a jockey.[6]

As the first important female jockey, Smith warranted a lengthy cover story in *Sports Illustrated* in the July 19, 1972, issue, written by the well-known sportswriter Frank Deford.[7] In 1973, her mounts earned a formidable $634,055 in 501 races, finishing in the money one-third of the time, and winning an incredible fifty-one times.[8] Her financial share was 10 percent. She based her riding style on that of Eddie Arcaro, the famous jockey.

Her relationship with Vanderbilt, thirty-two years her senior, was more than that of owner and jockey, but Smith contended, "I'm a good rider and win races. That is what is important. I'm legitimate." By 1977, her eighth year in racing, her earnings had slipped to a total of $180,822, but from having taken part in 169 races.[9] The next year she continued as an important jockey in a strictly man's world.

Her interdependence over the years with Vanderbilt had withstood a series of ups and downs. Following the sportsman's 1975 divorce, it appeared as though they would marry. Smith was frustrated, however, that her earnings didn't compare with those of the leading jockeys, such as Willie Shoemaker. She complained to a *New York Times* reporter, "All I ever ride are long shots. The male jockeys get the Cadillacs, and I get the Volkswagen—if I'm lucky.[10]

Reportedly, the Vanderbilt family had objected to Smith, believing she was after Alfred's money. Her love affair as well as her business dealings with Vanderbilt soon came to an abrupt end.[11]

Smith had developed a reputation as a loner and a fighter who would display a temper when she felt she had been treated unfairly. Fear was completely foreign to her. A strong and willful desire to succeed was paramount in her.

Astaire's and Smith's paths crossed several times in the intervening years at various racetracks. She had also enjoyed another dinner with him and Vanderbilt in Los Angeles in 1976. In 1977, she flew to Los Angeles to do a Shasta soft-drink television commercial. From the apartment she maintained in Arcadia, near Santa Anita, she sent flowers to Fred Astaire and asked him to have dinner with her. He had been a part of the horse-racing world for decades. Perhaps she felt he could be of help in her current plight.[12]

FRED'S CONTINUING INTEREST in Thoroughbreds had led to his flying East a few times over the years for the annual August sales meeting at Saratoga, New York. Horse races also take place, and therefore it is called Race Week. Astaire stayed with his longtime friend Jock Whitney at his home. Peter Duchin was in town leading his orchestra in a benefit performance at the newly opened Saratoga Arts Center in 1974. Fred and Peter's father, Eddy, had met at the Casino in Central Park during the early 1930s, where the Duchin band played, and became good friends.

One night after dinner, following their attending the yearling sales, Astaire, Whitney, "Shipwreck" Kelly, Duchin, and his wife, Cheray, returned to the Whitney home. After more than a little drinking, Kelly bellowed out to Astaire, "Astaire, what kind of dancer are you, anyway, for God's sake? You have a piano player right here with Peter. Sing us a song, goddammit!"

Peter Duchin recalled, "I am thinking, 'Jesus, I am going to play for Fred Astaire.' Fred didn't even look at me and said, 'Do you wanna do a few?' And I said, 'Sure, Fred, gosh, I'd love to. I would be honored.' It's a feeling I would experience with Fred, Arthur Rubinstein, and Lester Young—maybe a couple of others."[13]

Astaire and Duchin moved to the piano in the front hall. "This must have been about ten thirty," Duchin recalled. We started drinking a little bit of brandy and then quite a bit. Fred went from movie to movie, starting with *Top Hat,* and talked about each one of them, explaining how he and the choreographer had put the various numbers together. He grabbed Cheray and started dancing with her. She was in seventh heaven. He saw that she was a good dancer and was delighted with that. And Jock Whitney kept serving us brandy to keep us there. We went on until three in the morning.

"Fred's final song was 'One for My Baby.' He said, 'This is the way Frank [Sinatra] did it.' After one chorus, he stopped and said, 'This is the way I like to do it.' He put an elbow on the piano and rested his head in his hands. I slowed the tempo down to accommodate Fred. With a couple of gestures, and the flicker of his eyes, he supplied a vivid picture of a man who had plummeted from the heights of success to the depths.[14]

"As the song reached its conclusion, Whitney, with brandy snifter in hand, was crying. Even Shipwreck's eyes were wet. . . . I spotted Jock's valet, Eric, and some of the kitchen help, peaking out of the doorway that led up the back stairs." Duchin agreed that Astaire was one of the few entertainers whom society people actually revered. "I was born into it, he was not," Duchin said.

The outgoing and personable bandleader spoke of an unfulfilled idea of Fred's working with him on a book discussing all the many songs he had become associated with (much like the night in Saratoga), which would also feature arrangements of these songs that Duchin would write. "Fred said he would cooperate. We couldn't get the copyrights to be small enough so that it would be a viable idea. I called Irving Berlin myself. He was then in his eighties. I asked him if he would mind if I wrote a couple of arrangements of his songs. He said, 'Nobody writes arrangements and nobody publishes arrangements of any of my songs.' And I said, 'But this is a special thing with Fred Astaire.' His answer was 'Nobody.' "

IN JANUARY 1973, Fred was momentarily seen in an unusual vehicle, a movie called *Imagine,* which found Fred, along with Dick Cavett, playing a pair of Nebraskans (perfect casting) who attend a party in Riverdale, along with George Harrison and Jack Palance. This particular scene was directed by Jonas Mekas, the avant-garde filmmaker. The movie was made to promote John Lennon's memorable *Imagine* album. Lennon was the producer and director of the movie. Yoko Ono contributed the plot of sorts, which was a surreal, half-fiction, half-real-life study of a day in the life of John and Yoko.

The Film Society of Lincoln Center, in its annual gala honoring film greats, chose Fred as its second award recipient on April 30, 1973. At the press conference held at the St. Regis Hotel a few days before the gala, Fred was asked, "To millions of people you have always represented in your films the sophisticate, the debonair, the elegant. How would you say that compares with the real-life Fred Astaire?"

"I'd say," replied Astaire with a slight smile, "it's right on the nose." He also said, "You see, I never thought about bringing anything to dancing, or trying to say anything with dancing, or trying to be something arty. . . . I was just trying to make a buck. I never could take myself seriously. I'm really a rat if you want to know the truth."[15]

Some thirty-five film clips personally selected by Astaire, out of a possible two hundred, attesting to his dancing versatility, were shown. Anna Kisselgoff in the *New York Times* wrote, "Astaire and Rogers were always in love on screen. Their series of ten films has rightly been called, 'romance in chapters.' Chance and hard work had made Astaire the epitome of the 20th century artist. No other entertainer worked so well within the two vital art forms of this century—film and dance."

Seven years later, taking a retrospective look at these film clips, Kisselgoff made a further observation about the Astaire-Rogers team's choreography: "It was striking how similar the world of each duet was in each film. It was the ballroom duet in an empty space, filled entirely by two special people. All is variation on this theme. . . . But if the ballroom form is the keystone of the Astaire-Rogers duet, it is also used to explore an emotional relationship. Love in fact."[16]

At the gala, Fred was seated in a box with Dellie and several of their New York society friends. According to the gala's director and programmer, Wendy Keys, "He didn't want Ginger to sit with him in the box."[17] In the audience were Ginger Rogers, Cyd Charisse, Arlene Dahl, Rex Harrison, Danny Kaye, Josh Logan, Mayor John Lindsay, and Joan Fontaine, along with his close friends Allen Ludden and Betty White. Fred never forgot the magic that New York possessed. Broadway was where he and Dellie had received their first significant acclaim.

When he got up to accept the award and received a tumultuous ovation, he shoved his hands in his pocket—and showed his usual nervous twitch. He looked down at his shoes for a moment, then said, "Thank you so much. I've got to go easy to get this out. I'm overwhelmed. There's so much emotion here. This is the most exciting thing that's ever happened to me. I'm, I'm, I'm—here I go with the *I'm*s . . ." He introduced Dellie ("my little sister") and acknowledged his most prominent dancing partner, Ginger Rogers. He said, "When I was working with Ginger, it was like heaven on earth. She had all the talent anybody could have."

To make the evening complete, Fred insisted on having Count Basie and His Orchestra play for dancing at the champagne party that followed on the promenade of the New York State Theater with twelve hundred attendees. Sally Quinn, now a doyenne of Georgetown society but then a *Washington Post* reporter, observed that at the party the photographers naturally clamored for a picture of Fred and Ginger together. Ginger was brought over to Fred's table, smiling stiffly. They embraced as a large group of photographers clicked away, then pulled apart. In a telling exchange, Rogers said, "Oh, Freddie, darling, I'm so very proud of you." "Thank you," said Fred. Rogers asked, "Someday when I come to Los Angeles [she spent most of her time on her Medford, Oregon, ranch], can we have dinner together, maybe? Could we, may we, please?" Astaire nodded and smiled. "How do I get in touch with you?" she asked. Astaire again nodded and smiled. "Oh, well, don't worry," said Rogers, "I'll find someone who knows how to get in touch with you. I will call you." Then she moved away, blowing two kisses to her former dance partner.[18]

In a perfect example of going from the ridiculous (*Imagine*) to the sublime, Astaire's next film venture was the 1974 star-spangled study in MGM nostalgia, *That's Entertainment!*—a compilation of excerpts for the most part from its epic musicals. It was the perfect way to herald the studio's fiftieth anniversary. Fred joined such luminaries as Bing Crosby, Frank Sinatra, Gene Kelly, Elizabeth Taylor, Liza Minnelli, Debbie Reynolds, Jimmy Stewart, Mickey Rooney, and others in commenting on memorable scenes from their MGM heritage. Fred's numbers consisted of "Begin the Beguine" (from *Broadway Melody of 1940*), "The Babbitt and the Bromide" (from *Ziegfeld Follies*), "Sunday Jumps" (the hat-rack dance number from *Royal Wedding*), "Shoes with Wings On" (from *Barkleys of Broadway*), "You're All the World to Me" (the wall-and-ceiling dance from *Royal Wedding*), "Dancing in the Dark" (from *The Band Wagon*), and "By Myself" (also from *The Band Wagon*).[19]

In the film, Fred was dressed in a blue blazer, white shirt, striped tie, and flannels (which he called "the uniform")[20] while introducing the film clips in his favorite arms-crossed pose. In the background was the green railway coach, now peeling from neglect, in which he had arrived on the set that represented New York's Grand Central Terminal in *The Band Wagon*.

In a broader sense, the pathetic appearance of the railway car sadly symbolized what had happened to the once mighty MGM. Exposing its onetime majesty to a new film audience underlined that here was a studio with a brilliant past but, due to mismanagement at the top, no future.

Jack Haley Jr., the son of the Tin Man in *The Wizard of Oz,* as producer, spent considerable time in getting Fred to agree to address his past by appearing in the picture. In typical fashion, Fred insisted on doing twelve takes of his narration. Haley recalled, "Fred would think of something else he wanted to say about Gene Kelly, so he'd come back to the studio for another take. In the end I would say, 'Fred, this film has got to get to the theaters soon. You can't keep changing the narration.' Fred would say, 'Yes, Jack, I know. Just let me try one more thing.' "[21]

Haley added, "I think my father said it best. He said, 'Film is timeless. If you take Fred Astaire and Eleanor Powell dancing "Begin the Beguine," it's not dated. Excellence does not date, and that's an excellent number. People respond to excellence. They know that's good dancing, they know that's good music. So what if it is in black and white, and it's [almost] forty years old. It does not matter. It's exciting, and people appreciate it.' "[22]

To celebrate the world premiere of *That's Entertainment!* the studio threw a lavish party at the Beverly Wilshire Hotel that was guaranteed to deliver worldwide publicity for the film. A red carpet was extended from the now razed Beverly Theater across Wilshire Boulevard to the hotel a block away.

As an alumnus of several of the picture's movies, including *Seven Brides for Seven Brothers,* Russ Tamblyn was in attendance. The former dancer related, "All the MGM people went up to the ballroom, where tables were set with the names of the stars on little chairs. The tables were in alphabetical order. I sat next to Elizabeth Taylor, Jimmy Stewart, and Johnny Weissmuller [*Tarzan* was an MGM movie series at one time]. There was a moment when we were all called downstairs where Sammy Davis Jr. and Liza Minnelli introduced everybody. We were all standing on the cement stairwell looking downstairs. There must have been about ninety of us.

"Debbie Reynolds said something funny. Howard Keel sang a few notes. All of a sudden you could hear a tapping down there. Gene Kelly started to tap-dance on the stairwell. It was really funny, but the killer that shut everybody up was when Johnny Weissmuller suddenly let out his Tarzan scream. And then Gene got Fred to dance with Ginger Rogers."

For a few moments, a semblance of what the screen's first immortal dance team had created was reborn as they broke into a spirited fox-trot. Time hadn't changed their outward appearance that much. In a nostalgic coincidence, Rogers's multicolored dress was bedecked with feathers. This time, however, they caused no problems while they danced.

HIS STATURE AS THE LEADING STAR of movie musicals led to the "Fred Astaire Salutes the Fox Musicals" special that aired on October 24, 1974. Fred stated that "the key word to Fox musicals is 'variety.'" He emphasized the importance of rehearsal in the creation of great musicals.

The first film clip showed Ethel Merman belting out the title song from *There's No Business Like Show Business,* followed by one of Fred playing drums and then dancing in his only Fox musical, *Daddy Long Legs.* A potpourri of numbers by Jane Russell and Marilyn Monroe in *Gentlemen Prefer Blondes,* Maurice Chevalier with Ann Sothern in *Folies Bergère,* Astaire with Leslie Caron in *Daddy Long Legs,* Carmen Miranda and a group of girl dancers in *The Gang's All Here* (pointing up Busby Berkeley's contributions), and Barbra Streisand and Louis Armstrong in *Hello, Dolly!* were shown. One unusual film clip was of Rita Hayworth and Hermes Pan dancing together in *My Gal Sal* from 1942. Not surprisingly, Pan's dancing style resembled that of Fred Astaire. Astaire explained how important dance duets were to musicals and how the term "choreographer" really started with Agnes de Mille in *Oklahoma!* on Broadway.

Further clips of Sonja Henie, Betty Grable with Jack Haley, Shirley Temple, Janet Gaynor and Charles Farrell, Tony Martin, the Ritz Brothers, Lena Horne, the Nicholas Brothers, Susan Hayward, Martha Raye, and others seemed to belabor rather than highlight the importance of Fox musicals. In reality, they were simply not in the same league as the MGM musicals.

Astaire lamented the demise of the art form by saying, "Musicals have gone through many changes. They've lost their innocence." He closed the hour by giving tributes to Henry and Phoebe Ephron, Jean Negulesco, Johnny Mercer, and Leslie Caron for their work in *Daddy Long Legs.* The "Something's Gotta Give" number from *Daddy Long Legs* with Astaire dancing with the delightful Caron was shown to illustrate his ability as the master of the genre.

THEN IT WAS ONCE AGAIN back to playing a con man, this time in Irwin Allen's *The Towering Inferno,* for Fox. Allen had established himself as the master of the "disaster film" genre. He had most recently scored a substantial hit with *The Poseidon Adventure,* using a lengthy list of name actors that included Carol Lynley.

Astaire explained his raison d'être for continuing to work in films: "Any role I take is nothing I want to lecture about. . . . All that save-the-world jazz . . . I just want to knock 'em in the aisles with a good performance. I don't go for messageville. I always say this is my last picture, though I've been saying that for twenty years."

Fred's role in *The Towering Inferno* was really only an extended cameo. He was seen on camera less than fifteen minutes. This popular, well-produced movie was significant for two reasons: Fred did his last dance scene (albeit briefly) on film, this time with Jennifer Jones, who blended easily with him; and more significant, he was awarded the only Oscar nomination he ever received, for Best Supporting Actor. A performance by a prominent movie name in a splashy big box-office picture sometimes gets unwarranted attention from the Academy, especially when that star has previously been overlooked for Oscar consideration. One might correctly refer to it as a "sympathy nomination."

Allen stuck to his winning formula in *The Towering Inferno*. This time he had the financial backing of two studios, Twentieth Century–Fox and Warners, which provided him with a substantial budget and a long shooting schedule. The leads in the film were Steve McQueen and Paul Newman (each of whom was paid $1 million), along with Faye Dunaway ($100,000), Bill Holden ($200,000), Robert Wagner ($60,000), and Richard Chamberlain ($75,000). Astaire got $50,000. Even O. J. Simpson—as a security man no less!—was paid $30,000.[23] The disaster this time was an out-of-control fire that engulfs a newly constructed luxury apartment building in San Francisco, the tallest building in the world, during its opening-night party.

LYRICIST AL KASHA and his songwriting partner, Joel Hirschhorn, had won their first Oscar in 1973 for "The Morning After," sung by Maureen McGovern over the credits of *The Poseidon Adventure*. It became a #1 record. According to Kasha, they were preceded by nine other songwriting teams in submitting a song for the picture.

Kasha stated, "Johnny Mercer said to me, 'Write the philosophy of a picture. Don't tell the story, like "The Way We Were." ' He said, 'If you were writing that song, you would not say there is a Jewish girl meeting a Protestant boy. Write about the philosophy.' "

During production on *The Towering Inferno,* Kasha and Hirschhorn attended a meeting that also included Astaire and Bob Hastings, another actor in the picture. Not knowing who they were or that they were sitting behind him, Astaire asked, "Who are Kasha and Hirschhorn?" He was informed that they had won the Oscar for the previous Allen movie. Fred declared, "I heard that you were looking for a song. I can write something better than they can. I know I can."

Kasha recalled, "That made Joel and me a little nervous. Hastings explained that they had won the Oscar the previous year. He pointed out, 'Irwin is superstitious. I hear they've written a good song and that Maureen McGovern would sing it,'" whereupon Fred offered to sing it.

Kasha learned that Astaire (presumably with Tommy Wolf) had written a song and had sung it on a demo record. This information came from Lionel Newman, who headed the music department at Fox. Kasha said, "Newman told me, 'It was horrifying. It's just a terrible song. It had nothing to do with the picture.'"

Kasha and Hirschhorn's song "We May Never Love Like This Again" from *The Towering Inferno* won them their second Oscar.

FRED ADMIRED STEVE MCQUEEN'S WORK in *The Towering Inferno.* Fred said, "He was a great guy, Steve. He was a deep son of a gun. How unfortunate that he's no longer around, because he enjoyed himself while he was alive. . . . He was tough, and a bloody good actor when he was right. . . .

"Paul Newman is a rock. Bill [Holden] had been away, and I hadn't seen him for a while. It was great to work with those guys. . . . When you're in the middle of a group with good stuff going on, it's fun."[24]

Astaire's character (appropriately named Harlee Claiborne) was in one of the many horrifying wildfire scenes in the picture. He looked properly disheveled and grimy while dressed in black tie as water cascaded down upon him, causing his toupee to go slightly askew. (Sheila Allen, Irwin's wife, who had a small part in the movie, said Irwin actually directed this scene and several others.) Ava Astaire McKenzie informed me, "He [Fred] just loved this scene. He loved being drenched by that water, probably more than anything that he did in any other movie."

On Academy Awards night, April 8, 1975, Fred escorted Ava to the proceedings. They were seated next to Francis Coppola. Fred's restrained performance in *The Towering Inferno,* with his character ultimately becoming heroic, gave him a relatively good chance to take home the Oscar. This, however, was the year of *Godfather Part II*. Robert De Niro, Michael Gazzo, and Lee Strasberg were all nominated for their performances in arguably the most artistic sequel to a major hit ever produced. Fred's other competition was Jeff Bridges in *Thunderbolt and Lightfoot.* The winner was Robert De Niro. Coppola won as producer, cowriter, and director for *Godfather Part II.* Francis kindly told Fred, "I'm sorry," but Fred wasn't terribly let down. "It's a great compliment to be one of the five," he replied.[25]

As a consolation, he did win a British Academy Award, now known as the

BAFTA Award, as Best Supporting Actor, and a Golden Globe as well in the same category for his performance in *The Towering Inferno.*

WHILE IN LONDON that summer for the recording session that resulted in two albums, along with an album of duets with Bing Crosby, Fred consented to go on the leading English "chat show," hosted by Michael Parkinson. This is surely the best talk show appearance Fred ever made, mostly because of his making several candid admissions.

Backstage, before the show, the host discussed with Astaire his famous walk, which was once referred to as "that jaunty saunter with syncopated springs in the step."[26] He told Fred that John Wayne had said *his* walk was based on Astaire's. While imitating Wayne's and then Astaire's famous gaits, Parkinson fell down a flight of stairs!

At the outset of the show, Parkinson brought out that Astaire didn't enjoy being interviewed. As a result, Fred mentioned that the Hollywood Women's Press Club had once selected him as one of the least cooperative stars in one of its annual polls. In one of the few occasions he ever discussed his days in vaudeville, Fred spoke about the time when a dog act got the star dressing room while he and Dellie had to climb up a ladder to their dressing room.

He sang "A Foggy Day," which revealed that his voice was beginning to fade. He forgot one of the lines of the lyrics, but the rhythmic undercurrent of his singing was still there.

Parkinson spoke glowingly about the rapport Fred and Dellie had established with London audiences in the 1920s. Fred recalled how he couldn't at first understand the way English people talked because they spoke so fast and linked one word onto the next. Moving on to Dellie, he acknowledged that she loved parties and wasn't too concerned with rehearsing. He brought out that on the second night of *Funny Face* on Broadway, she came onstage tipsy. "She had been having a marvelous time. When she came onstage, she began by dancing in the wrong direction." He said that he had to push her around backstage to sober her up. "Her dignity was hurt, but she came back and did fine."

Turning to his film career, he said that in the famous golf dance scene in *Carefree,* he had to flatten his golf swing so that the cameraman could keep the ball in the shot. Taking a respite from discussing his film career, he sang his composition "City of the Angels," as his voice grew noticeably stronger. The small group, led by pianist and organist Harry Stoneham, backed him quite effectively. He said he was flattered that Mel Tormé, Frank Sinatra, and Tony Bennett had admired his singing, along with various jazz musicians, and appreciated the way composers liked the way he interpreted their songs.

Watching the film clip of the "Puttin' On The Ritz" number from *Blue Skies,* it was interesting how the camera angle elongated his slight frame. He mentioned how worried he was about the special effects in this memorable scene. He revealed that a technician was assigned to press a button to get the cane, which was embedded in the floor, to spring into his hands in sync.

Seeing the hat-rack dance again in *Royal Wedding,* he said he was surprised "at about a third of it." During Parkinson's interview, Fred's innate shyness, his prudishness, and the lack of warmth in his personality came through. These were prime ingredients that prevented him from coming across in a talk show format.

Ava was brought out by Parkinson to join them. It was her first time on camera. She told of her lyric contribution to "I Love Everybody," which Fred had just sung. She said she had never had any ambition to be a performer. Fred made it clear that he never wanted his children to become performers.

After Fred sang "A Fine Romance," when asked what her favorite numbers of her father's were, Ava said, "A Foggy Day," "One for My Baby," and "By Myself." As the credits rolled, Fred and Ava lovingly held hands.

DURING THE 1970S, soap operas became an important ingredient in pop culture, partly through the work of the resourceful producer Gloria Monty, who helped make *General Hospital* such a sensation. Fred and his mother, Ann Astaire, were very tuned in to this craze. They spent considerable time watching soap operas together. Their favorite shows were *As the World Turns* and *Guiding Light.*[27] Dellie had also become addicted to soap operas. They would seriously discuss the turn of events on the shows through daily phone calls. When he traveled, Fred was always intent on finding out just what had taken place on his favorite shows during his absence.

Unbeknownst to most people, Fred had also become a devotee of the syndicated TV show *Soul Train.* It gave him a thorough indoctrination into the dances of young people with a concentration on rhythm 'n' blues performers. But, in addition, it gave him a spirited workout as he danced to the contemporary music featured on the show.[28]

All of this frivolous activity appears symptomatic of an artist who was bored and lonely and whose only real solace came from his work. During the week in which he and Gene Kelly cohosted *The Mike Douglas Show,* out of nowhere he brought up how much he missed Phyllis. Her loss would never go away.

On July 26, 1975, Ann Geilus Astaire (Austerlitz) died of a stroke at the age of ninety-six. She had been a widow for fifty-one years. During her last years, she split her time between her New York apartment and Fred's home.

Two years earlier, Ann had fallen off a chair while examining some curtains that she felt needed replacing. She broke her hip, a serious injury for any elderly person. After pins were placed in her hip, the injury never healed correctly. She had had to use a walker, which annoyed her tremendously.[29]

Stanley Donen recalled, "One night, I went up to Fred's house to collect him and to go out to dinner. He said, 'Hold on, I'm just going to kiss my mother good-night.' Fred was then seventy-six."[30]

To the end, Ann was an important presence in her son's life. She continued to advise him on career decisions, whether he liked it or not. Visitors to their San Ysidro Drive residence were forever amazed by her beauty and dignity. No better tribute to her staggering importance in the life of her "Sonny" could be given than that of Stanley Green and Burt Goldblatt on the dedication page to their invaluable anthology, *Starring Fred Astaire*: "For Ann Geilus Astaire, who knew before anyone else."

Ann's death occurred during the midst of Fred's recording sessions with Bing Crosby in London. He didn't return home. Once again, he realized the show must go on. She was buried in the Astaire family plot at the Oakwood Memorial Park in Chatsworth, California.

Fred closed out 1975 with "Merry Christmas from the Crosbys" on CBS, in which he costarred with Bing and Bing's new family. Once again, the natural charm long displayed by the veteran troupers resulted in an easygoing hour. The producing team of Gary Smith and Dwight Hemion had already established themselves as old masters at this kind of variety show.

THAT'S ENTERTAINMENT!—produced by Jack Haley Jr. and executive-produced by Dan Melnick—was an unexpectedly huge hit for MGM, becoming the ninth-biggest-grossing film in its history. The studio vaults held many more sterling musical scenes to make up a sequel. Ergo, *That's Entertainment, Part II*. It wasn't difficult for Dan Melnick, the film's coproducer, along with Saul Chaplin, to get Gene Kelly to agree to appear with Astaire as essentially interlocutors in the movie. They introduced all of the segments instead of having many presenters as in the first film. Leonard Gershe wrote their narration.

Melnick, the veteran producer, said, "I went to Gene and said, 'You've get to do this,' and Gene went to Fred." Astaire agreed, but he had one stipulation: There was to be no dancing. Strangely enough, neither of the dance immortals was paid anything but Screen Actors Guild scale for their significant contributions to the movie. An additional payment in their names was donated to the Motion Picture Home.

One day, while rehearsing with Fred and Gene, Saul Chaplin watched as Fred suggested to Gene, "Don't you think we can do sixteen bars of dancing here?" "Both Gene and I were astonished and delighted," Chaplin said. "I just sat at the piano and stared straight ahead, hoping against hope that he wouldn't change his mind. In the film there are three or four scenes where they danced, and it was at Fred's suggestion."[31]

Making use of a mix-and-match format, following film footage of Gene performing "Be a Clown" with Judy Garland from *The Pirate,* Fred danced to the Cole Porter tune. After a clip of Astaire and Garland performing the title song from *Easter Parade,* Gene danced to a song called "Color Change," and later Gene did a solo dance to "Be a Clown." Astaire and Kelly collaborated on three Arthur Schwartz songs: "Shubert Alley," "Cartoon Sequence," and the film's finale, a new version of "That's Entertainment," with new lyrics by Howard Dietz. As the two danced across the screen, they were dressed in matching suits and derbies.

Kelly choreographed and directed their various song-and-dance spots. Fred later reflected, "He's a very hard worker, Gene. There was no monkeying around, like 'That's good enough for them.' He was very diligent about being on time and working in between shots. I used to say, 'Direct me! Go ahead and direct me.' He is a damned good director."[32]

In spite of the on- and offscreen chemistry between the aging dance masters, it was obvious they were well past their prime. The spirit was willing but their agility was sorely missing from the great days of yore. The director, Greg Garrison, who had directed both of them in television specials in the 1960s and admired them both, perhaps expressed it most succinctly when he said, "They couldn't hit the curveball any longer." Garrison also contended that while Astaire was precise as a singer, Kelly better captured the feeling of a song.

That time had taken its toll didn't seem to affect the public's enjoyment of *That's Entertainment, Part II.* This time Fred commented on film clips of his singing "That's Entertainment" (from *The Band Wagon*), singing and dancing "All of You" with Cyd Charisse (from *Silk Stockings*), "I Wanna Be a Dancin' Man" (from *The Belle of New York*), singing and dancing "A Couple of Swells" with Judy Garland as well as "Easter Parade," and "Steppin' Out with My Baby" (from *Easter Parade*), and "Bouncin' the Blues" (from *The Barkleys of Broadway*), in addition to his singing a duet with Red Skelton in *Three Little Words.*

"Gene and Fred had become very, very close in those years," said Dan Melnick.

"Gene would pick up Fred to have dinner because Fred had gotten very frail and didn't like driving at night. Gene was devoted to him and certainly did everything to make the songs not only capable of Fred's range, but also comfortable so that there was no strain. It was very sweet to see him almost at the seat of the master. He respected him because he knew he had led the way. He would lead him on like saying, 'Fred, tell Dan about . . .'"

Essentially, Astaire and Kelly were running the movie. Melnick as coproducer did everything a smart producer does to keep his stars happy. "I really made a point of getting very close to Fred during that period because I wanted him to feel comfortable enough to tell me if something was bothering him.

"I can remember one afternoon when Fred called me in my office at the studio and asked me, 'Are you going to be down here this afternoon?' and I said, 'Sure.' Every disaster scenario was going through my head. I went down, and he pulled me to his dressing room, which was a trailer set up off the set. He said, 'Now in this last sequence, should I wear this floral or this floral?' When I was a kid, I used to try and hold my pants up with neckties the way he did, and he's asking me a sartorial opinion!"

A screening of the final cut of the movie was held on the MGM lot for the studio employees. Melnick made sure that Jim Aubrey, who ran the studio, and whose reign was partly responsible for the continuing downfall of MGM, attended the screening. Aubrey had opposed the picture from the beginning. The response to the screening was overwhelmingly favorable, but Aubrey was still unconvinced, saying, "Sell it to television." Melnick went above Aubrey and approached Kirk Kerkorian, who for a few decades alternately bought and sold the studio. Kerkorian fortunately gave the proverbial green light for its release.

Based on the box-office performance of the original movie, a heavily increased publicity budget was assigned to *That's Entertainment, Part II.* In the campaign to sell the picture, Fred and Gene cohosted *The Mike Douglas Show,* on a visit to Hollywood from its base in Philadelphia, to do a week of shows stocked with former MGM stars.

Vince Calandra, who can boast of a fifty-year career in television production, was then a talent coordinator on the Douglas show. Calandra said, "I can still remember that when we went up to Fred's house to discuss what he is going to do on the show, he wore a blue shirt with an ascot under a blue cashmere sweater, slacks, and loafers with no socks." Accompanying Calandra were the show's bandleader, Joe Massimino, and Woody Fraser, the executive producer. Woody started the conversation with Astaire by saying how much he loved his performance in "Singin' in the Rain." Astaire politely offered, "I don't recall being in that movie."

On one of the Douglas shows, which took place outdoors on the MGM lot, Ava Astaire McKenzie was introduced by Mike Douglas, whereupon Fred explained again that Ava had helped him write the lyrics to "I Love Everybody"—"I love to rock / I love to swing / I love Alice Cooper / I love Madam Nu" [the Dragon Lady, the wife of the premier of South Vietnam]. Fred sang his song the way it deserved to be sung, with a decided verve.

After the taping of the final Douglas show, *Los Angeles Times* reporter Sally Davis wanted to get some comments from Astaire. An MGM publicist advised her, "Fred doesn't want to talk to anybody—he's had it." Astaire, later in the evening, explained his lack of enthusiasm by telling Davis, "Nostalgia is just not my bag. I live for today." Speaking of *That's Entertainment, Part II,* he said, "I'm glad people enjoyed it, but it didn't mean anything to me. I was a tap dancer then, and that's past. I don't do that anymore. You won't catch me with my feet in the sandbox again."[33]

Fred cheered up a bit when he was a guest on *The Tonight Show* on May 4, 1976. The Astaire/Kelly team again worked in tandem selling the movie. When Fred was introduced, he described Gene's and his dancing in the movie as "we were [just] trying to kid around." He then jokingly made the point of how difficult Gene was to work with. Their good-natured bantering could have been much more effective given two seasoned and witty veterans of the talk show circuit. The combination of Astaire and Kelly obviously didn't measure up in that area, however.

They relished their newfound attention from young people. On the eve of the picture's world premiere Fred remarked, "The kids get a crush on you, and they don't accept that you're old enough to be their grandfather or older. They see you in your old numbers and think you haven't gotten any older." About dancing, he said, "I can still do a lot of things. I could do a back out, but I'm afraid to. I don't want to throw myself out of gear."[34]

To keep the ballyhoo going, a contingent comprising Fred and Ava Astaire, Cary Grant, Gene Kelly, Kathryn Grayson, Marge Champion, Cyd Charisse, Johnny Weissmuller, and Saul Chaplin were brought to New York for the world premiere at the Ziegfeld Theatre. At the party following the premiere on May 9, 1976, the day before his seventy-seventh birthday, Fred blew out the candles on a huge cake.[35]

"I was Fred's seat partner at the Ziegfeld Theatre that night," Marge Champion remembered. "What I was most impressed with was when Gene Kelly was on the screen and did something, Fred muttered to himself—I don't think that he even thought that I heard him—but he was talking about how wonderful Gene was and how free and easy he was. When *he* came on the screen, he said things like 'Why don't you wipe that smile off your face.' He was putting himself down in the most astonishing way. How could this be happening when we all worshipped him!"

The next day the group flew to Cannes, where they were joined by French residents Leslie Caron and Georges Guétary. The film was shown at the 1976 Cannes Film Festival as the opening-night attraction.

Dan Melnick recalled, "It was about an eleven-hour flight. All of us were wearing sweats or whatever. Fred and Cary Grant, impeccably dressed—not a crease on them when they got off. Every reporter in the world was there when we unloaded on the tarmac at Nice Airport."

According to Rex Reed, at the party after the premiere of *That's Entertainment, Part II* at Cannes, "I said to him, like everybody else in the world, I've always wanted to dance with Fred Astaire. I mean, who doesn't? It's everybody's dream. He said, 'Well, it's never too late.' He said, 'Let's go around the floor.' I said, 'Well, the only problem is I only know how to lead.' And then he said, 'Well, I can tell you right now, after all those years of dancing with Ginger Rogers, I know how to follow. You lead, I'll follow.' All those people were watching, but no photographer. This was truly one of my great memories." Reed continued, "For him, it was never about the business, the art, the love, the camaraderie, the community. It was never about any of that. He worked very hard and expected everybody else to work very hard. And when he wasn't working, he went to the racetrack and was lonely. . . . I don't understand how a man can give so much of himself, and yet really be so unlike what he was giving to the world. The remoteness, the aloofness, seemed to carry through every aspect of his life."

AFTER THREE BOX-OFFICE HITS in a row that included an Oscar nomination, Fred's movie career was in the midst of a major revival. All of that went by the wayside in 1976 when he accepted the role of Daniel Hughes, a forlorn Bible-quoting ex-convict living in a decrepit trailer, devoted to training a pack of faithful Doberman pinschers, in *The Amazing Dobermans,* a Walt Disney release. Shot in Simi Valley, its low budget of $900,000 showed. Preceding it had been *The Doberman Gang* and *The Daring Dobermans,* both of which were profitable. *The Amazing Dobermans* wasn't.

The leads in the film were Barbara Eden, James Franciscus, and Jack Carter in a cheesy plot invoking a group of swindlers who almost succeed in taking over a circus only to have the reformed Hughes and his dogs save the day. Fred was quoted as saying, "They kept offering me sick old men. I won't play those kinds of people. . . . I enjoyed [*Dobermans*] probably more than any other picture."[36]

But he also said, "I can't think of a picture I ever regretted. I'm kind of stuck on this business," at a Disney luncheon given for the press at a Hollywood restaurant at which he shared the dais with Eden and Franciscus.

The only possible explanation for his appearing in this film was that this was a "family movie" and it would appeal to his grandchildren. He had previously been quoted as hating cruelty and violence in movies.[37] By this time, Freddie had three children, Peter three, and Ava two stepsons.[38] In his role in *The Amazing Dobermans,* he displayed genuine vulnerability, yet at times his inborn debonair quality got in the way.

The day after the film completed shooting Fred had the accident on a skateboard in his driveway and broke his left wrist. He had learned how to skateboard from watching his grandson Frederick, Freddie's son.[39] He was incapacitated for six weeks with his arm in a sling. The story of his injury was picked up by the wire services and was published in newspapers internationally.[40]

IN 1977, the lure of acting in a film in the western part of Ireland, near where Ava and Richard were living in Cork, caused Fred to accept the role of Dr. Scully in screenwriter and director Yves Boisset's *Un Taxi Mauve* (*The Purple Taxi*). His first line in the movie was, aptly, "I'm ageless. Everyone knows that," providing a perfect description of his role as the village doctor in a coastal town. Boisset's witty, sometimes shocking dialogue and brisk direction established the characters right away, photographed against a succession of picturesque landscapes with local charm. Interviewed on location, Fred said he was at a loss to explain much of the script. "I still don't know why the hell my character drives this purple taxi. By the way, did you know that purple is quite an Irish color? . . . While I've been here, I've bought a lot of purple neckties. You can't find them elsewhere."

He blanched at the writer Helen Lawrenson's profile of him that had run recently in *Esquire.* The veteran magazine writer had depicted Astaire as reticent and morose, snapping out angry monosyllables in answer to her questions. The ire in Lawrenson's article caused Fred to write the magazine's well-remembered editor, Harold Hayes. Astaire inquired why an interviewer with a drinking problem was let loose on him. In her piece, Lawrenson had mentioned that he never offered her a drink when she came to his home for the interview. He also complained that she had done little research on his childhood and speculated in her article that

Ann Astaire must have been a tough lady. Fred remarked, "If we hadn't lost her, boy, she'd have said to me, 'Sonny, don't let her get away with that.' "[41]

THE PURPLE TAXI got limited American distribution, which, in spite of its lack of commercial appeal, was too bad because it has some of Astaire's best acting. The disjointed plot was a brave attempt to show a group of people running away from their past. Charlotte Rampling's performance, which owed its inspiration to Lauren Bacall, carried the picture. Having Rampling and Philippe Noiret playing lovers was rather ridiculous. Several times, Peter Ustinov did the kind of scene-stealing that was long a trademark of his work. Astaire's last line in the movie, "Ireland offers a lush, seductive setting," supplied the essence of the film.

WHILE FILMING THE PURPLE TAXI, Fred had been quoted as saying, "I have no great ambition to hang on forever by my ears." After starring in two successive failed projects, he waited for the right vehicle. It was *A Family Upside Down,* billed as an "NBC Big Event." It was produced by Ross Hunter, who had been responsible for, among other films, the hugely successful Doris Day/Rock Hudson comedies and the *Airport* movies.

Michael Black, a former attorney, had begun representing Astaire at ICM after the retirement of Shep Fields, the onetime bandleader, known for his "Rippling Rhythm," who was the brother of Freddie Fields. Black's feeling was, "With all the things in which I was involved with him, I think the one that he was proudest of was *A Family Upside Down,* with Helen Hayes—and not because he won an Emmy Award. He told me, 'My mother would be so proud of me that I worked opposite Helen Hayes.' To him, she was this major, major actress, and the idea that he didn't have to dance but was cast as a dramatic actor was very important." As Black observed about Astaire's look in the film, "No one wears a cardigan sweater like Fred Astaire. Even with the wardrobe, they made him blue-collar and older than Helen, but he still had style." Black's comment had real validity, and at moments there was more than a trace of Fred's famous walk. More important, again his unmistakable brand of elegance seemed to occasionally get in the way of making him completely believable as a retired housepainter.

Hunter remembered, "One afternoon, I left the script off at Fred's home. He called me at one in the morning, saying, 'It's wonderful, but I've got dozens of questions to ask you.' We met the next day, and Fred was prepared with the script pages marked. We went over his questions one by one. . . . We talked for four hours, and at the end Fred agreed to do the movie."[42]

Fred insisted, however, on a week of rehearsal before shooting began. When he arrived for the first rehearsal, he had no reason to look at his script. He had memorized all his lines.[43] Helen Hayes, who could always be counted on to deliver an understated performance when the role called for it, was cast first. She played Astaire's devoted wife. "Fred was amazing," said Hayes, "After we started filming, he once stopped a scene because I had changed one word of dialogue." She reminisced about having had a date with Fred when she was starring on Broadway in *Coquette* and Leland Hayward was their mutual agent. Fred and Dellie were then appearing in one hit after another. "We went dancing at the Palais Royal. It's peculiar, but Fred never asked me to go dancing again."

Efrem Zimbalist Jr. recalled, "Ross Hunter called me about the movie. I had met Helen many times in New York. Astaire and I had never met, though. I had been [seated] near him at the Emmys." Zimbalist played Astaire's son in *A Family Upside Down,* who had to look after him while simultaneously being immersed in serious problems with his wife and son. Indeed it was "a family upside down." Zimbalist noted, "I always said you could count the roles that are outstanding on one hand. This was a lovely piece.

"I can remember that during rehearsal Fred would talk to the director, David Rich, and always refer to the character by saying, 'He would do this' and 'He says this,' rather than 'I should move here'—whatever it was, which sort of startled me. I hadn't heard that in years. I must say he had a wonderful sense of timing, and he knew to deliver a punch line." Zimbalist also noticed, "Fred liked and really opened up to the kid [Brad Rearden], who played my son and his grandson. The kid could ask him any question, and he would answer. That's how we found out about his life through the way he related to him. He had no idea how great he was. I mean, if he did, he didn't want to talk about it. He meant an awful lot in my life. I went to Yale and got thrown out twice. . . . I dressed like him, and I did a tap-dance thing at the theater in New Haven for a commercial for a milk company. I was convinced that I was Fred Astaire. . . . I must say he was the most stylish guy that ever came to Hollywood."

Gerald Di Pego, who wrote the teleplay, said that Ross Hunter originally approached him to develop a love story for a couple in their waning years. "I thought about that and came up with the premise for *A Family Upside Down,* based on how aging and illness can turn lives upside down so that the children take over the parenting role while the parents are losing their independence and struggling with this [problem]. It was about the importance of the quality of life over the quantity of life." For 1977, this kind of fare was certainly a departure from the television norm.

Di Pego said, "Ross delivered that wonderful cast that also included Patty

Duke and Pat Crowley. He even got Henry Mancini to score it. Fred was serious about his work, and he didn't want people to make a fuss about him. 'I'm just a crabby old guy from Nebraska,' he'd say. I never did see him crabby, though, but he could be kind of a shy loner."

An example of Fred's crabby behavior did take place during a photo session he had with Hayes. The photographer asked him to lean in closer to her. "I will not," he snapped. "You don't have to hang all over someone you love. I've always hated those photos. I think they're phony. These are two people who love each other deeply and have been married a long time, but they don't always display it. I don't like to see overt displays of affection, even among young people. It's in bad taste."[44]

FRED AND HAYES SANG Fred's 1956 composition, "Hello Baby," together while driving, which, from the start of the movie, established their closeness as a couple. Shortly after getting out of their car, Fred suffers a heart attack. The panic and bewilderment he portrayed on the screen showed real insight into what happens to a senior citizen who can no longer fend for himself and must depend on his children. The frustration of his having to move away from his beloved wife to a nursing home and to adjust was touchingly directed by David Rich.

Fred's character tells the attending doctor how he feels as if he had been in heaven but "a voice said, 'You're in the wrong place.'" It is then that Astaire's character suddenly related to his grandson. Hayes's way of expressing sentiment and tenderness toward Astaire is truly extraordinary. At the end of the story, she provides hope that her husband will survive. Throughout the drama, her underplaying helps keep the focus on Astaire.

Di Pego recalled, "I was on set the day we filmed the scene where his family takes him out of the rest home for a picnic in the park. The shot I remember so well is Fred leaving the car and walking, with the help of a cane and, I think, the boy playing his grandson, toward a tree where they were going to sit in the shade. He was acting quite frail because his character had had a heart attack. We got the shot, and the director said, 'Cut,' and that's when the magic happened.

"It was all very natural. On the cut, Fred straightened up and began to walk unaided and normally toward the tree for the next scene. Absently, as he walked, he began to twirl the cane. Nobody moved. The cast, the crew, we didn't look at each other, we just became very still, and we watched him. I'm still feeling emotional about it.

"What we were watching was history, his and ours, too. We were watching an icon, someone who had gotten inside of us and stayed there and was still there and still giving us his gift, just a glimpse of it, but reminding us, and showing just how deep the feelings were for this man. Image, dream that was Fred Astaire. It was just a moment and then gone, but I'll never forget it."

A Family Upside Down received five Emmy nominations. Astaire won Outstanding Lead Actor in a Drama or Comedy Special. He told the adoring audience, "My gosh, I never dreamed of this." Although Helen Hayes, Efrem Zimbalist Jr., and Patty Duke were also nominated, they failed to win.

EVEN AFTER AN ARTISTIC TRIUMPH like this, it was not easy for Michael Black to deliver good scripts to Astaire. Age was still the defining factor. Fred was also very definite about what he would and wouldn't do.

Black recalled, "He would say, 'I don't think that's for me!' If I said, 'They'll tailor it more for you and listen to you about what you don't like about it. I think you should be open to meet about it,' he still would not move off about it. He didn't want to live in the past. The opportunity to spend three months in Bora-Bora didn't appeal to him, which caused him to turn down the *Hurricane* that starred Mia Farrow. [Max von Sydow took the role.]

"The most telling thing that I learned," Black maintained, "was that he didn't have a secretary to handle the amount of fan mail that he got. Maybe his business manager's secretary would help him go over that stuff, but I ended up many times going up to his house with a box of mail to go over. I know he didn't like it when people asked him to send an autographed picture and they didn't include it in the mail. But if they included a self-addressed envelope and a picture, he would do it. He didn't keep pictures to give away.

"Even though he must have been in the house the entire day, he was always dressed great. He was a link to Hollywood that made me want to work there. I always laughed because he would cross his feet, and I would see the bottom of his shoes. It looked like the shoes were new. The only thing worn was on its toes.

"He didn't have a screening room in his home. Apparently, he went to the movies many times in the afternoon in Westwood. If the movie he saw was interesting, he would ask me questions about it. He wondered if certain things were true, like 'Is it true so-and-so is really making that much money for a movie?' He thought that the money he was hearing about that certain stars were making was unfathomable because when he had all that creative control and was one of the first to have 'pocket participation,' he wasn't as interested in the money as he was in demanding rehearsal time. That was more important to him."

SINCE FRED WAS RECEIVING so many honors during the 1970s, colleges and universities wanted to award him honorary degrees. This meant that he would have to show up to receive them, which he wouldn't do. Black remembered, "He laughed at those doctorate titles. I think Shep had gotten him an endorsement for a Cadillac. He liked that." Other requests for his endorsement included writing the foreword for several books, which he also declined to do.

On February 4, 1978, he attended a dinner honoring his NBC specials, given by the Academy of Television Arts and Sciences. His acceptance speech was brief: "I'm getting too old for this kind of thing. Thank you very much." The same year at a Century Plaza Hotel ceremony he accepted the National Artist Award from the American National Theatre and Academy.[45] It had previously been given to Broadway theatrical personalities such as Helen Hayes, the Lunts, and Katharine Cornell, among others.[46] But as Michael Black made clear, Fred didn't like being honored with a dinner. "He didn't like to be put upon and to have to sit there and be lauded." He turned down the AFI Life Achievement Award on that basis.

One afternoon, Fred called Black and said, "I would like you to come over. I want you to meet a friend of mine, Robyn Smith. She is here, and we have rabbits. They're just the cutest. Come over and have a drink."

"When I would come over to go over some things, Robyn would walk in. She knew it was business and wouldn't ask to be part of the meeting. She would walk through the house with the rabbit or do something or [say] 'I am going out for a ride' or 'Have fun.' He seemed *happy* with Robyn. No question. So that was very nice, very lovely. He would never share with me what he was doing socially, you know. He was old-school that way."

IN 1977, *Saturday Night Fever,* starring John Travolta with a score by the Bee Gees, brought a new dance craze to the screen: disco.

Overnight, white suits were suddenly in vogue, and musicals started being made again. Travolta starred in *Grease,* another big hit, followed by *Staying Alive,* which also highlighted Bee Gees songs. After that came *The Wiz, Thank God It's Friday, Can't Stop the Music, Grease 2,* and *Xanadu,* the latter in which Gene Kelly was tragically cast opposite Olivia Newton-John. The interest in musicals soon ended.[47]

The disco wave didn't at first wash with Astaire. "I was dancing like that years ago, you know," sniffed Fred. "Disco is jitterbug. It's not new. It's a combination of all the free-form dances—the kind where you don't have to work out a routine or, indeed, even find yourself a partner." Astaire was similarly underwhelmed by John Travolta. "What he did in those movie dance scenes was very attractive," allowed Astaire. "But basically, he's not a dancer."[48]

But Fred changed his mind about Travolta. They first met when Astaire telephoned him in 1979, after Travolta was nominated for a Golden Globe Award for his work in *Saturday Night Fever.* Astaire presented the award to him the night he won, and they had dinner shortly thereafter. This was also the first night that the gossip columnists took notice of Fred and Robyn being together.

John soon met Gene Kelly and learned that Fred and Gene were quite taken with him and referred to him as the Kid. "They were worried that no one was going to take the torch to keep that aspect of film alive and continue doing it at the level they had done it, meaning with the ballet behind it" was the way John described it.

Travolta continued, "After *Saturday Night Fever* and *Grease,* I went up to Fred's house. I met Robyn. She was lovely. I looked at the studio in the attic. I was invited to go and dance there. I also danced with Gene on occasion, and we would fool around and try to figure out some things.

"Fred had an effortlessness and elegant style that I admired. Gene Kelly in *American in Paris* had a power that I really liked. And I feel I combine the two in my work. If you looked at the walk down the street [in *Saturday Night Fever*] you'd say, 'This is more like Fred Astaire would be, yeah.' If you look at the solo dance, you'd say, 'It's more like Gene Kelly would do it.' The last dance in the movie where I was wearing a white suit and a black shirt, that was more like Fred."

Travolta found Fred "a man of thought and few words but tremendous care, responsibility, and thoughtfulness. I felt good being around him—comfortable, curious, and honored. He was reaching to spend time with me, so why would I misinterpret the quietness.

"He said that when he first saw my walk coming down the street, he immediately thought that would be the way he would have done it. And when I won the Oscar, I wore a white scarf. . . . He was impressed by that, saying that that was something he would have worn. I may have been inspired by both of these fabulous talents, but these two things weren't calculated. I got the walk from the school I went to in New Jersey that was more than fifty percent African-American."

In the summer of 2007, Travolta scored again as a dancer, only this time in drag, playing the chubby mother of a spirited teenager in the film musical *Hairspray,* which was adapted from the hit Broadway show. There was even a Fred and

Ginger number, which Travolta danced with Christopher Walken, who was also a trained dancer.

Travolta said he enjoyed discussing the strenuous preparation required for a dancing role. He paid tribute to the influence of Jack Cole on his dancing. "The guy never got the credit he deserved. Both Fred and Gene had done movies where they combined ballet and Jack Cole style. I did an homage to him in *Staying Alive*. I have a pride, and when you had people like Fred Astaire and Gene Kelly watching, you wanted to make sure you were good. They were primarily dancers, and I was primarily an actor who had a special talent for dancing, so I had to work that much harder."

I asked Travolta, "What do you think is the most important thing Fred Astaire gave to the dance in America?" He replied, "For me, it was for the first time an invitation to watch a man dance. And he inspired a man to want to dance, meaning that dancing always looked other than tribal—Scottish and English tribal dancing was always excepted—but a man in contemporary times, dancing in elegant ways, whether it was ballroom, jazz, or whatever, was looked at as not something you would be drawn towards. So he was an icon for people saying, 'I want to dance like Fred Astaire.'"

I mentioned that everybody thought he or she could be Fred Astaire. Travolta replied, "They wanted to be. They did the same with me when they watched *Saturday Night Fever*. They said, 'I want to be like John Travolta,' so it's an important thing because it moved men into an arena where they wouldn't normally go, and it made women happier because they want to dance with their man. And it makes it seem possible to do that. So I think what is important about Fred Astaire is that he has opened the door not just for other performers, but for the public to enjoy men dancing. And woman mainly would also enjoy it. It opened two audiences up."

EVEN FRED WAS TEMPTED by the disco craze. In 1979, an offer came in for Fred to appear as "special guest star" on the ABC-TV series *Battlestar Galactica*. Black suggested Fred shouldn't do it, but he said, "Mike, I like that show." It was another bow to his grandchildren, who watched the show. He costarred opposite Anne Jeffreys. Miriam Nelson, the well-regarded choreographer, who was married for several years to Gene Nelson, the dancing star of Warners' 1950s musicals, was signed to create a dance routine for the two.

Jeffreys accepted the role, which was relatively small, purely because "I always said I wanted to do something with Fred Astaire. I told the writer Don Bellisario that I would do it just so I could dance with Fred."

The two veteran stars, as a prince and a princess from another planet, first appeared as seatmates on the spaceship. Fred looked rather bizarre in an ascot (probably his suggestion), a vest, and space costume, which Anne Jeffreys described as a "modern student prince." The multiplotted episode once again found him in his by now patented role as a con man. After getting off the spaceship, Astaire and Jeffreys headed for a discotheque (very 1970s).

Jeffreys recalled, "At the discotheque, Fred was worried because we hadn't really rehearsed. I said, 'Fred, what's to rehearse? We do this, and we do that, and that's it.' And then he said, 'Well, uh . . . uh . . . I don't really want anybody to see my feet. I don't want to dance with my feet, and they'll expect a big dance number, and I don't want to do that because there isn't time to rehearse."

Miriam Nelson, Jeffreys's longtime friend, came to the rescue. Nelson said, "Well, now, we have a problem. I have an idea. You're on a dance floor at a discotheque." She moved the dance and the other dancers around them so that the camera would shoot Astaire and Jeffreys from the waist up or the chin up. She came up with what she called "handies" for the two actors to do things with their hands while they were talking, standing still, with just a movement of the hips, shoulders, and then hands. Fred quickly interjected, "I don't understand this."

Jeffreys saw how uncomfortable he was, noting, "He did not instantly remember something. It had to be rehearsed, rehearsed, and rehearsed." She said to him, "Fred, it's almost like patty-cake—right hand—clap—touch—down—left hand—right hand." Nelson went over it with Fred again. Finally, Fred caught on and said, "Oh, well, yeah, that will be okay." But as Jeffreys pointed out, "It was not within his realm of dancing."

"IF HE HAD PURSUED ME, I probably wouldn't have been attracted to him," Robyn Smith told Bob Thomas. "It was meant to happen because the last thing on *my* mind was wanting to get married. I had an open mind about it; I was hoping that I wouldn't get through my whole life without getting married. But if I never married, it wouldn't have bothered me."[49]

"My career was dwindling because I was getting older and finding it difficult to get good mounts. I had gone beyond the stage of getting a thrill by riding anything, because I had ridden good horses. The timing [for marriage] was good. It couldn't possibly have happened ten years before, when all I could think about was horses."[50]

"It got so I was spending a lot of money going out to California to see Fred. I'd have to be back for riding a day later, two days at the most. I was traveling out and back, staying in the best hotels and getting first-class service. I was doing it every other week. I think we both knew it was serious right away, almost. I told

Fred I liked him very, very much, and once he found that out, he started pursuing [me] a little bit."[51]

Hoagy Bix Carmichael remembered speaking to Astaire on the telephone one day in the late 1970s while visiting Los Angeles. "We had a casual conversation. All of a sudden he said, 'Hoagy, I am dating Robyn Smith.' . . . Maybe he was trying to tell me that he was probably going to get married. It was pretty obvious to me that life was again getting hard for him."

Robyn Smith was born on August 14, 1942 (rather than 1944 as she later said), as Melody Dawn Constance Palm in San Francisco. Her father was Bill Palm, and her mother was Constance Palm, then on her fourth marriage, who had already given birth to three other children.[52]

At the age of four, Melody suffered from erysipelas and was placed in a nursery along with her stepbrother, Fred. She was sent to the foster home of an Oregon lumberman named Orville Smith and his wife, Jane. Melody then became Caroline Smith. After a lengthy custody battle involving her mother, the Smiths, and Catholic Charities, Melody was returned to her original mother, who had married her fifth husband, Hartley Gordon. Shortly thereafter, Gordon died, and Caroline was sent to live with Frank Kucera and his wife in Gresham, Oregon.[53]

Caroline adopted the first name of Robyn when she moved to Hollywood after graduating from high school in Oregon. For six years she tried unsuccessfully to make it as an actress. For a while, she was enrolled at the workshop conducted by Columbia Pictures. She had an important benefactor in a significant 1960s Hollywood player, producer Martin Ransohoff, the president of Filmways. Ransohoff put her under contract to Filmways.[54]

Contrary to the biography that was submitted to the sportswriter Frank Deford, Robyn never majored in English, class of 1966, at Stanford University (nor did she ever attend Stanford or any other college). She blamed this error on an MGM publicist, but she had never worked at MGM.[55]

She never expressed any serious interest in animals, much less racehorses, until a man she was dating took her to Santa Anita for a day at the races. This inspired her to begin spending time around the Santa Anita stables. There she met a trainer named Bruce Headley, who allowed her to work with his horses during the morning at Santa Anita before she drove into Los Angeles to attend acting school.

Kjill Quale, a horse owner, gave her her first mount, Swift Yorky, on April 3, 1969, at Golden Gate Park near San Francisco. Gifted with the ability of a natural athlete and a tall, lanky body, she trained religiously to get down to and maintain a proper jockey's weight. Riding horses suddenly became what she was always meant to do with her young life.[56]

Looking back upon these years, one can scarcely miss Robyn's pattern of attaching herself to influential men who could help further her career, who were much older than she was. In the case of Fred Astaire, he at least shared a genuine passion for the sport of kings.

Underlying her hard-working quest to succeed was a woman who demanded that the world recognize her on her own terms. It is my feeling that an underlying sadness, a deep personal hurt, appears to stem from her years as a foster child, which has greatly influenced her life to the present in her steadfast decisions, sure that her way is the only way.

THE FIRST KENNEDY CENTER HONORS—"A Celebration of the Performing Arts"— were bestowed upon Marian Anderson, Fred Astaire, George Balanchine, Richard Rodgers, and Arthur Rubinstein in November 1978 and were seen on CBS. It has become the equivalent of a command performance by the queen of England.

Fred looked proud yet was still his usual reserved self at the White House when President Jimmy Carter hosted a reception for the nominees. To open the program at the Kennedy Center, José Ferrer quoted the novelist John O'Hara, who had said of Astaire, "He has the self-confidence of a lion tamer."

The debonair Douglas Fairbanks Jr., sporting a Palm Beach tan, called Astaire "an old and valuable friend." The camera caught Fred wearing sunglasses, to hide his feelings, while listening to the plaudits. Ginger Rogers, looking very blond, was spotted in the audience. A montage of the usual clips—"Top Hat," "Puttin' On The Ritz," "The Girl Hunt" ballet from *The Band Wagon,* and "Cheek to Cheek"—were interspersed with photos of Fred and Adele.

At the completion of the presentation, Fred stood bashfully, this time without his sunglasses, to bask in the thunderous ovation from the audience. But there was more: a contingent of dancers dressed in the gold costumes from *A Chorus Line,* the Broadway show he had seen and admired, sang specially written lyrics with such lines as "We think you're the greatest" while dancing to the song "One" from the show. This seemed to resonate with Fred more than anything—this was a heartfelt salute from his own kind.

Immediately following the Kennedy Center Honors, Fred flew to New York, where he was met by Robyn at 5:30 A.M. at Kennedy Airport. They embraced, oblivious to the stares of others in the terminal. The next afternoon they went over to see Jock Whitney, who was seriously ill. Taking Whitney's limousine, they went to Tavern on the Green for dinner.[57]

During dinner, Fred suggested they get married immediately. Robyn agreed. They fully realized this was nothing to take lightly. The direction of her career was a problem. A bigger problem was that Ava and Adele were not fond of Robyn. She suggested they not rush things.[58]

MICHAEL BLACK ACCOMPANIED FRED one night in June 1979 to attend the national company performance of Bob Fosse's *Dancin'* at the Ahmanson Theatre in Los Angeles. Included in the production was a tribute number called "For Fred." The male chorus line was appropriately attired in foulard ties as belts, which became apparent when they doffed their jackets at the culmination of an Astaire-like number that Fosse had choreographed.[59]

As Black recalled, "Fred was having trouble with his balance and held on to me. We were told to remain in our seats at the final curtain as they wanted him to come backstage afterwards. . . . The stage was still lit. The minute he let go of my arm, he became the Fred Astaire of 1948. He was on his toes dancing and did a little step and a bow, like a 'hats off to you.' He shook hands with everybody, and the minute he was out of that light, he got back on my arm. When we got to the car, we got in the backseat, and he just slumped. That took a lot out of him."

The tributes continued unabated. The other major theatrical choreographer of the time, Jerome Robbins, gave his impression of the "I'm Old-Fashioned" number that Fred had performed with Rita Hayworth in *You Were Never Lovelier,* complete with showing the film clip at the beginning of a neoclassical ballet that opened the 1983 New York City Ballet season. The clip received a spontaneous standing ovation.[60] Les Grands Ballets Canadiens at New York City Center staged an homage to Fred and Ginger by duplicating some of their foremost production numbers. Tommy Tune designed an unusual Fred and Ginger takeoff—visible from the knees down—in the Broadway musical *A Day in Hollywood/A Night in the Ukraine.* Arlene Croce called Tune's turn the cleverest tribute to Astaire [and Rogers] I have seen.[61]

New films revealed the Astaire influence. Martin Scorsese's *New York, New York* was inspired by the script of the Crosby and Astaire opus *Blue Skies.* In 1981, Steve Martin, with his costar Bernadette Peters, did a "Let's Face the Music and Dance" imitation in his second starring vehicle, *Pennies from Heaven.* Five years later, the famous Italian auteur Frederico Fellini created his own homage, entitled *Ginger and Fred.*

IN 1979, *The Man in the Santa Claus Suit* was produced by Lee Miller with Al Schwartz as coexecutive producer for Dick Clark Productions and ran as an NBC-

TV movie of the week. In the extensive cast were Gary Burghoff, John Byner, Bert Convy, Nanette Fabray, and Harold Gould. But what made this movie especially noteworthy was that Fred Astaire was the lead, playing eight roles: costume-shop proprietor, chauffeur, policeman, cabdriver, jeweler, floorwalker, choral director, and Santa Claus.

The Man in the Santa Claus Suit is a fairy tale. It was partially shot in New York, where a number of location scenes captured the bustling street life of the city. Fred enjoyed making the movie so much that he was talked into singing Charlie Fox's song "That Once a Year Christmas Day" over the titles.

The veteran director Corey Allen, a former actor, praised the way Astaire handled key early scenes in the movie. He described the scene where Gary Burghoff is seen purchasing a diamond ring on time payments from Astaire, the jeweler: "We shot it in New York in a large, narrow room that served as the jewelry shop. There was no place to block the camera shot behind Gary Burghoff's and Fred's shoulders. Fred was pure grace. He made you feel like behaving gracefully. He said, 'I want to be told when I'm doing something right. I am here to work, and this is a very difficult scene. I want to be told when I am doing something wrong!' He really captured me all the way through the picture."

Exactly twenty-six years after shooting this scene, Allen lamented that the jewelry-shop scene had incorrectly been edited. "Astaire and Burghoff were both shot over the same shoulder from both directions, which made the characters look away from each other," Allen explained. "It's the first thing film students learn. We had about one hundred and fifty years of experience on that film, and nobody caught it. Not Fred or any of the executives who came to the screening of the final cut."

The enthusiastic Burghoff remembered that during the shooting of this scene the assistant director, between takes, said to Fred, "Just about every newspaper in New York has learned that you are here, and they would like to do an interview with you if you would be willing to step outside on the sidewalk. I stepped aside. The assistant director didn't even know I was there. Fred said he would do the interview on one condition, and I listened intently because I wanted to know what conditions a great legend would have. He said, 'Only if my costar would go outside with me.' Isn't that something! He made sure that every photograph was taken with his arm around my shoulder. I never forget that graciousness and that kindness. . . . I am the last generation to work with Jimmy Durante and Fred Astaire—who could ask for anything more?

"When I heard that he was going to play Santa Claus, I was thinking of this thin man. But the thing was, his heart was the heart of Santa Claus. He had a warmth that was so great that it transcended his physical attributes. He personified in spades the essence of the Santa Claus symbol. . . . Fred Astaire knew a primary secret that all artists must learn: There is no freedom without discipline. He was just the best of the best.

"He was a gentleman. He would not get upset and was very patient. I had seen a thing that was wonderfully done called *The Life and Death of Peter Sellers.* A few seconds into the character you get that feeling—'Oh my God, that's him again.' Well, that's the feeling I got when I saw the finished product—'Oh my God, that's Fred again.' "

Al Schwartz possesses a unique personality for a TV producer. He is genuine and is much less interested in the froth involved in TV production than the quality of the final product. As vice president of Dick Clark Productions he brought the project to the company. Though retired, he still produces the popular Golden Globe Awards show.

Schwartz well remembered how *The Man in the Santa Claus Suit* became a viable TV movie. "Dick [Clark] had asked me to do some research on Christmas stories because that's what he thought NBC wanted. My background was primarily in variety specials and comedy. There were two basic Christmas movies that I liked: *Miracle on 34th Street* and *Tales of Manhattan,* where a tuxedo goes from person to person. So kind of relying on that idea, I went in and pitched an idea to NBC called *The Man in the Santa Claus Suit,* in which four people would come into a costume shop on Christmas Eve to rent a Santa Claus outfit."

In April, Schwartz signed Leonard Gershe, fresh from his triumph with *Butterflies Are Free* on Broadway, and who had written the screenplays for *Silk Stockings* and *Funny Face* and had also been involved with Astaire in *That's Entertainment, Part II.* Gershe took the original idea and adapted the premise of the popular seventies TV weekly series *The Love Boat,* which told several stories that would eventually intermingle, while creating the magic of the Christmas season. "The main character would influence the outcome of all of these people's lives" was the way Schwartz described the plot of the movie.

Gershe initially brought up the idea of casting Astaire, though Schwartz agrees that Mike Fenton, the casting director, might simultaneously have had the idea. "I know him, and maybe we can convince him to do this," Gershe said. When Schwartz and Gershe met with Astaire, he liked the project from the beginning and was intrigued about playing several characters.

Schwartz asked Fred to give him an old pair of his dancing shoes, which he presented to Dick Clark as a fiftieth-birthday present. This was an example of the relationship Schwartz and Astaire developed that continued throughout the project. As Schwartz described it, "Up to this time I had worked with a lot of stars. I did some things with Fred MacMurray and some other people that were movie stars that had crossed over to television. But Fred Astaire was a movie star."

Fred Silverman, then in charge of programming at NBC, wanted the movie to air just before Christmas, not a year later as originally planned. Gershe said he couldn't possibly deliver such a multifaceted script so quickly. He offered to bow out but offered to see that Fred remained committed. George Kirgo delivered the script in about two weeks, working from Gershe's outline.

Eddie Foy III, the grandson of Astaire's good friend from vaudeville Eddie Foy, was then vice president of casting at NBC. He made the deal for Astaire, paying him $250,000, which was more than the budget called for. As Lee Miller, the producer of the movie, explained, the network would pay the "breakage," the extra $150,000 for Astaire's salary for the lead role.

As shooting commenced in downtown Los Angeles, Schwartz remembered, "We didn't have the parts cast that were going to be done the next day. At the location, all of a sudden, the door opened, and in walked Fred Astaire. He wasn't called; he didn't have to be there. He just came down to introduce himself to everybody. That got us all going—crazy and enthused. I think he knew the pressure we were under because Leonard Gershe had told him. I think that motivated Fred."

Lee Miller recalled that the movie was shot over four weeks in November, including one week in New York. "The script supervisor told me we were eight minutes short when we went to New York. I thought, 'Let's put together a group of carolers and shoot them all over New York so that we can use them as a transition piece.' I called up Juilliard and ended up with a choral group. A couple of times Corey [Allen] worked it out so that we had the singers there when we were shooting in order that the actors would exit in front of the carolers.

"In a night scene on Thirty-fourth Street, a freight elevator rose up to the street level that contained a couple who is seen kissing while the twelve carolers sang 'Joy to the World.' Fred, as the choral director, smiled. This was his last shot in the scene. I thanked him for the experience of working with him. He pushed all that aside and said, 'If you are happy, I can go home now.' He walked away toward his trailer, which was maybe fifty feet away. Corey and I watched as he put on an overcoat and a scarf and he did a little time step and saluted. It was just another one of those little moments.

"We flew home on Thanksgiving Day and worked straight through. I hand-carried a print of the show to NBC thirty-six hours before airing. It has played maybe twenty times since then every Christmas somewhere," said Miller proudly.

Astaire conducted himself admirably in this movie, demonstrating versatility and believability in his eight character portraits. Only as a Macy's floorwalker in the men's department, a natural for him, was he Fred Astaire. No, he didn't bring an entirely new dimension to the various roles he played, but as a costume-shop proprietor and a jeweler, he showed that he could hold his own as a character actor.

AFTER THIS TRIUMPH, Fred resumed his relationship with Robyn. They began to be seen frequently at Hollywood dining establishments such as the Bistro, Matteo's, Ah Fong's, and even Old World, a health-foods restaurant. The press jumped on the story. Many accounts centered on Ava and Richard's, as well as Dellie's, opposition to Robyn. Their feelings toward her weren't purely a matter of money. All three of Fred's children had long since been set up with trust funds. They had also reportedly inherited $5 million each from their great-uncle Henry Bull's estate.

Jack Martin in the *New York Post* asserted that Fred had seen that Groucho Marx's and John Wayne's companions in their last years (Erin Fleming and Pat Stacy) had been ostracized socially and financially by the respective stars' families and wanted to protect Robyn.[62] Finally, columnist Liz Smith, who seems to understand celebrities better than any of her colleagues, wrote in the *Daily News,* "So why doesn't everybody just calm down and give America's greatest living entertainer a break."

PBS APPROACHED FRED to be the focal point of a documentary on the Fred and Ginger RKO era. He wouldn't agree to participate, but Gene Kelly, Ginger Rogers, Hermes Pan, Pandro S. Berman, and pianist Hal Borne commented on what was essential film history. Adele arrived to be interviewed, but turned down appearing on camera.[63] Joanne Woodward was the effective and understated host of *Fred Astaire: Puttin' On His Top Hat,* which aired on March 10, 1980.

Kelly opened the show by stating that Fred Astaire had established the history of dance on film. Kelly reminded the TV audience that talking pictures gave birth to the dance. As the clips unraveled, starting with the "Top Hat" number, I was struck anew by how much sheer personal enjoyment Astaire radiated from this and other spectacular numbers. He seemed to get more pleasure from them than from anything else he had ever done in his life. This was in addition to displaying his vast arsenal of dance steps in these routines. I also noticed how rarely Rogers's legs were seen on camera during the dance numbers; I assume the femininity of her frilly dresses won out over displaying her physical form.

Woodward introduced the often overlooked idea that Dellie may indeed have been Fred's best dancing partner. Dellie, in a voice-over, said, "He did better after I left him."

Some oft-told stories followed. Pandro S. Berman praised Ginger's pluck in going through the forty-seven takes that included the bleeding feet to get the prophetically titled dance number "Never Gonna Dance" on film. Ginger claimed she often had to participate in dance numbers with Fred in which she wore brand-new shoes that were still wet from being dyed. Woodward offered the perfect ending: "Never again would a dance team display such chemistry together."

PBS mounted a sequel to continue the Astaire dancing saga; four days later, *Change Partners and Dance* aired, again narrated by Joanne Woodward. In this, revelations about Astaire were heard, with the tone of the show similar to the first. The program showcased Fred's work with his dance partners at five different studios that followed his movies with Ginger Rogers at RKO.

Leslie Caron's astute observations were a keynote of the second Astaire tribute, along with Rudolf Nureyev's and Barrie Chase's comments. Still, such important Astaire partners as Cyd Charisse and Vera-Ellen were conspicuously absent from the interviews, as was Audrey Hepburn. However, the perceptive offerings of such master choreographers as Bob Fosse, Jerome Robbins, Hermes Pan, Roland Petit, and Eugene Loring added considerable insight into what separated Astaire from all the rest.

Caron said that as a novice dancer her mother had instructed her to go out and watch Astaire movie musicals to learn about time. Once she began working with him, she fully realized how diligent Fred was about maintaining the right tempo. She praised "the games with music" Astaire "transferred to the audience." She called the "Something's Gotta Give" number "perfection in dancing," which, when shown, proved to be just that.

Before they worked together in *Daddy Long Legs* she remembered that Fred told her that because of the disparity in their styles of dancing "you'll have to do my stuff. There's no way I can do your stuff." She also revealed that he admitted he disliked ballet because it would expose that he had such unusually large hands. (This excuse seems like a "packaged" rationalization.) Caron claimed that in the "Guardian Angel" number that her mentor Roland Petit created, Petit was able to successfully marry Astaire's style of dancing with hers.

Because of their diverse approaches to the dance, Petit contended he felt that he had little to offer in *Daddy Long Legs* until Astaire said, "I like you. I feel comfortable with you. I'll manage to do what I do. We'll work together."

A variety of famous talking heads rounded out this portrait. Nureyev called Astaire "the greatest dancer in American history" and also said, "He's an incredible drummer." Jerome Robbins vowed, "Fred Astaire infused our souls with the visions that he made. Fred was the reason I wanted to become a dancer and choreographer."[64]

Fosse stated that no white tap dancer had developed the kind of rhythm that Astaire had: "You never knew where he was going." He suggested that Fred's skill as a tap dancer came out of the years he had spent in musical comedy.

Fosse concluded the documentary by saying, "We owe Fred a lot," pointing out that anyone who merely went out to become a social dancer was influenced by him. This preceded a clip from *Blue Skies* of "Puttin' On The Ritz," as amazing when seen on television in 1980 as it was on film in 1946.

ONE AFTERNOON, while waiting for his car in a Beverly Hills parking lot, Fred came across Pandro Berman, who, after the RKO Astaire/Rogers musicals, went on to a distinguished career. They greeted each other warmly. Right away, Fred said to Berman, "Pan, I want to ask you something." "Sure, Fred, what is it?" replied the retired producer. "Well, I'm thinking of getting married again, to a girl who's much younger than I am. Some of my family and friends are against the idea. What do you think?"

"Do you love her?" asked Berman. "Yes, I do," said Fred. "Then what the hell do you care what other people say? They don't have to live with her. They don't have to live without her. You do. You have to make the decision. If you love her and you want to marry her, tell them all to go to hell."[65]

Fred also called Allen Ludden for advice, according to Betty White: "One night around dinnertime he called Allen and said, 'I have to talk to you. I am just going crazy. I am so nuts about this woman. My family doesn't like her.' I was not that particularly fond of Robyn myself, but she was a big animal person so that is where we connected.

"Allen dropped everything and went over to see Fred. When he came back, he said, 'He wants to marry this woman.' Allen had told him to go ahead if he was feeling it was that important to him. Allen was such a romantic. He said that it was amazing, Fred just poured it all out. Allen was not involved with the rest of the family. He could level with Fred. Fred knew that Allen had fallen in love with somebody [White] and wouldn't take no for an answer. I think he wanted to get some of that from Allen."

The retired producer Bill Self, who had become Fred's closest friend, was called by both Ava and Adele requesting that he intercede with Fred about his serious interest in marrying Robyn. "They thought she was after his money. I don't even know if I approved of it [his getting married] in many ways. I think in my heart I wished she hadn't married, or he hadn't married her. But I wasn't going to tell Fred that, and I wasn't trying to interfere in any way. . . . I never thought she was madly in love with him."[66]

Barbara Walters has long since developed a well-defined nose for a story. While in Hollywood working on one of her ABC Hollywood-interview specials, she heard from a reliable source that Astaire was planning to get married. She called him to request an interview. While describing what a delightful man she found him, she also readily acknowledged what a difficult interview he was: "In films, he had that great sardonic humor, but in person he was terribly shy. Unlike just about any other actor I've ever interviewed, he was extremely self-effacing, and not really very interested in talking about his own work. We did the interview at his home so that he would be more relaxed in talking to me."

In viewing the *20/20* segment, I couldn't help but notice how close Walters sat to Fred and how she put her arm through his as they walked around the swimming pool at Fred's home. "I do that with most of my interview subjects," she said. It seemed obvious that these were tricks of the interview trade. Walters was doing her utmost to make Astaire less introverted for her purposes.

Walters recalled, "He had known me from when he appeared on the *Today* show. That's where I had first interviewed him. In the course of the interview, he suddenly announced that he was in love with Robyn Smith and planned to marry her."

"She is a great girl," said Fred.

"Well, have you popped the question?" asked Walters.

"Yes, sure."

Walters wanted to know, "Would you wed soon?"

"I think so."

"What about the age difference?"

"I don't even think about it."

Walters said, "He asked me not to use this information since it was confidential. However, when the news came out that they were getting married, I had the interview with Fred talking about Robyn and [stating] his intention of marrying her. We ran it the next day."

Robyn made the point, "Once I knew we would eventually get married, I was very, very happy, and I didn't care when. Everything we did was natural; it was like we had been around each other all our lives. . . . It's a very unusual relationship, and if anyone would have said ten years ago that I was going to marry a man forty-seven years older [*sic*] than me, I would have said, 'Don't be ridiculous.' " She admitted, "I didn't think I was capable of love, not like this. But then I've always liked older men. . . . I looked for the father image, no question about it. There's nothing wrong with that. It's a normal thing if you haven't had a father.

I always was aware that I had that, but I didn't fight it. I went along with it. Fred's part-father to me, let's face it. But he's part-everything to me."[67]

On June 12, 1980, Fred and Robyn took out a marriage license at superior court in Santa Monica. Robyn paid the $23 fee. Fred quipped, "It would have been cheaper if we came in last week," noting that then governor Jerry Brown had recently raised the cost of a marriage license. Court clerk Hilda Mills said that they hadn't set a definite date for their wedding.[68]

Fred Astaire married Robyn Smith on June 24, 1980, at the Astaire home at 1155 San Ysidro Drive in Beverly Hills in a simple ceremony. Dellie, in her own inimitable manner, told close friends in New York, "He's just being fucking stupid." Neither the McKenzies nor Dellie attended the ceremony, although Freddie and his wife, Carol, did. Ava and Richard never set foot in the Astaire family home again. They stayed at a hotel when they came to visit Fred. Dellie never came to Los Angeles after that.

Six days after Fred's marriage to Robyn, coincidentally an intelligently conceived tribute to him, entitled "Puttin' On the Ritz," was produced in Carnegie Hall as part of the 1980 Newport Jazz Festival. The New York radio personality Bob Jones opened the concert by explaining that it was "not a retrospective," but just some favorite Astaire songs performed by the various artists.

Top-billed was Astaire's fervent admirer Mel Tormé, who opened the program with his own lyrics to the tune of "They All Laughed." Pianist George Shearing and baritone saxophonist Gerry Mulligan delivered other songs from the vast Astaire repertoire. Supporting acts were the singer Sylvia Syms; the trumpeters Clark Terry and Ruby Braff; the tenor saxophonist Stan Getz; and the alto saxophonist Lee Konitz.

Tormé was everywhere—dropping bon mots concerning Astaire's career, singing duets with George Shearing, playing piano behind Gerry Mulligan as the jazz great introduced the composition he had specially written for the evening, "I Just Want to Sing and Dance Like Fred Astaire," and concluding by singing a brace of Astaire tunes backed by a "tentette," a ten-piece band.[69]

ON SEPTEMBER 24, 1980, Fred was the recipient of ASCAP's Pied Piper Award, its highest accolade presented to a nonsongwriter (purposely overlooking Fred's own songwriting credits). It was a long overdue honor. After all, his singing and dancing over fifty years of ASCAP songs had made the organization substantial moneys and caused several of its songwriters to become household names. Hal David, in his first year of what turned out to be three terms as president of ASCAP, presided over the presentation.

"It was at our annual membership meeting at the Beverly Hilton," David recalled. "I thought if we could honor someone of great distinction that had a connection with us in one way or another, it would be a great thing. Karen Sherry was head of public relations at that point. . . . I don't recall if it was she or I who thought of Fred Astaire. Immediately, we concurred that it was a perfect choice.

"We wrote him and told him we would be very pleased if we could honor him at our membership meeting. He agreed to accept the award. All he wanted to be sure about was that it not appear on television. He gave us the impression that he felt that that would be taking advantage of him. Karen and I made plans to fly out to Los Angeles."

Sherry, now vice president and executive director of ASCAP, remembered that when the *Hollywood Reporter* received the press release concerning Astaire's Pied Piper Award, the publication requested that a photo be taken the day before the event to run with a front-page story the day after its actual presentation. "I contacted Michael Black, his agent, who gave me Mr. Astaire's telephone number. When I called, Mr. Astaire answered. I told him that I didn't mean to make things difficult for him, but that the *Hollywood Reporter* wanted a photo of the Pied Piper Award presentation to run on the cover. He said, 'I think that's a lovely idea. Why don't you come to my house the day before with Mr. Hal David at around ten thirty in the morning? Bring the photographer, and we'll be all set.' "

Sherry said, "Fred showed us around his house. The entryway was all marble and circular. That's where we had the picture taken. All the various rooms emanated from that circle."

David recalled, "He started to talk about Irving Berlin in particular and Gershwin and Porter. He spoke about how fantastic it was that Irving would trust him with his songs. He was in awe of those great songwriters. That's why he agreed to be honored."

In a moment of complete candor, Astaire told David, "I am a great admirer of your music because you do the one thing [that] I wish I could do, write great songs. If I could write great songs the way you do, the way Irving Berlin does— that's what I wanted to do all my life." David, in turn, praised Astaire for his significant artistic achievements.

Fred abruptly changed the direction of the conversation by saying, "But you know music has changed a lot." Sherry was astounded when Astaire turned toward her and remarked, "I imagine you are very up-to-date with contemporary music." David interjected, "Karen is very up-to-date and listens to everything." Astaire responded, "I'm very interested in what you think of Pink Floyd and Led Zeppelin." He discussed other groups and individual performers. He said that he listened to a lot of rock music. "I don't understand a lot of it, but I listen. I want to learn more about it," he said.

"We were with him about an hour and a half," Sherry recalled. "It was like he really didn't want us to leave. At a certain point, not wanting to impose, Hal finally said, 'Well, Mr. Astaire, this was really fantastic.'"

"On the day of the meeting, he arrived at the Hilton with Robyn," David remembered. "The photographers were five deep, and I had to say to them, 'You're blocking the membership.' Fred spoke about ten minutes, telling the audience of probably eight hundred how important songs had been in his life. He was very prepared."

Astaire may have enjoyed his musical heyday during the golden age of popular music, but in his constant attempts to remain au courant, he kept up with pop music, current performers, and various other forms of entertainment. He recognized that unlike in his performing years, when important songwriters wrote songs tailored to him, many contemporary musical artists wrote and performed their own material. And though he intensely disliked publicity and never retained a personal publicist, he fully understood the importance of the kind of meaningful publicity that the Pied Piper Award offered hm.

Robyn and Fred settled into a quiet married life. His bride, however, was not through with racing. After competing in Race Week at Saratoga, she still took occasional mounts that took her away from home. Fred looked ahead to the time when she would quit racing. He was afraid of her suffering a serious injury.

RICHARD MCKENZIE HAD TOUTED Peter Straub's novel *Ghost Story* to his father-in-law. Richard envisioned it as a possible starring vehicle for Fred. It was the story of four distinguished elderly gentlemen, long close friends, who had carried out a murder decades before that came back to haunt them.

Michael Black learned that Universal was fast-tracking the picture, hoping to put it into production in upstate New York in January 1981. Fred was seriously being considered for one of the four principal roles by the film's producer, Burt Weissbourd and its director, John Irvin. A deal was soon put together with Fred with tentative plans to release the picture at Christmastime 1981.[70]

In the meantime, Dellie was definitely fading. Her well-known zest for living was gone as a series of ailments had sapped her strength. In December 1980 she suffered a heart attack.[71] Robyn suggested to Fred that he spend Christmas with her at her home in Scottsdale.[72] His four days there would be the last time the onetime famous brother-and-sister team would ever be together.

CHAPTER THIRTEEN

THE MEMORY OF ALL THAT

W EATHER-WISE, upstate New York and Vermont in January can be a real horror story. The production of *Ghost Story,* another type of horror story, involved considerable outdoor shooting in icy conditions, which for veteran actors Fred Astaire (making his first theatrical film in four years), Melvyn Douglas, John Houseman, and Douglas Fairbanks Jr., at seventy-two the youngest, was especially dangerous. This same problem also faced Patricia Neal, Alice Krige, Craig Wasson, and the remainder of the cast of the Universal movie.

Fred developed a serious cold, and unfortunately Robyn was not there to minister to him. She was still fulfilling some racing commitments. Ava, however, arrived for a visit when filming began in Saratoga Springs, and Richard joined her for the end of Fred's work on the movie.[1] Fred had enjoyed several visits there in the past, but this time conditions were much different. Fred was older and not feeling well. His illness was visible in how drawn he looked on camera.

Marianne Moloney was a vice president of production at Universal. She had a background in publishing at Viking Press and as a literary agent at Ziegler Ross and was thus assigned to develop *Ghost Story.* Moloney signed Lawrence D. Cohen to write the screenplay. The budget for the movie was $16 million. The "favored nations" contract meant that the four principal actors were paid the same salary.

The vivacious Moloney, who was on location for the shooting, recalled, "We were dealing with these older actors who could only work for so many hours. The first night we were there, at the Saratoga Springs Hotel, Fred literally tap-danced down the marble stairway. At the bottom, he said, 'Thank God, I made it.' Everyone applauded because it was mischievous and nice. What struck me about all of them was the elegance, the perfection, and the humility. They all dressed for dinner every night. I remember Fred in red ascots. It was as though it was 1937 Hollywood."

Knowing how important it was to have the four relate to each other on-screen, as members of the Chowder Society, the director, John Irvin, arranged an initial dinner. "They barely knew each other," he said. "They were very boyish. There was a lot of banter and ragging—good and natural, of course, but not any observed rivalry. I must say they looked out for each other during the course of the movie.

"I called a rehearsal, the next day. I remember that Fred arrived ten minutes early. He sat there like a schoolboy, with all of his pencils sharpened, his notepad ready, his script on one side ready. Fairbanks Jr. was the last to arrive, twenty minutes later. He said, 'I'm sorry. I have been talking to the White House. I had to talk to the president.'"

The producer, Burt Weissbourd, recalled how Astaire "kept a very professional and kindly manner" throughout the production. "I remember one night he called me when we were shooting in Woodstock, Vermont. The cast was staying at the Holiday Inn. I went to see him. He said to me, 'Burt, I've been dancing around to keep warm.' He had this nice sense of humor. I also recall that he had trouble remembering his lines, but he hung in there. We worked out ways for him to get some help. It was a very happy time."

The "help" Weissbourd referred to was a young woman named Sue Peterson, hired as an assistant for Fred. That she was attractive led the *National Enquirer* to publish a ridiculous story about a supposed affair the two were having. Fred said, "How can they write stuff like that?" The publication had to have a juicy story emerge from a film with a name cast shooting on location in the dead of winter.

Patricia Neal, who played Astaire's wife in the film, said, "I remember that Fred was really very deeply in love with his wife, Robyn. He talked about her all the time and couldn't wait until he could talk to her at six thirty P.M. They spoke every day."

In the film, Neal had two scenes with him, including a touching moment sensitively depicting two elderly people in bed. This followed Fred's waking up from a nightmare about having been a participant in a murder, as a young man along with his cohorts, which was the central ingredient in the plot. Neal, too, enjoyed the camaraderie of working with the four older actors, all of whom she had previously known in Hollywood.

Irvin also noted, "They were very gung ho, but they were frail. That affected the way I shot the film. I could not do very long, continuous developing takes. I had to do short takes."

He also claimed, "All the special effects that I wanted, we never got them. Ned Tanen said, 'We have no time. All I can give you is maggots.' I said, 'Then, give me maggots.' I wanted things a little more subtle. The film is stylistically a little inconsistent. It's quite polished on one level and crude on the other. The crude part is as a result of having to smash to get it ready for release. I never felt the film was quite finished."

The genial director remembered that on the first day of shooting Astaire said to him, "I was just a hoofer. Adele, she was good. I am so happy to be acting. I am no Larry Olivier, but I like acting. I can do it. I did not like dancing."

"With Fred, I always wanted to put my arms around him and hug him, he was so likable but so unhappy," said Irvin. "He was lonely, and he was cold. He was limping badly because he had a skateboarding accident at home and was using a cane. The *National Enquirer* story was unhelpful, too."

Irvin had perfect recall of what had taken place on a movie he had directed a quarter of a century earlier. "I remember at one point I was having trouble with the crew. Fred was very tired. He went to his trailer. I knocked on the door, but he didn't respond. I opened the door. He looked very glum. I said, 'Fred, come on. Let's go to work.' He said, 'I can't sleep. I keep thinking about Ronnie.' I thought he was referring to the assistant director, who was very noisy, a cowboy. I said, 'You want to get out of here? I want to get out of here, but we have to shoot the scene first.' He said, 'No, no, my friend Ronnie Reagan. He is the president. Okay, he is no George Washington.' What he meant was that he could not believe that the guy who had been a friend of his could be the president of the United States. The idea of the presidency was a legend to him. It was beyond his imagination. It completely baffled him."

ON JANUARY 25, 1981, Dellie passed away in Phoenix. She had suffered a stroke on January 6 and never regained consciousness.[2] Ava was at her bedside when she died. The news absolutely devastated Fred. Douglas Fairbanks Jr. recalled, "I was with him when he got the news. I did my best to console him. They were an absolutely devoted pair."[3]

Fred's room was immediately adjacent to Fairbanks's. Randy Malone, Margaret O'Brien's manager, said that Fairbanks had informed him that Fred had requested that Fairbanks leave the door to their connecting rooms open. Fred said, "I don't want to be alone tonight." The next day he remarked to Craig Wasson, "I don't know how I'm going to go on without Adele. She was the most important person in my life." Dellie was buried at the Astaire family plot at the Oakwood Memorial Park in Chatsworth, California.

Immediately after Dellie's death, Astaire asked Irvin if he could be replaced. The movie, however, was already three weeks into the shooting. The director insisted, "Fred, we have gone too far. You look great, and you are great in the picture.

I don't really think you want to do that. You can finish this, please, for yourself, not for me." (Reportedly, Irvin asked Ava to remain until Fred's work was completed.)[4]

Evidently, the same thing had happened with Alec Guinness, when Irvin had directed him in *Tinker, Tailor, Soldier, Spy*. "Allie called me at four A.M. to say, 'I haven't found George Smiley.' He, too, had wanted to leave that movie," Irvin recalled. Guinness had been suggested for the role played by Astaire in *Ghost Story*.

"What Allie and Fred had in common was a total commitment to their work," said Irvin, "and a quest for the character's truth. I also think they were [both] quite modest and self-deprecating. In terms of their minutiae, the detailing and the nuance of their work, they were very similar. Without being a Method actor, Fred was very methodical."

DINING WITH FRED FREQUENTLY, Irvin got him to look back over his career. When he asked if he had ever got a bad review, Fred confessed, "*Bad* reviews, I got some terrible reviews! When I got bad reviews, I used to spend all day writing letters to those critics and then drive all over the Valley, Beverly Hills, and Santa Monica and put them in different mailboxes." The letters said, "How dare you say those things about Fred Astaire!" Irvin said, "He would write thirty to forty letters with different handwriting, different pencils, different pens, and different postmarks. I was thinking if Fred Astaire can get bad reviews, I don't feel too bad about mine."

Alice Krige, the South African actress, played Craig Wasson's love interest. She reported that Fred was given one day of mourning after Adele's passing, then he wanted to return to work. It was an extraordinary kind of fortitude and professionalism.

Krige said, "I don't think Fred ever lost the taste for acting. He did the film for the love of it. I think the adrenaline of having dinner and being around his contemporaries fueled his work. I can remember him as being animated, a lot more than I expected him to be."

Krige feels "*Ghost Story* did not have a central gravity. I felt it was a ship that was always trying to find its center. For me, however, it was a fascinating role because I got to play three versions of the same character."

On the final take of his last day of shooting, at one o'clock in the morning, Irvin said to Fred, "This is it."

Fred replied, "I am so happy. *Ghost Story*. I thought I was going home in a box."

Craig Wasson watched as Fred's assistant arrived to take him by the arm and escort him to his trailer. "Everybody applauded after the AD [assistant director] said, 'That's a wrap on Mr. Astaire.' Fred stopped and gestured for his assistant to let go of his elbow. He went dancing across the snow in a kind of pirouette, spinning his arms out. It wasn't perfect, but for a moment it was magic. Gracefully, he walked to his trailer, waved, and closed the door. Isn't that beautiful. Everyone was stunned. We were speechless." (Apparently, this bow-off gesture was something he practiced after the final shot in his last movies; it seems like still another residual from vaudeville.)

Wasson saw Astaire's exit as symbolic of what Astaire was really about. "He was so unprepossessing and so humble. It makes sense that Fred was more interested in the team of himself and Adele. If that meant Adele was the star, that was fine. It makes me think of what George C. Scott once told me: 'The story is always bigger than the storyteller, and a good actor serves the story, not himself.' Fred was the epitome of that. You could sense that he always was more interested in making sure that the final product was what he was contributing to, not himself."

Following up on that sentiment, Wasson was not adverse to admit, "If there had been more of Fred Astaire and the other three, it would have been a great movie. I know that's at my expense, but I wanted to see more of those guys. I played two parts that really ate up a lot of screen time."

John Houseman and Fred were extremely unhappy upon seeing the rough cut of the film. The focus had been changed from the old men to center on the love story with Wasson and Krige. The youth market had to be served. The studio remained firm in its decision that this was basically the cut the public would see.[5]

Perhaps the main reason for the picture's artistic failure was the casting of the young actors who were the counterparts of the four old men, who appeared in a key flashback sequence. There seemed to be no connection between the two generations, which made the murder that had been kept secret by the old men for many years puzzling and disconcerting. This deficiency threw off the narrative at a critical point just before the climax of the picture. John Irvin created an intense and scary atmosphere for much of the picture, but it lost its way at that moment.

Ned Tanen, who ran the studio at the time *Ghost Story* was in production, said, "I thought it was a really good property. I thought it had a chance, but I never kidded myself. You were not dealing with major stars. These guys had had great careers, all of them, and Fred phenomenal, but who in the audience cared? We had to make movies. It came in on schedule. I wish it had been more successful, but it was not. The problem may have been that it was impossible to sell four elderly men in a movie."

The movie grossed slightly over $27,371,000 domestically. With exhibition costs, distribution, marketing costs, etc., the film has never gone into profit.

Ghost Story marked the finale of Astaire's movie career. Vincent Canby of the *New York Times* had problems with the movie but wrote, "Mr. Astaire does his best work to date as a non dancer, non singer." Archer Winsten in the *New York Post,* however, believed, "The most depressing aspect of this film is to find such fine old stars stuck in a film of such little merit." Still, *Ghost Story* supplied a fitting close to a distinguished film career that had encompassed forty-three movies. Fred realized that now was the right time for him to retire.

He did appear in front of a camera one more time, though. The occasion was a 1985 TV commercial with Gene Kelly for Western Airlines. Together, they conveyed the idea that Western had more legroom on flights.

ALTHOUGH MICHAEL BLACK SAID that Fred was adamant about never allowing himself to be the guest of honor at a testimonial dinner, he agreed to be feted by the American Film Institute on April 10, 1981. It is generally considered the major annual dinner of its kind in the film industry. Bill Self said that George Stevens Jr., who produced the show, first asked him to intercede with Fred; obviously, he succeeded. Fred was the ninth recipient of AFI's Life Achievement Award. The dinner was held at the Beverly Hilton.

For one night only, Ava and Robyn declared a truce as they sat together at the large table of honor. Fred was seated in between them with Robyn on his right. Freddie and Carol sat to Ava and Richard's left. Hermes Pan, Bill and Peggy Self, and Michael Black were also seated at the table. Black believes, "Robyn wanted me at the table because she wanted someone to talk to. As the guest of honor, Fred entered separately through the room, and she was alone." When Astaire arrived, he was naturally in black tie, but with a bright pink sash tied around his waist.

Early on in the festivities, Fred approached John Irvin. He asked, "John, help me. I have to give a speech. What am I going to say?" Irvin tried to allay Fred's nervousness by saying, "Whatever you say, we all love you. It's gonna be wonderful. Don't worry," but of course Moanin' Minnie worried.

David Niven was the host for the evening, and a perfect choice. As David's son Jamie, the vice chairman of Sotheby's, recalled, "From my father's standpoint, Fred was his closest friend." A few years before, David had narrated an insightful radio series on Astaire's life for the BBC. His genuine affection for his old friend was evident throughout, as was his amusement over Fred's perfectionism.

David Niven represented the kind of man Astaire always wished he could be—droll, a more versatile actor, and someone who was at ease with people. According to Jamie Niven, this was in addition to David's frankness and his tenacity, which had been demonstrated when his career floundered after the war. Along with their mutual charm and debonair manner, they shared a common element of steely determination, David's emanating from the twelve years he had spent in the British army before and during World War II. Who can ever forget Niven's portrait of Phileas Fogg in *Around the World in Eighty Days* and his Oscar-winning performance playing a man in crisis in *Separate Tables*.

From the podium, speaking of Astaire, Niven began by relating candidly, "I can assure you the poor man is going through hell."[6] This was only one of many on-the-mark and amusing comments he made about Astaire during the evening.

While viewing the film clips of his movies, Black heard Fred making remarks. "He hadn't seen them for a long time. He was more interested in looking at his dance steps. It was like a director looking back upon his career. He was seeing what was still good and some that were not so good: 'I was pretty good in that,' 'I didn't know how good I was,' or 'Oh, I shouldn't have made that mistake.'"

Mikhail Baryshnikov was a surprise guest. A few years earlier, during a *60 Minutes* interview, the superlative Russian ballet dancer had mentioned his tremendous respect for Astaire. He soon received a letter saying, "Thank you for your most praiseworthy words about my work."

On his arrival onstage, Baryshnikov began by saying, "You are a disgrace." (As he explained to me, "I meant that he raised the bar for all of us.") His remark caused Astaire and the audience to gasp momentarily. He hesitated, then extolled Astaire's many virtues as a dancer and his overall importance to the profession.

Baryshnikov was seated at Jimmy Cagney's table and afterward finally met Astaire. "I was impressed. He was not shy at all. He looked directly into my eyes. It was a long stare, and I was so touched," Baryshnikov recalled.

Some confusion accompanied Ginger Rogers's not being in attendance. Niven read a telegram from Ginger congratulating Fred on his being honored by the AFI. She said, "It certainly was fun, Fred. When they put us together, it was a blessed event." She explained that unfortunately business in New Orleans prevented her from being there.

The display of film clips of Astaire, and tributes from his onetime dance partners, other dancers, and choreographers such as Cyd Charisse, Gene Kelly, Eleanor Powell, Barrie Chase, Jimmy Cagney, Audrey Hepburn, Hermes Pan, and Bob Fosse made it, as Niven said to his friend, "Freddy, I know it was hell for you, but it was heaven for us." Finally, Fred ambled to the stage, strolling through the audience. He didn't quite know how to handle Ginger's absence and fumbled his thank-you speech. He was, however, obviously quite moved by the tribute given him by his peers.

The old team did get back together when Fred and Ginger appeared together at UCLA at the unveiling of thirty years of RKO scripts, musical scores, and personal papers that were donated to the library. Rogers, as peppy as ever, said, "I could dance right here and now." Her more demure former partner said, "I guess it's a bit too crowded to do any steps here."[7]

NOW THAT ROBYN had finally retired from racing, neither she nor Fred had any career decisions to worry about. At first, Robyn's never having been married before and Fred's having been a bachelor for more than a quarter of a century caused some friction. They had lived together for only several months before they were married, but they shared interests in horse racing, gin rummy, pool, backgammon, and taking walks. Fred called her "baby"; she called him "darling."

Bill Self made it clear, "I was a big supporter of Robyn. Then later on she turned on me, and it seemed so unfair. I felt she gave Fred a social life. She got him to go out to dinner and generally got him out of the house. We would celebrate our birthdays and New Year's Eve together. We would go to the Bistro early for dinner after I would get a call from Robyn at the last minute asking me, "What are you doing tonight?"

Self remembered, "I saw Fred and Adele on Broadway in *The Band Wagon* when I was a child." He and Fred were first introduced to each other in the dining car on a train to New York in 1946, when Self was traveling with Spencer Tracy and Fred was with Phyllis. A decade later, they met again when the caddie master at the Bel-Air Country Club put them together to play a round of golf.

From playing golf together two or three times a week, they began a weekly Sunday-afternoon gin game that lasted for more than ten years. The game began at Bel-Air and subsequently moved to their homes. The competition even extended to New York when they were there together. Self said, "We continued when Robyn showed up in our lives until she kind of killed it. It was a very slow process.

"The gin game developed into a very nice friendship. I never treated him like a star. I think he appreciated that. We used to go to the fights and to Dodger games together. I felt I knew him very well. I felt privileged."

THE SHADOWS WERE LENGTHENING. On July 29, 1983, in Château-d'Oex, Switzerland, David Niven died from the dreaded disease ALS (amyotrophic lateral sclerosis), better known as Lou Gehrig's disease. The last time Fred saw him was at the AFI tribute. In October 1983, David Jr. and Jamie put together a memorial service in Beverly Hills. Cary Grant and Robert Wagner were among David's good friends who attended. Jamie said, "Fred was pretty frail at that moment. He was very teary and came and sat between the two of us. That was how close we all were and how close he was to our father. There would be no one else who would have that seat. In the middle of the service, he leaned over to me and said, 'Jamie, it should be the other way around.' I said, 'Oh, Fred, it's so nice you could be with us here.'"

MGM BEGAN PRODUCTION on *That's Dancing!*—which followed in the path set by *That's Entertainment!* and *That's Entertainment, Part II.* Released in early 1985, the film compiled dance scenes from the 1890s to Michael Jackson. The film's coproducers were David Niven Jr. and Jack Haley Jr. The dancer Ray Bolger introduced scenes of Fred dancing in such films as *Silk Stockings, The Band Wagon, Royal Wedding, The Gay Divorcée,* and *Swing Time.*

Niven dealt closely with both Astaire and Gene Kelly, who was the film's executive producer. Niven observed, "It was very tricky how to figure out how do you define Fred and Gene because they were both number one. We got a laugh by calling them 'number one and number one.'"

In Niven's opinion, "I think one looked better in tails, and one looked better in a dinner jacket. Gene in tails would not cut it; Fred in tails absolutely. A long torso [which Astaire had] looks better in tails because of the line. Gene looked like a thug, but he could do a more physical dance. He always gave the impression of looking much more macho, strong rather than graceful, which, of course, Astaire definitely was."

To promote *That's Dancing!* MGM's publicity department set up a *Life* photograph shoot that incorporated thirty living legends of the dance. It was scheduled for 2:00 P.M., right after the lunch Niven had shared with Astaire and Kelly at the commissary. As Niven and Astaire were walking down the studio street, Astaire's chauffeured car inched along behind them.

Looking at his watch and figuring they would be late, Niven said, "Fred, don't you think we should drive? The soundstage is four blocks away."

Fred said, "What are you trying to say?"

"Well, you're moving at the speed of a wounded snail. We are not going to make it. And quite honestly, without you the photograph would be a disaster."

Fred remarked matter-of-factly, "We then have two choices. Either they have to wait for me or I pick up the pace."

Niven remembered, "He said to me, 'People think I'm an old man. You say

"Move it, Fred," and I will move it.' And he did. He was a lesson in how to move. That was probably the last time I ever saw him."[8]

Two people who arranged photograph sessions around this time with Astaire stressed how Robyn tried to direct Fred on how he should pose for the camera. The first time was in 1983 when *Life*'s entertainment editor, Jim Watters, included Astaire in a layout of great stars of the 1930s. The other time was when the acclaimed photographer Ellen Graham was shooting him, some of which photos later appeared in Sarah Giles's book *Fred Astaire: His Friends Talk*.

When Graham began photographing Astaire in 1966, on assignment from *Harper's Bazaar* for an article entitled "The 100 Most Attractive Men in the World," she was suffering from a broken toe. "He was very sympathetic. I was charmed," said Graham. "We hit it off because then I photographed him for twenty years. He liked my pictures, and he liked me. Usually, if you are a photographer, and the person doesn't like you, that's the way to have a bad session, or no session. I shoot very fast, usually an hour or so. It makes the whole thing more fun.

"I photographed him for other books, other magazines from around the world. I did another book, *The Growling Gourmet,* in 1974, with celebrities and their dogs. He posed for that with his dog Allison." Viewing a good number of the portraits Graham did of Astaire, I saw they had a definite rapport. Graham said, "He was my idol. I would say he was elegant in everything he did."

When Graham photographed him in the 1980s, Robyn was there. "I would say they were an odd combination. I think he wanted somebody young and beautiful to take care of him." When she made suggestions during his last photo shoot, Graham remarked, "I don't think either of us paid any attention to her. She was trying to be helpful. He adored her so he wanted her there.

"I must say, Robyn did me one of the biggest favors anybody can possibly do. My mother was visiting with us. She was dying of cancer. I told Robyn her dream would be to have dinner with Fred. She arranged it. We went to the Bistro, and it made her so happy. That was the best thing anyone could have done for her and for me."

One of Graham's photographs of Astaire, reproduced in her book *The Bad and the Beautiful* shows Fred in clown face. "He made that face, and I had to have it. He just did it. The picture tells a lot."

Was it Camus who said that everybody over forty is responsible for his own face?[9] Astaire's face, since he drank moderately, smoked little, stayed away from drugs, and danced most of his life, was much the same until his final years. By then, his thinness and the natural ravages of age made a significant change. He would have never entertained the thought of having his teeth capped or having a face-lift as has become a common practice of aging stars. He once said, "An inventory of my face would disclose no feature that could be hailed as what the successful movie star should wear."

RICHARD MCKENZIE, during one of his and Ava's visits to see Fred, while staying at L'Ermitage Hotel, drove Fred home. Fred no longer drove at night. When he and Robyn went out together, she drove.

Richard would sometimes pick up Fred and Hermes Pan in front of Fred's house for them to have dinner with Ava and him at the hotel. He described the experience as "like having dinner with the two men from *The Muppet Show.* After they made such a display of 'helping' each other out of the car, and in the lift, Pan did a time step while Fred suspended himself up on the brass railing and kicked his feet in the air. I told them to behave themselves; this is a nice hotel, and we had reputations to consider if they hadn't. . . . When the door opened on me shaking my finger at Fred Astaire and Hermes Pan, nudging each other like schoolboys, the faces of departing diners waiting for the lift was something to behold."[10]

Looking back on this time, McKenzie wrote, "Like many others, since his marriage, we weren't invited to his house, and coming to us requires enormous effort on his part. I think he more enjoys telephone visits anyway."[11]

"Ava always tries to ring her dad when she thinks he will be in his bedroom and can see the telephone-button light flashing. . . . Lately, she relies mostly on kitchen channels to reach her father, though that isn't an easy solution . . . the staff changes with some frequency now."[12]

"Until a couple of years ago, Fred Astaire had the same private phone number for over thirty years. We don't know why it has changed after so long, but at least Fred knew about it, and we were informed of the fact. Then, slightly over a month ago, it was changed again, alarming information discovered when, unable to reach her dad on his own line, Ava rang the house and found that the number was no longer in service. She called her brother, and when he failed, too, he got in touch with the old family lawyer, who drove up to the house and found Fred walking around the driveway for exercise.

"Fred seemed unaware of the change. He gave his kids the information as soon as he had it himself. . . . It didn't occur to him so many old friends weren't alerted either. . . . We ran into the Pecks at a restaurant. Greg asked if we had Fred Astaire's new number. He said everyone was frantic, especially Robert

Wagner. We gave them the number, which Veronique promised to circulate. Ava rang RJ with it the next day."[13]

Wagner had his own opinion on what originally precipitated Robyn and Fred's getting together: "If I was a lonely man and a thirty-five-year-old woman came to me and would look after me, I think I would say, 'That's great.' Wouldn't you? I think we are all pretty vulnerable to that. . . . Fred said to me, 'Do you think people think that I'm a funny old man trying to get this young girl?' I said to him, 'It doesn't make any difference what anybody thinks. If you are in love with her, and if she is great for you, go for it.' Every one of us who were close to Fred supported him tremendously during that relationship. I don't think, however, that she was very supportive to Fred toward the end of his life.

"When Natalie [Wood] died, Fred was very helpful to me during this time. He was there for me. He was a very precious guy. He didn't stay locked up—he was very interested in what was going on. He was very open and courageous."

CAROL LYNLEY RECALLED SENDING Fred a bottle of Louis Crystal for his eighty-sixth birthday. "He called me and said, 'My doctors told me that I can't drink anymore.' I said, 'I heard it's good for washing your hair.' Humor was the key to our relationship. We never had an argument."

From talking to various people, I got the distinct impression that Ava had always hoped that her father would marry Lynley. The outgoing actress said to me Ava loved calling her "Mommy." Lynley and Ava are the same age.

Lynley became friendly with Barrie Chase through their both being close to Fred. "I actually knew Barrie before I met Fred. Toward the end of his life, I talked to Barrie and said, 'What we've got to do is rent a helicopter and drop pizzas on his property. I told him about our plans because he didn't want to go out and wouldn't eat. I guess that's the closest we ever had to an argument. He said, 'Don't you ever do that, sweetie,' which is what he always called me."

BILL SELF SAID, "He was becoming more and more of a recluse. He would talk to me of his other friends—Gregory Peck and Randolph Scott. He never put us all together. I was put in a compartment. I remember when he gave up golf. He was a very stylish player, shot around seventy-five. Then, he married Robyn, and she wanted to belong to Bel-Air. He gave up his membership. Robyn wanted to get a membership in her name. They said no way. Ladies do not own a membership. And then he started to play a little bit again, but he did not play well, and anything that he did not do well he didn't like. In fact, he also gave up drumming.

"He told me that he was giving up playing gin because he could not see the cards anymore. This may have been the reason or it may have been something else. Toward the end of our sessions, I didn't try to beat him anymore because I was afraid that he would get discouraged. I would still go visit him. We would basically watch some golf on television or have a drink.

"He once said to me, 'You know, the doctors think I am dying.' I said, 'Well, Fred, let's hope that's not true.' He was very aware. The last time I talked to him on the phone, I did get through to him, which was very shortly before he died. I said to him, 'I'm free if you want me to come over, visit or watch television or tell some jokes or do something.' And he said, 'Oh, Bill, not today. I have to sign a lot of papers. The lawyers are coming over.' "

Shortly thereafter, Self called to inform Astaire that he and his wife, Peggy, were going to Europe. "I said that we would love to see him before we left. He got off the phone and came back in a minute and said, 'Why don't you come up here and bring something.' I said, 'Great, I'll bring some Chinese food.' He said, 'That will be terrific.' So we did.

"He ate hardly anything. He said to Peggy, 'Robyn got [me] a nutritionist, and it's not worth it. It's not working.' I told Robyn, 'We won't go to Europe if you don't want us to.' She said, 'No, you should go, but please give me your itinerary because I may have to call you.' She couldn't have been friendlier. We said good-bye that night. It was the last time I ever saw him."

Jackie Mills saw Fred walking one day in Beverly Hills. He quickly parked his car and approached him. "This was about a month before he passed away. You could tell he was not a happy camper. He was sad. He wasn't Fred Astaire."

Bill Self recalled further, "I called him from Europe. I told him, 'Peggy and I went to dinner at the White Elephant in London, and the first person I saw was Ava and Richard.' We chatted about that. I thought nothing of that phone conversation."

On the Selfs' return to Los Angeles, Bill suddenly had a problem getting Fred on the phone. "That started to bother me. I said to Peggy, 'I think Fred is ill.' A few days later, I read in the newspaper that Fred had died in a hospital in Century City."

On June 12, 1987, Fred had been admitted to Century Hospital under the name of Fred Giles, suffering from a serious respiratory ailment.[14] It developed into pneumonia, and he was put on a respirator. He was transferred to the intensive care unit, where he passed away at the age of eighty-eight, on June 22, 1987. Robyn notified Freddie, who called Ava with the news.[15]

The next morning at 11:00 A.M. Robyn, with grief-reddened eyes, appeared for a ten-minute press conference at the Century Hospital. In his *People* cover story on Astaire, Brad Darrach reported, "As Fred became noticeably weaker, at 4:25 A.M., she [Robyn] lay down beside him to hold him. 'He died in my arms. That's the way he wanted it. He died holding on to me. . . . I loved him so much. . . . More than anything else. I respected him because he was such a good person,' she said."

Time magazine called Astaire "the Great American Flyer." Richard Schickel, in his piece, said, "His manner and his voice were basic to his success, creating an illusion of ordinariness. This was not unplanned. Nothing in the use of his only instrument—himself—ever was. A cool calculation of effects, a steely perfectionist in execution, he always affected astonishment over adulation."

In his *New York Times* front-page obituary, Dick Shepard said, "Astaire set standards for motion picture musical comedies that have rarely been made and never exceeded." He went on to write, "Mr. Astaire blithely danced his way into the heart of an America tormented by the Depression and edging toward World War II. His deceptively easy-looking light-footedness, warm smile, top hat, cane, charm and talent helped people to forget the real world that nagged at them outside the movie house." Vincent Canby offered, "Never before Fred Astaire, nor since his retirement, has dancing on film been more thoroughly understood and realized. We attend to his later performances as a dramatic actor with respect, but watching the nondancing, nonsinging Astaire is like watching a grounded skylark."[16]

Tom Shales, the longtime TV critic of the *Washington Post,* said of Astaire, "He danced where angels feared to tread. Nobody danced as well as Fred Astaire, of course, but nobody looked as comfortable dancing either. . . . There was a lot more to it than agility and finesse; Astaire was born to dance as some men are born to the priesthood."

The reaction to Astaire's death was immediate, and the comments from prominent people were effusive. Irving Berlin said, "He was the purest talent I ever worked with." Their frequent telephone conversations during Berlin's last decades when he never left his Beekman Place town house were one of the few joys he looked forward to, and now his old friend was gone.[17]

Ginger Rogers commented, "I just adored and admired Fred with all of my heart. He was the best partner anyone could ever have." President Reagan: "Nancy and I are deeply saddened by the loss of a very dear friend. . . . Fred was in every sense a superstar." Publicist Warren Cowan released Gene Kelly's statement: "Although we have lost one of the greatest dancers who ever lived, Fred Astaire will always be immortal and an inspiration to all dancers who come after him. He was a good, dear friend and a lovely man. God bless him!" Jack Lemmon said, "I've never known a man who carried the mantle of greatness with such dignity."

In his will, along with his wishes for a private funeral, he insisted that there be no memorial service. Astaire also made it clear that he was against having his life story being turned into a movie. From having starred in *The Story of Vernon and Irene Castle* and *Three Little Words* alone, he had seen firsthand how the life stories of musical greats had been transformed into baseless scripts that fit a pattern, complete with a mountain of unnecessary clichés.

Bill Self expected to hear from Robyn after Fred's death, but he didn't. He called her but couldn't get her on the phone. He got a call from Ava from Ireland, who informed him that when she had asked Robyn to call Bill after her father died, Robyn said, "We don't see Bill anymore. We don't have any relationship with him." Robyn had previously told Freddie that Bill had betrayed her by having dinner with Ava and Richard in London.

The Selfs were not invited to the funeral on June 24, the date of the seventh anniversary of Astaire's marriage to Robyn. Bill drove out to Oakwood Memorial Park where it took place. He was informed that the cemetery was closed for a couple of hours. He gained entrance by saying, "My mom is buried over there." He watched Fred's funeral service from behind a tree. Self thought to himself, "How sad, Fred's best friend is hiding behind a tree. It's a joke."

Robyn, two of Fred's three children, and their spouses (Peter and Janet were absent) were huddled around the grave along with Hermes Pan. The two ministers present were Monsignor James Callahan, an old friend of Fred and Hermes's, and the rector of All Saints Episcopal Church in Beverly Hills, which Fred had regularly attended. A Hebrew reading was included in the service.[18]

Self remembered that Robyn remained at the grave site after the burial. On Fred's grave the inscription read FRED ASTAIRE I WILL ALWAYS LOVE YOU MY DARLING THANK YOU. Self said, "When I saw it, and totally independent of talking to anybody, I said, 'Fred would have hated that. He would have had FRED ASTAIRE on it."

After Robyn and Freddie left the burial area, Self went over to pay his respects. In the intervening two decades, he has made twice-yearly visits to Fred's grave.

The day after the burial Robyn went to the track to ride. A few days later, she called and spoke to Peggy Self. She begged their forgiveness, explaining that she had been so upset by Fred's death that she hadn't behaved well. Peggy pointedly said, "Bullshit." Nevertheless, Self returned her call and went to see her. Robyn offered him any keepsake of Fred's he wanted. "I had brought back a card case from Florence, maybe five years earlier, which had the initials FA and BS on it. I foolishly declined her offer," Self admitted.

Ava and Richard headed for Carmel for a few days after the burial, then returned to Beverly Hills. Gene Kelly hosted a dinner at L'Ermitage for them, which was attended by Cyd Charisse and Tony Martin, and Hermes Pan. Another night was spent with RJ Wagner at Trader Vic's. Don Cook, one of their old friends, hosted a dinner for them that included other old friends such as Roddy McDowall, the well-liked actor. Finally they headed home to Cork.

Many letters of sympathy arrived for weeks afterward. One of them was addressed merely, "To the Daughter of Fred Astaire, Ireland."[19]

BUT IN THE IMMORTAL WORDS of the Hall of Fame, former New York Yankee catcher/philosopher Lawrence Peter "Yogi" Berra, "It ain't over till it's over." In life, Fred Astaire had been a major movie star; in death he was now an extremely valuable property.

When interviewed by Chuck Champlin in the *Los Angeles Times,* shortly after her husband's death, Robyn said, "Fred left me in charge, so to speak. He wanted me to protect him. He said he was tired of being used. . . . I'll do everything I can to carry out his wishes. I hope it doesn't make me look bad or seem like a power trip. But if it does, so be it."[20]

She mentioned how upset she was at the use of film clips of her late husband that were shown at the AFI Preservation Ball in Washington, about which she had not been consulted. However, the successful evening raised money for film preservation, something Fred would likely have endorsed.

Many years earlier, Fred had negotiated a financial interest in all of his studio movies for himself with the exception of *Second Chorus* and *Royal Wedding.* Robyn now had control of his image. She asserted herself by demanding previously unprecedented fees for use of film clips of Fred's movies in documentaries shown on television and later in videos.

A well-known Emmy-winning producer at PBS said, "I would love to do a Fred Astaire documentary, but what I had to pay for the use of one of Fred's dance numbers in a show I did a few years ago—it's just not worth it." The respected documentarian Peter Jones said that he gave up courting Robyn when she declined to respond to numerous letters.[21]

Richard Schickel said recently, "I think Astaire and Kelly were much more in people's minds a decade ago than they are now. I don't think that it helps that Mrs. Astaire is holding those movies so closely. Apparently, Astaire said to her, 'All I have to leave you is the legacy of my film roles.' And he had pretty good contracts that controlled his image, which again would be typical of his controlling nature. I think she slightly misunderstood him. He did not want her to be careful. I just stay away from Fred Astaire. You can't pay the fees she wants, which is too bad. It harms his immortality. . . . I wish that he would be more in the public consciousness than he is. It's not a problem for Kelly. MGM controls the movies. They come out in DVDs. Everything happens. It's fine."

Thomas A. White, the consultant to the Astaire estate, made the point, "If you were selling a Rolls-Royce, you wouldn't be selling it for the same price as a Pinto." Unfortunately, White neglected to mention that documentarians are rarely given Rolls-Royce budgets.

A film historian who studied the original RKO and MGM contracts with Astaire said, "In 1933, when Fred Astaire signed with RKO, nobody knew television would have cable networks with 'biography' television programs fifty years hence. It's a laughable idea.

"I interpreted that clause to mean that he wanted an assurance in writing that when his musical numbers were filmed, his body wouldn't be clipped, that you wouldn't see tap-dancing feet, that you would see the full face and figure."[22]

On October 5, 1989, Robyn sued Columbia Pictures for $25,000 for failure to pay profit payments on *You'll Never Get Rich* and *You Were Never Lovelier.* This was followed by legal action against the operators of the Fred Astaire Dance Studios chain for $100,000 for distributing a series of dance videos with Fred's name on them; the Ronby Corporation (the owners) claimed they had received permission in 1965 to use his name in connection with the dance schools. In 1990, Robyn sued CBS Records for back royalties, claiming a 1935 agreement with Brunswick Records (which had been absorbed by Columbia Records, which later became CBS Records, and is now Sony Records) guaranteed her 5 percent of retail sales, and demanding a full accounting. In September 1990, she sued Forbes Inc. for $250,000 for using a photograph of Fred sitting in a boat in an advertisement that contained the caption DON'T MISS THE BOAT.[23]

In 1992, when MGM produced *When the Lion Roars,* a three-part TV miniseries on the history of the studio, due to Robyn's disagreements with Ted Turner (who then owned the studio), examples of Astaire's work were conspicuously missing. In the third segment, which focused on the golden age of the MGM musicals, his importance was discussed, and he was seen in stills and newsreel footage, but when clips from his films were shown, they were of his costars. The overall impression was that he never was an integral part of MGM's successful musicals. This same sentiment extended to May 1994, when *That's Entertainment! III* was released. It contained only two brief scenes from *The Belle of New York,* a prime candidate for Astaire's most unimportant MGM musical.[24]

However, what really brought down the wrath of the press as well as prominent denizens of the Hollywood community occurred at the end of 1992. Ginger Rogers, at eighty-one, was one of the recipients of the Kennedy Center Honors that December. CBS showed the ceremony on December 20, with no film footage of Fred and Ginger dancing. Reportedly, Thomas A. White informed the show's producer, George Stevens Jr., that the fee for the use of four clips of Astaire and Rogers dance numbers would be $70,000. Stevens was outraged and, after lengthy negotiations, refused to go along with White's demand.

In the theater, on December 6, the night of the event, with Robyn's permission the audience saw such footage; the home audience, however, witnessed Rogers either dancing solo or in acting scenes from some of her dramatic movies. *People* referred to this flagrant discrepancy as "rather like presenting Allen without Burns."

Columnist Liz Smith wrote, "This is just staggering! Rogers is a legend. A grand part of her legend was her career as a partner to Astaire. In such a situation, with Rogers now infirm [she was confined to a wheelchair] and of a certain age, one would expect the widow Astaire to indulge in a burst of minor humanity and artistic generosity. Come on, Robyn Astaire, show us a little of Fred's legendary 'class.' "[25]

Ava was quoted in Robert Osborne's January 4, 1993, column in the *Hollywood Reporter* as saying, "My father entrusted Robyn to protect his name from exploitation. I'm only sad that she has used this power in such a misguided manner." Osborne lamented, "If such financial demands are made each time anyone wishes to include Fred Astaire in a film retrospective or documentary, his image could conceivably go into limbo in the years ahead. As great as Astaire was in the Hollywood scheme, penny-wise producers may decide to forgo the use of his image rather than pay huge fees to include it. His widow, rather than being a worthy 'keeper of the flame' of Fred Astaire's image, could possibly be responsible for obliterating it."

The famous author Dominick Dunne called Robyn's action "incredibly selfish. Dancing with Fred Astaire was what made Ginger famous."

People a month later covered the flap in some detail. The magazine revealed that Robyn had actually campaigned for Rogers by calling Stevens and suggesting she be awarded the Kennedy Center Honors. Ten days before the event, Robyn (she is a licensed pilot) flew her Glasair airplane, called *Fred,* to an overnight visit with Ginger in Rancho Mirage. They had previously collaborated in suing Nabisco for misuse of Fred's (and Ginger's) image.

Rogers said of Robyn, "I feel very sorry and very unhappy that this could have come to this situation. It certainly puts me and Robyn at sword's point, and I don't like that." Robyn was quoted as saying, equally sadly and with an edge of vehemence, "I really thought I was doing something nice for Ginger. But it was the worst thing I ever did."

Further, in explaining her decision to *People,* Robyn contended that the Kennedy Center wanted to retain the rights to the film clips in perpetuity. "When I heard the word 'perpetuity,' I refused. . . . What's the point in having control over the clips if you give them away?" Stevens denied what Robyn said. He said that the showing of the clips was intended for that night only. Robyn further denied she wanted any money for use of the clips. Her attorney, Steven Brown, claimed he requested documentation that the Kennedy Center is a nonprofit institution and further that his client wanted to see the contract the show had with the sponsor, General Motors. Brown said the Kennedy Center refused to adhere to his request, and as a result he considered the TV show a profit-making affair.

Rogers countered, "I just know the Kennedy Center is a nonprofit organization. If she doesn't, I don't know what rock she's been hiding under." George Stevens angrily stated "that the entire situation suggested a rather reclusive existence for someone whose husband was honored by the Kennedy Center—a presentation that was shown on TV."[26]

In a 1997 interview with Robyn in the *Los Angeles Times* by Irene Lacher, Robyn said that Stevens "had made good on his vendetta" against her. Stevens, on being faxed her statement, said, "Robyn Astaire's requests for money are well-documented, and the only person I have ever threatened to ruin is Saddam Hussein."

Ginger Rogers passed away on April 25, 1995, at her home in Rancho Mirage. The media deservedly devoted significant attention to the importance of what she and Fred Astaire had brought to film musicals. Their close compatriot Hermes Pan had died in Beverly Hills on September 19, 1990, highly respected to the end of his life for his valuable contributions to their incredible success.[27]

NOT EVERY USE of Robyn's husband's name resulted in controversy. On May 27, 1996, Robyn endorsed the fiftieth annual (1995–96 season) Astaire Awards by presenting statuettes to Savion Glover and Donna McKechnie for their achievements in theater dance.[28]

However, in 1997, by far the biggest row occurred, surrounding the use of the famous hat-rack scene in *Royal Wedding* and a cane and a mirror from *Easter Parade* in three television commercials. This time Robyn's taste, greed, and hypocrisy were severely questioned. Instead of Astaire's dancing with a hat rack, or the other props, through the magic of the computer he was shown prancing around with a Dirt Devil vacuum cleaner! This was especially surprising in that Robyn had told *People* that she had previously turned down numerous commercial pro-posals for the use of her late husband's image. This series of commercials, first seen by a huge audience during the Super Bowl telecast, were said to be highly lucrative for Robyn. One report said that they resulted in a total payment of $750,000 to the Astaire estate.

Perhaps after all she said and did, the *real* reason for agreeing to these tasteless commercials was, as she admitted to Irene Lacher, that she had spent more than a million dollars in legal fees. She said, "I've had to deplete much of my financial security over the years to prosecute infringers." Her bank account was replen-ished, but the dignity of Fred Astaire took a severe blow.

Ava's anger over the commercials was highly visible when portions of her letter to Mike Merriman, the CEO of the Royal Appliance Manufacturing Company, which makes Dirt Devil products, were quoted in *Time*. She told the veteran colum-nist Army Archerd of *Variety* that she was returning her own Dirt Devil vacuum cleaner to the company, "saddened that after [her father's] wonderful career, he was sold to the devil."

Robyn was quoted as saying that people should "lighten up," citing her hus-band's having appeared in *Battlestar Galactica* in a space suit with turned-up toes and had also danced with mops and brooms.[29] In her *Los Angeles Times* interview with Irene Lacher, Robyn said that when the Dirt Devil commercials began ap-pearing, TV journalists began saying, " 'Fred never would have approved this.' Wait a minute. They don't know me, and they sure as hell don't know Fred. I'm his wife, his closest confidant."

She said that she'd agreed to the Dirt Devil deal because she was given artistic control and because Fred had done various other commercials. "I know Fred would have done it. Period. I didn't change his work. All I did was substitute in each frame one of Fred's props for one of the Dirt Devil products. He'd take any-thing as a prop and dance with it. I think they're well done, and people love them."[30]

A commercials agent, who wished to remain anonymous, said he had spent hours discussing with Fred his feelings about doing commercials when he was alive. Fred declared that his 1980 commercial for Home Savings, in which he ex-plained what it took to be a perfectionist, represented his preference. "A voice-over followed saying, 'This message has been brought to you by Home Savings.' It was very soft. I would take issue with the fact that he would have done the Dirt Devil commercial. People have a fond memory of Mr. Astaire—and I think this denigrated it. . . . People think that someone was screwing over an icon without his knowledge."[31]

Freddie said, "I'm behind Robyn one hundred percent. I think my father knew how people exploited personalities after their death, and he didn't want that to happen to him. Protecting him is Robyn's job."

Robyn has long had a distinct way of doing things. She seems to be absolutely sure that her decisions are infallible. In this regard, she is not unlike the equally strong-willed George W. Bush. This has perhaps been predetermined by the self-confidence that stems from the success she has achieved as a jockey and as a pilot, in addition to her overcoming an extremely difficult childhood. However, making the right decisions concerning the legacy of a famous entertainer has little or nothing to do with what she has accomplished in these areas.

The money from Fred Astaire's estate has provided her with the only real security she has ever known. She acknowledged, "Without getting maudlin, I'd never been loved before." Speaking of her marriage to Astaire, she continued, "It was meant to be. I had no control over it, and neither did Fred. It was magical and wonderful, and I had him for seven years."[32]

Bob Thomas, who informed me that Robyn had helped convince Fred to agree to cooperate with him in his 1984 Astaire biography, has remained steadfastly loyal to Robyn. In Lacher's article, he called critics of Robyn "misdirected," particularly those who had failed to win her imprimatur for projects. He said, "They think maybe she was unreasonable in holding out her approval, but that's between her and them. That's business, and she can be just as tough as any shark in the world."[33]

Lacher reported how difficult it initially was to arrange her interview with Robyn, calling it "harder than scheduling an appointment with the Dalai Lama." Lacher eventually interviewed Robyn at her office at the Santa Monica Airport, after Robyn declined to meet with her at the home she'd lived in with Astaire. Lacher described Robyn as "wraithlike and intense with a tomboyish gait and the air of a younger Katharine Hepburn."[34]

MICHAEL BLACK, Astaire's last business representative, said, "I knew the man well enough to know that he didn't want to cut his nose to spite his face. He just didn't want to have his work being someone else's work. That's the artistic pride. The point is that he wanted to stand on his own two feet and not be compared to this or that.

"If he had said no to cohosting *That's Entertainment II* with Gene Kelly and Gene had done it solo—who's he hurting? His legacy. To have the Kennedy Center Honors to Ginger Rogers and not show his work with Ginger for her night is hurting his legacy because generations from now won't remember the great Fred Astaire."

Black did affirm that Robyn has fought hard to change California laws to protect the artist and his or her likeness. "There's no doubt about that," he said. "But I just felt she went overboard and was spearheaded more by greed."

IN JUNE 1999, Robyn hosted a gala centennial tribute to Fred, held at the Museum of Modern Art but sponsored by the Academy of Motion Picture Arts and Sciences. The Academy had its own tribute earlier, which included Robyn, Bud Yorkin, and others. Film clips were shown at MOMA to an audience that included Stanley Donen and Leslie Caron.

The most recent dustup took place on February 19, 2001, when Ava presented a salute to her father at the London Palladium, which included the participation of some of Fred's Hollywood cohorts, including Cyd Charisse and Tony Martin, Jane Powell, Ann Miller, Robert Wagner, and Elmer Bernstein. Performers from the West End re-created song-and-dance numbers from several classic Astaire movies. Astaire's last record producer, Ken Barnes, said, "It was magnificent. In all my thirty-five years in music and show business, I have never seen more dedication, more affection, or more love in one place, in one single evening."[35]

Robert Osborne, in the *Hollywood Reporter,* described what took place in putting the tribute together. It was part of the ongoing Ava/Robyn conflict. Once again, problems in the use of film clips arose. According to the coproducers of the evening's entertainment, Marcia Mitchell and Lynda Trapnell, Thomas A. White refused permission to Ava unless a credit line was given declaring that said clips were being shown 'by permission of Mrs. Fred Astaire.' Mitchell and Trapnell would not agree to this stipulation.

Robert Wagner was extremely disturbed that no clips were shown that evening. "What a shame Robyn couldn't have been more gracious. This was a charitable event; it wasn't televised nor planned to be. . . . If Fred were alive, he would be horrified [that] this happened. It's inconceivable that someone who knew Fred such a short time would deny permission to his own daughter having to do with her father's work. Putting up a roadblock of any kind was mean-spirited and in very bad taste. I'm all for protecting estates, and I think fees should be paid when outsiders are trying to make money off them. But here we're talking about a devoted daughter and a father she wanted to honor."

This naturally led to a confrontation between Robyn and Wagner. She threatened to sue him. Wagner said, "Go ahead," but nothing further transpired.

Thomas A. White wrote an irate letter to the *Hollywood Reporter,* claiming, "The producers themselves elected to delete a prepared clip montage from the program, then used that as an excuse to disseminate false claims."[36] Ava and her producers had their own version of the negotiation but chose not to respond.

After the controversy that has surrounded the use of Fred Astaire's legacy, I eagerly looked forward to having Robyn Astaire provide her thoughts on it. I therefore wrote a letter to Mr. White requesting an interview with her. Mr. White informed me that my request was denied because his client was writing her own book on her husband. It's interesting that Arlene Dahl, Leslie Caron, and Robert Wagner had either begun writing their memoirs or had just completed them at the time when I interviewed them to talk about their association with Fred Astaire.

Roger Mayer said, "It's also been my understanding that Robyn was working on a book on Fred." I learned that back in 1995 the English author Felix Shipmen had also requested an interview with Robyn and had been turned down on the same basis as me. In the intervening twelve years, however, Mrs. Astaire's projected book had not been published.[37]

Mayer told me, "I would have recommended to Robyn that she see you in order to give her side of things. She hasn't done any interviews on this subject in several years. I basically like Robyn, but I do think she has made some unfortunate decisions regarding Fred's estate. Since my retirement I seem to no longer be on the radar of Robyn or Thomas White."

Robyn never married again. She keeps busy as a pilot on large transport planes ferrying executives and cargo for a charter airline internationally. According to Jackie Mills, her mother, now elderly, is living with her in the Astaire home.

AS THE FRED ASTAIRE STORY draws to a close, I thought it might be appropriate to look at comments of a few dancers, film experts, and journalists for a detailed evaluation.

Russ Tamblyn remarked, "I think Fred's greatest contribution to musicals, to movies, and to dancers could be that he was heterosexual." Richard Schickel, however, believes, "Gene Kelly was even more heterosexual. . . . In Fred Astaire there was a kind of seamlessness to him. It was interesting, and it was masculine. . . . He was a man of some calculations, not handsome, but who compensated for it by being able to seduce a woman [on-screen] with intelligence, wit, and style, which made him fascinating to men, who could learn something from him, and which also made him attractive to women."

The writer Kirk Silsbee referred to Astaire as "kind of an American sphinx. As visible as he was in life and career, very few people knew the real Fred. Ability, transparency, and identity is very important to his story because the guy really did invent himself. He was a master of 'hide in plain sight.' One of the hallmarks of his art was that he didn't want anyone to see how hard he worked.

"In America, we don't have a monarchy, but in place of that we have celebrities, specifically entertainers. We don't like our monarchy to be aristocratic. We like them elegant, but we like them informal. We like them to be down-to-earth. Fred gave that illusion in his work. In his movies, he was the guy who looked like he was born in a tux but could hold his own in a crap game. The elegance was all quite studied."

Mikhail Baryshnikov, a quarter of a century after meeting Astaire in person, referred to him as "a male butterfly without the wings—the same kind of grace of a very young horse, so angular. He was also lucky to be built the way he was— very narrow hips. He was above his material most of the time, no matter what he did from very early on up to the TV specials. The dignity and that irony about himself he sort of superimposed on his life as an artist versus his aging. The older he gets, the humor has a quieter tone. He bitterly smiles at his own achievements. Only a great man can allow himself to do that.

"He was a perfectionist. He found a huge vertical diamond. . . . It takes a lot of hours to form a diamond. He was the most important dance figure in movie history."

Peter Bogdanovich was first a respected film historian before becoming a film director and documentarian. He noted, "There are a number of reasons that Fred Astaire would not be a star today. First of all, there is no studio system to foster and encourage this kind of talent. The guy was not particularly good-looking— balding, not particularly attractive. . . . The dance made him attractive. The studios also were in a position where they would take a chance on something like him because he was so good on Broadway. And then to develop vehicles for that, one after the other. Put him with Ginger. . . . At the height of the studio system, they knew how to do that. The pictures weren't great, but they work, some of them. That world doesn't exist anymore. The audience has become so jaded, and yet so less open, than they used to be.

"Somebody recently gave me the box of the Astaire/Rogers pictures. You can't believe what the dances are. They are just so extraordinary. They seem to fly. They are so ethereal and yet grounded. It's amazing work, and it's all about performance because the camera barely does anything except recording."

The outspoken but always insightful Stanley Crouch, who observed Astaire as a dancer, said, "I think that Fred was applauded for two reasons. One, he embodied this American feeling of rhythm. He was also influenced by the dance halls, vaudeville, and shows—the things he and his sister did together. But where he really exceeded everyone and seems to have created this enormous legacy that has not been filled by anyone else is that he was able to communicate such a wide emotional range in his dance—from the comic to the romantic. . . . See, that amazing thing about him is that he never really comes off as coy. Women would like to be astonished by a guy's sincere attention to them as people. . . . That's the way Fred's appeal remains and basically does not diminish."

Robert Osborne, the host of Turner Classic Movies, said "Fred Astaire was the most talented man we've ever had in the movies. I've always thought Judy Garland was the most talented woman. So that's why I've always thought that *Easter Parade* is one of the great jewels of the MGM library.

"Jane Powell said everybody in those days was a perfectionist—Judy, Katharine Hepburn. . . . They knew what was important or would someday be important. Fred had a sense of that. I think they knew it was longer than for a flash. With television today, we're so used to people just going on in a flash, and it's forgotten tomorrow.

"There are a handful that belong in the hierarchy. There's Bogart, Fred Astaire, Gene Kelly, Cagney, Bette Davis, Katharine Hepburn—there are maybe eight or nine people from that era who are true icons. They are known by people today and don't have to be explained. They're timeless and could be on Mount Rushmore. People would go by and know who they were."

Dominick Dunne, a kind of modern John Marquand in his unceasing interest in chronicling the lives of the rich and famous, said, "Fred always looked so stylish. You could not stop looking at him. For such a major star, if you talked to him, he listened to you and connected. He was unique. There is no replacement for him. There are some new Marlon Brandos, but there is no new Fred Astaire."

AFTER TWENTY YEARS OF ROBYN'S PRICING the use of film clips of her late husband's work out of the reach of all but a few documentarians, a real and serious danger exists that Fred Astaire will soon be forgotten by the public. There are no Astaire film-feature retrospectives as there once were during the last decades of his life. Yes, there are video collections of his work, but that is not enough. In view of all that, Ruta Lee, the actress and chairman of the Thalians, the long-established Hollywood charity organization, and an old friend of Fred's, said, "If I were given the opportunity, I would urge her [Robyn] to please share not the fiscal wealth but the talent wealth with more of those who give a damn about Fred Astaire."

It is certainly no secret that today young people in this country have lost all sense of history. No longer is its importance emphasized in schools as it once was. As Peter Bogdanovich said, "In America there is no tradition of tradition. There

is no respect for culture in this country." One of the ramifications of this unfortunate and troublesome turn of events is that Mick Jagger and Justin Timberlake
may soon be regarded as outstanding dancers, but Fred Astaire will be overlooked. Such a warped point of view would indeed be tragic!

WHAT FRED ASTAIRE ACCOMPLISHED in a remarkable professional career that
spanned an astounding seventy-four years is unlike that of any other entertainment
figure. He bridged the gaps that had heretofore existed between vaudeville,
Broadway, and the movies. With the help of Ginger Rogers, he established the
movie musical as a major force in the entertainment sphere. And a quarter of a
century later, when the public lost interest in that, he transformed his talents to
the small screen and triumphed anew.

He was always acutely aware of the constantly changing nature of show business. Foreseeing that the melodious form of music that he had long been such an
important exponent of had no future, he wisely chose to become a highly capable
character actor.

The length and breadth of Astaire's career is a testimonial to the combination
of hard work, drive, concentration—and superior talent. He never lost sight of
what he had accomplished and his overall importance, but he never lorded it over
anyone. He proved that once in a while good manners, good taste, and modesty
can actually exist within the realm of a superstar.

None other than actor Sean Penn recently wrote, "Sense of self, and the way
one shares it, is perhaps the most valuable and poetic gift in the arsenal of one's
life and craft."[38] This seems as apt a description of the *gift* Fred Astaire bestowed
upon us as one could find.

NOTES

1. Paying Dues

1. Tim Satchell, *Astaire: The Biography* (London, Melbourne, Auckland, and Johannesburg: Hutchinson, 1987), 1.
2. Foster Hirsch, *Otto Preminger: The Man Who Would Be King* (Alfred A. Knopf, 2007), 15–16.
3. Alessandro Garofalo, *Notes on the Austrian Roots of the Fred Astaire family* (Trieste, Italy: self-published, June 2004), and also quoted by Garofalo at the Fred Astaire Conference at Oxford in July 2008.
4. Natasha Fraser-Cavassoni, *Sam Spiegel* (New York: Simon & Schuster, 2003), 16.
5. Bob Thomas, *Astaire: The Man, the Dancer* (New York: St. Martin's Press, 1984), 12.
6. http://www.alsodances.net/biography/youth.htm.
7. Thomas, *Astaire,* 13.
8. Benny Green, *Fred Astaire* (New York: Excter Books, 1979), 7.
9. Fred Astaire, *Steps in Time* (New York: Cooper Square Publication Edition, 2000), 12.
10. Ibid.
11. Satchell, *Astaire,* 13.
12. Thomas, *Astaire,* 16–17.
13. Satchell, *Astaire,* 12–13.
14. Ibid., 15.
15. Astaire, *Steps in Time,* 12.
16. Satchell, *Astaire,* 18.
17. Michael Freedland, *Fred Astaire* (London: W. H. Allen, 1996), 5.
18. Peter Carrick, *A Tribute to Fred Astaire* (Salem, NH: Salem House, 1984), 18.
19. Satchell, *Astaire,* 18.
20. Ibid., 19.
21. Ibid.
22. Ibid., 20.
23. Ibid.

24. Astaire, *Steps in Time,* 12.
25. Roy Packard, *Fred Astaire* (New York: Crescent Books, 1985), 9.
26. Thomas, *Astaire,* 17.
27. John Mueller, *Astaire, Dancing: The Musical Films* (New York: Alfred A. Knopf, 1985), 3.
28. Thomas, *Astaire,* 20.
29. Packard, *Astaire,* 9.
30. Additional material cut from Astaire, *Steps in Time.*
31. Larry Billman, *Fred Astaire: A Bio-Bibliography* (Westport, CT: Greenwood Press, 1997), 3.
32. Lincoln Barnett, "Fred Astaire—He Is the No. 1 Exponent of America's Only Native and Original Dance Form," *Life,* 1941.
33. Billman, *Astaire,* 4.
34. Mueller, *Astaire,* 4.
35. Thomas, *Astaire,* 28.
36. Ibid.
37. Ibid.
38. Barnett, "Fred Astaire."
39. Thomas, *Astaire,* 26–27, 35.
40. Ibid.
41. Material not published in Astaire, *Steps in Time.*
42. Carrick, *Tribute to Fred Astaire,* 31.
43. Thomas, *Astaire,* 29.
44. Material not published in Astaire, *Steps in Time.*
45. http://www.alsodances.net/biography.
46. Satchell, *Astaire,* 36.
47. Dorothy Treloar, "It's a Great New Life for Me Now," *Motion Picture,* November 1975.
48. Carrick, *Tribute to Fred Astaire.*
49. Satchell, *Astaire,* 37.
50. Astaire, *Steps in Time,* 41–50.
51. Material not published in Astaire, *Steps in Time.*
52. Astaire, *Steps in Time,* 53.
53. Thomas, *Astaire,* 31.
54. Astaire, *Steps in Time,* 55.
55. Billman, *Astaire,* 5.

2. "The Runaround"

1. Fred Astaire, *Steps in Time* (New York: Cooper Square Press, 2000), 59.
2. Michael Freedland, *Fred Astaire* (London: W. H. Allen, 1976), 17–18.
3. Astaire, *Steps in Time,* 61–62.

4. Bob Thomas, *Astaire: The Man, the Dancer* (New York: St. Martin's Press, 1984), 35–36.

5. Michael Freedland, *Fred Astaire,* (London: W. H. Allen, 1976), 18.

6. Larry Billman, *Fred Astaire: A Bio-Bibliography* (Westport, CT: Greenwood Press, 1997), 6.

7. Freedland, *Fred Astaire,* 20.

8. Astaire, *Steps in Time,* 67–68.

9. Billman, *Fred Astaire,* 6.

10. *Astaire,* Thomas, 35.

11. Ibid., 36.

12. Thomas, *Astaire,* 35–36.

13. Astaire, *Steps in Time,* 72.

14. Billman, *Fred Astaire,* 6.

15. Astaire, *Steps in Time,* 74.

16. Thomas, *Astaire,* 36.

17. Stanley Green and Burt Goldblatt, *Starring Fred Astaire* (New York: Dodd, Mead, 1973), 18.

18. Billman, *Fred Astaire,* 6.

19. Thomas, *Astaire,* 37–38.

20. Astaire, *Steps in Time,* 13.

21. Bill Adler, *Fred Astaire: A Wonderful Life,* 1st ed. (Carroll & Graf, 1987), 41.

22. Green and Goldblatt, *Starring Fred Astaire,* 21.

23. Thomas, *Astaire,* 39.

24. Ibid.

25. Green and Goldblatt, *Starring Fred Astaire,* 21.

26. Billman, *Fred Astaire,* 7.

27. Peter Carrick, *A Tribute to Fred Astaire* (Salem, NH: Salem House, 1984), 24.

28. Astaire, *Steps in Time,* 86–87.

29. Thomas, *Astaire,* 41.

30. Billman, *Fred Astaire,* 7.

31. Freedland, *Fred Astaire,* 24–25.

32. Adler, *Fred Astaire,* 42.

33. Billman, *Fred Astaire,* 7.

34. Thomas, *Astaire,* 44.

35. Adler, *Fred Astaire,* 43.

36. Billman, *Fred Astaire,* 8.

37. Tim Satchell, *Astaire: The Biography* (London, Melbourne, Auckland, and Johannesburg: Hutchinson, 1987), 44.

38. Green and Goldblatt, *Starring Fred Astaire,* 27.

39. Thomas, *Astaire,* 48.

40. Green and Goldblatt, *Starring Fred Astaire,* 30.

41. Thomas, *Astaire,* 44.
42. Freedland, *Fred Astaire* 33.
43. Ibid.
44. Thomas, *Astaire,* 45.
45. Ibid., 47.
46. Ibid., 45.
47. Ibid., 49.
48. Satchell, *Astaire,* 45.
49. Billman, *Fred Astaire,* 9.
50. Benny Green, *Fred Astaire* (New York: Exeter Books, 1979).
51. Deena Ruth Rosenberg, *Fascinating Rhythm: The Collaboration of George and Ira Gershwin* (University of Michigan Press, 1991), 80.
52. Thomas, *Astaire,* 50.
53. Rosenberg, *Fascinating Rhythm,* 81.
54. Ibid., 99.
55. Thomas, *Astaire,* 51.
56. Ibid.
57. Rosenberg, *Fascinating Rhythm,* 111.
58. Laurence Bergreen, *As Thousands Cheer: The Life of Irving Berlin* (New York: Da Capo Press, 1996), 34.
59. Rosenberg, *Fascinating Rhythm,* 107.
60. Carrick, *Tribute to Fred Astaire,* 32.
61. Herbert G. Goldman, *Banjo Eyes* (New York: Oxford University Press, 1999), 103.
62. Ibid.
63. Sarah Giles, *Fred Astaire: His Friends Talk* (New York: Doubleday, 1988), 94.
64. Astaire, *Steps in Time,* 133.
65. Thomas, *Astaire,* 53.
66. Billman, *Fred Astaire,* 9.
67. Thomas, *Astaire,* 54.
68. Astaire, *Steps in Time,* 130–31.
69. Ibid., 138–39.
70. Thomas, *Astaire,* 55.
71. Satchell, *Astaire,* 67.
72. Ibid., 63.
73. Billman, *Fred Astaire,* 10.
74. Thomas, *Astaire,* 56.
75. Ibid., 56.
76. Green, *Fred Astaire,* 30.
77. Ibid., 28.
78. Thomas, *Astaire,* 57.
79. Ibid., 57.

80. Astaire, *Steps in Time*, 154.
81. Green and Goldblatt, *Starring Fred Astaire*, 32.
82. Green, *Fred Astaire*, 33.
83. Joel Whitburn, *Billboard Top Pop Hit Singles, 1890–1954* (Billboard Publication, Record Research, 1992), 37.
84. Thomas, *Astaire*, 59.
85. Ibid., 59.
86. Ibid., 59, 68.
87. Astaire, *Steps in Time*, 157.
88. Thomas, *Astaire*, 61.
89. Green and Goldblatt, *Starring Fred Astaire*, 32.
90. Green, *Astaire*, 36.
91. Ibid.
92. Carrick, *Tribute to Fred Astaire*, 35.
93. Ibid., 36.
94. Astaire, *Steps in Time*, 160.
95. Billman, *Fred Astaire*, 11.
96. Satchell, *Astaire*, 83.
97. Carrick, *Tribute to Fred Astaire*, 38.
98. Thomas, *Astaire*, 63–64.
99. Green and Goldblatt, *Starring Fred Astaire*, 34.
100. Satchell, *Astaire*, 84.
101. Ibid.
102. Ibid., 83–84.
103. Adler, *Fred Astaire*, 58.
104. Ibid.
105. Ibid.
106. Ibid.
107. Ibid.
108. Ibid., 59.
109. Ginger Rogers, *Ginger: My Story* (New York: HarperCollins, 1991), 79.
110. Ibid., 80–81.
111. Adler, *Fred Astaire*, 60.
112. Thomas, *Astaire*, 66.
113. Ibid.
114. Ibid., 67.
115. Adler, *Fred Astaire*, 60.
116. Green and Goldblatt, *Starring Fred Astaire*, 34.
117. Whitburn, *Billboard Top Pop Hit Singles, 1890–1954*, 37.
118. Lincoln Barnett, "Fred Astaire—He Is the No. 1 Exponent of America's Only Native and Original Dance Form," *Life*, 1941.

119. Jean Cox Penn, "Fred—Who Thinks of Himself as a Legend? I Never Did," *Los Angeles Times,* March 24, 1978.
120. Thomas, *Astaire,* 72.
121. Ibid., 70.
122. Ibid., 64.
123. Ibid.
124. Green, *Fred Astaire,* 45.
125. Thomas, *Astaire,* 64–65.
126. Satchell, *Astaire,* 89.
127. Ibid.
128. Ibid.
129. Ibid.
130. Tony Thomas, *That's Dancing!* (New York: Harry Abrams, 1984), 2.

3. In Search of a Partner

1. Tim Satchell, *Astaire, the Biography* (London, Melbourne, Auckland, and Johannesburg: Hutchinson, 1987), 95.
2. Peter Carrick, *A Tribute to Fred Astaire* (Salem, NH: Salem House, 1984), 39.
3. Larry Billman, *Fred Astaire: A Bio-Bibliography* (Westport, CT: Greenwood Press, 1997), 12.
4. Satchell, *Astaire,* 95.
5. Bill Adler, *Fred Astaire: A Wonderful Life* (Carroll & Graf, 1987), 84.
6. Fred Astaire, *Steps in Time* (New York: Cooper Square Press, 2000), 72.
7. Ibid., 73.
8. Satchell, *Astaire,* 96.
9. Billman, *Fred Astaire*, 12.
10. Ibid.
11. Satchell, *Astaire,* 97.
12. Bob Thomas, *Astaire: The Man, the Dancer* (New York: St. Martin's Press, 1984), 75.
13. Stanley Green and Burt Goldblatt, *Starring Fred Astaire* (New York: Dodd, Mead, 1973), 47.
14. Satchell, *Astaire,* 57.
15. William McBrien, *Cole Porter* (New York: Alfred A. Knopf, 1998), 148.
16. Ibid.
17. Satchell, *Astaire,* 18.
18. McBrien, *Cole Porter*, 147.
19. Joel Whitburn, *Billboard Top Pop Hit Singles, 1890–1954* (Billboard Publication, Record Research), 37.
20. Ibid.
21. Satchell, *Astaire,* 98–99.

22. Astaire, *Steps in Time,* 178.
23. Satchell, *Astaire,* 99.
24. Thomas, *Astaire,* 77.
25. Billman, *Fred Astaire,* 13.
26. Astaire, *Steps in Time,* 179.
27. Satchell, *Astaire,* 99.
28. Thomas, *Astaire,* 77.
29. Green and Goldblatt, *Starring Fred Astaire,* 33, 37.
30. Satchell, *Astaire,* 100.
31. Green and Goldblatt, *Starring Fred Astaire,* 33, 37.
32. Billman, *Fred Astaire,* 13.
33. John Mueller, *Astaire Dancing: The Musical Films* (New York: Alfred A. Knopf, 1985), 7.
34. Thomas, *Astaire,* 28.
35. Adler, *Fred Astaire,* 86.
36. Scott Eyman, *The Lion of Hollywood* (New York: Simon & Schuster, 2005).
37. Billman, *Fred Astaire,* 13.
38. Adler, *Fred Astaire,* 89.
39. Mueller, *Astaire Dancing,* 7.
40. Green and Goldblatt, *Starring Fred Astaire,* 53.
41. Astaire, *Steps in Time,* 182.
42. Green and Goldblatt, *Starring Fred Astaire,* 48.
43. Ibid.
44. Ibid., 49.

4. Fred and Ginger

1. Stanley Green and Burt Goldblatt, *Starring Fred Astaire* (New York: Dodd, Mead, 1973), 58.
2. Ibid., 58–59.
3. Bill Adler, *Fred Astaire: A Wonderful Life* (Carroll & Graf, 1987), 90.
4. Fred Astaire, *Steps in Time* (New York: Cooper Square Press, 2000), 185.
5. Larry Billman, *Fred Astaire: A Bio-Bibliography* (Westport, CT: Greenwood Press, 1997), 13.
6. Ibid.
7. Charles Higham, 1983, Beverly Hills, p. I-4, Oral History Collection of Columbia University.
8. Tony Thomas, *That's Dancing!* (New York: Harry Abrams, 1984), 92.
9. Green and Goldblatt, *Starring Fred Astaire,* 63.
10. Ibid., 64.
11. *Flying Down to Rio,* RKO Production Papers, Special Collection, UCLA Library.

12. Green and Goldblatt, *Starring Fred Astaire*, 65.
13. Hollywood Film Industry Oral History Project, "The Reminiscences of Fred Astaire," 1985, p. 11, Oral History Research Office, Columbia University, New York.
14. Green and Goldblatt, *Starring Fred Astaire*, 65.
15. Ibid., 67.
16. Arlene Croce, *The Fred Astaire and Ginger Rogers Book* (New York: Outerbridge & Lazard, 1972), 24.
17. Peter Carrick, *A Tribute to Fred Astaire* (Salem, NH: Salem House, 1984), 44–45.
18. Tim Satchell, *Astaire: The Biography* (London, Melbourne, Auckland, and Johannesburg: Hutchinson, 1987), 117.
19. AFI catalog of Fred Astaire films.
20. Carrick, *Tribute to Fred Astaire*, 45.
21. Sarah Giles, *Fred Astaire: His Friends Talk* (New York: Doubleday, 1988), 94.
22. John Mueller, *Astaire Dancing: The Musical Films* (New York: Alfred A. Knopf, 1985), 8.
23. *Flying Down to Rio*, RKO Production Papers.
24. Croce, *Fred Astaire and Ginger Rogers Book*, 136.
25. Green and Goldblatt, *Starring Fred Astaire*, 72.
26. AFI catalog from the Internet, *The Gay Divorcée*, 2.
27. Green and Goldblatt, *Starring Fred Astaire*, 73.
28. Wilfrid Sheed, *The House That George Built* (New York: Random House, 2007), 156.
29. Green and Goldblatt, *Starring Fred Astaire*, 72.
30. Roy Pickard, *Fred Astaire* (New York: Crescent Books, 1985), 41.
31. Croce, *Fred Astaire and Ginger Rogers Book*, 39.
32. Ibid., 89.
33. Billman, *Fred Astaire*, 14.
34. Croce, *Fred Astaire and Ginger Rogers Book*, 33–34.
35. Columbia University Oral History Project, "Interview with Fred Astaire," 1971, p. 13.
36. Pickard, *Fred Astaire*, 38.
37. Billman, *Fred Astaire*, 14.
38. Astaire, *Steps in Time*, 200.
39. Sheed, *House That George Built*, 132.
40. Croce, *Fred Astaire and Ginger Rogers Book*, 46.
41. Susan Lydon, "My Affair with Fred Astaire," *Rolling Stone*, December 6, 1973.
42. Sheed, *House That George Built*, 132.
43. Croce, *Fred Astaire and Ginger Rogers Book*, 49–50.
44. Ibid., 51.
45. Charles Higham, 1983, Beverly Hills, pp. I-5–6, Oral History Collection of Columbia University.

46. Satchell, *Astaire,* 125.
47. Gary Giddins, *Natural Selection* (New York: Oxford University Press, 2006), 110.
48. Green and Goldblatt, *Starring Fred Astaire,* 100.
49. Mueller, *Astaire Dancing,* 9.
50. Laurence Bergreen, *As Thousands Cheer: The Life of Irving Berlin* (New York: Da Capo Press), 344.
51. Bob Thomas, *Astaire: The Man, the Dancer* (New York: St. Martin's Press, 1984), 112.
52. Astaire, *Steps in Time,* 208.
53. Satchell, *Astaire,* 24.
54. *Steps in Time,* Astaire, 210.
55. Thomas, *Astaire,* 111.
56. John A. Wilson, "Irving Berlin Tips Top Hat to Fred Astaire," *New York Times,* November 19, 1976.
57. Green and Goldblatt, *Starring Fred Astaire,* 100.
58. Astaire, *Steps in Time,* 210.
59. Thomas, *Astaire,* 123.
60. Maureen Solomon, "Fred Astaire and Ginger Rogers at RKO" (American Film Institute), n.d.
61. Bergreen, *As Thousands Cheer,* 350.
62. Thomas, *Astaire,* 115.
63. Ibid., 119.
64. Ibid., 116.
65. Frederick L. Collins, "The Real Romance in the Life of Fred Astaire," *Liberty,* January 25, 1936, 32.
66. Satchell, *Astaire,* 133–34.
67. Ibid., 155.
68. Ibid., 135.
69. Ibid., 122–23.
70. Giles, *Fred Astaire,* 145.
71. Satchell, *Astaire,* 4.
72. Howard Thompson, *Fred Astaire: A Pictorial Treasury of His Films* (New York: Falcon Enterprises, 1975), 35.
73. Satchell, *Astaire,* 154.
74. Ibid., 137–38.
75. Billman, *Fred Astaire,* 14.
76. Thomas, *Astaire,* 118.
77. Virginia Hitchcock, *The Fred Astaire Story: His Life, His Films, His Friends,* (London: B.B.C., 1975), 36.
78. Edward Gallafent, *Astaire and Rogers* (New York: Columbia University Press, 2002), 51.

79. Croce, *Fred Astaire and Ginger Rogers Book,* 82–83.

80. Southern Methodist University Oral History Project, Pandro S. Berman, interviewed by Ronald L. Davies, August 22, 1978, p. 136.

81. Croce, *Fred Astaire and Ginger Rogers Book,* 83.

82. Astaire, *Steps in Time,* 214–15.

83. Croce, *Fred Astaire and Ginger Rogers Book,* 88–89.

84. Mueller, *Astaire Dancing,* 44.

85. Hitchcock, *Fred Astaire Story,* 36.

86. Mueller, *Astaire Dancing,* 107–8.

87. Ginger Rogers, *Ginger: My Story* (New York: HarperCollins, 1991), 102.

88. Jane Goldberg, "John Bubbles, a Hoofer's Homage," *Village Voice,* December 4, 1978.

89. Giles, *Fred Astaire,* 5.

90. Mueller, *Astaire Dancing,* 108–9.

91. Croce, *Fred Astaire and Ginger Rogers Book,* 107.

92. Charles Higham, 1983, Beverly Hills, pp. I-116–17, Oral History Collection of Columbia University.

93. Croce, *Fred Astaire and Ginger Rogers Book,* 107.

94. Richard Corliss, "Can Dance a Little," *Time,* November 16, 1981, 121.

95. Rogers, *Ginger,* 109.

96. Thomas, *Astaire,* 134–35.

97. Satchell, *Astaire,* 156.

98. Green and Goldblatt, *Starring Fred Astaire,* 149.

99. Southern Methodist University Oral History Project, Pandro S. Berman, interviewed by Ronald L. Davies, August 21, 1978, p. 12.

100. Thomas, *Astaire,* 139.

101. Ted Panken, *Playbill* program, November 2006.

102. Croce, *Fred Astaire and Ginger Rogers Book,* 120.

103. Green and Goldblatt, *Starring Fred Astaire,* 154.

104. Thomas, *Astaire,* 161.

105. Croce, *Fred Astaire and Ginger Rogers Book,* 120–21.

106. Stephen Holden, "Potato? Po-tah-to? Tomato?" *New York Times,* June 15, 2004.

107. Green and Goldblatt, *Starring Fred Astaire,* 158.

108. Carrick, *Tribute to Fred Astaire,* 89.

109. Croce, *Fred Astaire and Ginger Rogers Book,* 121.

110. Green and Goldblatt, *Starring Fred Astaire,* 189.

111. Pickard, *Fred Astaire,* 72.

112. Green and Goldblatt, *Starring Fred Astaire,* 160.

113. Alvin Yudkoff, *Gene Kelly* (New York: Back Stage Books, Watson-Guptill Publications, 1999), 41.

114. Richard L. Worsnos, "Thanks, Fred," *Editorial Research Reports,* April 29, 1974.

115. Green and Goldblatt, *Starring Fred Astaire,* 153.

116. Ibid., 152.

117. Allan Scott, "A Nice Life," in Patrick McGilligan, *Backstory: Interviews with Screenwriters of Hollywood's Golden Age* (Berkeley: University of California Press, 1986), 195.

118. *The Selected Nonfiction of John Gregory Dunne* (New York: Thunder's Mouth Press, 2006), 360.

119. Green and Goldblatt, *Starring Fred Astaire,* 164.

120. Thomas, *Astaire,* 137.

121. Satchell, *Astaire,* 147.

122. Thomas, *Astaire,* 143–44.

123. Ibid., 144.

124. Ibid., 145.

125. Green and Goldblatt, *Starring Fred Astaire,* 167.

126. Ibid.

127. Ibid., 170.

128. Thomas, *Astaire,* 160.

129. Ibid., 147.

130. Kevin Starr, *The Dream Endures: California Enters the 1940s* (New York: Oxford University Press, 1977), 150.

131. Ibid.

132. Thomas, *Astaire,* 148.

133. Thomas, *That's Dancing!,* 5.

134. Collins, "Real Romance," 32.

135. Thomas, *Astaire,* 151.

136. Ibid., 153.

137. Thomas, *That's Dancing!,* 9.

138. Hitchcock, *Fred Astaire Story,* 42–43.

139. Pickard, *Fred Astaire,* 70.

140. "Movie of the Week: *Carefree,*" *Life,* August 22, 1938.

141. Croce, *Fred Astaire and Ginger Rogers Book,* 147.

142. Green and Goldblatt, *Starring Fred Astaire,* 180, 185.

143. Hitchcock, *Fred Astaire Story,* 43.

144. Croce, *Fred Astaire and Ginger Rogers Book,* 50.

145. Pickard, *Fred Astaire,* 70.

146. Billman, *Fred Astaire,* 16.

147. Thomas, *Astaire,* 157.

148. Green and Goldblatt, *Starring Fred Astaire,* 192.

149. Solomon, "Fred Astaire and Ginger Rogers at RKO" 3, n.d.

150. Billman, *Fred Astaire,* 61.

151. *The Story of Vernon and Irene Castle,* RKO Production Papers, Special Collection, UCLA Library.

152. Croce, *Fred Astaire and Ginger Rogers Book,* 166.

153. Giles, *Fred Astaire,* 34.

154. Gerald Clarke, *Get Happy: The Life of Judy Garland* (New York: Random House, 2000), 240.

155. Giles, *Fred Astaire,* 34.

156. Ibid., 94.

157. Southern Methodist University Oral History Project, Pandro S. Berman, interviewed by Ronald L. Davies, August 21, 1978, p. 17.

158. Thomas, *Astaire,* 153.

159. Billman, *Fred Astaire,* 16.

160. Gallafent, *Astaire and Rogers,* 80.

161. Joyce Haber, "Astaire's Way to the Stars," *Los Angeles Times,* May 11, 1975.

5. Change Partners and Dance

1. Roy Pickard, *Fred Astaire* (New York: Crescent Books, 1985), 76.

2. Ibid., 79.

3. Tim Satchell, *Astaire: The Biography* (London, Melbourne, Auckland, and Johannesburg: Hutchinson, 1987), 162.

4. Fred Astaire, *Steps in Time* (New York: Cooper Square Press, 2000), 242.

5. Ibid., 241.

6. Pickard, *Fred Astaire* (New York: Crescent Books, 1985), 79.

7. John Mueller, *Astaire Dancing: The Musical Films* (New York: Alfred A. Knopf, 1985), 167.

8. Ibid., 176.

9. Stanley Green and Burt Goldblatt, *Starring Fred Astaire* (New York: Dodd, Mead, 1973), 310–11.

10. Pickard, *Fred Astaire,* 80.

11. Larry Billman, *Fred Astaire: A Bio-Bibliography* (Westport, CT: Greenwood Press, 1997), 16.

12. Mueller, *Astaire Dancing,* 167.

13. Joyce Haber, "Astaire's Way to the Stars," *Los Angeles Times,* May 11, 1975.

14. Bob Thomas, *Astaire: The Man, the Dancer* (New York: St. Martin's Press, 1984), 163.

15. Mueller, *Astaire Dancing,* 179.

16. Satchell, *Astaire,* 163.

17. Mueller, *Astaire Dancing,* 179.

18. Pickard, *Fred Astaire,* 85, 87.
19. Astaire, *Steps in Time,* 243–44.
20. Barbara Leaming, *If This Was Happiness: A Biography of Rita Hayworth* (New York: Random House, 1992), 55.
21. Ibid., 62.
22. Green and Goldblatt, *Starring Fred Astaire,* 226.
23. Thomas, *Astaire,* 171.
24. Peter Carrick, *A Tribute to Fred Astaire* (Salem, NH: Salem House, 1984), 165.
25. Mueller, *Astaire Dancing,* 187–88.
26. G. Bruce Boyer, *Fred Astaire Style* (New York: Assouline Publishing, 2004), 15.
27. Green and Goldblatt, *Starring Fred Astaire,* 232.
28. Ibid., 233.
29. Thomas, *Astaire,* 176.
30. Gene Lees, *Portrait of Johnny: The Life of John Herndon Mercer* (New York: Pantheon, 2004), 115.
31. Thomas, *Astaire,* 171.
32. Satchell, *Astaire,* 164.
33. Green and Goldblatt, *Starring Fred Astaire,* 232.
34. Thomas, *Astaire,* 174–75.
35. Ibid., 173.
36. Green and Goldblatt, *Starring Fred Astaire,* 239.
37. Ibid.
38. Ibid.
39. Mueller, *Astaire Dancing,* 217.
40. Green and Goldblatt, *Starring Fred Astaire,* 248.
41. Ibid., 249.
42. Ibid., 251.
43. Mueller, *Astaire Dancing,* 221.
44. Ibid.
45. Satchell, *Astaire,* 164.
46. Green and Goldblatt, *Starring Fred Astaire,* 255.
47. Leaming, *If This Was Happiness,* 74.
48. Thomas, *Astaire,* 176–80.
49. Satchell, *Astaire,* 168.
50. Thomas, *Astaire,* 176–80.
51. Billman, *Fred Astaire,* 17.
52. Green and Goldblatt, *Starring Fred Astaire,* 261–62.
53. Ibid., 263.
54. Mueller, *Astaire Dancing,* 228.
55. Green and Goldblatt, *Starring Fred Astaire,* 260.

56. Thomas, *Astaire,* 184.

57. Ibid.

58. Billman, *Fred Astaire,* 17.

6. The Dream Factory and Two Excursions to Paramount

1. Scott Eyman, *Lion of Hollywood: The Life and Legend of Louis B. Mayer* (New York: Simon & Schuster, 2005), 44.

2. Fred Astaire interview, conducted by Fred Davis, July 31, 1976, Southern Methodist University Collection.

3. Eyman, *Lion of Hollywood,* 4.

4. Ibid., 331.

5. Ibid., 355.

6. *Ziegfeld Follies* production notes by Arthur Freed, Arthur Freed Collection, Doheny Library, USC.

7. John Mueller, *Astaire Dancing: The Musical Films* (New York: Alfred A. Knopf, 1985), 242.

8. Stanley Green and Burt Goldblatt, *Starring Fred Astaire* (New York: Dodd, Mead, 1973), 276.

9. Mueller, *Astaire Dancing,* (New York: Alfred A. Knopf, 1985), 248.

10. Alvin Yudkoff, *Gene Kelly: A Life of Dance and Dreams* (New York: Back Stage Books, Watson-Guptill Publications, 1999), 140.

11. Tim Satchell, *Astaire: The Biography* (London, Melbourne, Auckland, and Johannesburg: Hutchinson, 1987), 167.

12. Ibid.

13. Clive Hirschhorn, *Gene Kelly: A Biography* (London: WH Allen, 1984), 117.

14. Peter Carrick, *A Tribute to Fred Astaire* (Salem, NH: Salem House, 1984), 108.

15. Roy Pickard, *Fred Astaire* (New York: Crescent Books, 1985), 99.

16. Green and Goldblatt, *Starring Fred Astaire,* 275.

17. Pickard, *Fred Astaire,* 44.

18. Dave Kehr, "Critic's Choice: New DVD's," *New York Times,* April 25, 2006, B3.

19. Mueller, *Astaire Dancing,* 250.

20. Ibid., 251

21. Fred Astaire, *Steps in Time* (New York: Cooper Square Press, 2000), 206.

22. Bob Thomas, *Astaire: The Man, the Dancer* (New York: St. Martin's Press, 1984), 186.

23. Dorothy S. Gaiter, "Adele Astaire, Dancer-Comedian, Dies," *New York Times,* January 26, 1981.

24. "Adele Astaire Urges Raw Cabbage as Diet; Her Daily Fare, Says the Ex-Dancer Here," *New York Times,* December 23, 1935.

25. Thomas, *Astaire,* 176–80.

26. Satchell, *Astaire,* 168.
27. Ibid., 169
28. Astaire, *Steps in Time,* 272.
29. Thomas, *Astaire,* 176–80.
30. Satchell, *Astaire,* 169.
31. *Ziegfeld Follies* production notes by Arthur Freed.
32. Interview with Marian McPartland, by Paul De Barros, August 19, 2006.
33. Thomas, *Astaire,* 176–77.
34. Michael Dregni, *Django: The Life and Music of a Gypsy Legend* (New York: Oxford University Press, 2004), 140.
35. Satchell, *Astaire,* 169.
36. Ibid.
37. Astaire, *Steps in Time,* 276.
38. Thomas, *Astaire,* 176–80.
39. Ibid., 182.
40. Satchell, *Astaire,* 171.
41. Mueller, *Astaire Dancing,* 254.
42. Green and Goldblatt, *Starring Fred Astaire,* 283.
43. Mueller, *Astaire Dancing,* 259.
44. Green and Goldblatt, *Starring Fred Astaire,* 281.
45. *Yolanda and the Thief* production notes by Arthur Freed, Arthur Freed Collection, Doheny Library, University of Southern California.
46. Mueller, *Astaire Dancing,* 253.
47. Kevin Starr, *Embattled Dreams: California in War and Peace, 1940–1950* (New York: Oxford University Press, 2002), 165.
48. Satchell, *Astaire,* 170.
49. Ibid., 174–75.
50. Ibid., 175–76.
51. Thomas, *Astaire,* 191.
52. Ibid.
53. Mueller, *Astaire Dancing,* 270–71.
54. Ibid., 273.
55. Thomas, *Astaire,* 193.
56. Green and Goldblatt, *Starring Fred Astaire,* 300–301.
57. Pickard, *Fred Astaire,* 104.
58. Thomas, *Astaire,* 193.
59. Mueller, *Astaire Dancing,* 263.
60. Satchell, *Astaire,* 174.
61. Ibid., 176.
62. Astaire, *Steps in Time,* 290.
63. Thomas, *Astaire,* 200.

64. Satchell, *Astaire*, 178.

65. Ibid.

66. Ibid.

67. Thomas, *Astaire*, 202.

68. Astaire, *Steps in Time*, 290.

69. Betsy Blair, *The Memory of All That: Love and Politics in New York, Hollywood, and Paris* (New York: Alfred A. Knopf, 2003), 128.

70. Astaire, *Steps in Time*, 291.

71. Eyman, *Lion of Hollywood*, 380.

72. Gerald Clarke, *Get Happy* (New York: Random House, 2000), 242.

73. Mueller, *Astaire Dancing*, 275.

74. Ibid., 277

75. *Easter Parade* production notes by Arthur Freed, Arthur Freed Collection, Doheny Library, USC.

76. Carrick, *Tribute to Fred Astaire*, 111.

77. Ann Miller with Norma Lee Browning, *Miller's High Life*, (Garden City, NY: Doubleday, 1972), 148.

78. Hugh Fordin, *MGM's Greatest Musicals: The Arthur Freed Unit* (New York: Da Capo Press, 1996), 231.

79. Clarke, *Get Happy*, 248.

80. Pickard, *Fred Astaire*, 110.

81. Clarke, *Get Happy*, 240.

82. Mueller, *Astaire Dancing*, 277.

83. Pickard, *Fred Astaire*, 111.

84. Larry Billman, *Fred Astaire: A Bio-Bibliography* (Westport, CT: Greenwood Press, 1997), 19.

85. Fordin, *MGM's Greatest Musicals*, 233.

86. *Easter Parade* production notes by Freed.

87. Astaire, *Steps in Time*, 293.

88. Stanley Crouch, *Considering Genius: Writings on Jazz* (New York: Basic Civitas Books, 2006), 225.

89. Eyman, *Lion of Hollywood*, 397.

90. *The Barkleys of Broadway* production notes by Arthur Freed, Arthur Freed Collection, Doheny Library, USC.

91. Clarke, *Get Happy*, 246.

92. Ibid.

93. Satchell, *Astaire*, 183.

94. Thomas, *Astaire*, 210.

95. Clarke, *Get Happy*, 249.

96. Green and Goldblatt, *Starring Fred Astaire*, 326.

97. Pickard, *Fred Astaire*, 115.

98. *Regards: The Selected Nonfiction of John Gregory Dunne* (New York: Thunder's Mouth Press, 2006), 327.

99. Mueller, *Astaire Dancing,* 296.

100. *The Barkleys of Broadway* production notes by Freed.

101. Ibid.

102. Green and Goldblatt, *Starring Fred Astaire,* 327.

103. Mueller, *Astaire Dancing,* 289.

104. Ibid., 298.

105. Satchell, *Astaire,* 283.

106. Pickard, *Fred Astaire,* 121.

107. Mueller, *Astaire Dancing,* 23.

108. Green and Goldblatt, *Starring Fred Astaire,* 345.

109. Pickard, *Fred Astaire,* 126.

110. Billman, *Fred Astaire,* 20.

111. Mueller, *Astaire Dancing,* 313.

112. Billman, *Fred Astaire,* 20.

113. Thomas, *Astaire,* 216.

114. Satchell, *Astaire,* 187.

115. *The Barkleys of Broadway* production notes by Freed.

116. Tony Thomas, *That's Dancing!* (New York: Harry Abrams, 1984), 15.

117. Green and Goldblatt, *Starring Fred Astaire,* 352.

118. Thomas, *Astaire,* 219.

119. Stephen M. Silverman, *Dancing on the Ceiling: Stanley Donen and His Movies* (New York: Alfred A. Knopf, 1996), 123.

120. Satchell, *Astaire,* 187.

121. Silverman, *Dancing on the Ceiling,* 125.

122. Satchell, *Astaire,* 188.

123. Silverman, *Dancing on the Ceiling,* 128.

124. Thomas, *Astaire,* 219.

125. Silverman, *Dancing on the Ceiling,* 130.

126. Ibid., 131.

127. Ibid.

128. Pickard, *Fred Astaire,* 132.

129. Silverman, *Dancing on the Ceiling,* 132.

130. Ibid.

131. Alan Jay Lerner, *The Street Where I Live* (New York: W. W. Norton, 1994), 89.

132. *Royal Wedding* production notes by Arthur Freed, Arthur Freed Collection, Doheny Library, USC.

133. Jane Powell, *The Girl Next Door and How She Grew* (New York: William Morrow, 1988), 123.

134. Silverman, *Dancing on the Ceiling,* 129.

135. Ibid., 130.

136. Pickard, *Fred Astaire,* 137.

137. Ibid.

138. Fordin, *MGM's Greatest Musicals,* 364–65.

139. Ibid., 365.

140. *The Belle of New York* production notes by Arthur Freed, Arthur Freed Collection, Doheny Library, USC.

141. Ibid.

142. Pickard, *Fred Astaire,* 138.

143. Ibid.

144. *The Band Wagon* production notes by Arthur Freed, Arthur Freed Collection, Doheny Library, USC.

145. Fordin, *MGM's Greatest Musicals,* 44.

146. *The Band Wagon* production notes by Freed.

147. Carrick, *Tribute to Fred Astaire,* 119.

148. Satchell, *Astaire,* 189.

149. Mueller, *Astaire Dancing,* 351, 354.

150. Fordin, *MGM's Greatest Musicals,* 411.

151. Thomas, *Astaire,* 225.

152. *The Band Wagon* production notes by Freed.

153. Vincente Minnelli and Hector Arce, *I Remember It Well* (Garden City, NY: Doubleday, 1974), 262.

154. Green and Goldblatt, *Starring Fred Astaire,* 385.

155. Charles Higham, "The Reminiscences of Fred Astaire," 1971, p. 36, Hollywood Film Industry Oral History Project.

156. Vincente Minnelli, quoted in Richard Schickel, *The Man Who Made the Movies* (New York: Atheneum, 1975).

157. Thomas, *Astaire,* (New York: St. Martin's Press, 1984), 225.

158. Mueller, *Astaire Dancing,* 357.

159. Fordin, *MGM's Greatest Musicals,* 411–12.

160. Ibid., 404.

161. Mueller, *Astaire Dancing,* 353.

162. Thomas, *That's Dancing!,* 24.

163. Thomas, *Astaire,* 223–24.

164. Pickard, *Fred Astaire,* 143.

165. Ibid., 145.

166. Satchell, *Astaire,* 192.

167. Green and Goldblatt, *Starring Fred Astaire,* 386.

168. Carrick, *Tribute to Fred Astaire,* 119.

169. Astaire, *Steps in Time,* 305–6.

170. Pickard, *Fred Astaire,* 147.

171. Satchell, *Astaire,* 193.
172. Thomas, *Astaire,* 231.
173. Ibid.

7. The Last of the Grand Old Musicals

1. Roy Pickard, *Fred Astaire* (New York: Crescent Books, 1985), 147.
2. John Mueller, *Astaire Dancing: The Musical Films* (New York: Alfred A. Knopf, 1985), 362.
3. Stanley Green and Burt Goldblatt, *Starring Fred Astaire* (New York: Dodd, Mead, 1973), 400.
4. Henry Ephron, *We Thought We Could Do Anything: The Life of Screenwriters Phoebe and Henry Ephron* (New York: W. W. Norton, 1977), 136.
5. Pickard, *Fred Astaire,* 147.
6. Mueller, *Astaire Dancing,* 370.
7. Green and Goldblatt, *Starring Fred Astaire,* 402.
8. Ibid., 403–4.
9. Larry Billman, *Fred Astaire: A Bio-Bibliography* (Westport, CT: Greenwood Press, 1997), 22.
10. Sarah Giles, *Fred Astaire: His Friends Talk* (New York: Doubleday, 1988), 187.
11. Mueller, *Astaire Dancing,* 367.
12. Giles, *Fred Astaire,* 79.
13. Tim Satchell, *Astaire: The Biography* (London, Melbourne, Auckland, and Do-hamburg: Hutchinson, 1987), 196.
14. Pickard, *Fred Astaire,* 147.
15. Satchell, *Astaire,* 195–96.
16. Ibid., 196.
17. Ibid., 196–97.
18. Ibid., 197.
19. Ibid.
20. Ibid.
21. Pickard, *Fred Astaire,* 155.
22. *Funny Face* production notes from Roger Edens Collection, Doheny Library, USC.
23. Pickard, *Fred Astaire,* 150–51, 155.
24. Stephen M. Silverman, *Dancing on the Ceiling: Stanley Donen and His Movies* (New York: Alfred A. Knopf, 1996), 222.
25. Ibid.
26. *Funny Face* production notes from Roger Edens Collection.
27. Pickard, *Fred Astaire*, 155.
28. Silverman, *Dancing on the Ceiling,* 222.
29. Ibid., 218.

30. Pickard, *Fred Astaire,* 155.

31. *Funny Face* production notes from Roger Edens Collection.

32. Silverman, *Dancing on the Ceiling,* 235.

33. Ibid., 236.

34. Liesl Schillinger, review of Donald Spoto's *Enchantment: The Life of Audrey Hepburn, New York Times,* October 1, 2006.

35. Pickard, *Fred Astaire,* 155.

36. *Funny Face* production notes from Roger Edens Collection.

37. Bob Thomas, *Astaire: The Man, the Dancer* (New York: St. Martin's Press, 1984), 235.

38. *Funny Face* production notes from Roger Edens Collection.

39. Mueller, *Astaire Dancing,* 382.

40. Silverman, *Dancing on the Ceiling,* 236.

41. Ibid., 239.

42. Giles, *Fred Astaire,* 196.

43. Silverman, *Dancing on the Ceiling,* 240.

44. Leonard Gershe material from the original liner notes to the Verve sound track LP of *Funny Face.*

45. Silverman, *Dancing on the Ceiling,* 241.

46. Philip Gefter, "Defining Beauty Through Avedon," *New York Times,* September 18, 2005, Style section, 6.

47. Silverman, *Dancing on the Ceiling,* 241.

48. Joe Goldberg material from the reissue liner notes to the Verve sound track CD of *Funny Face.*

49. Satchell, *Astaire,* 200.

50. Ibid.

51. *Funny Face* production notes from Roger Edens Collection.

52. Thomas, *Astaire,* 236.

53. Mueller, *Astaire Dancing,* 388.

54. Pickard, *Fred Astaire,* 159.

55. Green and Goldblatt, *Starring Fred Astaire,* 423.

56. Pickard, *Fred Astaire,* 159.

57. Green and Goldblatt, *Starring Fred Astaire,* 423.

58. Mueller, *Astaire Dancing,* 388.

59. Ibid., 310.

60. Billman, *Fred Astaire,* 22.

61. *Silk Stockings* production notes from the Arthur Freed Collection, Doheny Library, USC.

62. Mueller, *Astaire Dancing,* 388.

63. *Silk Stockings* production notes from the Arthur Freed Collection.

64. Mueller, *Astaire Dancing,* 392.

65. Myron Meisel, "Some Enchanted Evening," *American Film Magazine,* May 1988.
66. David Zeitlin, "I train just like a racehorse," *Life,* 1965–66.
67. Green and Goldblatt, *Starring Fred Astaire,* 432.
68. Charles Higham, "The Reminiscences of Fred Astaire," 1971, p. 35, Hollywood Film Industry Oral History Project.
69. Mueller, *Astaire Dancing,* 390.
70. Ibid., 388.
71. Higham, "Reminiscences of Fred Astaire," 34.
72. Mueller, *Astaire Dancing,* 399.
73. *Silk Stockings* production notes from the Arthur Freed Collection.
74. John Anderson, *Daily Variety,* January 19, 2006.
75. Mueller, *Astaire Dancing,* 390.

8. The Clothes That Made the Man

1. Lincoln Barnett, "Fred Astaire—He Is the No. 1 Exponent of America's Only Native and Original Dance Form," *Life,* 1941.
2. Sarah Giles, *Fred Astaire: His Friends Talk* (New York: Doubleday, 1988), 50.
3. Barnett, "Fred Astaire."
4. Ibid.
5. Giles, *Fred Astaire,* 56.
6. Ibid., 12.
7. Ibid., 48.
8. Barnett, "Fred Astaire."
9. G. Bruce Boyer, *Eminently Suitable* (New York: W. W. Norton, 1990), 55.
10. Michael Freedland, *Fred Astaire* (Grosset & Dunlap, 1977), 245.
11. *Listen,* January 19, 1979.
12. Giles, *Fred Astaire,* 53.

9. The NBC-TV Specials: Three Hits and a Miss

1. Fred Astaire, *Steps in Time* (New York: Cooper Square Press, 2000), 321.
2. Roy Pickard, *Fred Astaire* (New York: Crescent Books, 1985), 361.
3. Bob Thomas, *Astaire: The Man, the Dancer* (New York: St. Martin's Press, 1984), 247.
4. Ibid.
5. Ibid., 248.
6. Ibid.
7. Ibid., 249.
8. Ibid., 250.
9. Tim Satchell, *Astaire: The Biography* (London, Melbourne, Ackland, and Johannesburg: Hutchinson, 1987), 207.

10. Liner notes to *Easy to Dance with Fred Astaire* (Verve Records) by Don Freeman.

11. Astaire, *Steps in Time,* 323.

12. "Fred Astaire, Dancer," Associated Press Biographical Service, Sketch 4236, May 1, 1965.

13. Satchell, *Astaire,* 212.

14. Benny Green, *Fred Astaire* (New York: Exeter Books, 1979), 141.

15. Pickard, *Fred Astaire,* 163.

16. Robert Stone, *Prime Green: Remembering the Sixties* (New York: Ecco Press, 2007), 92.

17. Green, *Fred Astaire,* 141.

18. Steve Zee, "From Broadway to Hollywood and Back," *On Tap,* a publication of the International Tap Association, April/May/June 2005, 27.

19. Ibid.

10. The Perfect Singer and the Would-Be Jazz Musician

1. John S. Wilson, "Irving Berlin Tips Top Hat to Fred Astaire," *New York Times,* November 19, 1976.

2. Whitney Balliett, *Collected Works: A Journal of Jazz, 1954–2001* (New York: St. Martin's Press, 2002) 545–46.

3. Richard M. Sudhalter, "Fred Astaire Makes an Impression on New Disc," *New York Post,* March 22, 1980.

4. Gary Giddins, *Bing Crosby: A Pocketful of Dream, the Early Years, 1903–1940* (Boston: Little, Brown, 2001), 514.

5. Ibid., 254.

6. Ruth Prigozy, *The Life of Dick Haymes: No More Little White Lies* (Jackson: University of Mississippi Press, 2006), 60.

7. "A Grateful Farewell," *Los Angeles Times,* Calendar section, January 29, 2005.

11. The Character Actor Emerges as the Song-and-Dance Man Fades

1. Tim Satchell, *Astaire: The Biography* (London, Melbourne, Auckland, and Johannesburg: Hutchinson, 1987), 210.

2. Stanley Green and Burt Goldblatt, *Starring Fred Astaire* (New York: Dodd, Mead, 1973), 438.

3. Bob Thomas, *Astaire: The Man, the Dancer* (New York: St. Martin's Press, 1984), 261.

4. Ibid., 262–63.

5. Charles Higham, "The Reminiscences of Fred Astaire," Hollywood Film Industry Oral History Project, Oral History Research Office, Columbia University 1985, pp. 42–43.

6. Leonard Lyons, "The Lyons Den," *New York Post,* May 2, 1970.

7. Green and Goldblatt, *Starring Fred Astaire* 436.

8. Ibid., 439.

9. Larry Billman, *Fred Astaire: A Bio-Bibliography* (Westport, CT: Greenwood Press, 1997), 23.

10. Roy Pickard, *Fred Astaire* (New York: Crescent Books, 1985), 166.

11. Foster Hirsch, *Otto Preminger: The Man Who Would Be King* (New York: Alfred A. Knopf, 2007), 285.

12. Unpublished material from George Jacobs and William Stadiem, *Mr. S: My Life with Frank Sinatra* (New York: Harper Entertainment, 2003).

13. Richard McKenzie, *Turn Left at the Black Cow: One Family's Journey from Beverly Hills to Ireland* (Lanham, MD: Roberts Rinehart Publishers, 1998), 154.

14. Satchell, *Astaire,* 229.

15. John Anthony Gilvey, *Before the Parade Passes By: Gower Champion and the Glorious American Musical* (New York: St. Martin's Press, 2005), 79.

16. Higham, "Reminiscences of Fred Astaire," 42–43.

17. Lilli Palmer, *Change Lobsters and Dance* (New York: Macmillan, 1975), 296–97.

18. Green and Goldblatt, *Starring Fred Astaire* 483.

19. Thomas, *Astaire,* 268.

20. Ibid., 170.

21. Ibid.

22. Green and Goldblatt, *Starring Fred Astaire* 446.

23. Ibid.

24. Ibid.

25. Ibid., 447.

26. Laurence Bergreen, *As Thousands Cheer: The Life of Irving Berlin* (New York: Da Capo Press, 1996) 557–68.

27. Ronald and Allis Radosh, *Red Star over Hollywood* (New York: Encounter Books, 2006), 35.

28. *Time/Life* file of Doug Lindeman, June 23, 1987.

29. Charles Champlin, "Step Up and Meet a Dancing Man," *Los Angeles Times,* March 11, 1966.

30. Philip K. Scheuer, "The Gold at 'Rainbow' End," *Los Angeles Times,* October 20, 1968.

31. Green and Goldblatt, *Starring Fred Astaire,* 433.

32. Rebecca Winters Kugan, "Coppola, Take 2," *Time,* November 19, 2007.

33. John Mueller, *Astaire Dancing: The Musical Films* (New York: Alfred A. Knopf, 1985), 401.

34. Ibid., 403

35. Higham, "Reminiscences of Fred Astaire." 39–40.

36. Aljean Harmetz, "Astaire, Nearing 80, Is Still a Very Private Person," *New York Times,* May 8, 1979.

37. Green and Goldblatt, *Starring Fred Astaire,* 458–59.
38. Satchell, *Astaire,* 216.
39. Green and Goldblatt, *Starring Fred Astaire,* 458.
40. *Esquire,* August 1969, 26.
41. Satchell, *Astaire,* 278.

12. A Decade of Tributes

1. Leslie Bricusse, *The Music Man: The Life and Good Times of a Songwriter* (London: Metro Publishing, 2006), 241.
2. Tim Satchell, *Astaire: The Biography* (London, Melbourne, Auckland, Johannesburg: Hutchinson, 1987), 213.
3. Sarah Giles, *Fred Astaire: His Friends Talk* (New York: Doubleday, 1988), 114.
4. Ibid., 200.
5. Satchell, *Astaire,* 233.
6. Bob Thomas, *Astaire: The Man, the Dancer* (New York: St. Martin's Press, 1984), 292.
7. Frank Deford, "Beauty and the Beast," *Sports Illustrated,* July 19, 1972, 62.
8. Satchell, *Astaire,* 234.
9. Ibid., 235.
10. Thomas, *Astaire,* 299.
11. Satchell, *Astaire,* 235.
12. Ibid., 236.
13. Peter Duchin with Charles Michener, *Ghost of a Chance: A Memoir* (New York: Random House, 1996), 138–39.
14. Ibid., 289.
15. Sally Quinn, "He Hates White Tie and Tails," *Washington Post,* May 2, 1973.
16. Anna Kisselgoff, "The Old Movie Musicals," *New York Times,* March 3, 1980.
17. Robert Hofler, "Keys Unlocks Secrets to a 30-Year Icon Quest," *Daily Variety,* April 19, 2008, A4.
18. Quinn, "He Hates White Tie and Tails."
19. Satchell, *Astaire,* 283–84.
20. Richard McKenzie, *Turn Left at the Black Cow: One Family's Journey from Beverly Hills to Ireland* (Lanham, MD: Roberts Rinehart Publishers, 1998), 312–13.
21. Roy Pickard, *Fred Astaire* (New York: Crescent Books, 1985), 167.
22. Ibid., 180.
23. Irwin Allen Archive, UCLA Library.
24. Thomas, *Astaire,* 282.
25. Ibid.
26. Harry Haun, "Dancing Man," New York *Daily News,* April 12, 1981.
27. Thomas, *Astaire,* 288.

28. Richard L. Worsnos, "Thanks, Fred," Editorial Research Reports, Daily Service, April 29, 1974.
29. Satchell, *Astaire,* 231.
30. Giles, *Fred Astaire,* 89.
31. Pickard, *Fred Astaire,* 176.
32. Thomas, *Astaire,* 285.
33. Sally Davis, "With All the Huzzahs and Hoopla, Why Isn't Fred Astaire Laughing?" *Los Angeles Times,* May 8, 1974.
34. Robert Lindsey, "Astaire and Kelly in Spotlight Again," *New York Times,* May 10, 1976, 32.
35. Larry Billman, *Fred Astaire: A Bio-Bibliography* (Westport, CT: Greenwood Press, 1997), 25.
36. Lee Grant, "Another Straight Role for Astaire," *Los Angeles Times,* June 23, 1976.
37. Thomas, *Astaire,* 285.
38. Billman, *Fred Astaire,* 25.
39. Satchell, *Astaire,* 221.
40. Billman, *Fred Astaire,* 25.
41. Bart Mills, "Some Rampling and Astarical Euro Film-Making," *Los Angeles Times,* Calendar section, April 3, 1977.
42. Thomas, *Astaire,* 286.
43. Ibid.
44. "Shades of RKO days!" *People,* "Chatter," December 12, 1977.
45. Thomas, *Astaire,* 302.
46. Philip K. Scheuer, "Confession of an Ex–Song and Dance Man," *Los Angeles Times,* October 1, 1978.
47. David Rooney, *Xanadu* review, *Daily Variety,* July 12, 2007, 7.
48. "Chatter," *People,* April 18, 1979.
49. Thomas, *Astaire,* 299.
50. Ibid.
51. Ibid.
52. Satchell, *Astaire,* 237–38.
53. Ibid.
54. Deford, "Beauty and the Beast," 40.
55. Ibid., 39.
56. Ibid., 38–39.
57. Thomas, *Astaire,* 300.
58. Ibid., 300–301.
59. Ibid., 303.
60. Anna Kisselgoff, "City Ballet: A Premiere by Robbins," *New York Times,* June 18, 1983.
61. Thomas, *Astaire,* 303.

62. Jack Martin, "Why Fred Astaire Has His Heart Set on Marrying a Jockey Half His Age," *New York Post,* June 12, 1980.

63. Thomas, *Astaire,* 302.

64. John J. O'Connor, "TV: First of Salutes to Fred Astaire," *New York Times,* March 10, 1988.

65. Thomas, *Astaire,* 307.

66. Ibid.

67. Ibid., 307–8.

68. Phil Roura and Tom Poster, "Astaire and Smith Get Marriage License," *New York Daily News,* June 12, 1980.

69. John A. Wilson, "4 Sing Their Astaire Favorites," *New York Times,* June 30, 1980.

70. Thomas, *Astaire,* 308.

71. Satchell, *Astaire,* 247.

72. Thomas, *Astaire,* 308.

13. The Memory of All That

1. Richard McKenzie, *Turn Left at the Black Cow: One Family's Journey from Beverly Hills to Ireland* (Lanham, MD: Roberts Rinehart Publishers, 1998), 247.

2. Dorothy S. Gaiter, "Adele Astaire, Dancer-Comedian, Dies," *New York Times,* January 26, 1981.

3. *Time-Life* research file.

4. Larry Billman, *Fred Astaire: A Bio-Bibliography* (Westport, CT: Greenwood Press, 1997), 27.

5. Bob Thomas, *Astaire: The Man, the Dancer* (New York: St. Martin's Press, 1984), 313.

6. Tim Satchell, *Astaire: The Biography* (London, Melbourne, Auckland, and Johannesburg; Hutchinson, 1987), 250.

7. Ibid., 254.

8. Sarah Giles, *Fred Astaire: His Friends Talk* (New York: Doubleday, 1988), 44.

9. Mike Zwerin, *Parisian Jazz Chronicles: An Improvisational Memoir* (New Haven, CT: Yale University Press, 2005), 52.

10. McKenzie, *Turn Left at the Black Cow,* 301.

11. Irene Lacher, "From Ace Jockey to Fred's Baby," *Los Angeles Times,* August 17, 1997.

12. McKenzie, *Turn Left at the Black Cow,* 301.

13. Ibid., 302.

14. Billman, *Fred Astaire,* 27.

15. McKenzie, *Turn Left at the Black Cow,* 303.

16. Vincent Canby, "Astaire Persona: Urbanity and Grace," *New York Times,* June 23, 1987.

17. Laurence Bergreen, *As Thousands Cheer: The Life of Irving Berlin* (New York: Da Capo Press, 1996), 254.

18. McKenzie, *Turn Left at the Black Cow,* 314.

19. Ibid., 316–17, 319.

20. Charles Champlin, "Astaire's Last Partner Copes with Life After Fred," *Los Angeles Times,* June 8, 1988.

21. Irene Lacher, "Managing the Memories," *Los Angeles Times,* August 17, 1997, 8.

22. Ibid.

23. Billman, *Fred Astaire,* 27. The outcomes of these cases were not readily ascertainable except for the suit involving the Fred Astaire Dance Studios, which Robyn lost on appeal.

24. Ibid., 28.

25. Liz Smith, "Ginger Without Fred," *Los Angeles Times,* December 17, 1992.

26. "Keeping the Flame," *People,* February 22, 1993.

27. Billman, *Fred Astaire,* 28.

28. Ibid.

29. Bob Thomas, "Astaire's Widow Guards Legacy," Associated Press, May 31, 1998.

30. Lacher, "Managing the Memories," 8.

31. Ibid.

32. Lacher, "From Ace Jockey to Fred's Baby."

33. Lacher, "Managing the Memories," 8.

34. Ibid.

35. Robert Osborne, "One from the Heart: Daughter Ava," *Hollywood Reporter,* March 18, 2001.

36. Ibid.

37. Billman, *Fred Astaire,* 28.

38. Sean Penn, "Bruce Springsteen: The Legendary Singer Conveys Truth, Humor and a Timeless Sense of Self," *Time,* May 12, 2008.

INDEX